Management and Supervision in Law Enforcement

Sixth Edition

Kären Matison Hess, Ph.D.
President, Institute for Professional Development
Former Instructor, Normandale Community College
Bloomington, Minnesota

Christine Hess Orthmann, M.S.
Orthmann Writing and Research
Rosemount, Minnesota

With contributions by **Shaun E. LaDue, M.S.**
Chief of Police
Owatonna, Minnesota

Australia • Brazil • Japan • Korea • Mexico • Singapore • Spain • United Kingdom • United States

Management and Supervision in Law Enforcement, Sixth Edition
Kären Matison Hess, Christine Hess Orthmann

Vice President, Career and Professional Editorial: Dave Garza

Director of Learning Solutions: Sandy Clark

Senior Acquisitions Editor: Shelley Esposito

Managing Editor: Larry Main

Product Manager: Anne Orgren

Editorial Assistant: Danielle Klahr

Vice President, Career and Professional Marketing: Jennifer Baker

Marketing Director: Deborah S. Yarnell

Marketing Manager: Erin Brennan

Marketing Coordinator: Erin Deangelo

Production Director: Wendy Troeger

Production Manager: Mark Bernard

Senior Content Project Manager: Betty Dickson

Senior Art Director: Joy Kocsis

Photo Research: Terri Wright Design, www.terriwright.com

Production Editor: Sara Dovre Wudali, Buuji, Inc.

Library of Congress Control Number: 2010935151

ISBN-13: 978-1-4390-5644-8

ISBN-10: 1-4390-5644-7

Delmar
5 Maxwell Drive
Clifton Park, NY 12065-2919
USA

Cengage Learning is a leading provider of customized learning solutions with office locations around the globe, including Singapore, the United Kingdom, Australia, Mexico, Brazil, and Japan. Locate your local office at: **international.cengage.com/region**

Cengage Learning products are represented in Canada by Nelson Education, Ltd.

To learn more about Delmar, visit **www.cengage.com/delmar**

Purchase any of our products at your local college store or at our preferred online store **www.cengagebrain.com**

Notice to the Reader

Publisher does not warrant or guarantee any of the products described herein or perform any independent analysis in connection with any of the product information contained herein. Publisher does not assume, and expressly disclaims, any obligation to obtain and include information other than that provided to it by the manufacturer. The reader is expressly warned to consider and adopt all safety precautions that might be indicated by the activities described herein and to avoid all potential hazards. By following the instructions contained herein, the reader willingly assumes all risks in connection with such instructions. The publisher makes no representations or warranties of any kind, including but not limited to, the warranties of fitness for particular purpose or merchantability, nor are any such representations implied with respect to the material set forth herein, and the publisher takes no responsibility with respect to such material. The publisher shall not be liable for any special, consequential, or exemplary damages resulting, in whole or part, from the readers' use of, or reliance upon, this material.

Printed in the United States of America
1 2 3 4 5 6 7 14 13 12 11 10

BRIEF CONTENTS

CONTENTS

SECTION I
Management, Supervision, and Leadership: An Overview

v

SECTION II
Basic Management/ Personal Skills

CHAPTER 5

Decision Making and Problem Solving as a Manager | 134

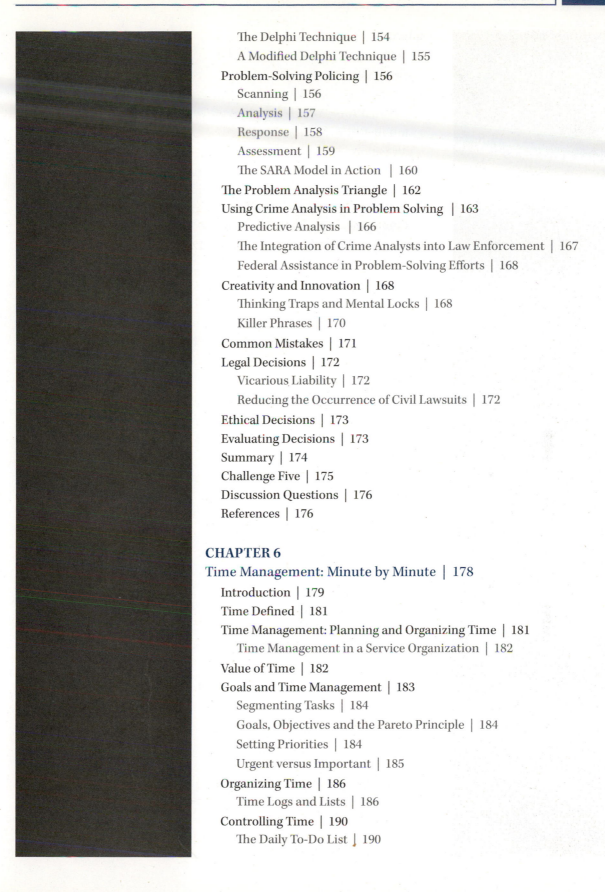

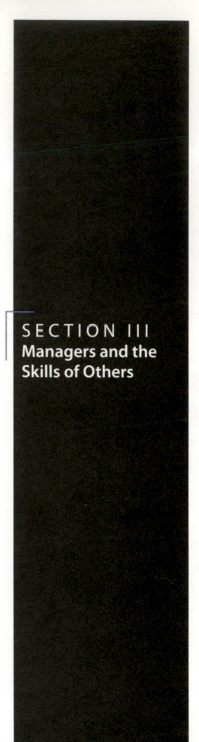

SECTION III
Managers and the Skills of Others

CHAPTER 7

Training and Beyond | 208

CHAPTER 8
Promoting Growth and Development | 250

SECTION IV
Managing Problems

CHAPTER 10

Discipline and Problem Behaviors | 320

SECTION V
Getting the Job Done . . . Through Others

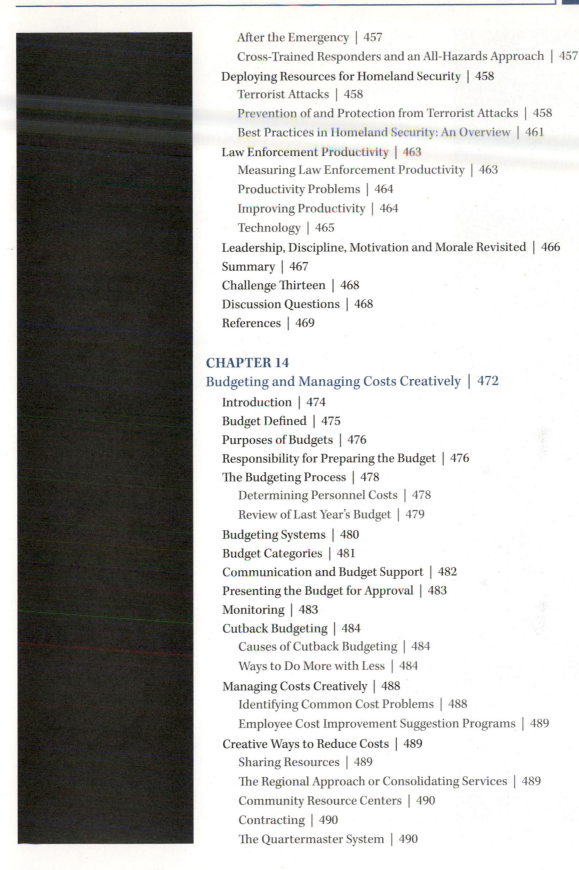

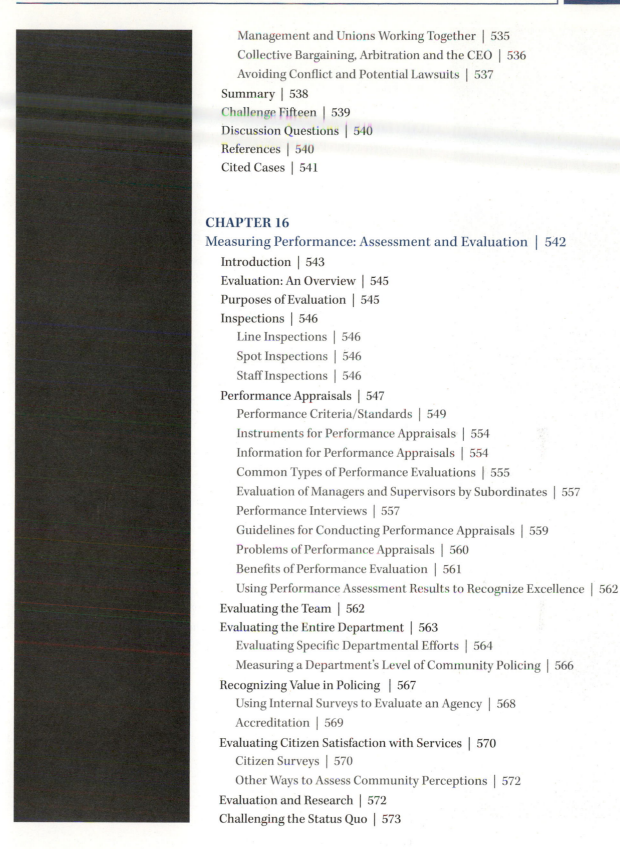

PREFACE

Welcome to the sixth edition of *Management and Supervision in Law Enforcement*. Based on feedback from students and instructors, we have made several changes in this edition, but we have retained our focus on writing a reader-friendly text that provides a comprehensive, up-to-date overview of management and supervision in law enforcement, blending theory and practice. The content applies to agencies of all sizes at all levels: local, county, state and federal. Many of the competencies discussed apply to anyone working in the criminal justice system, including courts and corrections.

KEY THEMES

Although significant changes have been made, three themes continue from previous editions. First, managers and supervisors need to move from an authoritative style to a participative leadership style—empowering all personnel to become contributing team members. Second, community policing and problem solving are key to preserving the peace and fighting crime. Citizens can become allies in both. Law enforcement cannot go it alone any longer. How community policing and problem solving affect management is illustrated throughout the text.

Third, change must be viewed as an opportunity rather than a threat. Managers must help their people grow and develop, and managers must continuously grow and develop, looking for new and better ways to accomplish their mission. As futurist Alvin Toffler asserts, "The illiterate of the 21st century will not be those who cannot read and write, but those who cannot learn, unlearn and relearn." This text is a beginning toward opening your mind to new ways of thinking and doing.

ORGANIZATION OF THE TEXT

Section I, Management and Supervision: An Overview, takes a broad look at management, beginning with the evolution of law enforcement and its influence on contemporary policing (Chapter 1). Next the organization of most law enforcement agencies is described, including how management is apparent at every level (Chapter 2). The section concludes with a discussion of the complementary roles of managing and leading (Chapter 3).

Section II, Basic Management/Personal Skills, focuses on basic skills that affect everything done by law enforcement managers at all levels. A critical basic skill that can make or break a law enforcement manager is skill in communication. Effective communication is at the core of effective management

(Chapter 4). The manager's role, by definition, includes decision making and problem solving (Chapter 5). How decisions are made and by whom are vital management questions. Among the most important decisions are those involving how time will be spent—the time of individual managers, officers and the agency as a whole (Chapter 6).

Section III, Managers and the Skills of Others, focuses on how managers can develop the numerous talents of their subordinates through participatory leadership. It first explains the importance of training (Chapter 7) and then suggests ways managers can go beyond training to fully develop the potential of all personnel (Chapter 8). Managers must build on the strengths of their people, accommodate their weaknesses and motivate their officers to be as effective as possible. Research has shown that tangible rewards such as pay raises and fringe benefits are not necessarily the most successful motivators. They are often taken for granted, making managing much more challenging. Managers who can develop and motivate their team members will make a tremendous contribution to the department and to the accomplishment of its goals, objectives and mission. In addition, many concepts basic to motivation are directly related to keeping morale high. Attending to employees' motivation and morale is critical to being an effective manager (Chapter 9).

Section IV, Managing Problems, discusses difficulties to be anticipated in any law enforcement organization. They are an inevitable part of the challenge of accomplishing work through others. Managers must recognize problem behaviors and use an appropriate combination of constructive criticism, discipline and incentives to correct the problems (Chapter 10). In addition, supervisors and managers will be faced with numerous complaints and grievances from their subordinates, their superiors and the public they serve. They or their officers may, in fact, be the objects of civil lawsuits. Effectively handling such matters requires great knowledge as well as skilled communication. Complaints, grievances, conflicts, disagreements, differences of opinions and outright confrontations may also occur and must be dealt with diplomatically by law enforcement managers (Chapter 11). Finally, all the preceding, plus the challenges inherent in law enforcement work itself, can result in extreme stress for supervisors, managers and subordinates. Reducing such stress and the hazards related to it are critical tasks for administrators (Chapter 12).

Section V, Getting the Job Done . . . Through Others, focuses on meeting responsibilities through effective leadership. People would rather be led than managed. Personnel must be effectively deployed and their productivity enhanced (Chapter 13). Other important decisions involve how resources other than time can be most effectively managed—that is, the ongoing task of budgeting, which directly affects what individual managers, their officers and ultimately the agency can accomplish (Chapter 14). The section then discusses the selection process and dealing with unions (Chapter 15). A final management responsibility is evaluating the efforts of the officers, managers and the entire department. Evaluation should be continuous and should include both formal and informal evaluation. The results should be used to help employees continue to grow and develop and to make the department more effective as well (Chapter 16). The section concludes with a discussion of the need for managers to be forward looking, considering what the future of law enforcement and the entire criminal justice system may hold (Chapter 17).

NEW TO THIS EDITION

The entire text has been completely updated, with over 475 references from 2007 or later. Among the other numerous additions to this edition are the following:

Chapter 1, Management, Supervision and Leadership

- New opening quote on management.
- Combined material from the fifth edition Chapters 1 and 2.
- Added COPS and PERF *"Good to Great" Policing*—lessons from business by Jim Collins and the Level 5 Leader.
- Added discussions on the personal characteristics of effective managers, micromanaging and common leadership errors.
- Stressed that management, supervision and leadership are important at all levels, including those just starting in law enforcement—patrol officers are managers, supervisors and leaders of the public they serve.

Chapter 2, The Organization and Structure of American Policing

- Combined material from fifth edition Chapters 1 and 3. Chapter 3, which was community policing, is no longer a stand-alone chapter but, rather, is incorporated into this one.
- New organizational charts.
- New discussion on post–9/11 policing and research on the effects of 9/11.
- Added material on CompStat policing, intelligence-led policing and evidence-based policing.
- Added discussion on partnering with universities to do research and the importance of reporting failures as well as successes.
- Added section on how these new policing styles affect new supervisors and managers.

Chapter 3, Mission and Management Functions

- Now includes remaining material from fifth edition Chapter 1 and 2.
- Added challenges faced by new managers, specifically those for new sergeants and first-line supervisors.
- Added discussions of the National Incident Management System (NIMS), management in law enforcement as a career and the importance of life-long learning.

Chapter 4, Communication: A Critical Management Skill

◉ Added "noise" (i.e., interference) in the communication process.

◉ Added next generation 9-1-1, the Gates/Crowley incident, medical conditions mimicking intoxication, improving internal communications via the Internet, the National Data Exchange (N-DEx), OneDOJ (Department of Justice) and Law Enforcement On Line (LEO).

Chapter 5, Decision Making and Problem Solving as a Manager

◉ New opening quote.

◉ Added discussions on emotional intelligence, predictive analysis, liability and discretion, CPTED.

◉ Added importance of data mining and crime analysis.

Chapter 6, Time Management: Minute by Minute

◉ Deleted several of the time log forms and added new technology to keep track of time use.

Chapter 7, Training and Beyond

◉ New Table 7.2—generations of police officers.

◉ New figures of the professional development matrix and the training criticality matrix.

◉ Added or expanded discussions on the importance of documenting training, failure to train litigation, the importance of using roll call for training, a new paradigm of learning, reality-based learning, CALEA training standards, the PTO versus the FTO, the learning organization and rethinking the traditional in-service training program.

Chapter 8, Promoting Growth and Development

◉ New discussions on legacy-based leadership, whistle blowing, building a culture of pride, how attitudes toward police are shaped, unintentional racial profiling; developing policies on officer off-duty misconduct, officers' lying, and professional courtesy, and succession planning.

◉ Added six research studies.

Chapter 9, Motivation and Morale

◉ Added a discussion on the shortage of staffing, partly as a result of the retirement of the baby boomers.

◉ Added the effect of the economic downturn of 2008 on staffing and retention.

- Added factors influencing retention and the use of contracts to improve retention.
- Added a discussion on signs employees may be considering leaving as well as a discussion on the importance of compassion for managers/leaders.

Chapter 10, Discipline and Problem Behaviors

- Added discussions on passive resistance and on off-duty misconduct.
- Added discussions on building a culture of discipline, bullying in the workplace, and the ACT method of negative discipline (accuracy, consistency and timeliness).
- New linear use-of-force continuum.
- Added education-based discipline.

Chapter 11, Complaints, Grievances and Conflict

- Added two new research studies on complaints.
- Added COPS publication: *Standards and Guidelines for Internal Affairs: Recommendations from a Community of Practice*, August 2009, including minimum standards for adjudication.
- Added information on the National Association for Community Mediation (NAFCM).
- New figure illustrating the complaint process and a new figure illustrating how an issue can flow through the system to become an Internal Affairs investigation.

Chapter 12, Stress and Related Hazards of the Job

- Added discussions on the CSI effect, death notifications, resiliency, sleep inertia and fitness for duty concerns of managers.

Chapter 13, Deploying Law Enforcement Resources and Improving Productivity

- Focused more on management/supervision.
- Added four research studies.
- Added discussions on sleep inertia, triage, scheduling software, cost-effectiveness of take-home vehicle programs and a model policy, citizens on radar patrol, Explorer posts, cross-trained responders and an all-hazards approach.

Chapter 14, Budgeting and Managing Costs Creatively

- Added discussion of the effect of the current economic crisis on law enforcement, including the two 2009 PERF studies and reports, as well as stimulus funds available to law enforcement agencies.

- Streamlined information on available grants.
- New topic of "going green to save green".
- Expanded discussions of asset forfeiture and privatization.
- Added a more complete discussion of the BCPA's Book 'Em sale, the funds raised and the resulting grants.
- Included the fiscal year of the federal government and of most police departments.

Chapter 15, Hiring Personnel and Dealing with Unions

- Discussed in greater depth the shrinking application pool and the difficulty in recruiting officers.
- Added discussions on recruiting immigrants, branding and the importance of the Internet in recruiting, including DiscoveringPolicing.org.
- Explained the ADA Amendment Act of 2008 and the changes it made to ADA.
- Updated legislative efforts to federalize labor-management relations (H.S. 413).
- Added *Ricci v. DeStefano* (2009) regarding affirmative action in hiring, including the distinction between disparate impact and disparate treatment.
- Added guidelines for managers when dealing with unions as well as recommendations for improving labor-management relations and avoiding conflict and lawsuits.

Chapter 16, Measuring Performance: Assessment and Evaluation

- Expanded discussion of fitness for duty standards.
- Added two new tables.
- Added discussions of the 10-star evaluation/recognition system, assessing the performance of new tactile and/or programs, assessing level of implementing community policing through the Community Policing Self-Assessment tool, the importance of accreditation and certification for forensic laboratories, units and personnel and the BJA's Smart Policing Initiative.
- Linked evaluation and assessment to evidence-based policing.

Chapter 17, Learning from the Past; Looking to the Future

- Added top ten trends shaping policing as well as the critical issues identified by the Police Executive Research Forum (PERF) over the past five years.
- Added two recent research studies on the relationship between drugs, gangs and violence.

- Added tension between local and federal agencies in several places, including the Ft. Hood shooting incident.
- Added discussion of local police response to the immigrant problem.

LEARNING AIDS

Management and Supervision in Law Enforcement, sixth edition, is a planned learning experience. It uses triple-strength learning, presenting all key concepts at least three times within a chapter. The more actively you participate, the better your learning will be. You will learn and remember more if you first familiarize yourself with the total scope of the subject. Read and think about the table of contents; it provides an outline of the many facets of law enforcement management and supervision. Then follow these steps as you study each chapter.

1. Read the objectives at the beginning of the chapter. These are stated as "Do you Know?" questions. Assess your current knowledge of each question. Examine any preconceptions you may hold.

2. Read the list of key terms and think about their possible meanings.

3. Read the chapter, underlining, highlighting or taking notes if that is your preferred study style. Pay special attention to all information that is highlighted. Also pay special attention to all words in bold print—these are the key terms for the chapter.

4. When you have finished reading the chapter, reread the "Do You Know?" questions to make sure you can give an educated response to each. If you find yourself stumped by one, find the appropriate section in the chapter and review it. Also define each key term. Again, if you find yourself stumped, either find the term in the chapter or look it up in the glossary.

5. Read the discussion questions and be prepared to contribute to a class discussion of the ideas presented in the chapter.

6. Periodically review the "Do You Know?" questions, key terms and chapter summaries.

By following these steps, you will learn more, understand better and remember longer.

NOTE: The material selected to highlight using the triple-strength learning instructional design includes only the chapter's key concepts. Although this information is certainly important because it provides a structural foundation for understanding the topics discussed, you cannot simply glance over the "Do You Know?" questions, highlighted boxes and summaries and expect to master the chapter. You are also responsible for reading and understanding the material that surrounds these basics—the "meat" around the bones, so to speak.

ANCILLARIES

To further enhance your study of management and supervision, these supplements are available:

Instructor Support Materials:

- **New to this edition,** the Instructor's Resource CD-ROM to accompany the text includes:
  - **Instructor's Manual**—Completely revised and updated by Joseph R. Budd of Brown Mackie College–Louisville, the Instructor's Manual for the Sixth Edition includes learning objectives, a chapter outline, a chapter summary, key terms and definitions, classroom activities, out-of-classroom activities, suggested answers to the challenge questions featured in the text for each chapter, and discussion questions.
  - **Computerized Test Bank**—The computerized test bank contains approximately 60 questions for each chapter in multiple choice, true/false, fill-in, and essay format.
  - **New to this edition, PowerPoint® lecture slides** are provided.
- **New to this edition,** the CourseMate Web site—For password-protected instructor resources, visit login.cengage.com, sign on using your single sign-on (SSO) login, and add this book to your bookshelf. This will give you access to:
  - The Instructor Companion Site that contains the Instructor's Manual, Test Bank, and PowerPoint® slides; and
  - The CourseMate Web site for students, which includes an interactive eBook and more. (See "Student Materials" list below for details)
- **WebTutor™ Toolbox on Blackboard® and WebCT®** A powerful combination: easy-to-use course management tools for whichever program you use—WebCT or Blackboard—and content from this text's rich companion Web site, all in one place. You can use ToolBox as is, from the moment you log on—or, if you prefer, customize the program with Web links, images, and other resources.

Student Materials

- **New to this edition: The CourseMate Web site** To access additional course materials including CourseMate, please visit www.cengagebrain.com. At the Cengagebrain.com home page, search for the ISBN of your title (from the back cover of your book) using the search box at the top of the page. This will take you to the product page where these resources can be found. The CourseMate website for this text includes:
- an interactive eBook, with highlighting, note taking and search capabilities
- interactive learning tools including:
  - Quizzes
  - Flashcards
  - Chapter-by-chapter critical thinking questions
  - Web links
  - and more!
- **The Criminal Justice Resource Center http://cj.wadsworth.com**—This Web site's "Discipline Resources" section contains links to popular criminal justice sites, Supreme Court updates, and more.

Additional Resources Available:

- **Careers in Criminal Justice Web site** academic.cengage.com/criminal justice/careers —This unique Web site helps students investigate the criminal justice career choices that are right for them with the help of several important tools:

- **Careers in Criminal Justice and Related Fields: From Internship to Promotion, Sixth Edition**—This book provides specific information on many criminal justice professions, helpful tips on resumes and cover letters, and practical advice on interview techniques.

ACKNOWLEDGMENTS

First we must acknowledge the late Wayne W. Bennett (d. 2004), lead author of the first two editions of *Management & Supervision in Law Enforcement*. Wayne was a graduate of the FBI National Police Academy, held an LL.B. degree in law, and served as the Director of Public Safety for the Edina (Minnesota) Police Department as well as Chief of Police of the Boulder City (Nevada) Police Department. He was also coauthor of *Criminal Investigation*, for the first few editions.

We would like to thank Tim Hess for his review of and contributions to the manuscript, Bobbi Peacock for her assistance on the photo program, and Richard Gautsch for developing the challenges for the text. In addition, a heartfelt thanks to the reviewers of the past editions of the text and their valuable suggestions: Timothy Apolito, University of Dayton; Tom Barker, Jacksonville State University; A. J. Bartok, Regional Law Enforcement Academy, Colorado; Bill Bourns, California State University–Stanislaus; Lloyd Bratz, Cuyahoga Community College; Gib H. Bruns, Arizona State University; Michael Buckley, Texas A&M University; Chris Carmean, Houston Community College–Northeast; David Carter, Michigan State University; Samuel L. Dameron, Marshall University; Dana Dewitt, Cadron State College; Hank DiMatteo, New Mexico State University; Bill Formby, University of Alabama–Tuscaloosa; Larry Gould, Northern Arizona University; Lori Guevara, University of Texas–Arlington; Joseph J. Hanrahan, Westfield State College; Robert G. Huckabee, Indiana State University; Alan Lawson, Ferris State University, Michigan; Muriel Lembright, Wichita State University; Stan Malm, University of Maryland; Robert L. Marsh, Boise State University; John Maxwell, Community College of Philadelphia; Robert G. May, Waubonsee Community College; William McCamey, Western Illinois University; Dennis M. Payne, Michigan State University; Carroll S. Price, Penn Valley Community College; Lawrence G. Stephens, Columbus State Community College; W. Fred Wegener, Indiana University of Pennsylvania; Stanley W. Wisnoski, Jr., Broward Community College; and Solomon Zhao, University of Nebraska, Omaha.

We would like to thank the following reviewers for their insightful suggestions for this sixth edition: Chris Carmean, Houston Community College; Thomas Chuda, Bunker Hill Community College (Boston, Massachusetts); George Franks, Stephen F. Austin State University; Richard Hough, University of West Florida; and Bobby Polk, Metropolitan Community College (Omaha, Nebraska). We are deeply indebted to them for their work. Any errors, however, are the sole responsibility of the authors.

Finally, a special thanks to our senior acquisitions editor, Shelley Esposito; and our product manager, Anne Orgren, at Delmar, Cengage Learning; photo researcher Terri Wright at Terri Wright Design; and our production editor, Sara Dovre Wudali at Buuji.

ABOUT THE AUTHORS

ABOUT THE AUTHORS

Kären Matison Hess holds a Ph.D. in English and instructional design from the University of Minnesota. She taught for 30 years at Normandale Community College and has presented workshops on report writing in law enforcement throughout the country. Other Cengage texts Dr. Hess has coauthored are *Community Policing: Partnerships for Problem Solving* (6th edition), *Constitutional Law* (5th edition), *Corrections in the 21st Century: A Practical Approach, Criminal Investigation* (9th edition), *Criminal Procedure, Introduction to Law Enforcement and Criminal Justice* (9th edition), *Introduction to Private Security* (5th edition), *Juvenile Justice* (5th edition), *Police Operations* (5th edition), and *Careers in Criminal Justice and Related Fields: From Internship to Promotion* (6th edition).

Dr. Hess is a member of the Academy of Criminal Justice Sciences (ACJS), the American Society for Law Enforcement Trainers (ASLET), the Bloomington Crime Prevention Association, the International Association of Chiefs of Police (IACP), the Minnesota Association of Chiefs of Police, the Police Executive Research Forum (PERF) and the Text and Academic Author's Association (TAA), in which she is a fellow and a member of the TAA Foundation Board of Directors.

Christine Hess Orthmann holds an M.S. in criminal justice from the University of Cincinnati and has been writing and researching in various aspects of criminal justice for over 20 years. She is a coauthor of *Community Policing: Partnerships for Problem Solving* (6th edition), *Corrections for the Twenty-First Century, Criminal Investigation* (9th edition), and *Police Operations* (5th edition), as well as a major contributor to *Constitutional Law* (5th edition), *Introduction to Law Enforcement and Criminal Justice* (9th edition), *Introduction to Private Security* (5th edition), *Juvenile Justice* (5th edition), and *Careers in Criminal Justice and Related Fields: From Internship to Promotion* (6th edition). She is a member of the Academy of Criminal Justice Sciences (ACJS), the American Society of Criminology (ASC), the Text and Academic Authors Association (TAA), and the National Criminal Justice Honor Society (Alpha Phi Sigma), and is a reserve officer with the Rosemount (Minnesota) Police Department.

ABOUT THE CONTRIBUTOR

Shaun E. LaDue, M.S., has been the chief of police of the Owatonna (Minnesota) Police Department since 2004. He was previously with the Bloomington (Minnesota) Police Department, having risen from a patrol officer in 1993 to

Commander of Special Operations and Patrol Administration, with various positions along the way including detective and school liaison officer. Chief LaDue has attended numerous leadership and management institutes as well as general professional development programs and specialized training courses. He has been actively involved in both communities he has served and is also actively involved in several professional organizations, including the Law Enforcement Executive Development Association (LEEDA), the International Association of Chiefs of Police (IACP), the Southern Police Institute Alumni Association (SPI), and the Minnesota Police & Peace Officers Association (MPPOA).

Management, Supervision and Leadership

The conventional definition of management is getting work done through people, but real management is developing people through work.

—Agha Hasan Abedi
Founder of the Bank of Credit and Commerce International

The watchwords of the new leadership paradigm are coach, inspire, gain commitment, empower, affirm, flexibility, responsibility, self-management, shared power, autonomous teams and entrepreneurial units.

—Donald C. Witham
Chief, FBI Strategic Planning Unit

DO YOU KNOW?

- ☉ What basic management skills are important?
- ☉ What four tools successful managers use?
- ☉ What personal characteristics most successful managers exhibit?
- ☉ What management style is best suited for law enforcement work?
- ☉ Who from the business world has helped shape management and how?
- ☉ What management by objectives is?
- ☉ What basic differences exist between managers and leaders?
- ☉ What theories of leadership have been researched?
- ☉ What leadership styles have been identified and their main characteristics?
- ☉ What constitutes effective leadership training?
- ☉ What the common mistakes made between management and leadership are?

CAN YOU DEFINE?

INTRODUCTION

Hundreds of management, supervision and leadership books exist as do numerous other learning opportunities: "Never in the history of law enforcement have we had more managers holding Bachelor's and Master's Degrees. Northwestern University's Center for Public Safety, the FBI National Academy, the Southern Police Institute and many other highly recognized institutions are educating and graduating police managers at a record pace" (Glennon, 2009).

And yet we still have managers and supervisors who cannot lead primarily because they do not see their own personal deficits. Glennon asserts (2009), "All the classes, theories, and techniques don't mean a thing if the personality can not conquer its shortcomings. Stubbornness, control issues, insecurity, obsessive-compulsive tendencies, selfishness, and fear all hinder leadership ability." He believes that to succeed, managers and supervisors have to accept that "understanding people, putting ego aside, and developing an organizational climate that encourages independence, creativity and trust is absolutely essential. The way to start is by honest evaluation." Such self-evaluation, combined with a working knowledge of the roles and responsibilities of management and supervision, an understanding of what makes a successful leader and a solid foundation of skills sets honed through proper professional development should put individuals on the road to success.

CHAPTER at a GLANCE

This chapter examines the complex role of the law enforcement manager, the challenges presented by management and the relationship between authority, responsibility and delegation. This is followed by an overview of the basic skills and tools required of an effective manager and the personal characteristics held by most successful managers. The next area of discussion is an analysis of the various management styles and influences from the business world, including ways to avoid micromanaging. Then the differences between managing and leading and the key characteristics of leaders are discussed. This is followed by a review of research on and theories related to leadership, the various leadership styles and the apparent need for change within law enforcement agencies, again with a perspective on leadership from the business world. Then the discussion turns to leadership training and development, common leadership errors and guidelines for effective leadership. The chapter concludes with a call for change in law enforcement management and leadership.

MANAGERS AND MANAGEMENT

To manage means to control and direct, to administer, to take charge of. **Management** is the process of using resources to achieve organizational goals. Law enforcement management is a process of deciding goals and objectives, adopting a work plan to accomplish them, obtaining and wisely using resources and making decisions that result in a high level of performance and productivity. Those who undertake these activities are managers. **Supervision** is making sure the activities are effectively implemented by those responsible for doing so. Supervisors are usually those who focus on the daily operations of a department and evaluate those who perform them. The most effective managers and supervisors are also leaders. Management and leadership are closely related. Effective management requires leadership, but leadership does not necessarily involve management. Leadership is discussed shortly.

Managers and supervisors control and direct people and operations to achieve organizational objectives. They are also jointly involved in planning, organizing, staffing and budgeting—topics that will be discussed in greater depth in later chapters. Many gray areas exist in the duties of managers and supervisors. This is increasingly true in organizations that have been "flattened" by eliminating some middle-management positions and empowering employees at the lowest level.

Managers must also support the development of *individual* responsibility and self-initiation, permitting all employees to achieve maximum potential while supporting organizational needs. The total individual member energy is transferred to the organizational energy needed for success.

management
the process of combining resources to accomplish organizational goals.

supervision
overseeing the actual work being done.

Authority, Responsibility and Delegation

Authority, responsibility and delegation are key factors in any organization. Without them organizations could not exist. *Authority* is the power to enforce laws, exact obedience and command. It is the legal right to get things done through others by influencing behavior. Formal authority comes from rank or credentials. Informal authority comes from friendships or alignments with others. *Responsibility* means being answerable, liable or accountable. Thus, managers have the authority to give commands, and subordinates have the responsibility of carrying out the commands. This authority-responsibility structure is in keeping with the paramilitary organization that traditional police management is modeled after.

Vernon (2007c, p.128) notes, "In the practice of leadership, to cultivate legitimate authority, you must follow the leader yourself. When you step out from under authority, you lose that power. The only exception involves a matter of principle, not simply preference. Legitimate authority does not demand followers violate laws or established principles."

In a democracy, authority is not always regarded as desirable. Even though managers may use it, and employees recognize management's right to do so, a limitation exists in the employees' mind-set as to how much is acceptable.

seagull management

manager hears something's wrong, flies in, makes a lot of noise, craps on everybody and flies away.

They expect some freedom of choice. Managers should never manipulate employees and should avoid **seagull management**. According to management guru Ken Blanchard, "[Seagull managers] hear something's wrong, so they fly in, make a lot of noise, crap on everybody and fly away" (1988, p.14). Managers need authority, but they should also share this authority by delegating effectively.

Delegation, or transferring authority, is a necessary and often difficult aspect of management because it requires placing trust in others to do the job as well as, or better than, the manager would do it. It is also a form of empowerment. Theodore Roosevelt once said "The best executive is the one who has enough sense to pick good people to do what he wants done, and self-restraint enough to keep from meddling with them while they do it." Yet many managers fail to delegate effectively because they believe "If you want something done right, you have to do it yourself."

Delegation is *not* passing the buck, shirking personal responsibility or dumping on someone. It is the way managers and supervisors free up time to get their work done while avoiding getting tied up in "administrivia." Managers can put their minds at ease when they delegate important tasks by carefully selecting the right person, thoroughly defining the task and specifying the qualifications for doing it well. The results, standards and deadlines should be clearly defined. Managers should also decide how much authority, support and time the officer will need.

Managers who find themselves wondering why their officers cannot take more responsibility or who feel they must drop every detail of every project into their officers' laps may not be delegating effectively. Key points to remember are

1. Stress the results, the final outcome, not details.

2. Turn employee questions around and ask for possible answers.

3. Establish measurable objectives.

4. Develop reporting systems.

5. Set realistic deadlines.

6. Recognize accomplishments.

It is not enough to delegate a task. The employee also needs the necessary authority to get the task done. To avoid problems, managers need to match tasks with one of three levels of authority:

1. *Recommending:* Assign an employee to research available options and present the manager with a recommendation of the best choice.

2. *Informing and implementing:* Assign an employee to research and choose the best option, inform the manager and be ready to implement it.

3. *Acting:* Give the employee the authority to act, if the manager is confident the employee can handle the task independently.

In addition to knowing how to delegate effectively, managers need several other basic management skills and tools.

BASIC MANAGEMENT SKILLS AND TOOLS

To be effective, managers at all levels must be skilled at planning, organizing, coordinating, reporting and budgeting. Equally critical, however, are people skills such as communicating, motivating and leading, as will be discussed throughout the text.

 Basic management skills include technical skills, administrative skills, conceptual skills and people skills.

Technical skills include all the procedures necessary to be a successful police officer: interviewing and interrogating, searching, arresting, gathering evidence and so on. Police officers who wish to be promoted to sergeants must have a solid foundation regarding these technical skills, although possessing such skills is not enough, in itself, to guarantee promotion.

Administrative skills include organizing, delegating and directing the work of others. These skills also include writing proposals, formulating work plans, establishing policies and procedures and developing budgets.

Conceptual skills include the ability to problem solve, plan and see the big picture and how all the pieces within it fit. Managers must be able to think in terms of the future; synthesize great amounts of data; make decisions on complex matters; and have broad, even national or global, perspectives. Managers must see the organization as a whole, yet existing within society. They must also have a sensitivity to the spirit—not just the letter—of the law.

People skills include being able to communicate clearly, to motivate, to discipline appropriately and to inspire. People skills also include working effectively with managers up the chain of command, as well as with the general public. The higher the management position, the more important people skills become. According to Blanchard (1988, p.14), "Successful managers use four tools to accomplish their goals."

 Successful managers have
- **Clear goals.**
- **A commitment to excellence.**
- **Feedback.**
- **Support.**

In addition to these basic skills and tools, effective managers usually possess personal characteristics that help them succeed.

PERSONAL CHARACTERISTICS

 Most successful managers are consistently self-confident and have a consistently positive attitude.

Consistency in these two characteristics is the key.

The Role of Self-Confidence

Most police supervisors and managers have been promoted into their positions because they possessed or had learned the necessary skills and tools. But with the excitement and pride of promotion often comes an instinctive tinge of self-doubt. Taking on a new level of management is a major challenge and involves risk. Though initially daunting, change can serve as a catalyst for growth.

Change often requires that a person use already acquired skills in a new context, which can be threatening. Asking a person to walk across a 6-inch wide board on the ground poses no threat. Put it 40 feet in the air, and the person is unlikely to take even the first step. To maintain a consistent level of self-confidence, seek the support of your peers, set goals for yourself in mastering the skills you need and get feedback.

Wallenda Effect

the negative consequences of fear of failure.

A lack of self-confidence can lead to failure and other dire consequences, a situation sometimes referred to as the **Wallenda Effect**. In 1968 tightrope aerialist Karl Wallenda said, "Being on the tightrope is living; everything else is waiting." He loved his work and had total confidence in himself. Ten years later he fell to his death. His wife, also an aerialist, said that he had recently been worried about falling. This was in total contrast to his earlier years, when all his energy was focused on succeeding.

Attitude

It has been said that it is not aptitude but attitude that determines your altitude. Henry Ford has been quoted as saying, "Whether you think you can or think you can't, you are right." People's attitudes most determine how effectively they can use their management skills and knowledge to lead their departments. Optimism can be a valuable attitude in many management scenarios. As General Colin Powell has stated, "It can be done. Perpetual optimism is a force multiplier." But the optimism should always be grounded in reality.

A positive attitude is vital for successful management. Closely related to how managers view themselves is the management style(s) they use and their attitudes toward their subordinates.

MANAGEMENT STYLES

Just as different managers use different types of authority and delegation, they also have varied personalities and management styles. Managers at any level may be sociable and friendly, firm and hard driving, or analytical and detail oriented. Several theories regarding management style have been developed, including those of Douglas McGregor, Rensis Likert, Chris Argyris and Robert Blake and Jane Mouton. Within each theory, "pure" or ideal types are described, but in reality management style should be viewed as a continuum, with "pure" types at the opposing ends. Table 1.1 summarizes the four theories about management style.

TABLE 1.1 Four Theories about Management Style

Theory and Originator	Basic Premise
Theory X/Theory Y—Douglas McGregor	Managers act toward subordinates in relation to the views they have of them. Theory X views employees as lazy and motivated by pay. The average worker has an aversion to work and does not want responsibility. Management's responsibility is to provide constant employee supervision and control workers through coercion, threats and punishment. Management makes all decisions and directs employees to carry them out. Theory X might have worked in the past, but with better-educated workers, it could create hostility. Theory Y views employees as committed and motivated by growth and development. They are willing workers who can be trusted to do a good job and given reasonable goals to accomplish. Employees should share in decision making. The humanistic approach reflected in Theory Y is more effective in today's work world. Management should encourage self-motivation and fewer outside controls. Decisions could be delegated. Employees would be responsive to management's goals if management set the proper environment for work.
Four-System Approach—Rensis Likert	System 1, similar to McGregor's Theory X, is the *traditional*, dictatorial approach to managing people. This system generally exploits employees and uses coercion and a few economic rewards. Communication flows downward from the top, and there is little to no feedback. System 2 is similar to System 1, except that economic rewards replace coercion. Some information on organizational development is permitted but not in opposition to management's control. System 3 is more liberal, uses employee initiative and gives employees more responsibility. System 4 is participative management (the complete opposite of System 1). Final decisions are made by management but only after employees have added their input. Communication flows back freely through the organization, and there is much feedback. Also includes team management, which is widely used today.
Mature Employee Theory—Chris Argyris	Organizations and individuals exist for a purpose. Both are *interdependent:* Organizations provide jobs, and people perform them. As individuals develop, they mature from passive to active and from dependent to interdependent. Individuals and organizations need to develop together in much the same way. They need to grow and mature together to be of mutual benefit. The work force has energy to be released if management recognizes it. An organization that restricts individuals and keeps employees dependent, subordinate and restrained will engender a work climate of frustration, failure, short-term perspective and conflict and will hinder employees from achieving the organization's mission.
Managerial/Leadership Grid Theory—Dr. Robert R. Blake and Dr. Jane S. Mouton	Describes five management styles as falling on a grid—the vertical (Y) axis measures "concern for people" (low to high) and the horizontal (X) axis measures "concern for results" (low to high). Lower right corner (high concern for results; low concern for people): *Authority–Compliance Management* style, the early autocratic, authoritarian approach. The manager is a no-nonsense taskmaster. Concern is for manager authority, status and operation of the organization. Employees have little say and less influence, and production is the only concern. This is also known as *Task Management*. Upper left corner (low concern for results; high concern for people): *Country Club Management* style. Managers are overly concerned with keeping employees happy at the expense of reasonable productivity. The work atmosphere is friendly and comfortable. Concern for employees is utmost; concern for productivity is limited. Lower left corner (low concern for results; low concern for people): the *Impoverished Management* style, which permits workers to do just enough to get by. Managers and employees put in their time and look ahead to retirement. Little real concern exists for employees or management. Little is expected and little is given. Minimal effort is made. The prevailing attitude: ignore problems and they will go away. In the center (moderate concern for results; moderate concern for people): *Middle-of-the-Road Management* style, with the manager showing some concern for both employees and management but in a low-key manner that is not really productive. The manager is a fence straddler, appeasing both sides, avoiding conflict and satisfying no one. Upper right corner (high concern for results; high concern for people): *Team Management* approach, suggested as the ideal. The manager works with employees as a team, providing information, caring about their feelings and concern, assisting, advising and coaching. Managers encourage employees to be creative and share suggestions for improvement. Employees are committed to their jobs and organization through a mutual relationship of trust and respect. Goals are achieved as a team.

Which Management Style to Select?

It was once thought that fist-pounding, authoritarian managers were the greatest achievers. People now believe that many styles of management or combinations of several can be effective. The management style selected depends on the individuals involved, the tasks to be accomplished and any emergency the organization is facing, such as a hostage incident, a multiple-alarm fire or an officer down.

Management styles might be depicted as falling along a continuum, with the task on one end, the people on the other end, and the time available to accomplish a goal determining where on that continuum the management style falls. If the task requires a great deal of time and will involve working with the same group of people throughout the duration, it is important to cater to group morale and manage more from the people side of the continuum. Take care of the people, and they will take care of the task/goal. In contrast, if time is short and the task will be over before morale becomes a factor, manage more from the task side of the continuum. Battles are won by task-oriented managers; wars are won by people-oriented managers.

No one management style is more apt than another to achieve the agency's mission. The selected style must match individual personalities and situations.

INFLUENCES FROM
THE BUSINESS WORLD

Peter Drucker and W. Edwards Deming had a great influence on approaches to management in policing.

During the 1940s, American economist, management specialist and consultant Peter Drucker (1909–2005) became influential, asserting that productivity was the result of self-starting, self-directed workers who accepted responsibility. He advocated a shift from traditional production lines to flexible production methods. Among his most quoted statements are the following:

- "Efficiency is doing better what is already being done."
- "There is nothing so useless as doing efficiently that which should not be done at all."
- "Today knowledge has power. It controls access to opportunity and advancement."
- "The individual is the central, rarest, most precious capital resource of our society."

Drucker developed and is credited with first using the term *management by objectives (MBO)* in the early 1950s.

Management by Objectives

 Management by objectives (MBO) involves managers and subordinates setting goals and objectives together and then tracking performance to ensure that the objectives are met.

Drucker's theory can be summed up as "Expect to get the right things done." Drucker also says, "Intelligence, imagination, and knowledge are essential resources, but only effectiveness converts them into results." The key to the MBO system is to get workers to participate in deciding and setting goals, both individually and in work groups. The performance achieved is then compared to these agreed-upon goals.

management by objectives (MBO) involves managers and subordinates setting goals and objectives together and then tracking performance to ensure that the objectives are met.

Total Quality Management

The pioneer in **total quality management (TQM)** was W. Edwards Deming (1900–1993), a management expert who assisted Japanese businesses in recovering and prospering following the end of World War II. In the 1980s Deming's ideas were taken up by American corporations as they sought to compete more effectively against foreign manufacturers. His quality-control methods focused on systematically tallying product defects, analyzing their causes, correcting those causes and then recording the effects of the corrections on subsequent product quality. The watchword of TQM is *zero defects.*

Although Deming's famous "14 Points" were originally aimed at business, several are applicable to the public sector as well—including law enforcement:

- Create constancy of purpose for improvement of product and service.
- Adopt the new philosophy.
- Improve constantly.
- Institute modern methods of training on the job.
- Institute modern methods of supervision.
- Drive fear from the workplace.
- Break down barriers between staff areas.
- Eliminate numerical goals for the work force.
- Remove barriers that rob people of pride of workmanship.
- Institute a vigorous program of education and training (Deming, 1982, p.17).

A concern regarding the TQM management style is that the emphasis on zero defects may hinder innovation and change. Although TQM may work well in manufacturing, its value to those in the service industries may not be as great because progress often demands risk taking and mistakes.

No matter what management approach supervisors and managers select, they should consciously avoid micromanaging subordinates.

total quality management (TQM)

Deming's theory that managers should create constancy of purpose for improvement of product and service, adopt the new philosophy, improve constantly, institute modern methods of training on the job, institute modern methods of supervision, drive fear from the workplace, break down barriers between staff areas, eliminate numerical goals for the work force, remove barriers that rob people of pride of workmanship and institute a vigorous program of education and training.

AVOIDING MICROMANAGING

micromanagement
oversupervising, providing oversight with excessive control and attention to details better left to the operational personnel.

Micromanagement is oversupervising, providing oversight with excessive control and attention to details better left to the operational personnel. As Gove (2008, p.26) explains,

> Micromanagers tend to dictate every detail of the work for which their subordinates are responsible, and they truly believe that their way is not only the best but also the only way to accomplish a goal. Rather than help, true micromanagers impede work progress and risk stifling the growth of subordinate officers as well as the police agency as a whole. . . .

> Micromanaged employees become disengaged from their work, leading to lower productivity, a behavior that spreads to colleagues. Consequently, motivation is lost, quality drops, and esprit de corps can be irreparably damaged.

Some well-meaning supervisors mistake micromanaging for mentoring. Only by recognizing this defective management style can supervisors work toward a more effective style. Among the symptoms of micromanagement are the following (Gove, p.28):

- Being overly critical of subordinates when reviewing work, finding something wrong every time—often referred to as the "red pen syndrome."
- Being easily irritated if decisions are made without their input.
- Spending an inordinate amount of time overseeing simple tasks.
- Seldom praising.
- Noticing that subordinates appear unmotivated and never take initiative.

Supervisors of micromanagers should not accuse them of this management style but, instead, help them identify the reasons they manage this way. Work with such managers to obtain a clear understanding of priorities, the importance of each task and which tasks need more careful oversight. Encourage them to avoid asking those they manage "why" questions and instead ask them how they might have done it differently. Allow honest mistakes and help them learn from those mistakes. In effect, become a mentor rather than a micromanager.

LEADING VERSUS MANAGING

In the 21st century, most people resist being managed. They seek leadership. Leaders solve problems, maximize potential with competent associates, take safe risks, take responsibility, move forward, lead by example and have vision. Managers may or may not be leaders, and leaders do not have to be managers. A true leader has the potential to influence from any position in the organization, formal or informal. Police administrators must be both skilled managers and effective leaders.

More than 20 years ago Drucker conducted a study of the Los Angeles Police Department and found: "You police are so concerned with doing things right that you fail to do the right things." In other words, the administrators were so concerned with managing that they failed to lead. He also noted that the preoccupation with doing things right fostered a climate that promoted for "the absence of wrongdoing rather than for the presence of initiative, innovation and leadership." Perhaps Drucker's best known quote is, "Managers do things

TABLE 1.2 Management versus Leadership

Management	Leadership
Does the thing right	Does the right thing
Tangible	Intangible
Referee	Cheerleader
Directs	Coaches
What you do	How you do it
Pronounces	Facilitates
Responsible	Responsive
Has a view of the mission	Has a vision of the mission
Views world from inside	Views world from outside
Chateau leadership	Front-line leadership
What you say	How you say it
No gut stake in enterprise	Gut stake in enterprise
Preserving life	Passion for life
Driven by constraints	Driven by goals
Looks for things done wrong	Looks for things done right
Runs a cost center	Runs an effort center
Quantitative	Qualitative
Initiates programs	Initiates an ongoing process
Develops programs	Develops people
Concerned with programs	Concerned with people
Concerned with efficiency	Concerned with efficacy
Sometimes plays the hero	Plays the hero no more

Source: Bill Westfall. "Leadership: Caring for the Organizational Spirit." *Knight Line USA*, May–June 1993, p. 9. Reprinted with permission of Executive Excellence, Provo, Utah. September 1992, p.11.

right; leaders do the right thing." Table 1.2 highlights several other differences between managers and leaders.

 A basic **difference** between **managers** and **leaders** is that **managers focus on tasks**, whereas **leaders focus on people**. Manage things; lead people.

However, if *management* is defined as the administrative ordering of things—with written plans, clear organization charts, well-documented objectives, detailed and precise job descriptions and regular evaluation of performance—few would deny that competent management is essential to any law enforcement agency. To be truly effective, those in positions of authority combine managerial and leadership skills. All leadership and no management would be as serious a problem as an imbalance in the other direction, a situation that currently exists in many police organizations.

Despite the tendency to disparage managers as "cold," "non-people-oriented" task masters, their abilities to solve problems and "get the job done" are essential to every aspect of successful police organizations (Borrello, 2009, p.64). Characteristics of effective managers including being well-organized and dependable, setting expectations, providing organizational direction, performing work that is tangible, serving as risk managers, accepting and defining reality, controlling human resources, enforcing and following the rules and providing directions that must be followed: "Managers may not be dynamic, charismatic, or influential, but without them, a police department would simply fail to operate. . . . A leader may be in the center of the spotlight, but it was a manager who researched the light, authored the proposal to purchase the light, and keeps the light serviced and operational" (Borrello, p.66). Fortunately, many effective managers are also competent leaders.

LEADERSHIP

leadership

influencing, working with and through individuals and groups to accomplish a common goal.

Leadership has been defined as "working with and through individuals and groups to accomplish organizational goals" (Hersey and Blanchard, 1977). Leadership generates an emotional connection between the leader and the led. Centuries ago, Chinese philosopher Lao Tzu observed, "The good leader is he who the people revere. The great leader is he whose people say, 'We did it ourselves.'" President and World War II Commanding General Dwight Eisenhower defined leadership like this: "Leadership: The art of getting someone else to do something you want done, because he wants to do it."

CHARACTERISTICS OF LEADERS

A leader in the purest sense influences others by example. "A leader is a motivator, coach, disciplinarian, mentor, encourager, restrainer, teacher, evaluator, team builder and role model. Successful leaders have the wisdom to assess the situation and determine the correct role or combination of roles needed for the movement. The priorities of our varied responsibilities can change in a moment, depending on the circumstances we face" (Vernon, 2009, p.48).

Effective leaders develop strong interpersonal relationships, working with and through other individuals and groups to accomplish the organization's goals.

© Jeff Greenberg/PhotoEdit

Leadership creates a special bond that has to be earned. To build and maintain credibility, it is necessary to clarify values, identify the wishes of the community and employees, build a consensus, communicate shared values, stand up for beliefs and lead by example.

A good leader knows being the boss does not mean bossing. Rather, it means giving employees the resources, training and coaching they need and providing them with information so they can see their organization's mission. It also means showing how what is important to the department is also important to them: "People are more likely to follow someone they sense is sincerely interested in helping them fulfill their goals" (Vernon, 2007a, p.48).

The self-confidence and positive attitude discussed earlier as important characteristics of effective managers should not be construed as synonymous with pride, which can often be a leader's greatest problem. Field (2009, p.62) describes two kinds of pride—good and bad: "Good pride represents personal dignity and self-respect. Bad pride is the deadly leadership sin of superiority that reeks of conceit and arrogance." Rather, a true leader exhibits humility. One way to show humility is to respect and rely on the knowledge held by those around you, regardless of their rank. Some subordinates are very experienced, having forgotten more than their new supervisors or managers will learn for months or years. The effective leader respects these subordinates' ideas and solicits their opinions (Vernon, 2008b, p.42).

Finally, effective leadership requires trust: "Every phase of leadership necessitates trust. Followers must trust the leader is taking them in the right direction. They must trust their leader will support their actions as long as they operate within the agreed-upon parameters. They must believe their leader will keep commitments. They must count on their leader's judgment. Perhaps most importantly, followers must expect their leader's motives are not self-centered, but rather, stem from the interests of those being led. In short, leadership and trust are inseparable" (Vernon 2007b, p.66).

RESEARCH ON AND THEORIES RELATED TO LEADERSHIP

Leadership has been studied over the past several decades from many different perspectives. Authorities on leadership have differing views on what they perceive to be the most important characteristics of leaders.

 Theories about leadership include the study of traits, the classic studies conducted at Michigan State and Ohio State Universities, the Managerial/Leadership Grid and situational leadership.

Trait Theorists

The first group of leadership researchers, the *trait theorists*, examined the individual. They looked at leaders in industry and government to determine what special characteristics or traits these people possessed.

Although many leadership traits have been identified, none dominate. Leadership trait theory was highly popular because it simplified the process of selecting leaders. Guaranteed leadership through possession of specific traits, however, was never fully realized because of the large number of traits identified and that no single person possessed them all. No criteria determined which traits were more desirable than others. Even possession of all the traits did not guarantee leadership success.

After many studies and experiments, trait theorists could not empirically document leadership characteristics. Researchers in the 1940s and 1950s turned their attention to the situations in which leaders actually functioned.

The Michigan State and Ohio State Universities Studies

Research conducted at Michigan State University and Ohio State University also provides insights into effective leadership. These studies determined that leaders must provide an environment that motivates employees to accomplish organizational goals.

The Michigan State study looked at how leaders motivated individuals or groups to achieve organizational goals and determined that leaders must have a sense of the task to be accomplished and the most favorable work environment. Three principles of leadership behavior emerged from the Michigan State study:

- Leaders must give task direction to their followers.
- Closeness of supervision directly affects employee production. High-producing units had less direct supervision; highly supervised units had lower production. Conclusion: Employees need some freedom to make choices. Given this, they produce at a higher rate.
- Leaders must be employee oriented. It is the leader's responsibility to facilitate employees' accomplishment of goals.

The Ohio State study on leadership behavior used similar methods and focused on two dimensions of leadership: initiating structure and consideration structure. **Initiating structure** looked at the leader's behavior in assigning *tasks*. It focused on leaders who assigned employees to specific tasks and asked them to follow standard rules and regulations. **Consideration structure** looked at establishing the *relationship* between the group and the leader. It focused on leaders who found time to listen to employees, were willing to make changes and were friendly and approachable. The Ohio study used these two variables—focus on task and focus on relationships—to develop a management quadrant describing leadership behavior.

initiating structure
looks at how leaders assign tasks.

consideration structure
looks at establishing the relationship between the group and the leader.

The Managerial Grid from a Leadership Perspective

Blake and Mouton developed their Managerial Grid from the studies done at Ohio State University and the Group Dynamics Leadership studies. Their classic Managerial Grid has been further developed into the Managerial/Leadership Grid, as summarized in Table 1.1.

Situational Leadership

Hersey and Blanchard (1977) in *Management and Organizational Behavior* took existing leadership theory a step further, contending that a style can be effective only when matched with the appropriate level of competence and commitment. They viewed leadership as an interplay between the amount of direction (task behavior) a leader gives, combined with the amount of relationship behavior a leader provides (the Managerial/Leadership Grid) *and* the readiness level that followers exhibit on a specific task the leader is attempting to accomplish through the individual or group.

Situational leadership specifies that initially workers need support and direction. As they become more task-ready, they need less direction and more support, to the point where even support can be reduced. The basic premise of situational leadership theory is that as the followers' readiness level in relation to task increases, leaders should lessen their direction or task behavior and simultaneously increase their relationship behavior. This would be the leaders' strategy until individuals or groups reach a moderate level of task-readiness.

As followers or groups move into an above-average level of readiness, leaders would decrease both their task behavior and their relationship behavior. At this point, followers would be ready from the task point of view and from the amount of relationship behavior they need. Once a follower or group reaches this level of readiness, close supervision is reduced and delegation is increased, indicating the leader's trust and confidence. Johnson (2009, p.37) advises, "The desire and ability to adjust is essential to success. Know your people. Discern what style works best within each unit and with each individual. Then tweak your leadership technique accordingly."

Transformational Leadership

The most recent form of leadership to be recognized is *transformational leadership*, which treats employees as the organization's most valuable asset. It is employee-centered and focused on empowerment. According to the Center for Leadership Studies (CLS): "Transformational leaders set high standards of conduct and become role models, gaining trust, respect and confidence from others; articulate the future desired state and a plan to achieve it; question the status quo and [are] continuously innovative, even at the peak of success; and energize people to achieve their full potential and performance."

An important aspect of transformational leadership is its employee orientation and how it seeks to empower people to make the fullest possible contribution to the organization. What is often lacking, however, is a model for effective *followership*. A leader cannot simply tell people they are empowered and expect them to instantly know how to perform. Employees need training, resources and authority if they are to be truly empowered.

As Bynum (2008, p.72) notes, "Transformational leadership theory is based on the principles of shared leadership, shared vision, and the continuing improvement of the individual." Briggs (2008, p.41) contends that the paramount element of transformational leadership is vision. Putting this vision into words and action is discussed in Chapter 3. At this point, consider the explanation of vision set forth by Vernon (2008a, p.59):

- Vision makes the future. It does not predict or anticipate the future, it creates it.
- Vision sets the standard, describing in detail the actions and qualities of behavior that will deliver desirable result.
- Vision describes uniqueness, what will make it stand out.
- Vision is idealistic and inspiring, calling its members to a noble, meaningful purpose.
- Vision is clarifying, giving specific direction like a roadmap or blueprint.
- Vision is challenging, motivating people to stretch beyond their comfort zone.
- Vision is not complex. It can be communicated simply yet is comprehensive enough to give clear direction and guidance.

Vernon concludes, "Authorities on the subject of leadership recognize that vision is one of the essential ingredients of being a successful leader."

The focus on leadership rather than management complements the move toward community policing and problem-solving policing because it stresses resolving problems rather than simply reacting to incidents. It encourages experimenting with new ways and allows honest mistakes to encourage creativity.

LEADERSHIP STYLES

Management literature has identified many leadership styles, several of which can be found in police organizations.

 Leadership styles include autocratic; consultative, democratic or participative; and laissez-faire.

Autocratic Leadership

autocratic leadership

managers make decisions without participant input; completely authoritative, showing little or no concern for subordinates.

Autocratic leadership is most frequently mentioned in connection with the past. Many early leaders inherited their positions. They were members of the aristocracy, and positions of leadership were passed down to family members through the centuries.

In early industrial production efforts, the boss was often a domineering figure. He (bosses were invariably men) was specifically chosen because he displayed traits associated with autocratic leadership. His authority was uncontested, and employees did what they were told out of fear. This style of management emerged in response to the demands of the Industrial Revolution, when masses of illiterate workers used expensive machinery and needed to follow explicit orders. Managers who used autocratic leadership made decisions without participant input. They were completely authoritative and showed little or no concern for subordinates. Rules were rules, without exception. This **mechanistic model** of management derived from the theories of Frederick Taylor (1856–1915), an American industrial engineer, sometimes referred to as the father of scientific management. This model divides jobs into highly

mechanistic model

divides tasks into highly specialized jobs where job holders become experts in their fields, demonstrating the "one best way" to perform their cog in the wheel (Taylorism); the opposite of the *organic model*.

specialized tasks where employees can become experts in their task. Taylor's influence on the organization of police departments is described in more detail in Chapter 2. Certain circumstances may call for autocratic leadership.

Consultative, Democratic or Participative Leadership

Consultative, democratic or participative leadership has been evolving since the 1930s and 1940s. Democratic leadership does not mean that every decision is made only after discussion and a vote. It means rather that management welcomes employees' ideas and input. Employees are encouraged to be innovative. Management development of a strong sense of individual achievement and responsibility is a necessary ingredient of participative or consultative leadership.

Democratic or participative managers are interested in their subordinates and their problems and welfare. Management still makes the final decisions but considers the input from employees. This leadership style is a good fit with the **organic model** of management: The model is flexible, participatory, democratic and science-based, and accommodates change. In contrast to the mechanistic model, which focuses on efficiency and productivity, the organic model focuses on worker satisfaction, flexibility and personal growth.

To better understand the differences between the mechanistic and organic leadership styles, compare the key concepts from each, summarized in Table 1.3.

Laissez-Faire Leadership

Laissez-faire leadership implies nonintervention and is almost a contradiction in terms. The idea is to let everything run itself without direction from the leader,

organic model

a flexible, participatory, science-based structure that will accommodate change; designed for effectiveness in serving the needs of citizens rather than the autocratic rationality of operation; the opposite of the *mechanistic model*.

TABLE 1.3 Authoritarian and Participatory Leadership Styles Compared

Authoritarian (Mechanistic) Style	Participatory (Organic) Style
Response to incidents	Problem solving
Individual effort and competitiveness	Teamwork
Professional expertise	Community orientation; ask customers what they want
Go by the "book"; decisions by emotion	Use data-based decision making
Tell subordinates	Ask and listen to employees
Boss as patriarch and order giver	Boss as coach and teacher
Maintain status quo	Create, innovate, experiment
Control and watch employees	Trust employees
Reliance on scientific investigation and technology rather than people	Reliance on skilled employees—a better resource than machines
When things go wrong, blame employees	Errors mean failed systems/processes—improve them
Organization is closed to outsiders	Organization is open

FIGURE 1.1
Continuum of
Leadership Styles

Source: Paul R. Timm.
Supervision, 2nd ed. St. Paul,
MN: West Publishing Company,
1992, p. 269

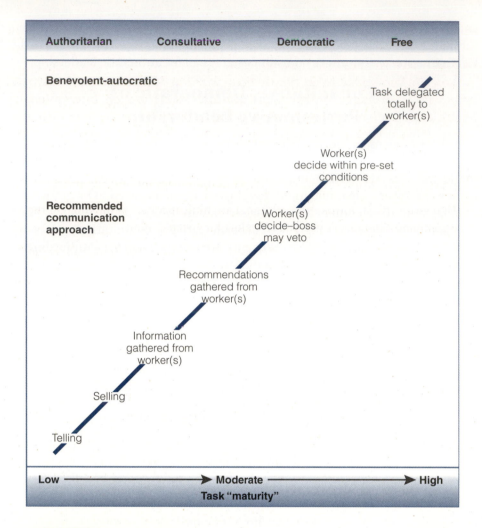

Authoritarian	Consultative	Democratic	Free

Benevolent-autocratic

Task delegated totally to worker(s)

Worker(s) decide within pre-set conditions

Recommended communication approach

Worker(s) decide–boss may veto

Recommendations gathered from worker(s)

Information gathered from worker(s)

Selling

Telling

Low ————————➤ Moderate ————————➤ High

Task "maturity"

who exerts little or no control. This style arises from the concept that employees are adults, should know as well as the manager what is right and wrong and will automatically do what is right for themselves and the organization.

Laissez-faire leaders want employees to be happy and believe that if employees are happy, they will be more productive. Employees *should* feel comfortable and good about their work, but this should be because they participate. Even when they participate, employees must still do the job and meet the organization's goals and objectives. Leaderless management, sometimes called free-rein leadership, may result in low morale, inefficiency, lack of discipline and low productivity. Figure 1.1 shows the continuum of leadership styles.

Implications

Research on leaders and leadership is abundant. Each theory offers something to the law enforcement manager. However, no one type of leader or leadership style will suffice in all situations. Leaders must often be autocratic in one situation and democratic or participatory in another. They must know when to make an immediate decision and when to make a decision only after input, discussion and consideration. Emergency situations rarely permit the opportunity for democratic or participatory decision making. Employees in nonemergency situations rarely respond well to autocratic leadership for routine task performance over the long term.

Leaders know what to do, how to do it, when to do it and with what type of employee, according to the demands of the individual situation. Internationally, leaders have been recognized because of the leadership abilities they displayed for a particular time, place and need. Put into another situation and time, they might not have become leaders. Regardless of the situation or time, Smith (2002) suggests several caveats related to leadership (Section II of this text presents many of these caveats in the context of management and supervision):

Use your wit to amuse not abuse. Laughing at others is hurtful. On the other hand, laughing at yourself is healing for you and others.

Acknowledge mistakes quickly and completely. The best leaders acknowledge their mistakes quickly, and take corrective actions to reduce the possibility of a similar mistake in the future.

Avoid "I don't trust you" phrases. Be careful about using phrases such as "I never want to be surprised," "Before you start anything, check with me first," and "When I am on the road, I will call in every morning for an update."

Welcome criticism. Understand that criticism and loyalty are mutually supporting.

Don't become a wind chime. Blowing with the wind by being politically agile will not gain you respect from those you lead.

Be a blame acceptor. If something goes wrong within your organization, be willing to accept the blame even though you personally may be only a tiny part of the failure.

Establish self-reinforcing relationships. Praise and support those who can move smoothly from competition to cooperation. The French have it right in their national motto: liberty, equality and *fraternity*.

Be a leader developer. A big part of leadership is mentorship. Help people develop their leadership skills. When these subordinates are promoted, they will be ready to take on the big job.

Find an anchor and hold on to it in the tough times. A spouse, children, friends, colleagues can help when you need advice, comfort, solace or support.

A PERSPECTIVE ON LEADERSHIP FROM THE BUSINESS WORLD

Jim Collins, whose book *Good to Great* (GTG) (2001) was on the best seller list for six years and has been translated into 29 languages, studied Fortune 500 companies to see if he could identify traits that separated the great companies and their executives from the lesser companies. He and his research team of 20 assistants spent 10.5 people-years researching these traits. His ideas aroused interest in the law enforcement community, the Police Executive

Research Forum (PERF) and its director, Chuck Wexler, who met with Collins to discuss adapting the research-based ideas further to fit law enforcement.

In 2005 PERF hosted, and the Office of Community Oriented Policing Services (COPS) sponsored, a conference on applying Collins' principles to law enforcement as well as to the public schools. The result was *From "Good to Great" Policing: Application of Business Management Principles in the Public Sector* (Wexler et al., 2007). Collins' findings will be discussed as they relate to topics discussed in this text. For now, consider a few of his key findings as they relate to attitude and leadership:

- Organizations do not become great because they are satisfied with being good.
- Greatness is not a function of circumstance. Greatness is largely a matter of conscious choice and discipline.
- Whether you prevail or fail depends more on what you do to yourself than on what the world does to you.
- Humility + will = a level 5 leader.

Collins defines "Level 5 leaders" as those capable of taking their organizations from good to great. Such leaders are "frantically driven, infected with an incurable need to produce results" (Wexler et al., 2007, p.5). Level 5 leaders were first and foremost ambitious, but their ambition was directed toward the company and its success, not to themselves. The Collins team found that Level 5 leaders did not exhibit large egos but rather were usually quiet and reserved, a paradoxical blend of personal humility and professional will.

Collins cautions that applying business principles to policing is fraught with challenges as the chief executive of a law enforcement agency does not measure "success" by profits and does not have the tight control of a CEO in the business world. In addition, activities in policing are very much in the public eye, unlike the inner workings of most businesses:

> Given the very public nature of policing and the high-visibility issues that police leaders must face, such as the use of force and the need for fairness in police officers' dealings with the citizens they serve, it can be argued that what police refer to as "command presence" is a critical trait. In fact, when a "defining moment" comes—a terrorism event or other catastrophe, a controversial police officer use of force, the killing of an officer, the kidnapping of a child—if a chief fails to rise to the occasion and speak in a very public, visible way, he risks losing credibility with the community and officers in his or her department. (Wexler et al., 2007, p.17)

Collins warns, "Good is the enemy of great." To make the transition to great, good leaders recognize that complacency can set in when things are going well.

LEADERSHIP TRAINING AND DEVELOPMENT

An appointment to fill a position on an organizational chart does not automatically make one a leader. By the same token, relatively few leaders are able to simply step into the role without needing to develop and refine their leadership skills and abilities.

The trend in the 21st century is to not tie leadership to rank, but rather to instill leadership qualities through the department, referred to as **dispersed leadership**. *Leadership in Police Organizations, Training Bulletin 2* (2005, p.1) describes the essentials of dispersed leadership:

- Shared understanding of what leadership means
- Commitment to shared goals and values
- Leaders at all levels of the organization
- Leaders leading differently at different organizational levels
- A way to develop leadership knowledge and skills throughout the organization
- A way to determine where you are as an organization and as individual leaders

The leader is developed through learned professional values, training and job experience over time. Leadership development perpetuates the mission, values and goals of the agency. Leadership training must develop character, technical skills and leadership knowledge and provide the chance to express this knowledge in ethically sound leadership behaviors. Figure 1.2 illustrates this leadership development system.

Leadership comes with the job of being a law enforcement officer, regardless of rank. In effect, all officers at all ranks are leaders at one time or another and need to have the appropriate skills. As the most visible form of government, people look to police for leadership. Every time a police officer puts on a uniform and goes into the field, people look to him or her for leadership.

Also of importance is developing new sergeants into leaders. They must be guided through the conversion from a law enforcement function to the role of supervisor and must learn to command as well as to delegate.

dispersed leadership

the 21st century trend to not tie leadership to rank, but rather to instill leadership qualities throughout the department.

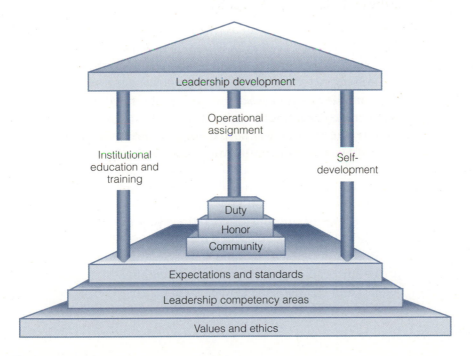

FIGURE 1.2
Leadership Development System

Source: DA PAM (Department of the Army Pamphlet) 350–358

Leaders who have adopted a specific leadership style can change that style through training. They can turn their weaknesses into strengths through studying, working with mentors or observing other leaders in action. Leaders are not born; they are developed. Task-oriented leaders can become people-oriented leaders. Changing leadership styles, however, is a slow, evolutionary process that can take years.

Leadership training before appointment is highly desirable. If that is not possible, it should happen soon after appointment. Each leader must be an individual, not a mirror image of the predecessor.

Leadership can be developed through comprehensive training programs, including participative management and team-building theory, motivational theory, communications and decision making.

COMMON LEADERSHIP ERRORS

Common management/leadership errors include preoccupation, indecisiveness, defending decisions made without full information and ignoring danger signs.

A subordinate who goes to the leader for a decision deserves the leader's undivided attention (Barlow, 2008, p.64). Giving less is rude, and making a decision when you are *preoccupied* makes it unlikely that the decision is given the thought it deserves.

Indecisiveness may result from preoccupation. Or it may be the result of lacking the courage to make a decision; this is what leaders are paid to do: "Strong leaders are willing to step up to the plate and make decisions. Many of them will be put in many situations where 'peer leaders' avoid making a decision. Unfortunately, by stepping up and making a decision for these peer leaders, strong leaders successfully allow them to disengage from their responsibilities. . . . Do not allow other leaders to force your hand to make decisions out of your area of responsibility" (Barlow, 2008, p.65).

Another common mistake is *defending a position without full information* or in a situation where circumstances have changed. If a leader takes a position that turns out to be bad for the organization, a simple admission of error can help the leader take a better position and gain the respect of others. *Ignoring danger signs* is yet another common mistake. Leaders may get so engrossed in the everyday minutiae of running organizations they forget the big picture. Barlow recommends that this can be avoided by adopting the concept of managing by walking around (MBWA) to know how things are functioning and to become aware of any problems that might be developing. Managers/leaders might also benefit from the following guidelines to improve their effectiveness.

GUIDELINES FOR EFFECTIVE MANAGEMENT AND LEADERSHIP

Several guidelines have been developed for effective management and leadership:

- Know your work and those you manage.
- Know how to get and maintain cooperation.
- Learn as much as possible about decision making.
- Learn as much as possible about how to be a leader.
- Learn how to give praise and constructive criticism.
- Learn to think positively; create rather than destroy.
- Learn to handle bad situations as well as good ones.
- Know when to discipline and when to be authoritarian or democratic/participatory.
- Help your employees improve themselves. Doing so will in turn improve you. Give them responsibility, tell them your expectations and provide instructions.
- Be honest with yourself and your officers. Expect honesty from them. Maintain integrity in yourself and demand it in others.
- Use your employees' abilities. They can provide new approaches to problems. Establish two-way communication to capture the vast amount of information contained within the group. Use participation to achieve greater acceptance of decisions.
- Do not oversupervise. Employees do not like managers constantly breathing down their necks.
- Remember that you are part of management, and never downgrade management or managers. If a problem exists, help solve it rather than creating a worse one.
- Keep your perception of your leadership abilities in line with subordinates' perceptions. Ask them what you can do better for them.
- If you call a meeting, make it worthwhile. Excessive meetings that provide a façade of participation are worse than no meetings. Every meeting should produce a result.
- Treat employees' mistakes as a teaching responsibility, not a punitive opportunity.
- Develop officers who differ with you, rather than clones. Develop officers who can compensate for your weaknesses. The tendency is to do the opposite.
- Be consistent. Be direct. Be honest. Be fair.
- Listen. Lead by example.
- Develop people skills.
- Be a risk taker.

MANAGEMENT AND LEADERSHIP— A CALL FOR CHANGE

Managers must pay attention to the new ideas and trends emerging from America's businesses: a commitment to people, the development of a people-oriented workplace and the belief that leadership can and does make a difference. Leadership in law enforcement historically depended on a strong, authoritarian chief. However, this style of leadership neglects everything known about people and their behavior. Coercion discourages creativity and risk taking and often causes people to rebel. President Eisenhower used to demonstrate this aspect of leadership with a simple piece of string. He would put the string on a table and say, "Pull it and it'll follow wherever you wish. Push it and it'll go nowhere at all." It is the same with people.

Although law enforcement is well known for being resistant to change, as futurist Alvin Toffler has said, "Change is not merely necessary to life. It is life." Managers must shift from telling and controlling the people they work with to developing and enhancing them. Managers must ask for subordinates' input before making critical decisions that affect them. Managers must also listen to their customers—the citizens—in new and more open ways. Managers must stop reacting to incidents and begin solving problems. They must permit risk taking and tolerate honest mistakes to encourage creativity and achieve innovation.

 ## SUMMARY

Basic management skills include technical skills, administrative skills, conceptual skills and people skills. Successful managers have clear goals, a commitment to excellence, feedback and support. Most successful managers are consistently self-confident and have a consistently positive attitude. Several management theories have evolved over time, yet no one style is more apt than another to achieve the department's mission. The selected style must match individual personalities.

Peter Drucker and W. Edwards Deming had a great influence on approaches to management in policing. Management by objectives (MBO) involves managers and subordinates setting goals and objectives together and then tracking performance to ensure that the objectives are met.

A basic difference between managers and leaders is that managers focus on tasks, whereas leaders focus on people. Manage things; lead people. Theories about leadership include the study of traits, the classic studies conducted at Michigan State and Ohio State universities, the Managerial/Leadership Grid, situational leadership and transformational leadership. Research has also identified several leadership styles, including autocratic; consultative, democratic or participative; and laissez-faire.

Leadership can be developed through comprehensive training programs, including participative management and team-building theory, motivational theory, communications and decision making. Common management/leadership errors include preoccupation, indecisiveness, defending decisions made without full information and ignoring danger signs.

CHALLENGE ONE

After five years as an officer, you were recently promoted to the rank of patrol sergeant by the new chief of the Greenfield Police Department. The chief tells you he is expanding the authority and responsibility of sergeants and is looking for strong leadership at the supervisor level. Many of the officers you are now supervising, including your old partner, have considerably more experience than you. Your old partner is a 20-year veteran and trained you as a rookie. You consider him a mentor and a good friend. You confided in each other when you had problems.

You were a popular officer and often attended social gatherings after your shift. You've declined several invitations since your promotion. Some officers are greeting you less cordially, and you hear talk that your promotion has changed you. Others openly wonder why your old partner was passed by for the promotion. Your old partner seems less friendly and sometimes questions your decisions at roll call. He often brings up things you did in the past and openly criticizes management.

1. The transition from officer to supervisor is difficult and sometimes isolating. Discuss some issues that complicate the transition.

2. What should you do as a new sergeant to prove to your officers that you haven't changed? Should you use your new authority to demand compliance and establish your position of authority over your old peers?

3. What is the best style of leadership for a new sergeant?

4. Do different situations require different leadership approaches?

5. Do different officers need different levels of direction and support?

DISCUSSION QUESTIONS

1. Who is a law enforcement manager?

2. What is the purpose of law enforcement management?

3. What does delegation mean? Can you delegate authority? Responsibility?

4. What changes do you foresee in law enforcement agencies management, supervision and leadership in the 21st century?

5. How do you develop yourself to be a law enforcement manager?

6. What is your definition of leadership?

7. What traits do you attribute to successful law enforcement leaders? If you had to select one most important characteristic of a law enforcement leader, which would you select?

8. Which style of leadership do you prefer? Which style do you perceive you use most of the time?

9. Of the common errors made by those who manage, supervise and lead, which has the potential for the most ill effects on a department?

10. What direction should law enforcement leaders take for the future?

11. What leadership traits do you possess? What leadership traits do you need to develop?

 REFERENCES

Barlow, Scott. "The 10 Deadly Errors of Leadership." *The Police Chief*, March 2008, pp. 64–67.

Blanchard, Ken. "Getting Back to Basics." *Today's Office*, January 1988, pp. 14, 19.

Borrello, Andrew. "In Defense of the Police Manager." *Law and Order*, March 2009, pp. 64–66.

Briggs, Douglas J. "Transformational Leadership as a Means to Ethical Behavior." *Minnesota Police Chief*, Spring 2008, pp. 40–41.

Bynum, Ray. "Transformational Leadership and Staff Training in the Law Enforcement Profession." *The Police Chief*, February 2008, pp. 72–81.

Collins, Jim. *Good to Great: Why Some Companies Make the Leap and Other's Don't*. New York: Harper Collins Publishers, 2001.

Deming, W. Edwards. *Quality, Productivity, and Competitive Position*. Cambridge, MA: Institute of Technology, Center for Advanced Engineering Study, 1982.

Field, Mark. "A Leader's Greatest Challenge." *Law and Order*, March 2009, pp. 62–63.

Glennon, Jim. "Inventories Can Be Managed, People Must Be Led." *PoliceOne.com*, October 5, 2009.

Gove, Tracey G. "Micromanagement: Dealing with RED PEN Supervisors." *The Police Chief*, August 2008, pp. 26–30.

Hersey, Paul, and Blanchard, Kenneth H. *Management of Organizational Behavior*, 3rd ed., Englewood Cliffs, NJ: Prentice Hall, 1977.

Johnson, Robert Roy. "Leadership Styles." *Law and Order*, 2009, pp. 36–37.

Leadership in Police Organizations, Training Bulletin #2. Washington, DC: International Association of Chief of Police and Community Oriented Policing Services Office, 2005, pp. 1–4.

Smith, Perry M. *Rules and Tools for Leaders*, Revised. New York: Penguin Group, 2002.

Vernon, Bob. "Do You Know Your Officers?" *Law Officer Magazine*, 2007a, p. 48.

Vernon, Bob. "Effective Leadership Requires Trust." *Law Officer Magazine*, August 2007b, pp. 66–68.

Vernon, Bob. "I Lead, Therefore I Follow." *Law Officer Magazine*, May 2007c, p. 128.

Vernon, Bob. "Developing Vision." *Law Officer Magazine*, December 2008a, pp. 58–59.

Vernon, Bob. "Humility in Leadership." *Law Officer Magazine*, 2008b, p. 42.

Vernon, Bob. "Changing Priorities." *Law Officer Magazine*, February 2009, p. 48.

Wexler, Chuck; Wycoff; Mary Ann; and Fischer, Craig. "'Good to Great' Policing: Application of Business Management Principles in the Public Sector." Washington, DC: Community Oriented Policing Services and the Police Executive Research Forum, 2007.

The Organization and Structure of American Policing

Good organizations are living bodies that grow new muscles to meet challenges.

—Robert Townsend
Corporate consultant

DO YOU KNOW?

- How law enforcement agencies were traditionally organized?
- What line and staff personnel are?
- What advantages and disadvantages are associated with specialization?
- What the chain of command does?
- What type of organization law enforcement managers should recognize?
- What the emerging law enforcement organization looks like?
- What five broad strategic or organizational approaches currently operate in contemporary policing?
- What community policing is?
- How traditional and community policing differ?
- What the two critical key elements of community policing are?
- If the core functions of policing change when community policing is implemented?
- What problem solving requires of the police?
- What the four principles of CompStat are?
- What the 3-I model of intelligence-led policing illustrates?
- Who may be important partners in evidence-based policing?
- What role failure plays in evidence-based policing?

CAN YOU DEFINE?

administrative services	integrated patrol
bifurcated society	intelligence-led policing
broken-window theory	line personnel
chain of command	paradigm
channels of communication	paradigm shift
community policing	proactive
CompStat policing	problem-solving policing
decentralization	pyramid of authority
evidence-based policing	reactive
field operations	staff personnel
field services	social capital
flat organization	span of control
fusion center	transactional change
hierarchy	transformational change
incident	unity of command
incivilities	working in "silos"

INTRODUCTION

An *organization* is an artificial structure created to coordinate either people or groups and resources to achieve a mission or goal. Organizations exist for many different reasons. One important reason is synergy and the concept that a group can accomplish, through teamwork, tasks and objectives that an individual could never do alone. For example, no single individual could have put a person on the moon, but an organization— the National Aeronautics and Space Administration (NASA)—was successful.

The need for organizing has been recognized for centuries. Since recorded time people have banded together into societies. Within these societies they have sought ways to protect themselves from nature and from those who would harm them or their possessions. They made rules, set up ways to enforce these rules and provided swift punishment to those who did not obey.

Law enforcement agencies provide their services to the political entity from which they derive their authority and responsibility. Providing services is their sole reason for existence. It is highly likely that newly created municipalities would expect *someone* to respond to their needs for the many services provided by police. Americans have come to expect and demand reasonably safe communities, so they demand law enforcement organizations. As such organizations develop, they resemble those already in existence in other communities because tradition and experience are enduring. Further, most present-day law enforcement managers inherited their organizations when they assumed their positions.

CHAPTER at a GLANCE

This chapter begins by describing the traditional formal law enforcement organization with which most citizens are familiar, including line and staff personnel, generalists and specialists and the typical hierarchy of authority. This is followed by a discussion of the informal organization as well as the emerging law enforcement agency. Next the approaches currently being used in law enforcement agencies along with traditional policing following the terrorist attacks of 9/11 are described. These include community policing, problem-solving policing, CompStat policing, intelligence-led policing and evidence-based policing. The chapter concludes with a look at the impact of contemporary policing approaches on the new supervisor or manager.

THE TRADITIONAL LAW ENFORCEMENT ORGANIZATION

The traditional organization of American law enforcement was greatly influenced by Sir Robert Peel (1788–1850), often called the "Father of Modern Policing," and included the following: Police must be stable, efficient and organized militarily. Police must be under governmental control. The deployment of police strength by both time and area is essential. Police headquarters should be centrally located and easily accessible. The test of police effectiveness is the absence of crime and disorder, not the visible evidence of police activity in dealing with these problems.

Also influential on American law enforcement was Max Weber (1864–1920), a German sociologist and economist, who helped establish the foundations of modern sociology. He considered bureaucracy to be the most important feature of modern society. Weber believed that business was conducted from a desk or office by preparing and dispatching written documents through an elaborate hierarchical division of labor directed by explicit rules impersonally applied. These rules were meant to design and regulate the whole organization on the basis of technical knowledge with the aim of achieving maximum efficiency. According to Weber one of the most fundamental features of bureaucracy was a highly developed division of labor and specialization of tasks. This was achieved by a precise, detailed definition of the duties and responsibilities of each position.

© Bettmann/CORBIS

New York City police officers in front of the 20th Precinct Station during the 1880s.

Also influential and living in the same period was Frederick W. Taylor (1856–1915), an American industrial engineer who is sometimes referred to as the father of scientific management. Taylor suggested that production efficiency in a shop or factory could be greatly enhanced by observing individual workers and eliminating wasted time and motion. The impact of his time and motion studies on mass production was immense, but they fostered resentment and opposition from labor. Taylor's book, *The Principles of Scientific Management* (1911), called for a small span of control, a clear chain of command, a tall organizational hierarchy and centralized decision making modeled after the military. These influences are visible in the traditional law enforcement organization.

 The traditional law enforcement organizational design is that of a pyramid-shaped hierarchy based on a military model.

Many have perpetuated the traditional organization, diagrammed in Figure 2.1, because it has worked.

Pre–World War II law enforcement agencies followed the industry pattern by placing maximum emphasis on the job and minimum attention on the human interrelationships of people filling the positions. Rigid rules and regulations were used excessively, along with frequent use and abuse of the threat of job loss. Individual needs were almost entirely ignored. Early law enforcement management was characterized by the general attitude of, "If you don't like the job, plenty of others want it."

Law enforcement organizations were simple. The typical **pyramid of authority** predominated with its **hierarchy** of authoritative management. Command officers and supervisors had complete authority over subordinates, and there was little opportunity for departmental appeal except through the courts. Communication flowed downward. Little or no specialization existed,

---

pyramid of authority

the shape of the typical law enforcement hierarchy, with the chief at the peak and having full authority, down through managers (captains and lieutenants) and supervisors (sergeants), to those who accomplish most of the tasks (officers).

hierarchy

a group of people organized or classified by rank and authority. In law enforcement, typically pyramid shaped with a single "authority" at the top expanding down and out through the ranks to the broad base of "workers."

FIGURE 2.1 The Traditional Law Enforcement Organization

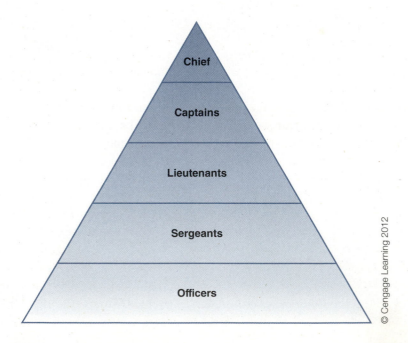

© Cengage Learning 2012

and training was nonexistent or minimal. Selection was based largely on physical qualifications, and most applicants had military experience.

Most personnel were assigned to foot patrol. Police radio communications systems and other technology were virtually nonexistent. University- or college-level training, training programs and even courses were unheard of. Ten-hour days and six-day weeks were common, accompanied by extremely low salaries. Flexibility was nonexistent, and fringe benefits were few. However, the law enforcement organization has evolved considerably

THE FORMAL ORGANIZATION

The *formal organization* is put together by design and rational plan. The essential elements of a formal organization are

- A clear statement of mission, goals, objectives and values (as discussed previously).
- A division of labor among specialists.
- A rational organization or design.
- A hierarchy of authority and responsibility.

Typical Divisions in Law Enforcement Agencies

Law enforcement agencies typically are divided into field and administrative services, with personnel designated as line and staff personnel.

 Field services, also called **field operations**, use **line personnel** to *directly* help accomplish the goals of the department. **Administrative services** use **staff personnel** to *support* the line organization.

Field operations' main division is the uniformed patrol. Larger agencies may have other divisions as well, such as investigations, narcotics, vice and juvenile. Line personnel fulfill the goals and objectives of the organization. This is what most people think of as law enforcement—the uniformed police officer on the street.

Field operations divisions are typically further broken into shifts to provide service within a framework of geographical space and extended time. Continuity of service must be provided between areas and shifts. Larger departments may divide the political entity they serve into distinct *precincts* or *patrol districts*, the geographical areas served by a given portion of the officers, essentially forming a number of smaller organizations subject to overall administration and operational command. Time traditionally was divided into three 8-hour shifts; today, however, it is fairly common for departments to use 10- or even 12-hours shifts, with some using a combination of 8-, 10- and 12-hour shifts. However a department structures its shifts, the point is that it does so to provide services continuously. Officers frequently rotate through these shifts. Personnel assigned to specific divisions and shifts vary depending on the community's size and service needs.

field services

directly help accomplish the goals of the department using line personnel; main division is uniformed patrol; also includes investigations, narcotics, vice, juvenile and the like.

line personnel

those who actually perform most of the tasks outlined in the work plan.

administrative services

supports those performing field services; includes recruitment and training, records and communication, planning and research and technical services.

staff personnel

those who support line personnel.

Administrative services, which are usually centralized, include recruitment and training, records and communications, planning and research and technical services. Staff personnel assist line personnel, including supervisors. The laboratory staff, for example, assists line personnel, acting as liaisons, specialists or advisory personnel. They are technical experts who provide specialized information. Legal staffs (city, county or district attorneys) act as legal advisors to all members of the agency.

Conflicts can and do arise between line and staff, particularly when staff attempts to act in a capacity beyond advisory or informational. Both line and staff are necessary components of the law enforcement organization. They must, however, be coordinated and controlled to achieve department goals.

Division of Labor: Generalists and Specialists

Law enforcement agencies, despite their organizational hierarchy, are basically decentralized units, with most decisions made at the level of patrol and investigations and that of the first-line supervisor. Even the authority to arrest is made at the lowest level of the organization. Most arrests are made by patrol officers, detectives and juvenile officers.

Law enforcement agencies cannot function without division of work and, often, specialization. Neither can they function without maximum coordination of these generalists and specialists. As the organization grows in size, specialization develops to meet the community's needs. The extent of specialization is a management decision.

Specialization occurs when the organizational structure is divided into units with specific tasks to perform. The patrol unit is assigned the majority of personnel and provides the greatest variety of tasks and services. Even though specialized units may be formed, the patrol unit often still performs some of these specialized units' tasks.

For example, patrol officers may investigate a crime scene up to the point at which they must leave their shift or area to continue the investigation. Or they may investigate only to the point of protecting the scene and keeping witnesses present or immediately arresting a suspect. At this point they may complete their report on tasks performed relating to the specific crime and either turn it over to another shift of patrol officers (other generalists) or to the investigative unit (specialists). Regardless of the division of tasks performed by generalist or specialist units, close communication about incidents must occur or problems develop.

Specialization creates a potential for substantially increased levels of expertise, creativity and innovation. The more completely an employee can perform a task or set of tasks, the more job satisfaction the employee will experience. When specialization is not practical, people must understand why the division of labor is necessary. It must also be clear where patrol's responsibility ends and that of the investigative unit begins.

The greater the specialization, necessary as it is, the greater the difficulties of coordination, communication, control and employee relationships. Conflicts and jealousies may arise, including an attitude of "Let the expert do it if he or she is going to get the credit."

Officers in a small agency must perform all tasks. They cannot afford the luxury of specialization. However, with more standardized training requirements and accreditation, all officers should, theoretically, achieve similar backgrounds for performing tasks, regardless of the size of the agency, although in reality, such training often lags many years behind when it should be attained, or it is lacking entirely. The major difference between small and large agencies is the frequency of opportunity presented to officers regarding specialization.

> **Specialization can enhance a department's effectiveness and efficiency, but overspecialization can impede the organizational purpose.**

Overspecialization fragments the opportunity to achieve the organizational purpose of providing courteous, competent, expeditious law enforcement services. The more specialized an agency becomes, the more attention must be paid to interrelationships and coordination.

The Hierarchy of Authority

The structure of most police departments, as noted, has traditionally been a semi-military, pyramid-shaped hierarchy with authority flowing from the narrow apex down to the broad base. This hierarchical pyramid is often graphically represented in an organizational chart.

An organizational chart visually depicts how personnel are organized within an agency and might illustrate how the agency fits into the community's political structure. Figure 2.2 shows the organization of the Owatonna (Minnesota) Police Department. This is typical of how police departments are organized in smaller cities.

The figure also shows how the police department fits into the city's organizational structure. This formal organization is generally supported in writing by rules and regulations, department operational manuals and job descriptions. All provide control and a foundation from which actions can be taken.

The larger the agency and the jurisdiction it serves, the more complex the organization and the chart depicting it. Figure 2.3, a chart of the Minneapolis (Minnesota) Police Department, shows how a large police department is organized.

Chain of Command

The **chain of command** is the order of authority. It begins at the top of the pyramid with the chief or sheriff and flows downward through the commissioned ranks in the agency—from deputy chief to captain to lieutenant to sergeant and finally to the patrol officer.

chain of command
the order of authority; begins at the top of the pyramid and flows down to the base.

> **The chain of command establishes definite lines of authority and channels of communication.**

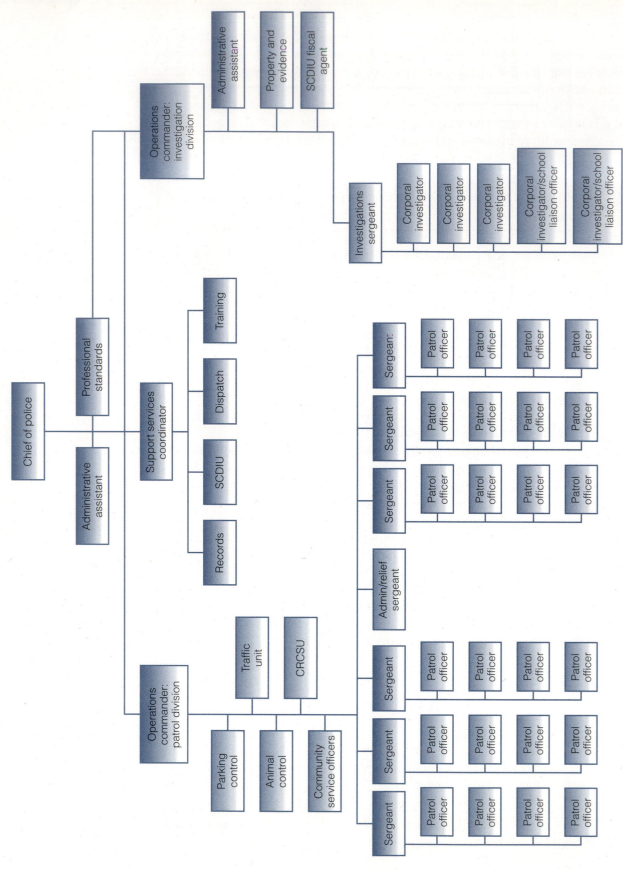

FIGURE 2.2 A Smaller Department Organizational Chart

Source: Shaun LaDue, Owatonna (Minnesota) Police Department

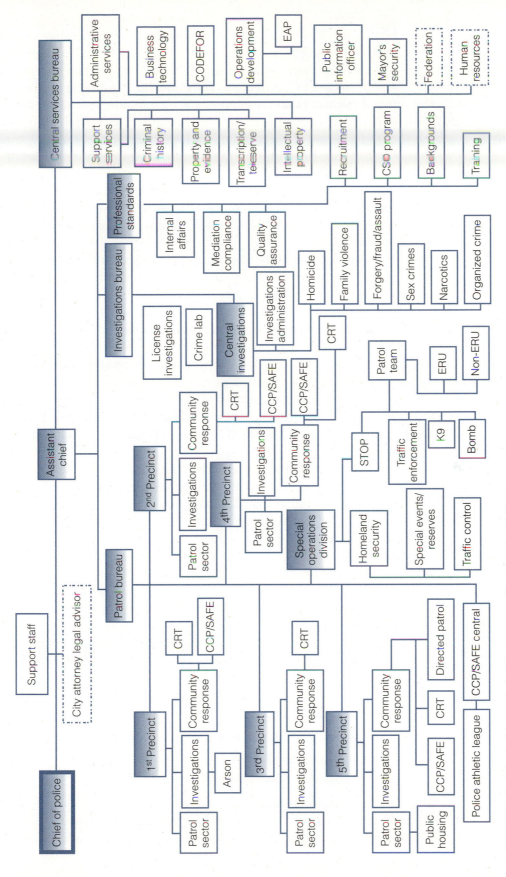

FIGURE 2.3 A Typical Large Police Department Organizational Chart

Source: Courtesy of the Minneapolis (Minnesota) Police Department

channels of communication

the official paths through which orders flow from management to personnel who carry out the orders; usually follow the chain of command.

unity of command

means that every individual in the organization has only one immediate superior or supervisor.

span of control

how many people one individual manages or supervises.

Each level must forward communications to the next higher or lower level. **Channels of communication** are the official paths through which orders flow from management to personnel who carry out the orders. Most companies set up these channels carefully and for good reasons. They are the "highways" for orders and communications to follow and keep everyone aware of events. They coordinate the organization into a whole, integrated unit instead of a series of parts. When an individual leaves these channels and takes a shortcut, he or she is apt to run into problems. For example, a patrol officer who takes a complaint directly to the chief rather than to the sergeant would probably fall out of favor in the department. Sometimes in law enforcement work, however, emergencies exist that cannot wait for information to be sent through the expected channels. This is one of the challenges of police work.

Another important part of the organizational design is **unity of command**, a construct that means every individual in the organization has only one immediate superior or supervisor. Unity of command is extremely important and needs to be ensured in most instances. Each individual, unit and situation should be under the control of one—and only one—person.

Yet another factor in most law enforcement organizations is the number of people one individual manages or supervises. The **span of control** refers to the number of people or units supervised by one manager. The span of control depends on the department's size, the supervisors' and subordinates' abilities, crime rates, community expectations and the political environment. Often the greater the span of control, the less effective the management or supervision.

However, technological advances involving communications with personnel in the field, higher levels of education and training and the extent of the empowerment and flattening of the organization may allow managers to increase their span of control and remain effective. Do not confuse span of control with how many people one person has authority over. The chief, for example, has authority over everyone in the department, but the chief's span of control extends to only those who report directly to him or her.

The span of control must be realistic. If too few people report to a manager, that manager may not be operating at optimum efficiency or effectiveness as a manager. If too many people report to a manager, that manager cannot do a good job with all of them. Within a law enforcement agency, the more levels in the pyramid, the smaller the span of control. A number of factors must be considered:

- Distance in space and time between manager and subordinate
- Difficulty of tasks performed
- Types of assistance available to the manager
- Amount of direction subordinates need
- Extent of subordinates' skill and experience

Each factor must be considered as personnel are assigned.

The formal organization groups people by task and responsibility and clearly delineates the chain of command and channels of communication.

As important as the formal organization of a police department is, as in any group, an informal structure also exists. The informal organization exists side-by-side with this formal organization and may be a truer representation of the way the department actually functions.

THE INFORMAL ORGANIZATION

Within any organization some people may emerge as leaders, regardless of whether they are in leadership positions. In addition, within any organization people will form their own groups—people who enjoy being together and perhaps working together.

 Managers should recognize the informal organization that exists within any law enforcement agency.

The *informal organization* operates without official sanctions, but it influences the agency's performance. It may help or harm the agency's goals, and it may support the organization or cause dissention.

Inasmuch as informal organizations are going to exist regardless of whether the supervisor likes them, it might be wise to view them as a positive force and use them to facilitate the department's work. This can be done by thinking of the informal leader not as a ringleader but as a person "in on things," one whose informal network can benefit the whole group.

THE EMERGING LAW ENFORCEMENT ORGANIZATION

Business and industry are undergoing sweeping changes in organization and management styles to remain competitive. Law enforcement agencies are also facing the need for change to meet the competition of private policing. Harr and Hess (2010) report that private security has become a "major player" in safeguarding Americans and their property. For example, as our elderly and business populations continue to occupy high-rise condominiums and office buildings, the reliance on private security will also increase, as law enforcement cannot practically be expected to patrol such structures.

Police departments and other law enforcement agencies must also compete with private security organizations for the bright, young college graduates entering the work force. No longer will law enforcement agencies be recruiting a majority of candidates with a military background. Instead agencies will be recruiting college graduates who will not accept authority blindly. Other changes are also evident in police departments across the country.

 The emerging law enforcement agency has a flattened organization, is decentralized and empowers its employees.

A Flattened Organization

flat organization
one with fewer lieutenants and captains, fewer staff departments, fewer staff assistants, more sergeants, and more patrol officers.

Like businesses, for the sake of efficiency, many police departments are turning to a **flat organization**, one with fewer lieutenants and captains, fewer staff departments, fewer staff assistants, more sergeants and more patrol officers. Typical pyramid organization charts will have the top pushed down and the sides expanded at the base.

Top-heavy organizational structures are no longer tolerated in business. Progressive firms are flattening their structure, restructuring top-heavy organizations and pushing authority and decision making as low as possible. Accompanying this change in organizational structure is decentralization.

A Decentralized Organization

decentralization
encourages flattening of the organization and places decision-making authority and autonomy at the level where information is plentiful; in police organizations, this is usually at the level of the patrol officer.

Successful businesses concentrate on soliciting ideas from everyone in their organizations about every facet of their operations. This approach can be applied to policing, especially in larger departments. **Decentralization** generally refers to a department's organizational structure and operations: It encourages flattening of the organization and places decision making at the level where information is plentiful, usually at the level of the patrol officer. Flattened, decentralized organizations empower line personnel.

Decentralization frees managers from spending all their time and intellectual energy on day-to-day operational matters, allowing them to concentrate more on strategies to improve the organization's capabilities to perform. Decentralization also improves operational decisions because they are made by those closest to the situation and challenges more people to be creative and take responsibility for the problems in their area. A likely result of decentralization is that officers will feel empowered.

Change Revisited

Some readers may be thinking, "If it ain't broke, don't fix it. What's wrong with the way the law enforcement agencies are organized? They have worked fine for the past 200 years." The short answer is, our society, and the world in which we exist, is significantly different than that of previous generations. Law enforcement must now deal with disruptive social, demographic and technological changes. America is growing increasingly diverse, with more minorities and more elderly people. Immigrants, legal and illegal, are streaming into our country. People with disabilities have entered into mainstream America following the passage of the Americans with Disabilities Act, and thousands of mentally ill people have been released from institutions, often becoming homeless. In addition, America is becoming a **bifurcated society** with more wealth, more poverty and a shrinking middle class. The gap between the "haves" and the "have nots" is widening. Other social and cultural changes include the weakening influence of family, church and school.

bifurcated society
a society in which the gap between the "haves" and the "have nots" is wide—that is, there are many poor people, many wealthy people and a shrinking middle class.

Personnel within police departments has also changed with newer generations having different views of what is important and representing more women and greater ethnic diversity. The laws police enforce have also changed, mostly in favor of criminals and against the police. Technology is revolutionizing law enforcement, affecting everything from crime scene investigations to law enforcement gear, weapons and police vehicles. Technology has a significant impact on supervisors' and managers' effectiveness. For example, scheduling has become an art in and of itself in law enforcement, particularly because of unions and increasing union rules. The dynamics of an organization is that if it is trying to be proactive and progressive, those leading it need to embrace technology.

Finally, the inability of law enforcement to win the "wars" on drugs and terrorism has shown that the police cannot fight crime and disorder by themselves. They need the help of the citizens within their jurisdiction. This need has become even greater after the tragic events of September 11, 2001. The fear and risk of terrorism affects all Americans. Combating this heightened threat to our national security requires a combined effort. The challenges facing law enforcement and our entire country necessitate reexamining our public organizations, including law enforcement.

These changes may require a **paradigm shift**, a dramatic change in how some basic structures are viewed. A **paradigm** is a model, theory or frame of reference. For example, in the early beginnings of our country, we were an agricultural society. The Industrial Revolution dramatically changed how we viewed our society. We have since shifted to an information-based society. Likewise, law enforcement appears to be undergoing a paradigm shift from an emphasis on crime fighting to an emphasis on order maintenance and peace keeping.

Law enforcement managers at all levels must reexamine past assumptions, consider future projections and think very carefully about the future of policing, law enforcement and the entire criminal justice system.

> **paradigm shift**
> a dramatic change in how some basic structure is viewed.

> **paradigm**
> a model, theory or frame of reference.

POST–9/11 POLICING

Schafer et al. (2009, p.263) studied the impact of September 11, 2001, on small municipal agencies and found that although homeland security has been the focus of ample rhetoric since the terrorist attacks, empirical research on actual effects has been lacking. They studied perceptions of risk, engagement in preparatory measures and perception of response capacities in Illinois and found only modest improvements in homeland security innovation in small departments in the first six years after 9/11: "Small agencies perceived their risk of a terrorist attack to be low. Whether the limited innovation was a function of minimal perception of risk is difficult to disentangle with cross-sectional data. Agencies reported struggling to secure training, equipment and other resources to enhance homeland security efforts, though open comments suggested variation in whether this was actually a cause for concern for agency representatives. When considered in light of extant literature on small police agencies, the findings suggest little has changed in the policing of Mayberry post-9/11" (pp.282–283).

Marks and Sun (2007) also studied the impact of 9/11 on organizational development among state and local law enforcement agencies and found, "Changes in internal structures, such as the creation of a counterterrorism unit, tend to occur only in larger metropolitan and state police agencies. Changes in organizational processes or operations tend to be far more universal and typically involve an increased collaboration among police departments, specifically greater openness toward information sharing" (p.159).

transactional change

various features of an organization may be altered, but the core framework is untouched; this evolutionary change intervenes in structure, management practices, and motivations.

transformational change

intervenes in an organization's mission, culture and leadership style.

Marks and Sun (2007, p.161) describe two types of change: transactional change and transformational change. In **transactional change** various features of an organization may be altered, but the core framework is untouched. This evolutionary change intervenes in structure, management practices and motivations—for example, creating a drug task force to deal with drug trafficking. The change is on the organization's periphery, unlikely to affect the organization's mission and culture.

Transformational change, in contrast, intervenes in an organization's mission, culture and leadership style. Marks and Sun's analysis following 9/11 found that "virtually all" of the organizational changes were transactional, perhaps because it is easier to change departmental policies and practices than to change deeply embedded cultures (2007, p.170). Another reason might be that changes in policing do not seem to occur unless the general public decides change is needed and supports such change. Often this change is sought when a critical incident or major event takes place. For example, "In the case of 9/11, the majority of the fault seems to have been placed on federal agencies, such as the FBI and CIA, for not preventing the attacks. Consequently, this may be why the majority of organizational change has occurred among these federal agencies and not the state and local police departments" (p.170).

In September 2009, the National Institute of Justice (NIJ) and the Harvard Kennedy School again held an Executive Session on Policing and Public Safety, offering *New Perspectives in Policing* (Sparrow, 2009). This session focused on five broad strategic or organizational approaches currently found in post-9/11 policing.

 Five broad strategic or organizational approaches currently operating in contemporary policing are community policing, problem-solving policing, CompStat policing, intelligence-led policing and evidence-based policing.

Sparrow (2009, pp.1–2) notes, "Police departments across the United States vary in how many of these approaches they have embraced and which ones. Moreover, implementations of any one of these strategies vary enormously from jurisdiction to jurisdiction and over time. As implementations mature, they tend to become more versatile and better adapted to local circumstances, departing from more standardized models originally imported or copied from other jurisdictions."

The impact of 9/11 on the organizational development of state and local law enforcement agencies resulted in a renewed focus on community policing and problem-solving policing as well as on other data-driven models. The overlap and interplay of these approaches is apparent, yet each approach offers its own contribution to policing and challenges to those who manage and lead within their agencies.

COMMUNITY POLICING

The September 11, 2001, terrorist attacks on America, while unquestionably horrific and devastating, had a positive effect by bringing even the most diverse, fragmented communities together in ways rarely seen before. The government's appeal to the nation's public to become "soldiers" in the effort to preserve our American way of life and to be increasingly vigilant about activities occurring in neighborhoods is a direct application of the community policing philosophy. All citizens are made to feel they have an important part to play, an implicit responsibility, in keeping themselves, their communities and their country safe from harm.

Community policing often operates side by side with traditional policing. Connell et al. (2008, pp.127–128) contend, "Community policing has been a dominant innovation in American policing for the past two decades. Scholars and police practitioners alike acknowledge the increasing influence of a community-oriented approach to policing."

Community policing is a philosophy that promotes "organization strategies, which supports the systematic use of partnership and problem solving techniques to proactively address the immediate conditions that give rise to public safety issues, such as crime, social disorder and fear of crime" (*Community Policing Defined*, 2009).

community policing

decentralized model of policing in which individual officers exercise their own initiatives and citizens become actively involved in making their neighborhoods safer; this proactive approach usually includes increased emphasis on foot patrol.

Several principles set forth by Peel foreshadowed community policing: "The duty of the police is to prevent crime and disorder. The power of the police to fulfill these duties is dependent on public approval and on their ability to secure and maintain public respect. The police should strive to maintain a relationship with the public that gives reality to the tradition that *the police are the public and the public are the police*."

As O. W. Wilson wrote in *Police Administration* (1950, p.420), "The active interest and participation of individual citizens and groups is so vital to the success of most police programs that the police should deliberately seek to

The majority of police work involves nonenforcement activities, including the provision of services such as giving information, working with neglected and abused children and providing community education programs on crime prevention, drug abuse, safety and the like. Here, an Austin, Texas, police officer distributes antidrug literature to kids.

© Larry Kolvoord/The Image Works

arouse, promote and maintain an active public concern in their affairs." Police officers must understand and be a part of this defined community if they are to fulfill their mission.

Community also refers to a feeling of belonging—a sense of integration, shared values and "we-ness." Where integrated communities exist, people share a sense of ownership and pride in their environment. They also have a sense of what is acceptable behavior, which makes policing in such a community much easier. Research strongly suggests that a sense of community is the "glue" that binds communities to maintain order and provides the foundation for effective community action. This is often referred to as social capital.

Social capital, is defined by Coleman (1990, p.302), who developed this concept, as "a variety of different entities having two characteristics in common: They all consist of some aspect of a social structure, and they facilitate certain actions of individuals who are within the structure." Coleman saw the two most important elements in social capital as being (1) trustworthiness, that is, citizens' trust of each other and their public institutions, and (2) obligations, that is, expectation that service to each other will be reciprocated.

Social capital exists at two levels: local and public. *Local social capital* is the bond among family members and their immediate, informal groups. *Public social capital* refers to the networks tying individuals to broader community institutions such as schools, civic organizations, churches and the like, as well as to networks linking individuals to various levels of government—including the police.

If citizens perceive low levels of physical disorder, they will feel safer. If citizens feel safe and trust one another, social capital is heightened. The higher the levels of public social capital are, the higher the levels of collective action will be. Adequate levels of social capital are required for community policing to work. Unfortunately, the communities that most need community policing are often the ones with the lowest levels of social capital.

Sociologists have been describing for decades either the loss or the breakdown of "community" in modern, technological, industrial, urban societies such as ours. Proponents of community policing in some areas may be missing a major sociological reality—the absence of "community"—in the midst of all the optimism about police playing a greater role in encouraging it. This absence of community is reflected in the broken-window theory set forth in a classic article by Wilson and Kelling (1982, p.31):

> Social psychologists and police officers tend to agree that if a window in a building is broken and is left unrepaired, all the rest of the windows will soon be broken. This is as true in nice neighborhoods as in run-down ones. Window-breaking does not necessarily occur on a large scale because some areas are inhabited by determined window-breakers whereas others are populated by window-lovers; rather, one unrepaired broken window is a signal that no one cares, and so breaking more windows costs nothing. (It has always been fun.)

The **broken-window theory** suggests that if it appears "no one cares," disorder and crime will thrive. Broken windows and smashed cars are very visible signs of people not caring about their community. Other more subtle signs include unmowed lawns, piles of accumulated trash, litter, graffiti, abandoned

social capital
a concept to describe the level or degree of social structure within a community and the extent to which individuals within the community feel bonded to each other. Exists at two levels (local and public) and can be measured by *trustworthiness*, or citizens' trust of each other and their public institutions and by *obligations*, or by the expectation that service to each other will be reciprocated.

broken-window theory
suggests that if it appears "no one cares," disorder and crime will thrive.

© Bob Daemmrich/The Image Works

One of the most common strategies used in implementing community policing involves getting neighborhood residents to organize for a common purpose. Here, concerned Neighborhood Watch citizens in Austin, Texas, meet with police regarding crime, drugs and gangs in their community.

buildings, rowdiness, drunkenness, fighting and prostitution, often referred to as **incivilities**. Incivilities and social disorder occur when social control mechanisms have eroded. Increases in incivilities may increase the fear of crime and reduce citizens' sense of safety, causing people to physically or psychologically withdraw and isolate themselves from their neighbors. Or increased incivilities and disorder may bring people together to "take back the neighborhood."

incivilities
signs of disorder.

Traditional and Community Policing Compared

Traditional policing is **reactive**, focusing on fighting crime and measuring effectiveness by arrest rates. A tenet of traditional policing is that crime is a police problem. In contrast, community policing is **proactive**, focusing on community problems and measuring effectiveness on the absence of crime and disorder. A tenet of community policing is that crime is everyone's problem.

reactive
simply responding to calls for service.

proactive
recognizing problems and seeking the underlying cause(s) of the problems.

Table 2.1 summarizes the differences between these two approaches to policing.

Reactive policing has a long-standing tradition. Community policing does not imply that officers will not respond to calls, just that they may respond differently. In addition, community policing is not "soft" on crime. Scheider (2008) clarifies,

Those who claim that community policing is soft on crime should ask themselves what is the ultimate goal of policing—to arrest offenders, or to reduce crime and social disorder problems and enhance trust in police? Of course,

TABLE 2.1 Comparison of Traditional Policing and Community Policing

Question	Traditional Policing	Community Policing
Who are the police?	A government agency principally responsible for law enforcement.	Police are the public and the public are the police; the police officers are those who are paid to give full-time attention to the duties of every citizen.
What is the role of the police?	Focusing on solving crimes.	A broader problem-solving approach.
How is police efficiency measured?	By detection and arrest rates.	By the absence of crime and disorder.
What are the highest priorities?	Crimes that are high value and those involving violence.	Whatever problems disturb the community most.
What, specifically, do police deal with?	Incidents.	Citizens' problems and concerns.
What determines the effectiveness of police?	Response times.	Public cooperation.
What view do police take of service calls?	Deal with them only if there is no real police work to do.	Vital function and great opportunity.
What is police professionalism?	Swift, effective response to serious crime.	Keeping close to the community.
What kind of intelligence is most important?	Crime intelligence (study of particular crimes or series of crimes).	Criminal intelligence (information about the activities of individuals or groups).
What is the essential nature of police accountability?	Highly centralized; governed by rules, regulations and policy directives; accountable to the law.	Emphasis on local accountability to community needs.

Source: Malcolm K. Sparrow. *Implementing Community Policing.* U.S. Department of Justice, National Institute of Justice, November 1988, pp.8–9.

most efforts to reduce crime and social disorder problems will involve arresting offenders (particularly high-volume repeat offenders) and arrests will always be an important and central function for police agencies; however, arrests in and of themselves should not be confused with the ultimate public safety and public satisfaction goals of policing. By calling for more strategic enforcement, by improving the understanding of crime and of the effectiveness of responses, by bringing in the resources of partners, and by developing innovative responses, community policing is not soft on crime, but rather, brings far tougher and smarter solutions.

Kelling (2009, pp.1, 3) also addresses the question of how to measure policing effectiveness, asserting, "You measure by the absence of crime and disorder, not by the numbers of arrests or police actions. . . . It is absolutely essential that we maintain community policing values as we face the coming [economic] crisis."

 The two key elements of community policing are partnerships and problem solving.

Partnerships

Partnerships are a cornerstone of community policing. Traditional policing expected the community members to remain in the background. Crime and disorder were viewed as police matters, best left to professionals. That meant most citizen–police interactions were negative contacts. Citizens' only

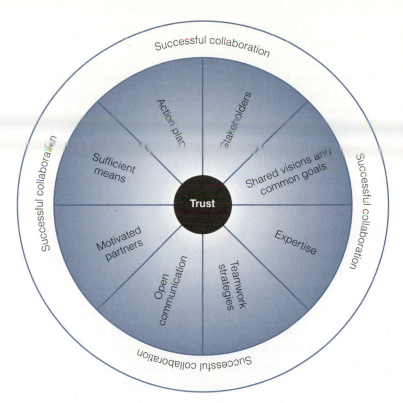

FIGURE 2.4 Core Components of a Successful Collaboration/ Partnership

Source: Tammy A. Rinehart, Anna T. Laszlo and Gwen O. Briscoe. *Collaboration Toolkit: How to Build, Fix, and Sustain Productive Partnerships.* Washington, DC, US Department of Justice, Office of Community Oriented Policing Services, 2001, p. 7.

opportunities to interact with officers came either when they were victims of crime, were involved in some other type of emergency situation such as a medical emergency, or were the subject of some enforcement action, such as receiving traffic tickets. A discussion of partnerships is beyond the scope of this book, but Figure 2.4 illustrates the core components of such partners. Note that, just as with management and leaderships, *trust* is essential.

Partnering with other city and county departments and agencies is important to problem-solving success. Sometimes described as **working in "silos,"** local government agencies and departments have traditionally worked quite independently of each other. Under community policing, appropriate government departments and agencies are called on and recognized for their abilities to respond to and address crime and social disorder issues. Fire departments, building inspections, health departments, street departments, parks and recreation departments and child welfare frequently are appropriate and necessary stakeholders in problem-solving initiatives. State and federal agencies may also assist. Examples of collaborative efforts include multi-jurisdictional initiatives such as Safe and Sober and other traffic safety campaigns, drug task forces, predatory offender task forces and, at the federal level, the National Incident Management System (NIMS).

working in "silos"

when local government agencies and departments work quite independently of each other. This lack of partnering with other city and county agencies hinders problem-solving success.

A Change in Core Functions?

Researchers Zhao et al. (2003) analyzed the changes in law enforcement organizational priorities related to three core functions of policing—crime control, the maintenance of order and the provision of services—during the era of community policing, by examining data from three national surveys of more than

200 municipal police departments conducted in 1993, 1996 and 2000. Zhao et al. found that police core-function priorities remained largely unchanged, but that the systematic implementation of community oriented policing (COP) programs reflects an all-out effort to address all three core functions at a higher level of achievement: "Our analysis showed that the extent of implementation of COP is a statistically significant predictor of all core functions of policing. On the basis of the analysis presented here, we argue that COP can be characterized as a comprehensive effort by local police simultaneously to control crime, to reduce social disorder and to provide services to the citizenry" (p.716). A basic difference, however, is that they no longer seek to do it alone, but rather through partnerships and problem solving.

 In most departments implementing community policing, the core functions remain, with the difference being that police no longer seek to accomplish these functions alone.

This earlier research supports the findings of Schafer et al. that the majority of changes implemented post–9/11 are transactional rather than transformational. Consider next the second core component of community policing which the Harvard group identified as one of the five approaches currently found across the country—problem-solving policing.

PROBLEM-SOLVING POLICING

Many practitioners equate community policing and problem solving. They are not, however, synonymous. As Wilson and Kelling (1989, p.49) note, "Community-oriented policing means changing the daily work of the police to include investigating problems as well as incidents. It means defining as a problem whatever a significant body of public opinion regards as a threat to community order. It means working with the good guys, and not just against the bad guys." Wilson and Kelling suggest that community policing requires the police mission to be redefined "to help the police become accustomed to fixing broken windows as well as arresting window-breakers."

problem-solving policing

management ascertains what problems exist and tries to solve them, redefining the role of law enforcement from incident driven and reactive to problem oriented and proactive.

Problem-solving policing focuses on determining the underlying causes of crime, fear of crime and disorder and identifying solutions. Such problem solving is often referred to as problem-oriented policing (POP). Eck and Spelman's classic work, *Problem-Solving: Problem Oriented Policing in Newport News* (1987), defines problem-oriented policing as "a departmental-wide strategy aimed at solving persistent community problems. Police identify, analyze and respond to the underlying circumstances that create incidents." This emphasis on *strategy* is one of the main features that distinguishes POP from COP. COP is a guiding philosophy and holistic approach to policing, whereas POP is a strategy for solving problems.

Goldstein (1990, p.20), who is credited with originating the concept of POP and coined the term, was among the first to criticize the professional model of policing as being incident driven: "In the vast majority of police departments, the telephone, more than any policy decision by the community or by management, continues to dictate how police resources will be used." The primary work unit in the professional model is the **incident**, that is, an isolated event that requires a police response. The institution of 911 has greatly increased the demand for police services and the public's expectation that the police will respond quickly.

Goldstein (1990, p.33) also asserts, "Most policing is limited to ameliorating the overt, offensive symptoms of a problem." He suggests that police are more productive if they respond to incidents as symptoms of underlying community problems. A problem is "a cluster of similar, related or recurring incidents rather than a single incident, a substantive community concern, and a unit of police business" (Goldstein, p.66). Once the problems in a community are identified, police efforts can focus on addressing the possible causes of such problems.

 Problem solving requires police to group incidents as a way to identify underlying causes of problems in the community.

Although problem solving may be the ideal, law enforcement cannot ignore specific incidents. When calls come in, most police departments respond as soon as possible. Problem solving has a dual focus. First, it requires that incidents be linked to problems. Second, time devoted to "preventive" patrol must be spent proactively, determining community problems and their underlying causes.

Problem-oriented policing is the result of 20 years of research into police operations converging on three main themes (Eck and Spelman, 1987, p.2):

1. Increased effectiveness by attacking underlying problems that give rise to incidents that consume patrol and detective time.

2. Reliance on the expertise and creativity of line officers to study problems carefully and develop innovative solutions.

3. Closer involvement with the public to make sure that the police are addressing the needs of citizens.

The goals of problem solving policing and aggressive enforcement are not mutually exclusive. The combination of these two efforts is called **integrated patrol**. As has been stressed, law enforcement agencies are expected to combat crime but are also being asked to look at causes for problems existing within communities and address them as well. Specific skills needed for effective problem solving are discussed in Chapter 5.

COMPSTAT POLICING

CompStat is a mid-level management-driven control structure that focuses on accountability and enforcement. "CompStat has become synonymous with progressive police management, and police departments large and small are adopting the principles of CompStat to identify crime problems, select tactics for dealing with specific crime situations and conduct relentless follow-up and assessment to learn about what works best" (Bond, 2007, p.6). The essence of

incident
an isolated event that requires a police response.

integrated patrol
the end goal resulting from the combination of the two elements of community policing and aggressive enforcement.

CompStat, which is short for "Computer Comparison Statistics," is that police cannot manage what they do not measure: "CompStat is pin-mapping on steroids. It simply helps to draw sharp attention to problem areas. It puts facts in the place of impressions" (Sanow, 2009, p.6).

Godown (2009, p.36) explains **CompStat policing** as "a method of management accountability and a philosophy of crime control." Noting its popularity in law enforcement agencies throughout the United States as well as in other countries, he adds (p.36),

> CompStat is not a quick-fix answer to crime but rather a process of organized problem solving that, when coupled with commitment and consistency, inexorably leads to the positive outcome of recurring incremental reductions in crime. . . .

> The CompStat process can be described as a two-pronged examination of police operations. The first prong looks outwardly at crime and its effects in the community, while the second examines the organization internally to identify best practices in managing such police personnel and risk management issues as sick time, use of force, pursuits, complaints, and accompanying municipal liability.

Godown (2009, p.38) identifies the four principles on which CompStat rests:

1. Accurate and timely intelligence: know what is happening.
2. Effective tactics; have a plan.
3. Rapid deployment; do it quickly.
4. Relentless follow-up and assessment; if it works do more, if not, do something else.

Again, as a method of problem solving, the emphasis of CompStat policing in on *strategy*.

 The four principles of CompStat involve accurate, timely intelligence; effective tactics; rapid deployment; and relentless follow-up.

The Columbia (South Carolina) Police Department implemented CompStat in an effort to address a series of armed robberies, placing the problem in the department's open forum and enabling a brainstorming and problem-solving session (Crisp and Hines, 2007). The goal was to capture the robbers by saturating the area with officers, pooling all available staffing and resources from other law enforcement agencies. The strategy involved sharing real-time crime reports, field reports and investigative reports, thus allowing the information to get to patrol officers within hours after an offense, enhancing officer awareness and increasing the possibility of apprehension. Additional strategic efforts involved enlisting the aid of the media to disseminate news of the robberies and informing community leaders, residents and merchants of the problem.

CompStat policing

a method of management accountability and a philosophy of crime control.

According to Crisp and Hines (2007, p.47), "Using the CompStat process, the police department tore down barriers to communication and information sharing between officers and units in the department and between the Columbia Police Department and other agencies. Where it used to take 30 days to create a BOLO (be on the lookout) advisory, it now took only 30 minutes because of reorganization and improved communications." Crisp and Hines (p.48) conclude, "The CompStat process has created an air of openness, seamless communication and enhanced teamwork in the department. It also improved relations with neighboring law enforcement agencies and community organizations. Most importantly, it has drastically reduced the incidences of crime within the city and increased the number of arrests." In short, "There can be little debate that CompStat processes in police agencies across the United Stated have revolutionized crime fighting and made communities safer" (Serpas and Morley, 2008, p.60).

This data driven approach has been applied to crime and traffic safety through a new concept called *predictive analysis* developed by recently retired Los Angeles Police Department Chief William J. Bratton. Predictive analysis will be examined in greater detail in Chapter 17.

The connection between CompStat and intelligence-led policing is obvious in that the first principle of the CompStat process is accurate, timely intelligence.

INTELLIGENCE-LED POLICING

There was a time in policing when *intelligence* was considered clandestine, obtained from confidential informants. Secrecy and silo-ing information were common practices. However, the events of 9/11 changed that view considerably. Information sharing is now expected, and competent analysis of this information to provide law enforcement with the intelligence they need to keep our communities safe is what intelligence-led policing (ILP) is about. **Intelligence-led policing** is a methodical approach to prevent, detect and disrupt crime, including terrorist activities. Early detection of crime trends through ILP allows police to be proactive in preventing continued crime instead of taking the traditional reactive, and less-effective, response to identified crime trends (Brewer, 2009, p.68). "Intelligence-led policing is a business model and managerial philosophy where data analysis and crime intelligence are pivotal to an objective, decision-making framework that facilitates crime and problem reduction, disruption and prevention through both strategic management and effective enforcement strategies that target prolific and serious offenders" (Ratcliffe, 2008, p.89).

In March 2002, the International Association of Chiefs of Police (IACP) and the Office of Community Oriented Policing Services (COPS) held a summit on criminal intelligence sharing in the United States, one result of which was development of fusion centers through the United States. A **fusion center**, according to the FBI, does not just *collect* information; it also *integrates* new data into existing information, *evaluates* it to determine its worth, *analyzes* it for links and trends and *disseminates* its findings to the appropriate agency in the best position to do something about it. Fusion centers pool the resources

intelligence-led policing

a methodical approach to prevent, detect and disrupt crime, including terrorist activities; uses early detection of crime trends to allows police to be proactive in preventing continued crime.

fusion center

an entity that pools the resources and personnel of multiple agencies into one central location to facilitate information sharing and intelligence development regarding criminal activities.

and personnel of multiple agencies into one central location to facilitate information sharing and intelligence development regarding criminal activities (Johnson and Dorn, 2008). Currently there are 70 fusion centers around the country—50 state and 20 regional—and some have expanded their focus from information on terrorism threats to include public safety matters and major criminal threats ("Fusion Centers," 2009).

In October 2007 the White House released the *National Strategy for Information Sharing*, intended to ensure that those responsible for combating terrorism and protecting local communities have timely, accurate information. The strategy works by

> Providing a framework for enhanced information sharing among federal, state, local, and tribal officials; the private sector; and foreign partners to aid their individual missions and to help secure the U.S. homeland.

> Describing the federal government's approach to supporting state and major-urban area fusion centers, as well as national efforts to fight crime and make local communities safer.

> Recognizing that as information-sharing capabilities are enhanced, it is imperative that the legal rights of U.S. citizens continue to be protected, especially in the area of privacy and civil liberties. (McNamara, 2008, p.46)

The *National Summit on Intelligence: Gathering, Sharing, Analysis, and Use after 9-11* (2009) reports that since 9/11, law enforcement agencies have made "great strides" in their ability to share intelligence, a capability considered critical to preventing terrorism. The report also concludes, however, that some agencies consider themselves too small or too remote to participate in criminal intelligence sharing: "The participants in the follow-up 2007 IACP Criminal Intelligence Sharing Summit made it clear that many of the nation's law enforcement agencies do not participate in the criminal intelligence sharing plan. . . . Too many state, local, and tribal agencies, it would seem, underestimate their importance to the criminal intelligence sharing process, overestimate the burdens of full participation, and/or remain unaware of how to contribute to the vital work of the plan."

Among the recommendations of the follow-up summit are the following (*National Summit on Intelligence*, pp.3–4):

- Every state, local and tribal law enforcement agency in the United States should strive to develop and maintain a criminal intelligence capability consisting of at least the following requirements: formal criminal intelligence awareness training for at least one sworn officer; training all levels of law enforcement personnel to recognize behavior indicative of criminal activity associated with terrorism; and defined procedures and mechanisms for communication with the nearest fusion center and/or a regional information sharing network.

- A nationwide marketing and training initiative should be designed to convince every law enforcement agency to participate in criminal intelligence sharing and make every law enforcement agency aware of the criminal intelligence resources available to it.

- All law enforcement organizations and agencies should explore potential partnerships in order to enhance analytical capacity within their agencies.
- The U.S. Department of Homeland Security, the Office of the Director of National Intelligence and the U.S. Department of Justice should work together to simplify and streamline security classifications.
- Law enforcement agencies should develop ways to measure the success of criminal intelligence sharing and recognize those individuals involved in that success.

McGarrell et al. (2007) present a model of intelligence-led policing as a framework for responding to terrorism but caution: "Applying the model only to terrorism would be unfortunate because of terrorists' involvement in such a wide variety of routine and preparatory crimes" (pp.151–152). They suggest that, in addition to taking an all-crimes approach, intelligence-led policing is most likely to be effective if it is focused on particular crime types, criminal organizations and terrorist threats of particular concern to a locality.

Ethical Considerations in Intelligence-Led Policing

Maintaining ethics and integrity is an ever-present concern and obligation of police. A department using ILP should "zealously endorse proactive investigative tactics" while maintaining "an equal vigilance toward protecting the privacy rights of innocent people and suspects alike" (Martinelli and Shaw, 2009, p.141). In this new ILP environment, a key acronym to bear in mind is CAP: common sense, audits and purges.

Schafer and Martinelli (2009, p.144) stress the importance in having intelligence unit supervisors rigorously review and amend intelligence data before allowing it to be passed on to other agencies: "In the intelligence field, 'Garbage in, Gospel out' refers to data included in an intelligence file although they have not been properly cross-checked or investigated for their veracity and reliability. The intelligence-led policing mantra must be 'corroborate, substantiate and validate.'"

According to Guidetti and Martinelli (2009, p.132), "A strategic framework ensures that all collection operations follow strict investigative guidelines set by commanders as opposed to relying upon individual officer's value-based decision-making. This cannot be over-emphasized enough because it protects valid intelligence-led policing initiatives from the overzealous, renegade acts of a few."

Guarding against Noble Cause Corruption

ILP is vulnerable to noble cause corruption, which refers to when a law enforcement officer breaks the rules (aka, the law), commonly violating the Fourth Amendment, in an effort to contain society's terrorists and criminals (Martinelli, 2009, p.124). This abuse of police power, in which the ends are used to justify the means, is a felony.

Such corruption may occur through reliance on suspicious activity reports (SARs), which have no mandatory prerequisite to establish probable cause or a criminal predicate nexus to generate reports. SARs, tips and leads, arrest reports and other sources are used by intelligence analysts to piece together tougher puzzle parts to thwart serious crime threats. They rely on their puzzle pieces being true, putting more faith in law enforcement-generated reports than in anonymous tips or leads. If an arrest is made, Martinelli stresses, "Today's street-level supervisors must emphasize the need to specifically articulate the probable cause facts of arrests so warrants may be issued and convictions successfully obtained" (Martinelli, 2009, p.124)

Intelligence-Led Policing in Action

A "Corruption Alert" from the FBI ("Potential Economic Stimulus Fraud," 2009) illustrates intelligence-led policing in action, stating that the FBI and Department of Justice are working with federal, state and local partners to get out in front of possible fraud and corruption associated with the American Recovery and Reinvestment Act (ARRA), which was signed into law in 2009 to inject $787 billion into the U.S. economy by providing jobs and other resources. The FBI states that most of those receiving funding are honest, but chances are good that some unscrupulous government officials and others might attempt to defraud the government and "line their own pockets," as occurred after Hurricane Katrina. Relying on past experience, the FBI anticipates that crime is most likely to occur among those with minimal or no reporting requirements and limited oversight: "The use of intelligence is key. . . . We are working now to head off potential problems by strategically collecting and analyzing intelligence to identify where we should be focusing resources." Programs pinpointed by the FBI that could be most vulnerable include transportation and infrastructure, education, energy/environment and housing. The alert concludes with a request that anyone who suspects fraud or corruption submit a tip electronically or through his or her local FBI office.

The 3-I Model

Ratcliffe (2008) explains crime analysis in the context of intelligence-led policing using a 3-I model to illustrate the purpose of crime analysis in the modern policing environment.

 The 3-I model of intelligence-led policing consists of _interpreting_ the criminal environment, _influencing_ decision makers and _impacting_ the criminal environment.

Interpreting the criminal environment is the first step in crime analysis, gaining a thorough understanding of the local environment in which criminals operate. Intelligence must then be actively directed to the decision makers, a step that involves first deciding who the key decision makers are and then deciding on the best way to influence their thinking, keeping in mind that such individuals might be outside the law enforcement environment. Finally, for an organization to be truly intelligence-led, the decision makers must use the intelligence they receive to positively affect the criminal environment. Like CompStat, "Intelligence-led policing requires a fundamental commitment to data collection and analysis. Too many departments react to headlines and political winds, at the expense of cold, hard facts" (Serrao, 2009, p.10). Taking this 3-I model one step further leads to the final strategy increasingly being advocated: evidence-based policing.

EVIDENCE-BASED POLICING

Although evidence-based policing (EBP) was first advocated by criminologist Lawrence Sherman in 1998, it is only recently being discussed and written about. EBP takes what is known about criminology and applies this "evidence" toward more cost-effective police policies and practices. In the context of EBP, the "evidence" does not pertain to a suspect's guilt or innocence but rather to "statistical and individual assessments of costs, risks and benefits" (Sherman, 2009). **Evidence-based policing** is a methodological approach that uses empirically derived evidence—what has been shown, through scientific research, to be effective—and applies it to real-world policing: "EBP is about monitoring and evaluating program outcomes and delivery processes, analyzing whether this is making a difference in people's lives, and making adjustments to improve and enhance outcomes. It is about training, so that services are administered effectively and consistently. It is about innovation, efficiency, fiscal responsibility, and ongoing communication—with partners, stakeholders, and researchers—about what works and what does not. It is about continuing to push for better results" (Rodriguez, 2008, p.1).

> **evidence-based policing**
>
> a methodological approach that uses empirically derived evidence—what has been shown, through scientific research, to be effective—and applies it to real-world policing.

From a law enforcement perspective, this change to empirical, evidence-based policy and practice represents a significant paradigm shift for which most agencies are not adequately prepared (Abrahamson and Taylor, 2007, p.3). Few agencies have the training or requisite resources to conduct scientific research during their day-to-day operations and apply it to decision-making about policies and practices. Because of this, many departments are partnering with colleges and universities.

Partnering with Colleges or Universities

 Students or staff at local or regional colleges or universities may be valuable partners for agencies wanting to participate in evidence-based policing.

For partnerships between police agencies and researchers to be successful, the participants need to identify and locate each other, specify mutually interesting projects, determine compensation and set ground rules clarifying expectations for how the project will proceed (Sanders and Fields, 2009, p.58). One important expectation to clarify is data use and attendant confidentiality or anonymity requirements. It is also important to have a clear but flexible timeline for projects, ensuring that researchers are aware of the real-life emergencies that may arise for a law enforcement agency and that may making meeting deadlines difficult. However, researchers, too, often have deadlines for journal articles or conference presentations and need to have their time and talents respected, especially if the researchers are donating their time.

Such partnerships can have long-term benefits for both groups (Sanders and Fields, 2009, p.61). For researchers the main benefit of a police partnership is access to a data source. Colleges and universities can also benefit from having contacts at a local police agency for internships and for future job opportunities. Police departments benefit by having researchers who are trained in statistical analysis evaluate the effectiveness of their programs, data gathering processes and the like.

Reporting Failure

More than a century ago Abraham Lincoln observed, "Men are greedy to publish the successes of their efforts, but meanly shy as to publishing the failure of men. Men are ruined by this one-sided practice of concealment of blunders and failures."

 Evidence-based policing must report successes and failures to reach its full potential.

It has been suggested that, in the criminal justice world, *failure* is a whispered word (Berman et al., 2007, p.7). For evidence-based policing to move forward, failure must be openly discussed to foster an environment promoting new thinking and testing of new ideas. "The expectation should be that failure is normal. Even with clear-headed designs, savvy implementation strategies, robust training, skilled staff, and committed executive leadership, some things are likely to go wrong. . . Even when a program is going relatively well, it is difficult to get anyone interested in writing about failure" (Immarigeon, 2008, p.43).

Throughout the chapters that follow, the preceding strategies will be referred to as currently practiced.

THE IMPACT OF CONTEMPORARY POLICING APPROACHES ON THE NEW SUPERVISOR OR MANAGER

Much of what has been written about police supervision and management is geared toward the more traditional contexts and formats of police organization. However, as policing styles have evolved, the changes have compelled a concomitant adjustment in the way supervisors and managers perform their jobs. These new expectations and requirements must be embraced by new police supervisors and managers if they are to be successful in their positions.

All of the contemporary strategic philosophies and approaches discussed—community policing, problem-oriented policing, CompStat-policing, intelligence-led policing and evidence-based policing—run fairly parallel and have only minor differences between them; as such, they all change the job responsibilities and skills sets of new supervisors in similar ways. When the culture of a police department is focused on problem solving, the patrol officer has more control over the work performed and an attendant increase in responsibility, but he or she also has a much higher level of autonomy, which can change the role of a police supervisor, manager or leader in several fundamental ways:

- Supervisors and managers must share power with subordinates by including patrol officers in the decision-making process.

- Equally important to sharing power is sharing in failure. It is not uncommon for mistakes to precede innovative results.

- Supervisors must understand and accept failure as a learning experience that is controlled by keeping a consistently positive attitude and leading by example. Positive attitudes provide the power to propel an organization toward attainment of goals and success.

- Supervisors and managers must be able to accept constructive criticism more so than ever before.

- Supervisors and managers must have a comprehensive grasp of the problem-solving process, including identifying, addressing and resolving problems. Vital to effective, long-term problem solving is the relentless follow up necessary to ensure that problems are permanently fixed. In the past, supervisors left the concern about future incidents to those on the next shift.

- Supervisors must serve as mentor, motivator and facilitator. What changes under these strategies is that the first-line supervisor acts more as a facilitator by pushing problem solving to the officer level and relinquishing power and decision making. This is a big change in supervision from the traditional model.

- Traditionally, supervisors did not need to spend much time with officers on calls, as patrol generally had the proper training and experience to manage most situations. However, with these new strategies for policing, supervisors must be more involved with the officers and the community on various issues within a neighborhood and or community. Consider, for example, gang-related issues. To fulfill the obligations of *accountability* in the CompStat strategy, supervisors may be asked to report on gang problems, which will require that they have a complete knowledge and understanding of the problem and are able to communicate what is being done about it. Supervisors will be reporting before their peers and will be expected to produce results. This involves an increase in skill sets in the areas of communication and reporting, specifically in the ability to create reports from data and respond accordingly. Supervisors will be expected to detect and rank problems by patrol districts and apply demographic data, crime reports, patterns and information regarding repeat or known offenders. In other words, they will need to know how to identify and solve a problem from start to finish, to produce results. Under the traditional model, once a problem was identified, it was typically passed on to another division or resource.

- Time management skills—supervisors and managers will need to be able to identify much earlier in the process when time and resources are needed to resolve an issue, and they must have the ability to coordinate resources to meet the demands of a community policing problem while maintaining resources required to respond to continuous calls for service. This requires an enhanced ability to prioritize and to multitask.

- Technology—Supervisors need now, more than ever, to have a solid set of technological skills and equally well-developed analytical skills to be able to understand and interpret data and respond accordingly. For example, being able to use software programs for electronic scheduling and knowing how to build in resources for problem solving, all while working within resource allocations and union contract–related issues.

- These strategies require a supervisor to better understand and focus on a more planned approach to attainment of departmental goals.

- Performance evaluations—the first-line supervisor is required to be engaged more than ever in day-to-day officer performance because data can now be made available to help support accountability.

To be successful and effective under these contemporary policing philosophies, a supervisor *must* be wholeheartedly "on board" and committed as never before. In the past, supervisors could get by with just being out there, doing their own thing. Community policing and problem-solving strategies are forcing the supervisor to be engaged because the officers are not going to be questioned; it is the supervisor more now than ever.

SUMMARY

The traditional organizational design is that of a pyramid-shaped hierarchy based on a military model.

Field services, also called field operations, use line personnel to *directly* help accomplish the goals of the department. Administrative services use staff personnel to *support* the line organization.

Specialization can enhance an agency's effectiveness and efficiency, but overspecialization can impede the organizational purpose. The chain of command establishes definite lines of authority and channels of communication. The emerging law enforcement agency has a flattened organization, is decentralized and empowers its employees.

Five broad strategic or organizational approaches currently operating in contemporary policing are community policing, problem-oriented policing, CompStat policing, intelligence-led policing and evidence-based policing.

Community policing is a philosophy that promotes "organization strategies, which supports the systematic use of partnership and problem solving techniques to proactively address the immediate conditions that give rise to public safety issues, such as crime, social disorder and fear of crime." Traditional policing is reactive; focusing on fighting crime and measuring effectiveness by arrest rates. A tenet of traditional policing is that crime is a police problem. In contrast, community policing is proactive, focusing on community problems and measuring effectiveness on the absence of crime and disorder. A tenet of community policing is that crime is everyone's problem. Two critical elements of community policing are partnerships and problem solving. In most departments implementing community policing the core functions remain, with the difference being that police no longer seek to accomplish these functions alone.

Problem solving requires police to group incidents as a way to identify underlying causes of problems in the community. The four principles of CompStat involve accurate, timely intelligence; effective tactics; rapid deployment; and relentless follow-up. The 3-I model of intelligence-led policing consists of interpreting the criminal environment; influencing decision makers and impacting the criminal environment.

Students or staff at local or regional colleges or universities may be valuable partners in agencies wanting to participate in evidence-based policing. Evidence-based policing must report successes and failures to reach its full potential.

CHALLENGE TWO

You are the new chief of the Greenfield Police Department. After 30 years of iron-fisted control, Chief Slaughter has retired. Slaughter believed in the military model of police management and a traditional crime-fighting policing strategy. He was fully entrenched in the war on crime and ran his department like an army unit. His book of rules and regulations was a foot thick, and he demanded absolute compliance. Decisions were made in the chief's office and passed down to the officers through layers of captains, lieutenants and sergeants. At Chief Slaughter's retirement ceremony, the mayor slaps you on the back and says, "You've got some big shoes to fill, son. That guy knew how to fight crime, and his officers never stepped out of line. Our crime rate was below the national average every year he was here." The City Council presents Slaughter the Meritorious Service Award for 30 years of crime fighting.

As a student of police history you realize that most police departments battle complex social problems and seldom march off to war. You know that crime rates are minimally influenced by crime fighting and are a poor indication of policing success. You also know that traditional organizational structures and policing strategies are slow to change and often are out of sync with one another. Most of your questions to the captains about department operations have generated the same response: "Because that's the way we've always done it. If it ain't broke, why fix it?"

You decide to visit with members of the community. A homeowner tells you that Chief Slaughter's officers do a great job of patrolling her neighborhood, but she's worried about the future impact of the deteriorating apartment complex across the street. She realizes it's not a police problem. The manager of a senior citizens' residence tells you that there hasn't been a crime reported in their neighborhood in over a year, but the residents are afraid to go out at night. He thinks it's the rumors that spread from crime reports on the television news. The business owners in the shopping center complain that customers are being driven away by kids skateboarding in the parking lot. They understand that the police have more urgent crime problems to fight. The high school principal praises the police department's stringent traffic enforcement before and after school. He wishes he could resolve the growing truancy problem as efficiently as the police handle traffic. None of the people you talk to is personally acquainted with a Greenfield police officer.

It appears the Greenfield Police Department is trapped in the traditional mode of policing. They rely on preventive patrolling and rapid response as their primary policing strategies

and seldom interact with the community. You review their mission statement and find it emphasizes the professional model of crime fighting.

1. What challenges are facing you as the new chief?
2. What type of data might be collected to address the identified problems?
3. What changes would you introduce in policing strategies?
4. What changes would you make in the organizational structure to enable the new strategy?
5. Identify some quality-of-life issues that are not being addressed by the crime-fighting strategy of Chief Slaughter.

DISCUSSION QUESTIONS

1. Is there a difference between the terms *pyramidal structure* and *hierarchy*?
2. What is the difference between unity of command and chain of command?
3. What forces are driving change in your community?
4. What does an organizational chart indicate?
5. How could you reorganize to force decision making downward? Is this desirable?
6. Which of the five strategies described appear to have the most promise?
7. Which of the five strategies seem most compatible with traditional policing?
8. Which of the five strategies seem most compatible with each other?
9. How would you describe the organization and strategic approaches being used in your police department?
10. What changes do you foresee in law enforcement agencies in the 21st century?

REFERENCES

Abrahamson, Doug, and Taylor, Bruce. "Evidence-Based Policing: Are We Ready, Willing and Able?" *Subject to Debate*, February 2007, pp.3, 5.

Berman, Greg; Bowen, Phillip; and Mansky, Adam. "Trial and Error: Failure and Innovation in Criminal Justice Reform." *Executive Exchange*, Summer 2007, pp.7–11.

Bond, Brenda J. "CompStat: Let's Focus on Communication and Coordination." *Subject to Debate*, September 2007, pp.6–7.

Brewer, Brad. "C.R.I.M.E. Fights Crime with Intelligence-Led Policing." *Law and Order*, May 2009, pp.68–74.

Coleman, J. *Foundations of Social Theory*. Cambridge, MA: Harvard University Press, 1990.

Community Policing Defined. Washington, DC: Office of Community-Oriented Policing Services, April 3, 2009.

Connell, Nadine M.; Miggans, Kristen; and McGloin, Jean Marie. "Can a Community Policing Initiative Reduce Serious Crime?" *Police Quarterly*, June 2008, pp.127–150.

Crisp, H. Dean, and Hines, R. J. "The CompStat Process in Columbia." *The Police Chief*, February 2007, pp.46–49.

Eck, John E., and Spelman, William. *Problem-Solving: Problem-Oriented Policing in Newport News*. Washington, DC: The Police Executive Research Forum, 1987.

"Fusion Centers." Washington, DC: Federal Bureau of Investigation Headline Archives, March 12, 2009.

Godown, Jeff, "The CompStat Process: Four Principles for Managing Crime Reduction." *The Police Chief*, August 2009, pp.36–42.

Goldstein, Herman. *Problem-Oriented Policing*. New York: McGraw-Hill, 1990.

Guidetti, Ray, and Martinelli, Thomas J. "Intelligence-Led Policing: A Strategic Framework." *The Police Chief*, October 2009, pp.132–136.

Harr, J. Scott, and Hess, Kären M. *Careers in Criminal Justice and Related Fields*, 6th ed., Belmont, CA: Wadsworth/Cengage Publishing, 2010.

Immarigeon, Russ. "What Does Not Work? Lessons from the Center for Court Innovations Failure Roundtable." *Criminal Justice Research Review*, January/February 2008, pp.43–44.

"Intelligence-Led Policing." Washington, DC: Bureau of Justice Assistance, no date.

Johnson, Bart R., and Dorn, Shelagh. "Fusion Centers: New York State Intelligence Strategy Unifies Law Enforcement." *The Police Chief*, February 2008, pp.34–46.

Kelling, George L. "Don't Let Budget Cuts Damage Your Commitment to Community Policing." *Subject to Debate*, June 2009, pp.1, 3.

Marks, Daniel E., and Sun, Ivan Y. "The Impact of 9/11 on Organizational Development among State and Local Law Enforcement Agencies." *Journal of Contemporary Criminal Justice*, May 2007, pp.159–173.

Martinelli, Thomas J. "Dodging the Pitfalls of Noble Cause Corruption and the Intelligence Unit." *The Police Chief*, October 2009, pp.124–130.

Martinelli, Thomas J., and Shaw, Lawrence E. "ILP Abbreviations for the ISE and NCISP Can Spell Trouble." *The Police Chief*, October 2009, pp.138–141.

McGarrell, Edmund F.; Freilich, Joshua D.; and Chermak, Steven. "Intelligence-Led Policing as a Framework for Responding to Terrorism." *Journal of Contemporary Criminal Justice*, May 2007, 142–158.

McNamara, Thomas E. "U.S. National Strategy for Information Sharing Release." *The Police Chief*, April 2008, p.46.

National Strategy for Information Sharing, Washington, DC: The White House, October 2007.

National Summit on Intelligence: Gathering, Sharing, Analysis, and Use after 9-11. Washington, DC: Office of Community Oriented Policing, July 3, 2009.

"Potential Economic Stimulus Fraud." Washington, DC: Federal Bureau of Investigation Corruption Alert; Headline Archives, September 17, 2009.

Ratcliffe, Jerry H. *Intelligence-Led Policing*. Cullompton, Devon, UK: Willan Publishing, 2008.

Rodriguez, Pamela F. "Understanding Evidence-Based Practice." *TASC News and Views* (Treatment Alternatives for Safe Communities), Winter, 2008, p.1.

Sanders, Beth A., and Fields, Marc L. "Partnerships with University-Based Researchers. *The Police Chief*, June 2009, pp.58–61.

Sanow, Ed. "Measure Equals Manage." *Law and Order*, June 2009, p.6.

Schafer, Joseph A.; Burruss, George W., Jr.; and Giblin, Matthew J. "Measuring Homeland Security Innovation in Small Municipal Agencies: Policing in a Post-9/11 World." *Police Quarterly*, September 2009, pp.263–288.

Schafer, Joseph A., and Martinelli, Thomas J. "The Privacy Police: Sense-Enhancing Technology and the Future of Intelligence-Led Policing." *The Police Chief*, October 2009, pp.142–147.

Scheider, Matthew. "Community Policing Is Not Soft on Crime." *Community Policing Dispatch*, July 2008.

Serpas, Ronal W., and Morley, Matthew. "The Next Step in Accountability-Driven Leadership: 'CompStating' the CompStat Data." *The Police Chief*, May 2008, pp.60–70.

Serrao, Stephen G. "Intelligence-Led Policing: Beyond the Fusion Center—Strategic Intelligence." *Law Officer Magazine*, July 2009, p.10.

Sherman, Lawrence. "Evidence-Based Policing: What We Know and How We Know It." Preview of an address to be presented at the Scottish Police College, October 1, 2009.

Sparrow, Malcolm K. *One Week in Heron City—A Case Study, Teaching Notes. New Perspectives in Policing*. National Institute of Justice and the Harvard Kennedy School Program in Criminal Justice Policy and Management, September 2009.

Taylor, Frederick W. *The Principles of Scientific Management*. New York: Harper Bros., 1911.

Wilson, James Q., and Kelling, George L. "The Police and Neighborhood Safety: Broken Windows." *The Atlantic Monthly*, March 1982, pp.29–38.

Wilson, James Q., and Kelling, George L. "Making Neighborhoods Safe." *The Atlantic Monthly*, February 1989, pp.46–52.

Wilson, O. W. *Police Administration*. New York: McGraw-Hill, 1950.

Zhao, Jhong (Solomon); He, Ni; and Lovrich, Nicholas P. "Community Policing: Did It Change the Basic Functions of Policing in the 1990s? A National Follow-Up Study." *Justice Quarterly*, December 2003, pp.697–724.

The Police Mission: Getting the Job Done

Supervisors serve as the keepers of the faith and the mentors of the young. Theirs is a quiet profession that combines the discipline of science with the aesthetic creativity of art. It is a curious paradox that at their best they are the least visible.

—Alonso

DO YOU KNOW?

- What should drive an organization?
- How goals differ from objectives and work plans? From policies and procedures?
- What the relationship between Collin's flywheel challenge and doom loop is?
- What typical levels of management exist in law enforcement?
- What management tools help coordination?
- Which transition from one management level to another is usually the most difficult and why?
- What essential functions chief executives perform?
- How strategic and tactical planning differ?
- With whom law enforcement executives typically interact?
- What the attributes of a high-performing team are?
- What two key components of the National Incident Management System (NIMS) are?

CAN YOU DEFINE?

doom loop

facilitators

flywheel challenge

goals

guiding philosophy

holistic management/leadership

incident command

interactors

interfacers

mission

mission statement

objectives

SMART goals and objectives

stakeholders

strategic planning

synergy

tactical planning

unified command

vetting

work plans

INTRODUCTION

Although police departments have changed substantially since their early beginnings in this country, they have always had a mission, whether stated or unstated. That police missions have always existed, however, should not be taken to mean they are permanent and fixed elements of law enforcement organization. Police missions change as departments and the communities they serve change.

CHAPTER at a GLANCE

This chapter begins with a discussion of the law enforcement mission, guiding philosophy and values, followed by an explanation of goals, objectives, work plans and policies and procedures. The discussion then takes an in-depth look at the functions performed at the various levels of police management, followed by an examination of holistic management/leadership. Next is a description of the team approach to policing at the local, state and federal level, including multiagency teams and task forces and the National Incident Management System (NIMS). The chapter concludes with a discussion of being new to a management position and law enforcement management as a career.

THE LAW ENFORCEMENT MISSION

A mission statement should clearly express the core purpose of an organization and its reason for existence: "Mission statements are instruments of organization communication. They have the ability to shape the attitudes and behavior of individuals in the organization. They also have the ability to shape the perceptions of the public" (DeLone, 2007, p.218). Traditionally, as the name implies, the mission was to enforce the law, that is, to fight crime and to keep the public safe. Today, however, many departments have changed their focus to providing services while other departments seek a combination of the two. It is important for departments to clearly articulate their **mission** or overriding, core purpose in writing.

 A **mission statement** is a written explanation of why an organization exists and is the driving force for that organization, providing a focus for its energy and resources.

mission

the reason an organization exists.

mission statement

a written explanation of why an organization exists and the driving force for that organization, providing a focus for its energy and resources.

Mission statements articulate the rationale for an organization's existence. A mission statement can be the most powerful underlying influence in law enforcement, affecting organizational and individual attitudes, conduct and performance. It provides focus for decisions.

This focus is illustrated well in a poster commonly found hanging in many managers' offices, showing an eagle and the adage: "If you chase two rabbits, both will get away" (anonymous). This adage refers to one of Jim Collins' (*Good to Great, GTG*) key principles called the *hedgehog* concept, based on the Greek parable about the fox, which knows many things, and the hedgehog, which knows one big thing (Wexler et al., 2007, p.7). Hedgehogs may appear to be slow and plodding, but they are blessed with a "piercing insight that allows them to see through complexity and discern underlying patterns," seeing what is essential and ignoring the rest, or what Collins refers to as the ability to recognize your strengths and understand what you are best at. This is perhaps the most difficult part of Collins' theory to apply to police work because police have a wide range of dictated responsibilities that fall under the heading of "public safety" (Wexler et al., p.35). Actually, the community often dictates, through calls for service, the functions of the police, and the hedgehog concept in this context can have a temporal or geographic applicability for certain agencies. The main point is to be focused—select a key priority and become the best at it, perhaps becoming a model for other department to emulate.

Mission statements are best developed by an appointed committee, representative of the larger organizational "whole" but not too large for individual participation. Developing the statement is only the first step. It must then be distributed, explained, understood and accepted by all department members. A mission statement is not automatically implemented or effective. It must be practiced in everyday actions and decision making by management and field personnel.

The mission statement of a law enforcement agency should be believable, worthy of support, widely known, shared and exciting to key stakeholders.

stakeholders

those affected by an organization and those in a position to affect it.

Stakeholders are those *affected by* the organization and those in a position to *affect it.* In a law enforcement organization, stakeholders include everyone in the jurisdiction. Two key questions to answer are (1) what do the stakeholders *want?* and (2) what do the stakeholders *need?* What people want and what they need are not necessarily the same. Stakeholders should, however, have input into what is provided for them.

An example of an effective mission statement is that of the Owatonna (Minnesota) Police Department:

> We are a value driven organization that serves the community by protecting life and property, preventing crime, enforcing the laws, and maintaining order for all citizens.

> In serving our community, we emphasize education of citizens, voluntary compliance, partnership with the community, visual presence in the community, and detection and apprehension of offenders.

> We achieve our mission through planning and problem solving, personal responsibility, customer orientation, fairness and equity, teamwork, and integrity above all else.

A mission statement such as this can both guide and drive an organization. Mission statements are usually part of an organization's overall guiding philosophy.

AN ORGANIZATION'S GUIDING PHILOSOPHY AND VALUES

guiding philosophy

the organization's mission statement and the basic values honored by the organization.

A **guiding philosophy** consists of an organization's mission statement *and* its basic *values*, the beliefs, principles or standards considered worthwhile or desirable. Consider, for example, the values set forth by the Owatonna (Minnesota) Police Department:

> In pursuit of our organizational mission, we are guided by the philosophy of Socrates, "We are what we repeatedly do. Excellence, therefore is a habit." Our Motto of "Exceeding Expectations Through Excellence in Policing" is carried out in the following ways:

- In the prevention, detection and suppression of crime and the relentless pursuit of offenders
- In providing quality service
- In recognizing the commitment, contribution, and importance of all our staff, citizens, and community partners
- In open, positive communication that encourages teamwork
- In the respect for, value of and equitable treatment of all individuals in our diverse community and our ongoing efforts towards our organization so that our organization adequately represents our community and the people we serve
- In being sensitive to the needs of victims of crime and other circumstances

- In using only the minimum force required to carry out our duties
- In educating others by the example we set
- In a commitment to continuous learning, improvement and innovation

Our values and ethics express the commonly held beliefs we must strive for in our daily operations. These beliefs govern our work behavior and actions and make them a reality.

Some readers may be thinking that mission statements and value statements are fine, but that they are simply words. How do such words get translated into action?

Our Declaration of Independence was a statement of the guiding philosophy of our country, but it did not establish how the United States should be structured or governed. This was accomplished through our Constitution and Bill of Rights. A statement of philosophy is meaningless without a plan or blueprint for accomplishing it. Goals, objectives, work plans and policies and procedures provide this blueprint.

GOALS, OBJECTIVES, WORK PLANS AND POLICIES AND PROCEDURES

Goals, objectives and work plans are interdependent. All three are needed to carry out an organization's mission.

Goals are broad, general, desired outcomes. **Objectives** are specific, measurable ways to accomplish the goals. **Work plans** are the precise activities that contribute to accomplishing objectives. Policies and procedures specify how the activities are to be carried out.

Goals

Goals are visionary, projected achievements. They provide guidelines for planning efforts. They are what in business would be called the *key result areas*. Goals provide the foundation for objectives and ultimately for work plans. Among the commonly agreed-upon goals of most law enforcement agencies are to enforce laws, prevent crime, preserve the peace, protect civil rights and civil liberties, provide services and solve problems. Specific problem-solving goals might be to promote community involvement in developing crime prevention strategies, reducing youth crime through the directed use of strategies and resources or ensuring that criminal investigations are conducted, prepared and presented in an effective, timely and thorough manner.

Two important principles that can take an organization from good to great, according to Collins, are the flywheel challenge and the doom loop (Wexler et al., 2007, p.8). The **flywheel challenge** asks managers to imagine a huge, heavy flywheel about 30 feet in diameter, weighing about 5,000 pounds

goals

broad, general, desired outcomes; visionary, projected achievements; what business calls *key result areas.*

objectives

specific, measurable ways to accomplish goals; more specific than goals and usually have a timeline.

work plans

the precise activities that contribute to accomplishing objectives; detailed steps or tasks to be accomplished.

flywheel challenge

asks managers to imagine a huge, heavy flywheel about 30 feet in diameter, weighing about 5,000 pounds mounted horizontally on an axle; then to further imagine that management's task is to get the fly wheel rotating on the axle as fast and long as possible, requiring time and the combined efforts of many people making many decisions and doing many things to get it going.

mounted horizontally on an axle. Further imagine that management's task is to get the flywheel rotating on the axle as fast and for as long as possible, requiring time and the combined efforts of many people making many decisions and doing many things to get it going. Making the transformation from good to great never happens instantly.

The opposite of the flywheel image is what Collins calls the doom loop, a cycle in which organizations are kept from becoming great. The **doom loop** is characterized by incessant restructuring, following fads, management by cheerleading without careful thought and especially inconsistency, constantly running after new ideas rather than making progress toward accomplishing the goals of the organization. In policing, reasons for the doom loop include the frequent change of police chiefs that creates inconsistent leadership in some departments, constant shifts in a community's priorities regarding demands for police service and the never-ending barrage of new technology available, requiring continuous training and upgrading, which can leave resource-deficient departments and progress-resistant officers at a distinct service disadvantage.

doom loop
characterized by incessant restructuring, following fads, management by cheerleading without careful thought, and especially inconsistency, constantly running after new ideas.

 The flywheel challenge encourages all within an organization to focus on priority goals. In contrast, the doom loop sees management as unfocused, inconsistent and following fads.

According to Collins, a more common reason for the doom loop is that managing crisis is common in policing, forcing hedgehog leaders to come up for air and attend to matters outside the burrow (Wexler et al., 2007, p.45). This need not stop the flywheel or result in the doom loom if managers at all levels recognize what is occurring and return to their focus on goals as soon as the crisis is dealt with. In the event of a crisis such as the September 11, 2001, attacks, it may require a reexamination of present goals.

"Good performance," says Ken Blanchard (1988, p.14), "starts with clear goals." The importance of goals cannot be overemphasized. Just as important, however, are the objectives developed to meet the goals. According to Blanchard, **SMART goals and objectives** are *s*pecific, *m*easurable, *a*ttainable, *r*elevant and *t*rackable. An example of a SMART goal is a 10 percent reduction in the number of injuries to persons involved in collisions because it accounts for all five facets. Failure to address any of the five aspects of a SMART goals lessens the effectiveness of that goal. For instance, to simply state a goal to reduce injuries is not being specific; a goal to eliminate all injuries is not attainable.

SMART goals and objectives
objectives that are specific, measurable, attainable, relevant and trackable.

Few people would argue about the value of these goals. The disagreements arise over which are most important and how resources should be apportioned. For example, providing how much service and of what kind, compared with how much enforcing of laws? It is also often difficult to determine which objectives might accomplish the goals.

Collins uses the term *Level 5 leader* to identify those leaders capable of taking their organization from good to great. Such leaders are "frantically driven, infected with an incurable need to produce results" (Wexler et al., 2007, p.5).

Objectives

Objectives are needed before work plans can be developed. They are much more specific than goals and usually have a timeline. Objectives are critical to planning, assigning tasks and evaluating performance. For example, one objective might be to reduce traffic accidents by 20 percent by the end of the year. Management by objectives (MBO) was introduced in Chapter 1. According to Peter Drucker, its originator, nine times out of ten, managers fail to think about their objectives, which compromises agency results.

Good objectives are clear and understandable, especially to those who will be responsible for carrying them out. They are also practical—that is, they are realistic and achievable. Personnel must have the knowledge, skill and resources to accomplish their objectives. Effective objectives deal with important matters. They should motivate and energize each person to perform at a high level individually and as a team member. Good objectives provide the basis for a department's work plans.

Work Plans

Work plans, sometimes called *tactical and strategic plans*, are the detailed steps needed to accomplish objectives. They are tied to a timeline and are an effective way to evaluate an organization's performance. To accomplish the objective of reducing traffic accidents, a department might, in January, establish the following work plans:

- Analyze where accidents are happening to determine their cause by July 1.
- Based on this analysis, take steps to correct identified problems by December 1.
- Conduct ten educational meetings regarding traffic safety for the public by June 1.
- Design and display five educational billboards regarding drinking and driving by April 1.

Policies and Procedures

"By definition, policy is a course of action, a guiding principle or procedure considered expedient, prudent or advantageous. By practice, the policies of a law enforcement agency dictate the protocol by which officers are expected to conduct their duties, often carrying with it the added responsibility of mitigating potential liability resulting from those duties" (Scoville, 2008, p.56). Policies and procedures minimize supervisory inconsistency and resulting confusion and attempt to get everyone in the department "on the same page" and "singing from the same sheet of music" (Means, 2007, p.10).

Policies and procedures are usually contained in a manual distributed to all personnel within the department. In addition to addressing legal and liability issues, policies and procedures need to incorporate the values of the department, requiring police managers to simultaneously be both realists and idealists. Realistic idealism recognizes what is possible given the existing situation while aspiring to high principles and a worthwhile mission.

Just what should be contained in a policy and procedures manual is controversial—should they provide rules or simply guidelines? It is impossible to write a rule that would apply to every set of circumstances that might be encountered. Nonetheless, "Law enforcement officers deserve clear and consistent guidance on what is expected of them. Such guidance empowers officers to work in ways that are organizationally acceptable and to avoid a wide range of pitfalls, including disciplinary actions and civil liability" (Means, 2007, p.10). Consider, for example, the policy of adherence to the chain of command: "The divide-and-conquer strategy is stopped dead in its tracks when there is but one place to go to get a decision" (Furey, 2007, p.46).

Although lawyers may suggest the inadvisability of having rules, as rules may adversely affect a department's ability to defend lawsuits, this problem can be resolved by having a conspicuous preface with appropriate wording acknowledging that rules are rules but that deviation from them occasionally be appropriate. For example (Furey, 2007, p.46):

> This manual contains both policies and procedures, both rules and guidelines. Employees are expected and required to adhere to the provisions of this document. However, no policy manual could ever anticipate all of the infinite situations that an employee could face in the course of organizational and human affairs.
>
> In the event that an employee reasonably and honestly believes that to follow a police or rule in this manual would cause an illegal, unjust, or significantly inappropriate outcome, the employee may be excused from adherence to the policy or rule in question.
>
> In the event that an employee perceives that such a situation exists and consequently chooses to deviate from the requirements of this manual, the burden will be on the employee to prove that the circumstances he or she faced made it unreasonable to follow policy or rules. If the employee can establish that such was the case, the employee's deviation from the policy or rule will be excused.

The paramilitary structure of law enforcement has led to public expectations of conformity and consistency in law enforcement, yet policies, typically written by administrators, often conflict with how officers need to react in the moment (Scoville, 2008, p.56). Policies are not created in a vacuum but rather through **vetting**, a process in which policies are evaluated, examined and investigated thoroughly and expertly by sergeants, department attorneys and other stakeholders: "The vetting cycle includes an assessment phase wherein the department evaluates the outcome of the policy: Has it accomplished its purpose? Does it need modification? Or is it fundamentally impractical?" (Scoville, p.60). The vetting process often leads to modifications in policy.

Scoville (2008, p.63) criticizes those departments that have volumes of policies and procedures, viewing this as a lack of trust in officers by those who oversee them, and hoping, "Perhaps one day, [supervisors] will allow greater leeway for officers to exercise their authority and greater latitude for the men and women who evaluate their discretion so that if they can't temper justice with mercy, then perhaps with a little common sense."

vetting

a process in which policies are evaluated, examined and investigated thoroughly and expertly by sergeants, department attorneys and other stakeholders

Common sense is also praised by Burch (2008, p.69), who states, "I believe common sense is the single important key to effective policing, and most of my colleagues seem to agree." Common sense refers to people who have "street smarts," use their "sixth sense," have good "gut feelings" or "gut instincts," or can trust a hunch: "These officers know policy and the law but use their common sense to their advantage and know where to draw the line" (Burch, p.69).

An additional controversy is whether policies should be long and detailed or relatively short and general (Means, 2008). General policies often fail to help officers understand how such policies apply on the street. Allowing such questions to be answered only through training or by the supervisor or leaving them up to the officer's discretion, leaves too much room for error and inconsistency in how the policies are carried out. Although it is impossible to anticipate every legitimate question an officer may have, a policy and procedures manual should answer as many question as possible within reason.

FUNCTIONS OF MANAGERS AT VARIOUS LEVELS

The organizational chart discussed in Chapter 2 is inanimate, like a house without people. The form and foundation exist and are necessary, but the structure is in no sense vital or exciting. Vitality and excitement come when the boxes in the chart are filled with people, men and women patrol officers, investigators, sergeants, lieutenants, captains and chiefs, interacting and working together to accomplish their mission—"to serve and protect." The organization accomplishes its mission through management directing and guiding employees and resources, both internal and external to the organization.

Managers in law enforcement face unique problems because of the continuous need for service, 24/7, 365 days a year. The highest-level manager, or chief executive officer (CEO), of the law enforcement agency obviously cannot be physically present for this extended period and must therefore rely on the organizational structure to permit other members to perform administrative and operational functions. In addition, challenges facing today's law enforcement administrators are enormous, including strained budgets and cutbacks, greater citizen demands and expectations for service and an increasingly diverse society.

Management typically has three levels:
- **The first-line level (sergeants, first-line supervisors)**
- **The middle level (captains, lieutenants)**
- **The top level (chief, sheriff)**

At each level of management, responsibilities include planning, organizing, controlling and leading. Although the same activities are performed at each management level, the activities flow downward with each management level interacting with its subordinates (Hesser, 2008, p.64).

The expression "rank has its privileges" is certainly true in law enforcement but where an actual rank designation carries its own power. An officer who abuses that power loses respect: "Rank without respect is an empty holster" (Johnson, 2007a, p.10). This comment should be kept in mind by managers at all levels as they perform their functions.

Coordination

Coordination ensures that each individual unit performs harmoniously with the total effort to achieve the department's mission.

Management tools for coordination include
- **A clear chain of command and unity of command.**
- **Clear channels of communication and strict adherence to them.**
- **Clear, specific job descriptions.**
- **Clear, specific goals, objectives and work plans.**
- **Standard operating procedures for routine tasks.**
- **An agency regulation guidebook.**
- **Meetings and roll calls.**
- **Informational bulletins, newsletters and memos.**

Coordinating efforts should be a part of an agency's work plan. Coordination is especially important in departments that are changing their focus from crime fighting to community policing and problem solving.

The specific functions performed at these basic levels of management vary considerably.

First-Line Supervisors

The two most influential positions in a law enforcement agency are the chief and the field supervisor or sergeant: "The sergeant is a direct link between the chief's view of the law enforcement mission and the way the officers do their jobs" (Miller, 2009, p.92). As such, the first-line supervisor is responsible for translating the organizational values, philosophies and strategies into officer performance and compliance (Hesser, 2008, p.66). Management consultant Drucker says, "Supervisors are, so to speak, the ligaments, the tendons and sinews of an organization. They provide the articulation. Without them, no joint can move."

Most first-line managers or supervisors are sergeants, who are responsible to the next highest rank in the organization unless their positions are specialized. Sergeants, having been promoted from the rank of patrol officer, often endure numerous challenges in adjusting to this new position.

Challenges for the New Sergeant

Before examining the specific functions of first-line supervisors, it is prudent to highlight some of the challenges new supervisors face simply because they are now in the position of managing individuals who were, until recently, their peers. This new working dynamic leads to the commonly held belief:

"The hardest promotional move in law enforcement is the move from patrol officer to first-line supervisor" (Nowicki, 2007, p.18). Officers promoted to sergeant from the rank and file must form a different relationship with their former coworkers, who are now their subordinates. They cannot simply be buddies, but they can still be friends who work for them (Sanow, 2008, p.6). If friendships continue, the appearance of favoritism must be avoided.

The transition to first-line supervisor is one of the most difficult in law enforcement, for this is when new supervisors begin to make decisions that separate them from their fellow officers.

Supervisors may not have the same camaraderie they enjoyed with members of the rank and file. They are now management and will not always be liked because they may have to make unpopular decisions. Supervisors will grow to dislike some of the officers in their command, and some of them will grow to dislike their supervisors, perhaps passionately. But supervisors simply must control any personal animosity that exists or arises (Oldham, 2007, p.10). Supervision is not a popularity contest.

Many new supervisors wonder whether they can, or even should, maintain the same social relationships with former peers—relationships that may have taken many years to develop—or whether that interaction must stop. Some officers may remind new supervisors of the pranks the new supervisors used to pull with them. Pretending these things didn't happen will kill a supervisor's credibility. The supervisor might reply, "I remember the crazy stuff we used to do, but those days are gone." Make it clear that the relationship has changed.

One of the most difficult aspects of becoming a sergeant is learning how to be an effective disciplinarian, particularly when it comes to circumstances involving a peer from the previous work group (the patrol officer unit). Another significant demand on a new supervisor is the ability to manage conflict. If day-to-day conflict can be managed, there is a greater likelihood of success.

New supervisors often face considerable stress and tension when they are positioned as a buffer between administration and line officers, making it important to find the balance necessary to work effectively between these two divisions of the organization. Another area that makes this transition so difficult is that a new first-line supervisor must determine how to deliver results through others. A related challenge is adapting to the responsibility of being held accountable for both positive results and negative outcomes. As a patrol officer, the individual was generally only responsible for his or her own work. As supervisors, however, they are required to accept and be responsible for the outcomes generated by those they supervise. Again, the difficulties of this transition are alleviated once the new supervisor finds a balance between attaining goals and developing people.

Consider the following supervisory skill set, which requires an ability by the new sergeant to accept and adapt to change more so than at any other point in this career:

⦿ Accountable for work, or lack thereof, performed by subordinates

⦿ Vulnerable to criticism—more so than in the last position

◉ Responsible for disciplinary actions

◉ Implementing agency policy that may run counter to personal opinions

◉ Requirement to work through conflict

◉ Need for effectiveness versus being popular

◉ Inability to be a close friend in lieu of serving as a supervisor

◉ Working more in isolation

As the conduit between the rank and file and the command element, supervisors are responsible for ensuring that orders are carried out, even if a policy is unpopular. A paramilitary structure is not a democracy, and policing has never been a job for those who cannot take orders (Oldham, 2009a, p.10).

Functions of the First-Line Supervisor

Supervisors' fundamental responsibility is to ensure that what needs to be accomplished during any given shift is accomplished effectively and legally. Supervisors are concerned with overseeing the day-to-day concerns of law enforcement officers—that is, overseeing the activities of all nonranking employees in the agency. Although the overall job description requires first-line supervisors to manage line personnel in the field and supervise patrol activities, more specific functions include

◉ Enforcing rules and regulations

◉ Maintaining discipline

◉ Training, guiding and mentoring others

◉ Conducting performance reviews—evaluating the work of others

◉ Coordinating work schedules

◉ Managing citizen complaints

◉ Performing tactical/critical incident decision making

◉ Conducting inspections

◉ Conducting roll call

First-line supervisors *planning activities* include analyzing operational data and information, forecasting, developing recommendations for changes, establishing programs and strategies, scheduling and budgeting at the service delivery level. Their *organizing activities* include balancing resources, delegating responsibility and authority and maintaining relationships. Their *controlling activities* include measuring performance, evaluating results and correcting undesirable performance. Their *leading activities* include influencing others, initiating projects, making decisions, communicating effectively, motivating employees and developing personnel (Hesser, 2008, p.66).

The sergeant is the first stop in line for almost everything in police work: the first supervisor to most scenes, the first one to know when an officer needs something, the first to yell when an officer makes a mistake, the first to talk to angry citizens who have been stopped for speeding, the first one officers run to when they are in trouble and the first one to jump to his or her officers' defense against the upper management. It is crucial for sergeants to know their officers so that they can spot those who are in trouble and those who are teetering on the edge of self-destructive behavior. Sometimes all that is needed is to listen.

One key area a sergeant should be aware of is the need for officers not to become "destructively obsessive" about their careers—fighting the good battle at the expense of other areas in their lives. Supervisors can show their officers, especially the younger officers, how important it is for them to be involved with the lives of their families. For married officers: "To become the partner your spouse needs and requires means you have to 'mind the store' and be sure that your spouse has everything needed to both survive and to thrive" (Oldham, 2008b, p.10).

A sergeant's first priority is to bring his or her officers home alive at the end of their shift: "Sergeants have a given function in the paramilitary world in which we all exist in law enforcement. It is our job to be sure that business is taken care of in the safest and most efficient manner possible" (Oldham, 2007, p.10). Sergeants must therefore strictly enforce officer safety practices and follow them themselves. If they teach that backup guns and body armor save lives, they should be wearing theirs, leading from the front on the calls with their officers. Officers would much rather hear "follow me" than "go do such and such."

"As law enforcement supervisors, it is us and the officers at their command who will be the first to be targeted, our civilians who will be the first to die. It is our communities that will suffer," says Oldham (2008c, p.24). Supervisors must learn as much as possible about the dangers they and their officers face. Fortunately training of all kinds is available.

Among the lessons supervisors need to teach their officers is to not run into a call without backup, yet many still do. Officers are taught not to park directly in front of an address when making a run, yet it happens often. They

© Joel Gordon

An NYPD Shift Captain conducts roll call and goes over the assignment duties and posts for police officers before the start of a protest march. Roll call can be an ideal time to remind officers of important safety measures.

have been lectured about noise and light discipline on approaches to calls, but this lesson also is often ignored (Oldham, 2009b, p.10). Often the more tenured officers are the "problem children," saying they've never had a problem with such actions.

Every supervisor should understand the acronym TTPE—training, tactics, procedures and equipment—which will help supervisors evaluate exactly how prepared they and their officers are to do the job when lives are in danger (Oldham, 2009c, p.10). It is critical that supervisors never place their officers in a position where they are required to exceed their capabilities simply to survive.

A sergeant is likely to be the first commander on the scene to deal with any incident. In chaotic situations, sergeants need to command, but must also remain calm. Sergeants are expected to step up and take charge when the shift needs it and to step back and allow their officers to run the show and grow in their capabilities when they do not need that firm, calming hand.

Supervisors frequently are not trained in the new skills they need. Initial training should concentrate on the "people activities" performed by supervisors, with particular emphasis on motivating others. General George Patton wrote in his battle journal, "Don't tell people what to do. Tell them what you want done and let them surprise you with their ingenuity." As Nowicki (2007, p.20) stresses, "A great street cop will not be a good supervisor unless he or she has these people skills." Night watch supervisors must be aware of the relative youth of their officers, many of whom are still trying to find their place; supervising these officers is a mix of being part mentor, part disciplinarian and all leader (Oldham, 2008a, p.105).

Supervisors also need to stay current with changes in the law rather than concentrating only on training in supervisory skills. They must not let their basic technical knowledge become stale and neglected and must continue to train in the areas they supervise: "Both the up-to-date officer and the out-of-date supervisor experience frustration over their information gap" (Rutledge, 2008, p.74).

New supervisors soon learn they are only as good as their officers and that their officers' performance often directly reflects on the supervisor's abilities. Weak supervisors spend a lot of time trying to cover up anything negative that happened on their watch; strong supervisors, in contrast, spend their energy finding out what went wrong and making sure it doesn't happen again.

A National Institute of Justice (NIJ) study, "Identifying Characteristics of Exemplary Baltimore Police Department First Line Supervisors" (Baltimore Police Department and Johns Hopkins University, 2001) identified sergeants considered exemplary and those considered less so. Among the vital traits identified by the focus group were character and integrity, knowledge of the job, management skills, communication skills, interpersonal skills, ability to develop entry-level officers, problem-solving and critical-thinking skills, effectiveness as a role model and as a disciplinarian and the ability to be proactive. The greatest difference between the exemplary sergeants and their less exemplary peers was in moral reasoning.

Another NIJ study (Engel, 2003) identified four distinct supervisory styles—traditional, innovative, supportive and active—and found the *quality*, or style, of field supervision more significantly influenced patrol officer behavior than did the *quantity* of supervision. According to the study, *traditional supervisors* expect aggressive enforcement from officers, are highly task oriented and expect officers to produce measurable outcomes, especially arrests and citations. *Innovative supervisors* tend to form relationships with their officers, to have a low level of task orientation and to hold more positive views of subordinates. They embrace community policing and problem solving and encourage their officers to embrace new philosophies and methods of policing.

Supportive supervisors protect subordinates from discipline or punishment perceived as "unfair" and provide "inspirational motivation." They are less concerned with enforcing rules and regulations and paperwork. They encourage officers through praise and recognition. *Active supervisors* embrace a philosophy of leading by example. They are heavily involved in the field alongside subordinates while controlling patrol officer behavior. In effect, they perform the dual function of street officer and supervisor. Officers with active supervisors spent more time on self-initiated activities, community policing activities and problem solving. The study concluded, "An 'active' supervisory style—involving leading by example—seems to be the most influential despite potential drawbacks. Indeed, active supervisors appear to be crucial to the implementation of organizational goals" (Engel, 2003, p.ii).

In an open letter to line supervisors, Trautman (2008) lists what he perceives to be the four most devastating, real-life flaws of supervisors: Fourth, failure to stay knowledgeable and develop those they lead. Third, not disclosing or taking actions to expose misconduct to administrators. Second, not being a role model for integrity. And the number one failure is wanting to be liked more than wanting to be a good supervisor.

Middle Management

Middle management usually includes captains and lieutenants. Captains have authority over all officers of the agency below the chief or sheriff and are responsible only to the chief or sheriff. Lieutenants are second in rank to captains. They are in charge of sergeants and all officers within their assigned responsibility, and they report to captains. Captains and lieutenants may perform the following functions:

- Inspecting assigned operations
- Reviewing and making recommendations on reports
- Helping develop plans
- Preparing work schedules
- Overseeing records and equipment
- Making appointments, demotions and promotions.

The role of middle management is, "To turn the values, philosophies, principles, policies and strategies into some form of action to achieve desired results" (Hesser, 2008, p.65). Their responsibilities include communicating accurately the values, philosophies, principles, policies and strategies of the department while being sensitive to the needs, issues and concerns of employees through positive interaction and communicating them to the executive level. Middle managers also coordinate the efforts of staff and peers to achieve operational objectives, organizing and assigning available resources for optimum results. In addition, they are expected to be sensitive to work and people conflicts and proactively seek solutions to resolve any such conflicts (Hesser, p.65).

Middle managers' *planning activities* include analyzing the internal climate, supporting data and information, forecasting, establishing objectives, scheduling, budgeting, developing strategies and establishing procedures at the division level. *Organizing activities* include establishing staffing levels, balancing resources, delegating responsibilities and authority and identifying needed skills and skill levels. *Controlling activities* include establishing performance standards, measuring performance, evaluating results and correcting undesirable performance. *Leading activities* include influencing others, initiating projects, decision making, communicating effectively, motivating employees, selecting people and developing personnel (Hesser, 2008, p.65).

The middle manager champions the leader's agenda to the troops and bears the responsibility of developing newly promoted sergeants. One of the most demanding middle management positions in larger departments is that of patrol district commander, essentially the chief in their own geographic area.

The captain's rank is generally the first time a supervisor is responsible for the entire operation, in the field and administratively, of a watch or unit (Johnson, 2008c, p.10). Often, captains want to make a good impression by suggesting they will make changes everyone has been wanting. However, new captains must be cautious not to make promises they are unable to keep. For example, a captain might want to promise some new equipment or offer relief from unpopular policies, but budget restrictions or labor agreements may make either of these impossible. Captains who have to renege on promises will appear impotent to affect change.

A middle manager's authority, like that of sergeants' authority, comes with the rank, but respect must be earned. Managers' communication styles, arguably one of a leader's most valuable assets, directly determine the respect they are given: "The arrogant manager who is both condescending and fails to listen is doomed to fail" (Johnson, 2008b, p.32). And as at any level of management, lieutenants and captains should not take things personally, which gives the other person power over them (Johnson, 2008a, p.10).

Middle managers should also be aware of the self-fulfilling prophecy phenomenon—more than 300 studies indicate that expectations clearly influence behavior (Johnson, 2007b, p.20). Effective captains can use this knowledge to shift a sergeant's focus from negative to positive by talking to the sergeant before taking any disciplinary action: "Self-fulfilling prophecies are really only a problem to the extent they are influenced by negative expectations and attitudes. To avoid damaging self-fulfilling prophecies, captains need to emphasize the positive and encourage high expectations. They must keep open minds and not rush to judgments about their supervisors' ability to resolve the situation to everyone's satisfaction" (Johnson, 2007b, p.23).

Furthermore, middle managers should not be afraid to allow emotional, personal connections with those under their command because research has shown that emotions precede thoughts and can affect what a person thinks "While awards are nice, officers need the emotionally sincere expression of heartfelt approval and appreciation for a job well done" (Johnson, 2007c, p.12).

Among the most important responsibilities of middle managers is assigning personnel—promoting, demoting, sometimes terminating. Business guru Collins is well known for his advice on this topic, noting that organizations who can go from good to great get the right people on the bus and the wrong people off the bus (easier to do in business than in law enforcement). To accomplish this, managers need to know those under their command. They also need to be aware of situations that may cause problems such as fraternization and workplace romances. Although manager-subordinate relationships with the rank and file within the work environment based on mutual respect and trust are desirable, all managers need to consider the implications and consequences of fraternization outside the workplace (Johnson, 2007b, p.21). Such consideration can minimize potential problems.

Johnson (2008d, p.10) cautions that simply prohibiting workplace romance is not realistic, but that situations can lead to serious problems, especially if one or both of those involved are married, suggesting that captains need to be prepared to address the concerns of those who have been betrayed as well as to deal with charges of harassment should the romance end badly. He notes that managers who interact regularly with their officers will usually be able to pick up on clues when something is amiss and proactively step in before the situation escalates.

Gebhardt (2007, p.29) addresses another area of importance to middle management, recommending that when middle managers are given a new project, they should not think they know it all. Such a "developmental vacuum" will show in the final product. Project managers should ask those below them for information and take advantage of others' experience—"from the rookie who offers a fresh perspective to the seasoned veteran who can perform the task in their sleep."

The Top Level—The Executive Manager

The executive manager, or the CEO, is the top official in any law enforcement agency. The title may be chief of police, director, superintendent or sheriff, but the authority and responsibility of the position are similar. The executive manager is either elected or appointed by the city council, the county commission or the city manager, subject to approval of the city council.

Executive managers have full authority and responsibility as provided by the charter provisions of their local jurisdictions. People appointed to this position are to enforce the applicable laws of the United States as well as state and local jurisdiction and all rules and regulations established by local government or the civil service commission.

Executive managers are responsible for planning, organizing and managing the agency's resources, including its employees. Executive managers are responsible for preserving the peace and enforcing laws and ordinances. The duties and responsibilities of executive managers often include

- Developing a mission statement.
- Formulating goals and objectives.
- Preparing an annual budget.

- Preparing and periodically reviewing agency rules and regulations and general and specific agency orders.
- Developing strategic long-term and tactical short-term plans for organizational operations.
- Attending designated meetings of the city council or other organizations.
- Preparing required reports for the governing authority or person.
- Coordinating with other law enforcement agencies.
- Participating in emergency preparedness plans and operations.
- Developing public relations liaisons with the press.
- Administering ongoing, operational financial processes.
- Developing training programs to meet local needs.
- Acting as a liaison with community agencies.
- Communicating through oral, written and technological means.

The role of the executive-level manager is to develop values, philosophies, principles, policies and strategies that are supported by the community and the department and that allow the department to fulfill its mission (Hesser, 2008, p.64). Responsibilities include viewing the department as a total entity operating in a larger environment and accurately assessing the department's and community's climate; establishing a vision and clearly defined mission and goals based on current needs and future forecasts; recognizing and adapting the department to internal and external forces for change; establishing mechanisms to recruit the most competent personnel, developing and promoting personnel to higher levels of responsibility and providing an atmosphere that encourages teamwork, mutual support and open sharing of information; and encouraging creative and responsible risk-taking with accountability (Hesser, p.65).

Planning activities include analyzing external climate, data and information; forecasting; establishing goals; scheduling; budgeting; establishing the mission, values, philosophy and principles; and developing policy at the department level. *Organizing activities* include developing department structure, establishing relationships and delegating responsibilities and authority. *Controlling* activities include establishing performance standards, measuring performance, evaluating results and correcting undesirable performance. *Leading activities* include influencing others, initiating projects, decision making, communicating effectively, motivating employees, selecting people and developing personnel.

Literature on management often conveys the image of an executive working at an uncluttered desk in a spacious office. The executive is rationally planning, organizing, coordinating and controlling the organization. After careful analysis the executive makes critical decisions and has competent, motivated subordinates readily available to offer insightful input. The executive has a full schedule but no unexpected interruptions. Timelines are met without problem.

Several studies, however, indicate that this is *not* a realistic portrayal. Actually, most executives work at an unrelenting pace, are frequently interrupted and are often more oriented to reacting to crises than to planning and executing. As one top-level manager said, "I dread any time I hear someone say,

'Chief, do you have a minute?' Inevitably that means they need at least half an hour." This challenge is discussed in Chapter 6.

The executive manager's roles in law enforcement differ from other levels of managers. Executive managers are responsible for the big picture, for accomplishing the department's mission through goals and objectives and for interacting with the community, its leaders, organizations and individual citizens, as well as the entire criminal justice system.

Essential Functions of Law Enforcement Executives

Acting in a *managerial* capacity, law enforcement executives serve as
- **Planners.**
- **Facilitators.**
- **Interfacers.**
- **Interactors.**

Planners Law enforcement managers must possess basic skills for planning—that is, the ability to set goals and objectives and to develop work plans to meet them. Whether managers personally formulate these goals and objectives or seek assistance from their staff, plans are essential. Law enforcement organizations cannot function efficiently without tactical and strategic planning.

Tactical planning is short-term planning. Strategic planning is long-term planning.

| **tactical planning** |
| short-term planning. |

| **strategic planning** |
| long-term planning. |

Tactical planning includes the year's work plans. Strategic planning, on the other hand, is futuristic planning. Some people may use the term *tactical* in an operational or military sense to refer to unusual situations in which combat might be expected. In law enforcement this might include serving warrants, conducting drug raids, dealing with hostage situations and the like. In this context tactical planning would mean planning designed to carry out a tactical operation. Tactical planning is most often necessary to provide the flexibility needed for change, determine personnel needs, determine objectives and provide organizational control and handle large incidents such as drug raids and special events such as sports competitions, popular concerts, large conventions and parades.

A meeting of line and staff personnel can determine the events for which tactical planning is necessary. Special problems can then be resolved and personnel needs assessed and assigned. A review of similar past events may require assistance from other police agencies in the area or state or federal aid. Tactical planning should be flexible because of changing conditions such as the number of people involved. Tactical plans are sometimes cast in the form of an action plan such as that shown in Figure 3.1.

Objective: _____
_____

Strategy: _____

What is known about the situation (+'s and −'s): _____
_____

What will be done? (Tasks)	Who will do it? (People)	When will it be done?	Resources needed	Evidence of accomplishment

© Cengage Learning 2012

FIGURE 3.1 Action Plan Sample Worksheet

Strategic plans, in contrast, focus on the future and on setting priorities: "Strategic planning is rooted in future-oriented, proactive thinking that anticipates change and adopts long-term strategies to meet the demands of that change. In other words, it is a 'master plan' for your law enforcement agency. It's also a management tool that will help your organization focus its energies appropriately" (Barishansky, 2009, p.40). Such planning should seek answers to four basic questions:

1. Where are we going (defined by mission and vision statements)?

2. How do we get there (defined by specific goals)?

3. What is our blueprint for action (the action steps for achieving the goals)?

4. How do we know if we are on track (assessment and revision)?

Before developing a strategic plan, many agencies conduct a S-W-O-T (strengths, weaknesses, opportunities and threats) analysis, examining the current state of the department as well as factors that might change that state. This analysis basically asks, Where are you right now? Where do you want to be?

Recall that strategic planning is long-term, large-scale, future-oriented planning. It begins with the vision and mission statement already discussed. Strategic planning is grounded in those statements and guided by the findings of the needs assessment. From here, specific goals and objectives and an accompanying implementation strategy and timeline are developed. What looks like a straightforward process can become extremely difficult as dilemmas arise and threaten the plan.

In addition to having a realistic timeline, the strategic plan must also be tied to the agency's budget. Without the resources to implement the activities outlined in the long-range plan, they are not likely to be accomplished. It is easy to get lost in the process with the plan becoming an end in itself. The strategic plan and the planning process are only a means to an end—delivering the future organization built on core values, agreed goals and an effective implementation process.

The strategic plan lays the foundation for the strategies that are to be used in implementing the community policing philosophy. Strategic planning provides several benefits, including clarifying future directions, establishing priorities, making decisions in light of their future consequences, developing a coherent and defensible basis for decision making, solving major organizational problems, improving organizational performance and building teamwork and expertise. In addition to planning, managers must be facilitators of those plans.

A department might decide to place more emphasis on the use of technological advances, including communications and technology training. It might decide to continue the same emphasis on the level of recruitment and in-service training for sworn personnel and to place less emphasis on the use of sworn personnel for nonsworn duties. The department might also identify new activities such as developing accurate job descriptions and career paths for all employees and eliminating other activities such as free services that most agencies charge for (e.g., fingerprinting, alarms, and computer entry).

Facilitators **Facilitators** assist others in performing their duties. Law enforcement managers at any level do not personally bring the agency goals, objectives and work plans to fruition. This is accomplished through a joint agency effort, as well as with the assistance of others external to the agency.

Rules, regulations, personal rapport, communications, standards, guidelines, logic, basic principles and direction all assist others in performing their duties. After managers have directed subordinates on what to do and how, managers should let their subordinates carry out their duties independently. Trust, honesty and integrity are important in the manager-subordinate work relationship. A 2009 *Police* magazine survey revealed that of the 1,997 respondents, 58.6 percent reported that the most important characteristic of a chief or sheriff was the ability to support the efforts of line officers in their duties. A distant second, at 24.9 percent, was a willingness to change policies and seek innovative practices. Almost all of the respondents agreed that being able to respect a chief or sheriff is much more important than likeability: "Police officers want a progressive, supportive top cop they can respect" (Basich, 2009, p.14).

Operating within this environment is constant change. All levels of management must recognize change and be flexible enough to adapt to its demands.

Interfacers Law enforcement executive managers must be **interfacers** who communicate with all segments of the agency, from chief deputy to patrol officer. They must have knowledge of communications and specialized staff activities and relationships and must understand the division of labor and the allocations of personnel.

Managers must set agency goals and work plans with input from all agency members. Managers are the interfacers between all actions of agency personnel and all other people and agencies in contact with these personnel. Like good drivers, they can look toward the horizon without losing sight of immediate concerns.

Interactors Law enforcement managers also must be **interactors** who work effectively with a number of groups. They act as the department's official

> **facilitators**
> assist others in performing their duties to meet mutual goals and objectives.

> **interfacers**
> coordinate law enforcement agency's goals with those of other agencies within the jurisdiction.

> **interactors**
> communicate with other groups and agencies: the press, other local government departments, the business community, schools and numerous community committees and organizations.

representatives to the press, other local government departments, the business community, schools and numerous community committees and organizations.

Figure 3.2 illustrates the interactions of a typical law enforcement executive and, to some extent, all law enforcement managers. This diagram shows that only one-fifth of the executive manager's role is with the law enforcement organization. Executive managers have political, community, interorganizational and media roles as well.

Each organization with whom the executive interacts sees the importance and conduct of the position from different viewpoints. Law enforcement managers must determine these varied expectations and develop goals and work plans to meet them effectively.

 Law enforcement executives typically interact with politicians, community groups, the media and executives of other law enforcement organizations, as well as individuals and groups within the agency itself.

FIGURE 3.2 The Role of the Law Enforcement Executive

Source: Witham, D. C., & Watson, P. J. (1983). "The Role of the Law Enforcement Executive." *Journal of Police Science and Administration,* *11*(1), 69–75.

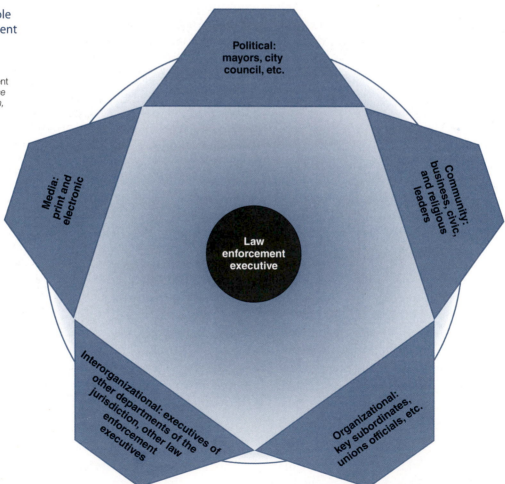

Attendance at intergovernmental staff meetings is mandatory. Law enforcement agencies need services and information exchange from engineering, finance, planning, building inspections and other departments, just as other departments need the police department's services.

Although media communications have some undesirable aspects, if reporters and law enforcement personnel establish honest, forthright rapport, they can establish generally good working relationships. Law enforcement needs the media as much as the media need law enforcement agencies. (Dealing effectively with the media is discussed in Chapter 4.) Personal contact with representatives of all groups develops an atmosphere of trust, integrity and respect for each other's duties and responsibilities.

On Becoming an Executive Manager

Robert Frost once said, "By working faithfully eight hours a day, you may eventually get to be boss and work twelve hours a day!" When a person first becomes a chief of police, whether selected from within the department or as an outsider, many rumors concerning the appointment will precede the new chief's first day on the job. New chiefs should call a department meeting as soon as possible. At this meeting they should openly state that they understand the officers' concerns and past loyalties but expect to earn their respect. They should also describe the working relationships they seek. Such an open meeting will help allay fears, squelch rumors, decrease suspicions and establish an early rapport with the staff and line personnel.

A chief's management style should be adjusted to the department's needs. Some important changes should be made as soon as possible, but lesser changes should be instituted slowly. Change is stressful for an organization as well as individuals. People will have different opinions about the need for change. A participative approach that invites input from all employees usually works best, as discussed later in the chapter. Decisions should be based on what is good for the community and the department, not on what pleases specific individuals or interest groups.

Whether the department is small or large, the chief of police holds a powerful position in the governmental structure and in the community. The position is also challenging, exciting and filled with barriers and pitfalls. Chiefs should allow time for contemplation, innovation and creative thinking. They must be both managers and leaders. Their responsibilities are heavy, but their rewards are great. If chiefs adopt a coequal management approach with the department's formal and informal leaders, they may find that their organizational philosophy will be accepted more readily, thus enabling the organizational changes to occur with less resistance.

Kushner (2009, p.50) advises, "Use the international, state, and local associations to network. Pick up the phone, call chiefs from surrounding agencies, and go meet them in person. Each one of us was the new guy at some time. You remember that old saying about the 'brotherhood of blue'? Well, it's been my experience that it exists even in the upper ranks of agencies." He also suggests that new chiefs take a class on media relations: "Don't try to starve the sharks. Learn how to feed them without being eaten."

A major goal of chief executive officers should be to establish a department in which success is expected and excellence is desired. As Theodore Roosevelt once said, "The best executive is the one who has sense enough to pick good men to do what he wants done, and self-restraint to keep from meddling with them while they do it." Ideally, the chief of police is also a leader within the community, particularly in interactions with the city council and the city manager without "playing politics."

Politics

Orrick (2007, p.1) describes politics as "the process of determining what governmental services are provided for our communities and how they will be funded." A survey of police chiefs has identified the "most discouraging, dissatisfying aspect of their job as being frustrated by working in the political environment and dealing with politicians" (p.1).

With a clear mission, goals and objectives, a department's day-to-day operations should *not* be influenced by *partisan* politics. However, chiefs must recognize that politics can influence how much funding the department receives and, thus, they must be able to maneuver successfully in the political environment. This environment consists of five interconnected components or conceptual arenas: (1) the police department (internal), (2) the public (external), (3) the media, (4) other agencies (both police and community or state partners) and (5) elected officials (Orrick, 2007, p.1). Note that these five elements very closely match those identified in Figure 3.2 as those entities with which a law enforcement executive must be skilled in handling.

The essential personal characteristics that enhance a person's ability to influence others to achieve a desired end are (Orrick, 2007, p.3)

- Political astuteness—the ability to read the signals from another person's mood, speech and body language and to adjust one's own behavior appropriately.
- Interpersonal influence—the ability to tell others what they need to know in a way they want to hear it, being flexible and open to alternative approaches.
- Networking abilities—the ability to interact with as many diverse groups, friends and alliances as possible.
- Sincerity—the ability to be perceived as truly seeking what is best for the agency, community and personnel.

Political interference may be a major cause of corruption in law enforcement in such areas as interference with hiring standards, promotions and transfers, discipline, adequate budget, fair enforcement of laws and work environment. The political nature of police administrative positions also requires chiefs to keep abreast of changes in legislation. Police administrators must become proactive in the legislative process to effectively serve their departments and communities. Police chiefs have a duty to ensure that the laws enacted are sensible and allow law enforcement agencies to successfully overcome the challenges confronting them and to effectively protect the citizens and communities they serve.

When considering what it takes to be a great manager and leader, it is also important to remember that every officer is also an individual and should be treated as such. This principle is at the heart of holistic management.

HOLISTIC MANAGEMENT/LEADERSHIP

The **holistic management/leadership** approach recognizes that both management and leadership skills are required for an agency to accomplish its mission. It recognizes the importance of teamwork, but it also recognizes that all those within the organization are complete individuals who have answered a special calling. Police officers feel a high sense of peer identification—no call has higher priority than a fellow officer in danger. Police officers can also take pleasure in the fact that they are readily identified by their uniforms and have certain powers above and beyond those of the average citizen.

The police manager/leader is responsible for ensuring that the officer does not lose this feeling of ego satisfaction (e.g., after a citizen has flashed an obscene gesture to the officer) and continues to develop this sense of belonging to a unique profession geared toward helping one's fellow human beings. The holistic management/leadership approach views law enforcement officers and support personnel as complete individuals who make up a *team*.

> **holistic management/ leadership**
>
> recognizes that both management and leadership skills are required for an agency to accomplish its mission and that all those within the organization are complete individuals who have answered a special calling and are part of the team.

THE TEAM APPROACH

Team building is the ultimate act of leadership. A team consists of two or more people who must coordinate their activities regularly to accomplish a common task. The team approach builds on the concept of **synergy**, that the group can channel individual energies to accomplish together what no individual could possibly accomplish alone—that the whole is greater than the sum of its parts.

Synergy is all around. Athletics provides countless examples of how a team, working together, can defeat a "superstar." Examples of synergy also come from the music world. Consider the power and energy produced by a topnotch marching band or symphony orchestra. Every musician must know his or her part. Individual players may have solos, but ultimately what is important is how it all sounds together. Anthropologist Margaret Mead has said of the value of collective efforts, "Never doubt that a small group of thoughtful, committed citizens can change the world. Indeed, it is the only thing that ever has."

"Effective leaders must be capable of putting together individuals of diverse backgrounds, personalities, abilities, training and experience molding them into cohesive, high performing teams. The leader's ability to form, develop and lead functional and effective groups is essential to accomplish the department's mission" ("Leadership in Police Organizations," 2007, p.14).

The Wilson Learning Corporation has identified eight attributes of high-performing teams (Buchholz and Roth, 1987, p.14).

> **synergy**
>
> occurs when the whole is greater than the sum of its parts; the team achieves more than each could accomplish as individuals.

Attributes of high-performing teams are
- *Participative leadership*—creating interdependency by empowering, freeing up and serving others.
- *Shared responsibility*—establishing an environment in which all team members feel as responsible as the manager for the work unit's performance.
- *Aligned on purpose*—having a sense of common purpose about why the team exists and the function it serves.
- *High communication*—creating a climate of trust and open, honest communication.
- *Future focused*—seeing change as an opportunity for growth.
- *Focused on task*—keeping meetings focused on results.
- *Creative talents*—applying individual talents and creativity.
- *Rapid response*—identifying and acting on opportunities.

Although Buchholz and Roth were speaking of teams in the business world, the same eight attributes are likely to be present in a high-performing law enforcement agency.

True leaders are not intimidated by outstanding team members. They do not fear for their jobs. They develop followers who will surpass them. Athletes, for example, will become coaches and train other athletes who will break their records.

One way to initiate action is to encourage employees at the lowest level to work together to solve their problems, with or without manager involvement. These are not highly organized, trained teams but rather groups of employees with a common problem who band together. They are organized informally from anywhere in the organization to focus on a specific problem or project. They are usually self-formed, self-managed and highly productive. When they have met the need, the group dissolves.

Many texts on team building use the analogy of a team and a flock of geese and what can be learned from their behavior in accomplishing the goal of migration.

⊚ Fact/Lesson: When a goose flaps its wings, it creates an uplift for the birds that follow. By flying in a "V" formation, the flock adds 71 percent greater flying range than if each bird flew alone. People who share common direction and sense of community reach their goals quicker and easier by traveling on the thrust of one another.

⊚ Fact/Lesson: When the lead goose tires, it rotates back into formation and another goose flies to the point position. It pays to take turns doing the hard tasks and sharing the leadership. People should depend on each others' skills, capabilities and unique talents and resources.

⊚ When a goose falls out of formation, it feels the drag and resistance and quickly moves back into formation to take advantage of the lifting power of the bird in front of it. People need to stay in formation with those headed where they want to go, accepting their help and helping others.

- The geese flying in formation honk to encourage those up front to continue their speed. In teams where there is much encouragement, the team's production is much greater. The power of encouragement can drive a team to success.

These same lessons apply to larger teams such as multiagency task teams and task forces as well.

Multiagency Teams and Task Forces

Multiagency teams are an important element of current-day policing. Among the cultural norms that impede interagency teams are case ownership, secrecy, organizational isolation and valuing individuals above the team. Communication protocols are the first necessity to overcome the barriers.

One of the most analyzed and publicized examples is the multijurisdictional DC sniper investigation, a case that involved more than 20 local, 2 state and at least 10 federal law enforcement agencies. During the three-week investigation, law enforcement executives as well as government leaders at the local, state and national levels grappled with questions about leadership and its role in solving crimes and addressing community fear.

The Sniper Task Force vested leadership with three individuals: Montgomery County Police Chief Charles Moose, Federal Bureau of Investigation (FBI) Special Agent in Charge (SAC) Gary Bald and Bureau of Alcohol, Tobacco, Firearms and Explosives (ATF) SAC Michael Bouchard. These leaders were responsible for leading the main task force and for five task forces within the jurisdictions affected as the case unfolded—the counties of Montgomery, Spotsylvania, Prince William, Fairfax and Central Virginia. Every task force leader managed information, kept chiefs informed and followed up on leads.

Among the lessons learned regarding leadership in a multijurisdictional task force, were

- Who is in charge as well as the scope and nature of their authority must be clearly established.
- The leaders of each task force should speak with one voice.
- Communication and meaningful information must flow both into and out of the task forces.
- The task forces should address six immediate tasks: (1) Make order out of chaos, (2) remain flexible and help others adapt, (3) focus on the entire agency, (4) let a competent workforce do its job, (5) provide personnel with the resources they need and (6) work with external stakeholders.

Thus far, the discussion has focused on the organization of local law enforcement. However, local agencies do not operate in a vacuum. They need to communicate and corroborate with other local jurisdictions; county, state and federal agencies; and other stakeholders, depending on the situation. To effectively do so, it is important to understand the concepts of the National Incident Management System (NIMS), including unified and incident command.

BEYOND THE LOCAL LEVEL: THE NATIONAL INCIDENT MANAGEMENT SYSTEM (NIMS)

The NIMS "provides principles to organize incident response in a uniform manner, collect and share information during an incident, and notify the public before and during an incident" (Mulholland, 2007, p.12). NIMS principles ensure that real-time information flows between participating agencies during an incident to develop a "common operating picture" to all jurisdictions/ disciplines.

 Two key components of the National Incident Management System (NIMS) are incident command and unified command.

incident command

an organizational structure designed to aid In managing resources during incidents.

Incident command is an organizational structure designed to aid in managing resources during incidents. The Incident Command System (ICS) is a standardized on-scene emergency management construct that integrates facilities, equipment, personnel, procedures and communications operations. ICS reflects the complexity and demands of single or multiple incidents, without being hindered by jurisdictional boundaries. It is used for all kinds of emergencies and applies to small as well as to large, complex incidents. In seeking to provide a framework for interoperability and compatibility, the NIMS is based on an appropriate balance of flexibility and standardization.

Several states have adopted ICS as their standard for emergency management, and others are considering adopting ICS. As ICS gains wider use, training should be provided for those who are not first responders (i.e., law enforcement, fire or emergency medical services personnel) who may be called on to function in an ICS environment.

To ensure coordination during incidents involving multiple jurisdictions or agencies, a single jurisdiction with multiagency involvement or multiple jurisdictions with multiagency involvement, the principle of unified command applies. **Unified command** allows agencies with different legal, geographic and functional authorities and responsibilities to work together effectively without affecting individual agency authority, responsibility or accountability (*National Incident Management System*, 2004, pp.11–12). Unified command coordinates the efforts of many jurisdictions and provides for and ensures joint decisions on objectives, strategies, plans, priorities and public communications.

unified command

allows agencies with different legal, geographic and functional authorities and responsibilities to work together effectively without affecting individual agency authority, responsibility or accountability.

BEING NEW TO A MANAGEMENT POSITION

This chapter has already discussed the challenges faced by first-time managers—those who find themselves wearing sergeant's bars and, for the first time, assuming authority over people who were previously their rank-and-file equals. But the adjustments to management and leadership positions do not end with that first promotion; they continue with each step up the administrative ladder. New skills must continuously be learned, new responsibilities must be taken on and new relationships must be formed.

New managers may be brimming with ideas on how to make the department better and eagerly anticipating getting on with it. However, before doing so, Perdue (2008, p.176) suggests that an individual in a new position should have a clear understanding of the department's past and culture, noting, "A police department's organizational culture is a deeply ingrained, personal aspect of its function that must not be trivialized." Just where does the new manager fit in this culture?

MISSION CRITICAL: Know the Mission, Vision and Core Values and Purpose of the Organization

A new supervisor, manager or leader should be focused enough to champion others to grow personally and professionally through compassion, perspective, belief in others' inherent goodness, integrity and enormous potential. The values in the above statement are leadership as service. The vision is people helping people reach more of their potential through well-rounded growth and that everything we do is inspired by our enduring mission. The mission is the compass for leadership decisions and the impact those decisions have on the stakeholders—a community's citizenry. Further, the mission becomes the criterion by which both you and the organization are measured against. In doing so, your department fulfills its commitment by providing the best and most professional service possible and strives to build a culture of trust, and open and honest dialogue, with community it serves and among the people it employs. Do you have a personal mission statement? Do you know your organization's mission statement—do you know the actual meaning of the words contained within your organization's mission, vision, and core values statements?

—*Chief Shaun E. LaDue*

New managers should also assess how well subordinates have been performing in the past. The quality of service being provided to the community can be determined by reviewing the history of complaints and commendations submitted to the department. If negative trends are noted, priorities should be established and then small, incremental changes should be made to give subordinates a chance to "buy into" the changes, actively participating in making their department better. Making too many changes too quickly can lead to employee resistance (Perdue, 2008).

Another suggestion is that managers in new positions review the department's policies and procedures, concentrating on those areas that most affect the new position, and then compare how well those written policies compare with actual practices (Perdue, 2008, p.177).

A final recommendation is that managers in new positions take time to develop a plan to deal with the community's quality-of-life issues from their level (Perdue, 2008, p.177). Such issues are often the most frequent calls for service and the biggest drain on police resources. The most important resource managers control is the officers who deliver basic police services. Managers/leaders at all levels should be the "torchbearers for this service-oriented mentality" (Perdue, p.177).

Collins' (GTG) research indicates that big-ego leaders often are least likely to have access to truthful information because they believe they know the answers and tend to surround themselves with subordinates who protect them from bad news. To create a culture in which the truth is heard and valued, Collins suggests,

- Lead with questions, not answers.
- Engage in dialogue and debate, not coercion.
- Conduct "autopsies" of mistakes without blame.
- Build "red flag" mechanisms that prevent you from ignoring the data (Wexler et al., 2007, p.33).

These recommendations apply to the chief executive as well as to all those at levels lower in the hierarchy of authority.

LAW ENFORCEMENT MANAGEMENT AS A CAREER

Deciding to become a law enforcement officer is an exciting career choice, but becoming a manager in law enforcement is even more challenging. It is an opportunity to develop personally and a responsibility to develop others. You can become a successful law enforcement manager in many ways.

- *Prepare and develop yourself for promotion.* Study, attend training programs, take correspondence courses, read trade journals, attend academic courses, use the public library and the law enforcement agency's library and listen to contemporaries. Be ready when opportunity arises.

- *Be available.* Once prepared, you become a valuable resource to the law enforcement organization. Assert yourself at appropriate times. Support your organization's goals and objectives. Participate in work programs. Volunteer to do more than others. Become so valuable to the organization's future that it cannot do without you. Become an information source who is willing to selflessly share information.

- *Support your manager.* An old adage advises, "If you want your manager's job, praise and support him or her because soon that person will move up the ladder. Be derogatory to your manager and he or she will be there forever." Complaining, continually finding fault and being negative or nonsupportive are fast tracks to organizational oblivion. You may accomplish a short-term goal, but in the long run you will destroy your career. Be supportive; if you criticize, make it constructive criticism. Be positive. Praise the good things happening.

- *Select an advisor or mentor.* These are people within or outside the police organization who can assist and counsel you. Advisors can point you in the right direction. They can be a sounding board.

- *Network.* Build connections and contacts with others in the same or similar position as you, both internal to the organization and externally in other law enforcement organizations. Do not forget that people doing the job right in front of you are a great resource for learning more about the job and associated responsibilities.

- *Be positive at and toward work.* Either like what you do or change to another job. Rarely can you excel at something you hate. Work longer, more diligently and more competently than anyone else in the organization. Before you know it, you will be an expert.

- *Nurture interpersonal relationships.* Management is getting things done through others. This is impossible to do without treating others as important. Working with others is one of the keys to success. Working alone is a long, hard road. Develop your interpersonal relationships. Combine their strengths with your weaknesses and their weaknesses with your strengths.

A commitment to supervision, management and leadership is a commitment to lifelong learning, even taking coursework away from home for extended periods. Simply getting the promotion you seek and showing up is not enough. Success at each level is determined by how much a person puts into the job outside his or her day-to-day responsibilities. Finally, remember Collins' emphasis on getting on the right bus in the right seat and not being afraid to fail (Wexler et al. 2007, p.23).

SUMMARY

A mission statement is a written explanation of why an organization exists and is the driving force for that organization, providing a focus for its energy and resources. Goals are broad, general, desired outcomes. Objectives are specific, measurable ways to accomplish the goals. Work plans are the precise activities that contribute to accomplishing objectives. Policies and procedures specify how the activities are to be carried out. The flywheel challenge encourages all within an organization to focus on priority goals. In contrast, the doom loop sees management as unfocused, inconsistent and following fads.

Management typically has three levels: the first-line level (sergeants, first-line supervisors), the middle level (captains, lieutenants) and the top level (chief, sheriff).

Management tools for coordination include a clear chain of command and unity of command; clear channels of communication and strict adherence to them; clear, specific job descriptions; clear, specific goals, objectives and work plans; standard operating procedures for routine tasks; an agency regulation guidebook; meetings and roll calls; and informational bulletins, newsletters and memos.

The transition to first-line supervisor is one of the most difficult in law enforcement, for this is when new supervisors begin to make decisions that separate them from their fellow officers.

Law enforcement executives are planners, facilitators, interfacers and interactors. They are responsible for both tactical and strategic planning. *Tactical planning* is short-term planning. *Strategic planning* is long-term planning.

In addition to these roles and responsibilities, law enforcement executives typically interact with politicians, community groups, the media, executives of other law enforcement organizations and individuals and groups within the law enforcement agency itself.

Attributes of high-performing teams are participative leadership, shared responsibility, aligned on purpose, high communication, future focused, focused on task, creative talents and rapid response. Two key components of the National Incident Management System (NIMS) are incident command and unified command.

CHALLENGE THREE

The Greenfield Police Department's new mission statement emphasizes a community policing philosophy. The new chief has increased the authority and the responsibility of sergeants to identify and solve problems affecting the quality of life in Greenfield. You are the evening shift supervisor and have learned that the residents of the Senior Citizens' Center are reluctant to venture out after dark. The center is located in a low-crime neighborhood adjacent to a public park with walking paths. Evening walks in the park used to be a popular activity for the seniors, but no one uses the park now. The center's owner tells you the residents are worried about all the crime they see on the news and read about in the paper. They are also concerned about thefts from their cars in the parking lot. He says rumors of criminal activity spread quickly through the center. The

owner provides classes every month on how to avoid being a crime victim. He also installed new security doors and cameras. Nothing seems to work.

You gather the officers on your shift to discuss the situation. They tell you there is no crime problem in the area of the center. The crime statistics support the officers. There has been one car window broken in the center's parking lot during the last year, and a few kids have been told not to skateboard through the lot on their way to the park. An officer remarks that the kids dress rather oddly and sport some strange haircuts, but they're good kids who stay out of trouble. Officers state that they patrol the area constantly and conduct frequent traffic enforcement on the street in front of the center. They flash their red lights to make sure the residents see them in the area. The officers tell you the residents have exaggerated the problem.

1. Is there a crime problem at the Senior Citizens' Center?

2. Is fear reduction a police problem?

3. What are some possible causes of fear of crime at the center?

4. What is missing in the current community–police relationship between the Greenfield Police department and the senior citizens?

5. How might the department's mission statement be changed—or should it?

DISCUSSION QUESTIONS

1. Are mission statements really vital or are they "window dressing?"

2. Is it possible for all members of police department to hold and support the same values?

3. How many goals are realistic for a department to have?

4. How many objectives do you believe are usually necessary to accomplish a goal?

5. Do you buy into Collins' concepts of the flywheel challenge and the doom loop?

6. What are the main challenges of becoming a new first-level manager? A mid-level manager? An executive manager?

7. How do the issues facing those doing strategic planning differ from those doing tactical planning? Can the two really be separated?

8. Do you agree with the attributes of a high-performing team as being the most important attributes or are others also important?

9. Does the police department in your community participate in multiagency teams or task forces? If so, how do they function?

10. Given the tremendous variation in size and location of law enforcement agencies across the country, is the National Incident Management System feasible or is it simply a model to be adapted to local circumstances?

REFERENCES

Baltimore Police Department and Johns Hopkins University. "Identifying Characteristics of Exemplary Baltimore Police Department First-Line Supervisors." August 20, 2001. (A locally initiated research project, property of NCJRS)

Barishansky, Raphael M. "What's Your Master Plan? Strategic Planning—It's Not Just for Business." *Law Officer Magazine*, August 2009, pp.40–44.

Basich, Melanie. "Who Is Your Ideal Chief?" *Police*, October 2009, p.14.

Blanchard, Ken. "Getting Back to Basics." *Today's Office*, January 1988, pp.14, 19.

Buchholz, Steve, and Roth, Thomas. *Creating the High-Performance Team*. New York: John Wiley and Sons, 1987.

Burch, Jay. "Letter of the Policy Versus Spirit of the Policy: The Loss of Common Sense in Policing." *Law and Order*, November 2008, pp.69–74.

DeLone, Gregory J. "Law Enforcement Mission Statements Post–September 11." *Police Quarterly*, June 2007, pp.218–235.

Engel, Robin Shepard. *How Police Supervisory Styles Influence Patrol Officer Behavior*. Washington, DC: U.S. Department of Justice, National Institute of Justice, June 2003. (NCJ 194078)

Furey, Barry. "Is That Your Final Answer? Consistency Is the Key to Supervision." *9-1-1 Magazine*, August 2007, pp.46–47.

Gebhardt, Chris. "Information Exchange: Listen to Your Officers and Turn Adversaries into Advocates." *Law Officer Magazine*, February 2007, pp.28–29.

Hesser, Larry M. "An Organizational Strategy Guide for an Effective Police Department." In *Police Chiefs Desk Reference*, 2nd ed. Washington, DC: Bureau of Justice

Assistance, and Arlington, VA: The International Association of Chiefs of Police, 2008.

Johnson, Robert Roy. "Power of Supervision." *Law and Order*, April 2007a, p.10.

Johnson, Robert Roy. "Self-Fulfilling Prophecy." *Law and Order*, October 2007b, pp.20–23.

Johnson, Robert Roy. "Supervising with Emotion." *Law and Order*, February 2007c, pp.10–14.

Johnson, Robert Roy. "Don't Take It Personally." *Law and Order*, April 2008a, p.10.

Johnson, Robert Roy. "Pride, Not Arrogance." *Law and Order*, October 2008b, p.32.

Johnson, Robert Roy. "Tips for the New Captain." *Law and Order*, August 2008c, p.10.

Johnson, Robert Roy. "Workplace Romances." *Law and Order*, June 2008d, p.10.

Kushner, William. "New Chief's Guide: Tips and Resources for the New Chief." *Law and Order*, February 2009, pp.50–51.

"Leadership in Police Organizations." *Big Ideas*, Spring 2007, pp.14–23.

Means, Randy. "Getting on the Same Page: Minimizing Supervisory Inconsistency." *The Police Chief*, October 2007, pp.10–11.

Means, Randy. "Rules Versus Guidelines." *Law and Order*, August 2008, p.12.

Miller, R. K. "Raising Leaders: Are Your New Supervisors Ready for the Job?" *Law Officer Magazine*, May 2009, pp.92–94.

Mulholland, David J. "NIMS: Information Sharing for Results." *The Police Chief*, November 2007, p.12.

National Incident Management System. Washington, DC: Department of Homeland Security, March 1, 2004.

Nowicki, Ed. "Training for Supervisors." *Law and Order*, June 2007, pp.18–20.

Oldham, Scott. "You Hate Me? I Hate You." *Law and Order*, January 2007, pp.10–13.

Oldham, Scott. "Fear Not the Darkness." *Law and Order*, March 2008a, pp.105–106.

Oldham, Scott. "Minding the Store." *Law and Order*, July 2008b, p.10.

Oldham, Scott. "Once Upon a Time. . . ." *Law and Order*, January 2008c, pp.24–26.

Oldham, Scott. "Advice for the New Sergeant." *Law and Order*, February 2009a, pp.10–12.

Oldham, Scott. "Run, Walk, Crawl." *Law and Order*, April 2009b, p.10.

Oldham, Scott. "Training, Tactics, Procedures, & Equipment." *Law and Order*, June 2009c, pp.10–12.

Orrick, Dwayne. "Maneuvering Successfully in the Political Environment." *Big Ideas for Smaller Police Departments*, Spring 2007, pp.1–8.

Perdue, Jimmy. "Lessons Learned: Advice for New Chiefs." *The Police Chief*, October 2008, pp.176–178.

Rutledge, Devallis. "Keeping Up with Case Law." *Police*, November 2008, pp.74–75.

Sanow, Ed. "Avoid New Manager Mistakes." *Police*, October 2008, p.6.

Scoville, Dean. "Rules of Engagement." *Police*, October 2008, pp.56–63.

Trautman, Neal. "An Open Letter to Line Supervisors." *Law Officer.com*, June 16, 2008.

Wexler, Chuck; Wycoff, Mary Ann; and Fischer, Craig. *"Good to Great" Policing: Application of Business Management Principles in the Public Sector.* Washington, DC: Community Oriented Policing Services and the Police Executive Research Forum, 2007.

CHAPTER FOUR

Communication: A Critical Management Skill

Developing excellent communication skills is absolutely essential to effective leadership. The leader must be able to share knowledge and ideas to transmit a sense of urgency and enthusiasm to others. If a leader can't get a message across clearly and motivate others to act on it, then having a message doesn't even matter.

—Gilbert Amaliuo

DO YOU KNOW?

- ◉ What the communication process involves?
- ◉ How much of a message is conveyed by body language and tone of voice rather than words?
- ◉ What the weakest link in the communication process is?
- ◉ What barriers can hinder communication?
- ◉ What directions communication can flow?
- ◉ What types of meetings departments typically have?
- ◉ How to make meetings efficient and productive?
- ◉ What powerful information sources are available from the FBI and the purpose of each?
- ◉ What four obstacles to sharing information among local, state and federal agencies are?

CAN YOU DEFINE?

abstract words
active listening
agenda
anticipatory benefit
body language
deconfliction
geographical diffusion of benefit
grapevine
interoperability
jargon
lines of communication
nonverbal communication
sound bite
vocoder

INTRODUCTION

Managers and supervisors are in the communication business. Of all the skills a manager, leader or supervisor needs to be effective, skill in communicating is *the* most vital. Estimates vary, but all studies emphasize the importance of communication in everyday law enforcement operations. Consider how much of a person's day is occupied with communication: conversations, television, radio, memos, letters, e-mails, text messages, faxes, phone calls, meetings, newspapers. Although technological advances have greatly expanded and speeded up communication capabilities, the communication process has not changed.

CHAPTER at a GLANCE

This chapter begins with a definition of communication and its importance to managers at all levels. This is followed by an examination of the communication process and its components. Next, barriers and obstacles to communication are discussed, followed by a discussion of communication enhancers. Then comes a look at internal communication, including meetings and newsletters and external communication, including dealing with the media and communicating with outside agencies and the public, followed by a discussion on communicating with the community. The chapter concludes by describing the various ways law enforcement agencies can share information and the types of obstacles often encountered in information sharing.

COMMUNICATION: AN OVERVIEW

"Communication is one of the most important skills in life. It is the key to building positive relationships and the essence of professionalism. Many 'people problems' are magnified because of the lack of effective communication skills. Problem-solving, decision-making and quality-improvement efforts are seriously hampered, if not impossible, if poor or ineffective communication skills are prevalent" (Hesser, 2008, p 34). Standards of performance for evaluating the effectiveness of communication include effective meetings, effective group processes, absence of conflict in the area of responsibility, effective problem solving and teamwork (p.34).

Hesser (2008, p.35) points out, "Our degree of ability to communicate will either evoke trust or distrust in those we lead. It will instill either confidence or fear. It will determine to a large extent how eagerly our followers will follow us." He presents a lengthy list of guiding principles for effective communication, including the following:

- The key to effective interpersonal communication: Seek first to understand, then to be understood.
- Think before you speak; select words that nurture rather than destroy.
- Words are meant to richly bless and empower. Words are not merely to inform but to transform.
- The art of listening well and speaking in appropriate ways are essential to effective leadership.
- Effective communication is about a variety of media, not just talking. One communicates with dress, facial expression, tone of voice, and by selecting whom to talk with, how often, how and when.

THE COMMUNICATION PROCESS

Communication is the complex process through which information *and understanding* are transferred from one person to another. This process may involve written or spoken words or signs and gestures. Communication involves more than sending an idea. Successful communication occurs when the receiver's understanding of the message is the same as the sender's intent. This sounds simple, but often it just does not happen.

Without effective communication, people do not know what is expected of them or how well they are doing. Consequences of not communicating well include low morale, increased workplace tension, reduced work quality and quantity, rumors and gossip, increased union disputes and sometimes even lawsuits. To understand how messages can become so muddled, consider the process of communication. The basic parts of the communication process are the message, sender and receiver. The process, however, is much more complex than this, as illustrated in Figure 4.1.

 The *communication process* involves a message, a sender, a channel and a receiver. It may include feedback.

FIGURE 4.1 The Communication Process

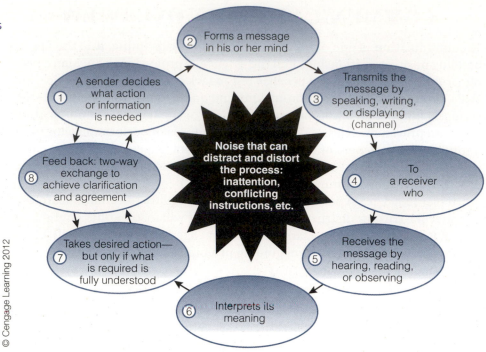

© Cengage Learning 2012

Often the sender is unaware that the encoding of the message may be inappropriate. For example, a physician might refer to a person using the abbreviation "S.O.B." To medical people this quite naturally means "short of breath." Laypeople, however, would likely decode it to mean something far different.

How effectively messages are conveyed depends on the following:

- Communication skills of the sender
- Clarity of purpose
- Effectiveness of the message itself
- Appropriateness of the channel used
- Receptivity and communication skills of the receiver
- Feedback
- Life experience and preexisting biases in either the sender or receiver

Shared frames of reference such as language, experience and cultural heritage are extremely important in communication. The narrower the shared frames of reference, the more likely miscommunication and misunderstanding will occur.

jargon

nonsense or meaningless language, often called *legalese*, for example, "party of the first part, hereafter referred to as . . ."; also, specialized language of a field, for example, perpetrator.

Making a Message Clear

The message should avoid **jargon**, which is the specialized language of a field, and evasive or "impressive" language. Consider the phrase "manually operated impact device"—military jargon for a hammer. In the business world, employee theft is referred to as "inventory shrinkage" and losing money as having a "net profit revenue deficiency." Law enforcement, too, has its share of jargon: "aforesaid," "alleged perpetrator," "a subject later identified as John

Doe," and "said officer proceeded to exit his squad." Especially troublesome is the use of 10-codes, used for more than 50 years by law enforcement and other first responders to communicate in shorthand over the radio. Efforts to phase out 10-codes with plain talk are being done under a directive from the U.S. Department of Homeland Security in an effort to have all public safety agencies simply speaking spoken words, as discussed later in the chapter.

Omit all empty words and redundancies. For example, use *asked* rather than *asked the question*; use *blue* rather than *blue in color*; use *February* rather than *month of February*. Be especially careful in using modifiers. They can result in embarrassing statements such as "Three cars were reported stolen by our police department yesterday," which could be read to mean the department stole the cars.

Avoid ambiguous or confusing words. For example, *subsequently*, which means "after," is often confused with or treated as synonymous with *consequently*, which means "as a result of." To say that an event happened *subsequently* to another simply means it occurred afterward, whereas using the term *consequently* implies one event caused another. This is a critical difference, especially in law enforcement, and one that can lead to erroneous reporting if used improperly. Therefore, use "after" or "as a result of."

Also pay attention to the emotional effect of certain words. Some words convey negative connotations, for example, *dirt bag*, *snitch*, *soused* and *slammer*. Be aware of such words and avoid using them when communicating professionally.

Avoid **abstract words** and generalities that blur messages and result in miscommunication. A department policy that prohibits *long hair*, for example, is subject to misinterpretation, lacking specificity, particularly between genders. Women might be allowed to have long hair, and a policy might state how the hair is to be "worn" while on duty. What does *at your earliest convenience* mean? It would be clearer to give the date by which you would like something done.

> **abstract words**
> theoretical, not concrete, for example, *tall* rather than *6'10"*.

E-Mail and Text Messages

E-mail is quickly becoming the most popular form of communication because it enhances the lines of communication between managers and employees and between coworkers of all levels. E-mail is not without its perils, however. E-mail can lead to virtual human relations, distancing people from one another unless organizations assume control with specific policies and procedures. The same problems can arise with text messages.

When managers depend on e-mail, face-to-face interaction diminishes, and personal relationships built on trust and teamwork suffer: Nothing can replace good interpersonal relations in any profession. Organizations that fail to preserve traditional internal communications risk losing critical organizational dynamics. E-mail also carries an inherent risk of misinterpretation because the word choice and "tone" used by the sender can cause the message to take a different path than intended. However, because law enforcement consists of multiple shifts throughout a 24-hour day, e-mail can be an effective way for supervisors or managers to communicate with each other when they are working different shifts. In fact, this may be the most efficient way to communicate, provided it is used properly.

A common problem with e-mail messages is that people often fail to proofread them. The quality of an e-mail reflects the professionalism of the sender. Take time to read your replies and messages before hitting the send button. Another peril is hitting the "reply to all" and forwarding messages to unintended people. When using the global address book, people may click on the wrong name and send information to the wrong person. In addition, many managers are too quick to click the *reply* button. If you find yourself engaged in an online back-and-forth dialogue, pick up the phone and have a real conversation. Finally, users of e-mail and or text messages need to recognize the tool they are using and make the necessary adjustments for how they send a message. For example, "lol" is not necessarily a good e-mail statement to use in day-to-day operations and communications, but as a text message it has a more effective use as people attempt to reduce the number of characters that they have to actually type on a PDA.

Nonverbal Messages and Body Language

nonverbal communication

messages conveyed by body language as well as tone of voice.

body language

messages conveyed by gestures, facial expressions, stance and physical appearance.

Nonverbal communication is how messages may be transferred without words. Entire books are written about **body language** and interpreting the mannerisms of other people, including eye contact or lack of it, facial expressions, leg and arm movements and so on. Ferrante (2009) recalls what he was told at an academy as a police recruit: "For every one person you see, 50 will see you." He says, "A warm smile, a helpful demeanor, and an open stance is useful when giving directions or taking a report from a victim."

> **Most communication between two people comes from body language and tone of voice.**

Research by Ray Birdwhistell (1918–1984), an American anthropologist who founded kinesics as a field of inquiry and research, showed that 10 percent of the message delivered is verbal and 90 percent is nonverbal. A similar percentage (93 percent) is often given by Dr. George Thompson, founder of the Verbal Judo Institute. Many nonverbal messages are obvious: a frown, a smile, a shrug, a yawn, tapping fingers, rolling eyes and so forth. Consider what the following nonverbal cues tell about a person:

- Walking—fast, slow, stomping
- Posture—rigid, relaxed
- Facial expression—wink, smile, frown
- Eye contact—direct, indirect, shifting
- Gestures—nod, shrug, finger point
- Physical spacing—close, distant
- Appearance—well groomed, unkempt

Use caution, however, when interpreting body language. Managers and supervisors should use nonverbal messages to their advantage, pay attention to the nonverbal messages being sent to them and carefully discern what the true intent of the message is.

Tone of voice can also greatly influence how communication is received. Consider the difference between a captain who asks a lieutenant, "What's your problem?," and one who asks, "How can I help you?" Consider how the first question might be interpreted if received in an e-mail. Again, keep in mind that those who communicate via e-mail to account for working separate shifts might have to wait many hours, or even days, for a response to this question, potentially adding to workplace tension.

In addition to speaking effectively, effective communication relies greatly on the manager/supervisor's ability to listen to what is being said.

Listening

Listening effectively can be the most fundamental, powerful communication tool of all. Listening skills are critical to the success of a manager, supervisor and leader. Unfortunately, "Listening is the most neglected form of communication" (Carlton, 2008, p.70). A manager who is formulating a response or developing a solution while a subordinate is talking is not hearing what is being said. Police work, first and foremost, will always be about people. Personal interaction is one constant for police managers. Developing listening skills ensures these interactions are positive, constructive and empowering.

 The weakest link in the communication process is _listening_.

Few people have taken courses in listening. We were taught to speak, read and write, but we simply _assume_ we know how to listen. Yet most people are _not_ good listeners. One reason is the gap between speaking and listening rates. The average person speaks at approximately 125 words per minute but listens at about 400 words per minute. This gap lets people daydream or begin to think about other topics.

Preoccupation is another common problem. Managers often "hear" the sounds but do not "listen" to the message; instead, they evaluate what they are hearing and concentrate on how they are going to respond. It is almost impossible to think, speak and listen at the same time. Other factors that affect listening include the manager's attitude toward the speaker or the topic, the location, the time available, noise and other distractions and lack of interest or boredom. Carlton (2009, p.85) provides a partial list of irritating communication habits to be avoided: "Interrupting, jumping to conclusions, finishing the speaker's sentence, inattentive behavior, poor posture, failure to make eye contact, changing the subject, making no comments, impatience, losing one's temper, playing with a pen, paper clip or other objects, and writing everything down."

An increasingly common distraction has become the phone, particularly the cell phone. Too often, when people are speaking face to face and a call comes in, there is a great, almost irresistible, urge to answer to phone, making the caller a higher priority than the person standing before you. Unless an urgent call is expected, common courtesy dictates that the call should be allowed to roll to voice mail and the face-to-face conversation should proceed uninterrupted. People need to prioritize the times when there is actual interpersonal interaction occurring and to not allow advancements in technology to control how they interact with one another.

A good listener looks at the speaker, is nonjudgmental, resists distracts, shows interest, asks questions and truly tries to understand the message being conveyed (Carlton, 2009, p.85). **Active listening** includes concentration, full attention and thought. To be an effective listener, look at the speaker. Think about the words and the implied message. Ask questions to clarify, but do not interrupt and remain objective. In addition, as Peter Drucker is fond of saying, "The most important thing in communication is to hear what isn't being said." It is often said that everyone talks, but few listen. The results when people do *not* listen can be disastrous. To determine how well you listen, take a few minutes to complete the listening test on the following page created by Fritz.

Recognize that in communication, receivers and senders of messages constantly switch roles. The effective communicator is skilled at speaking (or writing) and at listening (and reading). Another crucial element of effective communication is feedback.

active listening

includes concentration, full attention and thought.

Feedback

Without feedback, communication is one way. Feedback is the process by which the sender knows whether the receiver has understood the message. Two people may talk and yet neither may understand what the other is saying. Most feedback is direct and oral. Two people discuss something, one makes a statement and the other responds. Head nodding or shaking, smiling, grimacing, raised eyebrows, yawns—all are forms of feedback. The better the feedback, the better the communication.

BARRIERS TO COMMUNICATION

Communication barriers include
- **Noise.**
- **Time.**
- **Volume of information.**
- **Tendency to say what we think others want to hear.**
- **Certainty.**
- **Failure to select the best word.**
- **Prejudices (sender and receiver).**
- **Strained sender-receiver relationships.**

Noise is at the center of the communication process, as shown in Figure 4.1. Lee (2007, p.61) says, "Noise is sound that is not welcome. In law enforcement this can be defined as sound that disrupts messages or makes no sense to the

A Test of Listening Skills

When participating in an interview, discussion or group conference, do you:

		Usually	Sometimes	Seldom
1.	Prepare yourself physically by facing the speaker and making sure that you can hear?	_____	_____	_____
2.	Watch the speaker as well as listen to him or her?	_____	_____	_____
3.	Decide from the speaker's appearance and delivery whether what he or she has to say is worthwhile?	_____	_____	_____
4.	Listen primarily for ideas and underlying feelings?	_____	_____	_____
5.	Determine your own bias, if any, and try to allow for it?	_____	_____	_____
6.	Keep your mind on what the speaker is saying?	_____	_____	_____
7.	Interrupt immediately if you hear a statement you feel is wrong?	_____	_____	_____
8.	Make sure before answering that you've taken in the other person's point of view?	_____	_____	_____
9.	Try to have the last word?	_____	_____	_____
10.	Make a conscious effort to evaluate the logic and credibility of what you hear?	_____	_____	_____

Scoring

On questions 1, 2, 4, 5, 6, 8 and 10, give yourself: 10 points for each answer of *Usually*; 5 points for each answer of *Sometimes;* 0 points for each answer of *Seldom.*

On questions 3, 7 and 9, give yourself: 10 points for each answer of *Seldom;* 5 points for each answer of *Sometimes;* 0 points for each answer of *Usually.*

If your score is:

90 or more	You're a very good listener.
75–89	Not bad, but you could improve.
74 or less	You definitely need to work on your listening skills.

Source: *Think Like a Manager,* by Roger Fritz, PhD, president of Organization Development Consultants, 1240 Iroquois Drive, Suite 406, Naperville, IL 60563 (630) 420-7673. © 2003. Reprinted by permission.

What Happened to Communication in the Gates/Crowley Incident?

On July 16, 2009, at 12:45 A.M., a Cambridge, Massachusetts, radio dispatch went out about a call from a resident about a possible breaking and entering at their neighbor's house on Ware Street by "two males, unknown race" who might still be in the house. Off-duty Sgt. James Crowley was in the vicinity, so he responded to the call. He saw a man in the foyer, who also saw him. The man was the homeowner who had had trouble with his key. In fact, the man was nationally known Harvard Professor Henry Gates, who upon seeing the officer at the door expected him to inquire if he needed help. But the officer, knowing nothing of the man's reputation nor of the fact that he resided at the house, asked him to step outside. Crowley was White, Gates Black.

Because Crowley was on the porch, he did not answer at least three calls from dispatch, who, alarmed, dispatched six police cars to the scene. Gates refused to leave the house and told Crowley he didn't know who he was messing with. Crowley remained calm, while Gates, who continued to refuse to step outside or to produce identification, became indignant and began shouting at Crowley. Crowley arrested Gates and took him to police headquarters, where the professor was properly identified and released.

Professor Gates is a highly acclaimed Harvard professor who holds dozens of honorary degrees. He was just returning home after filming a documentary in China, was still weary from the 14-hour flight and was fighting a bronchial infection when he arrived home to find his front door jammed and feared someone had tried to break in.

Sgt. Crowley was described as the "antithesis of a racially biased officer, a trusted adviser of the Cambridge police commissioner and a new-generation officer indoctrinated with racial sensitivity, a role model who taught other officers on avoiding racial profiling" (Stockton, 2009, p.8). On national television, President Obama said that although he didn't have all the facts, the Cambridge police acted "stupidly." A national debate ensured.

What went wrong in this incident? What role did communication play? A national panel has been convened not to determine any wrongdoing but to focus on what actions could have created a better outcome. Consider this challenge to the panel while learning about management and communication.

circumstances at hand when present." Common noises in the law enforcement work environment that may affect radio communications include sirens, engine noise, explosives and gunshots, helicopters, barking dogs and officers shouting back and forth. Officers can get used to these noises and, not realizing how substantial the noise is, fail to communicate clearly. Furthermore, in stressful situations, one sense that shuts down is hearing (Lee, p.62). Yet another barrier to effective communication is that human voices sound and ears hear in analog, yet modern radios transmit in digital. Thus, for coherent communication to occur across the airwaves, human speech must first be changed from analog to digital to be transmitted through the technology and then converted from digital to analog when the signal reaches the receiver. This is done through a **vocoder**, a part of every digital radio. If background noise is louder than the speaker's voice, the voice may be overridden and come through as unintelligible.

vocoder
a device that is part of every digital radio that changes voices from analog to digital to be transmitted.

Time is important to everyone, especially law enforcement officers and managers. Communication systems have greatly enhanced the ability to pass information from one person or organization to another. Conversely, e-mails, faxes, text messages, blogs, tweets (Twitter) and other devices have deluged subordinates and managers alike with information. To cope, managers must be selective in what they personally take action on and what they delegate.

Another obstacle to communication is the tendency to say what we think others want to hear. This is especially true when the information is negative. This tendency can be dangerous because the person may form opinions or act on insufficient information.

A fifth obstacle is certainty, the unwavering belief that the information a person has is accurate: "My mind's made up; don't confuse me with the facts." This is illustrated by the young man who went to see a psychiatrist to learn to cope with being dead. This young man was certain he was dead, but no one would believe him. The psychiatrist, eager to help the man, asked him, "Do dead people bleed?" When the young man answered, "Of course not," the psychiatrist asked for the young man's hand and permission to stick his finger with a pin. The young man consented, and, as the psychiatrist expected, the finger bled. Amazed, the young man exclaimed, "I'll be darned. Dead people do bleed!"

Yet another obstacle is the varied meanings words may have. Select your words carefully to convey precisely what you mean. For example, in one department a police chief sent a memo to all officers asking for suggestions on how to improve retention. He received numerous ideas on how to help officers improve their memories. What he wanted, however, was thoughts on how to keep officers from quitting their jobs with the department.

Another important obstacle to communication is prejudice. Bias against a certain race, religion, nationality, gender, sexual preference or disability can create tremendous communication barriers. Usually such biases are based on stereotypes, which are overgeneralizations about a certain group of people.

This might also lead to a strained relationship between the sender and receiver, which can obstruct communication. Laine (2009, p.6) notes, "The very nature of their duties ensures that law enforcement officers will be placed in the center of situations that are typified by stress and hostility." This last barrier often arises when police have to take negative actions against an individual. This was graphically illustrated in the Gates/Crowley incident discussed.

The Gender Barrier

Despite decades of being conditioned to overlook differences between men and women, most gender-communication experts agree very real differences exist in the ways men and women communicate, possibly creating a gender barrier unless the differences are recognized and understood.

Credibility and authority are primary qualities men want most to project in their communication. They also tend to use fewer words, to "get to the point." Women, in contrast, often use qualifiers and are more likely to downplay their certainty, whereas men downplay their doubts. Table 4.1 summarizes other gender differences in communication.

Managers can learn to use the strengths of both genders in their communications. *Men can learn from women* to temper the talking head, replacing a monologue with dialogue and use inclusive language. Women tend to use inclusive words such as *we, our* and *us*, whereas men tend to say *I, me* and *mine* more often.

Women can learn from men to minimize qualifiers, "for example, "in my opinion" or "this might be better if." Don't personalize. Consider the difference between "I have a problem with your lack of initiative" and "The lack of initiative you have shown is troublesome." The first sentence inadvertently makes the problem about the speaker. Be more authoritative by minimizing digression, indecisiveness and equivocation.

TABLE 4.1 Conversational Styles: Gender Tendencies

Listening	
Male	**Female**
Irregular eye contact	Uninterrupted eye contact
Infrequent nodding	Frequent nodding
May continue another activity while speaking	Usually stops other activities while speaking
Interrupts in order to speak	Waits for pauses in order to speak
Questions are designed to analyze speaker's information	Questions are designed to elicit more information
Speaking	
Male	**Female**
Few pauses	Frequent pauses
May abruptly change topic	Connects information to previous speaker's information
Speaks until interrupted	Stops speaking when information delivered
Speaks louder than previous speaker	Uses same volume as previous speaker
Frequent use of "I" and "me"	Frequent use of "us" and "we"
Personal self-disclosure rarely included	Personal self-disclosure often included
Humor delivered as separate jokes or anecdotes	Humor interwoven into discussion content
Humor often based on kidding or making fun of others	Humor rarely based on kidding or making fun of others

Source: Peg Meier and Ellen Foley. "War of the Words." *Minneapolis Star Tribune, First Sunday,* January 6, 1991. Reprinted with permission of the *Star Tribune.*

Of special note is that, when communicating, men tend to not pause and to interrupt, whereas women tend to pause, allowing the male interruption. Such interruptions, even though unintentional, may create anger and tension. In addition, because men tend to speak until interrupted, they often dominate a conversation.

The Language Barrier

The most obvious barrier for individuals interacting with people from different cultures is often a language barrier. Executive Order 13166, signed August 11, 2000, and titled "Improving Access to Services for Persons with Limited English Proficiency," requires the federal government and grant recipients to take "reasonable steps to ensure that people with limited English proficiency (LEP) have meaningful access to the programs, services and information they provide." This is important because of the nation's changing demographics.

More than 47 million people in the United States speak a language other than English (Holt, 2008, p.54). Of those, about 19 million have LEP and nearly 2.6 million adults speak no English at all. U.S. census data from 2006 show that almost 20 percent of Americans speak a language other than English at home. About 9 percent are LEP, that is, they have a limited ability to read, write, speak or understand English. Add to this the number of LEP immigrants (legal and illegal) and the problem intensifies.

The U.S. Census Bureau projects that our country will become more racially and ethnically diverse during the next half century. Minorities, now roughly one-third of the U.S. population, are expected to become the majority in 2042, with the nation projected to be 54 percent minority in 2050. The non-Hispanic, single-race White population is projected to be only slightly larger in 2050 than in 2008, declining in overall population proportion from 66 percent in 2008 to 46 percent of the total population in 2050. The Hispanic population is projected to nearly triple during that same period, from 46.7 million to 132.8 million, effectively doubling the proportion of the total U.S. population claiming Hispanic ethnicity, from 15 percent in 2008 to 30 percent in 2050. The Black population is projected to increase from 14 percent to 15 percent and the Asian population from 5.1 percent to 9.2 percent ("An Older and More Diverse Nation," 2008).

Moore (2008, p.106) points out, "Dealing with individuals who do not speak English in the course of an emergency call can turn out to be a nightmare if a miscommunication takes place." Although overcoming language barriers may seem daunting, agencies can take cost-effective steps according to Shah et al. (2007). Holt notes that departments across the country are using a number of strategies to bridge the language gap, including hiring more bilingual officers, employing interpreters or translators and hiring companies that deliver telephone interpretation services. As technology advances and costs come down, a mainstream foreign language translator or a universal translator may be in the foreseeable future (Hansen, 2009, p.31). However, it will be some time before such a translator can properly interpret the subtle nuances of language and the meaning of tone behind the words transmitted.

A partnership was formed between the COPS Office and the Vera Institute to conduct a national assessment of best practices in "bridging the language divide." The assessment identified eight "best practices":

1. Clearly identify a need.

2. Build on what already exists.

3. Maximize resources.

4. Leverage partnerships with members of the nonprofit, business, academic and social communities.

5. Enlist volunteers.

6. Improve personnel skills.

7. Make the program permanent.

8. Use data to manage the program (Shah and Estrada, 2009).

The spoken language is not the only barrier. Gestures can also be misinterpreted. For example, making the "A-Okay" sign (a circle with the thumb and forefinger) is friendly in the United States, but it means "you're worth zero" in France, Belgium and many Latin American countries. The thumbs-up gesture meaning "good going" in the United States is the equivalent of an upraised middle finger in some Islamic countries.

The amount of eye contact also varies with different racial and ethnic groups. For example, in the United States, Caucasians maintain eye contact while speaking about 45 percent of the time, African Americans about 30 percent, Hispanics about 25 percent and Asians about 18 percent.

Medical Conditions Mimicking Intoxication

Dickinson (2009) stresses that officers need to be trained to recognize the difference between an intoxicated person and a medical emergency. Several medical conditions can mimic those of intoxication or drug impairment, including hypoglycemia (commonly associated with diabetes), a traumatic head injury, a stroke or epilepsy. Communicating with individuals experiencing a medical condition mimicking intoxication requires skill and patience. Officers should not be so focused on making a driving while intoxicated (DWI) arrest that they lose sight of this possibility.

COMMUNICATION ENHANCERS

Communication enhancers are often the opposite of actions that obstruct communication. To overcome the obstacle of communication overload, managers must establish priorities. Not all communications need to be available to all employees. The main criteria should be whether the employees need the information to perform assigned tasks and whether it would improve morale. Overloading employees with immaterial communications will restrict their performance and productivity. If a message promises further information, follow through. Use and encourage free and open two-way communication whenever possible. Emphasize brevity and accuracy.

Obstacles to communication are difficult to eliminate, but many can be minimized by concentrating on what you say and write. Communicating openly and clearly reduces informal communications such as the grapevine and rumor mill. When you look at the barriers within the communication process itself, certain guidelines become obvious.

Send clear messages. Say what you mean and mean what you say. Watch word choices. Consider the receiver of the message. Match nonverbal communication with the verbal message. Make sure messages are accurate and timely. Always be open, candid, honest and sincere.

Select the best communication channel. Focus on one-on-one, face-to-face communication, the most powerful channel available. Although this takes more time than a bulletin or memo, it is decidedly more effective.

Be open. Investigate options rather than steadfastly clinging to *the* solution. Effective managers work together toward solutions rather than choosing sides. In effect, people agree to disagree without being disagreeable.

INTERNAL COMMUNICATION

Lines of communication are inherent in an organizational structure. Just as authority flows downward and outward, so can communication. However, communication should also flow upward.

Communication may be downward, upward (vertical) or lateral (horizontal). It may also be internal or external. Most effective communication is two way.

lines of communication

similar to channels of communication; may be downward, upward (vertical) or lateral (horizontal) and internal or external.

Downward communication includes directives from managers and supervisors, either spoken or written. Managers who make it a practice to draw out the thoughts and ideas of their subordinates and are receptive even to bad news will be properly informed. Managers should communicate downward to subordinates with at least the same care and attention as they communicate upward to superiors. When time is limited and an emergency exists, communication often *must* flow downward and one way. In such cases, subordinates must listen and act on the communication.

Top-level law enforcement managers issue orders, policies, rules and regulations, memos, orders of the day and so on. These communications are delivered primarily downward and sometimes laterally. Communication from this level filters down and is understood by officers according to their knowledge, training, competence and experience.

Middle-level management and frontline supervisors also issue directives, roll-call information, explanations of directives from higher-level managers, information for department newsletters or roll-call bulletins, letters, memos and instructions. Again, such communication is distributed downward and laterally.

Upward communication includes requests from subordinates to their superiors. It should also include input on important decisions affecting subordinates. Effective managers give all subordinates a chance to contribute ideas, opinions and values as decisions are made.

Another critical form of upward communication is found in operational reports. The major portion of law enforcement operations is in the field at the lowest level of the hierarchy. Most investigations, traffic citations, arrests, form completion and other activities are at this basic level. These actions eventually travel both from the bottom up and laterally throughout the organization. Communication may take the form of reports, performance evaluations, charts, statistics, daily summaries or logs. All are extremely important.

Downward and upward communication are also called *vertical communication*. *Lateral* or *horizontal communication* includes communication among managers on the same level and among subordinates on the same level. Internal communication includes all of the preceding as well as messages from dispatch to officers in the field—among the most important communication of any law enforcement agency.

Subordinate Communication

Communicating with subordinates is an essential managerial responsibility. Managers and supervisors accomplish organizational goals through their subordinates. Employees want to know what is going on in the organization, to be "in the know." If employees do not know what the administration expects, they cannot support organizational goals and objectives.

A problem that commonly arises with new supervisors occurs when they attempt to communicate with subordinates about a new policy, procedure or work-related expectation that they, themselves, being new to management, do not completely understand. Communication can also be made less effective when a supervisor allows personal biases about a policy or procedure to taint the message they are delivering.

Supervisors and managers might consider addressing subordinates by their first names. If a manager knows he or she will be communicating with a subordinate later in the day, he or she should find out that person's first name and then ask the subordinate how he or she would like to be addressed.

The Grapevine

grapevine

informal channel of communication within the agency or department; also called the *rumor mill*.

In addition to the formal channels of communication established by an organization, informal channels also exist. Commonly referred to as the **grapevine**, or rumor mill, these informal channels frequently hinder cooperation and teamwork. Burch (2008, p.132) describes that he calls "verbal arsonists" who start a rumor or half-truth, spread it around a department as fact and then watch the "fire" of controversy that occurs. Such rumors can present a considerable challenge to management because they can greatly affect an organization's effectiveness and efficiency.

Managers and supervisors must realize that even if they *wanted* to stop the grapevine, they could not. Directing people to not talk about an issue often ensures that the word will spread more quickly. Thus it is important that managers make the grapevine work for them rather than against them.

The grapevine is strongest in organizations in which information is not openly shared. Employees begin to guess and speculate when they do not know—hence the rumors. One way to positively influence the grapevine is to provide staff with *all* information needed to function efficiently, effectively and happily. This includes letting people know the bad as well as the good. Do not let the grapevine beat you to informing people of bad news that affects them.

Burch (2008, p.134) has successfully used the Peer Leadership Group (PLG) concept to enhance employee-management communication. Employees choose their own committee of at least three members, but it can be as many as they want. No one from the supervisor ranks or above is allowed to be on the committee. The committee decides when or how often to meet and it creates its own rules. Any employee can bring an issue to the committee, which determines if action needs to be taken. Any department-related issue can be discussed, but the meeting should be more than just a gripe session. The PLG can address and resolve issues on its own without bringing them to the attention of command staff, or it can meet with the chief or a member of the command staff. No retaliation or retribution is threatened by supervisors, command staff or chief.

A PLG is *not* a replacement for existing protocols, nor does it bypass department general orders or directives. The PLG does not threaten the chain of command or offer employees a way to bypass any supervisor or command staff member. Regular personnel issues including training, discipline, policy and procedure continue to be handled through normal channels, and the PLG would not circumvent that process. The PLG is not a union or police association, and any issues involving those groups would likely be addressed within the rules and regulations of those entities (Burch, 2008, p.132).

Burch (2008, p.134) concludes that a PLG might help employees take ownership in their organization, feeling they are given a voice. A PLG can open the employee-management communication lines and help make an organization more effective and efficient, taking advantage of the great ideas many employees have.

Newsletters

Another way to keep lines of communication open is through newsletters. Newsletters can address the personal side of policing. For instance, newsletters can focus on achievements of people within the department, sworn and civilian; acknowledge and welcome new employees; and cover topics such as weddings, births, deaths and community activities and contributions. Newsletters can also be educational. For example, each issue could contain a column on tips for effective report writing. This form of communication should be delegated to someone within the department who has the interest and skill to undertake the responsibility.

Improving Internal Communication through an Intranet

"Law enforcement agencies face increasing amounts of communications clutter and must compile and store a large amount of data. Forms, manuals, job announcements and executive memos need to be made available to staff at all levels and in all locations" (Brown, 2008, p.32). One solution becoming increasingly popular is an intranet—a Web site inside a department's firewall serving the department's mission and unavailable to anyone else. An intranet can streamline a department's communications and records management system (RMS). Brown (pp.37–38) recommends that a department wishing to develop an intranet should get buy-in from advocates early in the process, preferably from chain-of-command going vertical. He also suggests consolidating the forms and manuals, getting the most current versions and making sure only the editors control any updating. An intranet enables better intradepartmental communication, and it can eliminate shelves of manuals and walls of file cabinets.

Communication at Meetings

It has been said that meetings are gatherings where minutes are kept and hours are lost. According to a *Wall Street Journal* report, the average CEO in the United States spends 17 hours a week in meetings that costs the company $42,500 per year (Jenkins and Visser, no date). A manager can go online and find several formulates for calculating the cost of a meeting. For example, you can download a meeting cost clock from meetings.com, enter the number of participants and their average hourly wage, and then, with a click, the meeting cost clock counter shows how much the meeting is costing each minute.

Too many meetings are held simply because they are part of the weekly routine or because other options (such as sending e-mails or memos) are ignored. Recall that one of the ways communication is often judged is by the effectiveness of the meetings held. Meetings serve important functions and need not be time wasters. The keys to successful, productive meetings are planning and effective communication.

 Departments typically have four types of meetings: informational, opinion seeking, problem solving and new-idea seeking.

Knowing what type of meeting to plan helps you set appropriate goals for the meeting. Every meeting should have a clearly defined purpose and anticipated outcome. Some meetings serve two or more purposes. Before scheduling a meeting, however, explore alternatives: Is group action needed? Could the desired results be accomplished by one-on-one interactions? A phone call? A memo? An e-mail?

One key to successful meetings is a carefully prepared **agenda** or outline, usually given to participants *before* the meeting. The agenda should have a time frame, including beginning and ending.

> **agenda**
>
> a plan, usually referring to a meeting outline or program; a list of things to be accomplished.

 Keys for effective meetings:
- **Prepare in advance—have an agenda.**
- **Start and stop on time.**
- **Stick to the agenda.**
- **Facilitate open communication and participation.**

Webb (2007, p.87), deputy chief of operations, describes how his agency's department meetings had become tedious and lacked input from frontline supervisors. He took some elements of the CompStat philosophy to combine with the department's existing tools and developed a new staff meeting format called the "staff presentation." Each supervisor was to take 10 minutes to address the staff meeting from a podium on a set format that included his or her response to an "Action Plan" the shift was currently implementing as well as problems or crime trends he or she was noticing, officers' outstanding performances, status of ongoing investigation or assignments and any other information the supervisor felt was important to address.

Interestingly, the recognition of outstanding performance recognized the same names from meeting to meeting, helping pinpoint which officers were performing on a high level. However, some names were never mentioned. Webb (2007, p.89) notes that their 20-minute staff meetings turned into an hour and a half–long meeting, but it was worth it:

> The preparation required for the staff presentation forced out information that would have not normally been shared. Sergeants and lieutenants were tracking and documenting what was occurring on their shift. They were keeping facts from incidents in order to fill the 10 minutes for their presentation and present the information professionally. It tightened up their supervision and leadership on their individual teams. Common threads between shifts (intelligence, problem residents, problem employee, etc) came out and were dealt with as a whole rather than piecemeal. This headed off problems before they got out of hand. From a command staff standpoint, the presentations brought out which supervisors were on top of things and which ones needed improvement.

An additional important benefit was that as time went on, the presenters' communications skills showed great improvement as did the listening skills of those in the audience.

Technology and Communication in the Field

Technology has greatly enhanced communication between the department headquarters and the officers in the field: "No longer is access to data in the field a perk; it's become a mission-critical necessity . . . Mobile technology empowers agencies to increase productivity, officer morale and community safety" (Bourre, 2007, p.84). Today's officers are more efficient by having available several remote database tools accessed through compact PDAs, wireless phones and laptops (Geoghegan (2009, p.40).

A Brief Word about 9-1-1 Systems

February 2008 marked the 40th anniversary of 9-1-1 service in the United States, a system designed to allow citizens in need of emergency assistance to dial a single number to reach a public safety answering point (PSAP) from which police, fire or ambulance service could be dispatched. Evolving from a system of landline telephones, conventional radios and notepads in 1969, today's PSAPs are often "sophisticated command and control centers equipped with digital phones, trunked radios, and computer-aided dispatch (CAD) systems with map displays and real-time unit tracing" (Pendleton, 2008, p.36). However, most 9-1-1 communications are sorely in need of modernization to remain effective: "The typical model today is still one of a small, standalone emergency communications systems using yesterday's analog technologies" (Scott, 2009, p.46). The challenges facing 9-1-1 include an aging infrastructure, tighter budgets and increased lag times between technological developments and system implementation (Eggers, 2009, p.37).

In response to these challenges many agencies are developing what is commonly referred to as "Next Generation 9-1-1" or NG9-1-1. An NG9-1-1 system must be able to handle the growing market penetration of mobile phones, Internet protocol (IP) and voice over Internet protocol (VoIP) telephony networks (Hall, 2009, p.70). A truly state-of-the-art next generation system must also move beyond the "one size fits all" rigidity and offer dynamic situation adaptability, flexibility, immediate and easy usability and intelligence—interacting successfully with other technologies (Bitner, 2009). The technology should also have real-time data-sharing capabilities, meaning that as data is entered at the local level, it is available at the desktop and in the field within *six seconds* (Johnston, 2009, p.17).

A special report in the *9-1-1 Magazine* ("Improved Public Safety," 2009, p.12) cautions, "The promise of improved public safety in this NG9-1-1 environment is only achieved through a balanced marriage of technology and operations." The article asks if NG9-1-1 will be defined by those who manage it or those who use it to get assistance to people in emergencies.

It is critical for managers to recognize that 9-1-1, even though it is a vital communication tool, exists almost exclusively in a reactive capacity, driven by citizen calls for service. Furthermore, police dispatchers are a vital communication link between the police bureaucracy and the public. Thus, it is worth giving a modicum of consideration to the place that 9-1-1 holds in terms of how information about crime and incidents is communicated from the public to the police and how police management structures response protocol to citizen calls for service.

Tactical Communications

"Communications are more critical to police operations than guns and ammo," says Scoville (2009, p.26). He notes, "The success or failure of tactical operations can come down to a matter of communication dependability." For example, when special weapons and tactics (SWAT) teams are called out to respond to school shootings or other community emergencies, the success of the response hinges heavily on the effectiveness of tactical communications.

Not all tactical communications depend on technology. In many instances, the successful handling of a call for service depends on the leadership and management skills of the first officer on the scene. Campbell (2009) gives as an example a "huge mess of a call" (a large wreck with possible fatalities, an active shooter at a public place, even a downed officer), and all available officers are dispatched to the scene. Dispatch is trying to get information to the officers from the callers on the line as arriving officers try to decide what needs to be done, and the situation becomes hectic. Two things usually happen. First, multiple officers continue to respond without direction, and two, a supervisor who has not yet arrived tries to direct the officers on the scene from his radio. Campbell suggests that the first responding officer should take charge by saying, "I'm in command!" These three words can calm a chaotic scene. The first responding officer is most likely to have firsthand information and make informed decisions. By saying, "I'm in command," this officer establishes himself or herself as a source for firsthand, real-time information and clarifies who is in charge. This also initiates the Incident Command System (ICS) or National Incident Management System (NIMS) as other emergency responders, such as fire and emergency medical services (EMS) personnel, arrive. And it allows the supervisor to concentrate on getting to the scene and avoid making uninformed decisions. When the supervisor arrives, he or she can go directly to the officer in charge and be quickly briefed.

As Stockton (2008, p.8) concludes, "No matter how fancy the technology, law enforcement must still rely on solid people doing good police work to make the right things happen." In other words, the people involved in communicating during an emergency are still the primary element of communication, regardless of the technological advancements available.

EXTERNAL COMMUNICATION

External communication includes all interactions with agencies and people outside the department, including the news media and citizen contacts. Law enforcement agencies must effectively interact with other components of the criminal justice system—that is, the courts and correctional services. Law enforcement agencies must also interface with other social services, as well as with other departments of the jurisdiction they serve, as noted in Chapter 3.

Communicating with Other Agencies

"The need to provide first responders with an improved system for interoperable communications remains an urgent national priority, despite the painful lessons of 9/11 and Hurricane Katrina" (Kane, 2009, p.52). **Interoperability** refers to the ability of public safety emergency responders to work seamlessly with other systems or products without special efforts.

In 2004 the Department of Homeland Security (DHS) announced the establishment of the Office for Interoperability and Compatibility (OIC) to oversee interoperability research and development, testing and evaluation, standards, technical assistance and grant guidance. One OIC program, SAFECOM, coordinates the efforts of more than 50,000 local, state, federal and tribal public safety agencies across the country working on communications interoperability. SAFECOM is committed to a bottom-up approach, defining interoperability needs locally. These same practitioners should guide the development and implementation of interoperability solutions. This makes sense given that more than 90 percent of the U.S. public safety communications infrastructure is owned and operated by localities and states with distinct needs.

interoperability
the ability of public safety emergency responders to work seamlessly with other systems or products without special efforts.

The importance of interoperability in the DC sniper case was evident where hundreds of local, state and federal police officers worked together to track down the suspects because of interoperable radio communications. The need for officers from different jurisdictions to communicate with each other can be hindered by the use of 10-codes referred to earlier in the chapter. Although some "codes" may be necessary for officer safety and for confidentiality, it is often recommended that most 10-codes be eliminated in favor of plain English (O'Toole and Reyes, 2008, p.74). Four "signal codes" that might be retained for intra-agency use include: (1) when an officer is in immediate danger; (2) when an officer needs assistance, but there is no immediate threat to the officer; (3) when an arrest has been made or will be attempted; and (4) when there is a need to convey confidential, sensitive or safety information (O'Toole and Reyes). Many agencies have also adopted the North Atlantic Treaty Organization (NATO) phonetic alphabet for radio use.

Wright (2008, p.44) contends that 21st century interoperability needs to go beyond radio to comprehensive communications interoperability: "The end goal is for first responders and other government personnel to be able to communicate using any communications device (new or legacy radio, smartphone, traditional phone, IP phone or softphone) with any media (voice, video, text messages, and data)." Communications interoperability provides greater situational awareness and enables a unified chain of command.

Although interoperability depends on technology, that is only one part of the interoperability problem; it also requires regulation and management. It has been suggested that only 20 percent of the interoperability solution lies in technical and regulatory issues, whereas 80 percent of the problem is in policy and management issues. Management issues involve getting departments and chiefs to agree on procedures to share channels and resources, terminology, response scenarios and mutual aid agreements. After the plans and agreements are developed, they need to be communicated to every level of the agencies and practiced regularly.

Communicating with the Media

The media can be friend or foe, depending on the effectiveness of the channels of communication. "For police leaders, the ability to communicate clearly is a necessity; communicating effectively with the public is an absolute necessity. The news media represent police leaders' most valuable tools for reaching that public" (Garner, 2009, p.52). Difficulties in dealing with the press usually arise from the need to balance the public's right to know, the First Amendment right to freedom of the press and the need of law enforcement agencies to protect the Sixth Amendment rights of those accused of crimes, as well as the privacy of crime victims, while maintaining the integrity of an investigation.

The police and reporter professions share much in common: both are highly visible, powerful institutions; both attract ambitious, strong-minded people with a strong sense of justice and a desire to help others; both are frequently criticized by the public they serve and are sensitive to that criticism; both can be highly defensive and feel misunderstood by their critics; both are sometimes secretive about their operations and their methods for gathering information; and both see themselves as vital to the public welfare (Garner, 2009, p.52).

At the Police Executive Research Forum (PERF) Annual Convention in 2008, a panel of news media experts convened to offer their views on police-media relations ("Reporters Offer PERF," 2008, p.4). One expert, who had been on both sides of the fence, having served with the New York City and Los Angeles Police Departments and the Federal Bureau of Investigation (FBI) as well as having had a stellar career in journalism at ABC News and winning nine Emmys, told the audience, "The first thing you need to know about reporters is that they are not your friends. The second thing you need to know is they are not your enemy. In large measure, they are what you make of them." His final advice to police chiefs was, "Get your good news out fast, and get your bad news out even faster."

Research done in Montana found many misperceptions by law enforcement community members regarding their relationship with the media as well as on how influential the media is in shaping the image of police (Tooley and Lande, 2009, pp.63–65):

> What the mainstream media report and what the public as a whole believes are not the same. The research revealed overwhelming support for police officers and their efforts to reduce crime and keep neighborhoods safe. On the street, however, it is easy for officers to believe that the opposite is true, because they generally do not come into contact with the supportive segment of the population. The same research indicates that many police officers do in fact feel distrusted and unappreciated. . . .

> The national survey results show that people typically disregard media reports when it comes to forming their own opinion of law enforcement officers. In reality, people's opinions are formed by their own experiences with law enforcement agencies. . . .

> In fact, data from the Montana State University public survey show that 77 percent of respondents stated that media coverage of law enforcement agencies did not change their opinion of police officers one way or another. Of the remainder, more people gained a more positive view of the profession through the media than a negative view.

Public Information Officers (PIOs)

All police officers should be prepared to interact with the media while handling a variety of incidents. However, in departments that can afford it, a public information officer (PIO) has the opportunity and responsibility to present the best possible image of the department: "Proficient and sophisticated PIOs are worth their weight in gold to police brass and the rank-and-file alike" (Paris, 2007, p.50). The PIO need not be a police officer, but should be someone who subscribes to the department's mission, knows the community well and is an excellent communicator. There are very specific courses and training related to media and PIO-related responsibilities that are beyond the scope of this chapter. Managers might consider designating an officer to be the official media "go to" person for the department and be sure that person receives the necessary training to maximize his or her effectiveness as a PIO.

News Releases

Call it a "news" release, not a "press" release. The preferred term is *news release* because radio and television reporters don't use presses. The news release should answer the six basic questions: What? Who? How? When? Where? and Why? with the most important or newest information in the first paragraph. A news release should be written as a **sound bite**, which, simply put, is good, solid information stated clearly and briefly.

sound bite

good information stated briefly; two essential elements are (1) that it contain good, solid nuggets of information, not speculation or opinion, and (2) that it is short.

News Conferences and Interviews

The public is interested in what law enforcement does—good and bad. Agencies should hold a news conference when a high-profile crime or other incident of great public interest occurs. Other occasions that might warrant a news conference are if help from the public on a major case is needed, if the public needs to be informed of an ongoing danger, if new crime prevention or other programs are being launched or if administrators want to answer serious allegations of law enforcement misconduct. Finally, holding a news conference to announce major promotions within the department or when the administrators are honoring employees or citizens with significant awards can enhance a department's public image.

If the interview is planned in advance, the interviewee is advised to remember the Rule of the 7 Ps: "Proper Prior Planning Prevents Pathetically Poor Performance" (Rosenthal, 2008, p.6). To prepare, the interviewee can do the "Double Nickel" taught in media courses at the FBI: Write down the 5 questions you hope the reporter will ask, and then the 5 questions you pray won't be asked. Then write brief answers to all 10 (Rosenthal, 2008).

When the media contact involves a major breaking event or "big news" story, the police representative should never talk about things they know

© Brian Snyder/Reuters NewMedia Inc./CORBIS

Montgomery County (Maryland) Chief Charles Moose answers questions from reporters at a briefing at police headquarters. In 2002, Montgomery County was the site of five shootings attributed to the Washington-area snipers.

nothing about, bluff or lie, make assumptions, "beat round the bush," use police jargon, say "no comment" (implying more is known) or ever speculate (Paris, 2007, p.51). This should usually be within two hours. After US Airways Flight 1549 Captain Sullenberger put his disabled aircraft down on the Hudson River, US Air CEO Parker provided an excellent example of dealing with the media: (1) He dealt with the media right away. (2) He was empathetic, expressing concern about the victims and the community and their commitment to make things right, saying a response team and hotline had been set up to help them and their families. And (3) he dealt with facts and information, not what he thought. He refused to speculate, and he urged the media to avoid speculation (Rosenthal, 2009, p.6). Although this example is from the business world, these same recommendations hold true for police officers and administrators responsible for dealing with the media during a crisis.

Publicity as a Means to Prevent Crime

Some research suggests that publicizing crime prevention efforts increases the offenders' perceptions of the risks involved in perpetrating crime. Publicizing such efforts before they go into effect can have an **anticipatory benefit**—that is, criminals may be deterred even before the efforts are implemented. According to their findings, the most frequently used publicity was newspaper articles (90 percent), followed by leaflets, letters and cards (62 percent). The strategies used by participants in their research are summarized in Table 4.2.

Another interesting effect sometimes seen when a major crime prevention program is announced is **geographical diffusion of benefit**, where

> **anticipatory benefit**
> criminals may be deterred even before the efforts are implemented.

> **geographical diffusion of benefit**
> properties immediately adjacent to the intervention implemented also experienced a reduction in burglary.

TABLE 4.2 Number of Schemes Undertaking Different Forms of Publicity

Publicity Type	% of schemes (n)
General publicity	
Radio interviews (local/national)	33% (7)
Newspaper articles (local/national)	90% (19)
Television appearances (local/national)	24% (5)
Leaflets/letters/cards	62% (13)
Posters	38% (8)
Publicity directed at offenders(e.g., Christmas cards)	14% (3)
Stickers (e.g., neighborhood watch or smartwater)	19% (4)
Significant community meetings explaining the scheme	43% (9)
Informal information or scheme to community offenders	14% (3)
Stand alone publicity campaigns	57% (12)
Surveys (including fear of crime, alleygating, target hardening)	33% (7)
Other (any other form of publicity)	43% (9)

Source: Shane D. Johnson and Kate J. Bowers. "Opportunity Is in the Eye of the Beholder: The Role of Publicity in Crime Prevention." *Criminology and Public Justice*, Vol. 2, No. 3, 2003, p.505. Reprinted by permission.

FIGURE 4.2 Bull's-Eye Resource Budgeting Strategy and Publicity

Source: Shane D. Johnson and Kate J. Bowers. "Opportunity Is in the Eye of the Beholder: The Role of Publicity in Crime Prevention." *Criminology & Public Justice*, Vol. 2, No. 3, 2003, p.519. Reprinted by permission.

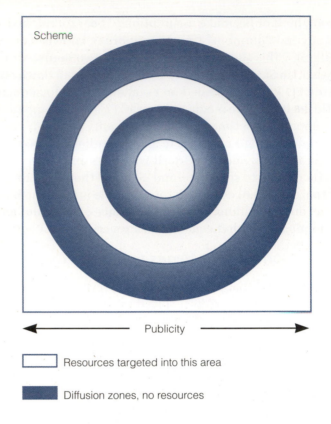

Scheme

◄──────── Publicity ────────►

☐ Resources targeted into this area

■ Diffusion zones, no resources

properties immediately adjacent to that where the intervention was implemented also experienced a reduction in crime. A cost-effective way to target resources may be to employ a kind of bull's-eye resource targeting approach, dividing an area into concentric zones and resources targeted into every other zone, as shown in Figure 4.2. In addition, news release campaigns may be more effective if done in bursts rather than continuously, as the effects of such campaigns commonly extend beyond the time they are active.

Sipes and Mentel (2009) describe how the Fugitive Safe Surrender (FSS) effort used the media to encourage individuals wanted for nonviolent felony or misdemeanor crimes to voluntarily surrender to faith-based leaders and law enforcement in a place of worship, giving them a chance to resolve their warrants and get on with their lives. Implemented by the U.S. Marshals Service in six cities, more than 6,000 people surrendered, with most returning home the same day they surrendered, either after receiving a new court date or having their charges adjudicated on the spot. In addition to traditional forms of communicating with the public, the FSS effort used social media such as podcasts and blogs to connect with its audience.

COMMUNICATING WITH THE COMMUNITY

Emergency notification systems (ENS) are a vital component of emergency preparedness and response plans (Ladin, 2009, p.31). A discussion of ENS is beyond the scope of this text, but it should be recognized that ENS cannot do what social networking text messaging alert systems can do—reach more than 250 million Americans in the palms of their hands (Neman, 2009, p.20). No matter what the emergency is, residents will look to law enforcement for reassurance and guidance. This is true of public health emergencies as well as natural disasters or any other emergency. It is important to "establish trust-based, two-way communication within the agency, between the agency and the community, and between the law enforcement and other local agencies before an emergency strikes" (Brito et al., 2009, p.4).

Every contact with the public is a public relations contact. It is critical that all members of the agency, especially those in positions of authority, present a positive image and communicate effectively. This is true whether officers are giving directions or answering a call from citizens with a raccoon in their chimney. It is true whether traffic officers are issuing a ticket or the chief of police is addressing a Rotary Club or the local parent-teacher association (PTA). An established reality in businesses regarding customers is that satisfied people tell their stories to at least 3 other people, whereas dissatisfied individuals will tell, on average, 10 others about a negative experience.

Annual Reports

One effective way to keep the public informed about the operations of a police department is to publish an annual report. Long recognized as effective business communication tools, annual reports can also serve law enforcement agencies. They might include the department's mission statement; a brief biographical overview of department members with names, photos, academic degrees, dates of hire, dates of most recent promotion and special duties; departmental information and statistics; a summary of projects and projected programs; a budget statement; an outline of ongoing interaction with the fire service, emergency medical care providers, scuba and rescue units or any emergency support group in your community; and a closing, which may include statements of appreciation and remarks about the "state of the department."

The Internet

Many agencies are using the Internet's social media outlets such as Facebook, MySpace, Twitter and YouTube to reach and draw the public to the department's Web site. That Web site can inform viewers where to direct tips or communication with the department. However, "Agencies keeping up with social media run the risk of spreading themselves too thin" (Wethal, 2009, p.6). A suggestion is to track which sites are most popular in a jurisdiction or that hold the most useful data and limit an electronic beat to those sites: "Prioritizing sites and electronic time is vital to making the best use of online portals" (Wethal, p.6).

No tool is currently more efficient than the Internet when it comes to providing citizens with information about criminal activity. This type of external communication can be extremely beneficial to departments willing to invest the time and minimal expense to develop a Web site. The Internet can

Many police departments now have their own Web sites like this one for Santa Monica, California. Internet communications help link law enforcement agencies with each other and the public.

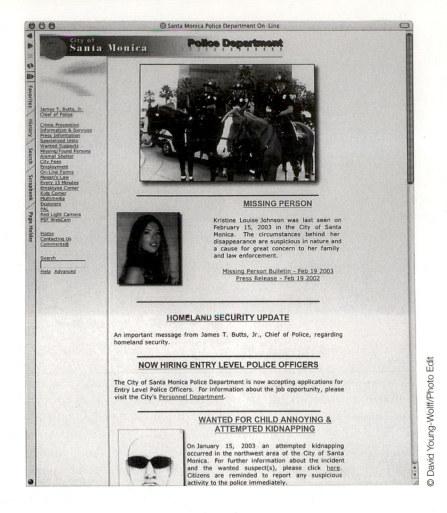

© David Young-Wolff/Photo Edit

also help law enforcement agencies communicate more effectively with each other. Valuable information may be accessed and shared on department Web sites. Police Web sites are used to display most wanted lists, crime statistics, employment information news releases, links, copies of crime reports and permits.

Departments might go beyond posting information to using the Internet as a proactive tool for obtaining information about neighborhood conditions, solving problems, building partnerships and evaluating the department's performance.

The importance of information sharing has been evident throughout this chapter. Next, briefly consider sources of information available to law enforcement agencies throughout the country.

INFORMATION SHARING THROUGH N-DEX, ONEDOJ AND LEO

Managers, especially supervisors, need to be aware of the information sources available to officers in the field.

The FBI has made available to local, state and tribal law enforcement agencies three powerful information sources: N-DEx, OneDOJ and LEO.

The Criminal Justice Information Services (CJIS) Division of the FBI administers the Law Enforcement National Data Exchange (N-DEx) system, the primary purposes of which are to solve crimes and fight terrorism. Information is provided to N-DEx by various law enforcement agencies, which retain control over this information by deciding what data to share, with whom and under what circumstances. N-DEx is not a replacement for individual agencies' information-sharing systems nor is it an intelligence-sharing system: "Its purpose is to be the thread that binds together the current patchwork of disparate criminal justice information-sharing systems into one that is exponentially more powerful" (Lindsey, 2009, p.22).

The OneDOJ Initiative is another valuable information-sharing tool that allows state, local and tribal law enforcement partners to obtain information from all of the Department of Justice's investigative components—the FBI; the Drug Enforcement Administration; the Bureau of Alcohol, Tobacco, Firearms and Explosives; the U.S. Marshals Service; and the Bureau of Prisons—with a single query (Hitch, 2007, p.26).

Law Enforcement Online (LEO) provides law enforcement officers with access to N-DEx, One DOJ, the FBI's Virtual Command Center (VCC), a national alert system and a variety of other information-sharing services. Members of LEO can log on from anywhere in the world, any time, with a single sign-on procedure and have access to information-sharing services such as chat, secure e-mail between LEO members, special interest groups, e-learning modules and an e-library (Lindsey, 2008, p.82). Despite all the information-sharing advances being made, obstacles to such sharing still exist.

OBSTACLES TO INFORMATION SHARING

Four obstacles to sharing information among local, state and federal agencies are technical, logistic, political and ethical.

The technological obstacle of lack of interoperability has been discussed. Logistic obstacles include data entry. If intelligence officers spend all their time entering data, they have no time for anything else. Political obstacles include finances and roles and relationships with the FBI and with the state police. Probably the most serious impediment to establishing a national interconnected antiterrorism database is the issue of "who pays for this?" The ethical obstacles include the issue of profiling and open records legislation. Another major obstacle to information sharing is withholding of information.

Some information received by an agency such as the FBI is classified. Rules of federal procedure and grand jury classified material are two other limitations to what or how much information can be shared. In response, the FBI has launched the State and Local Law Enforcement Executive Clearance Initiative, which is based on a long-running FBI program designed to help state and local law enforcement executives obtain security clearances to receive classified information. This initiative might help prevent local law enforcement officers from interfering with a terrorism investigation.

No law enforcement officer wants to compromise an existing investigation or conduct a conflicting case. To avoid this problem, departments might develop a local networking module with local, state and federal law enforcement agencies to discuss investigative and enforcement endeavors, including a deconfliction protocol. **Deconfliction** is the process of detecting and preventing potential conflict and can be used with declassified and confidential investigations. It necessarily involves shared communication of sensitive information.

deconfliction

avoiding conflict when working with other agencies during an investigation; deployed with declassified and confidential investigations.

A FINAL WORD ABOUT COMMUNICATION

Police executives typically identify one characteristic that serves as a common denominator among successful supervisors and managers—the ability to identify and use communication. Communication is a vital element in every aspect of a police manager's day-to-day responsibilities. Using communication to build relationships within the workplace is the foundation for innovation and effectiveness.

Supervisors and managers spend a large part of their working hours engaged in tasks that can be identified as communicating. They are engaged in the organizational culture, mission, vision, goals, strategic objectives, employee performance and the professional development of their subordinates. Those supervisors and managers who fully understand and use the wide variety of resources available to facilitate the communication process will experience the greatest opportunities within any law enforcement organization.

SUMMARY

The communication process involves a message, a sender, a channel and a receiver and it may include feedback. Most communication between two people comes from body language and tone of voice. The weakest link in the communication process is *listening*.

Communication barriers include noise, time, volume of information, tendency to say what we think others want to hear, certainty, failure to select the best words, prejudices (of the sender and receiver) and strained sender-receiver relationships. Communication may be downward, upward (vertical) or lateral (horizontal). It may also be internal or external. Most effective communication is two way.

Departments typically have four types of meetings: informational, opinion seeking, problem solving and new-idea seeking. Meetings may be informational, opinion seeking, problem solving or new-idea seeking. For more effective meetings: (1) prepare in advance—have an agenda, (2) start and stop on time, (3) stick to the agenda and (4) facilitate open communication and participation.

The FBI has made available to local, state and tribal law enforcement agencies three powerful information sources: N-DEx, OneDOJ and LEO. Four obstacles to sharing information among local, state and federal agencies are technical, logistic, political and ethical.

CHALLENGE FOUR

Chief Slaughter loses his temper at a contemptuous labor meeting with the patrol officers' union. As Slaughter cools off in his office, he realizes some of his comments were out of line. He's actually a good-hearted guy who backs his cops. Chief Slaughter recently attended a conference where a vender was selling hats with special reflective pink brims. The vender quoted impressive statistics concerning the added safety the hats provide to officers. Chief Slaughter knows he's going to have to squeeze his tight budget to buy the hats, but it's his way of demonstrating his concern for his officers and their safety. After his outburst at the labor meeting, he thinks this will be a good time to show them he cares.

Chief Slaughter dictates a memo and has his secretary post it in the glass case outside the roll call room. He leaves for the weekend.

"New hats with reflective pink safety brims will be distributed to the entire department next week. The hats will be worn by all officers. By order of Chief Slaughter."

On Monday morning Chief Slaughter was greeted by disgruntled cops and a grievance.

1. Is there a problem in the communication process between Chief Slaughter and his officers?

2. Do you think Chief Slaughter used the most effective channel of communications for his message?

3. Was timing important?

4. Are there some inherent problems in communications between unions and administrations?

5. Suggest a better channel for communicating the Chief's message.

DISCUSSION QUESTIONS

1. Why is communication ability so important to law enforcement managers?

2. How would you compare and contrast the various channels of communication?

3. Which is more difficult, written or spoken communication? Why? Which do you prefer?

4. What are the main obstacles to communication in your law enforcement agency?

5. What types of communication exist in your agency? What is the value of each?

6. What types of feedback are available in a typical law enforcement agency?

7. How is nonverbal communication used in law enforcement? How is such nonverbal communication depicted on television programs about law enforcement?

8. What methods do you use as an active listener?

9. What is the key role of the first-line supervisor as a communicator in a law enforcement agency?

10. What public figures do you consider to be effective communicators? What characteristics make them so?

REFERENCES

Bitner, Amy. "Next Generation State-of-the-Art Emergency Alerting Systems." *9-1-1 Magazine*, June/July 2009, pp.39–40.

Bourre, Mike. "Five Things You Need to Know about Keeping Your Officers Connected." *Law Enforcement Technology*, August 2007, pp.84–89.

Brito, Corina Sole; Luna, Andrea Morrozoff; and Sanberg, Elizabeth Lang. *Communication and Public Health Emergencies: A Guide for Law Enforcement*. Washington, DC: Bureau of Justice Assistance and the Police Executive Research Forum, August 2009.

Brown, Ralph. "Inside a Law Enforcement Intranet." *Law Enforcement Technology*, April 2008, pp.32–38.

Burch, Jay. "Peer Leadership Group for Employee-Management Communications." *Law and Order*, October 2008, pp.130–134.

Campbell, Bill. "Three Words Can Help Calm a Chaotic Scene." *PoliceOne.com News*, October 16, 2009.

Carlton, Jerry. "Listen and Survive." *Tactical Response*, May/June 2008, pp.70–72.

Carlton, Jerry. "Listen and Survive." *Law and Order*, May 2009, pp.84–85.

Dickinson, Eric. "Just Another Drunk—Or a Medical Emergency?" *Law Officer Magazine*, May 2009.

Eggers, Ron. "9-1-A: The 9-1-1 Industry Alliance." *9-1-1 Magazine*, June/July 2009, pp.37, 41.

Executive Order 13166, "Improving Access to Services for Persons with Limited English Proficiency," signed August 11, 2000. http://www.hud.gov/offices/fheo/FHLaws/EXO13166.cfm

Ferrante, David L. "Choose Your Words Carefully." *PoliceOne.com News*, June 19, 2009.

Garner, Gerald W. "Surviving the Circus: How Effective Leaders Work Well with the Media." *The Police Chief*, March 2009, pp.52–57.

Geoghegan, Susan. "Telecommunications Technology in Policing." *Law and Order*, January 2009, pp.40–45.

Hall, Betty. "One Year Later: The NET 911 Act of 2008." *Law Enforcement Technology*, July 2009, pp.70–75.

Hansen, Peter. "Speak Easy." *Law Officer Magazine*, July 2009, pp.28–31.

Hesser, Larry M. "Communication" in *Police Chiefs Desk Reference*, 2nd ed. Washington, DC: Bureau of Justice Assistance and Arlington, VA: International Association of Chiefs of Police, Published by McGraw-Hill Learning Solutions, 2008.

Hitch, Vance. "OneDOJ: The Storefront for Federal Law Enforcement Information." *The Police Chief*, April 2007, pp.26–31.

Holt, Greg. "Mobile Language Interpretation Program." *Law and Order*, July 2008, pp.54–56.

"Improved Public Safety with Next Generation 9-1-1." *9-1-1 Magazine*, June/July 2009, pp.12–14.

Jenkins, Jon, and Visser, Gerrit. "Meetings Bloody Meetings." International Association of Facilitators, no date. Accessed October 15, 2009. http://www.iaf-world.org

Johnston, Fred. "Real-Time Data Sharing." *9-1-1 Magazine*, June/July 2009, pp.16–18, 40.

Kane, Kevin. "Radio Communications Bandwidth Melting Pot." *Law Enforcement Technology*, February 2009, pp.52–56.

Ladin, Marc. "Emergency Notification Systems: Past, Present and Future." *9-1-1 Magazine*, April/May 2009, pp.31–33.

Laine, Russell B. "Law Enforcement and Public Perception: Race, Ethnicity, and Community Policing." *The Police Chief*, September 2009, p.6.

Lee, Robert E., Jr. "Compensating for Noise in Law Enforcement Communications." *The Police Chief*, September 2007, pp.58–63.

Lindsey, Jeffrey C. "Law Enforcement Online: A Powerful Partner for Information Sharing." *The Police Chief*, May 2008, p.82.

Lindsey, Jeffrey C. "N-DEx Implementation Update: Ready and Able." *The Police Chief*, August 2009, pp.20–24.

Moore, Carole. "Lost without Translation." *Law Enforcement Technology*, October 2008, pp.100–107.

Neman, Shane. "Notification Systems: Emergency Communications and Text Messaging." *9-1-1 Magazine*, June/July 2009, pp.20–21, 35.

"An Older and More Diverse Nation by Midcentury." Washington, DC: *U.S. Census Bureau News*, August 14, 2008.

O'Toole, William C., and Reyes, Eddie. "Making a Successful Transition to Common Radio Language." *The Police Chief*, May 2008, pp.72–75.

Paris, Chris. "Lights, Camera, Action." *Law Officer Magazine*, March 2007, pp.50–55.

Pendleton, Steve. "Information Overload and the 9-1-1 Dispatcher." *9-1-1 Magazine*, April 2008, pp.36–40.

"Reporters Offer PERF Chiefs Hard-Boiled View of Media Relations." *Subject to Debate*, May 2008, pp.1, 4-5.

Rosenthal, Rick. "Interview Successes for Trainers." *ILEETA Digest*, July/August/September 2008, p.6.

Rosenthal, Richard. "Media Relations Lessons from Flight 1549." *ILEETA Digest*, January/February/March 2009, p.6.

Scott, Michael. "Entering the Next Generation: Vendor-Driven Technologies That Will Affect Your Comm Center." *9-1-1 Magazine*, January–March 2009, pp.26–28, 46.

Scoville, Dean. "Sound Tactics." *Police*, August 2009, pp.26–30.

Shah, Susan, and Estrada, Rodolfo. *Bridging the Language Divide: Promising Practices for Law Enforcement*. Washington, DC: Community Oriented Policing Services and the Vera Institute of Justice, February 1, 2009.

Shah, Susan; Rahman, Insha; and Khashu, Anita. *Overcoming Language Barriers: Solutions for Law Enforcement*. Washington, DC: Community Oriented Policing Services and the Vera Institute of Justice, 2007. (NCJ 217863)

Sipes, Leonard A., Jr., and Mentel, Zoe. "Using Social Media to Protect Public Safety." *Community Policing Dispatch*, April 2009.

Stockton, Dale. "Keep It Compatible." *Law Officer Magazine*, July 2008, p.8.

Stockton, Dale. "A Harvard Education." *Law Officer Magazine*, August 2009, p.8.

Tooley, Michael, and Lande, Brian J. "The Media, the Public, and the Law Enforcement Community: Correcting Misperceptions." *The Police Chief*, June 2009, pp.62–67.

Webb, David. "Make Your Staff Meetings Count." *Law and Order*, July 2007, pp.86–90.

Wethal, Tabatha. "The Electronic Beat." *Law Enforcement Technology*, September 2009, p.6.

Wright, Morgan. "Crisis Collaboration: Beyond Radio." *9-1-1 Magazine*, July 2008, pp.44–46.

CHAPTER FIVE

Decision Making and Problem Solving as a Manager

Good management is the art of making problems so interesting and their solutions so constructive that everyone wants to get to work and deal with them.

—Paul Hawken

DO YOU KNOW?

- What fosters a decision-making, problem-solving environment?
- What levels of decision making exist?
- What kinds of decisions managers must make?
- What functions may be served by the brain's left and right sides?
- What basic methods are commonly used to make decisions or solve problems?
- What levels of the agency benefit from group participation in decision making?
- How brainstorming can be most effective?
- What more complex methods are often used to make decisions or solve problems and what each involves?
- What the SARA Model problem-solving process includes?
- What common thinking traps exist? Mental locks?
- What "killer phrases" are and how to deal with them?
- What other considerations decision making and problem solving include?

CAN YOU DEFINE?

Abilene Paradox
convergent thinking
creative procrastination
cross flow
cross tell
data mining
Delphi technique
divergent thinking
force-field analysis (FFA)
GIGO
groupthink
impact evaluation
left-brain thinking
magnet phenomenon
modified Delphi technique
nominal group technique (NGT)
process evaluation
qualitative data
quantitative data
right-brain thinking
vicarious liability
whole-brain thinking

INTRODUCTION

Decision making and problem solving are primary responsibilities of law enforcement personnel at all levels. Most law enforcement managers developed their decision-making skills in the field as patrol officers. They made important decisions regularly, but their decisions were usually based on clear department policies and procedures. The decision to arrest someone, for example, was made many times. If something new occurred, the first-line supervisor might be directed to the scene for a decision. Even this decision was comparatively easy because standards existed and the supervisor had to consider only alternatives to the established procedure.

Because of the discretion they had as patrol officers, most law enforcement managers are comfortable making decisions as long as guidelines exist. There is little time to problem solve if someone

135

is shooting at you. Often, however, law enforcement managers encounter unique problems that call for problem-solving and decision-making skills.

Officers who adopt problem solving as their most important goals tend to see these as their supervisors' goals also and spend more time engaged in problem-solving activities. Organizations must provide time, information and rewards for problem solving by its officers.

CHAPTER at a GLANCE

This chapter begins by describing a decision-making, problem-solving environment and the kinds of decisions managers must make. Next, research on how the human brain processes information and modes of thinking is explored. Then basic methods for making decisions or solving problems are described, including participatory decision making, brainstorming, focus groups and groupthink. This is followed by descriptions of several more complex approaches to decision making, including a seven-step decision-making/problem-solving process, force-field analysis, the nominal group technique and the Delphi technique. Next is a discussion of problem-oriented policing (POP), the decisions made in this process and a look at the problem analysis triangle. Then a discussion of creativity and innovation and how they help in solving problems is presented, followed by a discussion of how creativity can be hindered by thinking traps, mental locks, killer phrases and common mistakes in decision making/problem solving. The chapter concludes with a brief discussion of legal issues, ethics in decision making and problem solving and criteria for evaluating the decisions reached.

A DECISION-MAKING, PROBLEM-SOLVING ENVIRONMENT

The environment that promotes decision making and problem solving must encourage diversity and disagreement. Managers should seek out those of a different mind-set to foster healthy debate. However, they should be careful to prevent a debate from escalating to an argument.

 Diversity, disagreement and risk taking help foster a decision-making, problem-solving environment.

Managers must make decisions and take risks. It comes with the job. German author Johann Wolfgang von Goethe has said, "Daring ideas are like chessmen moved forward; they may be beaten, but they may start a winning game." As noted previously, risk taking can be of great benefit. Consider the following exchange:

A new supervisor asked his captain what the secret of his success was.

The captain replied, "I can sum it up in two words: right decisions."

"How do you make those right decisions?" the sergeant asked.

"I can sum that up in one word: experience," replied the captain.

"And how does someone get that experience?" the sergeant asked.

To which the captain replied, "Two words: wrong decisions."

KINDS OF DECISIONS

Decisions may deal with problems that are trivial or critical, short term or long term, personal or organizational. They may also be categorized by the level in the organizational hierarchy at which they are made. The executive level mainly deals with conceptual problems and alternatives, middle management most frequently makes administrative decisions and first-line supervisors most frequently make operational decisions.

 Decisions may be *strategic*—executive level; *administrative*—middle-management level; or *operational*—first-line level.

Applying a business plan model, consider how the nature of decision making differs by the level of police personnel involved:

- Decisions by *executive*-level personnel may concern reduction in the overall crime rate
- Decisions by *mid-level* personnel may be directed at reduction of violent, property, drug-related and youth crimes
- Decisions by *first-line* personnel may center on the implementation of a Neighborhood Safety Project

From these examples, it should be clear to see how strategic, administrative and operational decisions differ.

Decisions at all levels involve individual skills and life experiences, organizational policies, different managerial styles and a certain amount of risk taking. Decisions may also be categorized by who carries them out.

 Decisions may be command, consultative or consensual.

A *command decision* is one that managers make on their own, with little or no input from others. For example, the chief of police decides to give an award to an officer.

A *consultative decision*, in contrast, uses input and opinions from others. The final decision is still made by the one in charge but only after considering others' input. For example, a lieutenant in charge of organizing a Neighborhood Watch program might ask for ideas from other officers and citizens, and he may consult other agencies that already have such a program. The lieutenant then makes decisions about the program based on this input. Managers will gain greater acceptance of and support for their decisions if they seek input from all levels and other stakeholders and weigh that input before making their final decisions.

A *consensus decision* is made democratically by a group. It is a joint decision often made by committee members. For example, training priorities for the year might be decided by a committee established for this purpose. This committee might operate independently or seek input from others in the organization.

Law enforcement organizations regularly make all three kinds of decisions. One key to effectiveness is that the individuals involved know what kind of decision they are making. For example, a situation in which a manager makes it very clear that he or she alone is going to decide an issue is quite different from a situation in which the manager *appears* to seek input from others but is only making a gesture. Likewise, if employees believe they are to decide an issue, but the final decision is *not* what they recommended, the entire decision-making process may be undermined.

Before looking at specific methods of decision making and problem solving, consider the thinking process and how it functions. Managers are expected to use their heads—their brains. Most managers have attained their present positions because of this ability, which is equated with intelligence or mental ability. They also have traditionally relied upon logic and reason to solve problems, but whole-brain research suggests that this may not always be the most appropriate approach.

WHOLE-BRAIN RESEARCH

Two thousand five hundred years ago, Hippocrates suggested that our emotions come from the head, not the heart. Twenty-five years ago Nobel Prize–winning neuroscientist, Roger Sperry, conducted research on what happens when parts of the corpus callosum, which connects left and right hemispheres of the brain, is cut. Some of the work was done on animals, and some occurred on humans who had had their corpus callosum cut for medical reasons, often as a treatment for epilepsy. Sperry's research established that the right and the left sides of the brain each have their own thoughts and memories and *process information differently*.

 Left-brain thinking processes *language* and is primarily *logical*. **Right-brain thinking** processes *images* and is primarily *emotional*.

left-brain thinking
primarily using language and logic.

right-brain thinking
primarily using images and emotions.

Brain research also indicates differences in the way each side of the brain processes information. The left side usually processes information sequentially, logically and rationally in linear fashion. It also controls skilled movements. The right side usually processes information spatially, intuitively, holistically and emotionally. The left side uses reasoning; the right side, imagination and creativity. Researchers have discovered that

1. Right-hemisphere processes add emotional and humorous overtones important for understanding the full meaning of oral and written communication.

2. Both hemispheres are involved in thinking, logic and reasoning.

3. The right hemisphere seems to play a special role in emotion. If students are emotionally engaged, both sides of the brain will participate in the educational process, regardless of subject matter.

When dealing with problem-solving, decision-making situations, our educational system and our culture tend to place more value on those factors associated with the left brain: logical, rational, objective, sequential and so forth. Our organizations, public and private, also rely heavily on rational, logical and analytical approaches to problems. Further, most effective law enforcement managers are precise, methodical and conservative. They seek to preserve the status quo—to keep things on an even keel.

The logical approach was perhaps more appropriate when organizations were less complex and change was less frequent. Our complex, rapidly changing modern society, however, requires the ability to use *both* logic and creativity in problem solving and decision making—that is, **whole-brain thinking**. There is no "better" side. Most managers are familiar with the role of logic in decision making and problems solving. Recently, however, *emotional intelligence* has been receiving attention in law enforcement.

whole-brain thinking
using both the logical left side and the emotional right side of the brain together for best results.

Emotional Intelligence

Fitch (2009, p.104) defines *emotional intelligence* (EI) as "the ability to recognize and manage one's emotions, as well as those of others." He describes the ABC's of emotions like this:

Activating events are the people, things or other assumed stressors in an officer's life. It could be a motorist who refuses to sign a citation, a citizen who "pays your salary," or a supervisor who wants things done a certain way. The person or event prevents the officer from meeting a goal, which can lead to frustration and, ultimately, anger if not managed properly.

Beliefs and self-talk are statements that officers tell themselves about the activating events in their lives. The first type of beliefs and self-talk are rational, adaptive, and supportive. They help cope with frustration, find workable solutions, and soothe negative emotions. In contract, the second type of beliefs and self-talk are irrational, maladaptive, and hurtful. Predictably, the latter type often leads to frustration, anxiety, and poor decision making.

Consequences are what result from an officer's beliefs and self-talk. Depending on the statements involved, emotional consequences can include anger and depression or more positive responses, such as satisfaction or happiness.

Fitch (2009, pp.106–107) suggests that most officers are unaware of their self-talk and allow negative patterns to develop. These negative, irrational and unhealthy beliefs must be replaced with positive, healthy, realistic self-talk. A first step in replacing negative self-talk is to recognize individual "hot buttons." Officers and managers who recognize their triggers ahead of time can prepare themselves mentally and emotionally for these events (Fitch, p.108). They should also be aware of how they physically react as they become angry and make adjustments in what they are telling themselves.

Individuals with emotional self-awareness can prevent simple incidents from growing out or proportion. These individuals show a high level of impulse control, staying composed and refraining from aggression, hostility and irresponsible behavior (Turner, 2009, p.100). Individuals with a high level of emotional intelligence are optimistic, looking for the bright side of situations and recognizing that emotions are like germs, in that they are transmissible and contagious (Turner).

Emotional intelligence can positively influence both logical and creative decision making and problem solving. Because most managers are more familiar with and reliant on logic, it will be addressed first.

BASIC METHODS FOR MAKING DECISIONS OR PROBLEM SOLVING

An important management tool is a decision-making process, that is, a systematic approach to solving a problem. This chapter describes several decision-making processes that can be tailored to fit specific law enforcement department problems.

 Basic methods for making decisions range from using intuition and snap decisions to using a computer, with a systematic individual or group approach falling in between.

Intuition

Intuition is insight. It is knowing without using any rational thought process. The subconscious makes decisions based on intuition. Intuition crosses the left and right hemispheres, integrating facts and feelings. Decisions may be the slow, rational, analytic result of deliberate reasoning or the rapid emotionally based result of intuition.

Officers frequently act intuitively in policing, but find it difficult to explain. They instinctively read and react to danger signals based on training and experience. It is an uneasy feeling, a gut reaction, a sixth-sense that results in law enforcement officers perceiving danger signals and reacting accordingly. Some have called this phenomenon the "Pucker Factor," although other euphemisms exist. Whatever it is called, it refers to an officer's ability to just *know* that an individual poses a threat, without either of them ever having to say a word.

Glennon (2007) states, "From a law enforcement perspective this phenomenon is in constant play on many levels: evaluating witnesses, sizing up a given situation and rooting out lying suspects. But it is never more important than when it processes the communication cues of potential assaults. . . . Veteran officers especially are experts at spotting body language signals and verbal cues that are precursors to nefarious intent." Glennon (2008a) suggests that this instinctive communication doesn't come from the prehistoric "reptilian" part of our brain, but rather involves a cognitive function that processes unconscious thought at lightning speed. Glennon (2008b) describes several "telegraphed" indicators of hostile intent such as clenching the fists or teeth that managers can also use to "read" the emotional state of those they interact with. Managers use intuition in many ways also, sometimes just having a hunch or gut feeling that a decision has to be made and made quickly.

Snap Decisions

At times managers must be decisive. It is not always possible to obtain all available information. Do not expect every decision to be perfect. Perfectionists find it difficult to make decisions because they never have sufficient information.

General Colin Powell uses what he calls the P-40-70 Rule whenever he has to be decisive. P stands for the probability of success, and the numbers indicate the percentage of information acquired. He goes with his gut feeling when he has acquired information in the 40 to 70 percent range. If time is critical, he makes the decision with only 40 percent of the information needed. According to Powell, if he waited until he had all the information, he would never make a decision; he'd always be waiting for another piece of information. It has been said that it is better to be boldly decisive and risk being wrong than to agonize at length and be right too late.

Learning to make snap decisions prudently can be extremely beneficial. A not-so-great snap decision may have better results than a good decision made slowly. This is because any kind of movement often brings a new perspective that makes the right decision more obvious.

Being decisive often inspires support from subordinates and superiors. It also lets managers feel in control. Having a list of 10 unsolved problems sitting on their desks can cause anxiety and stress. Many problems and decisions should be made quickly and decisively. Others can be delegated or not even made. Know when to slow down and proceed with caution, and remember that you can change your mind.

Delegating Revisited

Delegation sends the decision-making process to a subordinate. The manager is removed from the process at this point until it is time to report the results. Delegation is an excellent motivating technique and gets the job done at the level of those with firsthand knowledge of the problem.

When you delegate, establish a timeline. Delegated tasks should be concise and clear. You must also give authority along with a level of responsibility. Effective managers make sure decisions are made at the lowest level possible. They offer assistance but encourage independence. The skills needed to delegate effectively were discussed in Chapter 2.

Not Deciding

Not to decide *is* to decide. In some instances, any decision is better than none. But in other instances, such as a life-threatening situation, a wrong decision or a delayed decision, may have disastrous results. Effective managers know when they do not have to make a decision. They use **creative procrastination**—providing time for a minor difficulty to work itself out. In other instances, the "if it isn't broken, don't fix it" thinking trap works to keep managers from getting bogged down in trivia.

creative procrastination
delaying decisions, allowing time for minor difficulties to work themselves out.

Using Technology for Decision Making

A few decades ago law enforcement had limited technological assistance. Managers were truly independent decision makers with little support. The advent of sophisticated software and data banks for crime analysis has greatly changed this situation. A vast array of technology is available to assist decision making at all levels.

At the operational or line level, squad cars now have computers that give patrol officers instant access to information. By tracing a license number directly from the patrol car, officers may know the history of the vehicle they are stopping before they approach it. The driver's identification and past record can also be instantly checked. This is important to personal safety and decisions about whether to arrest.

At the management level, administrative programs help with allocating personnel, budgeting, scheduling shifts, analyzing reports (such as CompStat reports) and many other functions. Software programs also provide statistical information as well as analysis of this information and may even suggest implications and alternatives. It is critical for a new supervisor to "buy into" the analysis of data for predicting crime and to lead by example. This is a significantly different task than being told by a supervisor what to do. In other words, new managers and supervisors must be proactive and assist executive management with the buy in and culture change as it relates to intelligence-led policing if the department is to truly reap the benefits of technology in decision making.

Among the data files being maintained are arrests, traffic citations, stolen property/vehicles records, crash reports, calls for service, Uniform Crime Report (UCR) summary or disposition data, alarms, personnel, criminal histories, inventory, evidence, warrants, field interviews, payroll, driver's license information, summonses, linked files for crime analysis and vehicle registration. These files are often used for data mining.

Data mining uses advanced computational techniques to explore and characterize large data sets. Data-mining applications include crime analysis, deployment, risk assessment, behavioral analysis, homeland security and Internet/infrastructure protection, transforming information into knowledge.

> **data mining**
>
> an automated tool that uses advanced computational techniques to explore and characterize large data sets.

Even with computer support, however, managers must adapt the information and knowledge to suit current circumstances and arrive at independent decisions. Anyone who works with management information systems must remember the watchword of computer users: "garbage in/garbage out," or **GIGO**. Computers cannot replace experience and expertise, but they can enhance them. Such situations can clearly present a challenge for new supervisors, who do not possess a wealth of experience and expertise from which to draw. This is where a strong analytical skill set can pay dividends for new managers.

> **GIGO**
>
> computer acronym for "garbage in, garbage out."

Computer programs can also help review goals and objectives. Based on the experience of other organizations, computer programs can project alternatives, one or more of which may apply to a situation. From these alternatives, managers can make more informed decisions. Regional information systems, or those that give more than one agency or entity access, are becoming more common.

Wexler et al. (2007, p.40) report that Collins (*Good to Great "Policing"*) and his research team found: "Technology was not a prime cause of either greatness or decline among the companies they studied. . . . [h]owever, . . . the GTG executives thought differently about technology than did the leaders of the merely good companies. While the great companies made pioneering use of selected technologies, the technologies were not adopted for their own sake and did not drive the direction of change." The technologies were used to support the organization's mission.

Using information systems in crime analysis for problem solving policing is discussed later in the chapter. The discussion continues now with other forms of decision making.

Participatory Decision Making (PDM)

A participatory management environment often leads to increased and better decision making. In participatory decision making (PDM), employees of the organization have a say in the decision-making process. Employees prefer PDM largely because decisions often directly affect them. They also bring a diversity of backgrounds and experiences to the decision-making process.

PDM provides more input about the number and content of alternatives because of the participants' varied experience and background. Opportunity for innovative ideas also increases. Shared input fosters better acceptance of and commitment to the final decision. Upward and downward organizational communication also increases, as does teamwork.

The participative manager outlines the problems and leaves the development of alternatives to subordinates. This encourages creativity by the participants and improves the quality and quantity of the decisions they send to the manager. The group may obtain synergistic results when the process of working together enhances sharing and functional competition. With PDM, conflict is considered an asset, and individuals who do not "go along" are viewed as catalysts for innovative ideas and solutions.

Although obtaining consensus may be more difficult with PDM, it can be achieved if participants avoid arguing to win as individuals and keep their focus on reaching the best judgment of the whole group. Group members must also accept responsibility for both hearing and being heard, so that everyone's input receives consideration. Finally, group members should remember that the best results stem from a combination of information, logic and emotion—including participants' feelings about the information and decision-making process. Such participation will positively affect value judgments as well as the final decision.

An entirely participative decision-making process, however, may be difficult to establish because of lack of training on how to work together. It is difficult for officers to include themselves in the process if it has not been past practice to do so. If people are used to being told what to do, they may feel awkward when given a chance to participate. A certain amount of confusion and hesitancy may exist initially. It is even more difficult for autocratic managers to give up their decision-making authority.

In addition, discussion and agreement are time consuming. Further, not all decisions *should* be democratic or participatory. Some decisions must be immediate, and others cannot be resolved by agreement. Sometimes, a final decision can be made only after top management considers the alternatives.

Nonetheless, if possible, decisions should involve those who will be affected by them. The synergy of a group of decision makers can often produce results that a single person or even many people working independently would be unable to produce. Further, implementing the selected alternative will be easier because it is more likely to be accepted. *People tend to support what they help create.* Morale is improved, and participants feel commitment and loyalty.

 All levels of the organization benefit from group participation in the decision-making process.

In any law enforcement organization, newer officers can bring fresh approaches and ideas, but these must be balanced by both work-related and life experience.

Although full department meetings are difficult to schedule because of multiple shifts, input from all officers can be obtained through shift discussions and a joint meeting of first-line supervisors with middle and executive management. Full department meetings should be called only for critical matters or to communicate a decision.

Polzin and Yantovsky (2009) report on a study showing that "the neglect of police unions has seriously impeded understanding of American policing, particularly with respect to basic police management, innovation and reform." They point out that issues such as budget cuts, privatization and civilianization, recruitment, health care and benefits affect everyone in the department, making it logical that union representatives and management need to work together in decision making. To that end, the first National Joint Police Union-Management Symposium was held in October 2008, sponsored by the Michigan State University Schools of Labor and Industrial Relations and Criminal Justice and the U.S. Department of Justice Office of Community Policing Services. The weeklong symposium gave police union and management leaders an opportunity to get to know one another and to discuss the challenges each faced and what changes might benefit both. One outcome was identification of characteristics of both successful and unsuccessful change efforts, summarized in Table 5.1

A valuable outcome of the symposium was the recognition that a joint approach to addressing issues of mutual concern is more enduring than is the more traditional adversarial approach and that successes coming from such a joint process are often magnified by increased trust between union and management leaders (Polzin and Yantovsky, 2009).

Although participatory leadership styles support group decision making, disadvantages might also arise, such as wasted time, shirked responsibilities, a tendency toward indecisiveness and costly delays. One common type of participatory decision making is brainstorming.

TABLE 5.1 Successful vs. Unsuccessful Change Efforts

Successful Change Efforts	Unsuccessful Change Efforts
Use data to understand problems and needs and to support the options or plans being implemented	A perception that the change was just one among many that received little or no follow-through; the flavor-of-the-month syndrome
Communicate change to all affected	Bad timing
Be honest with each other and build trust	Failure to achieve input from those affected or with expertise to bear
Learn from past efforts and utilize feedback	Failure to achieve buy-in from those affected
Ensure that change is inclusive, eliciting involvement from those affected	Lack of flexibility
Have enough time for the process to work; stakeholders should be patient	Poorly thought out
Consistent with other goals	No or poor communication
Have a flexible implementation process	Fear-resistance not addressed
Incorporate follow-up plans	Insufficient will/lack of follow-through
Accomplish through a joint labor-management process	The resources needed to support change were not provided or sufficient

Source: Michael Polzin and Tamara Yantovsky. "Police Labor Relations: Interest-Based Problem-Solving and the Power of Collaboration." *Community Policing Dispatch*, September 2009.

Brainstorming

Most people are familiar with the concept of brainstorming, but the practice is often not as effective as it might be. Brainstorming is a method of shared problem solving in which members of a group spontaneously contribute ideas, no matter how wild, without criticism or critique. It is creative, uninhibited thinking designed to produce ideas, generate alternatives, suggest solutions and create plans. Alex Osborn, the originator of the brainstorming technique, established four rules:

1. No one is permitted to criticize an idea.

2. The wilder the idea, the better.

3. The group should concentrate on the quantity of ideas and not concern itself with the quality.

4. Participants should combine suggested ideas or build on others whenever possible.

Although brainstorming must be unfettered, it is not unstructured, as many believe. Participants should be prepared. They should know in advance the problem they will address. A leader should keep the ideas flowing and make sure no criticism or evaluation of ideas occurs. Group size should be limited to no more than 15 participants, and they should sit at a round or U-shaped table. If not led properly, a brainstorming session can backfire and leave a bad taste in the mouths of those who participated, negatively affecting all future efforts to get volunteers to step up and be a part of the change process.

One key to an effective brainstorming session is to write all ideas on a flip-chart. As pages become filled, tape them to the walls so the group will see the flow of ideas and be motivated to continue. All brainstorming sessions should have a definite ending time so a sense of urgency prevails. Most sessions should be limited to 20 to 40 minutes. Time is *not* unlimited.

During brainstorming, it is critical that **divergent thinking** (right brain) occur before **convergent thinking** (left brain). Divergent thinking is free flowing, creative, imaginative and uninhibited. Convergent thinking, in contrast, is evaluative, rational and objective.

divergent thinking

free, uninhibited thinking; includes imagining, fantasizing, free associating and combining and juxtaposing dissimilar elements; opposite of *convergent thinking*.

convergent thinking

focused, evaluative thinking; includes decision making, choosing, testing, judging and rating; opposite of *divergent thinking*.

To make brainstorming sessions effective:
1. **Ensure that participants are prepared.**
2. **Write down *all* ideas.**
3. **Allow *no* criticizing of ideas.**
4. **Have a definite ending time.**

After the brainstorming session, move to the critical judgment phase, where ideas are reviewed, synthesized, added and subtracted, evaluated and prioritized. Brainstorming can be a powerful decision-making, problem-solving tool. Another participatory approach is to use focus groups.

As these officers brainstorm, they generate many creative solutions to a problem. Their ideas are as broad and radical as possible and are developed rapidly. Creativity has free rein.

© Michael Newman/PhotoEdit

Focus Groups

The police-community collaboration emphasized in many departments can be facilitated by using focus groups to help in decision making and problem solving. Focus groups usually consist of people from the educational community, the religious community, Neighborhood Watch groups, business groups and professional groups, as well as ordinary citizens, who express their opinions about certain issues. The groups are directed by a moderator or facilitator and are meant to collect broad information on a specific topic in an open, personal environment.

Groupthink

Although involving coworkers, citizens and outside agencies is a cornerstone of community policing, hazards do exist, one of which is *groupthink*. **Groupthink** is the negative tendency for group members to submit to peer pressure and endorse the majority opinion even if individually it is unacceptable. Groupthink is more concerned with team play and unanimity than with reaching the best solution. Group members suppress individual concerns to avoid rocking the group's boat. Groupthink is especially hazardous to law enforcement organizations because of the feeling of "family" that exists. Officers support one another, and sometimes a feeling of "them versus us" exists between law enforcement organizations and those they are hired to "serve and protect."

Even life-and-death decisions can be affected by groupthink. It can be difficult to speak up and say that safety concerns indicate that a tactical operation should be delayed, to refuse to go into a barricaded suspect incident with insufficient personnel or wait for a back-up unit on a domestic call.

groupthink
the negative tendency for members of a group to submit to peer pressure and endorse the majority opinion even if it individually is unacceptable.

Abilene Paradox

begins innocently, with everyone in a group agreeing that a particular problem exists; later, when it comes time to discuss solutions, no one expresses a viewpoint that differs from what appears to be the group's consensus, even though many secretly disagree with it; finally, after the solution has been implemented, group members complain privately about the plan and look for someone to blame for its development.

The **Abilene Paradox** is an expression coined by author Jerry Harvey after a trip to Abilene while visiting his in-laws in a small town in west Texas in the 1950s. On a stifling hot afternoon during the visit, Harvey and his wife and her family decided to take a trip to Abilene, 53 miles away, in a car with no air conditioning, to a restaurant they didn't like and ate a not-so-great meal. They returned home late that afternoon, arguing about who had suggested such a bad idea in the first place.

Although everyone had agreed to take the trip, no one had really wanted to go; they each kept their reservations to themselves. They all considered themselves to be victims of someone else's poor decision to travel to Abilene, even though any of them could have objected. They had fallen victim to what Harvey called the Abilene Paradox.

An Abilene Paradox begins with everyone in a group agreeing that a particular problem exists. But when they discuss solutions, no one expresses an idea that differs from what seems to be the group's consensus, even though they disagree with it. Then, after the solution has been implemented, group members complain about the solution and look for someone to blame for its implementation.

An example of how this might happen in a police department is a police chief concerned about racial profiling calls a meeting, and nearly every supervisor present agrees there is a problem and knows how he or she would solve it. The chief, however, upon hearing consensus that the problem exists, declares that the only solution is to record every officer's traffic stops and other citizen contacts. Any officer detaining a disproportionate set number of non-Whites would automatically undergo an internal investigation. The chief asks for comments, but because no one speaks up, everyone, including the chief, takes the silence to mean approval and the new policy goes into effect. Months later, after many internal investigations, tickets and arrests are down. Driving under the influence (DUIs) and residential burglary are up, and citizens are complaining about officers' rudeness. Line officers, supervisors, managers and commanders complain about the racial profiling policy—but only to each another—a prime example of the Abilene Paradox of groupthink.

How can groupthink be avoided? It should be stressed during meetings that individual problems and concerns about a decision should be made known. Create a heterogeneous group representing a broad range of interests. Have the chief or upper management hold back opinions until others have a chance to present their ideas. Brainstorm. Beware of premature decisions—have separate meetings for identifying alternatives and making the final decision.

MORE COMPLEX DECISION-MAKING/ PROBLEM-SOLVING PROCESSES

Whether decisions are made by a group or an individual, often a more complex process is used.

More complex decision-making/problem-solving processes include the seven-step decision-making/problem-solving approach, force-field analysis, the nominal group technique, the Delphi technique or a modified form of the Delphi technique. These approaches often include brainstorming.

The Seven-Step Decision-Making/ Problem-Solving Process

Many decisions can be effectively made and many problems effectively solved through a seven-step process.

Decision making often follows these seven steps:
1. Define the specific problem.
2. Gather all facts concerning the problem.
3. Generate alternatives.
4. Analyze the alternatives.
5. Select the best alternative.
6. Implement the alternative.
7. Evaluate the decision.

Define the Problem

The logical first step is to identify the problem. It must be located, defined and limited before you can seek solutions. Those involved need to agree it is a priority problem that needs to be solved. Take care not to confuse a problem with its *symptoms*. For example, patrol officers may be coming to work late or calling in sick more often. These could be symptoms of a deeper problem—low morale. The problem, not the symptoms, must be addressed.

Another important determination is whether the decision to be made is a large, organizational decision or a small, departmental one. If it is only a small problem, perhaps a command decision is most appropriate. All too often myriad minor decisions rob managers' time that should be spent on more pressing problems.

Gather the Facts

All available relevant data must be reviewed, including facts that may not support existing policies. *Good to Great* guru Collins contends one thing is certain: "You absolutely cannot make a series of good decisions without first confronting the brutal facts" (Wexler et al, 2007, p.32). No organization is perfect. Recognize weaknesses. Determine existing standards, policies and rules that may affect the problem. If possible, consult everyone involved. Experience in dealing with identical or similar problems helps greatly. Sometimes experts are needed. Other times a problem may fall within department guidelines and require very little research. Take the time needed to be thorough. Avoid snap decisions for critical or recurring problems.

Generate Alternatives

Put the alternatives on a flipchart or white board. The following questions can generate alternatives: Is there a new way to do it? Can you give it a new twist? Do you need more of the same? Less of the same? Is there a substitute? Can you rearrange the parts? What if you do just the opposite? Can you combine the ideas? Can you borrow or adapt?

The military uses the phrases *cross tell* and *cross flow* when talking about borrowing or adapting ideas. If one unit goes through an inspection, they **cross tell** what they learned to all the other units so those units do not make the same mistake. If they encounter a problem they have never seen before, they send out a **cross flow** message stating the problem and asking the other units if they have encountered the same thing and, if so, what they did about it. This helps in two ways. If other units have not seen the problem, they can have a heads up that the problem exists. If they have encountered the problem, they can share what worked—or did not work. There is no need to reinvent the wheel.

cross tell

one department alerts other departments about a mistake revealed during inspection.

cross flow

message stating a problem and asking other units if they have encountered the same thing and, if so, what they did about it.

Analyze the Alternatives

What are the likely consequences of each alternative? Among the many factors to consider in analyzing the alternatives are how they fit with the agency mission statement and goals, cost, personnel required, resources available, staff reaction, long-range consequences, union contract provisions, ethical considerations and problems that may arise as a result of the decision. Time and resources may limit the alternatives or control the outcome.

What are the risks involved in deciding? In not deciding? In selecting a different alternative? In being wrong? Thomas Edison was quoted as saying he did not fail to make a storage battery 25,000 times. He simply knew 25,000 ways not to make one.

Select the Most Appropriate Alternative

Choosing the right alternative is the heart of decision making. For normal problem-solving situations, one alternative eventually appears as the best solution. For situations in which all look equal, the choice is more difficult. Most alternatives have advantages and disadvantages. Make a chart with two columns. List each alternative and its corresponding advantages and disadvantages. They may be equal in number, but assign a weight to each point. Use the total points as part of your final decision.

Determining alternatives and evaluating them is often difficult. It may require experience, knowledge, training, creativity, intuition, advice from others and even computer assistance. The more input available, the better the decision.

Implement the Alternative

Implementation is usually the most time-consuming phase of the decision-making process. It involves several steps and should be carefully planned. Who will do the implementing? What resources are needed? When will implementation occur? A critical first step is communicating the decision to everyone involved. Ideally, those involved will have taken part in the decision-making process and will already be familiar with the options and the reasons a particular option was selected.

If a decision is a command or a consultative decision, communication is vital. Effective managers keep their people in on what is happening and enlist their support from the earliest possible minute. Support those implementing the solution. Follow up to see that needed support is continually provided. Seek feedback at all stages of the implementation.

Evaluate the Decision

How effective is the alternative selected? Did it accomplish the expected result? Solve the problem? Evaluation provides information for future decisions. If the solution does not prove effective, learn from the experience. It does little good to brood over solutions that do not work. It does even less good to attempt to place blame.

The primary purpose of evaluation is to improve—to learn what alternatives work and maintain and strengthen them and to learn what alternatives do not work and to change them. Evaluation is discussed in greater depth later in this chapter.

The Steps Applied

Assume that an organizational goal is to reduce vehicle crashes by 10 percent. The *problem* is increased traffic crashes. The major *cause* of the problem is motorist driving behavior. How can police action resolve the problem by reducing crashes by a sustainable 10 percent?

Once the problem is clearly stated, the next step is to use crash records to obtain data concerning frequency, location, day of week, time of day and causes. Computer software programs can provide data analysis and instant information.

After information is compiled, alternatives are identified. Alternative A might be to increase radar enforcement to reduce the speed of vehicles because crashes are increasing not only in frequency but also in severity. Increased speed of vehicles involved in crashes results in increased severity. Alternative B might be to station a squad car at high-crash intersections as a deterrent during the day of the week and time of day that crash occurrence is highest. Alternative C might be to add road signs to warn drivers of the crash problem. Alternative D might be to provide additional traffic patrol officers to increase enforcement of traffic violations and increase deterrent visibility. Alternative E might be to station officers in high-crash locations and have them hand out cards to motorists stopping at stop signs. The cards inform the drivers of the crash problem, locations and things they can do to help. Alternative F might be to implement a combination of the preceding options. Alternative G might be to do nothing.

Next, the alternatives must be analyzed so the best ones can be selected and implemented. Alternative A is accepted, and radar enforcement is increased in selected areas of high crash frequency. Alternative B is eliminated because of time consumption and lack of sufficient vehicles. Alternative C is accepted, and engineering is directed to install signs at the proper locations. Alternative D is eliminated because it requires funds that are not available. Alternative E is eliminated because it would take time to develop and print the card, and the officers do not think this is good use of their time. Alternative F is accepted by default, as more than one of the proposed solutions is implemented. Alternative G is ruled out because measures *are* needed to reduce crashes.

The final step is evaluation, which is done six months later. It was determined that crashes were reduced by 5 percent, half the original goal. The results were disseminated to all police department members and the engineering department. A team of volunteers met to determine why the goal was not achieved, what worked and what didn't work.

Force-Field Analysis (FFA)

force-field analysis

identifies forces that impede and enhance goal attainment; a problem exists when the equilibrium is such that more forces are impeding goal attainment than enhancing it.

Force-field analysis (FFA) is a problem-solving technique that identifies forces that impede and others that foster goal achievement. Forces that impede goal achievement are called *restraining forces*; those that foster it are called *driving forces*. When the forces are in balance, the situation is said to be in *equilibrium*. In a problem situation, the balance becomes tipped and the equilibrium shifts negatively, with more restraining forces than driving forces. Force-field analysis is illustrated in Figure 5.1.

 Force-field analysis identifies factors that impede and enhance goal attainment. A problem exists when the equilibrium is upset because more factors are impeding goal attainment than enhancing it.

In force-field analysis, you can state the problem as an undesirable situation, then list and label each force as high, medium or low (H-M-L) to indicate the strength. The final step is to devise a plan to change the equilibrium. Select specific

FIGURE 5.1
Force-Field Analysis

Source: Michael J. Evers and George Heenan. "Balancing Act: Optimizing Strategies and Projects for Success." *Minnesota Business*, March 2002, p.16.

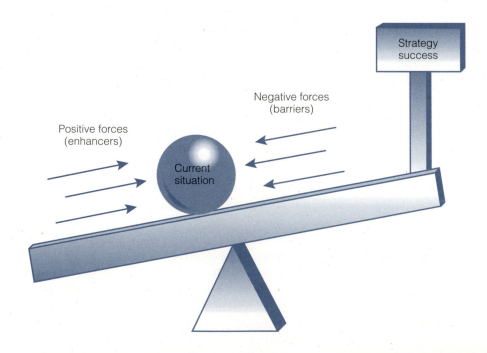

TABLE 5.2 Sample Force-Field Analysis

Problem: Increasing Drug Abuse in Our Community	
Restraining Forces	**Driving Forces**
Lack of finances	Increase in drug arrests
Lack of organization/coordination	Church groups
Lack of school cooperation	Parental concerns
Lack of church cooperation	Suicide rate
Lack of available personnel	Increase in drug use
Public apathy	Teen pregnancies
Parental drug use	Fatal accidents
Drug sales profits	
Recommended Action Plan	
Create a specialized narcotics unit.	
Initiate a 24-hour "hotline."	
Pass an ordinance creating a drug-free zone of 1,000 feet around any school.	
Conduct educational programs such as DARE in the schools.	
Conduct parenting classes.	
Conduct drug-free workplace programs.	
Start a newsletter to be sent to all residents in the community.	
Confiscate all property involved in drug arrests.	
Create an Anti-Drug Abuse Council.	
Hire a drug counselor for those who cannot afford one.	

Source: From KOSSEN. *Supervision*, 2E. © 1991 South-Western, a part of Cengage Learning, Inc. Reproduced by permission. www.cengage.com/permissions

ways to reduce the restraining forces and other ways to increase the driving forces. The entire analysis can be put into a chart, as shown in Table 5.2.

The Nominal Group Technique (NGT)

Research has found that some people work better by themselves than in a group. To take advantage of this and still capture the synergy of a team approach, the nominal group technique was developed to produce more and better ideas.

 The **nominal group technique (NGT)** is an objective way to achieve consensus on the most effective alternatives by ranking them.

nominal group technique

an objective way to achieve consensus on the most effective alternatives by using an objective ranking of alternatives.

It works like this:

1. Divide the staff or people involved into groups of six to nine.

2. Have each person write down as many ideas for solving the problem at hand as they can—without talking to anyone. Allow 5 to 15 minutes for this step.

3. Go around the group and have each person, including the leader, read one item from his or her list while the leader writes the ideas on a flip-chart. No evaluation of the ideas is allowed.

4. Continue going around the room until all ideas are posted. If more than one person gives the same idea, place a tally mark behind it.

5. After all the ideas are posted, allow questions to clarify the ideas, but no evaluation.

6. Hand out note cards and have everyone rank the five best ideas, with "1" being the best.

7. Collect the cards and take a break. Total the rankings for each idea and divide by the number of people in the meeting. Then write on the flipchart the five ideas with the highest scores.

8. Reconvene the group and have them discuss the five ideas. Usually one best idea will emerge from this discussion.

This technique works well to obtain input from everyone, but it is also very time consuming. It should be reserved for important problems that truly require a consensus decision.

The Delphi Technique

Delphi technique

a way to have individual input; uses open-ended questionnaires completed by individuals; answers are shared, and the questionnaires are again completed until consensus is achieved.

The **Delphi technique** was developed in the 1960s at the Rand Corporation. Like the nominal group process, the Delphi Technique is a way to have individual input result in a group effort. Rather than calling a meeting, management sends questionnaires to those who will be involved in the decision making. Figure 5.2 illustrates a typical Delphi questionnaire.

Management then circulates the answers to all participants, who are asked to again complete the questionnaire considering the various answers. This continues until a consensus is reached. Usually, three or four cycles are enough.

> The Delphi technique uses questionnaires completed by individuals. Answers are shared, and the questionnaires are again completed until consensus is reached.

FIGURE 5.2
Typical Delphi Questionnaire

> **Survey on options for combatting the drug problem**
>
> As an officer on the street, you are closest to the drug problem our agency is battling. We would appreciate your suggestions on possible approaches to this problem. Please take a few minutes to answer the questions that follow. Your answers will be confidential, but all answers will be shared with all other members of the patrol division.
>
> 1. How can we increase community drug education?
> _____
> _____
>
> 2. What are the three main drug abuse problem areas?
> _____
> _____
>
> 3. What should we do to reduce the drug problem in our community?
> _____
> _____

Delphi is actually a thoughtful conversation in which everyone gets a chance to *listen*. Groups often debate rather than problem solve. The Delphi technique removes the need for winning points or besting the opposition.

A Modified Delphi Technique

The Delphi technique can be modified to take away the open-endedness. This **modified Delphi technique** presents a questionnaire that contains policy statements representing key issues to be decided and a response column with three choices: Agree with, not certain but willing to try and disagree with. Those who do not agree are asked to indicate the changes they would recommend that would make the statement acceptable. This is Phase 1. Figure 5.3 shows an example of how this might look.

Phase 2 shows the number replying with each option for each statement and the choice each respondent circled. Respondents are then asked to reconsider their original responses and make any changes they want based on the responses of others. Figure 5.4 shows how this might look.

Phase 3 is a tally of the responses in Phase 2 and a summary of the actions to be taken for each item, based on those responses. Many of these decision-making methods are also appropriate for a department using problem-solving policing. Considerable overlap can be seen between the two processes.

> **modified Delphi technique**
>
> uses objective rather than open-ended questions.

FIGURE 5.3
Phase 1 of the Modified Delphi Technique

1. For each statement below, check the column that best reflects your position: 　A　Agree with 　B　Not certain but willing to try for a year and evaluate 　C　Disagree with 2. For each column where you check C, indicate in the space below the statement how you would like it amended. You may also comment if you checked A or B.			

Suggested action	A	B	C
To increase community drug education we should: 1. Start a school DARE program. 　Comment: _____			
2. Publish in local papers a series of articles by community leaders. 　Comment: _____			
3. Highlight drug abuse literature at the library. 　Comment: _____			
To reduce the drug problem in our community we should: 4. Increase the number of police. 　Comment: _____			
5. Begin a community-wide anti-drug abuse council. 　Comment: _____			
6. Provide stiffer penalties to drug dealers and users. 　Comment: _____			

FIGURE 5.4
Phase 2 of the Modified
Delphi Technique

Following is a tally of responses to the drug questionnaire and suggested changes that we would like you to respond to. As before, for each statement and change, check the column that best reflects your position:
A   Agree with
B   Not certain, but willing to try for a year and evaluate
C   Disagree with

Suggested action	A	B	C
To increase community drug education we should:			
1. Start a school DARE program.	5	3	3
Change: Also have parenting classes.			
2. Publish in local papers a series of articles by community leaders.	4	4	3
Change: Also articles by victims and cops.			
3. Highlight drug abuse literature at the library.	3	3	5
Change: Distribute literature through civic groups and the schools as well.			
To reduce the drug problem in our community we should:			
4. Increase the number of police.	6	5	0
Change: Increase in areas known to have high rates of drug dealing.			
5. Begin a community-wide anti-drug abuse council.	4	4	3
Change: Members appointed by chief of police.			
6. Provide stiffer penalties to drug dealers and users.	5	1	5
Change: For dealers only. Counseling for users.			

© Cengage Learning 2012

PROBLEM-SOLVING POLICING

Problem-solving policing (often referred to as problem-oriented policing) has become extremely popular in many departments and, as noted in Chapter 2, often goes hand-in-hand with community policing. However, the distinction between problem solving and community policing is apparent in many departments. Table 5.3 summarizes some key distinctions that may occur between the two approaches.

The approach used in problem-oriented policing is typically the SARA model.

The SARA model problem-solving process involves four steps (Eck and Spelman, 1987):
1. **Scanning (identifying the problem)**
2. **Analysis (looking at alternatives)**
3. **Response (implementing an alternative)**
4. **Assessment (evaluating the results)**

Scanning

Scanning refers to identifying recurring problems and prioritizing them to select one problem to address. The scanning step incorporates the first two steps in the seven-step decision making, problem-solving process: define the

TABLE 5.3 Selected Comparisons between Problem-Oriented Policing and Community Policing Principles

Principle	Problem-Oriented Policing	Community Policing
Primary emphasis	Substantive social problems within police mandate	Engaging the community in the policing
When police and community collaborate	Determined on a problem-by-problem basis	Always or nearly always
Emphasis on problem analysis	Highest priority given to thorough analysis	Encouraged, but less important than community collaboration
Preference for responses	Strong preference that alternatives to criminal law enforcement be explored	Preference for collaborative response with community
Role for police in organizing and mobilizing community	Advocated only if warranted within the context of the specific problem being addressed	Emphasizes strong role for police
Importance of geographic decentralization of police and continuity of officer assignment to community	Preferred but not essential	Essential
Degree to which police share decision-making authority with community	Strongly encourages input from community while preserving ultimate decision-making authority to police	Emphasizes sharing decision-making authority with community
Emphasis on officers' skills	Emphasizes intellectual and analytical skills	Emphasizes interpersonal skills
View of the role or mandate of police	Encourages broad, but not unlimited, role for police, stresses limited capabilities of police, and guards against creating unrealistic expectations of police	Encourages expansive role for police to achieve ambitious social objectives

Source: Michael S. Scott. *Problem-Oriented Policing: Reflection of the First 20 Years.* Washington, DC: U.S. Department of Justice, Office of Community Oriented Policing Services, 2000, p.99.

specific problem and gather all facts concerning the problem. Basic questions to address at this stage include

- Who is affected by the problem?
- What harms are created by the problem and what is expected of the police?
- What factors contribute to the problem?
- How often do they recur?
- How are they similar?

Table 5.4 illustrates potential sources of information for identifying problems obtained through scanning.

Analysis

Analysis examines the identified problem's causes, scope and effects. It includes determining how often the problem occurs and how long it has been occurring, as well as conditions that appear to create the problem. Analysis also should include potential resources and partners who might assist in understanding and addressing the problem.

The analysis phase incorporates the third, fourth and fifth steps of the seven-step process: generate alternatives, analyze the alternatives, select

TABLE 5.4 Potential Sources of Information for Identifying Problems

Crime Analysis Unit—Time trends and patterns (time of day, day of week, monthly, seasonal and other cyclical events) and patterns of similar events (offender descriptions, victim characteristics, locations, physical settings and other circumstances).
Patrol—Recurring calls, bad areas, active offenders, victim types, complaints from citizens.
Investigations—Recurring crimes, active offenders, victim difficulties, complaints from citizens.
Crime Prevention—Physical conditions, potential victims, complaints from citizens.
Vice—Drug dealing, illegal alcohol sales, gambling, prostitution, organized crime.
Communications—Call types, repeat calls from same location, temporal peaks in calls for service.
Chief's Office—Letters and calls from citizens, concerns of elected officials, concerns from city manager's office.
Other Law Enforcement Agencies—Multi-jurisdictional concerns.
Elected Officials—Concerns and complaints.
Local Government Agencies—Plans that could influence crimes, common difficulties, complaints from citizens.
Schools—Juvenile concerns, vandalism, employee safety.
Community Leaders—Problems of constituents.
Business Groups—Problems of commerce and development.
Neighborhood Watch—Local problems regarding disorder, crime and other complaints.
Newspapers and Other News Media—Indications of problems not detected from other sources, problems in other jurisdictions that could occur in any city.
Community Surveys—Problems of citizens in general.

Source: John E. Eck and William Spelman. *Problem Solving: Problem-Oriented Policing in Newport News.* Washington, DC: Police Executive Research Forum, 1987, p.46. ©1987 Police Executive Research Forum. Reprinted with permission by PERF.

the best alternative. Goldstein's (1990, p.ix) range of possible alternatives includes

- Concentrating attention on those who account for a disproportionate share of a problem.
- Connecting with other government and private services.
- Using mediation and negotiation skills.
- Conveying information.
- Mobilizing the community.
- Using existing forms of social control in addition to the community.
- Altering the physical environment to reduce opportunities for problems to recur.
- Increasing regulation, through statutes or ordinances, of conditions that contribute to problems.
- Developing new forms of limited authority to intervene and detain.
- Using the criminal justice system more discriminately.
- Using civil law to control public nuisances, offensive behavior and conditions contributing to crime.

Response

Response is acting to alleviate the problem, that is, selecting the alternative solution or solutions to try. The response step parallels the sixth step in the seven-step process: implement the alternative. This may include finding out what other communities with similar problems have tried and with what success, as well as looking at whether any research on the problem exists. Focus groups might be used to brainstorm possible interventions. Experts might be enlisted. Several alternatives might be ranked and prioritized according to difficulty, expense and the like. At this point goals are usually refined and the interventions are implemented. Often the most common response to complex issues of crime and disorder involves increased use of conventional law enforcement strategies such as enforcement.

Brown and Scott (2007, p.3) identify six factors to assess before beginning any implementation response: internal support; external support, including partner organizations, the community and the local media; leadership; communication; resources; and staffing. They (pp.1–2) also list four reasons implementation may fail:

1. The problem was inaccurately identified.

2. The problem was insufficiently or inadequately analyzed.

3. The response was improperly or insufficiently implemented.

4. Responses did not have the desired effect.

Assessment

The final phase of the SARA model is assessment. It should be stressed, however, that assessment should be ongoing during the response or implementation phase of the project. *Assessment* refers to evaluating how effective the intervention was. Was the problem solved? If not, why? The assessment phase in the SARA model parallels the seventh step of the seven-step process: evaluate the decision. Data collected throughout the evaluation process provides information that helps determine whether earlier stages should be revisited to improve the response. Figure 5.5 illustrates the problem-solving process and evaluation.

Assessment should include both qualitative and quantitative data. **Qualitative data** examines the excellence (quality) of the response—that is, how satisfied were the officers and the citizens. This is most frequently determined by surveys, focus groups or tracking of complaints and compliments. Qualitative data is often referred to as *soft* data because it is based heavily on subjective opinions. In contrast, **quantitative data** examines the amount of change (quantity) as a result of the response. This is most frequently measured by pre/post data. Quantitative data is referred to as *hard* data because it can be objectively assessed numerically or ranked by orders of magnitude. Qualitative data *describes* whereas quantitative data *defines*.

Assessment should also include process and impact evaluations. **Process evaluation** determines whether the response was implemented as planned, whereas **impact evaluation** determines whether the problem declined. Table 5.5 provides guidance in interpreting the results of process and impact evaluation.

The SARA model of problem solving stresses that there are no failures, only responses that do not provide the desired goal. When a response does not give the desired results, those involved in problem solving can examine the results

---

qualitative data

examines the excellence (quality) of the response—that is, how satisfied were the officers and the citizens; most frequently determined by surveys, focus groups or tracking of complaints and compliments.

quantitative data

examines the amount of change (quantity) as a result of the response; most frequently measured by pre/post data.

process evaluation

an assessment to determine whether the response was implemented as planned.

impact evaluation

an assessment to determine whether a problem declined.

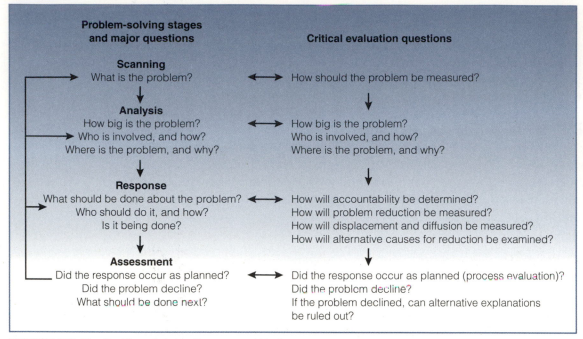

FIGURE 5.5 The Problem-Solving Process and Evaluation

Source: John E. Eck. *Assessing Responses to Problems: An Introductory Guide for Police Problem-Solvers.* Washington, DC: Office of Community Oriented Policing Services, 2002, p.6.

FIGURE 5.6

Interpreting Results of Process and Impact Evaluations

Source: John E. Eck. *Assessing Responses to Problems: An Introductory Guide for Police Problem Solvers.* Washington, DC. Office of Community Oriented Policing Services, 2002, p.10.

Process Evaluation Results

	Response implemented as planned, or nearly so	Response not implemented, or implemented in a radically different manner than planned
Problem declined	Evidence that the response caused the decline	Suggests that other factors may have caused the decline or that the response was accidentally effective
Problem did not decline	Evidence that the response was ineffective, and that a different response should be tried	Little is learned. Perhaps if the response had been implemented as planned, the problem would have declined, but this is speculative

Impact Evaluation Results

and try a different response. Other communities might benefit from what was learned. The difference between simply handling a call and solving a problem is illustrated in Table 5.6.

The SARA Model in Action

An example of problem-oriented policing in action and implementing the SARA model is seen in the 2001 winner of the Herman Goldstein Excellence in Problem-Oriented Policing Award, the California Highway Patrol (CHP), for its Corridor

TABLE 5.5 Handling a Call versus Solving a Problem

Handling a Call	versus	Solving a Problem
Call-/case-driven response		Problem-driven response
Temporary/transient result		Longer lasting/permanent result
Less effort/energy required/expended		More effort/energy required/expended
Less imagination applied		More imagination applied
Limited results expected by officers		Less limited results expected by officers
Little collaboration with others		Much collaboration with others
Response driven by limited information		Response driven by much information

Source: Terry Eisenberg and Bruce Glasscock. "Looking Inward with Problem-Oriented Policing." *FBI Law Enforcement Bulletin*, July 2001, p.4.

Safety Program. The program used the SARA model to address a high rate of fatal accidents on an infamous stretch of rural highway in California, the roadway where actor James Dean was killed in the late 1950s, dubbed "Blood Alley."

Scanning

Scanning was rigorous, with 550 qualifying roadway segments examined. Three years of collision and victim data were reviewed to minimize any statistical anomalies. To be included in the selection pool, potential corridors had to pass through or be adjacent to an urban area and fall under the jurisdiction of the CHP. Segments with fewer than five deaths in three years were also eliminated. Based on statistical rankings and input from local experts, State Route 41/46 was selected.

Analysis

The CHP formed a multidisciplinary task force. The task force found that much of the corridor was quite remote, largely without cellular phone service and having too few call boxes. Call response times for emergency services depended on the emergency medical services (EMS) unit with jurisdiction over the area, sometimes not the closest unit. The roadway lacked adequate shoulders and medians, and existing signage was confusing and inadequate, as were existing passing and merging lanes. Being an east-west route, glare was a problem during sunrise and sunset. Various roadway curves also contributed to poor visibility.

The task force also found that the primary collision factors spoke to the presence of aggressive driving and of impatient drivers behind large, slow-moving vehicles who made unwise passing decisions. The top five collision factors were unsafe turning, driving on the wrong side of the road, improper passing, driving under the influence and unsafe speed. The task force also suggested that many involved in collisions were local farm workers with limited English skills who were unfamiliar with California rules of the road.

Response

Proposed solutions fell into four categories: enforcement, emergency services, engineering and education. Special *enforcement* operations were implemented and funded through federal traffic safety grants. Ultimately officers worked

2,922 overtime hours, offered assistance and services to motorists 2,837 times and issued 14,606 citations.

Additional *emergency* roadside call boxes were installed. A CHP helicopter was permanently assigned to the roadway, and agreements were reached with emergency service providers that the closest units should respond to collision scenes without regard to jurisdictional boundaries.

Several *engineering* changes were made in the roadway. Raised-profile thermoplastic striping was installed where passing was allowed in one direction. In no-passing zones, a widened center median with rumble strips and thermoplastic striping was installed. Outside shoulders were treated with rumble strips. Several signing, striping and maintenance projects were completed. "Stop Ahead" warning signs were posted at key intersections, and chevron signs were installed to warn of impending curves.

A variety of *educational programs* and materials involved the local media, businesses, government and residents in reminding motorists to drive safely.

Assessment

The efforts were quite successful, with fatal collisions reduced by 10 percent and injury collisions reduced by 32 percent. Over the five years of available data, it is estimated that the safety initiatives have saved 21 lives and prevented 55 injuries.

THE PROBLEM ANALYSIS TRIANGLE

The Community Oriented Police Services (COPS) Center for Problem Solving Web site provides a problem analysis triangle that is useful when thinking about recurring problems of crime and disorder. The triangle assumes crime or disorder results when (1) likely offenders and (2) suitable targets come together in (3) time and space in the absence of capable guardians for the target, as illustrated in Figure 5.6 (sometimes referred to as the crime triangle).

Crime prevention through environmental deign (CPTED) focuses on efforts the third side of the triangle—the place where crime occurs. It seeks to reduce opportunities for crime to occur by controlling access and providing opportunities to see and be seen. CPTED is very consistent with problem solving policing in four ways (Zahm, 2007. pp.5–6):

1. It considers a broad array of problems, not just crime.

2. It requires a systematic analysis of crime events and conditions and factors that contribute to opportunities for crime.

3. It results in a set of programs or strategies that are proactive and tailored to the problem and the location.

4. It engages an array of citizens, government agencies and local institutions, each of which has a role to play in defining the problem and deciding on an appropriate solution as well as some accountability for long-term improvements.

CPTED is designed to answer four questions that parallel the four steps in the SARA problem-solving model: (1) What is the problem? (2) Why here? (3) What

FIGURE 5.7
The Problem Analysis Triangle

Source: Craig D. Uchida, Shellie Solomon, Charles M. Katz and Cynthia Pappas. School-Based Partnerships: A Problem-Solving Strategy. US Dept of Justice, Office of Community Oriented Policing Services (COPS), 2006: page 3.

can be done to solve the problem? And (4) How well are we doing? (Zahm, 2007, p.11). Crime analysis can be invaluable in answering these questions.

USING CRIME ANALYSIS IN PROBLEM SOLVING

Osborne (2009) suggests that, as a society, we put more thought and effort into analyzing sports that we do analyzing crime. An analogy can be drawn between sports and crime fighting, with crime prevention being the defensive team (proactive) and catching the bad guys the offensive team (reactive). Both are needed. Unfortunately, the law enforcement team is handicapped by its opponents (offenders) not having to follow any rules, a factor that, ironically, defines and justifies the "game" in the first place. Therefore, a law enforcement team needs analytical support staff dedicated to provide the information needed to win and keep on winning. A key staff member on this team is the coach. Osborne suggests that we need coach-leaders at all levels of management. Some team members are in the field, but the management staff needs to provide the support, including sound crime analysis.

Paletta and Belledin (2008, p.36) point out, "Patrol commanders should be able to answer two questions: What are the biggest crime problems in the community, and what is the department doing about this? This is the foundation of the CompStat philosophy." Without such information "you don't know what you don't know" (Paletta and Belledin). The need to answer these two questions has led to the need for crime analysis.

According to Burch and Geraci (2009, p.22), "The use of timely and accurate localized data to drive law enforcement operations toward more efficient and effective resource deployment is the benchmark for 21st-century policing. The cornerstone of initiatives designed to achieve this benchmark is the use of mapping technologies that allow unbiased evaluation of crime 'hot spots' as well as the ability to deploy resources both spatially and temporally to increase effectiveness." As Casady (2008, p.40) points out, "Police officers have been sticking pins in maps as long as there have been police officers and maps. In many respects, high-tech wizardry only serves to accomplish the same task faster—identifying geographic crime patterns."

A 2008 PERF survey, *Violent Crime in America: What We Know about Hot Spots Enforcement* (2008), identified the most widely used antiviolence strategy to combat violent crime. For almost all of the violent crimes, using mapping to identify hot spots and problem solving was most frequently used. For homicide/shooting, mapping was used by 77 percent, with targeting known offenders considered most effective; for robbery, mapping was used by 93 percent, with directed patrol perceived as most effective; for aggravated assault, mapping was used by 82 percent, with directed patrol again being considered most effective. For gang violence, targeting known offenders was the most commonly used strategy (89 percent), which was also perceived as most effective. Problem analysis and problem solving came in third as being most commonly used by 86 percent; for drug violence, targeting known offenders again was most commonly used (90 percent), with buy and bust and reverse stings considered most effective (pp.4–8).

An effort related to identifying hot spots is that undertaken by the COPS office to identify risky facilities. Clarke and Eck (2007, p.3) note that the risky facility theory postulates that only a small proportion of any specific type of facility accounts for the majority of crime and disorder problems. Their rule of thumb is that about 20 percent of all facilities in a community will account for 80 percent of the problems, noting that this 80/20 rule is not specific to crime but is almost a universal law. Although risky facilities can show up as hot spots on crime maps—for example, school, hospitals and train stations— they present an important analytical opportunity to compare the risky facilities with other like facilities (p.11).

When identifying hot spots and risky facilities, it is important to be aware of the magnet phenomenon. The **magnet phenomenon** occurs when a phone number or address is associated with a crime simply because it was a convenient number or address to use. A magnet telephone is one that is available when no other telephones are—for example, a telephone in a convenience store that is open all night and on weekends. Victims of or witnesses to a crime in the area may use that telephone to report the crime, even though the store was not the scene of the crime. Similarly, a magnet address is one that is easy for people to give, for example, a high school or a theater. High numbers of calls from one location can give skewed results because the assumption is often made, for record-keeping purposes, that the location of the call is also the location of the incident.

Five focus group meetings consisting of patrol, supervisors, crime analysts and commanders were conducted to gather input on how crime analysis is currently being used in patrol work (Scalisi, 2009). The focus groups identified several key themes, including the following:

◉ Distinguishing between information and analysis—for analysis to be useful, it must be actionable.

◉ Distinguishing between "looking at" and "using" crime analysis.

---

magnet phenomenon

occurs when a phone number or address is associated with a crime simply because it was a convenient number or address to use.

- Focus on short-term and long-term activity—while patrol focuses on short-term activity, the command structure can focus on patrol responses on long-term problem areas.
- Clear vision and purpose for crime analysis—the purpose and use of crime analysis should be supported from the chief command structure.

Bruce and Ouellette (2008, p.30) expand on the first key theme:

Effective crime analysis relies on standard processes that transform good data into effective law enforcement actions. All of the process models of crime analysis, whether the traditional "crime analysis process" (collect, query, identify, analyze, disseminate, respond and evaluate); the SARA model (scan, analyze, respond, assess); or the "intelligence cycle" (collect, process, analyze, disseminate, respond) suggest a smooth progression through each of the steps in the process. But not all of the transitions require equal effort, and the most difficult in any of the processes is the transition between analysis and response. It is here that the analyst loses direct control over the process and must pass the baton to the operational units. The operational units, for their part, end up having to work with whatever the analyst passes them, regardless of its quality or operational relevance. There are, then, two major potential breakdowns in the process:

- *No actionable information.* Either the agency's crime analysis unit does not provide the type of information decision makers need or the information is incorrect or insufficient.
- *Inadequate follow-up.* The analysis unit provides actionable information, but the agency has no processes in place to use it for its intended purposes.

Osborne (2008, pp.40–41) reports how the Police Foundation coordinator of research and crime mapping looks at crime analysis in three distinct parts:

First, successful units use technology by employing and supporting well-trained analysts. Successful units ensure their analysts understand various concepts, such as geographic information systems (GIS) and problem solving various strategies, such as problem-oriented policing and community-oriented policing, and the theoretical underpinnings of crime, etc. . . .

Second, successful units have a comprehensive understanding of the technology itself and can tailor it to their agency's needs. . . .

Third, successful units use GIS technology to understand and identify crime patterns and trends, and repeat and serial offenders; create analytical products to support investigation, crime suppression and crime prevention strategies; and to inform their communities about crime and disorder problems.

Crime analysts and their supervisors should recognize that using crime analysis to prevent future crimes can be more effective than using it for investigative strategies: "Many law enforcement agencies might not be using crime analysis technology to its full potential. Analysts can help formulate and evaluate the strategies used to intervene in crime patterns, and they can be advocates for responses that move beyond merely responding to crime after the fact and instead work to prevent crime" (Casady, 2008, p.40). This is the premise behind the predictive model for policing.

Predictive Analysis

"Advanced predictive analytics could be the next generation problem-solving tool for the policing profession," asserts Mills (2009, p.60). "Predictive analytics combines existing technologies like computers, crime analysis and well-developed police reporting techniques and adds a few newer technologies such as artificial intelligence, universally shared data and borrowed technology from the consumer industry to build a system that is capable of predicting crime before it happens" (Mills, p.60).

Mills (2009, p.64) gives the example of the use of this approach by the Richmond (Virginia) Police Department in 2003. Richmond experienced random gunfire problems every New Year's Eve. They had tried several strategies to address the problem without success. However, information provided by the crime analysis unit included a plan to strategically place officers where analysts expected history to repeat itself, and it did. Richmond experienced a 49 percent reduction in gunfire complaints on New Year's Eve and a 26 percent reduction on the following days. Forty-five weapons were seized, and an unanticipated benefit was a $15,000 reduction in overtime expenses.

NEW TECHNOLOGY: ShotSpotter

In its first month of operation in Minneapolis, the Minneapolis Police Department's new ShotSpotter gunfire detection system has helped police make several arrests, recover guns and respond quickly to shots fired calls.

ShotSpotter, which is now live in about two square miles of south Minneapolis, detects gunshots using multiple sensors, triangulates the position of the gunshot with great accuracy and immediately alerts 911 operators, who can quickly dispatch police.

In one month since the system came on line in December 2006, ShotSpotter has triggered dispatches to 69 suspected gunshot locations. Most dispatches are made in less than one minute after the shot is detected. Those alerts have helped lead to

- Three felony arrests
- Three misdemeanor arrests
- Two recovered guns
- A recovered stolen car
- Information used in homicide, robbery and shooting investigations

ShotSpotter is just one way Minneapolis is using new technology, in addition to more cops, to make neighborhoods safer. The city's budget provides for $2 million in public safety technology funding over the next two years. New security cameras along Bloomington Avenue and in Cedar Riverside are already helping deter crime, allow better police response and provide valuable evidence for prosecutors.

By March 2007, ShotSpotter will also be operating in two square miles of north Minneapolis. Although the total area that will be covered by ShotSpotter accounts for less than 10 percent of the city's geographic area, those four square miles account for more than 50 percent of the city's shots fired calls to 911. That means the technology is going where it's needed most.

In addition to providing 911 dispatchers and police with better tools to respond to shots, it is expected the technology will eventually deter would-be criminals from committing gun violence. When police are able to respond quickly to shots fired calls, even when they're not called in to 911, the word spreads that if you fire a gun in these neighborhoods, anytime, Minneapolis Police will know and be on the scene fast.

Source: "ShotSpotter Success—Minneapolis Police Get Results with New Technology." News Release. January 30, 2007. Minneapolis, Minnesota. Online: http://www.ci.minneapolis.mn.us/ newsroom/200701/20070130-nr_SpotShotter.asp

The Philadelphia Police Department is using Spike Detector, an early warning system that puts user-defined crime parameters in place and automatically detects statistically significant changes in clusters of incident events. If a deviation is detected, officers and command staff are immediately notified via e-mail about a newly detected hot spot (Theodore, 2009). Incident information is integrated with location data in formulating a response: "Instant notification means management officials receive accurate and timely intelligence when it's available; they can then more rapidly deploy response tactics and follow up and assess results" (Theodore, p.60).

The Integration of Crime Analysts into Law Enforcement

From the preceding discussion, the importance of crime analysis and those who perform it is obvious. However, like dispatchers, crime analysts work behind the scenes and often go unappreciated. An online survey of crime analysts found that although most analysts felt management was fairly supportive of their work, a majority reported the level of support and appreciation they received from patrol officers was middle of the road, at best: "The results raise concerns about whether patrol officers understand what analysts do, which in turn leads to additional concerns about whether the skills and training of analysts are being used to their fullest capacities" (Taylor et al., 2007, p.154).

Police managers who wish to benefit from the advances made in crime analysis must ensure that their crime analysts are properly inducted into the police environment and that their analytical work is fully integrated into departmental operations: "[Crime analysts] will then be able to take their proper role as central members of the team in problem-solving projects" (White, 2008. p.1). Bruce and

Ouellette (2008, p.34) stress, "For all law enforcement leaders, sending the message that crime analysis really matters must be an organizational imperative."

Federal Assistance in Problem-Solving Efforts

Several federal agencies can assist in problem analysis, including the Office of Community Oriented Policing (COPS), the National Institute of Justice (NIJ), the Bureau of Justice Statistics (BJS) and the National Criminal Justice Reference Service (NCJRS). These agencies can provide funding and training as well as publish case studies and provide examples of innovation. As noted at the beginning of this chapter, innovation and creativity are also of great importance in law enforcement.

CREATIVITY AND INNOVATION

Creativity is a process of breaking old connections and making useful new ones. It often is synonymous with innovation and involves originality. One strategy for law enforcement managers to develop more creativity is to increase interaction with corporate leaders and other administrators outside criminal justice. Police management has been evolving for decades and has been described as conservative and traditional. Techniques such as participatory management, team approaches and quality circles are foreign to many police managers, who need to be alert to management changes in the corporate world. Some corporate techniques cannot be adapted to the police environment, but others can. Exposure to new ideas and thoughts stimulates the mind.

Some police administrators reject new programs or ideas because they did not originate with them or because the idea came from the rank and file. Many newspapers regularly publish columns by management experts, much of which is adaptable to police management. Many of the concepts presented in this text came from corporate America.

We are all born as potentially creative people. By the time we are adults only a very few of us have overcome all the messages our society sends that stifle individuality and creativity. Think about school and what you were taught: Dogs cannot be colored purple; give the "right" answer; do not make a mess; do not be different; stay in line; be quiet; raise your hand if you want to talk; and so on. In other words, conform. Our own habits can also stifle creativity.

Thinking Traps and Mental Locks

Thinking traps are habits people fall into without recognizing what they are doing.

 Common thinking traps include
1. **Being stuck in black/white, either/or thinking.**
2. **Being too quick in deciding.**
3. **Making decisions based on personal feelings about the proposer of an idea.**
4. **Being a victim of personal habits and prejudices.**
5. **Not using imagination.**

Being stuck in black/white, either/or thinking. People caught in this trap think that if one answer is bad, the other must be good. This kind of thinking causes people to miss intermediate solutions. Brainstorming many alternatives will help overcome this trap.

Being too quick in deciding. People in this trap jump to conclusions before they hear all the facts or have all the evidence. Avoid this trap by listing all possibilities and delaying decisions until each has been discussed.

Making decisions based on personal feelings about the proposer of an idea. Some people tend to support only what their friends propose. To overcome this, decide that you will listen for the facts and keep your feelings out of your decision.

Being a victim of personal habits and prejudices. "We've always done it that way" thinking can keep programs from moving forward. You can avoid this trap by asking questions such as, Who else can we serve? How can we do it differently? What more might we do?

Not using imagination. People who fall into this trap are too tied to data and statistics. They do not risk using their intuition. To bypass this trap, practice brainstorming and creative thinking—think laterally, horizontally and vertically. Take the risk of going with your hunches.

To illustrate the tendency to get stuck in a thinking rut, try the "Scottish Names" game on a colleague. (Note: It is more effective if done orally because the solution is obvious when written like this.) Without mentioning the idea that these words might be considered last names, ask a colleague to pronounce M-A-C-T-A-V-I-S-H; then M-A-C-D-O-U-G-A-L; then M-A-C-C-A-R-T-H-Y. Finally, ask them to pronounce M-A-C-H-I-N-E-S. If they respond "MacHines," they have become a victim of preconditioned thinking, a common thinking trap.

The mind easily gets stuck in patterns. Creativity consultant von Oech (1983) calls such thinking traps *mental locks*. He suggests that sometimes we need a "whack on the side of the head" to jar ourselves out of ways of thinking that keep us from being innovative.

 Mental locks **that prevent innovative thinking include**
1. **The right answer.**
2. **That's not logical.**
3. **Follow the rules.**
4. **Be practical.**
5. **Avoid ambiguity.**
6. **To err is wrong**
7. **Play is frivolous.**
8. **That's not my area.**
9. **Don't be foolish.**
10. **I'm not creative.**

The right answer. Most people will have taken in excess of 26,000 tests before they complete their education. Such tests usually focus on "right" answers. According to von Oech (p.22), "Children enter elementary school as question marks and leave as periods."

That's not logical. People need to learn to dream, create and fantasize. Both "soft" and "hard" thinking are needed. It is like making a clay pot. Clay that is not soft enough is difficult to work with. Once the pot is shaped, however, it must be fired and made hard before it will hold water. Metaphors such as this can help in problem solving as well.

Follow the rules. Parents teach their children to stay inside the lines when they color. People do rely on patterns to analyze problems, but this can sometimes be a hindrance.

Be practical. As von Oech (p.54) notes,

> Because we have the ability to symbolize our experience, our thinking is not limited to the real and the present. This capability empowers our thinking in two major ways. First, it enables us to anticipate the future. . . .

> Second, since our thinking is not bound by real world constraints, we can generate ideas which have no correlate in the world of experience. . . .

> I call the realm of the possible our "germinal seedbed." . . . Asking "what-if" is an easy way to get your imagination going.

Avoid ambiguity. A story told by von Oech involves former FBI director J. Edgar Hoover. Hoover wrote a letter to his agents, and as he was proofreading it, he decided he did not like the way it was laid out. He wrote a note on the bottom to his secretary, "Watch the borders," and asked her to retype it. She did and then sent it to all the agents. For the next few weeks, FBI agents were put on special alert along our Canadian and Mexican borders. Ambiguity should usually be avoided. When thinking creatively, however, ambiguity can help. Ask, How else might this be interpreted?

To err is wrong. This is similar to the first mental lock—that there is a "right" answer. View mistakes as learning opportunities and as a part of risk taking. If you are made of the right material, a hard fall will result in a high bounce. Mistakes or failures can be positive. Henry Ford viewed failure positively: "Failure is the opportunity to begin again more intelligently." And, as suggested in Chapter 3, failures or negative results should be as widely shared as successes.

Play is frivolous. According to von Oech (1983, p.97), "Necessity may be the mother of invention, but play is certainly the father." He urges that people not take themselves too seriously, especially when engaged in innovative thinking.

That's not my area. In our complex society, specialization is a fact of life. Sometimes, however, a person outside the area in which a problem exists is better able to generate possible solutions. It is not always the "experts" who come up with the best ideas.

Don't be foolish. In the Middle Ages, kings often had "fools" as part of their court. A major role these fools played was to ridicule the advice the king's counselors gave him, a forerunner of the devil's advocate role in today's society.

I'm not creative. This can become a self-fulfilling prophecy. If you think you cannot do something, you probably will not be able to. Conversely, the power of positive thinking has been proven time after time.

Killer Phrases

Closely related to thinking traps and mental locks are certain "killer phrases" people tend to use that limit the creative participation of *others* in the group.

Killer phrases are judgmental and critical and serve as put-downs. They stifle creativity.

Among the more common killer phrases are the following: It's not our policy. It's not our area. We don't have the time. We'll never get help. It's too much hassle. That's too radical. It won't work. Be practical. It costs too much. We've never done it that way before. Be realistic. Where did you come up with that idea? This isn't the time to try something like that. It's okay in theory, but I don't think we're ready for it yet. You don't really think that would work, do you? Get serious. If it ain't broke, why fix it?

To handle killer phrases, recognize them, describe to the group what is happening and then challenge the group to discuss whether the killer phrases are true. Encourage the group to remain open to all ideas.

Organizations that promote creativity and innovation provide more freedom to think and act, recognize ideas and provide ample opportunities for communication as well as for private creative thinking. They also invest in research and experimentation and permit ideas from outside the organization. Gray (2009, p.74) suggests, "[Managers] can inspire creativity and innovation by sharing information on problems, removing obstacles, creating a climate of mutual respect and collaboration and quickly rewarding acts of creativity and innovation. Use visual tools in employee group settings to display complex information, because this inspires creative problem solving. The agency may have less funding, but the human creative potential within the agency is not restricted."

COMMON MISTAKES

Common mistakes in problem solving and decision making include spending too much energy on unimportant details, failing to resolve important issues, being secretive about true feelings, having a closed mind, making decisions while angry or excited and not expressing ideas. Managers who reject information, suggestions and alternatives that do not fit into their comfortable past patterns can severely limit their decision-making capabilities. Inability to decide, putting decisions off to the last minute, failing to set deadlines, making decisions under pressure and using unreliable sources of information are other common errors in problem solving and decision making. Without the willingness to change, to reach out or to go farther, you cannot be creative or innovative.

Each of these common errors has an alternative, positive approach. For example, rather than making multiple decisions about the same problem, that is, reinventing the wheel, managers should establish standard operating procedures for recurring problems. When doing so, they must also consider whether what they establish is both legal and ethical.

LEGAL DECISIONS

Most civil lawsuits brought against law enforcement officers are based on Statute 42 of the U.S. Code, Section 1983, also called the Civil Rights Act. This act, passed in 1871, was designed to prevent the abuse of constitutional rights by officers who "under color of state law" deny defendants those rights. The act states,

> Every person who, under color of any statute, ordinance, regulation, custom, or usage, of any State or Territory, subjects, or causes to be subjected any citizen of the United States or other person within the jurisdiction thereof to the deprivation of any rights, privileges, or immunities secured by the Constitution and laws, shall be liable to the party injured in an action at law, suit in equity, or other proper proceeding for redress.

In other words, Section 1983 says that anyone acting under the authority of the law who violates another person's constitutional rights can be sued. This includes law enforcement officers. It now may also include their supervisors, their departments and even their municipalities. Such lawsuits may involve First Amendment issues such as freedom of speech, religion and association; Fourth Amendment matters pertaining to arrest and detention, search and seizure and use of force; Fifth Amendment issues involving interrogation and confessions; Sixth Amendment concerns regarding the right to counsel; and Fourteenth Amendment claims of due process violations. It is important for law enforcement officers to understand Section 1983 because it is often the basis for a civil action against police.

 Law enforcement officers and managers must consider whether discretionary actions are within the law.

Vicarious Liability

vicarious liability

makes others specifically associated with a person also responsible for that person's actions.

Vicarious liability makes others specifically associated with a person also responsible for that person's actions. The vast majority of lawsuits naming supervisory officers are attempts to get to more, wealthier and better-insured defendants through vicarious liability.

The most frequent civil lawsuits against police involve false arrest or imprisonment, malicious prosecution, use of unnecessary or excessive force, brutality, wrongful death, failure to protect and negligent service.

Reducing the Occurrence of Civil Lawsuits

According to Means (2007, p.33), "Nothing whatsoever reduces legal problems and liability risks in law enforcement like good interpersonal communications skills. We all know officers who can go into a biker bar, make an arrest and leave with a friend. Other officers could start a fight in a Quaker Friends meeting." The critical need for effective communication spills into every aspect of police work and will not be discussed further here even though it is one vital way to avoid lawsuits.

Ultimately, the risk of civil liability rests on the individual actions of each police officer. Police departments can develop extensive policies and procedures to help ensure that their officers act in a way that will deter civil lawsuits. Hess and Orthmann (2011, pp.450–451) offer the following ways departments can protect against lawsuits.

Protection against lawsuits includes
- **Effective policies and procedures clearly communicated to all.**
- **Thorough and continuous training.**
- **Proper supervision, discipline and standards of accountability.**
- **Accurate, thorough police reports.**

In addition to being legal, decisions should also be ethical.

ETHICAL DECISIONS

Ethical considerations are important in decision making.

A decision may be logical, creative and legal, but is it also ethical—morally right? Many problems facing law enforcement decision makers involve ethical issues. For example, are issues of fairness or morality involved? Who is affected? Will there be victims? What are the alternatives? Does it clearly violate a moral rule? Does the decision accurately reflect the kind of person/department you are or want to be? How does it make you and your department look to the public? To other law enforcement agencies? Ethics in law enforcement is discussed in Chapter 8.

EVALUATING DECISIONS

When decisions have been made, they can be evaluated against the following checklist. Is the decision

1. Consistent with the agency's mission? Goals? Objectives?

2. A long-term solution?

3. Cost effective?

4. Legal?

5. Ethical?

6. Practical?

7. Acceptable to those responsible for implementing it?

SUMMARY

Diversity, disagreement and risk taking help foster a decision-making, problem-solving environment. Decisions may be strategic—executive level; administrative—middle management level; or operational—first-line level. Decisions may also be classified as command, consultative or consensual.

Decision making and problem solving involve thinking. Whole-brain research suggests that left-brain thinking processes *language* and is primarily *logical*. Right-brain thinking processes *images* and is primarily *emotional*. Both processes (that is, whole-brain thinking) are needed.

Basic methods for making decisions range from using intuition and snap decisions to using a computer, with a systematic individual or group approach falling in between.

All levels of the police department benefit from group participation in the decision-making process. Many approaches to problem solving seek solutions through brainstorming. To make brainstorming sessions effective, ensure that participants are prepared, write down *all* ideas, allow *no* criticizing of ideas and have a definite ending time.

More complex decision-making/problem-solving processes include the seven-step decision-making/problem-solving approach, force-field analysis, the nominal group technique, the Delphi technique or a modified form of the Delphi technique. These approaches often include brainstorming.

The seven-step approach involves defining the problem, gathering the facts, generating alternatives, analyzing the alternatives, selecting the best alternative, implementing the alternative and evaluating the decision.

Force-field analysis identifies forces that impede and enhance goal attainment. A problem exists when the equilibrium is upset because more forces are impeding goal attainment than enhancing it. The nominal group technique is an objective way to achieve consensus on the most effective alternatives by ranking them. The Delphi technique uses questionnaires completed by individuals. Answers are shared, and the questionnaires are again completed until consensus is reached.

The SARA model problem-solving process involves four steps: scanning (identifying the problem), analysis (looking at alternatives), response (implementing an alternative) and assessment (evaluating the results).

Often synonymous with innovation, creativity can be hindered by thinking traps, mental locks and killer phrases. Common thinking traps include being stuck in black/white, either/or thinking; being too quick in deciding; making decisions based on personal feelings about the proposer of an idea; being a victim of personal habits and prejudices; and not using imagination. Mental locks that prevent innovative thinking include insisting on the "right" answer and the following opinions/statements: that's not logical; follow the rules; be practical; avoid ambiguity; to err is wrong; play is frivolous; that's not my area; don't be foolish; and I'm not creative.

Killer phrases are judgmental and critical and serve as put-downs. They stifle creativity. To handle killer phrases, recognize them, describe to the group what is happening and then challenge the group to discuss whether the killer phrases are true. Encourage the group to remain open to all ideas.

Law enforcement officers and managers must consider whether discretionary actions are within the law. Protection against lawsuits includes effective policies and procedures clearly communicated to all; thorough and continuous training; proper supervision, discipline and standards of accountability; and accurate, thorough police reports. Ethical considerations are important in decision making.

CHALLENGE FIVE

Lt. Johnson is in charge of the patrol division of the Greenfield Police Department. While reviewing activity logs and police reports, he detects an increase in residential burglaries during the previous month. The burglaries are being reported on the afternoon shift when residents return home from work. Most of burglaries are occurring in one neighborhood. Lt. Johnson calls the afternoon patrol supervisor to inquire about the burglaries. The supervisor tells him he is aware of the problem and has been assigning officers to patrol the neighborhood. The supervisor notes that the burglaries are all on Thursdays and Fridays, but adds, "It's like trying to find a needle in a hay stack."

Lt. Johnson contacts the investigations supervisor and learns that he is also aware of the increase in burglaries. The supervisor tells Johnson that they have fingerprints from several of the burglaries, but no suspects. He speculates it might be kids because most of the losses are cigarettes, liquor and small amounts of cash.

When Lt. Johnson talks to the day patrol supervisor, he learns that the supervisor isn't aware of an increase in burglaries because none have been reported during his shift. The supervisor says they have been dealing with loitering and disorderly conduct problems at the shopping center. He says high school kids are hanging around the video arcade during the day, and he plans to meet with the high school principal to figure out why these kids aren't in school.

Lt. Johnson realizes that patrolling and reactive investigations usually have a minimal effect on preventing burglaries. He decides on a new approach.

1. How might Lt. Johnson address the burglary problem more effectively?

2. If Lt. Johnson decides on a problem-solving approach, who should he include in his group of problem solvers? Be creative.

3. Can you suggest how inviting the high school principal, the owner of the local arcade and residents from the neighborhood where the burglaries are occurring might be helpful?

4. Suggest a single problem that may be causing other problems in the community.

5. How could this problem-solving group be used in the future?

DISCUSSION QUESTIONS

1. Compare and contrast command, consultative and consensual decisions. Which do you prefer?

2. Do you support the findings of whole-brain research? If not, what problems do you see?

3. Can you give an example of when intuition has been important in a decision you have made?

4. Are you comfortable making snap decisions? If so, about what? If not, why not?

5. What would your model of decision making look like?

6. Who would you involve in the decision-making process?

7. How important do you think creativity and innovation are in dealing with typical problems facing law enforcement?

8. How might you engage in "creative procrastination"?

9. Of the systematic approaches to problem solving, which seems the most practical to you?

10. What is the greatest problem you think law enforcement is facing today? What approaches would you use to attack it?

REFERENCES

Brown, Rick, and Scott, Michael S. *Implementing Responses to Problems.* Washington, DC: Community Oriented Policing Services, July 2007.

Bruce, Christopher W., and Ouellette, Neil F. "Closing the Gap between Analysis and Response." *The Police Chief,* September 2008, pp.30–34.

Burch, James H., II, and Geraci, Michael N. "Data-Driven Approaches to Crime and Traffic Safety." *The Police Chief,* July 2009, pp.18–23.

Casady, Tom. "Beyond Arrest: Using Crime Analysis to Prevent Crime." *The Police Chief,* September 2008, pp.40–42.

Clarke, Ronald V., and Eck, John E. *Understanding Risky Facilities.* Washington, DC: Community Oriented Policing Services, April 4, 2007.

Eck, John E., and Spelman, William. *Problem-Solving: Problem-Oriented Policing in Newport News.* Washington, DC: Police Executive Research Forum, 1987.

Excellence in Problem-Oriented Policing: The 2001 Herman Goldstein Award Winners. Washington, DC: National Institute of Justice, Community Oriented Policing Services and the Police Executive Research Forum, 2001, pp.5–14.

Fitch, Brian D. "Emotional Intelligence: Practical Advice for Law Enforcement Officers." *The Police Chief,* 2009, pp.104–111.

Glennon, Jim. "Intuition on the Street: Harnessing the Power of the Sixth Sense." *PoliceOne.com,* December 13, 2007.

Glennon, Jim. "Intuition on the Street, Part 2: Rationalizing the Irrational." *PoliceOne.com,* January 15, 2008a.

Glennon, Jim. "Intuition on the Street, Part 3: Pre-Attack Indicators: Conscious Recognition of Telegraphed Cues." *PoliceOne.com,* March 12, 2008b.

Goldstein, Herman. *Problem-Oriented Policing.* New York: McGraw-Hill Publishing Company, 1990.

Gray, John L. "Leadership during Difficult Budget Times." *The Police Chief,* June 2009, pp.74–76.

Hess, Kären Matison, and Orthmann, Christine Hess. *Police Operations,* 5th ed. Clifton Park, NY: Delmar/Cengage Publishing Company, 2011.

Means, Randy. "The Greatest Liability Reduction Tool." *Law and Order,* December 2007, pp.32–33.

Mills, Eric. "An Ounce of Prevention." *Law Enforcement Technology,* September 2009, pp.60–65.

Osborne, Deborah. "Crime Analysis: Best Practices from 6 Agencies." *Law Officer Magazine,* September 2008, pp.36–42.

Osborne, Deborah. "Analysis Is Your Ally." *LawOfficer.com,* June 2, 2009.

Paletta, Kevin, and Belledin, Stacy. "Finding Out What You Don't Know: Tips on Using Crime Analysts." *The Police Chief,* September 2008, pp.36–39.

Polzin, Michael, and Yantovsky, Tamara. "Police Labor Relations: Interest-Based Problem-Solving and the Power of Collaboration." *Community Policing Dispatch,* September 2009. http://www.cops.usdoj.gov/html/dispatch/September_2009/labor_relations.htm

Scalisi, Nicole J. "The Role of Crime Analysis in Patrol Work: New Developments." *Community Policing Dispatch,* June 2009.

Taylor, Bruce; Kowalyk, Apollo; and Boba, Rachel. "The Integration of Crime Analysis into Law Enforcement Agencies: An Exploratory Study into the Perceptions of Crime Analysts." *Police Quarterly*, June 2007, pp.134–169.

Theodore, Jesse. "Predictive Modeling Becomes a Crime-Fighting Asset." *Law Officer Magazine*, February 2009, pp.58–61.

Turner, Timothy W. "Understanding the Benefits of Emotional Intelligence for Officer Growth and Agency Budgets." *The Police Chief*, August 2009, pp.94–102.

Violent Crime in America: What We Know about Hot Spots Enforcement. Washington, DC: Police Executive Research Forum, May 2008.

von Oech, Roger. *A Whack on the Side of the Head: How to Unlock Your Mind for Innovation.* New York: Warner Books, 1983.

Wexler, Chuck; Wycoff, Mary Ann; and Fischer, Craig. *"Good to Great" Policing: Application of Business Principles in the Public Sector.* Washington, DC: Community Oriented Policing Services and the Police Executive Research Forum, June 2007.

White, Matthew B. *Enhancing the Problem-Solving Capacity of Crime Analysis Units.* Washington, DC: Center for Problem-Oriented Policing, February 2008.

Zahm, Diane. *Using Crime Prevention through Environmental Design in Problem-Solving.* Washington, DC: Community Oriented Policing Services, August 2007.

CHAPTER SIX

Time Management: Minute by Minute

> *Time management is a question not of managing the clock but of managing ourselves with respect to the clock.*
>
> —**Alec MacKenzie**
> Time management expert

DO YOU KNOW?

- ☑ What time management is?
- ☑ What the greatest management resource is?
- ☑ What is at the heart of time management?
- ☑ How the Pareto principle applies to time management?
- ☑ How to learn where your time is actually going?
- ☑ What helps you manage time minute by minute?
- ☑ What the most common external time wasters are?
- ☑ What the learning curve principle is and how it relates to time management?
- ☑ What three words can prompt you and others to use time effectively?
- ☑ What the most common internal time wasters are?
- ☑ What an effective time manager concentrates on?
- ☑ What priorities and posteriorities are?
- ☑ What the 5P principle is?
- ☑ How to control the paper flood?
- ☑ How paperwork can be handled most efficiently?
- ☑ What the results of overdoing it might be?
- ☑ How to physically make time more productive?

6

CAN YOU DEFINE?

face time
5P principle
highlighting
learning curve principle
narrow eye span
Pareto principle
Parkinson's Law
posteriorities
priorities
procrastination
regression
scanning (reading skill)
single handling
skimming
subvocalization
tickler file system

INTRODUCTION

Voltaire, an eighteenth-century French philosopher, posed the following riddle (*Zadig: A Mystery of Fate*):

> What of all things in the world is the longest and the shortest, the swiftest and the slowest, the most divisible and the most extended, the most neglected and the most regretted, without which nothing can be done, which devours all that is little and enlivens all that is great? *The answer—time.*

Nothing is longer, since it is the measure of eternity.

Nothing is shorter, since it is insufficient for the accomplishment of our projects.

Nothing is more slow to him that expects; nothing more rapid to him that enjoys.

In greatness, it extends to infinity; in smallness, it is infinitely divisible.

All men neglect it; all regret the loss of it; nothing can be done without it.

It consigns to oblivion whatever is unworthy of being transmitted to posterity, and it immortalizes such actions as are truly great.

With each promotion you receive comes an increase in your duties and responsibilities, with no increase in the number of hours in a day or extra days in the week.

CHAPTER at a GLANCE

This chapter begins with definitions of time and time management, as well as a discussion of the value of time. It then examines the importance of goals in effective time management and ways to organize your time to meet these goals. Identifying how to use time more efficiently necessitates knowing how time is currently spent, so the function of time logs is described in detail. Next, the chapter discusses the importance of controlling time through use of a to-do list to make certain that priorities are set and then met through scheduling. This is followed by a look at common time abusers or unproductive time and how you might control this. One important step in managing time is controlling the paper flood and information load so common in law enforcement management. Also important is retaining what you need to remember. The chapter concludes with a discussion of how you can be most productive without overdoing—the ultimate goal of effective time management—including the physiology of productivity.

TIME DEFINED

Time can be defined as the period between two events or during which something exists, happens or acts; it is thought of in terms of measurable intervals. Time is most often used in the legal sense to identify specific events. For example, "The crash occurred on January 26, 2003, at 1304 hours." In the everyday, practical sense we measure time in years, months, weeks, days, hours, minutes and seconds. We also use many devices to measure time, the most popular of which are clocks, watches and calendars.

Despite much philosophizing and debate about time, it remains elusive, mysterious and difficult to define. Albert Einstein determined that time is one dimension of the universe and that it is relative. (Two weeks on vacation is not the same as two weeks on a diet.) It is finite, instant, constant and, in a sense, an illusion. Einstein once said, "The only reason for time is so that everything doesn't happen at once." Your time belongs to you and no one else. How you spend your time is your decision. Once used, it can never be regained. Once you have read this paragraph, the time you took to read it is lost forever.

Imagine for a moment that you have a special bank account and that every morning it is credited with $1,440. Whatever amount you do not use each day, however, is taken out of the account. No balance can be carried over. Naturally you would try to use every bit of that $1,440 each day and to get the most out of it. You *do* have such a bank—a time bank. Every morning when you get up you have a 1,440-minute deposit that you can either invest wisely or squander. You cannot save it for tomorrow. Sleep *does* count as a wise investment.

TIME MANAGEMENT: PLANNING AND ORGANIZING TIME

Personal growth guru Stephen R. Covey contends, "Time management is really a misnomer—the challenge is not to manage time, but to manage ourselves" (1989, p.150). Time management is a primary responsibility of law enforcement managers and involves a duty to use both their own time and employees' time productively. Time management is best accomplished through organization, planning and review. Most law enforcement managers and their subordinates work 40-hour weeks. Some departments schedule five 8-hour days, others four 10-hour days, some use still another type of schedule. Regardless of how the shifts are structured, each officer has approximately 2,000 working hours annually (allowing for two weeks of vacation). A 20-year law enforcement career has 40,000 assigned working hours, without overtime. Organizing and planning these assigned work hours determines both personal and public benefit: "Do not count time, but make time count." Although this chapter focuses on work time, the suggestions apply to time away from the job and keeping a healthy work/life balance as well.

Successful law enforcement managers at all levels get more done in less time when they develop and follow efficient techniques for using assigned time. They have a sense of time importance and a sense of timing. Managing time involves managing yourself and your daily life. It does not necessarily mean working longer or faster. Trying to do everything is not managing. Time management is committing yourself to making quality use of your time to accomplish what is important. It has been said that the bad news is that time flies; the good news is that you're the pilot.

 Time management is planning and organizing time to accomplish your most important goals in the shortest time possible.

Managers can assess how well they are controlling their time by asking themselves the following questions:

- Do I find myself completing tasks at the last minute or asking for extensions?
- Do I have to take work home or stay late to get it done?
- Am I stressed about deadlines and commitments (both at work and at home)?

Time management is a tool to move people from where they are to where they want to be. This means planning ahead. Do not think day by day but rather think in terms of the current year. Similar to setting New Year's resolutions, effective managers determine what the most important objectives to accomplish in the year ahead are. They then divide these objectives into months, then the months into days.

Time Management in a Service Organization

Effective time management often is evaluated based on the amount of tangible product produced—*this much* time spent produced *these* results. However, service organizations such as law enforcement agencies have inherent responsibilities that are time consuming yet not explicitly action-oriented and that yield few tangible results. Nonetheless, these responsibilities are vital to effective customer service, citizen satisfaction and community protection. Such tasks include consoling victims, talking with citizens, having a physical presence in high crash locations, following leads in a criminal investigation in which the actual monetary loss was low and so forth. To reiterate, effective managers/leaders focus more on people than on tasks. This may appear incongruous with the focus on "tasks to be accomplished" in this chapter, but to have time for their people, managers need to *make* the time. This chapter focuses on ways to do so.

VALUE OF TIME

Time has value. To realize the value of one minute, ask a person who just missed a train. To realize the value of one second, ask a person who just avoided a crash. To realize the value of one millisecond, ask the person who won a silver medal in the Olympics.

What is your time worth to you? Have you ever determined in dollars how much your time is worth? Divide your annual salary by the number of annual work hours, usually 2,080 hours. For example, if your annual salary were $50,000, your hourly rate would be $24. If you add in your fringe benefits, your total annual compensation would be much more than that. Your time is valuable and should not be squandered.

When law enforcement managers were asked if they felt they had enough time to do what their jobs demanded, the majority said they did not have enough time and could use more hours in the workday. This is *not* a viable solution to time problems. Managers have the same amount of time allotted to Helen Keller, Michelangelo, Thomas Edison, Albert Einstein and whoever the mangers most admire for their accomplishments.

It is ironic that managers who exercise good time management and complete their duties are often given extra responsibilities. In this situation managers who fail to use time wisely are, in effect, rewarded.

Time is the greatest management resource.

All other resources can be increased, but time is fixed. If a person could gain 2 more productive hours a day, times 5 days per week, times 50 working weeks, that would be 500 hours or 3 extra *months* for each person in the department.

Returning to the definition of time management as "planning and organizing time to accomplish your most important goals in the shortest time possible," the logical place to begin developing good time management is with *goals*.

GOALS AND TIME MANAGEMENT

The importance of goals to an organization has already been stressed. Goals are at the heart of efficiency and time management. It is a waste of time to do very well what you do not need to do at all.

At the heart of time management are *goals*.

To effectively guide action, goals should be written in specific terms; be given a time frame; be measurable, important and aligned with the department's organizational goals; and be challenging yet achievable. Devising work plans with SMART (*s*pecific, *m*easurable, *a*ttainable, *r*elevant and *t*rackable) goals and objectives was discussed in Chapter 3.

Ask yourself, "What is the most valuable use of my time right now?" You can answer this only by looking at the department's goals and objectives and what you must do to accomplish them. Time management needs to be both short and long range. Think in terms of the year, the month, the week, the day and the precise moment.

Segmenting Tasks

Some time-management consultants advocate setting up a **tickler file system** consisting of the following 45 files:

- 2 files, one each for the next 2 years beyond the current year
- 12 files, one for each month of the current year
- 31 files, one for each day of the current month

One reason time management is so difficult is the human tendency to want to accomplish everything at once. Time management requires that time be managed—that is, organized and divided.

Some important activities may be best set aside until the following year. Simply knowing they are in the upcoming year's file clears your mind of worrying about them for the present. You may put off many activities one or more months. Put them into the appropriate monthly file. At the end of the month, take the next month's file and divide the activities into the days available. At the end of each day—and this is a key to time management—take the next day's file and plan how to accomplish the activities slated for that day.

Goals, Objectives and the Pareto Principle

As you consider goals and objectives, the **Pareto principle** comes into play. Alfredo Pareto was an Italian economist who observed that 20 percent of the Italian population owned 80 percent of the wealth. This and similar observations led Pareto to the conclusion that results and their causes are unequally distributed. The percentage is not always 80/20, but it is usually close. Consider the following:

- Twenty percent of your activities may produce 80 percent of your accomplishments.
- Twenty percent of your officers may constitute "problem" officers who account for 80 percent of the department's problems.
- Twenty percent of your officers may be considered "outstanding" officers who account for 80 percent of your department's successes.
- Effective leaders pay attention to the 20 percent and concentrate on improvement in those areas.

 Effective time management uses the Pareto principle to identify the 20 percent (*few*) *vital tasks* that will account for 80 percent of the desired results. It also identifies and places as low priority the 80 percent (*many*) *trivial tasks* clamoring for attention.

This is similar to the 80/20 rule used in identifying risky facilities, discussed in Chapter 5. Figure 6.1 illustrates the Pareto principle.

Setting Priorities

Time is very important to police departments. In fact, response time presents an interesting time-management situation. Although research shows that response time has limited effect on arrest rates, it is important for citizen

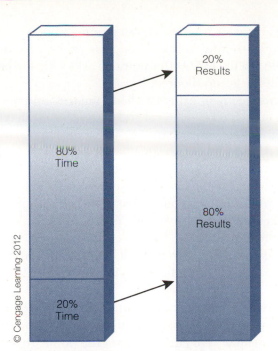

FIGURE 6.1 The Pareto Principle

© Cengage Learning 2012

satisfaction and citizens' perceptions of police performance. *Most* departments have to prioritize calls. In some cities, during certain days of the week or times of the day, there may be a backlog of 5 to 10 calls. Field officers have to prioritize calls for service according to severity and importance. Investigators set priorities for cases to follow up, based on the information furnished by the preliminary investigation report. Field officers' and investigators' responses are reactive. They have little or no control over the types of services required on any specific shift; they have only data based on experience. As departments become more proactive, time management will become more relevant.

Habit number 3 of Covey's *The 7 Habits of Highly Effective People* is "Put first things first" (1989, p.148). Putting first things first is about keeping balance in one's life by adhering to a simple principle of time management: organize and execute around priorities (Covey, p.149). Whatever the circumstance, highly effective people live and are driven by the principles they value most, by the sense of purpose they pursue and by the responsibilities that their key roles demand of them (Covey, 1989). Setting priorities requires that the urgent is differentiated from the important.

Urgent versus Important

President Lyndon Johnson once noted, "The trouble with our country is that we constantly put second things first." This, unfortunately, is often true of managers as well. Managers often spend too much time on urgent things and not enough time on the important things. Gresham's Law of Time Management says, "The urgent drives out the important." The little stuff, phones, meetings, interruptions and the like keep managers from getting to the long-term tasks that need doing.

The importance of prioritizing is well illustrated by the story of the time management expert who was speaking to a group of high-powered overachievers. He set a 1-gallon Mason jar on a table along with a dozen fist-sized rocks and carefully began placing the rocks into the jar one at a time until it was filled to the top. At this point he asked, "Is the jar full?"

Everyone in the group shouted, "Yes."

The time management expert replied, "Really?" and reached under the table. He pulled out a bucket of gravel and dumped it in, shaking the jar to cause the pieces of gravel to work themselves down into the spaces between the big rocks. He asked the group once more, "Is the jar full?"

"Probably not," one person in the group answered.

"Good," the expert replied, reaching under the table for a bucket of sand. He dumped the sand into the jar, and it went into all the spaces left between the rocks and gravel. Once more he asked, "Is the jar full?"

"No," the group shouted.

Again he said, "Good." Then he took a pitcher of water and began to pour it in until the jar was filled to the brim. Then he asked the group, "What is the point?"

One eager young man raised his hand and said, "No matter how full your schedule is, if you try really hard, you can always fit some more things in it."

"Sorry," the speaker replied. "That's not the point. This illustration teaches us that if you don't put the 'big rocks' in first, you'll never get them all in."

So tonight, or in the morning, when you are reflecting on this short story, ask yourself, "What are the 'big rocks' in my life?" Then put those in your jar first.

ORGANIZING TIME

Law enforcement managers can easily visualize the time available for each workday and may plan for the week, but few managers at any level plan beyond a month. Seldom do people think of their law enforcement careers as 40,000 hours. After a career is over, it is a rare law enforcement manager who does not look back and say, "I could have accomplished a lot more."

This chapter presents several ways to organize and plan time. Select the method you like best or devise your own. The system you use does not matter, only that you do something to make your time more productive. The first step is to know how you are actually spending your time.

Time Logs and Lists

A time log is a detailed list of how you spend your time each day. Keeping time logs and lists will show you how you actually use your time. Maintain such logs and lists only until you see which activities actually fill your work time.

 Keeping a daily log or time list tells you how you really spend your time, as opposed to how you perceive you spend it.

Until goals are established and can be adjusted to the actual daily use of time, a great disparity often exists between what people *think* they do and what they *actually* do. Some time experts suggest that a time log be made once a year for several days to a week. When your job changes, make a new time log.

Sample Time-Use Logs

The chart in Figure 6.2 asks you to list your starting time for the workday and the ending time of each task you perform. For example, if you start at 8:00 a.m. and your first task is to make a to-do list, which takes 10 minutes, your task ends at 8:10 and you are ready for the next task, which may be returning telephone calls. The difference between the times is the total task time. Figure 6.3 lists goals and objectives without regard to actual time use.

With the wide variety of technology available today to keep track of time commitments (e.g., versatile and powerful electronic calendars than can synch from a laptop to a cell phone), it can be relatively straightforward for a manager to record how time is being spent and analyze it later to see which tasks are consuming what quantity of time (Figure 6.4).

Approximately 50 percent of your time should be spent on priority 1 goals, 40 percent on priority 2 goals and 10 percent on priority 3 goals. Variations of these percentages will occur with levels of manager responsibility. The executive manager may spend 60 to 65 percent of time on priority 1 goals; command or middle-level managers, 40 percent; and first-line supervisors, 30 percent.

Determine actual time use for a designated period (perhaps a week). Then review the list and make decisions regarding delegating, shortening time devoted to certain tasks or eliminating a task. If the manager position should change, keep a new time log. Later compare the actual time logs with the lists of goals and objectives for the position, and make adjustments to bring both lists into one actual time plan. You will need to make adjustments, but once you have learned to make a time-use plan, making changes will be easy.

Daily use of time

Date _____ Rank or position _____

Arrival time at work _____

End time _____ Task performed _____ Evaluation

_____
_____
_____
_____
_____
_____
_____
_____
_____
_____
_____
_____
_____

This is a task chart, not a goals chart.
List each task in detail.
Mark down time task ended.
Continue listing tasks and end time for entire day.
At end of day, review and evaluate each task as either acceptable or to be delegated, lengthened, shortened or eliminated. Notice at the end of the day the time spent on tasks that were acceptable or to be delegated.

FIGURE 6.2 Sample Log for Daily Use of Time

FIGURE 6.3 Sample Daily Priorities and Goals List

Daily priorities and goal list

A. Priority 1 (most important)
1 _____ 5 _____
2 _____ 6 _____
3 _____ 7 _____
4 _____ 8 _____

B. Priority 2 (necessary, but less important)
1 _____ 5 _____
2 _____ 6 _____
3 _____ 7 _____
4 _____ 8 _____

C. Priority 3 (least important)
1 _____ 5 _____
2 _____ 6 _____
3 _____ 7 _____
4 _____ 8 _____

At the end of the day, compare this list with the time-use log. Think about what you actually did and what your priorities were. Eventually bring the two into one daily work plan.

From your time log, you should be able to identify what is considered *unproductive* time, focusing on bad work habits. Most people have at least one bad work habit. Many have several. Analyze time logs to identify time wasters.

Law enforcement managers should list their 5 to 10 top time wasters and then make a plan to overcome them. In fact, time wasters could be a training focus or the topic of a staff meeting. Changing bad time habits requires a desire to change. You must put the new habits into daily practice until they are firmly a part of your work routine and continue to practice them until the old habits disappear.

Using the Time Logs

A time log gives you an idea of what you do at work, but you do not always know if you make the most productive use of your time. This is especially true of management positions.

Patrol officers promoted to sergeant do not continue to perform the same duties; in departments where sergeants have eight or more patrol officers to manage, sergeants will find that managing the officers is a full-time occupation. In some larger departments sergeants may have as many as 25 officers to manage, a severe test for the first-line supervisor. Sergeants need to know how time is actually being used.

Moving up the ladder of command, lieutenants and captains will not perform the same functions they performed as sergeants. Likewise, police executives (chiefs, superintendents or sheriffs) will not perform the same duties as the command level. Each level will find the time log a valuable tool for providing an accurate picture of time use.

Without a time log you do not know where time goes, how much time is spent on what duties and how frequently activities occur. Usually only a small portion of the day is uncommitted, but how is it used? A time log shows where it actually goes. After you make revisions, the time log should match the

Pinewood City Police Department
Event Unit Summary—Last 24 Hours
Run Time: 11/16/2009 6:03:27

Unit ID	Officer Name				
7104	GUPTA, ASHWIN P				
Event Number	**Priority**	**Incident Type**	**Dispo**	**Dispatch Time**	**Address**
LOW091115033260	3	L/PROP	RPT	8:30:18	159 24 ST NE
LOW091115033266	3	L/MISC	C	9:58:20	26 ST NE&7 AV NE
LOW091115033269	3	L/BKGROUND/PRIN	C	10:19:26	204 PEARL ST E
LOW001115000273	1	L/TRAFFIC STOP	RPT	11:02:12	OAK AV S&SCHOOL ST W
LOW091115033276	1	L/MEDICALS	C	12:40:14	1105 FRONTAGE RD W
LOW091115033279	1	L/MEDICALS	C	13:24:17	284 CEDAR COVE LN NW
LOW091115033281	1	L/MEDICALS	C	14:27:53	195 24 PL NW
LOW091115033284	3	L/PROP	RPT	15:34:03	830 20 ST NE

Unit ID	Officer Name				
7106	JOHNSON, ANDREW J				
Event Number	**Priority**	**Incident Type**	**Dispo**	**Dispatch Time**	**Address**
LOW091115033256	1	L/ALARM	FAN	6:34:35	125 18 ST SE
LOW091115033308	3	L/CHECK PREMISE	C	23:11:30	320 HOFFMAN DR NW
LOW091116033312	2	L/DISTURB/PARTY	RPT	0:11:55	811 BIXBY RD SE
LOW091116033318	3	L/CHECK PREMISE	C	4:30:03	496 NORTH ST W
LOW091116033319	3	L/CHECK PARK	C	4:36:10	350 SCHOOL ST W
LOW091116033321	3	L/CHECK PREMISE	C	5:10:34	2449 ROSE ST
LOW091116033324	3	L/MEDICAL LIFT	C	5:22:57	324 CEDARDALE DR SE

Unit ID	Officer Name				
7117	MENDEZ, GABRIELLA A				
Event Number	**Priority**	**Incident Type**	**Dispo**	**Dispatch Time**	**Address**
LOW091115033270	3	L/JUVENILE	C	10:24:44	20 ST NE&PRAIRIE LN NE
LOW091115033276	1	L/MEDICALS	C	12:40:14	1105 FRONTAGE RD W
LOW091115033279	1	L/MEDICALS	C	13:24:17	284 CEDAR COVE LN NW
LOW091115033282	1	L/ALARM	RPT	14:34:49	722 ACADEMY ST E

Unit ID	Officer Name				
7132	ROBINSON, TYRONE				
Event Number	**Priority**	**Incident Type**	**Dispo**	**Dispatch Time**	**Address**
LOW091115033288	3	L/TRAFFIC DETAIL	C	17:26:10	MAIN ST E&SCHOOL ST E
LOW091115033290	1	L/DOMESTIC	C	17:46:13	270 22 ST NW
LOW091115033291	3	L/DISTURB/PARTY	S	18:03:03	444 FAIRVIEW ST NW
LOW091115033292	3	L/BKGROUND/PRIN	C	18:40:43	204 PEARL ST E
LOW091115033293	2	L/CIVIL/ASSIST	S	18:46:58	123 RIVERSIDE AV NW
LOW091115033294	3	L/BKGROUND/PRIN	C	18:58:08	204 PEARL ST E

Unit ID	Officer Name				
7133	FISHER, JILL J				
Event Number	**Priority**	**Incident Type**	**Dispo**	**Dispatch Time**	**Address**
LOW091115033287	3	L/TRAFFIC DETAIL	C	17:16:25	MAIN ST E&SCHOOL ST E
LOW091115033289	1	L/TRAFFIC STOP	CI	17:26:38	PHELPS ST E&TRUMAN AV SE
LOW091115033290	1	L/DOMESTIC	C	17:46:13	270 22 ST NW
LOW091115033295	1	L/TRAFFIC STOP	CI	19:03:53	22 ST SE&CEDAR AV S
LOW091115033296	3	L/ANIMAL CALL	C	19:13:05	2680 7 AV NE
LOW091115033297	3	L/ANIMAL CALL	C	19:29:26	439 ADAMS AV NW
LOW091115033301	3	L/ACTION	C	20:23:50	544 MURRAY ST SE
LOW091115033302	3	L/ACTION	C	20:38:44	350 SCHOOL ST W
LOW091116033312	2	L/DISTURB/PARTY	RPT	0:11:55	811 BIXBY RD SE

Unit ID	Officer Name				
7135	HANG, TONG V				
Event Number	**Priority**	**Incident Type**	**Dispo**	**Dispatch Time**	**Address**
LOW091115033259	3	L/MISC	C	8:22:08	100 CLARK DR NW
LOW091115033261	3	L/EXTRA PATROL	C	8:43:56	1285 KILWORTH DR NW
LOW091115033262	3	L/MISC	C	8:58:55	300B STATE AV NW
LOW091115033265	3	L/MISC	C	9:42:34	100B ROSE ST E
LOW....115..3267	3	L/M...			

FIGURE 6.4 Screen Capture of an Electronic Time Log

Source: Owatonna (Minnesota) Police Department.

desired time allotted for specific goals and objectives. You have then achieved effective time management.

After logging your time, ask, What am I doing that I don't really have to do? What am I doing that someone else could do? What am I doing that I could do more efficiently? What activities or events are the biggest time wasters for me? How can I eliminate them? What am I doing that wastes others' time? How can I change? When are my productivity peaks and valleys throughout each day? When do I tackle high-priority projects? How often am I interrupted? Why? Can I control or reduce the number of interruptions?

Your daily log should help you determine when you are at your peak. You can then schedule high-priority work during your peak working hours, and use your low-energy periods for low-priority work such as filing, catching up on reading and returning nonemergency phone calls.

Objections to Time Logs

The most common objection to keeping time logs is, "I don't have time." It does take time, but the payoff is worth it. Others claim that time use varies from day to day. Again true, yet patterns do exist. Some say their days are already full. Some object to putting what they do on paper. And you may agree and choose not to use this approach. In some instances these objections are only excuses to continue with time-wasting habits.

The time log is simply one tool to help you determine whether a workday is full of the right tasks. If the tasks are wrong for the position, you can delegate, eliminate or otherwise change them. If all the tasks are right and the assigned work schedule is full, you have achieved good time management.

Every manager's time is broken up by diversions, unexpected distractions and interruptions of all types. It is realistic to allocate time for these. Knowing when and how frequently interruptions occur helps you reduce the time you spend on them. Also plan some time during the day for creative thinking about your job.

CONTROLLING TIME

The first step in controlling time is to ensure that you are accomplishing the tasks that must get done.

The Daily To-Do List

Although it is not necessary to continuously keep a daily log, it *is* critical to plan each day's time. This is best done the night before. Simply write down everything you should accomplish the following day. Then prioritize the items as follows:

A   Acute or critical—must be done.

B   Big or important—should do when A is finished.

C   Can wait—nice to do if time allows.

D   Delegate.

E   Eliminate.

The military approach thinks in a longer time frame using the following designations: ! = do ASAP; A = do within the next few days; B = do within the next week; C = do within the next month; and L = long term (anything over a month to complete).

MacKenzie (1972) also describes five categories for activities:

- Important and urgent (for example, budget due next week)
- Important but not urgent (getting physically fit)
- Urgent but not important (a meeting you are expected to attend—politically important, but not task related)
- Busy work (cleaning files rather than starting on a project)
- Wasted time (sitting in traffic with no audiocassettes or cell phone)

Of these five categories, the biggest problem is usually the important but not urgent task. Such tasks tend to be put off indefinitely. To integrate long-term tasks into your daily schedule without adding overtime, break it down into small, manageable steps and set interim deadlines on your calendar. Build in a set amount of time each day to work on the project. Otherwise, a month or so later, you'll wish you had started earlier.

 The daily to-do list may be the single most important time management tool. It helps you manage minute by minute.

If you make a to-do list *the night before*, you have a jump on the next day. Sleep will come easier, and this in itself can reduce stress and tension. Do not make the list too full. Leave some time for planning and for those unexpected things that inevitably arise.

Consistently write out your to-do list in one place each day. It does little good to make a list and then to lose it on a cluttered desk. Covey advises, "The key is not to prioritize what's on your schedule, but to schedule your priorities."

SCHEDULING

Morgenstern (2000/2001, pp.94–96) has a somewhat more detailed approach to the to-do list that prioritizes the items in the list and specifies when tasks will be completed and how much time they will take. She uses a SPACE formula for each item on the to-do list: "Space is an acronym that stands for Sort tasks, Purge whatever you can, Assign a time, Containerize the time needed to do the task and Equalize."

To *sort* the tasks, estimate the amount of time each will take. When doing so, keep in mind the "Times Three" rule; that is, it generally takes three times longer to do something than you think. Be realistic. With a realistic time for each task, *purge* the list by determining whether someone else might be able to do the task faster or better. Noncreative, repetitive tasks and special projects can usually be easily delegated. Next *assign a time*; for example, work on a major project from 10:00 a.m. until noon. The trick is to *containerize* the time needed; that is, start and end when you scheduled. Don't procrastinate; don't allow interruptions; and don't let it drag on. Containerizing also helps conquer the need for perfection. The last step is to *equalize*, refine, maintain and adapt the schedule as needed: "Time management is not a stagnant process. It is a constant interaction between your goals and the changing rhythms and tempos of life" (Morgenstern, 2000/2001, p.96).

Another technique to scheduling your time is presented in *Time Management* (2005, pp.31–32):

◉ Schedule only part of your day. This is crucial for managers and becomes more important as you move into the higher management echelons. Leave some time open to deal with crises, opportunities, the unexpected and that tried-and-true approach to management, walking around.

◉ Schedule your highest-priority work first.

◉ Consolidate tasks such as e-mail, paperwork and phone calls when possible.

◉ As the week progresses, move uncompleted priority tasks to future open times.

Time Management (2005, p.54) suggests as a rule of thumb to include half the number of things you think you can do in a day and to be exceptionally diligent to keep urgent but unimportant and low-priority tasks off your schedule unless someone in authority requires you to perform them.

The Time Map

Morgenstern (2000/2001, p.92) also suggests that managers make use of time maps: "To make sure you leave enough time for the activities that support your personal big picture, you will need to draw up what I call a time map—a visual diagram of your daily, weekly and monthly schedule. It's a powerful tool. Instead of feeling that you have to act on every request the minute it crosses your path, you can glance at your time map, determine when you have time and schedule it or skip it."

Other Methods of Organizing Time

The Franklin Day Planner is a time-management notebook used by people all over the world and an option for busy law enforcement managers. Another option is to turn your car into a training center and use your driving time to listing to training CDs. If you live to be 77 and drive 10,000 miles a year, you'll spend *three years* of your life in your vehicle. Yet another option is to do the least-liked tasks first. It is natural to avoid things you do not want to do. The trouble is, when you waste energy avoiding the bad things, you may lose your ability to get anything else done. One suggestion for predominantly right-brained managers is to jot each task to be accomplished on color-coded notes and stick them around the desk.

Time Management (2005, p.37) cautions, "Schedules and day-planners work well for people whose jobs are highly structured, and less well for people, particularly higher-level managers, whose work is fragmented. People with less structured jobs can make the most of time-management tools by building more free time and flexibility into their schedules."

After you have identified, prioritized and scheduled the necessary tasks, the next step is to find the time to do them by identifying unproductive time or time abusers.

TIME ABUSERS: COMBATING UNPRODUCTIVE TIME

Murray (2008, p.74) comments, "Each day people waste time as though it's an inexhaustible resource. Worse, they bemoan its shortage while squandering it." Managers in law enforcement experience the same unproductive time problems found in other professions. Time abusers tend to develop into time-use monsters if not controlled.

Develop an image of time respect. Managers often contribute to their own demise by trying to solve too many problems for others when they should be solving their own. Some of this time abuse is normal and must be accepted as part of a manager's job. Generally, time abusers can be divided into external—generated from outside—and internal, or self-generated.

External Time Wasters

Among the most common outside or external time wasters are *interruptions*. Managers are interrupted approximately every 8 to 10 minutes. Controlling and reducing these interruptions is important to save time and to maintain continuity of thought.

 Among the most common external time abusers are the telephone, the e-mail chime, people who "drop in," nonessential meetings, socializing and "firefighting" or handling crises.

The Telephone

The telephone offers several advantages. You save time when you make a call instead of traveling. You also have more control over the timing of a telephone conversation than you do over a personal visit.

However, the telephone also heads the list of time wasters. Allowing too many calls, permitting conversations to last too long, failing to screen incoming calls, failing to keep conversations purposeful and allowing calls to interrupt quality creative time can be devastating to productivity. Keep a telephone time log if you find the telephone to be a problem.

Avoid getting caught playing telephone tag. Leave a time to receive calls and find out when individuals you are trying to call will be available. Consider leaving your e-mail address on your voice mail message. This gives you greater control of your time and eliminates small talk. In addition, you can print out your e-mail messages. When making calls, plan what you are going to talk about and stick to the subject. Eliminate as much small talk as possible, using a timer if necessary.

Screen your calls through a secretary, a receptionist, caller ID or an answering machine that can be monitored. Always answer the phone with paper and pencil in hand. Write down the name of the person who is calling and take careful notes. This will save time later.

Always have your calls held during your most productive, creative times and during important meetings, whether they are one-on-one or in a larger group. One effective time saver is to "batch" your calls. This relates directly to what is known as the learning curve principle.

learning curve principle

states that grouping similar tasks together can reduce the amount of time each takes, sometimes by as much as 80 percent.

 The **learning curve principle** states that grouping similar tasks together can reduce the amount of time each takes, sometimes by as much as 80 percent.

According to the learning curve, each time you repeat the same task, you become more efficient. Telephone calls are one responsibility for which the learning curve can help manage time.

Voice mail can compound the problem, however. Some managers arrive in the morning, check their voice mail and are greeted with, "You have 37 new messages." Not a good way to start the day, but a reality in many departments.

The secret is to reduce the disadvantages of telephones and multiply the advantages. Telephone companies have films you can use or trainers who can meet with your staff and point out the most efficient use of telephones.

The E-Mail Chime

The e-mail chime or the message "You've got mail" can also be a distraction. Most type-A personalities cannot hear the chime or message without checking to see who just e-mailed them. *Time Management* (2005, p.52) calls this the Pavlovian e-mail response and suggests that the chime or message be turned off to eliminate this distraction.

Drop-In Visitors

Put limits on the visits of people who just stop in without an appointment. Be polite but firm. At times you may need to simply close your door when priorities demand that you have time alone.

Hang a "Privacy, Please" sign on your door during periods when you need uninterrupted time. Arrange specific times when others know your door is "open." Communication is, after all, critical to good management, but it also needs to be managed. Meet others outside your own office, giving you greater control over ending a conversation.

Stand up when someone enters your office, and conduct the conversation with both of you standing. Such conversations tend to be brief. Keep socializing to a minimum. Get to the topic that brought the drop-in visitor to your office and stick with that topic. If the person who stops by for a business reason asks, "Got a minute?," consider looking at your watch and saying, "Actually I have exactly five minutes. What can I do for you?" The drop-in will assume you have something important to attend to and will probably respect your time.

If a drop-in visitor stays on, you might try saying, "One more thing before you go . . ." Or you might take the person out in the hall to show him or her something—anything. Of course, you may arrange for a coworker to interrupt you with an "emergency" if a drop-in visitor stays longer than a specified time.

Be honest. You might simply say, "I've enjoyed our talk, but I really must get *back to work*." That simple phrase will be a clue to the visitor to leave and will serve as a prompt to you.

The words *back to work* will prompt you and others to keep on task.

Meetings

As much as 50 percent of managers' time may be spent in meetings, and of this, 50 percent of the time is often wasted. Think about the hourly rate of each person attending and be sure the department is getting its money's worth, as discussed in Chapter 4. Wasted time includes the time in the meeting and the time spent winding up a particular task before the meeting, traveling to and from the meeting and then getting back on task.

Organizations might consider designating someone to be a "meeting attender," to go to meetings and make brief written reports. This would create more paperwork but take less time than you attending the meeting. This practice could be useful for informational meetings that do not require the manager's personal participation. Avoid nonessential meetings, and do not call them yourself.

If your sole purpose for attending a meeting is to make a presentation, find out what time the presentation is expected, arrive a few minutes before that time, make the presentation and then excuse yourself. If you find yourself at a nonproductive meeting, it can be most efficient to simply excuse yourself and leave. Use common sense, however, especially if the meeting was called by and is being chaired by your superior.

Socializing

Socializing is a factor in inefficient phone calls, encounters with drop-in visitors and meetings. Relationships are very important, and socializing is an important part of relationships. However, socializing should be confined to coffee breaks, lunch or before and after work. The phrase mentioned earlier, "I've got to get *back to work*," reminds coworkers that you are not getting paid to socialize.

"Firefighting": Dealing with Crises

Law enforcement managers can expect to confront the unexpected daily. It comes with the job. Allow time in each day for these crises so you can deal with them calmly and rationally. Anticipate what might occur and have policies developed. Is the department likely to receive a bomb threat? To undergo a natural disaster? To be overrun by gang members?

If a crisis occurs for which no policy exists, get the facts, remain objective and think before acting. Then, when time permits, develop a policy for the situation should it arise again.

Internal Time Wasters

Not all time wasters come from the outside. Meetings, for example, may be external or internal. Many internal time wasters are self-imposed or the fault of colleagues.

Among the most common internal time wasters are meetings, drop-in employees, procrastination, failure to set goals and objectives, failure to prioritize, failure to delegate, personal errands, indecision, failure to plan and lack of organization.

Effective meetings were discussed in Chapter 4.

Drop-In Employees

Being available to employees is an important part of being a supervisor or manager. However, just as drop-in visitors can disrupt a manager's day, so can drop-in employees. Henry Ford, the automobile pioneer, made a practice of conferring with managers and employees in their offices rather than his own. As he explained, "I've found that I can leave the other fellow's office a lot quicker than I can get him to leave mine."

Procrastination

procrastination

putting things off.

Procrastination is putting off until tomorrow what has already been put off until today. For some people the greatest labor-saving device is tomorrow. Do not delay things. Get them done. Get right to work on priorities.

Cadets at the Air Force Academy are taught two laws of procrastination to impress upon them the folly of such delays: First law: If you wait until the last minute, things take only a minute to get done; second law: The sooner you get behind, the more time you allow yourself to catch back up.

One reason for procrastination is fear that if you do it, it will be wrong. Set a goal and think only of the goal. So what if you make a mistake? The person who makes no mistakes usually makes nothing at all! Think, "I can do it, and do it now." Motivational speaker Zig Ziglar gives members of his audiences a round piece of wood bearing the word *tuit*. He chides them that they can no longer say they will do something when they get "around to it" because they already have one.

The following techniques might help combat procrastination:

◉ Start with your most unpleasant task to get it out of the way.
◉ Set aside half an hour a day to work on a given project—schedule the time to do it.
◉ Do not worry about doing a task perfectly the first time through.
◉ Work briskly. Speed up your actions.

Another effective way to avoid procrastination is to set deadlines and let others know about them. If others are counting on you to have a task completed by a specific date, chances are you will do it. Accept 100 percent responsibility for completing tasks on time. Help others to do likewise. Finish tasks. Procrastination is one of your worst enemies.

Although you want to overcome the human tendency to procrastinate, you should learn to practice creative procrastination. Creative procrastination is putting off those things that do not really matter. If you can put tasks off long enough, they probably will not have to be done. A simple example of this is sending holiday greeting cards. If you really do not feel an urgent need to send them and if you can procrastinate long enough, the holiday will pass and so will the need to send them—at least this year.

Failure to Set Goals and Objectives and to Prioritize

Too much of each day is spent by people, managers included, doing very well things they do not need to do at all.

 Effective time managers concentrate on doing the right thing, rather than on doing things right.

The temptation is to clear up all the small things first so the mind is clear for the "big stuff." What often happens is that the whole day is taken up with the small stuff. Or doing the small stuff saps so much energy that little is left for the big stuff. Too many managers become bogged down in routine activities.

How do you differentiate between the trivial many and the significant few—those 20 percent described in the Pareto principle? Consider how combat triage officers divide the wounded into three groups:

- ⊙ Those who will die no matter what—make comfortable.
- ⊙ Those who will live no matter what—give minimal medical attention.
- ⊙ Those who will survive only with medical attention—focus attention here.

The same can be done within law enforcement agencies. Think of the consequences of what you do. Will accomplishing a given task have a positive payoff? Prevent a negative consequence? What will happen if you *do not* get a specific task done? Clearing away the trivial tasks to leave room for single-minded concentration simply does not work. It has no payoff. *You never get to the bottom of the stack.*

 Effective managers set priorities—tasks that they must do, have a big payoff and prevent negative consequences. They also set posteriorities—tasks that they do *not* have to do, have a minimal payoff and have very limited negative consequences.

Many managers excel at setting priorities but have no grasp of setting posteriorities. A day has only so many hours. For each new task a manager takes on, one task should be cut out. To continue to take on new responsibilities

priorities

tasks that must be done, have a big payoff and prevent negative consequences.

posteriorities

tasks that do not have to be done, have a minimal payoff and have very limited negative consequences.

without delegating or eliminating others is courting disaster—often in the form of burnout.

A Chinese proverb states, "One cannot manage too many affairs; like pumpkins in the water, one pops up while you try to hold down the other." Effective managers know how to say no. In fact, one of the most potent time management tools is the simple word *no*. When they cannot say no, effective managers know how to ask for help and to delegate.

Failure to Delegate

Many managers think that the only way something will get done right is to do it themselves. Such managers need to ask who did it before me and who will do it after me? The effective manager is one who can be gone for a few days or even weeks and everything continues smoothly during the absence. If you do not learn to delegate, there will never be another person trained to perform the work in times of crisis.

As recommended in Chapter 1, delegate whenever possible. Train subordinates, trust them, set limited and clear expectations, provide the necessary authority for delegated tasks and give credit when they have completed the task. Delegation gives strength to the delegator and the person delegated to. It is not an abdication of responsibility.

Delegation moves organizational communication downward. Delegation must be based on mutual trust, acceptance and a spirit of cooperation between all parties. In addition, subordinates must be empowered to do the delegated tasks.

Put delegated tasks in writing with set time limits. Keep records and follow through. Do not overdelegate to the same few workers. Delegation helps people develop and spreads responsibility throughout the organization so goals and objectives are more easily attained.

Personal Errands

Only in emergencies should personal errands be attended to during on-duty time. It does not leave a good impression to see law enforcement managers on personal errands during working hours. This practice can be very damaging to the department if not taken seriously—damaging public relations and subordinate respect and discipline. Managers must lead by example.

Indecision

Subordinates have a reasonable expectation that managers will make final decisions, especially on high-priority issues. Indecisiveness indicates a lack of self-confidence and is most frequently caused by fear of making a mistake. Approach mistakes as learning experiences; the biggest mistake may be never making a mistake. Understanding the decision-making processes described in Chapter 5 can make this managerial responsibility less threatening.

Failure to Plan

The saying goes, "Most people don't plan to fail; they simply fail to plan." Managers must learn to recognize problems and determine their causes, or time will be lost. Working the hardest or doing the most work is not necessarily the best answer if the work you choose is not of value. The average person will spend more time planning a vacation than planning a career.

 The **5P principle** states, Proper planning prevents poor performance.

5P principle
proper planning prevents poor performance.

Planning the use of time may save time threefold, perhaps more. If you do not take time to plan to do it right, you may have to find time to do it over.

Lack of Organization

Desk signs may *incorrectly* proclaim, "A cluttered desk is the sign of genius." If you cannot see the top of your desk, it is cluttered. Do not get rid of the clutter by putting it in the drawer. Take some action to get rid of it. Out of sight does *not* necessarily mean out of mind. Set aside time once a week to eliminate clutter.

Keep in mind that big messes start with little piles. Put things away right after you are done with them. This will keep the desk uncluttered, you will know where to find things if you need them again and you will avoid a big clean up at the end of a project.

Of course, the right-brained reader might be thinking, "If a cluttered desk reflects a cluttered mind, what is an empty desk a sign of?" The following suggestions may help your office organization:

- Keep on your desk only the project you are currently working on.
- Keep reference books organized and in easy reach but off your desk.
- Keep office supplies such as paper clips in your desk.

In addition to keeping your desk and office organized and neat, keep your projects organized. Use organization charts and flowcharts to graphically portray your goals and objectives, work plans and schedules. Use tickler files to find information faster. Know where and how to find needed information.

A Caution

Remember that people are more important than schedules and plans. Put a priority on people, not on going through that pile on your desk and checking things off a to-do list.

CONTROLLING THE PAPER FLOOD AND INFORMATION LOAD

Knowledge is doubling every two and one-half years. One issue of the *New York Times* conveys as much information as a person living in the sixteenth century would obtain in a lifetime. The information age places tremendous demands on everyone, especially managers. Managers cannot ignore the paper flood because much of it is information vital to doing an effective job.

Police managers must control paperwork or it will control them. Set aside time to deal with necessary forms and paperwork, and abide by the "single handling" philosophy.

© Michael Newman/PhotoEdit

 Control the paper flood by using single handling for most items, improving reading skills, delegating or sharing some reading tasks and adding less to the paper flood yourself.

Managers must control paperwork or it will control them. Law enforcement tasks generate extensive paperwork because of the legal requirement to document information. Reports are a large time problem. The sheer volume of reports makes them time consuming to read and difficult to absorb.

In addition to service and offense-related reports, managers deal with mountains of other printed information. Effective managers have a system for handling everything that lands in their "in" baskets, whether from an internal or external source. One system that works for many includes four categories:

1. Throw it away—opened or unopened depending on the return address.

2. Route it to someone else (delegate).

3. Take action on it.

4. File it for later action or reference.

single handling

not picking up a piece of paper until you are ready to do something with it; applies particularly to the daily stack of mail.

This system incorporates **single handling**, that is, not picking up a piece of paper until you are ready to *do* something with it.

 Handling paperwork only once—single handling—increases efficiency tremendously.

Once printed information is picked up, take action: toss it, pass it on, file it or act on it. The system works best when a specific time is allotted to handle paperwork. Remember the learning curve and the efficiency of "batching"

tasks, or doing similar tasks at the same time. Single handling also applies to emails. In addition, color coding e-mails helps to visually prioritize what needs to be looked at immediately. E-mails from superiors might be in red. Subfolders might be created to store e-mails relating to the same subject. E-mails can also be grouped by open issues and closed issues. Managers who receive 20, 30 or more e-mails a day need some system to keep their e-mails organized.

Organize the printed information you refer to often. Information that you use every day can be condensed on file cards, put into a PDA, added to personal directories, address books and calendars; written on to-do lists; or placed in action files or reference files. Use computer files or microfilm to retain information for long periods in an easily accessible, retrievable form. Prepare master indexes to locate such stored information.

Controlling the paper flood and information load increases your decision-making capabilities, permits planning and lessens the sense of guilt when you do not complete all tasks on schedule. Have a specific place to put everything that comes into your office. Have a working file for frequently used files where they can be reached without leaving your chair.

Another way to control the paper flood is to improve reading efficiency. Learn the difference between **scanning**—reading material rapidly for specific information; **skimming**—reading information rapidly for the main ideas—and actually reading. Scan or skim most reports and publications; read only those of interest and importance. Go through your business reading pile at a quick, even pace, scanning for any time-sensitive material. Assess what you can take in quickly, what you don't need to know and what you need to read in more detail. Read in greater detail the items that are truly worth your attention. Keep and label only the clippings you want filed. Or copy them to read during downtime.

Three behaviors that slow down the reading process are subvocalization, regression and narrow eye span. **Subvocalization** is moving the lips or the tongue to form the words being read, a habit formed when one is learning to pronounce letters of the alphabet and which can slow down adult readers. Talking speed averages 120 to 180 words per minute, which is also the speed of readers who subvocalize. Such reading needs to be speeded up. Normal reading is about 250 words per minute. Managers need to read 300 to 500 words per minute. Subvocalization can be stopped by keeping the lips together and placing the tongue against the back of the teeth when reading. This trains the brain to read and understand words without physically forming them.

Regression is looking back over previously read material, which slows normal reading. To eliminate regression, use the hand or finger sweep. As you read left to right, use the finger as a target to follow.

Narrow eye span occurs when a person focuses on one word at a time rather than taking in groups of words and phrases in one look. Adult eye span is between two and three words. To eliminate narrow eye span, search for your name in a magazine or a newspaper. Practice taking two lines at a time as fast as you can and searching back and forth. This is what you do when you look for a name in the phone book. It is necessary to increase reading speed and reading comprehension. This comes only with practice.

---

scanning

reading material rapidly for specific information.

skimming

reading information rapidly for the main ideas, usually the first and last paragraph, the first sentence of all other paragraphs and the captions of any charts or figures.

subvocalization

the contraction of the tongue and other speech-related organs made during learning to pronounce each letter of the alphabet; becomes ingrained and can slow down adult readers.

regression

looking back over previously read material.

narrow eye span

occurs when a reader focuses on one word at a time rather than taking in groups of words or phrases in one look.

Time spent taking a speed-reading course pays huge dividends because it will enhance your ability to scan information with greater comprehension. As you improve your reading skills, also improve your writing and speaking skills. Use fewer, more precise words.

Delegate reading or divide it among those who are good readers and interested in participating. It is inefficient for several people in the organization to be reading the same outside sources of information. Try having people volunteer to be responsible for a given source, such as *The Police Chief, Law and Order, Law Enforcement News, and Police*, national news sources such as *Time* and *Newsweek* and local publications. The person who does the reading can highlight specific items of interest and route them to others within the department. Another way to share the information is to give brief updates at roll call or during regularly scheduled meetings.

Increase your computer skills, also. Many books and training sessions on using computers are available. Computers tremendously increase the ability to retrieve and coordinate information.

Use a PDA and carry it with you at all times so you can record your thoughts. This is an advantage at meetings, when talking to others (including the media) and in other impromptu situations. It saves time as well as ideas.

Finally, do not add to the problem yourself. Some managers like to create paperwork because it gives a sense of personal power and fulfills a desire to influence others. Resist that impulse. Before you add to the paper flood, consider: Might a phone call work as well as a letter or memo? If you must write, is it as brief as possible? Who *really* needs copies? Can it be routed instead? Do you need copies of reports you are receiving? If not, ask to be taken off the distribution list. When you receive written material, if you foresee no further use for it or it will be available somewhere else, do not file it. Have a good reason for every contribution to the paper flood created, circulated or filed.

RETAINING WHAT YOU NEED TO REMEMBER

Some information can be filed and retrieved when needed. Other information, however, should be retained in your mind. Forgetting has been called the relentless foe. Forgetting takes its greatest toll during the first day after learning something. To slow forgetting you must transfer the information from your short-term memory to long-term memory by *doing* something with it. This might include mentally asking yourself a question about something you have read and answering it, verbally summarizing an important concept to a colleague, highlighting the concept or taking notes on an article.

Highlighting is the memory method of choice for most college students, and it is an effective way to transfer information from short-term to long-term memory *if* it is done correctly. Unfortunately, most people simply highlight what they want to remember as they read. This is very ineffective and often results in almost the entire article being highlighted. To highlight effectively, read the entire article (or chapter) first. Then ask, "What is most important about what I have just read?" Then go back and highlight *after* you have

highlighting
using a special pen to graphically mark important written information; should be done after the initial reading of the information.

finished thinking about what you have read. This is a highly effective way to improve retention.

PRODUCTIVITY—THE BOTTOM LINE

Effective managers use their time wisely to boost their productivity. Time management and productivity are integrally related. "Work smarter, not harder" is a truism. Simply putting in your time will not make you productive. In fact, the term **face time** has come into vogue in describing the time people spend coming in early or staying late to impress their superiors. It is the equivalent of classroom "seat time." Sometimes the longer people work, the more tired and unproductive they become.

 Overdoing it is harmful to your health and often hazardous to the quality of your work.

The most frequent complaint of law enforcement managers is that there are too many interruptions and too many duties and tasks to be performed to accomplish the higher-priority goals of the position. They are unable to control their time to the extent necessary and are constantly operating in a crisis management environment. It is mandatory, however, to establish control to accomplish priority tasks and to make time for creativity, long-term planning and short-term goal innovation; to try new ideas; to accept increased responsibilities; and to make better decisions.

Time is the most important and the scarcest resource managers possess. The organized use of your and all your personnel's time creates a productive department. Control time as you would budget dollars. How you spend time relates to how you can provide more or better law enforcement service. A capable time manager is easily recognized. Time management is one factor that moves employees up the organizational ladder.

With the future probability of fewer rather than more budget dollars, time will become even more important. Because each member of the law enforcement department is interrelated with total department time, the possibility of decreased personnel in ratio to workload will make time an even scarcer resource. This increased demand can be met only by efficient use of available time.

You cannot make time, but you *can* use available time better. Cyril Northcote Parkinson, a British humorist, summed it up neatly in his famous **Parkinson's Law**: "Work expands so as to fill the time available for its completion." Consider posting Parkinson's Law on the bulletin board for a week.

THE PHYSIOLOGY OF PRODUCTIVITY

Although this chapter has focused on working smarter, not harder, that does not preclude the option to work *faster*. Pacing is a matter of habit. Many people walk slowly, talk slowly, think slowly and write slowly. You can physically take control of time and accomplish tasks within the time you have.

---

face time

time spent in the agency or department long after a shift ends and on weekends when not on duty to make sure you are seen putting in extra time by those with the power to promote you.

Parkinson's Law

the principle that work expands to fill the time available for its completion.

Speed yourself up. Walk briskly. Talk crisply. Write rapidly. Read quickly.

You can actually save several minutes each day by simply walking, talking, reading and writing faster. Break out of old habits. Show that time is important by making the most of it. High performance has much more to do with perspiration than with inspiration. Speeding up physically will carry over to your mental state. You will be constantly reminded that you have a finite amount of time to accomplish your goals and objectives. However, do not let time rule your life.

 ## SUMMARY

Time management is planning and organizing time to accomplish your most important goals in the shortest time possible. Time is the greatest management resource available. At the heart of time management are goals—what you want to accomplish. Effective time management uses the Pareto principle to identify the 20 percent (few) vital tasks that will account for 80 percent of the desired results. It also identifies and places as low priority the 80 percent (many) trivial tasks clamoring for attention.

Keeping a daily log or time list tells you how you really spend your time, as opposed to how you perceive you spend it. The daily to-do list may be the single most important time-management tool. It helps you manage minute by minute.

Among the most common external time abusers are the telephone, people who "drop in," nonessential meetings, socializing and "firefighting" or handling crises. The learning curve principle states that if you do a group of similar tasks together, you can reduce the time they take, sometimes by as much as 80 percent. In addition, the words *back to work* can prompt you and others to keep on task.

Among the most common internal time wasters are drop-in employees, procrastination, failure to set goals and objectives, failure to prioritize, failure to delegate, personal errands, indecision, failure to plan and lack of organization. Effective time managers concentrate on doing the right thing, rather than on doing things right.

Effective managers set priorities—tasks that they must do, have a big payoff and prevent negative consequences. They also set posteriorities—tasks that they do *not* have to do, have a minimal payoff and have very limited negative consequences. The 5P principle states, Proper planning prevents poor performance. Control the paper flood by using single handling for most items, improving reading skills, delegating or sharing some reading tasks and adding less to the paper flood yourself. Handling paperwork only once—single handling—increases efficiency tremendously.

Overdoing it is harmful to your health and often hazardous to the quality of your work. Speed yourself up. Walk briskly. Talk crisply. Write rapidly. Read quickly.

CHALLENGE SIX

Sgt. Kelly supervises the Greenfield Police Department's investigative division. Ten investigators report to her. Sgt. Kelly starts each day assigning cases to investigators and reviewing completed cases that investigators have placed in her in basket. She has high standards of performance and expects high-quality investigations and reports from her detectives. Sgt. Kelly meticulously reads each completed case file and enters the disposition into the department's computerized records system. She returns to the assigned investigator cases not meeting her expectations. She spends several hours each day assigning and reviewing cases and reading reports.

Sgt. Kelly spends a disproportionate amount of time dealing with the reports of two of her investigators. One investigator is new on the job and very inexperienced. His reports are poorly organized and difficult to read. He usually has completed the necessary work but does not communicate it clearly in his reports. The other investigator is experienced but tends to take investigative shortcuts. His reports are well written but very brief and incomplete. Sgt. Kelly suspects he is not making all the contacts necessary to conduct a thorough investigation.

The other investigators do an excellent job with their cases, including their reports.

Sgt. Kelly is frustrated that she spends so much time in her office reading cases and does not have time to supervise in the field. She feels bogged down and detached from the community. She inherited the practice of reading all the completed cases and entering the dispositions from her predecessor.

1. Is Sgt. Kelly making best use of her time?

2. How can Sgt. Kelly address the specific needs of the problem investigators?

3. Should Sgt. Kelly stop reviewing cases and trust that her investigators are doing a good job?

4. Is there a more efficient method to review cases that would take less time?

5. Should Sgt. Kelly be entering disposition data into the department's computerized records systems?

6. Sgt. Kelly learned to manage her time from the previous detective supervisor. She respected his supervisory skills and appreciated his mentoring, but she is questioning whether the way he used his time is effective for her. Is it acceptable for her to change the way she uses her time?

DISCUSSION QUESTIONS

1. Do you personally use some type of time list or log? A to-do list? Compare yours with those of others in the class.

2. What is the most unproductive time of your workday?

3. What are your greatest time wasters? Compare yours with those of others in the class.

4. What time-management ideas presented in this chapter seem most workable to you? Least workable? Why?

5. How do you determine whether a meeting is necessary? Plan the agenda of a meeting? Control a meeting?

6. What examples of Parkinson's Law can you cite in your life or experience?

7. How much of your time is used for paperwork, including correspondence, planning, analysis, reading in-house publications and improving yourself?

8. How would you prioritize your work time?

9. How does the discretionary time of police officers working in departments using the community policing philosophy differ from those using a more traditional approach?

10. What examples of the Pareto principle have you experienced?

REFERENCES

Covey, Stephen R. *The 7 Habits of Highly Effective People*. New York: Simon & Schuster, 1989.

MacKenzie, R. Alec. *The Time Trap*. New York: AMACOM, 1972.

Morgenstern, Julie. "Taming the Time Monster." From *Time Management from the Inside Out*. New York: Henry Holt and Company, 2000. Book excerpt in *Forbes Small Business*, December 2000/January 2001, pp.87–96.

Murray, Ken. "The Value of Time: Changing the Status Quo." *Law Officer Magazine*, April 2008, pp.74–75.

Time Management: Increase Your Personal Productivity and Effectiveness. Boston, MA: Harvard Business School Press, 2005.

CHAPTER SEVEN
Training and Beyond

Wisdom and courage through knowledge and skill.

—International Law Enforcement Educators
and Trainers Association (ILEETA) Digest tag line

DO YOU KNOW?

- How training and educating differ?
- What the manager's single most important objective should be?
- What two areas related to training are most commonly involved in civil lawsuits?
- What are keys to avoid civil liability related to training?
- What three variables affect learning?
- What the three general categories of learners or learning styles are?
- What the key to determining the material to teach and test is? What this is called?
- What three areas training can focus on?
- What principles of learning are important?
- What instructional methods can be used?
- What instructional materials are available?
- What LETN is?
- What other training options exist?
- Of the training models typically used for recruits, which appears most effective?
- Where on-the-job training can occur?
- What the most common type of on-the-job training for new recruits is?
- What external training options available are?
- When training should be done?
- What the training cycle consists of?

CAN YOU DEFINE?

andragogy
content validity
eclectic
field training officer (FTO)
Firefighter's Rule
formative assessment
interval reinforcement
prerequisites
rote learning
summative assessment

INTRODUCTION

In the first three decades of the 20th century, law enforcement was simple. A police officer often relied on physical brawn to keep the peace and political connections to keep the job. Little formal training was required. However, the days of handing an officer a badge and a gun and putting him or her on the street are long gone. The individual most responsible for this change was August Vollmer, who entered law enforcement by accident in 1905 when, at the age of 29, he was elected town marshal in Berkeley, California. He soon moved to the position of chief and inherited a department that was in shambles.

Although Vollmer had little formal education, he founded the Berkeley Police School in 1908,

209

and recruits were receiving more than 300 hours of training by 1930. This later became the University of California–Berkeley School of Criminology, providing specialized training and orientation for individuals hired to be police officers. He motivated them to train others. Vollmer reached more audiences than any other officer in history. One of his protégés, O. W. Wilson, carried on his efforts to make training a priority for police officers.

Today the importance of training is recognized as a fundamental duty of law enforcement managers. Police supervisors, managers and leaders must understand and accept that training is primarily about managing and reducing risk associated with the positions of both the officer and the supervisor. As risks are constantly changing and evolving, and skills once honed are subject to atrophy if not practiced and updated, the need to provide ongoing training is a critical responsibility of management. Similarly, individual officers are responsible for seeking training opportunities and recognizing that continuous learning is a necessity for those who wish to advance in the law enforcement career. Among the benefits of a quality police training program are increased productivity, greater commitment from personnel, reduced lawsuits, more efficient use of resources and better delivery of services.

 ## CHAPTER at a GLANCE

This chapter stresses the need for continuous improvement in police professionalism. It begins by examining the differences between training and educating and then turns to a discussion on the importance of training as a management function, including a look at training philosophy and the two areas related to training most commonly involved in civil lawsuits. This is followed by a description of the learning process, including variables that affect learning and principles of learning, particularly as applied to adults. Next the chapter explores instructional methods and materials and looks at levels of training standards and on-the-job training. The chapter then examines training at the various levels, including how external training is used. In addition to basic certification instruction, a manager must determine ongoing training needs and prioritize subjects to be included. The next discussion emphasizes the importance of ongoing training, the ideal training cycle, evaluation and the benefits of effective training programs. The chapter concludes with a brief discussion of the learning organization.

TRAINING VERSUS EDUCATING

Learning theorists make a distinction between training and educating. *Training* is often viewed as a lower form of learning, dealing with physical skills, the type of instruction that takes place in vocational schools and on the job in law enforcement agencies. After completing a training session, participants may be awarded a certificate or a license.

Education, in contrast, concerns knowledge and *understanding,* the kind of instruction that occurs in colleges and universities. After completing a specific educational program, participants may be awarded a degree. Some law enforcement agencies pay employees higher salaries if they have attained specific levels of education. Some require a two-year degree, and some states, such as Minnesota and Texas, are considering legislation that would require officers to hold a four-year degree before being hired.

 Training generally refers to vocational instruction that takes place on the job and deals with physical skills. *Educating* generally refers to academic instruction that takes place in a college, university or seminar-type setting and deals with knowledge and understanding.

Using this distinction, a law enforcement agency might train its personnel to shoot firearms and educate them on the laws of deadly force. It might train personnel in high-speed pursuit techniques and educate them on when high-speed pursuit is to be conducted. Usually both training and education are needed, and they often overlap.

Some have suggested that officers should first receive a comprehensive law enforcement education and then be trained in police work, often under the watchful guidance of a field training officer (FTO). This text does not concern itself further with the distinction between training and education. Because the term *training* is most commonly used in law enforcement—for example, organizations have training departments and a budget line item for training—this term is used throughout this text to refer to both training and education.

TRAINING AS A MANAGEMENT FUNCTION

Training is a major management function. A department's efficiency and effectiveness are directly related to the amount and quality of training it provides. Training ensures that subordinates have the necessary skills to perform well, making the manager's job that much easier. For new recruits, training reduces the time they need to reach an acceptable performance level. Training also tells subordinates that the agency and the manager are interested in their welfare and development.

Training Philosophy

A written statement of training *philosophy* should articulate management's attitude toward training, the extent of resources to devote to it and the training's purpose and expectations. The training philosophy should reflect that managers are essentially assigned to develop personnel, the most expensive portion of the law enforcement budget.

 Developing human resources (i.e., people) should be managers' single most important objective.

Included in the training should be a thorough understanding of a department's policies because everything an officer does is dictated by these policies. The philosophy must also be consistent with the state's training requirements and with state and federal law.

Managers must be directly involved in training from determining needs through evaluating the program. The role of law enforcement managers in training depends on the level of the manager. Executive-level managers make the final decisions about the kind of training program needed and the groups to be involved. Middle-level management usually prepares the training program and helps determine training needs. First-line supervisors determine the needs of their officers and specialized personnel because they are closest to everyday operations.

Managers must also assure that complete records are maintained of the training provided by the department as well as training and certifications officers obtain on their own. Software programs can help training administrators create, store, manage and share training records, giving greater accountability to local police departments and academies to ensure personnel are consistently trained, tested and recertified: "In response to the tougher training standards, law enforcement agencies are insisting upon technology that offers quicker data entry of training information into databases, steady notification of upcoming recertification expirations, more individualized training reports that can be generated instantly and easier creation and tracking of personnel records that can be searched, updated and shared more efficiently" (Galvin, 2007, p.38).

Documentation of training provided by the department to groups should include the course goals and objectives, lesson plans, copies of handouts, test documents and scores reviews of tests, attendance, instructor competency, safety rules and procedures (if applicable), AV materials used, remedial training, certification, and other criteria an agency deems appropriate (Nowicki, 2008, p.20). Again, software is available to facilitate such documentation.

Training and documentation improves productivity and reduces liability.

Training and Civil Liability

Being sued is always a possibility in police work, with such suits often aimed at the training officers received or failed to receive. When budgets need to be cut, training is often one of the first items to go: "Training is considered nonessential—a luxury that's affordable in good times, but something no one will miss when the dollars get tight" (Rutledge, 2009, p.68). However, the price agencies pay after they cut training is often much higher than the cost of continued training would have been: "Officers who fall behind on core training and who stop getting regular updates on recent case law become a civil liability to themselves and their employers" (Rutledge, p.68).

 Two areas often involved in civil lawsuits are failure to train and for trainees' injuries sustained during training.

Failure-to-Train Litigation

Failure-to-train liability can arise from an organization's failure to train managers, supervisors, field training officers and other instructors in what their job positions require; failure to develop subordinates; failure to train managers in what their subordinates are learning; failure to provide annual in-service training; failure to require attendance at training programs; and failure to evaluate training needs (Carpenter, 2009). The landmark case in failure-to-train suits is *City of Canton, Ohio v. Harris* (1989). Geraldine Harris was arrested by the Canton police and taken to the police station. When they arrived at the station, the officers found her on the floor of the patrol wagon and asked if she needed medical attention. Her reply was incoherent. While inside the station, she fell to the floor twice, so the officers left her there to prevent her from falling again. No medical assistance was provided. She was released to her family, who called an ambulance. She was hospitalized for a week with severe emotional illness and received treatment for a year. She sued the city for failure to provide adequate medical attention while she was in custody. She won, with the Supreme Court ruling that a municipality might be held liable for deliberate indifference for failure to train.

Another illustrative example is the case of *Davis v. Mason County* (1991), in which five deputies were sued for using excessive force when making arrests, with the plaintiffs alleging that the sheriff and county had been deliberately indifferent to their duty to train. The judgment against Mason County included $528,000 in compensatory damages, $320,000 in punitive damages against the individual deputies and $323,560 in attorney's fees. The appellate court ruled, "The training that the deputies received was woefully inadequate, if it can be said to have existed at all." This failure to train ended up costing the county $1,171,560. Rutledge (2009, p.71) concludes, "The cost of training is a relative bargain, compared to the price of neglecting it."

The Supreme Court in *Board of County Commissioners v. Brown* (1997) suggests liability for failure to train *a single officer*. A plaintiff's attorneys may search an individual defendant officer's training records to find some deficiency related to their client's claimed injury and hire an expert to identify these training deficiencies. Lawyers routinely begin their investigation by requesting the training records and evaluations of an officer being civilly sued.

Undoubtedly, police departments should review high-risk liability incidents and provide adequate training to avoid liability claims being upheld. Among the most common actions and incidents leading to a lawsuit against an officer and agency are officer-involved shootings, any use of force, pursuits, police vehicle accidents, detentions, arrests, searches, special weapons and tactics (SWAT) operations and K-9 operations. Other areas of liability concern sexual harassment and discrimination. An area less frequently mentioned

cases

in failure-to-train lawsuits is civil rights litigation. Federal courts have ruled that a supervisor who directs subordinates to violate a person's constitutional rights can be held individually liable, if the supervisor knew of and allowed the subordinate's unconstitutional behavior or if the supervisor tolerated past and ongoing misbehavior.

 Keys to avoiding civil liability related to training are to provide first-rate training, to thoroughly document such training and to require thorough reports on any incident that could lead to a lawsuit.

Civil Liability for Injuries Sustained during Training

Firefighter's Rule

states that a person who negligently starts a fire is not liable to a firefighter injured while responding to the fire.

Police trainers usually cannot be held civilly liable for trainees' injuries during training. This exemption is based on an established legal defense known as the *Firefighter's Rule* and *assumption of risk*. The **Firefighter's Rule** states that a person who negligently starts a fire is not liable to a firefighter injured while responding to the fire. This rule has long been fully applicable to police officers if an officer is injured confronting a risk or conduct that occasioned his or her response or presence. Today most courts accept the following definition of the Firefighter's Rule: "Public safety officers have no claim for injuries suffered during the performance of their duties on the premises of a hazard, even if intentionally created," as is often the case in training sessions. The *assumption of risk* defense bars liability if a person is injured as a result of the normal dangers associated with an activity a person voluntarily engages in, for example, extreme sports. Law enforcement is a risky business, and those who chose public safety as careers are assumed to have accepted the attendant risks.

That training is essential for the safe, effective dispatch of police services is clear and uncomplicated. What is less explicit, however, is how such training should be structured and presented to be of most benefit.

VARIABLES AFFECTING LEARNING

Research on how people learn most effectively suggests that three variables are critical.

 Three variables affect learning:
- **Individual variables**
- **Task or information variables**
- **Environmental or instructional variables**

Individual Variables

The first consideration is who the learner is. Among the important individual variables are the learner's age, sex, maturation, readiness, innate ability, level of motivation, personality and personal objectives. The astute supervisor will be knowledgeable about each factor in each subordinate. Questions to ask regarding individual learners include, What is the officer's current skill level? What has the officer already learned? How far, realistically, can one expect this officer to progress in a given time? How motivated is this officer?

The typical law enforcement agency now has multiple distinct generations, each with its own individual defining characteristics, motivations, expectations and learning preferences. Table 7.1 summarizes the characteristics of these generations. Most Boomers have either already retired or are nearing retirement age, and most officers actively employed by police departments are of the Generation X cohort (Werth, 2009, p.42). Millennials or Generation Yers, however, have begun to permeate the police profession as officers, trainers, supervisors and soon-to-be administrators, and this generation will continue to constitute the bulk of new police recruits throughout the next decade.

In addition to differences existing within individual students based on when they grew up, Miller (2008, pp.90–93) describes the attitudes trainers may encounter in their training session, most of which are self-explanatory: the veteran (been there, done that), the prisoner (mandatory attendance), the saboteur (knows more than the trainer) and the challenged student (has difficulty grasping the material). Some argue these generational differences are presenting significant challenges to trainers and supervisors, as never before has the gap between the generation "in charge" and those that follow it been so wide (Harrison, 2007, p.150).

Supervisors have limited control over individual variables, but they must be sensitive to their importance. They must also be careful of stereotyping individuals. The information in this section is meant to provide only a guide.

Learning Styles

People's preferred way of learning can differ.

 The three general categories of learners, or learning styles, are visual, auditory and kinesthetic.

Visual learners learn best through seeing. They like to read and take notes. They appreciate handouts. Auditory learners learn best through lecture. They feel the need to speak and welcome classroom discussion. Kinesthetic learners want to apply what they are learning, to take a hands-on approach to learning. They appreciate role playing, scenarios and simulations.

Adult Learners

Research and common sense suggest that adults learn differently from children. The principles of adult learning, known as **andragogy**, should be considered in training programs. Adults differ from children in motivation, interest, values, attitudes, physical and mental abilities and learning histories. Adult learners also have more life experiences, fear of failure and greater expectation of immediately using the learning. Because of more advanced cognitive abilities, adults should not be given the "right" answer to a given

andragogy
principles of adult learning

TABLE 7.1   Generations of Law Enforcement Officers Compared

Born*	Age in 2010	Name(s)	Most Common Position in 2010	Defining Characteristics	Learning Preferences & Training Needs
1984–2002	8–26	Millennials, Generation Y, Generation Next, Nexters, Gamers, Net Generation	Attending academies Patrol officers A few are new supervisors	Most diverse generation. Heavily concerned about the terrorist attacks of 9/11, the war in Iraq and the global economic crisis. Media has taught them that they can, and must, challenge the status quo. Are often seen by employers as having a disturbing lack of basic skills but are extremely technologically savvy. Able to multitask well. Have a casual attitude toward employers, expect instant gratification and seek fun and flexible work. They do not want to learn anything that does not have an immediate application to their present situation.	Learn by trial and error. Have trained on games in which the learning paradigm is different—they learn by failing; failure is not seen as an embarrassment but rather a badge of honor and an essential part of learning. Learning must be fast-paced and kept moving. Use a variety of methods. Minimize lectures, as this group is generally unresponsive to lecturing. Go lighter on theory and heavier on practical application. Encourage nonlinear thinking and teamwork. The more information and choices provided, the more likely they will stay engaged.
1961–1983	27–49	Generation X	Coming into power, with increasingly higher levels of management and supervision as they age	Grew up in times of troubling social events and turmoil. Often cynical: "I'll believe it when I see it." They know from watching their parents that jobs don't last forever. A common philosophy is Work to live, not live to work. This generation wants a balanced work-life schedule, including time for family.	Like question and answer sessions. Enjoy games and activities. Seek creative, challenging options. Trainer must earn their respect.
1943–1960	50–67	Baby Boomers	Upper management Nearing retirement	Many view Millennials as decision-challenged, sheltered, socially inept and ethically bankrupt. They may also feel threatened by Millennials and because of their computer and technology skills.	Receptive to lectures. Like problem solving in a nonauthoritarian environment.
1900–1942	68 & Older	Traditionals, Veterans, the Silent Generation	Mentor Volunteer	They are rule followers. **Very few members of this generation are still actively employed in policing.**	Enjoy stress-free, unhurried learning environment. Respond best to experienced instructors. Learned by memorization and practice, practice, practice. Some are computer-phobic.

* Different sources give different age ranges, but these appear to be the averages.

problem but rather encouraged to think through a problem and to develop an appropriate response.

Task or Information Variables

Task or *information variables* relate to *what* is to be learned. This might involve knowledge, skills or attitudes. The basic curriculum for recruits must be valid and job related. The first step in validation is to conduct a job analysis defining both the tasks that constitute the job and the knowledge, skills and abilities an individual must possess to perform the job effectively. To establish **content validity**, the direct relationship between tasks performed on the job, the curriculum and the test must be established.

content validity

the direct relationship between tasks performed on the job, the curriculum or training and the test.

 Job analysis is the key to determining the content to teach and test. When content relates directly to the tasks to be performed, it is considered valid. Tests that measure competence in these tasks are then also valid.

The next step is translating worker requirements into training and learning objectives. The result of these efforts is that police recruits are exposed to a curriculum that truly prepares them for a law enforcement career.

 Training can focus on knowledge, skills or attitudes.

Knowledge is often equated with book learning, theory and education and includes facts, ideas and information. This is referred to as the cognitive approach. The steps involved in loading and firing a gun or in obtaining information and then writing a report are usually first presented as facts—information. Officers are expected to apply most of the knowledge presented to them.

Skills generally involve applying knowledge. This is referred to as the behavioral approach. Skills may be technical or motor skills, such as firing a gun, or conceptual skills, such as actually writing a good report.

Attitudes are the most difficult to deal with through formal training. They are influenced primarily by the positive and negative examples set by managers, supervisors and others in the department. Officers may learn in training sessions that stress is a hazard of law enforcement work and that pessimism and cynicism are other occupational hazards. They may feel they are immune to stress, just as they may think they are immune to getting shot. This "it can never happen to me" syndrome so frequently attributed to law enforcement officers is not effectively dealt with through knowledge-centered training sessions.

Relevant questions about task or information variables include, How meaningful is the task or information? How difficult is it? How similar is it to tasks and information already mastered? How pleasant or unpleasant is the task? How is the instruction organized or presented?

Supervisors have great influence over this variable because they can try to ensure that the task or information being taught is seen as relevant, practical and indeed essential. Probably the most important variable, however, is the last one: how the instruction is organized or presented.

Environmental or Instructional Variables

Environmental/instructional variables refer to the *context* in which the training is provided. Common sense suggests that officers will learn better in a comfortable setting where they can see and hear what is happening and distractions are limited. The training environment should provide ample space and lighting, or low or no lighting if dealing with a nighttime issue; afford comfort and safety; be distraction free; and present an atmosphere where students can succeed.

Involving students in training is more difficult and time consuming and requires more teaching skill, creativity and a greater depth of instructor knowledge. However, it is widely accepted that application is an integral part of the training process. People learn by doing. Practical applications might include case studies and scenarios with role playing, small-group activities, field trips and individual student performances (discussed shortly).

Common sense also suggests that the more practice officers get with a given task, the more proficient they will become. Of particular concern are those high-risk/low-frequency types of events, such as high-risk traffic stops. Because such incidents, for most patrol officers, do not commonly occur on a daily basis, the skills and techniques for handling these calls can perish over time. Thus the need to routinely provide training to keep the skills needed for infrequent events as sharp as possible.

Another critical factor is whether officers are practicing techniques correctly. All too often practice does *not* make perfect; it makes an incorrectly practiced procedure *permanent* and therefore counterproductive.

Knowledge of results, or feedback, also greatly enhances learning. Feedback motivates and helps ensure that the correct learning has occurred. Incentives may be related to staying alive, becoming an exemplary officer, promotions, pay raises, threats or any number of factors. Chapter 9 deals with incentives and motivation.

Implications

Given the variables affecting learning, the bottom line is this: *There is no one best way to instruct*. The most effective instruction is adapted to the individual officers; the specific knowledge, skill or attitude being taught; and the setting in which the training occurs.

PRINCIPLES OF LEARNING

As discussed, officers will exhibit a variety of learning styles. Several principles of learning have been stated or implied in the preceding discussion. They are summarized as follows:

Principles of learning:

- Base training on an identified need.
- Tell officers the learning objective.
- Tell officers why they need to learn the material.
- Make sure officers have the necessary background to master the skill (the **prerequisites**). Provide a way to acquire the prerequisites.
- Present the material using the most appropriate materials and methods available. When possible, use variety.
- Adapt the materials and methods to individual officers' needs.
- Allow officers to be as active and involved as possible during training.
- Engage as many senses as possible.
- Break complex tasks into simple, easy-to-understand steps.
- Use repetition and practice to enhance remembering.
- Give officers periodic feedback on their performance.
- Whenever possible, present the "big picture." Teach an understandable concept rather than relying on simple memorization or **rote learning**.

prerequisites
necessary background needed to master a given skill.

rote learning
memorization, not necessarily with understanding.

A New Paradigm of Learning

The "old" paradigm of learning focuses on providing instruction through quality teaching, delivering knowledge from trainers to students; trainers work independently in isolation. The "old" paradigm views students as passive entities to be filled by trainers' knowledge, which comes in chunks and is objective. Criteria for success include enrollment growth, program additions and quality of entering students.

The "new" paradigm focuses on quality student learning based on specified learning outcomes and integrating intellectual and personal skills. Students are active constructors, discoverers and transformers of their own knowledge, which comes in frameworks to be grasped by the learner. Criteria for success include quality of learning, improved job performance rate, increasing retention rate and increasing job satisfaction.

Familiarity with the basic principles of learning will help trainers express key concepts more effectively and enable trainees to absorb such concepts more fully.

Effective Trainers

Opinions vary as to what makes an effective trainer. Certainly personality comes into play. Miller (2009a, pp.56–59) offers the following as necessary characteristics to be an effective trainer:

- Is well-versed in the topic
- Is committed

- Communicates effectively and knows the learning process
- Is perceptive and supportive
- Uses appropriate humor
- Delivers the message and walks the talk
- Makes sure training is goal-oriented and safe

Additional traits include affability and the capacity to encourage students to ask questions, avoiding the approach of being a drill sergeant, an all-knowing type or a "my-way-or the highway" instructor (Frederick, 2008, p.87). Finally, effective trainers, recognizing the different individual learning styles likely to be present in a diverse group of trainees, possess flexibility in their teaching styles and provide more than one learning method for each concept presented.

Trainers must remain current on the ever-changing challenges in law enforcement as well as changes in the laws they are sworn to uphold. In addition, effective trainers use recruits' experiences and involve them in setting their own educational objectives. Further, effective trainers recognize that learning is not a spectator sport and use active learning in the training. Effective trainers also give feedback promptly—knowing what a person knows and does not know sharpens learning. Trainers also emphasize time on task and communicate high expectations. Finally, trainers must respect diverse talents and ways of learning.

Having looked at basic principles of effective training, next consider some common mistakes trainers make and some unsafe teaching styles and practices.

Training Pitfalls

The most common training mistakes include

- Ignoring individual differences, expecting everyone to learn at the same pace.
- Going too fast.
- Giving too much at one time.
- Using tricks and gimmicks that serve no instructional purpose.
- Getting too fancy.
- Lecturing without showing.
- Being impatient.
- Not setting expectations or setting them too high.
- Creating stress, often through competition.
- Delegating training responsibilities without making sure the person assigned the task is qualified.
- Assuming that because something was assigned or presented, it was learned.
- Fearing subordinates' progress and success.
- Embarrassing trainees in front of others.
- Relying too heavily on "war stories."

Retention

People retain 10 percent of what they read, 20 percent of what they hear, 30 percent of what they see, 40 percent of what they see and hear, 60 percent of what they discuss with others, 70 percent of what they experience personally, 80 percent of what they discover and solve individually or in groups and 95 percent of what they teach to someone else. Figure 7.1 illustrates the correlation between various modes of learning and the percentage of information retained.

A key learning principle regarding retention is that of interval reinforcement. **Interval reinforcement** means presenting information several times, perhaps as follows:

First time:	During the introduction of a lecture
Second time:	In the middle of the lecture
Third time:	At the end of the lecture in a summary or review
Fourth time:	In a quiz a few days later, perhaps at roll call
Fifth time:	During a review session a week later
Sixth time:	In an application of the information

> **interval reinforcement**
> presenting information several times, with breaks between the repetition.

Notice that the information is repeated with intervals between the repetitions. Studies have shown that if learners are presented information once, they remember only 10 percent after 30 days. If, on the other hand, they are exposed to the same information six times, they remember 90 percent after 30 days (Figure 7.2).

The *law of primacy* states that things learned first are usually *learned best*. The *law of recency* states that things learned last are *remembered best*. The implication is that key concepts should be presented early in the training and summarized at the conclusion of the training. These principles have a direct bearing on the instructional methods and materials used during training.

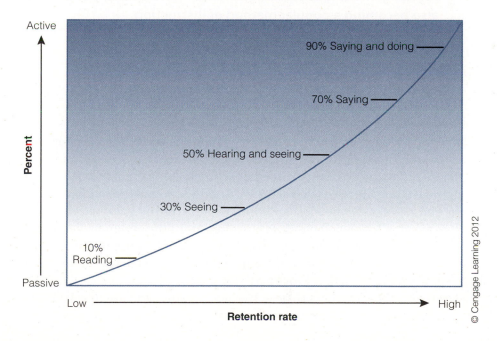

FIGURE 7.1
Retention Curve

© Cengage Learning 2012

FIGURE 7.2
Interval Reinforcement

Source: Robert W. Pike. *Creative Training Techniques Handbook.* Minneapolis, MN: Lakewood Books, 1989, p.15. Used with permission of Robert W. Pike, President, Creative Training Techniques International, Inc., Eden Prairie, MN.

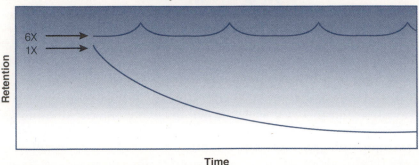

The key = interval reinforcement

| 30 days | 1 X | <10% |
| 30 days | 6 X | >90% |

INSTRUCTIONAL METHODS

Many training methods are available. Which to select depends on the time available, the kind and amount of training needed, how many officers need to be trained and the cost.

Often, a combination of instructional methods works best, with the methods selected being dependent on what is being taught. An **eclectic** approach to training blends the best teaching approaches to meet students' needs. Students would more easily transfer new skills into use if given theory, demonstration, practice, feedback and ongoing coaching.

eclectic

blending the best teaching approaches to meet students' needs.

 Instructional methods include lecture, question/answer sessions, discussion, videoconferencing, demonstration, hands-on learning, role playing, case studies and simulations, including digital game-based learning. Online learning and training is also becoming a popular method of instruction.

Lecture, direct oral presentation, is the traditional way to instruct. It is efficient, can be used with large numbers of people, is cost effective and is well suited to conveying large amounts of information. Unfortunately, lecture is sometimes overused and sometimes abused. Lectures should be short and supplemented with as many visual aids as possible.

Question/answer, or Q & A, sessions are of two basic types: Learners ask the instructor questions or the instructor asks the learners questions. Some lecturers will invite listeners to interrupt with questions that come to mind during the lecture. This is usually an effective way to break the monotony of a lecture, and it is usually the most appropriate place for the information. Other lecturers ask that listeners hold their questions until the end to make certain they cover all the information. The disadvantages of this approach are that people often forget their questions, the questions seem irrelevant later in the lecture or people are in a hurry to leave.

Discussions allow learners to be active participants and are usually motivating. Effective discussions require a skilled leader, usually the supervisor or trainer, to guide the discussion, keep it on track, control the amount of time devoted to each topic, ensure balanced participation by learners and summarize the key points at the end. Incident reviews of how specific cases were handled make excellent topics for discussion. The strengths and weaknesses of the cases can be identified and discussed, as can other approaches that might have been equally or more effective.

Videoconferencing is simultaneous, interactive audio and video communication involving a trainer and learners from several different sites. Although videoconferencing has advantages, the cost of purchasing the equipment is substantial and lengthy booking dates may be required for a multipoint hookup.

Many skills can be taught most effectively through *modeling* or *demonstrating* how to do something, such as how to give cardiopulmonary resuscitation (CPR), handcuff a suspect or frisk someone. Smith (2008a, p.72) notes, "Most things in life are best shown and practiced if they require doing. This is especially true of those things that are of great liability to both us and our agencies." An effective demonstration should explain each step as it is slowly done, noting the purpose of the skill as well as hazards or problems to be anticipated. Questions should be allowed during the demonstration. The demonstration is repeated at normal speed as many times as needed until everyone understands. Often, after a demonstration, learners are asked to do the procedure that was demonstrated.

Hands-on learning, actually doing what is required on the job, is an ideal form of training. It motivates learners and transfers to the real world. Whenever possible, theoretical information should be followed by some kind of actual performance.

Recalling the retention curve, people retain 10 percent of what they read compared with 90 percent of what they say and do. Sometimes, however, the real thing is not possible. In such instances, role playing can be very useful.

As the name implies, *role playing* casts people into specific parts to act out. For example, one student might take the role of an arresting officer and another that of the person being arrested. Sometimes specific scripts are provided. Other times, just the general situation is described. Role playing is one of the most frequently used training tools, with recent surveys showing more than 80 percent of law enforcement agencies using some form of role playing in their training. It has become a "mainstay" in crisis negotiation skills training and evaluation. In role playing the actors learn from doing and from class criticism. The watchers learn from what they see and from finding strengths and weaknesses in the performance. Role playing is especially useful in making officers more sensitive to how others feel and how their behavior affects others.

Case studies are detailed analyses of specific incidents used to instruct. They may be printed to read or delivered orally describing atypical emergency or adversarial events that could occur within the trainees' normal workday, typically followed by a series of discussion points. As Smith (2008b, p.96) points out, "war stories" can be effective teaching tools: "Nothing beats experience." He explains that when a student asks him what he would do in a given situation, he's not comfortable telling them what to do, but he is comfortable telling them what they shouldn't do based on his experience. Case studies and war stories are used in the same way as scenarios.

Away from the Desk

The Owatonna (Minnesota) Police Department (OPD) has made a commitment of providing continued development to every officer. Each year two in-service days are scheduled for the entire department. These in-service days are mandatory training requirements for all sworn personnel as well as all civilian personnel.

The first of the two training days is held in January and focuses on the current year's business plan. The department's goals and objectives are reviewed as a group. Next, the patrol officers are separated into groups based on their patrol districts and aligned with their direct supervisors. During this exercise, each group formulates how their platoon is going to achieve the established goals and objectives, setting forth measurable outcomes and making sure their approach is aligned with the department's mission and vision statements. When this exercise is complete, the platoons/patrol district officers are brought together to present their plans to the larger group. Finally, during this session a panel of officers and administrators from another department is brought in to compare and contrast these operations plans. The goal is for OPD officers to have a plan on how they will participate in meeting established goals and objectives. Further, it is equally important for them to hear how another department is addressing these issues and that, in fact, other departments are expected to do the same. This experience is used both as a team building exercise as well as an opportunity for individuals to have input into operation plans to help meet the expectations of the community.

The second annual in-service training day is devoted specifically to legal updates and case studies. The county attorney presents new case law as well as changes to existing case law. In addition, a focused breakdown is conducted on three to five major cases that took place in the jurisdiction in an effort to learn how the department can improve in certain areas that the county attorney found upon final prosecution of the case. The second half of this in-service is dedicated to specialized initiatives and involves presentations by guest speakers who are considered experts in the areas the department has identified as needing attention and that it is working on within the community to enhance its effectiveness.

I cannot underestimate the value of the time and effort spent on bringing the department together to facilitate groupthink, teamwork and approaches to better effectiveness and efficiency.

—*Chief Shaun E. LaDue*

Scenario-based training is well-suited for senior and special courses, especially for criminal investigations. For example, scenario-based training can be used for interior and exterior crime scenes, for conducting interviews of suspects on videotape, for homicide and sexual assault investigations data entries and for drafting search warrants based on a crime scene scenario.

Courtesy of Owatonna Police Department

New multimedia technology is used in the continued training of law enforcement officers. Driving simulators, such as this, help officers hone their behind-the-wheel skills in a risk-free environment.

Griffith (2008, p.49) recommends that because police officers need to use all their training the field, scenarios should incorporate multiple skills. A scenario might start with a traffic stop going through all the procedures needed to conduct it properly and to prevail when the stop goes bad, including proper arrest and cuffing procedures.

Simulations, imitations of a process, are another effective means of training. Simulation training has been used by law enforcement since the 1950s and includes such areas as driving; handcuffing, takedowns and other force options; and crisis resolution. Simulations are devised to immerse participants in life-like events to elicit probable responses. Improvements in technology, such as portable use-of-force simulators with high-tech audio and video, have created more realistic training experiences (Griffith, 2007, p.36). Judgment evaluation simulators can provide real-world critical incident experience.

Simulation is a valuable tool but never a replacement for good instruction, which can make the difference between life and death for an officer who, within seconds, has to make a critical decision. And although simulations can be a powerful training option, simulators used improperly or inappropriately can program officers to behave in ways that make them unlikely to win a confrontation on the street.

Digital game–based learning allows experimental learning in the safety of cyberspace. It is most effective in areas that might be dangerous, costly or catastrophic if actually reenacted. In effect, it allows officers to "play it out before they live it out."

Bertomen (2009, p.87) notes that the new generation of learners have trained on video games for years. They play a game until they reach a certain level they cannot accomplish, then re-spawn or are resurrected to continue to play. In effect, they learn by failing: "The learning paradigm is different. For the new generation, failing is an essential part of learning."

Video games can help officers hone their decision making skills (Kozlowski, 2008). Such games do not teach physical skills, for example putting a round through the center of a target. Rather, they provide practice in deciding whether or not to fire the round in the first place. Video games remove the physical motions, allowing users to focus on cognitive decision making. The video game doesn't teach what the right decision is, but rather teaches how to make the right decision.

Online learning and training are becoming popular options for many agencies around the country. For example, the Minnesota Counties Insurance Trust (MCIT) has collaborated with the League of Minnesota Cities, the Minnesota Chiefs of Police Association and the Minnesota Sheriffs' Association to offer online training for law enforcement officers through a program called Police Accredited Training OnLine (PATROL). PATROL provides training on the latest and most critical legal developments that expose officers and their organizations to risk, including executing search warrants or the role of school resource officers in interviewing school children.

Reality-Based Training

Training should be conducted in the most realistic setting as possible. According to the psychological principle known as state-dependent learning, "A subject who learns something will best recall their learning when in the same state of mind as when they learned" (Murray, 2007a, p.60). To law enforcement this means that if skills are taught in a contextual setting and are stressful enough without overwhelming students or ingraining a fear response, students will have better "access" to those skills under stressful conditions in similar settings. For example, training on how to intervene in a domestic violence incident should be done in an apartment-like setting, which could be set up in the simulation area of a regional training academy and furnished inexpensively with items from a local Salvation Army. Active shooter drills, which became mandatory for police departments in the wake of the Columbine High School shootings, are another example of reality-based training, where various public service agencies partner with schools and other institutions to practice lockdown techniques and other procedures for effectively responding to an active shooter scenario.

Risk aversion, the normal animal or human response of moving away from a source of pain, is also addressed in reality-based training. Referring to the adage, "Pain improves the memory of the slow learner, " Murray (2008a, p.60) notes fault in how early high-priced simulators actually could ingrain inappropriate or tactically unsound behaviors because there was no pain penalty for failure. Instead, a little beeper would sound or the video screen would flash, "You Lose," feedback that hardly corrected inappropriate behaviors. However, the advent of recreational paintball and other simulated battle games provided an interesting study on risk aversion, as Murray describes how striking it was to see military and law enforcement communities come up against the recreational players and lose: "In actuality, those who had ostensibly been trained in weapon craft had not been tested in battle—a completely different animal. The salient difference was the use of projectiles that caused pain on impact. Pain eliminated questioning a hit and provided an incentive for avoiding projective impact" (2008a, p.60). He cautions that the use of pain can be overdone, moving toward a hazing approach, and that carried to extremes, pain can program the participants for failure. There is little point in practicing failure. Training must always end on a positive note with the students winning. Indeed, the purpose of reality-based training is to test the plan, not the people: How will you respond in a particular scenario? What is your plan? The plan of action is what needs to be practiced.

Murray (2008b, p.98) recommends active interaction between a student and a trainer during a scenario, what he calls "pressing the pause button" or a "tactical time-out." These interventions should occur if a student is not effectively acting in a logical or tactical fashion, if the scenario seems stuck, or if it is headed in the wrong direction. Finally, reality-based training programs must be properly documented; if is not, it is deemed by the courts to have not occurred (Murray, 2007b, p.78).

Individual or Group Training

Instructional methods also include consideration of whether the training should be individual or group. Such decisions are based on similarities of officer behavior and schedules.

The individual, mentor, coach or FTO approach is a tradition within most local agencies and has been considered effective. Individual training is important and can be highly motivating, but it is also very costly.

Group training has the advantage of giving everyone in the group the same basic knowledge and approach. Because law enforcement officers must often rely on each other, sometimes without time or opportunity to discuss what action to take, group training is more likely to produce a consistent and expected unspoken reaction. And if each group member is trained to perform a specific way under a specific set of circumstances, officer safety is greatly enhanced. Group training is also more cost effective than individual training. Some topics are important for everyone within the agency to receive training on. In such instances training must be arranged to cover all shifts.

In addition to being familiar with instructional methods, trainers also need to know what instructional materials they might use.

INSTRUCTIONAL MATERIALS

 Instructional materials include printed information; visuals; bulletin boards; audiocassettes, videocassettes and DVDs; television programs; and computer programs.

FIGURE 7.3
The Power of Visuals

Source: Robert W. Pike. *Creative Training Techniques Handbook.* Minneapolis, MN: Lakewood Books, 1989, p.34. Used with permission of Robert W. Pike, President, Creative Training Techniques International, Inc., Eden Prairie, MN.

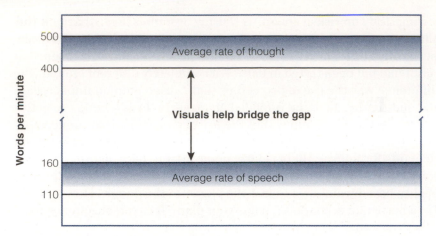

Printed materials are by far the most common and most widely used, including policies and procedures manuals, instruction books for new equipment and reading materials for specific training programs they will be attending. Printed materials are uniform, flexible and inexpensive. They can also be impersonal and boring.

Appropriate *visuals*, including PowerPoint presentations, flowcharts, graphs and maps, can enhance learning and help reduce barriers of time, space and language. A picture is much more effective than words alone, and words and pictures together are even more effective. One reason visuals are so powerful is they fill a gap between the rate of speaking and listening, as Figure 7.3 illustrates.

Bulletin boards also can be effectively used for instruction but need to be kept separate from those used for noneducational purposes, such as those provided for department members wanting to sell used guns, cars or furniture, as well as to post jokes, cartoons and announcements. *Audiocassettes, videocassettes and DVDs* are becoming increasingly popular and affordable instructional media, offering a wealth of opportunity to learn new skills from instructors who may not be available locally.

Educational television also has much to offer on general topics such as communication skills, dealing with people and cultural awareness.

 The Law Enforcement Television Network (LETN) is a private satellite television system that provides current programs on a variety of law enforcement subjects; it is available through subscription.

LETN programming is planned to reach each shift with identical information, providing uniformity of training. It is difficult if not impossible for local departments to provide training on each shift unless the shift managers or supervisors do the training. This usually means it is not presented the same way to each shift.

Learners using *computer training programs* are more active than when simply reading, listening to or viewing materials. The programs allow learners to proceed at their own pace, and most provide immediate feedback on the accuracy of responses. Many programs allow learners to skip material they can show they already know.

OTHER TRAINING OPTIONS

 Other organizations available to assist with training include the National Association of Field Training Officers (NAFTO), the Federal Law Enforcement Training Center (FLETC), the National Center for State and Local Training, the Southern Police Institute, the Federal Bureau of Investigation (FBI) National Academy and the FBI itself.

NAFTO was chartered in 1991 to advance the interests of field training officers in all areas of criminal justice. The FLETC, which is now a component of the Department of Homeland Security (DHS), seeks to provide high-quality, state-of-the-art law enforcement training for a broad spectrum of participating agencies in a cooperative, interagency manner. The Office of State and Local Training (OSL), a division within FLETC, was established in 1982 to provide training in advanced topics and develop specialized law enforcement skills. The Southern Police Institute is another training resource that offers an administrative officer course.

A major training program is the FBI National Police Academy. The FBI sustains all costs for sessions. The academy started in 1935 and is located on the U.S. Marine Base at Quantico, Virginia. The academy lasts 11 weeks and is offered four times a year. Each session includes 250 selected personnel. In addition, the FBI holds schools ranging from one hour to three weeks for local and state law enforcement officers.

Departments can also use local resources such as health professionals for training on stress, AIDS and the like; English teachers for assistance in report writing; and local attorneys for updates on new laws. The Federal Emergency Management Agency (FEMA), which became part of the DHS in 2003, can provide courses on terrorism, disaster response and similar topics.

TRAINING STANDARDS

Standards for police training, how much is needed and what it should consist of, have been controversial since the early 1800s when Robert Peel set forth his principles of reform. Compared with other professions, law enforcement does not require extensive formal training. Attorneys receive more than 9,000 hours of instruction, and physicians receive more than 11,000 hours. Officers receive 400 to 800 hours.

In 1967 the President's Commission on Law Enforcement and the Administration of Justice recommended that Peace Officer Standards and Training (POST) commissions be established in every state. These boards were to set mandatory minimum requirements and provide financial aid to governmental units to implement the standards. POST commissions now exist in every state to set requirements for becoming licensed as a law enforcement officer.

Among the specific charges of the POST commissions are

- Establishing mandatory minimum training standards (at both the recruit and in-service levels), with the authority to determine and approve curricula, identify required preparation for instructors and approve facilities acceptable for police training.

- Certifying police officers who have acquired various levels of education, training and experience necessary to adequately perform the duties of the police service.

The Commission on Accreditation for Law Enforcement Agencies (CALEA)

The Commission on Accreditation for Law Enforcement Agencies (CALEA) was created in 1979 as a credentialing authority through the joint efforts of the International Association of Chiefs of Police (IACP), the National Organization of Black Law Enforcement Executives (NOBLE), the National Sheriffs' Association (NSA) and the Police Executive Research Forum (PERF).

Chapter 33 of the CALEA training manual deals with training and career development and states, "Training has often been cited as one of the most important responsibilities in any law enforcement agency. Training serves three broad purposes. First, well-trained officers are generally better prepared to act decisively and correctly in a broad spectrum of situations. Second, training results in greater productivity and effectiveness. Third, training fosters cooperation and unity of purpose. Moreover, agencies are now being held legally accountable for the actions of their personnel and for failing to provide initial or remedial training" (*Standards for Law Enforcement Agencies*, 2006, p.33–1).

Whether an agency elects to seek the time-consuming and expensive CALEA accreditation or not, their standards can serve as guidelines in areas which an agency is updating its training programs.

Core Competencies

Means (2008, p.16) notes, "Arguably, nothing goes further toward risk management and liability prevention than assuring critical knowledge and proficiencies, i.e., the core competencies that underlie safe, effective and lawful police work." A survey of more than 400 law enforcement agencies identified 15 activities officers perform, called *core competencies*: police vehicle operations, use of force, report writing, problem-solving skills, legal authority, officer safety, ethics, cultural diversity, conflict resolution, local procedures, leadership, civil rights, community-specific skills, communication skills and self-awareness. Many of these core competencies are included in the requirements for basic certification in many departments.

Basic Certification Instruction

Some agencies require a certificate or license before they will hire an individual. Others prefer to do the training themselves. In some instances state

TABLE 7.2 Recommended Basic Training Curriculum

Topic*	Number of Hours	Percent of Total Course
Introduction to the Criminal Justice System	32	8
Law	40	10
Human Values and Problems	88	22
Patrol and Investigation Procedures	132	33
Police Proficiency	72	18
Administration	36	9
TOTAL	**400**	**100**

*The specific subjects included in each topic were as follows:

Introduction to the Criminal Justice System: An examination of the foundation and functions of the criminal justice system with specific attention to the role of the police in the system and government;

Law: An introduction to the development, philosophy, and types of law; criminal law; criminal procedure and rules of evidence; discretionary justice; application of the U.S. Constitution; court systems and procedures; and related civil law;

Human Values and Problems: Public service and noncriminal policing; cultural awareness; changing role of the police; human behavior and conflict management; psychology as it relates to the police function; causes of crime and delinquency; and police-public relations;

Patrol and Investigation Procedures: The fundamentals of the patrol function including traffic, juvenile, and preliminary investigation; reporting and communication; arrest and detention procedures; interviewing; criminal investigation and case preparation; equipment and facility use; and other day-to-day responsibilities;

Patrol Proficiency: The philosophy of when to use force and the appropriate determination of the degree necessary; armed and unarmed defense; crowd, riot, and prisoner control; physical conditioning; emergency medical services; and driver training;

Administration: Evaluation, examination, and counseling processes; department policies, rules, regulations, organization, and personnel procedures.

Source: *Report on Police* (1973). Standard 16.3, p.394.

Source: Terry D. Edwards. "State Police Basic Training Programs: An Assessment of Course Content and Instructional Methodology." *American Journal of Police*, Vol. 12, No. 4, 1993, p.27.

statutes specify a certain level of education and training before a person can become a law enforcement officer. One such state is Minnesota, whose POST board accredits colleges to provide the academic subjects (education) and a skills program. The objectives are divided into five categories: (1) practical applications and techniques, (2) the criminal justice system: civil and criminal law, (3) community policing, (4) victims and victims' rights and (5) leading, managing and communicating.

Individual agencies can expand the minimum requirements to better address their local interests and needs. Table 7.2 provides a recommended basic training curriculum, as well as the specific subjects included in each topic.

Many departments, especially the larger ones, have their own training academies for new recruits, tailored to their specific policies and procedures.

ACADEMY TRAINING FOR NEW RECRUITS

By the end of 2006, 648 state and local law enforcement academies were providing basic training to entry-level recruits in the United States. In addition to basic recruit training, 87 percent provided in-service training for active-duty officers and for officers in specialized units such as K-9 or SWAT units. A majority also provided training for first-line or higher supervisors (57 percent) and field training instructors (54 percent) (Reaves, 2009, p.1).

In 2005, an estimated 57,000 recruits entered basic training programs, which averaged 19 weeks. The average amount of classroom training was 720 hours, including firearms training (60 hours), self-defense (51 hours), health and fitness (46 hours), patrol procedures (40 hours), investigations (40 hours), emergency vehicle operations (40 hours), criminal law (36 hours) and basic first aid (24 hours). Eighty-six percent of those entering the program completed it and graduated from the academy (Reaves, 2009).

Training Models Used

The two most common models used in entry-level law enforcement training academies are the academic model and the paramilitary model. Many academies still use the paramilitary format for entry-level law enforcement training, but such institutions are under constant pressure to change to a more humanistic, academic type of training. Opponents of this type of training assert that it is outdated, it reinforces brutality and rough behavior, it is detrimental to recruiting efforts and it is generally considered to be unnecessary in training someone to be a police officer (Gundy, 2007, p.23). Yet an entrenched rationale exists for the continuation of this paramilitary model:

> These training institutions still use the paramilitary format because it is a method of training law enforcement officers. This style of training is easily criticized because it is much more difficult to complete and has been in existence longer than the more modern approaches to law enforcement training and certification.

> The longevity of this type of training alone is a testament to the effectiveness and acceptability of this style of training in the law enforcement community. There certainly is no arguing with the end product, a highly disciplined, fully functional and physically fit police officer that is capable of making decisions, as well as follow instructions.

> The paramilitary style of academy training is based on the military model because most police departments have a hierarchy (Gundy, 2007, p.23).

 Of the training models typically used for law enforcement recruits, experts recommend a blend of the paramilitary and the academic.

Most law enforcement training experts recognize the need for both approaches because the type of people becoming officers has changed. Fewer have military backgrounds—more have college educations. The traditional boot-camp approach using stress in academy training flies in the face of what is known about how adults learn. Modern adult learning principles and self-image psychology suggest that applying pressure to create a stressful response before training is *counterproductive*. Applying extreme pressure before training is as ineffective as giving new recruits handguns and expecting them to qualify before firearms training.

The academic model, in contrast, trains recruits in the necessary knowledge and skill areas. They have little or no staff contact outside the formal training. A weakness of this model is that it fails to indoctrinate recruits into the law enforcement culture, an important part of their overall training. No matter which model or combination of models is used, safety must be a prime consideration.

Safety

Two basic steps must be taken to take to ensure students' safety: designating a safety officer and establishing safety guidelines (Miller, 2009b, p.59). The safety guidelines should mandate that instructors have the proper credentials, that the students be given clear directions on the training to be given and any risks involved, that the facility and equipment be inspected before the training and that a readily identifiable extensive medical trauma kit be available on site.

ON-THE-JOB TRAINING

The most common and frequent training in law enforcement agencies is on-the-job training.

On-the-job training (OJT) may occur during field training, mentoring, in-house training sessions or roll call.

Field Training

Field training may take several forms. It might consist of rotation, which provides opportunity for additional knowledge and increased competence in a specialized area. Rotating through various specialties provides opportunity for more of the total-person approach to learning.

The most common type of on-the-job training for new recruits is done by the field training officer (FTO).

field training officer (FTO)

an experienced officer who serves as a mentor for a rookie, providing on-the-job training.

Not all law enforcement officers make good FTOs; therefore, all FTOs should be carefully selected and then thoroughly trained before instructing others. Rookie officers are assigned to an FTO who teaches them "the ropes." Recruits depend on their FTO and usually have a strong desire to please, fit in and be accepted. Although FTO programs vary from state to state, most have four primary goals (1) to apply classroom learning to real situations on the street; (2) to familiarize rookies with their beat; (3) to guide, train, monitor and evaluate; and (4) to be a role model.

The FTO approach has changed very little during the past 40-plus years and is in need of a training model that includes more contemporary approaches to policing, especially in agencies that have adopted community and problem-based learning and leadership principles (Pitts et al., 2007, p.114). In 1999 the Community Oriented Policing Services (COPS) Office provided a $300,000 grant to the Reno, Nevada, Police Department (RPD) to collaborate with the PERF to develop a new postacademy training program. From 1999 to 2001 the RPD worked with experts across the nation, surveying more than 400 police and sheriff's departments to determine what they needed in a field training program. The result was the Police Training Officer (PTO) program. With another $200,000 grant from COPS, the PTO program was implemented within the RPD and later in five other locations. Pitts et al. (p.115) explain the differences between an FTO program and the PTO program:

> The goal of the PTO program is to provide a foundation for lifelong learning that prepares new officers for the complexities of policing today and in the future. This approach is very different from traditional police training methods, which emphasize mechanical repetition skills and rote memory capabilities; by contrast, the focus of the PTO program is on developing an officer's learning ability as well as leadership and problem-solving skills. Although applied skills (e.g., weaponless defense, shooting, and defensive tactics) are essential, they constitute only one set of skills for contemporary policing. In addition to the advantages already mentioned, the PTO approach is also highly flexible, able to be tailored to each agency's needs; furthermore, because of its flexibility, it may be adjusted to meet future police training challenges.

Coaching or counseling, both forms of one-on-one field training, can also take place on the job as the need arises, as can mentoring.

Mentoring

"Mentoring is a mutually beneficial relationship in which a knowledgeable and skilled veteran officer (a mentor) provides insight, guidance and developmental opportunities to a lesser-skilled and experienced colleague (a protégé)" (Sprafka and Kranda, 2008, p.46). Mentoring is invaluable for those in both FTO and PTO programs because it provides a noncritical resource to a new officer. In other words, mentors do not critically evaluate officers as do FTOs; thus the new officer has considerably more latitude in asking questions and discussing topics that might otherwise not be approached with a FTO.

Having a mentoring program can be of value in recruiting, retention, and personnel leadership development. New sergeants may be mentored by seasoned lieutenants, new lieutenants by seasoned captains and up the chain of command. So who mentors the chief? This challenge has been addressed by a partnership of several state associations, the IACP New Police Chief Mentoring Project (IACP Mentoring project). This national project matches newer chiefs with experienced chiefs from agencies of similar size to learn how they achieved success and resolve similar problems ("State Associations of Chiefs of Police," 2008, p.33).

Jetmore (2008, p.70) notes that over the years he had several "magnificent" mentors who saw police work as a way of life, not just a job. They lived by a code of honor and had a clear sense of responsibility to pass the baton. Jetmore recommends that seasoned investigators mentor patrol officers and new detectives, and not just to teach them the technical aspects of criminal investigation, but to help improve their relationships with patrol officers: "Investigators, especially those in supervisory or command positions, should routinely liaison with their counterparts in the patrol division to work on building patrol/investigator relationships" (Jetmore, p.72). As mentors, they can help investigators improve their professional demeanor, communication style, work ethic and department. They can also explain internal and external politics, when to make an issue out of something and when not to and the like.

An additional area where mentoring can be beneficial is in helping outsiders assimilate into the department: "With the frequency in which officers are switching agencies, it is only logical that there are many new folks within departments throughout the country who are feeling like strangers in a foreign land" (Cartwright, 2009, p.50). Although the work is probably the same, every organization has its own cultures and peculiarities. A system should be in place to help outsiders assimilate rather than being left to their own devices. Assigning a mentor is an ideal way.

In-House Training Sessions

In-house or in-service training sessions are frequently used in local law enforcement departments. Specific portions of a shift may be set aside for training, which is repeated for each shift. Often trainers with the necessary knowledge, skills and ability to teach can be found within the department.

Consultants are used occasionally, although perhaps not as often as departments would like because of the expense. Consultants are used for their expertise and ability to look at problems without local bias or obligations.

© Mikael Karlsson/Arresting Images

Training can take place in the field when experienced officers, who have been through the same situations as new officers, can share information, provide solid instructions and give constructive criticism to the new recruits.

In areas where several law enforcement departments exist in proximity, it is sometimes cost effective to share training. One department, for example, might be known for its outstanding work on community relations. Another might be known for its expertise in investigating gang-related criminal activity and another for its work with juveniles. These departments might share their expertise during in-service training sessions.

Relationships might also be established with local, state and federal agencies to exchange instructors and perhaps materials on special problem areas such as drug investigations. They might also include prosecutors and courts, the coroner's office, private security consultants and social services personnel.

The traditional in-service training program designed around an 8-hour classroom day, with 50-minute classes and breaks, deserves rethinking. A suggested a new model comprises three "revolutionary components: (1) critical topics addressed in critical time, (2) a self-directed training program, and (3) a shortened training schedule" (Connolly, 2008, p.21). Not all topics require 50 minutes, and some require more. An in-service day should reflect this, with instructors being "on deck" in the event a session runs short. To give attendees an extended break equates to a waste of time for officer-students who would rather get on with the next session. Breaks should be scheduled for midmorning and midafternoon.

The second innovation allows officer-students to preselect at least part of their training program from a roster of potential classes packaged in full- or half-day groupings, with mandated topics delivered separately. With this innovation, officers attend classes in which they are actually interested. The final innovation recalls the adage, "The mind can only absorb what the seat can endure." Physical and mental fatigue sets in during 8 hours of instruction, with officers not really learning much after two or three o'clock.

Roll Call

Roll call, the short period before each shift when officers check in and receive their briefing before going on duty, can be a popular, economical time to provide training. Although roll call generally lasts only 10 to 15 minutes, it is well suited to short topics of specific, immediate interest to the frontline officer, particularly topics regarding safety. Such heightened officer interest and immediate applicability increases training success. Furthermore, training in short bursts is much more effective than long sessions for some subjects. Used wisely, those 15 minutes a day can add up to an extra 40 hours a year of training.

Grossi (2009, p.28) observes, "First- and second-line supervisors don't have to be certified trainers to teach." He (p.30) notes, "You don't have to be a pursuit-driving instructor to hand out copies of your department's pursuit policy. . . . A discussion led by an enthusiastic supervisor, coupled with some informative handouts can make for a great roll-call training session on police pursuits. Training is everyone's responsibility; don't leave it solely up to your training unit."

Because training is, at its core, concerned with risk management, it can be particularly beneficial to focus roll call on low-frequency/high-risk events or situations as a matter of continuous learning and of policy and procedure review. Examples of low-frequency/high-risk incidents include high speed pursuits, officer involved shootings, suicide by cop, bomb threats, active shooters and search and seizure-related issues. Identifying these training needs is discussed shortly.

Various online resources are available that provide training applications suitable for roll call. Some of these applications are formatted in distinct, short (five minutes or less) lesson packets with training clips and cover topics ranging from ethics to off-duty conduct to officers' obligations to provide medical assistance following a use-of-force incident.

TRAINING AT THE MANAGEMENT LEVEL

Management on-the-job training can consist of using actual past department problems and requesting managers to offer solutions. These problems are related to the department in which the manager operates. Of particular importance is effective training for newly promoted sergeants, as discussed in Chapter 3. If new sergeants are not provided with training in the skills needed to mange others, the result can be a breakdown in communication and job performance between the new supervisor and upper management and between the new supervisor and subordinates (Sharp, 2009, p.67). This promotion is a critical and challenging adjustment for the officer who, for the first time, must supervise others. Supervisors should be trained in the same topics in which their line officers receive training.

A number of approaches to management training are available. Some departments rotate the manager through divisions, giving them a total "cross-training" type of department experience. Other departments do not use rotation, and once managers are appointed, they remain in that position until their next promotion or retirement. Stagnation often reigns in such agencies. New managers may be assigned to experienced managers, who act as mentors.

Large city departments often provide their own management training, tailored to their special problems and needs. Smaller agencies use a combination of methods: lecturers from federal, state and local law enforcement agencies or special management seminars. Smaller departments may band together in training groups to share resources.

For many agencies, retirements come in clusters as officers who graduated together from the academy retire together, resulting in a significant loss of knowledge: "This mass exodus of human capital and loss of key personnel constitute a unique challenge for succession planning efforts" (Putney and Holmes, 2008, p.166). Another challenge in those departments with a paramilitary structure and its vertical chain-of-commend is the isolation of functions performed in top-level positions such as budgeting or policy making: "A newly promoted individual replacing a retiree faces a steep learning curve in a paramilitary organization where information is often secured at certain levels and in various functional areas" (Putney and Holmes, p.167). The Leadership Development Program implemented at the North Carolina State Highway Patrol provides a fairly comprehensive training curriculum for new managers, included developing competencies in communication skills, decision making, working relationships, innovation and change, leadership integrity/vision, coaching skills, use of strengths of others and self and team development (Putney and Holmes, p.169).

Management and supervisory training is available externally at the federal, state and local levels. External law enforcement management courses are available through the International City Managers Association, the IACP and the American Management Association. Courses are also available through local universities and colleges. Figure 7.4 illustrates a tool to track the professional development of police supervisors, managers and administrators. Note the diversity and length of training programs.

EXTERNAL TRAINING

Attendance at training sessions and seminars outside the department is costly, but it introduces officers to new ideas and subjects not available locally. External training provides the opportunity to meet officers from other departments and to share and appreciate the universal nature of some law enforcement problems. The real value in this type of training is the perspective that is gained by networking outside of one's home agency and learning other ways to be efficient and successful in the delivery of public services.

Possibilities for external training include local college courses; the FBI; the Northwestern Traffic Institute; the IACP; the Bureau of Alcohol, Tobacco and Firearms; the Drug Enforcement Agency; and the U.S. military branches of service. Officers should document in writing their participation in such external training.

External training may take the form of college classes, seminars, conferences, workshops, independent study and distance learning or e-learning.

Colleges and universities offer a wide variety of courses on subjects not taught by law enforcement departments. The department may pay for the tuition, fees, books and other costs, or officers may pay for them. In either case, such training usually takes place during officers' off-duty hours and may be impractical for many officers with an already overloaded schedule. Other options including seminars, conferences and off-site workshops offer attendees perspectives from other departments, but may pose scheduling problems.

Pick up any law enforcement journal and the opportunities available for training through seminars, conferences and workshops become immediately apparent.

Costs for seminars, workshops and conferences vary greatly, ranging from free (not very common) to hundreds of dollars per participant. Travel costs are also often involved. Nevertheless, this is sometimes the most effective alternative for obtaining needed expertise in a given topic. Many service clubs, such as Rotary, Kiwanis and Optimists, may financially assist law enforcement agencies with such educational opportunities.

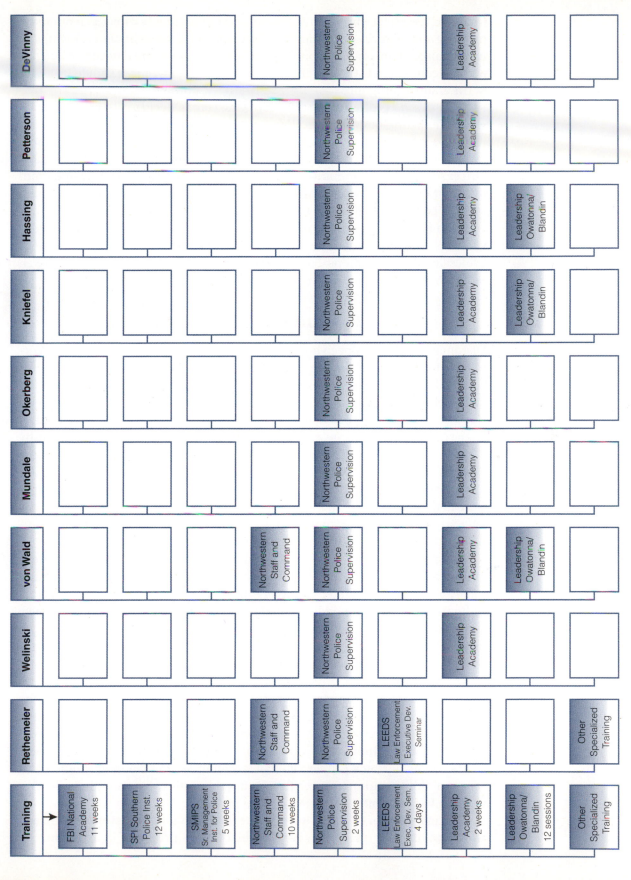

FIGURE 7.4 Professional Development Matrix

Source: Owatonna (Minnesota) Police Department

Conferences for professional law enforcement organizations also offer sessions on a wide variety of topics and have the added advantage of allowing the interchange of ideas among professionals from around the country. If budgets allow, attendance at state-level and even national conferences should be a part of the training program.

Who to send is often a key question. One way to decide is to consider who would make the best in-service instructor. Officers who attend conferences, workshops or seminars should be expected to share the information gained, usually by putting on a training session. Doing so may enhance the instructor officer's professional reputation, and it may be valuable in establishing credibility in court as an expert witness. Most of all, this enhances the agency's reputation as one that employs quality people and trains them well.

Even if the budget will not allow officers to attend conferences and conventions, the information from them is often available through publications of professional organizations. For many officers independent study is the answer, often through distance learning.

Distance or E-Learning

Distance learning has been around for many decades, beginning with the correspondence courses popular in the 1950s and 1960s. Distance learning has come a long way since then. The Internet has transformed distance learning into e-learning, making available an ever-expanding number of online courses that use interactive processes such as online discussions, audiovisual conferences and demonstrations and almost immediate feedback on work sent by e-mail and the Web. Many colleges offer complete degree programs online. Two distinct formats exist: some programs offer real-time, instructor-led online learning (synchronous) in which all participants are logged on at the same time and communicate directly with each other; in contrast, other programs have students sign on at their convenience and interact with teachers and students intermittently with a time delay (asynchronous).

E-learning is well established in university settings. A U.S. Department of Education study found that during 2006–2007, 66 percent of the two- and four-year colleges offered e-learning options, with a total enrollment of 12.2 million students nationwide (Schanlaub, 2009, p.37). Results of an intensive study comparing e-learning to classroom learning revealed, "The classroom group reported higher motivation and positive feelings concerning the instruction than did the online group. The bottom line, however, indicated that 'online training is as effective an instructional method as classroom training, and more efficient than classroom training. No meaningful learning differences occurred between the two groups, but online training was completed in almost half the time of classroom instruction and at a lesser cost'" (Schanlaub, pp.37–38). These findings provide powerful justification for e-learning opportunities considering a primary goal of law enforcement training should be to reduce liability and increase officer and public safety by providing effective training to police officers.

E-learning offers several advantages, including login systems that track who is taking the training as well as the officer's progress. In addition, the course content is consistent and up-to-date, it provides minimal adverse effects on the work schedule and brings cost savings to the training budget. On the downside, e-learning demands more self-discipline in meeting deadlines and completing assignments and provides little or no hands-on experience for technical classes. E-learning is just one way for officers at all levels to continue to learn throughout their career.

ONGOING TRAINING—LIFELONG LEARNING

Before getting the job, as a rookie, upon promotion to sergeant and beyond—throughout a law enforcement career—training should be ongoing: "A good police officer never stops learning on the job and off" (Petrocelli, 2009, p.16). Regardless of the methods used, training must be continuous because people fail to remember a high percentage of what they learned. In addition, new subjects continually arise that must be learned, including new laws and court decisions: "Law enforcement is an ever-evolving profession. We must be as proactive about our education as we are about making arrests, and current training is essential to that mission. Even though many departments have cut their training budgets, the innovative officer still has many low-cost options available for good police training" (Petrocelli, p.19). FLETC, mentioned earlier, is one of the best resources for free law enforcement training.

 Officers' training should be ongoing—lifelong learning.

Among the basics requiring periodic review are report writing, cultural diversity, Fourth Amendment and constitutional requirements and ethical dilemmas, in addition to the obvious and perishable skills of firearms qualification and self-defense. Management should work with trainers to periodically assess even established in-house training programs such as firearm training.

The Training Cycle

Because effective training is ongoing, it can be viewed as a cycle.

 The training cycle consists of need identification, goal setting, program development, program implementation, program evaluation, then back, full circle, to assessment of need based on the evaluation.

Need Identification

Training programs must emphasize actual individual and department goals. Needs come to light from officers' conversations, supervisors' and managers' observations, complaints, officers' suggestions and other sources. Training needs of officers at various levels of experience can be determined in a number of ways. Among the most common are

- Reviewing new statutes that affect police operations and investigations.
- Taking department surveys.
- Reviewing reports and noting deficiencies.
- Reviewing internal and external complaints as well as lawsuits against the agency.
- Analyzing specific law enforcement functions.
- Interviewing line officers, detectives, managers and supervisors.
- Getting input from other agencies and the community.

These various methods of identifying training needs are likely to indicate which subjects are considered priorities, as well as various types and levels of training needed in any given department.

As mentioned several times in this chapter, training is primarily about managing or reducing risk, and low-frequency/high-risk situations present a certain training need for all departments. A training criticality matrix (Figure 7.5) is a useful tool for assessing potential training topics. The vertical axis of the matrix identifies the frequency with which an event or procedure occurs (from seldom to often); the horizontal axis indicates the value of the consequences of poor performance because of deficiencies in officers' collective knowledge, skills and abilities (from modest to dire). Bradley (2009, p.29) explains the priority levels and the implications for training:

> Quadrant A: Little opportunity for performance-based assessment or reinforcement by supervisor. Situation should be simulated for training and performance evaluation.
>
> Quadrant B: Frequently occurring, although consequences could be serious, or infrequently occurring, but consequences are not very severe. Selection for periodic retraining may be based on supervisor feedback and calculated "return on investment."
>
> Quadrant C: Frequently occurring with minimum consequences. Periodic retraining is usually unnecessary. Proficiency in this activity is monitored and reinforced by supervision. . . .

The risk manager will recommend training investments be focused first on the procedures or activities that intersect on quadrant A. Annual training to address topics relevant to quadrant B would be considered second. . . . If the assumptions regarding frequency, criticality and supervisors' roles are correct, the risk manager would recommend little or no training resources by expended for matters in quadrant C.

Examples of events or procedures falling within the four quadrants include (Bradley, 2009, p.29)

- Quadrant A (low frequency, high risk): shooting under low light conditions, administering CPR, using shock-control devices
- Quadrant B_1 (low frequency, low risk): splint broken arm/leg, administering blood-alcohol concentration (BAC) test on driving while intoxicated (DWI) suspect, transporting an injured individual to a medical facility performing liquor license scrutiny

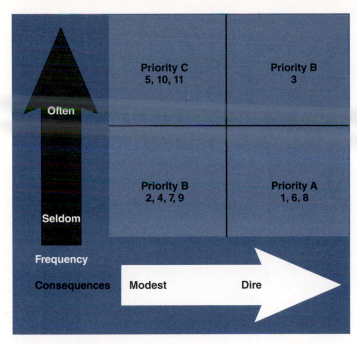

Quadrant A: Little opportunity for performance-based assessment or reinforcement by supervisor. Situation should be simulated for training and performance evaluation.

Quadrant B: Frequently occurring, although consequences could be serious, or infrequently occurring, but consequences are not very severe. Selection for periodic retraining may be based on supervisor feedback and calculated "return on investment."

Quadrant C: Frequently occurring with minimum consequences. Periodic retraining is usually unnecessary. Proficiency in this activity is monitored and reinforced by supervision.

1 Shoot under low light conditions
2 Splint broken arm/leg
3 Conduct car stop
4 Administer BAC test on DWI suspect
5 Issue parking ticket
6 Administer CPR
7 Transport injured to medical facility
8 Use of shock-control device
9 Perform liquor license scrutiny
10 Complete vehicle accident report
11 Distribute anti-crime literature

FIGURE 7.5 Training Criticality Matrix

Source: Patrick L. Bradley, "Designing the Annual Training Curriculum: a Team Effort." *The Police Chief,* November 2009, pp.26–31, IACP.

- Quadrant B_2 (high frequency, high risk): conducting a traffic stop
- Quadrant C (high frequency, low risk): issuing a parking ticket, completing a vehicle crash report, distributing anticrime literature

Once a specific need has been identified, goals for meeting that need should be set.

Goal Setting

As with any type of goal setting, training goals should reflect specific training objectives that are specific and observable, are measurable with a set criteria and have a clear timeline for achievement: "The instructional goal simply makes an umbrella statement about what it is you're trying to accomplish with the training" (Molnar, 2009a, p.16).

Program Development

After the needs have been identified and the goals and objectives specified, the actual training program must be developed or, for existing programs, revised based on the needs assessment. This usually includes determining the subject matter and objectives; selecting the most appropriate method(s); selecting/writing materials, audiovisual aids and tests; selecting the instructor and attendees; and scheduling the attendees.

Managers, by their position, should be constantly providing individual, on-the-job training, helping subordinates grow and develop. Managers may also schedule more formal training sessions and present information themselves. They may seek assistance from an expert within the department. Or they may bring in someone from outside the department. Whether managers do the actual training or not, they are responsible for ensuring it is effective and meets their subordinates' needs. The ultimate responsibility is theirs.

Program Implementation

Implementation is where it all comes together and the program is put into action. Often, however, implementation does not go as planned. Most programs face implementation challenges, and the ability of project planners to respond effectively to these challenges often marks the difference between a successful program and one that fails to achieve its goals (Cissner and Farole, 2009). Identifying what is not working is just as important as identifying that which is. But researchers are often reluctant to admit failures. The Center for Court Innovation has identified four key issues that can make or break a new initiative: (1) engaging in comprehensive planning, (2) identifying key stakeholders, (3) responding to emerging challenges and (4) recognizing the need for leadership (Cissner and Farole, p.2).

Program Evaluation

Like training, evaluation should be continuous. The officers' grasp of the material should be tested in the classroom and on the job. Such evaluation will help determine whether further training is needed in a specific area. Clearly stated performance objectives are critical to program evaluation, allowing students to understand what is expected and instructors to know what the evaluation parameters are (Molnar, 2009b, p.18). They also make it easier to create and track evaluation documents. Remember: "If it isn't documented, it didn't happen."

formative assessment

uses informative gathered during instruction to adjust and improve program content and training.

Two ways to determine a student's learning success are formative assessment and summative assessment (Molnar, 2009c, p.16). **Formative assessment** uses informative gathered during instruction to adjust and improve program content and training. **Summative assessment** involves tests given at the end of a predetermined period that assesses proficiency: written exams, end-of-week quizzes, end-of-training exams.

With the preponderance of technology now playing a significant role in policing, proficiency testing in this area is vital, to ascertain that officers know how to properly use the technology they have been provided. However, this area has been neglected by many managers and supervisors, particularly those who have more time on the job and who, perhaps, lack a high degree of comfort in using such technology themselves.

summative assessment

involves tests given at the end of a predetermined period that assess proficiency: written exams, end-of-week quizzes, end-of-training exams.

In addition to evaluating if learners have been successful, trainers should consider having the trainees complete an evaluation of the session, responding to such questions as

- How effective was the instructor?
- How interesting was the session?
- How relevant was the material?
- How was the pacing of the session?
- What did you like most about the training?
- What could be improved?

Trainees should then be observed to see if they apply their new knowledge and skills on the job. One effective nontest way to evaluate training effectiveness is to compare officers' performance before and after training. This can be accomplished through their immediate superior's observations, as well as by asking the attendees if the training was valuable in their job. Other before-and-after information that might reflect the effectiveness of training can be obtained from records of complaints, grievances, absenteeism, turnover and the like.

Cost and Facilities

The money budgeted for training varies greatly from department to department. In addition to costs for instructors and materials, the cost of officers' salaries during training should also be factored in. Training costs can be cut by sharing resources with other departments, cohosting training, using FBI programs, seeking scholarships for officers to attend training and seeking sponsors for officers.

The type of training, method of instruction and audiovisuals will affect the physical facilities needed. The facility should be conducive to learning and to two-way communication. It should be well lit and well ventilated, contain adequate seating and writing surfaces and have good acoustics. Depending on the size of the group, a small, wireless microphone may be necessary to allow the trainer freedom of movement.

BENEFITS OF EFFECTIVE TRAINING PROGRAMS

Training programs can benefit individual officers, supervisors, managers, the entire department and the community. Benefits for individual officers include improved chances for career success, increased motivation, improved morale, increased productivity, greater feelings of self-worth, reduced chances of injury on the job, greater confidence, pride, improved work attitudes and increased job satisfaction.

Among the many benefits supervisors of those trained might enjoy are getting to know officers better, furthering their own advancement and career, gaining more time, establishing better human relations, increased confidence in officers' abilities, increased flexibility, increased creativity, fewer discipline problems and mistakes, and improved discipline.

Many benefits enjoyed by individual managers also benefit the entire agency. In addition, the organization and ultimately the community benefit from training in more efficient, effective officers; increased quantity and quality of work; reduced turnover, absenteeism, waste, complaints and grievances; greater public support; and increased departmental pride.

THE LEARNING ORGANIZATION

A learning organization is one in which talented people are provided with growth opportunities that keep them learning and that can help recruitment as well as retention (Cartwright, 2008, pp.72–75). Such an environment can be characterized by three indicators.

First, how do individuals view their current assignments? Do they view the organization as a system where every action taken affects other parts of the system rather than limiting their field of vision to their specific assignments? Second, how do individuals view their coworkers? Is there a balance between competition and cooperation, both of which are important for organizational health. Without dialogue, command staff could fall into groupthink, discussed in Chapter 5. Third, how do individuals interpret the "processes" in the agency. Are they open to change? Is there an atmosphere where ignorance is not considered weakness and where continuous, lifelong learning is not just encouraged but is viewed as a fundamental value? Is there a willingness to learn from one another, to continually strive to improve the processes and avoid the faulty thinking of relying on what has worked in the past? Cartwright (2008, p.75) contends

> Developing a learning organization is an investment in people, and investments take time to mature. However, if true leaning takes place, the return is immeasurable. . . .

> In a learning organization, more people throughout the agency will have a voice. Also, members will be more inclined to identify their individual purpose in the grand scheme of things. In a healthy organization, that voice and purpose will serve the overall goals of the agency. It will be reflected in employee retention as well as provide law enforcement a competitive edge for the diminishing pool of talent for which the public sector must compete. Once the door is unlocked to learning, the possibilities are endless, the vision becomes clear, and the direction is full steam ahead!

SUMMARY

Training generally refers to vocational instruction that takes place on the job and deals with physical skills. Educating generally refers to academic instruction that takes place in a college, university or seminar-type setting and deals with knowledge and understanding.

Developing human resources through ongoing training should be managers' single most important objective. Two areas often involved in civil lawsuits are failure to train and for trainees' injuries sustained during training. Keys to avoiding civil liability related to training are to provide first-rate training, to thoroughly document such training and to require thorough reports on any incident that could lead to a lawsuit.

Three variables that affect learning are individual variables, task or information variables and environmental or instructional variables. The three general categories of learners, or learning styles, are visual, auditory and kinesthetic.

Job analysis is the key to determining the content to teach and test. When content relates directly to the tasks to be performed, it is considered valid. Tests that measure competence in these tasks are then also valid. Training can focus on knowledge, skills or attitudes.

Important learning principles include the following: base training on an identified need; tell officers the learning objective; tell officers why they need to learn the material; make sure officers have the necessary background to master the skill (the prerequisites) and provide a way to acquire the prerequisites; present the material using the most appropriate materials and methods available; when possible, use variety; adapt the materials and methods to individual officers' needs; allow officers to be as active and involved as possible during training; engage as many senses as possible; break complex tasks into simple, easy-to-understand steps; use repetition and practice to enhance remembering; give officers periodic feedback on how they are performing; and whenever possible, present the "big picture"—teach an understandable concept rather than relying on simple memorization or rote learning.

Instructional methods include lecture, question/answer sessions, discussion, video-conferencing, demonstration, hands-on learning, role playing, case studies and simulations, including digital game-based learning. Online learning and training is also becoming a popular method of instruction.

Instructional materials include printed information; visuals; bulletin boards; audiocassettes, videocassettes and DVDs; television programs; and computer programs. The Law Enforcement Television Network (LETN) is a private satellite television system that provides current programs on a variety of law enforcement subjects; it is available through subscription.

Other organizations available to assist with training include the National Association of Field Training Officers (NAFTO), the Federal Law Enforcement Training Center (FLETC), the National Center for State and Local Training, the Southern Police Institute, the FBI National Police Academy, and the FBI itself.

Of the models of training typically used for law enforcement recruits, experts recommend a blending of the paramilitary and the academic. On-the-job training may occur during field training, mentoring, in-house training sessions or roll call. The most common type of on-the-job training for new recruits is done by the field training officer, or FTO. External training may take the form of college classes, seminars, conferences, workshops, independent study and distance or e-learning.

Officers' training should be ongoing—lifelong learning. The training cycle consists of need identification, goal setting, program development, program implementation, program evaluation, then back, full circle, to assessment of needs based on the evaluation.

CHALLENGE SEVEN

Captain Hayley is responsible for the annual training plan for the Greenfield Police Department. During Chief Slaughter's crime-fighting tenure, Captain Hayley scheduled frequent training for all officers in the use of firearms, defensive tactics and enforcing criminal statutes. He scheduled training in pursuit driving and emergency medical response on a two-year rotation. Specialized training was provided to individual officers on an "as needed" basis. The training was usually conducted in an academy setting.

Chief Slaughter required his officers to train and qualify with their firearms every month—three times more often than required by POST. As a result, the department won the state shooting competition 10 years in a row. During those 10 years, Greenfield officers have fired their weapons on duty only to dispatch injured animals. Ammunition and officer overtime for training at the firearms range were the largest expenditures in the department's training budget.

The new chief has asked Captain Hayley to develop a training program with more emphasis on developing human resources and community policing. He suggested that some of the funds devoted to firearms training be used for other training.

1. Was the training provided by Chief Slaughter job related and appropriate for the tasks performed by his officers?

2. Captain Hayley should consider some fundamental changes in the training program if he wants to emphasize a community-policing strategy rather than a crime-fighting strategy. How might the blend of training verses educating change?

3. Suggest three specific topics for Captain Hayley's new training curriculum that relate to community policing.

4. The new chief is encouraging a participative management style within the department. In the past, the captains and Chief Slaughter determined the department's training needs. How can Captain Hayley reflect the department's new direction in how he selects training?

5. Training resources are often limited. POST-required and liability-driven training can consume a significant portion of the budget. What innovative training techniques might Captain Hayley explore to save money and ensure high-quality training? Describe three possible innovations.

6. If Captain Hayley reduces firearms training and adds communications training, he is likely to face resistance from the officers. Why? How can he circumvent a dispute over this change in the training curriculum?

 ## DISCUSSION QUESTIONS

1. How would you compare and contrast training and education?

2. Which instructional methods do you think are most effective? Least effective?

3. Which instructional materials do you think are most effective? Least effective?

4. What is the role of the employee in self-development?

5. When would you use a group or conference method of training?

6. When would you use external training programs?

7. What are the major considerations in developing a law enforcement training program?

8. What would you include in a law enforcement training philosophy statement?

9. What five subjects do you consider most essential for a management development training program?

10. What training could be conducted during a cutback budgeting period and still provide reasonable training?

 ## REFERENCES

Bertomen, Lindsey. "Using Drones: For Today's Generation the Training Paradigm Has Changed." *Law Enforcement Technology*, September 2009, pp.85–89.

Bradley, Patrick L. "Designing the Annual Training Curriculum: A Team Effort." *The Police Chief*, November 2009, pp.26–31.

Carpenter, Michael. "Law Enforcement Liability Concerns." *Police and Security News*, November/December 2009, pp.14–19.

Cartwright, George. "A Learning Organization." *Law and Order*, September 2008, pp.71–76.

Cartwright, George. "Mentoring for the Transition." *Law and Order*, April 2009, pp.50–52.

Cissner, Amanda B., and Farole, Donald J. Jr., *Avoiding Failures of Implementation.* Washington, DC: Bureau of Justice Assistance, June 2009.

Connolly, John. "Rethinking Police Training." *The Police Chief,* November 2008, pp.18–22.

Frederick, Steve. "What Makes a Good Instructor?" *9-1-1 Magazine,* November/December 2008, pp.86–87.

Galvin, Bob. "Know When to Retrain?" *Law Enforcement Technology,* October 2007, pp.38–47.

Griffith, David. "Sound and Vision." *Police,* June 2007, pp.36–39.

Griffith, David. "Teaching to the Test." *Police,* March 2008, pp.46–50.

Grossi, Dave. "Roll-Call Training Tactics." *Law Officer Magazine,* March 2009, pp.26–30.

Gundy, Jess. "Paramilitary Training in Police Academies." *Law and Order,* June 2007, pp.22–30.

Harrison, Bob. "Gamers, Millennials, and Generation Next: Implications for Policing." *The Police Chief,* October 2007, pp.150–160.

Jetmore, Larry F. "Show the Way." *Law Officer Magazine,* March 2008, pp.70–74.

Kozlowski, Jonathan. "Video Games: Not Just Jumping for Coins." *Law Enforcement Technology,* March 2008, pp.10–16.

Means, Randy. "Integrating Training." *Law and Order,* June 2008, pp.16–19.

Miller, R. K. "Classroom Characters." *Law Officer Magazine,* August 2008, pp.90–97.

Miller, R. K. "Characteristics of a Good Instructor." *Law Officer Magazine,* January 2009a, pp.56–59.

Miller, R. K. "Safety First: Two Components of a Safe Training Environment." *Law Officer Magazine,* March 2009b, pp.58–62.

Molnar, J. P. "Training by Design, Part 1." *Law Officer Magazine,* March 2009a, pp.14–18.

Molnar, J. P. "Training by Design, Part 2." *Law Officer Magazine,* April 2009b, pp.14–18.

Molnar, J. P. "Training by Design, Part 3." *Law Officer Magazine,* May 2009c, pp.16–24.

Murray, Ken. "It's a State of Mind." *Law Officer Magazine,* September 2007a, pp.60–63.

Murray, Ken. "The Paper Trail." *Law Officer Magazine,* August 2007b, pp.76–80.

Murray, Ken. "Risk Aversion: The Pros and Cons." *Law Officer Magazine,* February 2008a, pp.60–61.

Murray, Ken. "Training Tips." *Law Officer Magazine,* August 2008b, pp.98–102.

Nowicki, Ed. "Managing a Training Unit." *Law and Order,* November 2008, pp.20–25.

Petrocelli, Joseph. "Continuing Police Education." *Police,* September 2009, pp.16–19.

Pitts, Steven; Glensor, Ronald W.; and Peak, Kenneth J. "The Police Training Officer (PTO) Program: A Contemporary Approach to Postacademy Recruit Training." *The Police Chief,* August 2007, pp.114–121.

Putney, Deanna M., and Holmes, Cordelia L. "Designing a Law Enforcement Leadership Development Program." *The Police Chief,* October 2008, pp.166–171.

Reaves, Brian A. *State and Local Law Enforcement Training Academies, 2006.* Washington, DC: Bureau of Justice Statistics Special Report, February 2009. (NCJ 222987)

Rutledge, Devallis. "Saving Money through Training." *Police,* May 2009, pp.68–71.

Schanlaub, Russ. "Online Training." *Law and Order,* April 2009, pp.36–43.

Sharp, Kelly. "The Importance of Training New Sergeants." *Law and Order,* March 2009, pp.67–70.

Smith, Dave. "The Long Road to Utah." *Police,* December 2008a, p.72.

Smith, Dave. "The Value of 'War Stories.'" *Police,* October 2008b, p.96.

Sprafka, Harvey, and Kranda, April H. "Institutionalizing Mentoring in Police Departments." *The Police Chief,* January 2008, pp.46–49.

Standards for Law Enforcement Agencies, 5th ed. Fairfax, VA: Commission on Accreditation for Law Enforcement Agencies, Inc., 2006.

"State Associations of Chiefs of Police Partner to Provide Mentoring Resources for New Chiefs." *The Police Chief,* January 2008, pp.33–37.

Werth, Eric P. "Adult Learning: Similarities in Training Methods and Recruits Learning Characteristics." *The Police Chief,* November 2009, pp.42–45.

CITED CASES

Board of County Commissioners v. Brown, 520 U.S. 397 (1997)
City of Canton, Ohio v. Harris, 489 U.S. 378 (1989)

Davis v. Mason County, 502 U.S. 899 (1991)

ADDITIONAL RESOURCES

Lexipol—www.lexipol.com—According to the company's web site: Lexipol [is] the country's leading provider of risk management resources for public safety organizations … [with] services includ[ing] web based policy manuals and procedure manuals that contain solid, realistic, ongoing and verifiable training.

CHAPTER EIGHT

Promoting Growth and Development

If we all did the things we are capable of, we would astound ourselves.

—Thomas Edison

DO YOU KNOW?

- What the workplace culture is?
- What norms are and why they are important?
- Where an officer's first loyalty must lie?
- How managers can shape the workplace culture?
- What the Johari Window describes?
- What a necessary first step for growth and development is?
- What touchstone values and daily values are and how they are related?
- What a balanced performer manager is?
- What stages of growth people typically go through?
- How someone might develop a positive image?
- In what areas of cultural awareness law enforcement officers need development?
- What ethics entails and how to develop ethical behavior?
- What the key elements of corrupt behavior are?
- Why it is important to help officers grow and develop?

CAN YOU DEFINE?

balanced performer managers

balancing

code of silence

cultural awareness

daily values

ethics

ghosting

holistic personal goals

integrity

Johari Window

norms

racial profiling

touchstone values

unconditional backup

INTRODUCTION

Law enforcement managers have two obligations as developers: developing themselves and developing their subordinates. These are normally accomplished simultaneously. Because managing is getting work done through others, you will get the best from subordinates by developing their abilities. This is not always accomplished by being the "good guy." It is pleasant to have good interpersonal relationships with all workers, but it is not always possible. There are times for praise and times for discipline.

CHAPTER at a GLANCE

This chapter begins by discussing job descriptions and the workplace culture. Discussed next are the importance of developing positive interpersonal relationships and of goal setting. This is followed by a look at balanced performer managers and how they might empower those who report to them. Then the discussion turns to the stages of growth employees go through, approaches to developing positive attitudes, a positive image, cultural awareness and a sense of ethics and integrity. The chapter concludes with a discussion of the long-range importance of developing personnel; how managers can be motivators for change; and how they might evaluate the workplace climate for growth, development and change within their department.

JOB DESCRIPTIONS

A job description is a detailed, formally stated summary of duties and responsibilities for a position. It usually contains the position title, supervisor, education and experience required, salary, duties, responsibilities and job details. Job details make a specific position different from all others in an organization. Patrol officers' duties are different from those of detectives. Likewise, the duties of sergeants, lieutenants and chiefs differ.

Job descriptions are not limiting or restrictive. They are simply minimum requirements, and the job description should make this clear. Employees who can expand these tasks or do them differently and better should be encouraged to do so. Job descriptions provide the basis for getting work done and for setting expectations and standards for evaluating job performance.

Tasks must be broadly stated and leave room for growth, change and expansion. Job descriptions should also be reviewed at least annually, when some tasks may be eliminated and others added. For example, after September 11, 2001, many departments shifted resources from the war on drugs to the war on terrorism. Law enforcement managers must respond to this national interest.

All law enforcement personnel have opportunities to expand their tasks and perform them better. Any law enforcement task can be done better, with greater total effect. Managers need to use every available resource to develop the best in each individual and the team. One key is a positive work culture.

THE WORKPLACE CULTURE

The workplace culture is evident in any organization. Visit a high-powered law firm and you are likely to encounter a well-dressed staff member who greets you quite formally. Visit the local newspaper, and you are likely to encounter a casually dressed staff member who greets you quite informally. Further, within many workplace cultures, subcultures exist. Within an advertising agency, for example, the sales force may dress up, whereas the creative staff may favor T-shirts and blue jeans. Each workplace develops its own culture.

 The workplace culture is the sum of the beliefs and values shared by those within the organization, which formally and informally communicate their expectations.

These beliefs and values are a type of "collective conscience" by which those within the group judge each other. Vernon (2008, p.76) explains the importance of an organization's cultural values to managers:

> Organizational culture is recognized as a powerful force that impacts the behavior of its members. Leaders who want to exert powerful influence on their followers work hard to establish a culture that supports their values. The culture of an organization is often a more powerful influence on the behavior of its members than the explicit orders and directives coming from above.
>
> Organizational culture is derived from customs, rituals and values of the organization, the organization's history and how an organization's members interact with one another and with those outside the organization.

The Police Culture

Young men and women entering law enforcement are usually idealistic and ready to make a difference in the world. They are eager to learn and emulate veteran officers. This transformation of the police officer's identity and self-image may be more radical than in many other fields. Research shows that police recruits enter the profession with high ideals and standards. However, with exposure to the occupation, attitudes and values may undergo significant change and soon differ from attitudes of the general population.

Many officers become furiously loyal to others in the department and begin to see a separation between themselves and society. They perceive, and often rightly so, that their very lives depend on supporting one another. This perspective is a defining element of the police culture. Whether it is called the Blue Wall, the Thin Blue Line, the Brotherhood or something else, it all means the same. If you carry a badge, you're family. Every individual is bound by the oath taken when they become police officers. This simple pledge transcends positions and rank, gender and race. It inspires **unconditional backup**—physically, psychologically, emotionally and ethically binding recruits to the core ideals of the profession.

The police culture has been extensively written about and is sometimes described as isolationist, elitist and authoritarian. Within some departments there is no clear mission statement, and conflict occurs between officers who see themselves as crime fighters and those who prefer the social-service role emphasized in community policing, as discussed in Chapter 2.

Table 8.1 describes five distinct groups of officers identified by research. The first two groups describe what is often thought of as the traditional officer. Within a law enforcement agency, most or all of these groups can be found. Which group predominates will determine the dominant culture of that agency, which will also be reflected in its norms.

Norms

What is important within any department is expressed as norms.

 Norms are the attitudes and beliefs held by the members of a group.

Norms are, in effect, what is "normal." Most people do not want to be considered "abnormal," so they do and say what others expect of them, for example:

- Do the job the way you're told.
- It's okay to be late.
- Never give so many citations that you make your colleagues look bad.

These norms are enforced by putting pressure on those who do not conform. Norms can hurt or help managers. Negative work norms can destroy morale and decrease performance; positive norms can heighten morale and improve performance. Two norms common in many police departments are a fierce loyalty to one another and the accompanying **code of silence**, the unwillingness to reveal any misconduct by fellow officers, discussed later in the chapter.

---

unconditional backup

dictates that other officers must take action, get involved and back each other up physically, psychologically, emotionally and ethically.

norms

attitudes and beliefs held by a group of individuals.

code of silence

encourages officers not to speak up when they see another officer doing something wrong.

TABLE 8.1 Attitudinal Expectations for Group Formation

	Group 1: Tough-Cops	Group 2: Clean-Beat Crime-Fighters	Group 3: Avoiders	Group 4: Problem-Solvers	Group 5: Professionals
Citizens	(–) citizens are hostile and uncooperative	(–) citizens are unappreciative	(–) citizens do not understand the police	(+) help citizens get to the root of problems	(+) maintain positive rapport with citizens
Supervisors	(–) supervisors are unsupportive	(–) supervisors are unsupportive	(–) or (+/–) pacify supervisors to keep out of trouble	(+) especially in more community policing departments	(+) value supervisory approval
Procedural guidelines	(–) they do more harm than anything	(+) value these due process safeguards	(–) viewed as obstacles	(–) too restrictive, impede efforts to solve problems	(+) accept the limitations placed on them
Law enforcement	(+) narrow role orientation that only includes law enforcement	(+) very rigid law enforcement orientation	(–) or (+/–) believe in only handling unavoidable (i.e., serious) crimes	(–) or (+/–) not the most important/ defining function for an officer	(+) accept this role, though not rigid or inflexible
Order maintenance	(–) if handle, do so informally (not regarded as real police work)	(+) as long as they can handle them formally (i.e., ticket or arrest) part of role	(–) would only create more work	(+) expansive role orientation in handling citizen problems	(+) value roles beyond crime fighting
Community policing	(–) not real policing	(–) may impede their efforts to fight street crime	(–) would only create more work	(+) expansive role orientation	(+) expansive role orientation
Aggressiveness	(+) believe in aggressive style of patrol, part of image	(+) believe in aggressive style of patrol in controlling all illegality	(–) only increases chances to get into trouble	(–) usually only results in negative consequences for citizens	(–) or (+/–) exception rather than the norm
Selectivity	(+) believe in handling only real (i.e., serious) violations formally	(–) believe in pursuing and handling all forms (i.e., minor and serious) of illegal behavior	(+) believe in handling only unavoidable serious offenses that, if not handled, would bring undue negative attention to them	(+) discretionary informal judgment (over strict law enforcement) valued in handling problems	(–) handle full range of offenses, though do not feel the need to handle all formally (i.e., ticket or arrest)

Note: (+/−) indicates neutral attitudes.
Source: From Eugene A. Paoline, III. "Shedding Light on Police Culture: An Examination of Officers' Occupational Attitudes." *Police Quarterly*, June 2004, p.211. Reprinted by permission.

The Us vs. Them mentality is usually present within the minds of those who participate in the code of silence. The code of silence and the Us vs. Them phenomenon often bond together. The result is intense loyalty, a positive feature of the police culture if it is loyalty to principles.

 An officer's first loyalty must be to defend the Constitution and laws of the United States, his or her state constitution and laws and local laws.

Changing the Workplace Culture

The most effective way to transform the organizational culture of a law enforcement agency into an atmosphere that embraces loyalty to principle above all else is a combination of leadership, role modeling and training.

Managers can shape the workplace culture by
1. **Identifying existing norms.**
2. **Evaluating the norms—do they work for or against the department's mission?**
3. **Encouraging positive norms and trying to eliminate negative ones through modeling and training.**

The best subculture in an organization might be held up as an example from which others can learn. Do not expect change overnight—it may take several months. Perhaps most important, live the culture you want. Walk the talk.

Within the workplace culture, managers and their subordinates can grow and develop personally and professionally. The culture must expect, encourage and reward growth. Establishing a nurturing workplace culture depends on developing positive interpersonal relationships.

DEVELOPING POSITIVE INTERPERSONAL RELATIONSHIPS

Developing good manager–subordinate relations requires fairness, trust and confidence on everyone's part. It is not always the formal relationships, important as they are, that establish a rapport between manager and subordinate. It is a two-way feeling of respect, regard and trust.

Consider the employee who says, "I would do anything for the boss I have now. He demands a lot, but he is fair, and I trust that he will do what he says." More than likely this employee's manager has emotional maturity, displays confidence without being overbearing, knows his and the subordinate's job, would not ask the subordinate to do anything he would not do, expresses confidence in the subordinate and deals with the subordinate with compassion. Mutual respect develops when both manager and subordinate deal with each other in the same way.

Sutton (2007, pp.47–48) notes, "Unfortunately, fate or providence all too often places an officer who is in the formative stage of career evolution within the supervisory orbit of an unqualified, uncaring or incompetent sergeant. This can have far-reaching effects that seep into the future of a law enforcement organization." He gives as an example a management meeting he attended as a sergeant with other sergeants and their lieutenant. One sergeant complained about the attitudes of the young cops in his squad. The lieutenant said he had overheard a member of that squad complaining about his sergeant in a bar a few days before. To Sutton's surprise, the sergeant was not embarrassed but was pleased and said with a grin, "Well, there you go, LT. Now you know I'm doing my job, don't you? The more those little bastards hate me, the more work I'm getting out of them." The sergeant believed he was an effective leader, but in reality the legacy he left officers who came under his command was one of hate, distrust and failure. Sutton (p.48) explains that managers at each level of an organization leave a legacy. He contends,

> Law enforcement leadership begins at the field-training officer level and continues to the head of the organization. As a leader, you have a responsibility

to create an environment in which the needs of the organization and the needs of the employees meld together to accomplish the mission. The mission is not just getting the job done, but having a workforce that wants to get it done right.

Legacy Based Leadership is simple. You must understand that each interaction with another human being is like a microcosm of life itself. It has a beginning, a life span and an end. Knowing that you control what people think about you when you walk away is at the core of controlling your legacy.

Leadership is both an honor and a privilege. You owe it to those who follow you to leave a legacy of justice, unity and compassion.

Self-Disclosure and Feedback

An important part of developing relationships is for managers to get to know each member of the work unit better and, in the process, get to know themselves better. A model termed the **Johari Window** (named after the authors Joe and Harry) illustrates how people can learn more about others and themselves. The model is based on the premise that everyone has four parts to their identity, as Figure 8.1 illustrates.

> **Johari Window**
> a model to illustrate how people can learn more about others and themselves.

Your *open self* is what you know about yourself and what you show to others. Your *hidden self* is the secret part that you do not share with others. Your *blind self* is the part of you that others can see but you do not know about yourself. Your *undiscovered* or *subconscious self* is the part of you that neither you nor others have yet discovered.

 The Johari Window describes four parts of identity: the open self, the hidden self, the blind self and the subconscious or undiscovered self.

According to this model, through the process of self-disclosure and feedback—that is, honest interaction with others—you can widen the area of openness, reduce the hidden and blind parts and learn something about your undiscovered self. Honest, open interaction with subordinates can help *everyone* within the workplace culture grow and develop. The direction this growth and development takes depends on the goals that are set.

Goal Setting

The importance of organizational goals has been discussed. Within organizational goals, managers should include growth and development, both individual and organizational. Remember that goals are targets: specific, measurable outcomes with a timeline.

 Personal and organizational goals are a necessary first step for growth and development.

FIGURE 8.1

The Johari Window

Source: From TIMM/STEAD. *Supervision*, 2E. © South-Western, a part of Cengage Learning, Inc. Reproduced by permission. www.cengage.com/permissions

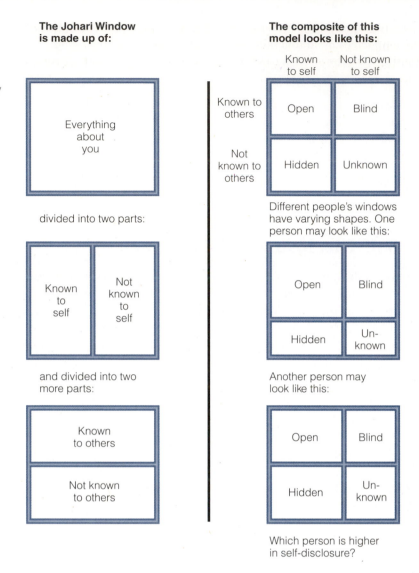

The Johari Window is made up of:

Everything about you

divided into two parts:

Known to self

Not known to self

and divided into two more parts:

Known to others

Not known to others

The composite of this model looks like this:

	Known to self	Not known to self
Known to others	Open	Blind
Not known to others	Hidden	Unknown

Different people's windows have varying shapes. One person may look like this:

Open	Blind
Hidden	Un-known

Another person may look like this:

Open	Blind
Hidden	Un-known

Which person is higher in self-disclosure?

Goals should be (1) stated positively, (2) realistic and attainable and (3) personally important. A personal goal states what, when and how much. The *what* is the specific result to achieve. The *when* is the target date by which the goal will be reached. The *how much* is, whenever possible, a quantifiable measure. Law enforcement managers may set a goal of "talking to their subordinates about organizational and personal problems." They may help subordinates set their goals, which should be discussed and then written down. A specific period should be established to accomplish the goals, and progress should be reviewed at the end of that period.

An example of an unrealistic goal would be that all officers become expert sharpshooters. Varied levels of shooting ability exist. A more realistic goal would be that all officers take firearms range practice and qualify.

Goal setting, goal achievement and ultimate performance are directly related. It is exciting to realize that few people use more than 20 to 30 percent of their potential. People have few limits except those they impose on themselves. The 4-minute mile was considered impossible—until Roger Bannister ran it. The 7-foot high jump and the 17-foot pole vault are other examples of the impossible achieved.

Untapped potential exists in managers and their people. The task is to create an exciting workplace in which people want to grow and develop and are helped to do so.

Holistic Goal Setting

Although managers are not technically responsible for their subordinates' off-the-job activities and aspirations, people have much more to them than their jobs. Indeed, a common problem of law enforcement officers is that their jobs become all-encompassing, overshadowing other important aspects of life. Effective managers consider themselves and those they manage as "total" people. **Holistic personal goals** should include the job/career and any other areas of importance such as financial, social, avocational and the like. In Covey's *7 Habits of Highly Effective People* (1989, p.270), "job" is but one of six critical areas, and the most effective employees are those who balance their mental, physical, social, spiritual and family goals with their work goals. Managers will naturally be most concerned with the career/job-related goals such as learning new skills, but should take care not to foster a lopsided workplace culture focused entirely on career/job goals. The other areas are also important and should be considered part of any growth and development program.

> **holistic personal goals**
>
> include all aspects of a person's life: career/job, financial, personal, family/relationships and spiritual/service.

Goals and Values

Closely related to goals are the values you hold—what is important to you. What are your key result areas—broad categories people often talk about as important? Figure 8.2 lists 20 key result areas commonly identified.

Rank from 1 to 10 (1 being the most important) what you want. These are your **touchstone values**. Then rank how you actually spend the majority of your time, energy and money day to day. These are your **daily values**. How do the rankings compare?

> **touchstone values**
>
> what people say is important to them.

> **daily values**
>
> how people actually spend their time and energy.

 Touchstone values, what people say is important to them, and *daily values,* how people actually spend their time and energy, need to correlate.

Achievement (sense of accomplishment)	**Physical health** (attractiveness and vitality)
Work (paying own way)	**Emotional health** (handle inner conflicts)
Adventure (exploration, risks, excitement)	**Meaningful work** (relevant/purposeful job)
Personal feedom (independence, choices)	**Affection** (warmth, giving/receiving love)
Authenticity (being frank and genuinely myself)	**Pleasure** (enjoyment, satisfaction, fun)
Expertness (being excellent at something)	**Wisdom** (mature understanding, insight)
Service (contribute to satisfaction of others)	**Family** (happy/contented living situation)
Leadership (having influence and authority)	**Recognition** (being well known; prestige)
Money (plenty of money for things I want)	**Security** (having a secure, stable future)
Spirituality (my religious beliefs/experiences)	**Self-growth** (continuing development)

FIGURE 8.2

Key Result Areas Achieved through Touchstone and Daily Values

Source: David G. Lee, Senior Consultant with Personal Decisions, Inc. of Minneapolis, MN. Reprinted with permission.

Often what people value and what they spend the majority of their time on conflict. For example, a person may have family as his or her Number 1 touchstone value, yet have work as the Number 1 daily value. Managers and those they manage need to examine their touchstone and daily values and seek a closer correlation between them.

An example of conflict between what people say they value and how they behave on the job is seen in an officer who claims loyalty to constitutional principles and to the department's value, yet falsifies a use-of-force report for him- or herself or a coworker; this officer has established that his or her highest loyalty is to convenience and self-interest (Shults, 2009). To counter such disparity, individuals should write a personal mission motto: "Without a clear reminder of what you really believe and live for, the expediency of the moment may prevail and betray your higher aspirations. . . . A visible cornerstone for your primary, ethics-defining loyalty can have refreshing preservative value" (Shults, 2009). For many in law enforcement, at whatever level, from officer to chief, a personal mission motto might be "Maintain Balance."

BALANCED PERFORMER MANAGERS AND EMPOWERMENT

It cannot be repeated often enough: The most effective managers are those who accomplish priority tasks through their people. Managers who do everything themselves, no matter how well the tasks are done, are *not* effective managers, as Figure 8.3 illustrates. Managers who concentrate on excelling themselves, on climbing up through the ranks rather than helping their subordinates to excel, are not balanced performers. Nor are the managers who do little or nothing themselves, relying on subordinates to carry the load but without providing an example for them to follow.

FIGURE 8.3
Balanced Performer

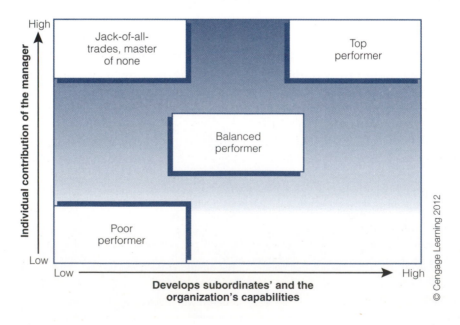

© Cengage Learning 2012

Managers who contribute their efforts to accomplishing department goals while developing their subordinates into top performers are superior balanced performer managers who empower others.

balanced performer managers

develop subordinates' and an organization's capabilities, empower others.

Managers who empower allow subordinates to grow to their fullest potential.

STAGES OF GROWTH

The stages of growth in a manager–employee relationship can be compared to that of a parent and child.

 The three stages of growth are dependent, independent and interdependent.

The first stage is the *dependent* stage. Rookies are initially learning the job and are very dependent on others. They watch, follow and need direction. The manager's role at this stage is usually to *tell* them what to do.

As officers grow, develop and gain confidence, they become more *independent*, just as adolescents learn to be less dependent on their parents. The manager's role at this point is to allow more freedom and give more responsibility. Traditionally, managers who brought their people to this level felt they had done their job—moving their subordinates from dependence to independence.

More progressive managers, those who use participative leadership approaches, take their subordinates one step further, moving them to being *interdependent*. The role of the manager shifts to that of a collaborator—similar to the relationship of a parent to an adult son or daughter. In such a relationship, levels of trust, cooperation and communication are high, producing synergy, where the whole is greater than the sum of its parts.

One major problem for supervisors is adjusting techniques for handling personnel on the same shift who have diverse experiences. Supervising an officer with 10 years' experience demands different approaches than would be used with a new recruit. Veteran officers have knowledge, experience and self-confidence that rookies lack. Supervisors should seek input on decisions from these veteran officers, giving credit where merited, praising good work and mentoring rather than managing. Supervisors should not unknowingly punish veteran officers by overloading them because of their experience.

Education is one important way to move employees from dependence to independence and finally to interdependence. All members of the police department should be encouraged to continue their education through special seminars, undergraduate and graduate courses, in-service training, research, writing and teaching, as discussed in Chapter 7.

Career currency includes enhancing one's professional skills or helping others augment their skill sets. Here a civil disturbance unit (CDU) police officer (left) trains other members of the Washington DC police force at the Metropolitan Police Training Center in Lorton, Virginia.

© Reuters/CORBIS

DEVELOPING POSITIVE ATTITUDES

Effective managers are upbeat and positive. They see opportunities in setbacks. They encourage risk taking and are supportive when mistakes happen. And they encourage these attitudes in their subordinates.

Personality problems can be more devastating to employees than can poor work performance. Managers must help certain employees to develop—those who are loners, who are sarcastic, who talk incessantly about themselves, who constantly complain or who have other personality problems. Directing them to outside counseling may be necessary. Managers have a responsibility to deal with problems in employee attitudes. Dealing with problem behaviors is the focus of Chapter 10.

Officers' attitudes are important personally, but they are also crucial to the public's perception of officers in general and the department they represent.

DEVELOPING A POSITIVE IMAGE

How people see themselves is their self-image. How others see them is their public image. The two often differ, as the Johari Window illustrated earlier. A critical part of a subordinate's development is creating a positive public image. As Will Rogers noted, "You never get a second chance to make a good first impression." This is particularly true for law enforcement officers, who often have only one contact with individual citizens. Officers in a large city who make a traffic stop, for example, are unlikely to ever see that particular driver again. How they approach the driver, what they say and do, is the image the driver will retain of the officer. It may also become the image that driver has of the entire law enforcement organization.

Managers must help subordinates learn to make favorable impressions whenever and wherever possible. Because law enforcement officers are so visible, they leave an impression even when they make no contact, merely by the way they patrol, their appearance, their manner and their attitude. Their uniforms, their badges, their guns—all signify authority and power. Add mirrored sunglasses, handcuff tie tacks and a swaggering walk, and a negative image is likely to be conveyed. Law enforcement officers should be encouraged to consider how they look, how they walk and how they talk to the public, especially when in uniform.

 Law enforcement officers who have a professional appearance and act with competence and courtesy will leave a favorable impression with the majority of the public.

In 2005, 43.5 million people had face-to-face contact with the police (primarily in traffic stops), and 9 of 10 citizens felt the officer or officers behaved properly during their encounter (Durose et al., 2007, p.1). But that leaves 10 percent who held a different view. Managers, through their training and supervision, can shape the relationship between residents and officers working the streets. Basich (2008, p.54) points out, "People who have never worn the badge can never truly understand what it is to be a police officer. Sometimes this lack of understanding leads to unrealistic expectations. Other times it leads to outright hatred for anyone in uniform." However, "Given the astonishingly high standard that Americans expect of their cops, it's surprising that most people have a positive view of law enforcement" (Basich, 2008, p.54).

A positive image will be greatly enhanced by treating all citizens fairly and equally. This often requires officers to recognize their personal biases and to deal with them. Much of officers' images are shaped by how they treat those who are different from themselves, be it a gender, racial or economic difference.

Five studies funded by the National Institute of Justice explored factors influencing public satisfaction with the police and found that satisfaction is shaped by demographic variables, neighborhood crime conditions and experiences with the police—whether firsthand or indirect: "Race was not found to directly determine level of satisfactions. Instead, researchers concluded that race, due to its correlation with other demographic variables, neighborhood crime rates and experiences with police, was an indirect influence on the level of satisfaction with the police" (Horowitz, 2007).

Attitudes toward police are also influenced by perceptible signs of crime and disorder in their neighborhood—prostitution, graffiti, speeding, loitering—not the violent crimes often assumed to worry citizens: "Officers should actively seek contact with citizens within circumstances designed to identify and attend to specific neighborhood problems that citizens believe are important. Addressing the identifiable concerns of the community . . . would improve public attitudes toward the police in problem neighborhoods" (Bridenball and Jesilow, 2008, p.174).

Sergeants are well advised to remind officers that what is routine for the police may well be the most traumatic event citizens have even been through, and that the difference between a good officer and a great officer is compassion. As one patrol sergeant regularly told his officers, "Treat everyone like they're going to be your next door neighbor tomorrow" (Stockton, 2007, p.8). Although officers may need to yell at a noncompliant citizen or a suspect who is lying prone on the pavement, the advice is simple: "Try to treat people the same way you would expect a fellow officer to treat your brother, sister, best, friend, etc., *if they were contacted under the same circumstances*" (Stockton, 2007, p.8).

Supervisors should also remind their officers that their actions may likely be recorded by camera phones "wielded by an increasingly video-savvy public" (Erpenbach, 2008, p.40). Supervisors should also strive to develop cultural awareness and sensitivity in themselves and those they supervise.

DEVELOPING CULTURAL AWARENESS AND SENSITIVITY

Cultural awareness is another critical area of development for law enforcement personnel.

cultural awareness

understanding the diversity of the United States, the dynamics of minority–majority relationships, the dynamics of sexism and racism and the issues of nationalism and separatism.

> **Cultural awareness** means understanding the diversity of the United States, the dynamics of minority–majority relationships, the dynamics of sexism and racism and the issues of nationalism and separatism.

Some of the difficulties arising from cultural differences were discussed in Chapter 4. Officers need to appreciate diversity both within their departments and in their communities. Most people understand and accept that our society is multicultural. Although the United States has been called a melting pot

Cultural awareness is a critical area of development for law enforcement personnel. Officers must appreciate the racial, ethnic and cultural diversity that exists within their communities. One way is for local patrol officers to interact with the people of their neighborhoods, like these white officers who are greeting black residents at a block party during a National Night Out event in Austin, Texas.

© Bob Daemmrich/PhotoEdit

of people from all parts of the world, it is more like a salad bowl, where some enjoy majority status and others are viewed as minorities. In a sense, law enforcement officers are in a better position than many to understand minority status because they may view themselves as being in the minority, isolated from the mainstream of society

An important aspect of cultural awareness is understanding and respecting gender differences as well as differences in sexual preference. Cultural awareness also means identifying and respecting the rights of specific separatist/nationalist groups currently active in American society, including the Ku Klux Klan, the American Nazi Party, neo-Nazi skinheads, the Aryan Brotherhood/White Supremacists, Posse Comitatus, the National Socialist Party, the Black Muslim Movement, the American Indian Movement (AIM) and the Jewish Defense League (JDL). When such groups engage in terrorist activity, such as the 1995 bombing of Oklahoma City's Murrah Federal Building, it may be difficult to remain objective. When hate groups' words translate into criminal actions, they have gone well beyond exercising their civil rights.

Another challenge is immigrants who settle in poor neighborhoods that have high crime rates and may therefore be associated with crime. Law enforcement personnel must guard against stereotyping such immigrants as criminals simply because they live in crime-infested neighborhoods. Such stereotyping may lead to racial profiling.

Racial Profiling

Racial profiling is any police-initiated action that relies on the race, ethnicity or national origin rather than the behavior of an individual or information that leads the police to a particular individual who has been identified as being or having been engaged in criminal activity. Allegations of racial profiling are among the most serious threats to the legitimacy of law enforcement in the United States (Miller, 2007, p.248). The *Sourcebook of Criminal Justice Statistics 2003* (2003, p.126) reports that 53 percent of Americans believe racial profiling occurs when motorists are stopped on roads and highways, and only 31 percent believe such profiling is justified. The literature is filled with studies confirming the "crime" of driving while Black (DWB) or driving while Hispanic (DWH).

The Supreme Court decision in *Whren v. United States* (1966) affirmed that police officers can stop vehicles if they have reasonable suspicion of a traffic violation, even though they have no evidence of criminal activity. The officer's intent or pretext for stopping the vehicle is irrelevant. This decision places officers under pressure to have clear, bias-free policies regarding citizen stops. It is interesting to consider that before 9/11 most Americans condemned racial profiling, but since then, the majority of Americans approve of using profiling to identify terrorists.

Profiling as a Legitimate Law Enforcement Tool

The problem of racial profiling has, at its center, the fact that *profiling* has been a valuable tool in policing for decades. At airports, law enforcement and security personnel are taught to watch for certain traits—paying for a ticket in

racial profiling
any police-initiated action that relies on the race, ethnicity or national origin rather than the behavior of an individual or information that leads the police to a particular individual who has been identified as being or having been engaged in criminal activity.

cash, no luggage, nervousness, etc.—to alert them to drug dealers. It might be appropriate to rename "profiling" to "building a case" with race simply part of most suspect descriptions.

The courts generally support race being included as one of several factors in identifying suspects. In *United States v. Weaver* (1992), a Drug Enforcement Administration (DEA) officer stopped and questioned Arthur Weaver because he was a roughly dressed, young Black male on a direct flight from Los Angeles who walked rapidly from the airport toward a cab, had two carry-on bags and no checked luggage and appeared nervous. Weaver was carrying drugs and was arrested, but he challenged the legality of the officer's intervention. The Eighth Circuit Court of Appeals upheld the officer's conduct, explaining,

> Facts are not to be ignored simply because they may be unpleasant—and the unpleasant fact in this case is that he [DEA agent] had knowledge, based upon his own experience and upon the intelligence reports he had received from Los Angeles authorities, that young male members of the African American Los Angeles gangs were flooding the Kansas City area with cocaine. To that extent then, race, when coupled with the other factors [the agent] relied upon, was a factor in the decision to approach and ultimately detain [the suspect]. We wish it were otherwise, but we take the facts as they are presented to us, not as we would wish them to be.

The Department of Justice as well as academia and legal scholars support the use of race during investigations when it's one of several factors given by a victim (Scarry, 2008, pp.22–23). Despite such court support, officers must be educated on how to avoid *unintentional* racial profiling based on personal bias.

Unintentional Racial Profiling

Moule (2009, p.321) provides the following explanation of unintentional racial profiling:

> In the blink of an eye, unconscious bias was visible to me, an African American. A man saw my face as I walked into the store and unconsciously checked his wallet. On the street, a woman catches my eye a half block away and moves her purse from the handle of her baby's stroller to her side as she arranges the baby's blanket. In the airport, a man signals to his wife to move her purse so it is not over the back of her chair, which is adjacent to the one I am moving toward. What is happening in these instances? Are these actions general safety precautions? Is so, why did the sight only of my brown face, not the others who moved among these individuals, elicit these actions?

> I believe these are examples of "blink of the eye" racism. Such unconscious biases lead to unintentional racism: racism that is usually invisible even *and especially* to those who perpetrate it. Yet most people do not want to be considered racist or capable of racist acts because the spoken and unspoken norm is that "good people do not discriminate or in any way participate in racism."

Moule (2009, p.326) concludes, "Individuals need to become less focused on feeling very tolerant and good about themselves and more focused on examining their own biases." Fridell and Laszlo (2009) note that social psychologists have shown that "implicit" or "unconscious" bias can affect what people perceive and do, even those who consciously believe themselves to be nonprejudiced: "It may manifest among agency command staff who decide (without crime-relevant evidence) that the forthcoming gathering of African-American college students bodes trouble, whereas the forthcoming gathering of White undergraduates does not." Fridell and Laszio note that six decades of considerable research has identified an implicit bias linking minorities to crime, even in people who are "consciously tolerant." Welch (2007, p.276) also reports, "The stereotyping of Blacks as criminals is so pervasive throughout society that 'criminal predator' is used as a euphemism for 'young Black male.'"

Law enforcement personnel must become aware of their unconscious biases so they are able and motivated to activate controlled responses to counteract them. To this end, a Community Oriented Policing Services (COPS)–supported academy curriculum, "Racially Biased Policing Training," is being developed in two forms, one for recruits and one for supervisors (Fridell and Laszlo, 2009).

It might be best to avoid the term *racial profiling* because profiling has a legitimate place in law enforcement, and replace it with *racially biased policing*, which has no place in law enforcement. One approach to identifying whether racially biased policing is occurring is to collect data on police-initiated stops of citizens. Most frequently this refers to traffic stops. In 1999 Connecticut was the first state to pass legislation requiring every municipal police agency and the state police to collect data on race for every police-initiated traffic stop. Such data collection presents supervisory challenges, including training officers to collect appropriate data, overcoming resistance to the practice, manipulating data and altering effective policing procedures. It behooves supervisors to address concerns of improper police action early, modify regulations and procedures accordingly and provide adequate training to officers *before* the federal government steps in and issues a consent decree that legally requires a change in departmental policy and subjects a department to rigorous federal oversight, often for many years. Such consent decrees have been issued to numerous police agencies throughout the country during the past decade, including Pittsburg, Pennsylvania; Cincinnati, Ohio; and Los Angeles, California—frequently as the result of alleged civil rights violations against citizens by police officers.

Resistance against legislation mandating data collection may result in **balancing**, unfairly stopping unoffending motorists to protect officers from the "statistical microscope" individually or collectively. The rationale is simple. If an officer stops a minority driver, he or she has to stop a certain number of White drivers to make the numbers come out right. This results in a great deal of unproductive work and may generate citizen complaints. **Ghosting**, falsifying patrol logs, might also occur to make the numbers come out right.

Supervisors should watch for and correct any such practices before they result in formal complaints against the department. Supervisors face a significant challenge to maintain morale in implementing a practice viewed by many officers as an insult and to maintain productivity while ensuring appropriate data is collected.

Before leaving the discussion of racism, consider the observations of Marcou (2009), who notes that bigotry goes both ways and that many officers

balancing

unfairly stopping unoffending motorists to protect officers from the "statistical microscope" individually or collectively.

ghosting

falsifying patrol logs to make the numbers come out right to avoid charges of racial profiling.

out there are "Officers of no color," who "pride themselves on trying to police with a sense of fairness, but they face bigotry every day. They are treated rudely, prejudged and even physically attacked because of their color—not the color of their skin, but the color of their uniform. Every 'Officer of no color' has had to bear the burden of ugly words. Every 'Officer of no color' has been called 'stupid' or 'racist' or much worse by people they protect and serve." Managers need to prepare their subordinates for this and help subordinates develop their emotional intelligence.

In addition to helping subordinates develop a positive attitude, a positive image and cultural awareness and sensitivity, managers should foster a strong sense of integrity and ethical behavior.

DEVELOPING A SENSE OF ETHICS AND INTEGRITY

ethics

standards of fair and honest conduct.

Ruby Ridge, Waco, O. J. Simpson, Rodney King, Abner Louima—these names and others have had the law enforcement community reeling from attacks on its integrity and ethical standards. **Ethics** refers to the rules or standards of fair, honest conduct. Ethics has become a primary focus in almost every profession and is the topic of countless articles, seminars and workshops. **Integrity** refers to steadfast adherence to an ethical code.

integrity

steadfast adherence to an ethical code.

Ethical behavior is that which is "moral" and "right." Law enforcement personnel must develop high ethical standards both on and off duty.

According to Klockars (1983, p.427), "Some areas of human conduct develop their own distinct ethics while others do not." He suggests that special codes of ethics are developed if the area

- Has some special features making it difficult to bring under the domain of general, conventional ethics. Police, for example, can use force, even deadly force, and may lie and deceive people in their work.
- Involves issues of concern not just to those who practice them, but also to others. They involve moral controversy.
- Involves certain types of misconduct that cannot or perhaps should not be controlled by other means.

Law enforcement fits all three conditions, partly because of its great discretionary power.

A multitude of personal, departmental and external forces shape the dynamics of police integrity that ultimately affect each police officer's career (Figure 8.4). Personal forces that affect police personnel include economy/ personal finances, diversity issues in the department, family values/moral literacy, experience with aggressive police tactics, the police subculture, community response to police activities and presence, frustration with the criminal justice system, peer influence and alcohol/drug abuse. Departmental forces that affect police personnel include the promotion system, leadership, reward

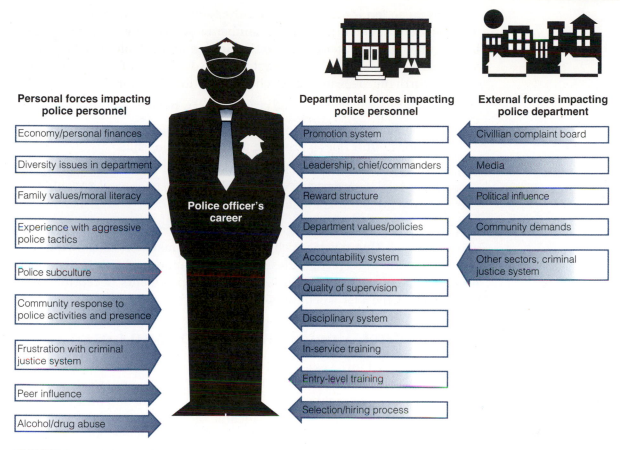

Personal forces impacting police personnel

Economy/personal finances

Diversity issues in department

Family values/moral literacy

Experience with aggressive police tactics

Police subculture

Community response to police activities and presence

Frustration with criminal justice system

Peer influence

Alcohol/drug abuse

Police officer's career

Departmental forces impacting police personnel

Promotion system

Leadership, chief/commanders

Reward structure

Department values/policies

Accountability system

Quality of supervision

Disciplinary system

In-service training

Entry-level training

Selection/hiring process

External forces impacting police department

Civillian complaint board

Media

Political influence

Community demands

Other sectors, criminal justice system

FIGURE 8.4 Dynamics of Police Integrity

Source: Stephen J. Gaffigan and Phyllis P. McDonald. *Police Integrity: Public Service with Honor.* U.S. Department of Justice. January 1997, p.92.

structures, departmental values/policies, the accountability system, the quality of supervision, the disciplinary system, in-service training, entry-level training and the selection/hiring process. These departmental forces are influenced in part by external forces that affect the entire agency, such as civilian complaint boards, news media, political influences, community demands and other sectors of the criminal justice system (courts and corrections).

To clarify the expectations regarding officer ethics and integrity, most law enforcement departments have a formal code of ethics, often framed and hanging on the wall. Such codes usually have at least three important themes:

- Justice or fairness is the dominant theme. Officers are not to take advantage of people or accept gratuities.
- Because of the importance of the law and the officer as tools of the Constitution, law enforcement behavior must be totally within the bounds set by the law.
- At all times, law enforcement officers must uphold a standard of behavior consistent with their public position.

A code of ethics helps officers make decisions lawfully, humanely and fairly. However, ethics is not about what we say; it is about what we do. To determine whether an action is ethical, consider the following questions: Is it legal? Is it the best solution for the greatest number of people? How would you feel if it were made public? Does it follow the Golden Rule? Would you like such a decision directed at you? Is it the right thing to do? Blanchard and Peale (1988, p.27) set forth the following "ethics check" questions:

1. Is it legal? Will I be violating either civil law or company policy?

2. Is it balanced? Is it fair to all concerned in the short term as well as in the long term? Does it promote win–win relationships?

3. How will it make me feel about myself? Will it make me proud? Would I feel good if my decision was published in the newspaper? Would I feel good if my family knew about it?

Fair or not, the conduct of law enforcement personnel is expected to be above reproach. One area in which officer conduct may be called into question is in whether they accept gratuities. Table 8.2 summarizes the main arguments for and against accepting gratuities. In some departments, accepting gratuities is considered a form of misconduct.

Misconduct, Unethical Behavior and Corruption

Police misconduct involves a broad spectrum of behavior including mistreatment of offenders, discrimination, illegal search and seizure, violation of suspects' constitutional rights, perjury, evidence planting and other forms of corruption. Unethical behavior may include taking overlong breaks, abusing sick time, arriving late for work, falsifying time sheets, lying, tampering with evidence, compromising an investigation, being disrespectful to the public, drinking on the job and the like.

TABLE 8.2 Arguments for and against Gratuities

Allowing Gratuities
• They help create a friendly bond between officers and the public, thus fostering community-policing goals.
• They represent a nonwritten form of appreciation and usually are given with no expectation of anything in return.
• Most gratuities are too small to be a significant motivator of actions.
• The practice is so deeply entrenched that efforts to root it out will be ineffective and cause unnecessary violations of the rules.
• A complete ban makes officers appear as though they cannot distinguish between a friendly gesture and a bribe.
• Some businesses and restaurants insist on the practice.

Banning Gratuities
• The acceptance violates most departments' policies and the law enforcement code of ethics.
• Even the smallest gifts create a sense of obligation.
• Even if nothing is expected in return, the gratuity may create an appearance of impropriety.
• Although most officers can discern between friendly gestures and bribes, some may not.
• They create an unfair distribution of services to those who can afford gratuities, voluntary taxing or private funding of a public service.
• It is unprofessional.

Source: Mike White. "The Problem with Gratuities." *FBI Law Enforcement Bulletin*, July 2002, p.21.

AWAY FROM THE DESK—Can Cracking Down on Gratuities Be a Career Killer?

Several years ago, a suburban Minnesota police department promoted an individual from within its ranks to that of police chief. Shortly after accepting the position, the new police chief embarked on a mission to notify the local businesses in the department's jurisdiction that his officers were *not* allowed to accept gratuities of any sort. This issue had been identified by the new chief as a problem that had been going on for some time and that the previous administration had either neglected to identify or had chosen to ignore. The new chief vowed to make good on correcting this problem now that he was in a position to do so.

A letter was mailed to all affected businesses and other places within this policing jurisdiction known to have provided officers with gratuities. The officers soon learned of the letter their new police chief had sent out, and the culture in this agency soon began to shift. The once popular up-and-coming new administrator became decidedly unpopular among his subordinates, and further decisions and policy changes were met with significant resistance.

Several years later this police chief became interested in another career opportunity in a neighboring suburb. The new department he sought to lead was somewhat larger, and the compensation was certainly much greater. During the selection process, the five finalists' names were released. Officers within the larger department began to use their network to compile information about each of the final candidates. Inevitably, several officers learned of the actions this chief took within his current department to deal with the problems surrounding gratuities. Part of the selection process also included a hiring recruiter, who met with a preselected group of officers to learn about what they felt they needed in their new police chief. This group of officers presented information indirectly to the recruiter that worked against this candidate, as they were certain they did not want a new chief who was going to take away their gratuities.

Managers, supervisors, administrators and leaders at all levels are expected to hold subordinates to professional standards and help guide colleagues toward attaining high levels of professionalism. Gratuities are perceived in some departments as being the first step in compromise, placing officers on a slippery slope of corruption. Knowing that your actions as a manager, supervisor, and very possibly the police chief could have an unintended outcome outside the current workplace culture and, frankly, could impact a future promotion, what would you do in the situation described above?

—Chief Shaun E. LaDue

Corruption goes beyond unethical behavior in that it is done for personal gain. Consider the following definition of *corruption*: "A violation of integrity through the abuse of one's role or position, or the influencing of a person in authority for personal benefit or the benefit of another" (Vernon, 2009, p.68). The Knapp Commission, the Mollen Commission, the Christopher Commission, the Rampart Board of Inquiry—all found myriad instances of unethical behavior and extensive corruption in the police departments investigated.

 The key elements of corrupt behavior are that the conduct (1) is prohibited by law or rule, (2) involves misuse of position and (3) involves a reward or personal gain for the officer.

In examining the underlying causes of corruption, usually one or more factors are observed: lack of legitimate accomplishments; anger (feeling being treated unfairly), lack of character, lack of team spirit, short-term goal orientation, lack of understanding negative results and greed (Vernon, 2009). Rarely does an officer suddenly decide to turn into a "rogue cop"; rather, officers often make "a series of small compromises that [end] up bringing them to the same shameful position" (Vernon, 2009, p.68).

The Slippery Slope

Sherman's *slippery slope of corruption* posits that police corruption begins with a lowering of ethical expectations and values to attain a gratuity of minor value, for example, accepting a free cup of coffee. Although this action in itself is most likely harmless and inconsequential as a corrupting force, it may over time produce a snowball effect, leading an officer to accept gratuities of larger magnitude. Furthermore, such practices often lead those providing the "freebies" to expect preferential treatment by recipient officers. In Vernon's words, "A chain of seemingly insignificant compromises gradually moves you from integrity to corruption" (2009, p.68).

Noble Cause and Ends versus Means

Another facet of unethical behavior concerns the noble cause corruption dilemma, in which officers believe unlawful means are justified when the result is the protection of human life or some other noble cause. Unquestionably, law enforcement officers face difficult decisions daily.

Because officers are granted awesome coercive authority, it is imperative that police officers exercise their power responsibly and ethically. When confronted with the really "bad guys," it may be tempting to take advantage of this power and the discretion granted to not administer "street justice." It takes moral courage and strong ethical principles to resist the "ends justifying means" pitfall: "In policing, catching the bad guy is used as a justification for illegal wiretaps, planting evidence, swearing to false information in affidavits supporting arrest and search warrants, using verbal and physical abuse and other misuses of police authority" (Jetmore, 2008, p.106). However, "Regardless of the motive or intent, there's *never* a justification for police officers to break the law or use unethical methods to enforce it" (Jetmore, pp.106–107).

Above the Law

The public understands that the police are granted special privileges and exceptions from obeying the law. Officers can exceed speed limits, violate traffic controls and carry concealed weapons in the line of duty. During the socialization process, some officers receive the message they are special and above the law. However, "equality under the law" is the foundation of the American criminal justice system. Officers who believe they are above the law subvert the essence of our criminal justice system.

Bad Apples or a Bad Barrel?

Often the argument is heard that just as a few "bad apples" can ruin the entire barrel, so a few bad cops can ruin the entire department. Garrett (2007, p.6) takes this analogy one step further, noting, "A few bad apples tarnish the image of the entire profession." Managers must examine their department and find ways to promote integrity and ethical behavior. However, identifying and dealing with "bad apples" in a police department is often a difficult mandate for management, as evidenced by results of a nationwide survey that found 52.4 percent of police officers either agree or agree strongly that "It is not unusual for a police officer to turn a blind eye to improper conduct by other officers" (Rothwell and Baldwin, 2007, p.605). In addition, 61.0 percent either disagree or disagree strongly that "police officers always report serious criminal violations involving abuse of authority by fellow officers."

A study of whistle-blowing found two variables to be the most consistent predictors of whistle-blowing: a policy mandating the reporting of misconduct and supervisory status (Rothwell and Baldwin, 2007). A mandatory reporting policy was related to almost all measures of willingness to blow the whistle but none of the measures of frequency of whistle-blowing, indicating that whistle-blowing is easier to do in the abstract than in reality: "Willingness is one thing; actual whistle-blowing is another." Whistle-blowing, especially of minor violations, may be hindered by informal sanctions such as ostracism by other officers. And the sanctions for not reporting misconduct may be nonexistent. Supervisory status, however, may have serious consequences for supervisors, as reporting of violations of policy is an expected and accepted behavior for supervisors. Rothwell and Baldwin's research also found: "Contrary to popular belief, the results also show that police are slightly less inclined than civilian public employees to subscribe to a code of silence."

The Code of Silence

Quinn (2004), in his highly acclaimed *Walking with the Devil: The Police Code of Silence,* cautions,

> As terrible as it is, there is no escaping the Code. It is as inevitable as your childhood diseases and just as necessary. Each stinging battle with the Code will be either an inoculation of the spirit and an opportunity to grow stronger or a crippling injury to your integrity. Regardless of the outcome there will be vivid images you can't erase from your memory. There will always be the mental and physical scars to remind you of your battles.

But, each encounter can leave you better prepared both physically and mentally for the tough challenges ahead, if you are willing to admit you're not superman, and you recognize your "dark side" for what it is. Because only when we know the Code of Silence for what it is can we gain some control over it. Either way, you won't escape unscathed because at some point in time you are going to "Walk with the Devil" in order to get the job done. (p.27)

Every day is a new challenge and ethical police conduct is often an uphill battle. Even the best of cops have days when they want to give up and do whatever it takes to put a child molester, baby murderer, or other lowlife in prison. When you sit inches away from these scum and they brag about the truly horrific things they have done to an innocent it's easy to abide by the Code—if that's what it takes. When the evidence isn't perfect, you just use a little creative report writing and this guy will never harm another person again. Illegal searches, physical abuse, or even perjury, you know you will be in the company of many good cops who have done the same. But are they really good cops?

The choice of being a "Peace Officer" means there will be many battles in solitary combat with other cops and with yourself. You will not win them all—you cannot—the cards are stacked against you. There will be no medals, awards ceremonies or cheering crowds for the battles you do win. But there will be honor and integrity—in your life and in your work. (pp.13–14)

Misconduct, unethical behavior (including the code of silence) and corruption are far more likely to cut short an officer's career than is a bad guy with a knife in the alley.

Promoting Ethical Behavior and Integrity

Many factors contribute to officers sliding down the slippery slope, and upper management must be proactive about issues that might cause such slippage: "Department leaders can spell the difference. And they can make this difference, primarily, by modeling their integrity and by establishing a personal relationship with their officers in which trust and respect are the foundation. When the captain is perceived as someone who can be trusted, an officer contemplating wrongdoing or facing an ethical dilemma can be comfortable going to the supervisor for advice" (Johnson, 2007, p.12).

Often personal problems such as substance abuse or gambling addiction lead officers astray. The manager who listens and takes an interest in subordinates will become aware of such problems and help officers get the help they need before the problems escalate.

As a symbolic statement of commitment to ethical behavior, the International Association of Chiefs of Police (IACP) has recommended a Law Enforcement Oath of Honor:

On my honor, I will never betray my badge, my integrity, my character, or the public trust.

I will always have the courage to hold myself and others accountable for our actions.
I will always uphold the Constitution and community I serve.

Sutton (2009) believes most people entering law enforcement do so out of a sense of purpose and patriotism and are committed to the ideal of what the badge represents. Management must build on that commitment by creating a culture of pride:

> A culture of pride is actually a simple concept. It begins with each one of us realizing that we are important not only as individuals and as members of a noble profession but also in how we play a vital role in the lives of others. Once we accept that fundamental truth about ourselves, we need to look at our colleagues and coworkers and regard them with the same respect. Ultimately, it's a belief in what one stands for and pride, of the healthy, expansive sort, that keeps a person from dishonoring themselves and their profession.
>
> What exactly is this sense of pride? It's that same feeling one gets at graduation from a law enforcement academy. It's the feeling of a crisp new uniform and a starched shirt and the weight of a shiny new badge on your chest. It's the feeling of an awesome responsibility coupled with a soaring belief that we, the new officer, can meet whatever challenges we face. There is no feeling like it, no greater sense of optimistic pride. This is the feeling we all, as experienced law enforcement officers, need to strive to recapture. We must seek to cloak ourselves in ethical pride for it is there that we are most invulnerable to our baser instincts. . . .
>
> At the organization level, each of us can play a critical role in building up the pride in our agency. From the cop on the beat taking a little extra time to make sure his or her uniform is clean and pressed to the top administrator making sure his or her personnel is properly equipped and provided with both technical and personal support, are all ways to instill, foster and promote pride.

In addition to promoting a culture of pride, numerous departmental policies and procedures have been shown to help foster an environment of ethical behavior and officer integrity. One area in which policies might be useful, if not legally prudent, is defining *off-duty police misconduct*: "A failure to educate subordinates regarding the agency's expectations of off-duty conduct could be defined as a neglect of duty on the part of the police administration" (Martinelli, 2007, p.40). A fine line exists between balancing an organization's right not to employ an officer who engages in unethical behavior versus the officer's right to off-duty privacy. If an officer is terminated for off-duty conduct "unbecoming an officer," a lawsuit might occur that can cost taxpayers thousands of dollars (Martinelli, p.41). Usually an agency can win such a suit if it can prove a nexus between legal off-duty misconduct and the officer's job performance and how it might affect the public's trust in the agency itself.

Another area in need of a clear policy is that of *lying*. It is accepted that police may lie during interrogations or when undercover, but a clear line can and should be drawn between sanctioned lying and prohibited lying:

> That clear line could be that police officers found to have lied intentionally in an official document such as a police report, statement, or affidavit or in an official proceeding such as an internal affairs investigation, administrative hearing, or in court will be terminated as a matter of public policy, as such officers

cannot work effectively and should therefore not be allowed to work within the law enforcement profession.

Until such public policy is adopted by the state in which an agency is located, the best way to encourage honesty is to have a clear code of conduct stating that officers who are untruthful will be subject to termination for a first offense and to implement this code standard in a consistent manner (Spector, 2008, p.12).

The rationale for such a policy can be found in *Brady v. Maryland* (1963), where the Supreme Court ruled that a prosecutor must release information favorable to an accused upon request (exculpatory information). If an officer with a history of untruthfulness is called to testify in a criminal proceeding, the prosecutor is legally and ethically obligated to disclose this history of untruthfulness to defense counsel, preventing the officer from providing useful service as a law enforcement officer.

In October 2009 the Police Executive Research Forum (PERF) held a town hall meeting to discuss sanctions against officers who lie. The entire October 2009 issue of the PERF's newsletter, *Subject to Debate*, was devoted to interviews with more than 20 chiefs of police on the subject. The overwhelming majority favored a zero-tolerance policy toward lying. However, in some jurisdictions, such as in Boston, the chief cannot terminate an officer for lying because of the heavily unionized environment and because of rules on "past practices"; the chief could give only long suspensions. When Boston Commissioner Davis came out with a widely publicized new policy stating that anyone caught lying in a police report, in testimony in court or before an Internal Affairs board will be fired, the union characterized it as the most severe and extreme policy in the nation ("PERF's Town Hall Meeting," 2009, pp.1–7). Following are representative views from around the country:

◉ Cops have been getting a pass on lying for a long time (Boston Commissioner Davis, p.1).

◉ We're telling supervisors: don't cover for officers (St. Louis Chief Isom, p.2).

◉ Our officers realize lying for a colleague puts them at risk (Nashville Chief Serpas, p.2).

◉ I had to say, "No more leniency in minor cases" (Aurora, Colorado, Chief Oates, p.3).

◉ I'm tired of hiding liars I can't fire (Montgomery County, Maryland, Chief Manger, p.3).

◉ Little lies are like broken windows (Retired Chief Olson, p.5).

◉ Sergeants are critical to dealing with lying (White Plains, New York, Commissioner Straub, p.5).

Miami Chief Timoney, however, cautions that some cases are tough judgment calls and gives as an example two young officers who got involved in a brawl in front of a nightclub. They did everything right, including using the necessary force to make an arrest. However, they did not check off the box on the arrest report indicating they had used necessary force, requiring another form to be prepared. It was 2 a.m., and they wanted to go home. The man who was arrested filed a complaint saying the officers had roughed him up, and when it went to Internal Affairs, they denied using force. A day later the officers and their lawyers asked for a second chance and told the truth. They were suspended for several months—a classic case of the cover-up being worse than the crime. Timoney ("PERF's Town Hall Meeting," 2009, p.7) points out, "You can create bright lines to say what will get you fired, and most of the time they will work, but about 10 or 15 percent of the time, it's just a difficult call and you have to use your experience and best judgment."

Yet another area in which a clear policy can promote ethical behavior is *professional courtesy* and department expectations. Professional courtesy involves providing free or discounted services to others in the profession, a long-standing and common practice in the medical and legal professions. In law enforcement, it may also involve someone in law enforcement "looking the other way" when a fellow officer breaks the law. Wolfe (2009) notes, "Some would say an officer letting another go is 'professional courtesy.' My definition differs. To me 'professional courtesy' means that when you are in my jurisdiction you conduct yourself so that your behavior doesn't require that I come into contact with you. You act like a professional and show me courtesy by not placing me in the position of having to deal with you. In return I do the same for you." A clear policy on professional courtesy is another way to promote ethical behavior.

In addition to clear policies, training on making ethical decisions at all levels in a department is needed. Trautman (2009), director of the National Institute of Ethics, asserts, "Law enforcement does a shameful job of preparing cops to make difficult ethical decisions." He also states, "As a profession, instructors seldom train about moments most likely to destroy officers and leaders rarely discuss the subject." He notes that an ethical dilemma, such as whether to be honest with your sergeant about a mistake you made, can be a career-ending moment.

THE LONG-RANGE IMPORTANCE OF DEVELOPING PERSONNEL

 Developing individuals and team players is important because most future law enforcement managers will come from the lower levels of the organization.

If officers are not self-developed or developed by managers at all levels, where will future managers come from? This is where succession planning comes in: "Succession planning is the process of reviewing the agency for leadership talent, identifying possible successors and then providing those individuals with the training, mentoring and support they need to prepare themselves for critical roles within the organization when vacancies occur" (Bratton, 2008, p.1). Although succession planning is often considered in the chief executive's position, it is essential to identify and prepare leadership at all levels of the agency. Effective succession planning includes

- Conducting internal agency surveys to determine areas of strength and areas for improvement.
- Encouraging and providing leadership training for command staff and line supervision.

- On-the-job training in special-duty assignments such as acting shift commander and allowing line officers to rotate preparing and conducting roll call briefing.
- In-service situational leadership training.
- Courses on budgets, computer skills, writing and instructor training.
- Mentoring staff by discussion, training and formal presentations with the chief to city administrators and businesses (Bratton, 2008, pp.1–2).

Bratton (2008, p.2) cites Collins' mantra from *Good to Great* that leaders need to have the right people on the bus and in the right seats to be a successful organization. Bratton suggests that one way to determine which officers are right for the bus and for what seats is to look for forward-looking individuals who are open to change. Consideration should also be given to employee's personnel files: evaluations, training records, awards or accomplishments and discipline.

Law enforcement organizations are similar to all other organizations. They constantly change. If they are to flourish, they must embrace change and make it work for them. Sometimes change occurs in a revolutionary manner, but most often it is evolutionary. Law enforcement managers at all levels play a significant role in this process, which may involve change in the organizational structure, its goals and its objectives; its members; or in the community it serves. Change involves alteration of attitudes and work behavior as individuals, as team members and as members of the department.

Evaluating the Climate for Growth, Development and Change

Law enforcement managers who want to evaluate their workplace culture and its conduciveness to growth, development and change can use the brief survey in Figure 8.5.

Evaluate your organization		
1. Inflexible: discourages the new and unusual	1 2 3 4 5 6 7	Open to new ideas; receptive _____
2. Focused on present or past	1 2 3 4 5 6 7	Future oriented; anticipates future _____
3. No way to train further or develop new skills	1 2 3 4 5 6 7	Many opportunities to learn new skills _____
4. Individual effort more important than group effort	1 2 3 4 5 6 7	Cooperative efforts, participation in group is important _____
5. Little planning and communication	1 2 3 4 5 6 7	Active planning, with involvement of others _____
TOTAL		_____

If your organization scored between 5 and 19, it is *not* conductive to growth and development. If your organization scored between 20 and 29, the growth and development environment is positive but needs improvement. A score of 30 and above indicates that your organization values growth and development.

© Cengage Learning 2012

FIGURE 8.5 Evaluate Your Organization Survey

SUMMARY

The workplace culture is the sum of the beliefs and values shared by those within the organization, which formally and informally communicate their expectations. Norms are the attitudes and beliefs held by the members of a group. An officer's first loyalty must be to defend the Constitution of the United States, his or her state constitution and laws and local laws.

Managers can shape the workplace culture by identifying existing norms, evaluating the norms and encouraging positive norms and trying to eliminate negative ones through modeling and training. The Johari Window describes four parts of a person's identity: the open self, the hidden self, the blind self and the subconscious or undiscovered self.

Personal and organizational goals are a necessary first step for growth and development. Touchstone values, what people say is important to them, and daily values, how people actually spend their time and energy, need to correlate.

Managers who contribute their efforts to accomplishing department goals while developing their subordinates into top performers are superior balanced performer managers who empower others. The three stages of growth are dependent, independent and interdependent. Law enforcement officers who have a professional appearance and act with competence and courtesy will leave a favorable impression with the majority of the public.

Cultural awareness means understanding the diversity of the United States, the dynamics of minority–majority relationships, the dynamics of sexism and racism and the issues of nationalism and separatism.

Ethical behavior is that which is "moral" and "right." Law enforcement personnel must develop high ethical standards both on and off duty. The key elements of corrupt behavior are that the conduct (1) is prohibited by law or rule, (2) involves misuse of position and (3) involves a reward or personal gain for the individual. Developing individuals and team players is important because most future law enforcement managers will come from the lower levels of the organization.

CHALLENGE EIGHT

As the new police chief of the Greenfield Police Department, you expected some resistance from officers during the transition from a crime fighting philosophy to a community policing philosophy. Several veteran officers oppose the change. Most younger officers are willing to try community policing and enjoy interacting with the community. Unfortunately, they worry about being rejected by the veteran officers. Most younger officers do not want to buck the prevailing police culture and informal hierarchy.

Officer Blake, a senior officer and vocal opponent of community policing, is an informal department leader. You decide to ride along with him on a patrol shift. He's an honest guy who tells you exactly what is on his mind. Officer Blake was the department shooting champion and unhappy with the cutbacks in firearms training. He thinks the old way of doing things was working just fine. They kept people in line, and the crime rates reflected it. He tells you that community policing is social work, not police work, and that his job is making arrests and keeping the streets safe.

As you listen to Officer Blake, he patrols a park where a group of young Asian men are gathered. He drives by slowly and stares at them. They look down, not making eye contact. Officer Blake looks at you and says, "I don't trust those guys. They're up to something." Officer Blake drives through the parking lot and back past the young men. "I always make sure they know I'm watching them." The young men begin playing soccer.

Officer Blake's next stop is Ruby's Bar and Grill. Several other squads are parked in front of the building. You learn this is their regular break location and that coffee is free, food is half price and a booth is reserved for cops.

1. How would you encourage the new officers' enthusiasm for community policing and help them buck the prevailing culture?

2. Is Officer Blake a good candidate to be a mentor for a new officer?

3. Officer Blake is clearly entrenched in the crime fighting mode of law enforcement. How would his encounter with the young men in the park affect your department's public image?

4. Isolating police officers in squad cars creates a barrier to good communications and can thwart cultural awareness. How could an emphasis on community policing have changed this encounter?

5. As a new chief attempting to implement a community policing strategy, how would you address the issue of gratuities?

 # DISCUSSION QUESTIONS

1. How would you describe an ethical person? Who might be role models in our society?

2. What would you include in a job description for a law enforcement officer? A sergeant? A chief or sheriff?

3. What norms would you like to see in a law enforcement agency?

4. What do you consider the five most important touchstone values listed in Figure 8.2?

5. What are your three most important touchstone values? Your three most important daily values? Do they correlate? If not, what should you do?

6. What ethical problems have you faced in your life?

7. How are unconditional backup and the code of silence related?

8. How prevalent do you believe racial profiling is in your community? Your state? The country?

9. Should officers accept gratuities? If so, what is acceptable?

10. What skills would you like to further develop? How important would this be to your law enforcement career?

REFERENCES

Basich, Melanie. "A Love-Hate Relationship." *Police*, April 2008, pp.54–57.

Blanchard, Kenneth, and Peale, Norman Vincent. *The Power of Ethical Management*. New York: William Morrow and Company, Inc., 1988.

Bratton, Randy S. "Succession Planning and Staff Development." *Big Ideas for Smaller Police Departments*, Fall 2008, pp.1–5.

Bridenball, Blaine, and Jesilow, Paul. "What Matters: The Formation of Attitudes toward the Police." *Police Quarterly*, June 2008, pp.151–181.

Covey, Stephen R. *The 7 Habits of Highly Effective People*. New York: Simon & Schuster, 1989.

Durose, Matthew R.; Smith, Erica L.; and Langan, Patrick A. *Contacts between Police and the Public, 2005*. Washington, DC: Bureau of Justice Statistics Special Report, April 2007. (NCJ 215243)

Erpenbach, Mary. "The Whole World Is Watching." *Law Enforcement Technology*, February 2008, pp.40–47.

Fridell, Lorie, and Laszlo, Anna T. "Reducing Biased Policing through Training." *Community Policing Dispatch*, February 2009.

Garrett, Ronnie. "Eyes Wide Shut." *Law Enforcement Technology*, August 2007, p.6.

Horowitz, Jake. "Making Every Encounter Count: Building Trust and Confidence in the Police." *NIJ Journal*, January 2007.

Jetmore, Larry F. "Investigative Ethics." *Law Officer Magazine*, August 2008, pp.104–108.

Johnson, Robert Roy. "When Good Cops Go Bad." *Law and Order*, August 2007, p.12.

Klockars, Carl B. *Thinking about Police: Contemporary Readings*. New York: McGraw-Hill, 1983.

Marcou, Dan. "Officer of No Color." *PoliceOne.com News*, July 24. 2009.

Martinelli, Thomas J. "Minimizing Risk by Defining Off-Duty Police Misconduct." *The Police Chief*, June 2007, pp.40–45.

Miller, Kirk. "Racial Profiling and Postmodern Society: Police Responsiveness, Image Maintenance, and the Left Flank of Police Legitimacy." *Journal of Contemporary Criminal Justice*, August 2007, pp.248–262.

Moule, Jean. "Understanding Unconscious Bias and Unintentional Racism." *Phi Delta Kappan*, January 2009, pp.321–326.

"PERF's Town Hall Meeting Focuses on Sanctions against Officers Who Lie." *Subject to Debate*, October 2009, pp.1–7.

Quinn, Michael W. *Walking with the Devil: The Police Code of Silence* (*What Bad Cops Don't Want You to Know and Good Cops Won't Tell You*). Minneapolis, MN: Quinn and Associates, 2004.

Rothwell, Gary R., and Baldwin, J. Norman. "Whistle-Blowing and the Code of Silence in Police Agencies: Policy and Structural Predictors." *Crime & Delinquency*, October 2007, pp.605–612.

Scarry, Laura L. "Racial Profiling or Good Policing?" *Law Officer Magazine*, May 2008, pp.22–24.

Shults, Joel F. "The Moral Imperative of Loyalty." *PoliceOne.com News*, August 3, 2009.

Sourcebook of Criminal Justice Statistics—2003. Washington, DC: Bureau of Justice Statistics, 2003. (Latest print version available) [NOTE: This source went to an online-only version in 2003 and is continuously updated at various times throughout the year.] Accessed September 13, 2010. http://www.albany.edu/sourcebook/.

Spector, Elliot. "Should Police Officers Who Lie Be Terminated as a Matter of Public Policy?" *The Police Chief*, April 2008, pp.10–12.

Stockton, Dale. "Is the Boss Looking?" *Law Officer Magazine*, October 2007, p.8.

Sutton, Randy. "What Legacy Will You Leave Behind?" *Law Officer Magazine*, August 2007, pp.44–48.

Sutton, Randy. "Policing with Honor." *PoliceOne.com News*, May 25, 2009.

Trautman, Neal. "Surviving Ethical Dilemmas: Overcoming the Moments Most Likely to End Your Career." *LawOfficer.com*, June 15, 2009.

Vernon, Bob. "Organizational Culture." *Law Officer Magazine*, August 2008, p.76.

Vernon, Bob. "Corruption: A Personal, Incremental Struggle." *Law Officer Magazine*, August 2009, pp.68–70.

Welch, Kelly. "Black Criminal Stereotypes and Racial Profiling." *Journal of Contemporary Criminal Justice*, August 2007, pp. 276–288.

Wolfe, Duane. "Defining 'Professional Courtesy.'" *PoliceOne.com News*, June 5, 2009.

 CITED CASES

Brady v. Maryland, 373 U.S. 83 (1963)
United States v. Weaver, 506 U.S. 1040 (1992)

Whren v. United States, 517 U.S. 806 (1966)

CHAPTER NINE

Motivation and Morale

Ability is what you are capable of doing. Motivation determines what you do. Attitude determines how well you do it.

—Lou Holtz

DO YOU KNOW?

- What motivation is?
- What theories of motivation have been proposed by Maslow? Herzberg? Skinner? Vroom? Morse and Lorsch?
- Which kind of reinforcement is more effective and when reinforcement should occur?
- What the most common external motivators are?
- What internal motivators include?
- How the law enforcement job can be made more interesting?
- What morale is?
- What factors might indicate a morale problem?
- What factors might be responsible for morale problems?
- Who is most able to improve or damage individual and department morale?
- How morale might be improved?
- What promotions should be based on?
- What three phases an assessment center typically uses for law enforcement personnel?
- Whether promotions should be from without or within?

CAN YOU DEFINE?

contingency theory
expectancy theory
Hawthorne effect
hierarchy of needs
hygiene factors
morale
motivation
motivator factors
negative reinforcement
positive reinforcement
Pygmalion effect
reinforcement theory
self-actualization
self-fulfilling prophecy
two-factor theory

INTRODUCTION

Why do some law enforcement officers arrive at work ahead of time, eager to perform? Why do others arrive just in the nick of time? Why do some perform at a high level without direction and others need constant direction? Why are some upbeat and others chronic complainers? What motivates such behavior?

Consider the following conversation between two officers, one who had just completed an especially frustrating shift. One officer asked the other, "Why do we come here day after day and put up with this crap?" The other officer thought for a moment and then answered, "I don't know. I think it has something to do with house payments." Most people do need to work to survive. What will make them also enjoy their work and do their best? What will motivate them?

CHAPTER at a GLANCE

This chapter begins with an examination of the turnover problem in law enforcement and how to retain good employees. The remainder of the chapter looks at motivation and morale, two keys to officer retention. First motivation and self-motivation are defined. Next the motivational theories of Maslow, Herzberg, Skinner, Vroom and Morse and Lorsch are discussed. This theoretical discussion leads into a more practical examination of the causes and symptoms of an unmotivated work force followed by a discussion of external, tangible motivators and internal, intangible motivators. This is followed by a look at the law enforcement career as a motivator and the benefits of motivated personnel.

The discussion then turns to morale and its definitions, both individual and organizational. Next indicators of morale problems are presented, along with a discussion of some reasons for such problems. The chapter concludes with specific suggestions for building morale and a discussion of the relationship between promotions and morale.

OFFICER RETENTION, MOTIVATION AND MORALE

Law enforcement agencies throughout the country are experiencing increased rates of staff turnover, a problem that is approaching critical levels for many agencies. Where the applicant-to-hiring ratio used to be 100-to-1, now it is 10-to-1 or less in many cases (Burch, 2008, p.80). Stockton (2007, p.10) states, "The perfect storm of police staffing is upon us. Nearly every agency in this country is having difficulty meeting its most basic staffing needs, and it's going to get worse before it gets better. From the smallest departments to the massive New York Police Department (NYPD), agencies are going short, often by hundreds of officers."

Many agencies are seeing an unprecedented exodus of experienced personnel because of career timing and enhanced retirement benefits. An entire generation of officers is reaching their 50s and 60s, so retirement is considered the primary reason underlying the staffing crisis (Griffith, 2008, p.45). Other reasons include poor pay and poor working conditions, the weakened economy and a significant number of sworn officers serving in the wars in Iraq and Afghanistan.

In addition, smaller departments become training grounds for officers who move on to larger better paying departments. Just the average cost of training a new recruit at an academy is $16,000 (Reaves, 2009, p.1), and the problem intensifies as officers receive additional training. It can cost approximately $80,000 to train a new officer from point of hire to the three-year mark, the point at which an officer becomes effective. Losing even two officers to lateral transfers can amount to a $160,000 "donation" to neighboring communities, a gift many departments cannot afford to absorb (Griffith, 2008, p.50). "Retention costs can be tallied as separation costs, recruitment costs, selection costs, new-employee costs, and other 'soft' costs such as those that departments incur when they must 'stack' calls and forgo proactive policing work because of staffing shortages, All told, failure to retain an officer can result in $100,000 in additional costs for a department" (Wilson and Grammich, 2009, p.19). Replacement costs are not a line item on the budget and are hard to articulate when explaining the cost-benefit of retention efforts: "As a rule of thumb, agencies should consider that the replacement cost is two to five times an officer's annual salary" (Orrick, 2009, p.24).

In addition to the costs of losing officers, agencies with higher turnover and therefore less experienced officers often suffer reduced productivity, lower quality service delivery, more frequent complaints and more lawsuits.

Factors Influencing Retention

The greatest factor outside the department influencing officer retention is the economy (Orrick, 2008, p.177). People leave for other opportunities because they can. Their skills, especially problem solving and communication skills, are highly valued in larger departments as well as in the business world.

Within the department, the most frequently cited reason by police executives of why officers leave is salary. Other factors include poor supervisors or leadership, poor job fit, higher-ordered needs, dysfunctional organizational cultures, generational differences, lack of career growth or better opportunities, inadequate feedback, inadequate recognition, inadequate training and inadequate equipment (Orrick, pp.178–179).

Although police executives often believe inadequate pay is the biggest reason for officer departure, studies indicate a more influential factor on whether an officer leaves or stays is the officer's immediate supervision: "People don't quit jobs, they quit bosses" (Wilson and Grammich, 2009, p.19). And a *Gallup Management Journal* survey of about 200,000 workers from 36 organizations across 21 different industries found: "Employees do not leave 'companies.' They leave managers and supervisors" (Fitch, 2008, p.100).

Use of Contracts to Improve Retention

Dickinson (2008, p.54) reports what he calls a "disturbing trend" in some departments, the use of contracts that require officers who leave an agency before a specified number of years to pay back the cost of their training, including the cost of their academy tuition, room and board: "Employment contracts are one of the most common and potentially damaging strikes to employee morale and retention. . . . If a contract alone forces an unhappy officer to stay, that officer's attitude and work ethic may deteriorate further and create collateral damages throughout the department."

Signs Employees May Be Considering Leaving

As individuals mature, they go through many transitions—such as having a child, purchasing a new home, getting married or divorced—that may be linked with other changes including job changes. Additional signs employees may be considering other job opportunities include the following (Orrick, 2008, p.182):

◉ Expressing prolonged disappointment about being passed over for transfer or promotion.

◉ Perceiving that a close friend who has gone to another job has better opportunities.

◉ Reviewing personnel and training records to update their resumes.

◉ Making inquiries of human resources about early retirement or transfers of benefits.

Managers who think a subordinate may be thinking of leaving should make an extra effort to communicate with the subordinate to understand the situation and attempt to rectify any complaints the subordinate has.

Retaining good officers is a key concern and challenge of police managers. Effective motivation and a climate of high morale are vital to retention efforts and are a primary responsibility of supervisors and managers. The goal of supervisors and managers at all levels should be to build a department with high-quality professionals who want to stay for many years because of the quality of the department, good working conditions and the opportunity to be part of a successful team (Burch, 2008, p.80). If an officer does leave, an exit interview should be conducted to determine the cause(s).

MOTIVATION DEFINED

"Work motivation is the energetic force behind the form, intensity, and persistence of an employee's behavior. It is the force that helps explain why officers pursue certain goals, how they attempt to accomplish those goals, how hard they will work to do so, and the degree of adversity they are willing to overcome" (Fitch, 2008, p.102).

 Motivation is an inner or outer drive to meet a need or goal.

> **motivation**
>
> an inner or outer drive or impetus to do something or to act in a specified manner; an inner or outer drive to meet a need or goal.

Self-motivation is derived from within an individual. Outer motivation is provided from external sources to influence an individual or to furnish a reason for another person to do a desired act in a desired way. A *motive* is an impetus, an impulse or an intention that causes a person to act, individually or collectively with others, in a directed manner.

Motivation and *morale* are terms often used in management but not easily defined or understood. Lack of motivation is often the reason for low morale. Research psychologists have outlined factors that affect motivation and morale. Incentives must be worthwhile to employees, they must be reasonably attainable and employees must feel a sense of responsibility to achieve them. In modern police terms, employees must be empowered. Motivation requires a sense of well-being, self-confidence and accomplishment. To keep levels of motivation and morale high, managers must give recognition.

Can managers motivate their subordinates? According to some, motivation can come only from within. A story from business helps illustrate the point. A young salesperson was disappointed because he had lost an important sale. Discussing it with the sales manager, the man lamented, "I guess it just proves you can lead a horse to water, but you can't make him drink." To which the sales manager replied, "Your job isn't to make him drink. It's to make him thirsty." Managers can create an environment that will motivate people by creating opportunities for success and recognizing accomplishments.

SELF-MOTIVATION

When employees know an agency's goals and choose to help meet them, this is self-motivation. Fortunately for management, most employees want to do a good job. It is management's job to help and to provide additional motivation when needed. For example, an officer who works long after the shift is over to make certain a victim is adequately taken care of may be rewarded by being given time off during the next shift. Many incentives other than monetary ones encourage employees and cost nothing. They take little time, yet are seldom used. Most employees have pride in their work. They want to satisfy themselves and their employers.

Self-motivated law enforcement officers work for personal job satisfaction. Law enforcement work gives them a sense of accomplishment and personal value. Self-motivated officers are dedicated to their work and make every hour on the job count.

Job satisfaction remains a basic reward of working, even though not many employees would mention it as a benefit. Recreation and time for home life, children and rest are equally important. Self-motivated employees are more apt to work toward organizational as well as personal goals because the melding of both provides even more job satisfaction.

Not all jobs provide an enjoyable environment. Many people work only to make a living, to provide security for their families and to supply the funds to enjoy the other things in life. Many work at jobs they do not like. Not all law enforcement officers like their work. Managers need to be motivators in these situations.

Many theories of motivation have been developed based on extensive research of employees in the work environment. These studies reveal that although monetary rewards are a necessary part of jobs, money is not the major consideration as long as it is basically adequate for living.

MOTIVATIONAL THEORIES

Each individual has needs, even though a person may not have a list of needs or even have consciously thought about them. These needs make each of us what we are and cause us to do what we do. Each individual takes action to meet these needs.

The 1960s saw the development of many theories about motivation. Knowledge of these theories helps us understand what people can do for themselves and what managers can do for employees. The results of studies by human-behavior researchers apply as much to law enforcement as to any other profession.

Hierarchy of Needs—Maslow

Abraham Maslow conducted one of the best-known studies of human needs in 1962. He concluded that every human has five basic needs, which he assembled into a hierarchy, as Figure 9.1 illustrates. At the base of the hierarchy are *physiological needs*: air, food, water, sleep, shelter and sex. It is mandatory that at least air, food, water and sleep be satisfied or a person could not function or proceed to the next level. Some segments of the world's population live their entire lives just trying to satisfy this level of need. Shelter could be added to the list because it is more than merely a place to sleep; it is protection from the elements.

hierarchy of needs

Maslow's motivational theory that people have certain needs that must be met in a specific order going from basic physiological needs to safety and security, social, esteem and self-actualization needs.

 Maslow's **hierarchy of needs** is, in the order they need to be met, physiological, safety and security, social, esteem and self-actualization.

The second level, *safety and security*, includes protection from serious injury and death, freedom from fear and a clear authority structure. Humans function better in an environment free from fear. It has long been known that children need a set of standards even though they tend to rebel against them. Adults also need a set of standards, an authority structure, even though they, too, sometimes rebel. People want a level of certainty, to know where they stand.

The Five-level Model

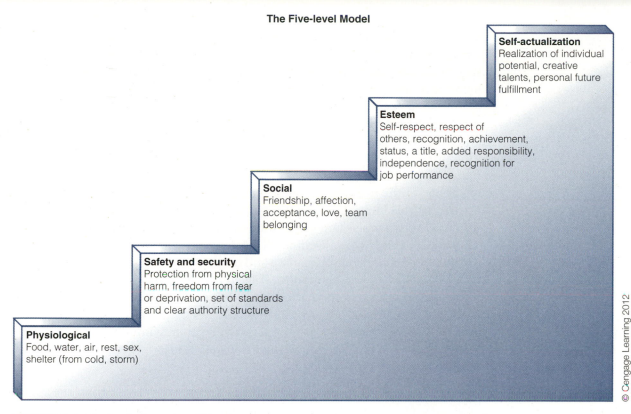

Self-actualization
Realization of individual potential, creative talents, personal future fulfillment

Esteem
Self-respect, respect of others, recognition, achievement, status, a title, added responsibility, independence, recognition for job performance

Social
Friendship, affection, acceptance, love, team belonging

Safety and security
Protection from physical harm, freedom from fear or deprivation, set of standards and clear authority structure

Physiological
Food, water, air, rest, sex, shelter (from cold, storm)

© Cengage Learning 2012

FIGURE 9.1 Maslow's Hierarchy of Needs

This translates at work to safety from accidents, a reasonable promise of job security and an opportunity for increases in pay and promotions.

The third level, *social*, includes friendship, love, affection and group and team belonging. These are important needs for everyone. Workers want peer acceptance, approval, sharing and friendship.

The fourth level, *esteem*, includes self-respect, respect and recognition from others, achievement, status, a title, added responsibility, independence and recognition for job performance.

The fifth level, *self-actualization*, refers to meeting individual goals and fulfilling one's potential, including expressing creative talents. **Self-actualization** is what you can do when all the other needs are satisfied. It is fostered by the chance to be creative and innovative and by having the opportunity to maximize skills and knowledge.

According to Maslow's theory, people's wants are always increasing and changing. Once an individual's basic (primary) needs have been satisfied, other needs take their place. The satisfied need no longer acts as a motivating force. If a number of needs are unsatisfied at any given time, an individual will try to satisfy the most pressing one first. Maslow believed that all levels of needs probably exist to some degree for individuals most of the time. Rarely is any one need completely satisfied, at least for long. Hunger, for example, may be satisfied after eating, but it emerges again later.

Maslow's need theory is popular because it makes sense. People can identify these needs in their own lives. In addition, the needs can be seen operating

self-actualization

refers to meeting individual goals and fulfilling one's potential, including expressing creative talents.

on the job. In many jobs, including law enforcement jobs, the first two levels of needs are automatically provided. Safety, for example, is extremely important in law enforcement. The law enforcement organization must do everything possible to ensure its officers' safety—and the officers should know what steps have been taken.

Satisfied needs do not necessarily become inactive needs. If law enforcement officers receive salary increases, they may raise their standard of living and then another salary increase is as welcome as the first.

Law enforcement organizations may meet the needs of the group but not of individuals. For example, with a minimal number of promotions, other means of satisfying the need for recognition must be found. Managers can play an important role in providing on-the-job authority structure. They can provide respect through praise and recognition for tasks well done.

Managers can help subordinates meet even the highest goals, fulfilling individual potential through training and on-the-job educational opportunities. Officers seek challenging opportunities to provide service to the community. If their performance is good, they expect fair compensation and rewards. The agency should provide clear goals that have been mutually agreed upon, and officers should expect to meet those goals, both individually and as a group. Maslow's five levels of needs and their translation into specific job-related factors are illustrated in Figure 9.2.

FIGURE 9.2
Maslow's Levels of Needs and Job Factors

Complex	Self-actualization	• Challenging job • Creativity • Achievement in work • Advancement • Involvement in planning • Chances for growth and development
	Esteem	• Merit pay raises • Titles • Status symbols/awards • Recognition (peer/boss) • Job itself • Responsibility • Sharing in decisions
	Social	• Quality supervision • Compatible coworkers • Professional friendships • Department pride/spirit
	Safety/security	• Safe working conditions • Sound department policies • Protective equipment • General salary increases • Job security • Feeling of competence
Basic	Physiological	• Heat/air conditioning • Base salary • Cafeteria/vending machine • Working conditions • Rest periods • Efficient work methods • Labor-saving devices • Comfortable uniform

© Cengage Learning 2012

© Joel Gordon

An important need is that of social acceptance by one's peers and a sense of belonging among coworkers. Here, officers from various law enforcement agencies throughout Florida satisfy not only their need to build social bonds with each other but also to participate in a charitable cause; running to raise funds for the Special Olympics in Putnam County, Florida.

Understanding officers' needs is a critical part of managers' abilities to motivate their subordinates. Some research has shown that age is fundamentally related to need orientation, with older police officers and those with higher educational levels requiring greater autonomy and control over their environment to achieve job satisfaction (Stojkovic et al., 2008, p.118). Furthermore, as the policing paradigm has shifted from traditional to community policing, managers have found it increasingly necessary to pay attention to the public service needs of newer officers and their desires to feel as if they are serving an important function in the community. A great challenge exists in meeting the self-esteem and self-actualization needs of officers, and managers and supervisors who are able to create work environments that encourage creativity, problem solving and decentralized decision making are more likely to be successful in maintaining a motivated workforce.

New officers are often socialized and indoctrinated on the dangers inherent in law enforcement and focus their attention on going home at the end of the shift without being complained about, disciplined, sued, injured or killed. Service and problem solving, not combat, should be the focus of academy instruction and socialization for new officers. Such a shift in focus would be in keeping with the motivational theory set forth by Herzberg.

Two-Factor Hygiene/Motivator Theory—Herzberg

Another behavioral psychologist, Frederick Herzberg, developed the **two-factor theory**, or the hygiene/motivator theory. Herzberg's theory divides needs that require satisfaction through work into two classes: hygiene factors and motivator factors.

two-factor theory

Herzberg's motivational theory that employees' needs can be classified as hygiene factors (tangible rewards that can cause dissatisfaction if lacking) and motivator factors (intangible rewards that can create satisfaction).

hygiene factors

tangible rewards that can cause dissatisfaction if lacking.

motivator factors

intangible rewards that can cause satisfaction.

 According to Herzberg's two-factor theory, **hygiene factors** are *tangible rewards* that can cause *dissatisfaction* if lacking, whereas **motivator factors** are *intangible rewards* that can create *satisfaction*.

Dissatisfaction and satisfaction are not two ends of a continuum because people can experience lack of dissatisfaction without necessarily being satisfied.

Tangible rewards pertaining basically to the hygiene factors do *not* provide satisfaction. They simply prevent dissatisfaction. Having officers who perform only because they are not dissatisfied is seldom conducive to high performance. Providing more tangible rewards is highly unlikely to accomplish better results.

The hygiene factors are similar to Maslow's lower-level needs. People assume these factors will be met. If they are not, people will be dissatisfied. Company policies, job security, supervision, a basic salary and safe working conditions are extrinsic factors that do not necessarily motivate people to do better work. They are expected.

Herzberg's hygiene factors help explain why many people stick with jobs they do not like. They stay because they are not dissatisfied with the tangible rewards such as the pay and the retirement plan even though they are definitely not satisfied with the work itself.

Industry found that when many of the wage increases, fringe benefits, seniority and security programs were initiated, they did not substantially reduce the basic problems of low productivity, high turnover, absenteeism and grievances. Herzberg claimed that approach was wrong. Instead, jobs should provide greater control over outcomes of work, have clearly established goals and have more to do rather than less. Figure 9.3 shows the relationship between Maslow's hierarchy of needs theory and Herzberg's two-factor theory.

As Herzberg (1978, p.49) pointed out, "A man whose work possesses no contentment in terms of self-fulfillment, but exists exclusively to fulfill the purposes of the enterprise or a social organization, is a man doomed to a life of human frustration, despite a return of animal contentment. You do not inspire employees by giving them higher wages, more benefits, or new status symbols. It is the successful achievement of a challenging task which fulfills the urge to create.... The employer's task is not to motivate his people to get them to achieve; he should provide opportunities for people to achieve so they will become motivated."

Herzberg's theory, like Maslow's, does not consider differences in people, for the same motivators will not motivate everyone. Law enforcement managers, for example, will find that not all patrol officers are motivated by the same needs. Managers have to adjust motivational approaches to the individual.

Most employees still believe that satisfying work is more important than increased salary and advancement, *if* the basic salary is adequate. The job itself—law enforcement work—is a good example: The work is satisfying because what officers do is meaningful to them and to the community they serve. Most law enforcement officers are *not* in it for the money.

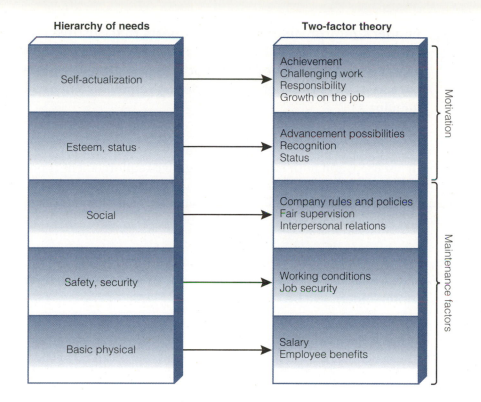

FIGURE 9.3
Comparison of Maslow and Herzberg

Source: From KOSSEN. *Supervision*, 2E. © South-Western, a part of Cengage Learning, Inc. Reproduced by permission. www.cengage.com/permissions

Reinforcement Theory—Skinner

Extremely influential writings by B. F. Skinner suggest that behavior can be shaped and modified using positive and negative reinforcement. Skinner's pioneering work in behavior modification was first described in his book *The Behavior of Organisms*, published in 1938, and expanded in *Walden Two*, published in 1948. A key conclusion of Skinner's research is that behavior is a function of its consequences. The ethics behind modifying behavior became highly controversial in the 1960s. Nonetheless, Skinner's theories *are* still relevant to managers, are implicit in the motivational theories just discussed and seem to be simple common sense.

In reinforcement theory, employees' behavior can be increased through the use of either positive or negative reinforcement. **Positive reinforcement** increases the likelihood that a behavior will occur in the future by introducing an appealing or pleasurable stimulus as a consequence of that behavior. This is the typical "reward cycle" scenario, where hard work by an employee results in positive recognition by superiors, which *should* lead to more hard work, which can result in a pay raise or promotion, which fosters the desire to keep working hard, and so on. **Negative reinforcement** is also designed to increase a given behavior, but it works by removing an unwanted stimulus instead of adding a wanted one (think of mathematics, with "positive" adding to a value and "negative" taking away from it). For example, most vehicles today are equipped with a seat belt chime that sounds incessantly until the driver buckles up. Thus, the behavior of wearing a seat belt is reinforced by an action that makes the chime stop.

positive reinforcement

increases the likelihood that a behavior will occur in the future by introducing an appealing or pleasurable stimuli as a consequence of that behavior.

negative reinforcement

increases a given behavior by removing an unwanted stimulus as a consequence of that behavior.

reinforcement theory

Skinner's motivational theory that behavior can be modified by using positive and negative reinforcement.

Skinner's **reinforcement theory** suggests that positive reinforcement increases a given behavior by providing a desirable stimulus as a consequence of that behavior; negative reinforcement increases a given behavior by removing a negative stimulus..

Use of both positive and negative reinforcement is readily seen on the job. Often both are used, and both make sense. Negative reinforcement is not to be confused with punishment. They are *not* the same. Reinforcement aims to strengthen or increase the likelihood of a behavior; punishment attempts to weaken or decrease the likelihood of a given behavior.

Reinforcement is usually more effective than punishment is. Also, the closer in time to the behavior, the more effective the reinforcement will be.

What is the problem with punishment? With a history as old as the human race, it is the belief that the harsher the punishment, the greater its effectiveness in changing behavior. Many managers, including those in penology, still adhere to this belief.

The means to inflict punishment have changed, with the whip, the rack and the stock falling into disfavor. Today's punishments are more subtle but have the same effect. Punishment-oriented managers might use techniques such as criticizing or ridiculing someone in public, ignoring a job well done, withholding needed information or avoiding discussion on an expected promotion or raise.

Although the punishments have changed, the problems associated with using a punishment-oriented management style have not. First, and perhaps most important, punishment can cause a get-even attitude. This can take the form of "fight"—where the employees cause problems by what they say or do. Or it can take the form of "flight," where the workers "quit but stay." They simply put in the required time and do as little as possible.

A second problem is that managers have to be constantly watching over employees. If vigilance is relaxed, the negative behavior is likely to recur. A third problem is that subordinates may come to associate punishment with the manager's presence and may dread seeing the manager coming around. They may become defensive every time the manager appears.

Yet another problem with punishment is that sometimes any kind of attention, even punishment, is considered more positive than being ignored. Teachers are well aware of this phenomenon with "problem" students who act up merely for the attention they get when they do. Law enforcement officers who crave acknowledgment of their existence by their superiors may feel that criticism is preferable to being totally ignored.

Another principle of reinforcement theory that managers need to consider is the time factor. Many incentives once thought to be powerful motivators are delayed—and scheduled. A good example is the paycheck. A law enforcement officer may conduct an excellent investigation on the first of the month but not be paid until the fifteenth of that month. In such cases, the paycheck is not seen as related to the investigation.

That is why incentives such as praise and recognition, given *immediately*, can be powerful motivators. Positive reinforcement can be highly motivating, but the theory also has some disadvantages. It does not consider human needs and tends to simplify behavior and rewards. It does not consider that employees may be motivated by the job itself, may be self-motivated or may consider rewards as manipulation, which they will eventually reject. Failing to reward can lead to decreased production, and failing to punish poor performance can reinforce that behavior.

Expectancy Theory—Vroom

Victor H. Vroom's expectancy theory looks at options employees have on the job. It combines some features of the preceding theories and advances the ideas that employees believe good work on the job will lead to high job performance and that high job performance will lead to job rewards.

Regardless of the chief individual motivating factors, if employees believe that performance will lead to satisfying motivational needs, they will work hard. Naturally, employees must be able to perform. According to Vroom's theory of motivation, employees become motivated to take action when the following three-step process takes place:

1. A motivating factor—a need to satisfy or goal to achieve—exists that is important to the employee.

2. The employee believes that by putting in the required or requested effort, the job can be performed.

3. The employee believes that by successfully performing the job as requested, the need will be satisfied or the goal will be achieved.

Employees have an effort expectancy and a performance expectancy. If managers clearly define the tasks and help employees with direction and skill training to perform the job, effort expectancy will rise. Managers can help achieve performance expectancy by providing means of satisfying individual needs.

Managers must know what opportunities specific jobs offer before they can use them as motivational opportunities for employees. These may be money, opportunity for educational or job growth, praise or peer recognition. Expectancies vary even with individuals doing the same job. Expectancy theory integrates ideas about employee motivation.

expectancy theory

Vroom's motivational theory that employees will choose the level of effort that matches the performance opportunity for reward.

 Vroom's **expectancy theory** suggests that employees will choose the level of effort that matches the performance opportunity for reward.

For example, if a law enforcement officer investigating a crash that happened one-half hour before shift change realizes that completing the investigation will take an hour, he or she can complete it, ask another officer to take over the investigation or do a poor job by leaving the investigation before obtaining the needed information.

The officer knows doing the complete job will receive recognition by the sergeant. He or she knows asking someone else to complete the investigation will lead to complications in obtaining facts and completing reports. He or she knows that leaving the scene without information for proper reporting will be reason for reprimand. The officer will probably choose to put in the extra time and complete the report because the rewards are a better expectancy than a reprimand. It will also look better on his or her record. The officer should also understand that making repeated comments to those involved in the crash that "this is on my own time" are negative and may result in a complaint. On the other hand, the satisfaction of a job well done and the good inner feeling that results may be motivating in themselves.

Contingency Theory—Morse and Lorsch

Closely related to the expectancy theory is the contingency theory developed by John J. Morse and Jay W. Lorsch. They built on Herzberg's motivation and maintenance factors in their research on how an organizational task fit affects and is affected by task performance and employees' feelings of *competence*. The four key components of the contingency theory are the following:

◉ People have a basic need to feel competent.

◉ How people fill this need varies and will depend on how the need interacts with other needs and the strengths of those needs.

◉ Competence motivation is most likely to exist when task and organization "fit."

◉ Feeling competent continues to be motivating even after competence is achieved.

contingency theory

Morse and Lorsch's motivational theory that suggests fitting tasks, officers and agency goals so that officers can feel competent.

 Morse and Lorsch's **contingency theory** suggests fitting tasks, officers and the agency's goals so that officers can feel competent.

Contingency theory further suggests that highly structured tasks might be performed better in highly structured organizations that have a management structure that resembles Douglas McGregor's Theory X approach (introduced in Chapter 1). Conversely, highly unstructured tasks might be performed better in more flexible organizations whose management structure resembles the Theory Y approach. In law enforcement work, both kinds of tasks occur. Consequently, flexibility in management style becomes very important.

Motivational theory has important implications for law enforcement managers and supervisors. No matter which theories they believe have the most credence, managers must understand that certain external, tangible motivators and certain internal, intangible motivators are important in accomplishing goals through others.

CAUSES AND SYMPTOMS OF AN UNMOTIVATED WORK FORCE

Causes of an unmotivated work force might include overwork, downsizing, endless restructuring, boredom, frustration, promotions—who gets them and why—work conditions and the court system. *Symptoms* of an unmotivated officer include absenteeism, constant complaining, lack of care for equipment, lack of respect for other officers, lack of respect for rules and regulations, low morale, sleeping or loafing on duty, slovenly appearance and tardiness. Dealing with these symptoms is the focus of the next section. In addition to recognizing the causes and symptoms of lack of motivation, managers must also understand and know how to use the knowledge that certain external, tangible motivators and certain internal, intangible motivators are important in accomplishing goals through others.

EXTERNAL, TANGIBLE MOTIVATORS

Although external motivators no longer have the power they once had, they are expected. As Herzberg's theory states, basic needs must be met or dissatisfaction will result. This is not to say that lack of dissatisfaction will be motivating. It is likely, however, to keep people on the job and to keep them from counterproductive behavior.

Among the most common external motivators or tangible rewards are salary, bonuses, insurance, retirement plans, favorable working conditions, paid vacation and holidays, titles and adequate equipment.

The Compensation Package

The law enforcement profession is not known for its great salaries. Nonetheless, money is important to most employees. They want and need enough salary to be comfortable and to meet their basic financial responsibilities. Some officers work two jobs until they have the amount of money they consider necessary. It is true that money talks. What managers must remember, however, is that it says different things to different people.

Although pay in the law enforcement profession is not at the top of the scale, the entire compensation package is usually competitive. One important factor is an equitable procedure for raises. In a well-managed department, employees would not have to ask for raises. They would know what to expect— and when—in return for their performance and dedication. Given the hazardous nature of law enforcement work, the compensation package should include health, disability and life insurance.

Working Conditions and Schedules

Employees expect adequate heat, light, ventilation and working hours. They also expect a well-maintained squad car and up-to-date equipment. Having a desk or a private office can also be rewarding. Inadequacies in working conditions can cause great dissatisfaction.

The work environment can have a great impact on morale. People appreciate working in a clean, attractive and healthy environment. Some plants might be brought in to brighten up the offices. Seasonal decorations can help add to appropriate holiday spirit. Attractive artwork can liven up otherwise drab hallways.

In addition, flexible hours and job-sharing opportunities, when possible, are attractive motivators to many officers, especially those trying to balance the job with family life.

Security

Although this may seem like an internal reward—or motivator—many aspects of security are indeed external, tangible and expected. Among them are fair work rules, adequate grievance procedures, reasonable department policies and discipline and seniority privileges. Some aspects of the compensation package such as insurance and retirement plans also meet basic security needs.

Social

Like the need for security, employees' social needs can fall within the external, tangible category when such things as parties, picnics, breaks and social gatherings are considered. Opportunities to mix with one's peers and superiors, sometimes including spouses, may be very rewarding.

Status

The need for status can also be partially met by external, tangible rewards such as privileges, titles, private offices, awards and other symbols of rank and position. These external, tangible factors are sometimes called *maintenance* factors. Provided in adequate quantity and quality, they merely prevent dissatisfaction. The best managers can hope for is a "fair day's work for a fair day's pay." To get subordinates to truly perform, managers usually need to provide internal, intangible motivators as well.

INTERNAL, INTANGIBLE MOTIVATORS

Internal, intangible motivators can spark employees to give their best effort to accomplish individual and department goals

 Internal motivators or intangible rewards include goals, achievement, recognition, self-respect, opportunity for advancement, opportunity to make a contribution and belief in individual and departmental goals.

Goals and Expectations

Goals need to be set and met. Specific goal setting results in greater accomplishment. Goals should make officers reach to their levels of competence. Different goals are often needed for individual officers. The reason some students fail in school is because goals are too easy and they become bored. On the other hand, the same goals may be too high for other students to achieve and they become frustrated. Students who achieve to their level of competence will be motivated.

The highly touted management by objectives (MBO) relies on clear, meaningful goals, both for individual officers and for the organization. Goals establish future direction of effort. Accomplishing goals provides room for creativity, innovation, diversity and a sense of accomplishment.

Operational goals should be set by first-line and middle managers, with the participation of patrol officers. Goals should be consistent and communicated. Realistic goals, proper resources to do the job, employee communication and a personal and organizational sense of accomplishment all play a major role in law enforcement motivation. Closely related to goals are expectations. To illustrate the importance of expectations, recognize the **Pygmalion effect**: What managers and supervisors expect of their officers and how they treat them largely determine their performance and career progress.

> **Pygmalion effect**
>
> what managers and supervisors expect of their officers and how managers treat officers largely determine officers' performance and career progress.

> There are hundreds of ways to motivate people, some good and some truly awful. . . . but the most effective way rests on one bottom-line principle: "Raise the expectations of others!" Whatever it is you do, your actions must raise a subordinate or employee's expectations of himself so that he or she can accomplish more than their current self-assessment gives them credit for. Once people believe they can do more and are properly encouraged, trained and given the responsibility to do so, they will often surprise themselves and you. Robert Browning, the English poet, once said, "A man's reach must exceed his grasp." As a supervisor, your responsibility is to inculcate a new belief system into your people. Raising expectations is not forcing your expectations on others or holding them accountable to the same. Rather it is planting the correct motivational seed in the employee's mind that he is capable of much more than he now believes. (Thompson and Walker, 2007, p.105)

Encouragement and Praise

Encouragement can be extremely motivating. Consider the story of a group of frogs traveling through the woods. Two fell into a deep pit. All the other frogs gathered around the pit and, upon seeing how deep the pit was, told the two they would never get out and would die there. The two frogs ignored their comrades and tried to jump out while the other frogs kept telling them to stop wasting their energy. Finally one frog paid attention and simply gave up, fell down and died. The other frog continued to jump as hard as he could despite his comrades yelling at him to stop the pain and suffering. This just made him jump even harder, and he finally jumped out. Amazed, his comrades asked him why he kept jumping. To which the frog replied he was deaf and thought they were encouraging him.

The lessons to be learned: (1) Destructive words to someone who is down can be what it takes to kill them. (2) Encouraging words to someone who is down can lift them up and help them make it through the day.

Thompson and Walker (2007, p.114) point out, "As a motivator, praise is one of the most powerful tools we can use, but it must be presented correctly. What do we know about praise? First, it must be believable, credible and appropriate to the situation and person. It also needs to be timely and, if at all possible, public, where others can hear it." They (p.155) share their "secret" for effective praise: *be specific*. General praise such as "Good job" is meaningless. They give as an example, a lieutenant who said to one of his officers: "Hey, George, I really appreciate the care you took out there watching the perimeter. Officer safety is important and you were alert and ready." Specific praise is powerful because it teaches the subordinate what you want and respect. It also reinforces employee values and skills.

Achievement, Recognition, Growth and Advancement

Achievement is a motivator. It can be a series of small accomplishments or one accomplishment that ultimately grows to a larger one. It can be a task done well for the first time, something done better than before, a higher score or committing fewer errors.

Recognition is also a motivator, whether it comes from peers or managers. Recognition is most effective if it can be related to a person's personal qualities rather than to the performance itself. For example, rather than saying "Good job on solving the XYZ case," emphasize the personal qualities involved, such as, "I admire your determination to keep working on the XYZ case until you got it solved."

Recognize accomplishment. Too often managers fail to use this reward that costs nothing. Recognition of something well done, offered at the time of accomplishment, is a powerful motivator: "Thank you for working overtime to get that report to me." "I have just reviewed your case report. It is excellent and reflects a lot of thought." The options for providing recognition are numerous, as accomplishments can be highlighted in weekly or monthly departmental news bulletins, posted on department or city web sites or announced at annual award ceremonies. Yet some employees report that their managers have never complimented or praised them in an entire year. Some managers cannot bring themselves to praise subordinates either because it is not in their nature or they are too busy.

The importance of recognition was established by the well-known experiment conducted from 1927 to 1932 by Elton Mayo at the Western Electric Company's Hawthorne Plant in Cicero, Illinois. This study's major finding was that almost regardless of the experimental manipulation used, the workers' production improved. One reasonable conclusion is that the workers were pleased to receive the researchers' attention, a phenomenon that became known as the **Hawthorne effect**. Production increased not as a consequence of actual changes in working conditions introduced by the plant's management but because management showed interest in such improvements. (The Hawthorne effect also needs to be considered when research is being conducted.)

Hawthorne effect

workers are positively affected by receiving attention, which affects research efforts.

In addition to recognition, employees want growth and advancement in their jobs. These do not have to be promotions or pay raises. They can even be little things: giving personal responsibility for a task, giving a title, showing concern for employees' health and welfare or giving deserved praise for a not-so-important task done well. All can contribute to a critical motivator: self-esteem.

Self-Esteem

Self-esteem involves self-confidence, a feeling of self-worth. As individual tasks are successfully accomplished, self-esteem builds. A sincere compliment by another person on your ability to perform a task also builds self-esteem. It is law enforcement managers' responsibility to build self-esteem in their team. The more self-esteem individuals in the agency have, the higher the organizational esteem will be. Recall Maslow's hierarchy of needs and, specifically, the fourth level labeled *esteem*.

Officers with low self-esteem will perform low-level work. If they have been told they are incompetent, they probably will not perform well. This has been referred to as a **self-fulfilling prophecy**. People tend to behave and eventually become what they think others expect of them. Law enforcement managers need to apply the implications of the self-fulfilling prophecy to everyday employee/law enforcement task performance. As one poster reads, "Every job is a self-portrait of the person who did it. Autograph your work with excellence."

Officers' perceptions of themselves and other people directly influence how the officers conduct themselves in public. This is important because law enforcement is a "people" profession. Officers' attitudes directly influence how they handle other people. Officers with low self-esteem are overly concerned with themselves because they fear failure and know they are not functioning as well as they should.

Managers can build individual self-esteem in the following ways:

- Do not embarrass subordinates, especially in front of others.
- Recognize and build on individual accomplishments.
- Give praise for things done well at the same time as you give criticism for things not well done.
- Give personal attention.
- Ask employees' opinions on problems.
- If an employee gives an opinion or suggestion, act on it in some way. Do not ignore it.
- Help individuals develop to their potential.
- Give employees breathing room for ideas, creativity and innovation.
- Give special task assignments.
- Get to know employees as individuals.
- Give certificates of appreciation when deserved.
- Truly listen.
- If employees express ideas, write them down in their presence.

> **self-fulfilling prophecy**
> the theory that people live up to expectations—if people believe they can do a job, they usually can, but if people believe they cannot do a job, they usually cannot.

- If someone has complimented an officer, pass it on.
- Assign part of the next departmental meeting to different officers.
- Share important information. Let everyone be "in the know."
- Acquire a piece of equipment that will help officers do a better job.

A Feeling of Importance

Managers must let their subordinates know they count. One manager used the following memo to let his employees know how valuable they were:

> "You Arx A Kxy Pxrson" Xvxn though my typxwritxr is an old modxl, it works vxry wxll—xxcxpt for onx kxy. You would think that with all thx othxr kxys functioning propxrly, onx kxy not working would hardly bx noticxd; but just onx kxy out of whack sxxms to ruin thx wholx xffort.

> You may say to yoursxlf—"Wxll I'm only onx pxrson. No onx will noticx if I don't do my bxst." But it doxs makx a diffxrxncx bxcausx to bx xffxctivx an organiza-tion nxxds activx participation by xvxryonx to thx bxst of his or hxr ability.

> So thx nxxt timx you think you arx not important, rxmxmbxr my old typxwritxr. You arx a kxy pxrson.

> (*Pasadena Weekly Journal of Business*, 155 S. El Molino Ave., Suite 101, Pasadena, CA, 91101. Reprinted by permission.)

One of the best ways managers and supervisors can let their people know they are important is to *listen* to them. Chapter 4 emphasized the role listening plays in communication. Law enforcement managers who truly listen to their subordinates will learn a great deal about their needs and feelings. The more managers know about their officers and their needs, the more managers can help officers meet those needs.

The more managers concentrate on the person talking to them, the more they show how much they value that person. Psychiatrists usually spend most of a patient's time listening. They understand this primary need of the patient to unburden, to let it all out. At the same time they learn a tremendous amount of information about the patient.

Effective listening is an *active* form of communication. You must work at it. Physically show your attentiveness. Ask questions. Clarify. Take notes. Main-tain eye contact. If you do not believe that listening is active, the next time someone tries to tell you something, do not pay attention; excuse yourself and start to make a phone call; or simply look away from the person, in no way en-couraging them to continue the conversation. The person will immediately be able to tell that you are not interested.

Being Involved, Included and "In" on Things

The importance of participative management has been discussed. The more employees feel a part of a department, the harder—and better—they will work. Orrick (2009, p.25) notes, "During periods of financial retrenchment, ru-mors of staffing cuts and reorganizations often take on a life of their own. Their existence unnecessarily perpetuates fear and adversely impacts morale when staff members spend valuable time venting and worrying about their own economic condition. Leaders must open multiple lines of communications with officers to keep them informed of steps being taken to address the financial challenges and how they will impact that person." To establish and maintain involvement, use a team approach and encourage suggestions.

Compassion

Because officers learn to steel themselves in dealing with suffering, misery and human depravity, they are often considered in danger of losing their compassion, creating a void that may then become occupied by cynicism and depression (Johnson, 2009). Managers need to "constantly dispel the notion so prevalent in law enforcement that it is 'us versus them.' We are them. We are a part of the communities we serve. If they suffer, so do we. Empathy generates compassion" (Johnson, 2009, p.10). Managers must lead the way to ensure their officers retain their compassion:

> It is in the best interest of the department and the public that police officers are compassionate, understanding and empathetic. True police leaders know that helping officers retain their humanity is essential to their psychological well-being.

> To this end, leaders must first and foremost model compassion. All interpersonal interactions between captains and the rank and file should be demonstrations of dignity, professionalism, care and concern. Such an example will be reflected in the attitudes and behavior of those under their command.

> In addition to leading by example, captains need to personally address their officers about the destructive impact of lost compassion. The resulting cynicism is contagious, and those most disheartened can easily influence their fellow officers. . . .

> Point out the simple observable fact that the officer with no compassion, and thus a disdainful interactive style, will more likely encounter physical resistance from offenders. An uncaring demeanor also frequently results in citizen complaints and disciplinary action.

> Most importantly, though, caring police leaders ensure that their officers understand the damage done to the emotional health of those who lose their compassion. (Johnson, 2009, p.10)

THE LAW ENFORCEMENT CAREER AS A MOTIVATOR

Law enforcement work itself can be a motivator. Many officers find that law enforcement tasks, in and of themselves, are a basis for self-motivation. When a law enforcement applicant appears before an interviewing board and is asked, "Why do you want to be a law enforcement officer?" the answer is invariably a variation of "Because I like to work with people," or "I want to provide a service, and I think law enforcement work is an opportunity to do that."

Herzberg identified several factors that could lead to dissatisfaction on the job, including inadequate pay, difficult work schedules, inadequate benefits, poor working conditions and the like. Herzberg also noted that job satisfaction is primarily a reflection of personal growth factors in one's workplace assignment. He identified three primary sources of job satisfaction: (1) the importance of the work itself, (2) the sense of responsibility while doing the work and (3) the feeling of recognition for that work.

Law enforcement entails a great variety of skills: handling an automobile, using weapons, conversing with all types of people, interviewing and interrogating, using computers and computerized information, setting up case investigations and so on. Everything law enforcement officers do provides task significance. They have a high degree of autonomy in their decisions and actions. Decisions are often instantaneous and permanent. In addition, their actions are highly visible because of their uniforms. This visibility should provide motivation to do the best possible job at all times.

Personal growth can be achieved by providing opportunities for departmental training, seminars, college classes or public talks to civic organizations and youth groups. These types of job enrichment opportunities can also provide a higher degree of self-motivation and self-control in performing law enforcement tasks in emergencies, without close manager control. Personal growth and development is the focus of Chapter 8.

The law enforcement job is generally not perceived as boring and routine. If it becomes that way, it is generally the officer's fault because ample opportunities exist to make it more exciting. Even routine foot and vehicle patrol should not be boring. Many exciting things happen on a shift or at least have the potential for happening.

The importance of interesting work is illustrated by the story of a man visiting Mexico who found in a little shop a very comfortable, attractive, reasonably priced handcrafted chair. Extremely pleased, the tourist asked the shop manager if he could make him a dozen chairs just like it. The Mexican nodded and, obviously displeased, said, "But the señor knows that I must charge much more for each such chair."

The tourist, astonished, exclaimed, "More? In the United States if you buy in quantity, you pay less. Why do you want to charge me more?"

The reply, "Because it is so dull to make twelve chairs all the same."

Managers should make the law enforcement job itself more interesting and challenging for officers, provide goals and make challenges out of routine work. Law enforcement tasks can be studied and made more interesting. Assignments can be made more efficiently and with greater variety to make the total job more satisfying. Community policing offers an opportunity to make a difference.

Giving more responsibility, providing opportunity for employees to perform the job without being directly told what to do, treating each employee according to his or her own needs—these actions are motivating.

Law enforcement work can be made more interesting and motivating in three important ways:
- **Job rotation**
- **Job enlargement**
- **Job enrichment**

Job Rotation

Job rotation can make the job more challenging. Job rotation also serves as a training opportunity and provides variety—an opportunity to understand the total law enforcement job. Different things happen on the day shift than on the night shift or middle shift. Job tasks are different in the patrol, detective, juvenile, narcotics and administrative divisions.

Job rotation is often done on a temporary basis. Such cross-training provides a better understanding of the total law enforcement effort and gives supervisors more flexibility to deal with absences and requests for vacations. Job rotation also prepares officers for promotions and can serve as a motivator as such officers begin to feel competent doing new and different tasks.

Job Enlargement

Job enlargement adds responsibilities, such as making a survey of vehicle licenses to determine the number of outsiders in the community, that can provide helpful information for the department, other departments or the community. Increasing the number of tasks may be perceived as a threat. Given the right training and tools, officers should perceive job enlargement as motivating, giving them renewed interest in and enthusiasm for law enforcement work.

Job Enrichment

Job enrichment is similar to job enlargement, except that in job enrichment the focus is the *quality* of the new jobs assigned rather than the quantity. Job enrichment emphasizes adding variety, deeper personal interest and involvement, increased responsibility and greater autonomy. Job enrichment is appropriate for any highly routine job.

For some officers, however, job enrichment might also be perceived as threatening. Some officers do not want enrichment. They do not need more challenges because they may already be working to capacity. They may be comfortable in their routine, or they may be burned out.

Not all officers will want to do all law enforcement tasks. Maybe they are satisfied with routine tasks. The lower level of tasks may satisfy their needs of security, money and group belonging. Even if given the opportunity for change, they may prefer one division over another. Not all officers want promotions. They would rather be responsible for only what they do, not for getting results from other people.

Job Satisfaction and Community Policing and Problem Solving

One benefit often attributed to community policing and problem solving is that officers are more motivated and morale is heightened. This is a result of officers feeling they are making a significant difference in the community. Officers in departments embracing community policing report greater job satisfaction.

AWAY FROM THE DESK:
The Leader as Motivator

An organization with a culture of achievement is one where professional excellence is expected and where there is commitment to performance and accountability. It is our people who drive this culture by being professional, motivated and flexible in their approach. Police leaders are results-oriented, innovative, fair, passionate about policing and responsive to change. The goal of motivation is to bring about a certain behavior in a worker, and this behavior is beneficial not only to the organization but also the worker. Motivation creates a two-way street where the goal is seen as desirable by both the agency and the officer.

An individual's qualities do not create a culture—the organization must also foster a climate where superior public service is standard practice, partnerships and collaboration are expected and supported, respect is freely given and accountability is expected and accepted. This organizational climate becomes effective when all individuals commit to these requirements. While many people commit daily, we all need to adopt this approach of maintaining pride and motivation in our personal achievements as well as being a part of a motivated workplace on an ongoing basis.

The goal is to create a work culture in which goals are easily identifiable, where there is room for growth, and where officers feel secure and appreciated, as well as properly rewarded. What motivates one person may have little to no effect on another. Also, what motivates one person in one situation may not motivate the same person in another situation. For example, not all officers understand the need for roadway safety and traffic enforcement initiatives as part of their day-to-day responsibilities. In particular, an officer who has served for several years often will not prioritize this responsibility. It is therefore the responsibility of leadership to communicate the importance of roadway safety through educational programs and enforcement efforts that produce impact. This can be done only when the entire organization makes it a priority and when its officers share motivation to make a positive and sustaining impact on the community served.

Being *motivated* is being committed to high standards of performance and service delivery. In serving your community, there is no room for complacency. The community deserves the best services we can provide, and we must, therefore, aspire to do better.

—*Chief Shaun E. LaDue*

BENEFITS OF MOTIVATED PERSONNEL

The benefits of having highly motivated personnel are numerous—less sick leave, better coverage, more arrests and better investigations. In fact, most of the numerous benefits listed in Chapter 7 as resulting from an effective training program would also result from effective motivation. With both effective training and motivational programs, these benefits are highly probable. The price of not paying attention to motivation is often low morale and a generally negative environment.

MORALE: AN OVERVIEW

An office poster designed to inspire employees to greater efforts reads, "You can— if you will!" Beneath it, someone had scrawled, "And you're canned if you won't!" Both sayings relate directly to morale and employees' attitudes toward their jobs. This brings to mind the military aphorism: "The beatings will continue until morale improves."

 Morale is a person's or group's state of mind, level of enthusiasm and amount of involvement with work and with life.

> **morale**
>
> a person's or group's state of mind, level of enthusiasm and involvement with work and with life; how employees feel, in contrast to discipline, which is how employees act.

Morale can make or break an individual or an organization. As Napoleon observed, referring to his army, "An army's effectiveness depends on its size, training, experience and morale . . . and morale is worth more than all the other factors combined."

Morale is *always* present. It might be high, low or on an even keel, but it exists perpetually. Management's responsibility is to keep morale as high as possible and to be alert to signs that it may be dropping. The morale of individuals, work units and an entire agency concerns managers and supervisors.

Achieving high morale is a complex challenge, with different problems depending on the department's size and leadership style. Even within the same agency, morale, as it relates to job satisfaction, can differ from one position to another.

Morale is somewhat elusive and difficult to define. Individuals and organizations differ greatly, and what would induce high or low morale in one might be the opposite in another. Good or poor morale is generally attributed to individuals, whereas high or low morale characterizes the entire organization.

Good or high morale is a *can-do* attitude. As Admiral Ben Morrell says, "Morale is when your hands and feet keep on working when your head says it can't be done." The right kind of persistence *does* pay. Coaches stress the importance of that "second effort" in winning games. The willingness to make another try when the first one fails distinguishes the average player and employee from the star. A Chinese proverb proclaims, "The person who says it cannot be done should not interrupt the person doing it."

Douglas MacArthur, the general so instrumental in helping win World War II, might never have gained his status without persistence. When he applied for admission to West Point, he was turned down, not once but twice. He persisted, however, applied a third time, was accepted and marched into history.

Morale can be measured by observing the actions and statements of employees. Are they positive and upbeat? Do people take pride in their work? Are they supportive? Or are they negative? The quality of officers' work will be affected as much by their morale as by their skills. Effective managers know that people's job performance is directly related to how they feel about the job, themselves, their peers, their managers and their agency.

Although improved morale will not always increase employees' effectiveness and productivity, it puts employees in the frame of mind to be productive. Given good supervision and good working conditions, employees with high morale will be extremely effective.

INDICATORS OF MORALE PROBLEMS

Knowing where an agency stands is the first step in improving morale. Good managers are always alert for changes in work attitudes that may indicate trouble. Among the most common indicators of morale problems are a noticeably less positive attitude, loss of interest and enthusiasm, negativism and lack of respect. Other indicators are excessive absenteeism, sick leave and turnover; longer lunch hours or breaks; and coming in late and leaving early. Still other indicators include low productivity, less attention to personal appearance, increasing numbers of grievances and complaints and a rise in the number of accidents.

Indicators of low morale include lack of productivity, enthusiasm and cooperation; absenteeism; tardiness; grievances; complaints; and excessive turnover.

Managers may recognize these red flags in individual officers, or they may be pervasive throughout the department. In the latter case, the manager faces a much greater challenge. A first step is to identify *why* morale might be low. Seldom is the answer simple or singular.

To identify causes of morale problems, some managers distribute a survey that includes questions such as the following (to which respondents anonymously answer strongly disagree, disagree, uncertain, agree or strongly agree):

1. This is a good department to work for.
2. My supervisor understands me.
3. My supervisor listens to my concerns.
4. I have the training I need to do a good job.
5. I have the equipment I need to do a good job.
6. I am proud to be a member of this department.

Such a survey helps identify areas that might be causing morale problems and lets employees communicate their feelings and know that these feelings are important to the department. However, the survey results must be *used*. Employees who think the department is insensitive might use a lack of follow-through to support their contention.

Surveys are not the only way to identify factors contributing to a morale problem. Managers who communicate well with their subordinates can often discover problems simply by having an open-door policy and listening to what people say. The closer managers are to their employees, the easier it will be for them to recognize a negative change in morale before it becomes disruptive.

REASONS FOR MORALE PROBLEMS

The underlying causes of morale problems are not always easy to determine. Individual morale can be low and the organizational morale high, or the reverse can be true. Some people point out that morale is related to happiness and well-being. Others say it is more related to work benefits. Still others believe it is a philosophical problem of self-fulfillment. In general, employees who work toward organizational goals are deemed to have high morale, and those who do not are deemed to have low morale.

If a law enforcement agency has inadequate, nonequitable salaries and fringe benefits; lacks modern equipment; and does not provide adequate resources, morale is likely to be low. Measures must be taken to correct these inadequacies. If all these factors are met and morale is still low, the problem is probably centered in individual needs. Most of the blame for low morale can be placed on controllable factors such as poor management, internal politics and favoritism by supervisors.

 Causes for low morale include poor management, job dissatisfaction and failure to meet important individual needs.

In many departments, what drives officer morale down is an uncaring police administration and rude or disrespectful supervisors. When individual morale is low, employees should first examine themselves. Mental attitudes toward superiors, fellow workers and the public have a great deal to do with job satisfaction.

Another important cause of low morale is job dissatisfaction. Among the job-related factors contributing to low morale are lack of administrative support; ineffective supervision; lack of necessary equipment or training to perform effectively; lack of promotion opportunities; political interference; corruption within the department; the criminal justice system itself, which may appear to be a revolving door for criminals; and the image of the police frequently portrayed by the media.

In addition, police wages and salaries have never been high, although the total benefit package and sense of job security have always made the job desirable. Given that police endure a high level of stress, most certainly face an abnormal risk of injury or death on the job and have a higher rate of burnout than most workers, police positions are underpaid.

Perception, the angle from which people view things, makes a tremendous difference in what they see. For example, the difference between a cute little mischief maker and a juvenile delinquent is whether the child is yours or someone else's.

TABLE 9.1 Worker and Supervisor Ratings Compared

Job Conditions	Worker Rating	Supervisor Rating
Full appreciation of work done	1	8
Feeling "in" on things	2	10
Sympathetic help on personal problems	3	9
Job security	4	2
Good wages	5	1
Work that keeps you interested	6	5
Promotion and growth in company	7	3
Personal loyalty to workers	8	6
Good working conditions	9	4
Tactful disciplining	10	7

Source: William B. Melincoe and John P. Peper. *Supervisory Personnel Development*. California State Police Officers Training Series, #76, Sacramento, CA, p.87. Used by permission, California Highway Patrol, Sacramento, CA.

A story about a young couple who opened a salmon cannery in Alaska also illustrates this point. They were having a hard time selling their salmon, despite an extensive advertising campaign. The problem was that their salmon was grey, not the pink salmon customers were used to. They pondered the problem for several days and then had a brainstorm. They changed the can's label, putting in bold letters right under the brand name "The only salmon guaranteed not to turn pink in the can." It worked.

A similar situation exists in how subordinates rate certain job factors and how managers rate the same factors. Consider the survey results summarized in Table 9.1. Full appreciation of work done and feeling "in" on things led the workers' list of job conditions that matter most. These same factors were at the bottom of the supervisors' ratings, indicating a significant disconnect between what employees regard as important and what supervisors *think* their employees regard as important. Similarly, good wages were at the top of the supervisors' list and in the middle of the workers' list. Such information is critical for managers to know.

BUILDING MORALE

Key considerations in building morale include salary, the quality of supervision, organizational and public support, physical conditions at work and favoritism.

 The individual most able to raise or lower individual and department morale is the manager/supervisor through leadership and open communication.

Improving morale requires certain attitudes on the manager's part. First, managers must believe that subordinates *can* grow and change—they can improve their attitudes/morale given the right circumstances. Managers must be like the tailor, who, according to George Bernard Shaw, is the "only person who behaves sensibly because he takes new measurements every time he sees me."

Second, managers must be open and honest with their subordinates, treat them with respect and seek to understand them. Finally, managers must understand themselves. They must recognize their own prejudices, their own strengths and weaknesses, their own obstacles to high morale and their critical role as a model for others.

The story is told of the Reverend Billy Graham visiting a small town and asking a young boy how to get to the post office. After receiving directions, Dr. Graham invited the lad to come to the church and hear him explain to the townsfolk how to get to heaven. The boy declined, saying, "I don't think so. You don't even know how to get to the post office."

Credibility is crucial. Managers who seek to build morale must exhibit high morale themselves. Only then can they hope to raise the work unit's morale. Several options for morale building are available to managers and supervisors.

Options for building morale include
- **Being positive and upbeat.**
- **Setting clear, meaningful goals and objectives.**
- **Setting appropriate standards.**
- **Being fair.**
- **Making no promises that cannot be kept.**
- **Providing the necessary resources.**
- **Developing organizational and personal pride.**
- **Providing a sense of participation—teamwork.**
- **Treating each person as an individual.**
- **Giving deserved recognition.**
- **Criticizing tactfully.**
- **Avoiding the "boss" attitude.**
- **Communicating effectively.**

People enjoy working with a cheerful, optimistic boss. Like magnets, people are drawn to the positive and repelled by the negative. An upbeat attitude is contagious—as is a negative attitude.

You have heard it before, but goals and objectives are at the heart of most management areas, and this certainly includes morale. Companies with the least employee turnover and the highest morale are those that have successfully communicated the company's mission and goals. Law enforcement executive managers should set department goals and objectives with the input of their subordinates—and this includes the line officers. The moment officers get the feeling they are not sharing in the department's goals, in what is going on, morale will drop, productivity will decrease and serious problems will arise.

Reasonable, clear, fair employee standards for conduct and behavior also should be established, published and made known. Employees expect this, and the law enforcement organization cannot function without these standards. As obvious as it may sound, it is critical that managers be fair in all aspects of the job. Most employees do not mind reasonably strict rules and procedures if they make sense and apply equally to everyone. Fairness is a common denominator for increased employee morale.

Likewise, managers should never promise things they cannot deliver. They should not be overly optimistic, trying to please their subordinates or telling them what they want to hear simply to keep them happy. It is very tempting to do so and to hope that things will work out for the best, but this can lead to problems.

Law enforcement employees need resources to do a good job and to feel good about themselves and what they do. Training is essential. All employees need to feel competent in the tasks for which they are responsible. Training also needs to be ongoing so officers are up to date. Their equipment should also be current and in good working condition.

The appearance of the station, the squad cars and insignia on the door, identification or name signs on each room in the station, desk name signs, uniforms that leave a favorable impression—all reflect morale. Many of these are not expensive, but they can make a significant difference in how officers feel about themselves and their organization.

Organizational and personal pride are closely related. Employees like to work for an organization they can be proud of. All law enforcement organizations have individual identities based largely on management goals and objectives. Bring up the subject of department and personal pride at staff and department meetings. Do not just think you are the best; really work at being the best. Often, competing in intradepartmental competitions such as sharpshooting, physical fitness or intradepartmental sports can contribute to a feeling of pride. These can also foster a sense of participation, another factor contributing to high morale.

Despite an emphasis on teamwork, every employee is an individual and must be recognized as such. Call employees by the names they prefer, including nicknames in appropriate situations. Take an interest in their problems. Employees who have problems at home cannot function at full efficiency on the job. Although managers cannot usually *do* anything about such problems, they can lend a sympathetic ear.

Too many law enforcement managers criticize when things go wrong but fail to praise when things go right. However, show judgment in giving credit and praise, as it can be carried to extremes so that subordinates come to rely on it for every task they complete. Such people are like the little boy who said to his dad, "Let's play darts. I'll throw and you say 'Wonderful.'"

A wise manager once said, "That criticism is best which sounds like an explanation." It is easy to be critical. The real management challenge is to come up with constructive alternatives. Several other considerations are important when criticism is necessary.

- Be certain of the facts. Do not make mountains out of molehills.
- Correct in private; praise in public.

- Be objective and impersonal. Do not compare one officer unfavorably with another.
- Ask questions; do not accuse. Allow those you are correcting to explain themselves.
- Focus on the action that needs correcting, not on the individual officer. Emphasize what is to be done, not what is wrong.

The legitimate purpose of criticism is *not* to humiliate but to help subordinates do better next time. Remember that criticism is seldom as effective as praise in changing behavior. Before managers give a person a "kick in the pants," no matter how much it is deserved, they should raise their sights and *try* to give a pat on the back instead.

Managers should also avoid the "boss" attitude, striving to be friendly yet businesslike and to think of "We" instead of "I." When appropriate, they should smile and be enthusiastic.

Finally, and most importantly, managers must communicate effectively: Employees want to know what is going on and how they are doing. Employees cannot act or react in a vacuum. Department newsletters, letters of commendation, constructive criticism, news releases, department bulletin boards, personal conversations, department or staff meetings—all are forms of communication.

It is demoralizing for officers to hear inside information from news media rather than from their superiors. It is essential that police administrators keep their officers informed. Among the ways to do this are newsletters, attending roll call, going on ride-alongs and simply walking around the department, sometimes referred to as management by walking around (MBWA). Administrators who take this approach should be prepared to hear negative comments, especially at first.

PROMOTIONS AND MORALE

Management positions within the law enforcement profession are more limited than in almost any other profession. This can cause severe morale problems. The promotion process must be fair, and those who want promotions must be helped in their quest.

Not everyone is management material. Those who are not should be guided into seeking satisfaction on the job in other ways, perhaps in developing a specialty the agency needs. The future of law enforcement agencies rests in making the best use of personnel. Those who are best suited for management—who have leadership qualities and communication skills—are those who should be promoted.

 Promotions must be fair and based on management qualities, not on technical skills or seniority.

Written examinations have been the most frequently used technique to make promotional selections of mid- to lower-level police positions. Any examination should be validated for the type and size of the agency using it. Written examinations, oral examinations and on-the-job performance ratings can be used for promotional decisions.

Most law enforcement agencies use a civil service examination, both written and oral. It is common to require minimum or maximum ages, terms of service, specific types of experience and other criteria for eligibility to take the examination. Most merit systems provide similar examinations. Final selection of the top three candidates (or any preestablished number) is made from the written and oral examinations. The Civil Service Commission, the city manager, the mayor with the city council's approval or the law enforcement chief executive officer then makes the choice.

Promotion panels often consider formal education level, amount and type of specialized training, specific skills, length of employment, previous evaluations, productivity or performance levels, personal appearance, department awards and recognition and discipline/reprimand history.

Assessment Centers

A trend is to use an assessment center to select those eligible for promotion, especially at the upper levels. Properly designed and administered assessments are more reliable than traditional testing methods for evaluating supervisory, managerial and administrative potential and can be adapted to all types of positions and assignments.

The multifaceted, structured process used in an assessment center can take the guesswork out of finding the right person for a job opening. Furthermore, a properly planned and implemented assessment center will be seen as a fair, objective process for promoting the most qualified officer. However, used incorrectly, an assessment center can become "stigmatized" as unreliable and unfair and could result in civil litigation. Examples of the methods used in assessment centers are contained in Table 9.2.

The total assessment typically is organized into three phases.

 Assessment centers use three phases:
1. Testing: written examination, verbal screening and psychological testing
2. Oral board interview, situational testing, leaderless group discussion and individual psychological interview
3. Polygraph examination, background check, physical examination and officer/staff interviews

During the second phase, candidates confront hypothetical problems that managers typically encounter. At the end of the second phase, candidates are ranked using the information from the first two phases. A predetermined number are selected in rank order to complete the third phase.

Whether an assessment center is used or the promotions are done inhouse, whenever possible it is usually best to promote from within the agency. This is not always easy. Sometimes this decision is not up to the immediate

TABLE 9.2 Typical Management Assessment Center Methods

Method	Description	Example Traits Analyzed
Management game or simulation	Participants perform in a simulated setting, sometimes with a computer simulation, make necessary decisions and analyze the results.	Organizing ability, financial aptitude, decision making, efficiency under stress, adaptability and leadership capacity
Leaderless group discussions	Participants in a group with no formally appointed leader are asked to solve a business problem.	Aggressiveness, persuasiveness, verbal skills, flexibility and self-confidence
In-basket exercise	A mail in-basket for an ill executive is given to the participants to analyze, to set priorities and to take action on.	Organizing ability, decision making under stress, conceptual skills, ability to delegate and concern for others
Role playing	Participants are asked to take the roles of hypothetical employees, as in a performance evaluation interview.	Insight, empathy to others, human and technical skills and sensitivity to others
Psychological testing	A series of pencil-and-paper instruments is completed by the participants.	Reasoning, interests, aptitudes, communication tendencies, leadership and group styles, motivation profile and the like
Case analysis	Participants are given a case to analyze individually and present to a group of evaluators.	Verbal ability, diagnostic skills, conceptual skills, technical skills and so on
In-depth interviews	Participants are interviewed by raters—usually after some of the above exercises have been completed—regarding a variety of personal interests, skills and aptitudes.	Verbal ability, self-confidence, managerial skills, commitment to career and so on

Source: International City Managers Association, 1120 G. Street, NW, Washington, DC, p.253. Reprinted by permission.

supervisor or manager. But studies and common sense show that passing over qualified personnel to bring in an outsider almost invariably erodes morale.

 When possible, law enforcement administrators should promote from within to improve overall morale.

Seeing colleagues receive a promotion can be highly motivating for those who also want to be promoted and can improve department morale. Another morale booster is to provide police/family programs for officers.

Police/Family Programs

The police career is difficult to keep separate from officers' personal lives. Tasks and experiences are often intermixed with family well-being. Job stress is often family stress: "Studies have shown that law enforcement officers who experience ongoing stress are more likely to display anger, distance themselves from their family members, and have unsatisfactory marriage and family relationships" (Westphal and Openshaw, 2009, p.48).

Ironically, the very distrust that keeps officers alive and serves them well on the street can become the undoing of their personal lives (Nowicki, 2008, pp.21–22). In addition, traumatic experiences do not end with the termination of the shift or on arriving home. Incidents that result in shooting a suspect or end with an officer being injured or killed on duty are endured by the family as well as by the officer. Families often experience the ups and downs of law enforcement just as the officers do: "Many officers bring home their struggles with the job, especially if they are involved in critical incidents. Even if an officer attempts to keep the struggles away from the home life, the family senses problems or feels the officer is distant" (Nowicki, p.23). Officers' daily interactions with the seamy side of life and with problem people may cause a distorted, unbalanced view of society. In severe cases this can lead to alcoholism, drug abuse, separation, divorce or even suicide.

Police family members often have no more understanding of the police job than the average layperson. Family training in communication and cultivating caring relationships can help spouses achieve a realistic understanding of the police job. Ideally this is done through programs specifically developed for police families. A number of police departments have experimented with police-spouse seminars to explain work shifts; police jargon; salaries; fringe benefits; types of police incidents; types of people police come in contact with; police equipment; police training; and panel discussions on selected subjects, with the panel consisting of officers, spouses and experts on the subject. Expectations and fears of officers and their spouses are discussed freely. Spouses often form support groups that meet regularly or when a crisis arises.

If the budget does not allow for such programs, and if the department has a citizen's academy, spouses might be encouraged to attend that academy. "Ultimately, a family can be either a great support or an ongoing pressure for officers" (Johnson and Huffman, 2008, p.34). Family programs can foster the support officers need.

SUMMARY

Motivation is an inner or outer drive to meet a need or goal.

Maslow's hierarchy of needs is, in the order they need to be met, physiological, safety and security, social, esteem and self-actualization. According to Herzberg's two-factor theory, hygiene factors are tangible rewards that can cause dissatisfaction if lacking, whereas motivator factors are intangible rewards that can create satisfaction.

Skinner's reinforcement theory suggests that positive reinforcement increases a given behavior by providing a desirable stimulus as a consequence of that behavior; negative reinforcement increases a given behavior by removing a negative stimulus. Reinforcement is usually more effective than punishment is. Also, the closer in time to the behavior, the more effective the reinforcement will be.

Vroom's expectancy theory suggests that employees will choose the level of effort that matches the performance opportunity for reward. Morse and Lorsch's contingency theory suggests fitting tasks, officers and the agency's goals so that officers can feel competent.

Among the most common external motivators or tangible rewards are salary, bonuses, insurance, retirement plans, favorable working conditions, paid vacation and holidays, titles and adequate equipment. Internal motivators or intangible rewards include goals, achievement, recognition, self-respect, opportunity for advancement, opportunity to make a contribution and belief in individual and departmental goals. Law enforcement work can be made more interesting and motivating in three important ways: job rotation, job enlargement and job enrichment.

Morale is a person's or group's state of mind, level of enthusiasm and amount of involvement with work and life. Indicators of low morale include lack of productivity, enthusiasm and cooperation; absenteeism; tardiness; grievances; complaints; and excessive turnover. Causes of low morale include poor management, job dissatisfaction and failure to meet important individual needs.

The individual most able to raise or lower individual and department morale is the manager/supervisor through leadership and open communication. Options for building morale include being positive and upbeat; setting clear, meaningful goals and objectives; setting appropriate standards; being fair; making no promises that cannot be kept; providing necessary resources; developing organizational and personal pride; providing a sense of participation—teamwork; treating each person as an individual; giving deserved recognition; criticizing tactfully; avoiding the "boss" attitude; and communicating effectively.

One important factor affecting morale is promotions. Promotions must be fair and based on management qualities, not on technical skills or seniority. Some law enforcement agencies use assessment centers to determine promotions. Assessment centers use three phases: (1) testing: written examination, verbal screening and psychological testing; (2) oral board interview, situational testing, leaderless group discussion and individual psychological interview; and (3) polygraph examination, background check, physical examination and officer/staff interviews. When possible, law enforcement administrators should promote from within to improve overall morale.

CHALLENGE NINE

After several months on the job as the Greenfield police chief, you observe a lack of motivation and low morale among a core group of officers. They are resistant to the concept of community policing and just want to be left alone to do "real" police work—arresting crooks. During the previous administration, officers received monthly awards for making the most arrests and writing the most traffic citations.

One of your captains tells you the disgruntled officers are influential in the department's informal hierarchy. Some are veterans who have taken promotional exams but were never selected. Others never even took the exams. The captain says they are skilled officers who could have been promoted if they had worked harder and better prepared themselves. He thinks their lack of success has left them bitter.

The captain suggests you issue a directive ordering the entire department to implement one community policing project each month. Those who do not comply will be progressively disciplined. He thinks the threat of discipline will motivate the disgruntled officer to accept community policing.

1. As the Greenfield Police Department chief, what changes would you implement to improve morale and increase motivation among officers not pursuing supervisory positions?

2. Is resistance to change a sign of low morale and lack of motivation?

3. What affect will your captain's suggested directive have on the department?

4. How can community policing improve morale?

5. How does your role (police chief) as a motivator differ from the role of a sergeant as a motivator?

DISCUSSION QUESTIONS

1. What motivates you?

2. What do you consider your basic needs? Write down the top five.

3. What are five motivators that make you do better work?

4. What would not motivate you?

5. Do you agree or disagree with the following statement: "It is not possible to motivate anyone." Why?

6. What makes your on-the-job morale go down? Go up?

7. What are some ways to give personal recognition for a job well done?

8. What job conditions make you feel best?

9. How do morale and motivation interact?

10. If you could make one change in your life that would improve your morale, what would that change be?

REFERENCES

Burch, Jay. "Recruiting Character." *Law and Order*, September 2008, pp.80–83.

Conroy, Dennis. Personal correspondence regarding reinforcement, 2006.

Dickinson, Eric. "Get 'Em & Keep 'Em: Recruiting and Retention for Small Departments." *Law Officer Magazine*, October 2008, pp.52–56.

Fitch, Brian. "Motivation: Rethinking the Supervisor's Role." *Law and Order*, March 2008, pp.100–106.

Griffith, David. "The Thinning Blue Line." *Police*, January 2008, pp.44–51.

Herzberg, Frederick. "The Human Need for Work." *Industry Week*, July 24, 1978, pp.49–52.

Johnson, Horace, and Huffman, Jerry. "Kentucky Develops Orientation for New Law Enforcement Families." *The Police Chief*, May 2008, pp.34–36.

Johnson, Robert Roy. "Compassion in Command." *Law and Order*, October 2009, p.10.

Nowicki, Ed. "Training Police Family Members, Part 2." *Law and Order*, May 2008, pp.20–23.

Orrick, Dwayne. "Recruiting and Retention." In *Police Chiefs Desk Reference: A Guide for Newly Appointed Police Leaders*, 2nd ed., edited by International Association of Chiefs of Police and U.S. Bureau of Justice Assistance. Boston: McGraw-Hill Learning Solutions, 2008, pp.175–183.

Orrick, Dwayne. "Talent Management in a Slow Economy." *Law and Order*, May 2009, pp.24–25.

Reaves, Brian A. *State and Local Law Enforcement Training Academies, 2006*. Washington, DC: Bureau of Justice Statistics Special Report, February 2009. (NCJ 222987)

Stockton, Dale. "Our Police Staffing Crisis." *Law Officer Magazine*, April 2007, p.10.

Stojkovic, Stan; Kalinich, David; and Klofas, John. *Criminal Justice Organizations: Administration and Management*, 4th ed. Belmont, CA: Thomson Wadsworth, 2008.

Thompson, George J., and Walker, Gregory A. *The Verbal Judo Way of Leadership: Empowering the Blue Line from the Inside Up*. Flushing, NH: Looseleaf Law Publications, Inc., 2007.

Westphal, Gary, and Openshaw, Linda. "Law Enforcement Healthy Marriage and Family Project." *The Police Chief*, January 2009, pp.48–50.

Wilson, Jeremy M., and Grammich, Clifford A. *Police Recruitment and Retention in the Contemporary Urban Environment: A National Discussion of Personnel Experiences and Promising Practices from the Front Lines*. Santa Monica, CA: The RAND Corporation, 2009.

Discipline and Problem Behaviors

Discipline is the bridge between goals and accomplishments.

—Jim Rohn
Motivational speaker and entrepreneur

DO YOU KNOW?

- How morale and discipline differ?
- What the purpose of discipline is?
- What a fundamental management right is?
- What the foundation for most disciplinary actions is?
- What the 10/80/10 principle is?
- How a problem employee is characterized?
- What types of personalities might be likely to result in problems?
- How managers can deal with problem people?
- What behavior problems managers must deal with?
- What a primary rule for the timing of discipline is?
- What should be considered when assessing penalties?
- What steps progressive discipline usually involves?
- What balance of consequences analysis is?
- What consequences are most powerful?
- How managers can use the balance of consequences?
- What the PRICE Method consists of?
- How much time effective praise and reprimands might require?
- What ratio of praise to blame is usually needed?
- What strokes managers can use?

CAN YOU DEFINE?

appeal
comprehensive discipline
decoupling
discipline
general orders
gunnysack approach
insubordination
marginal performer
negligent retention
nonactor liability
passive resistance
progressive discipline
reprimand
sexual harassment
summary discipline/punishment

INTRODUCTION

Managers are challenged in the area of discipline as in no other. Values have changed, and court decisions have supported more liberal views of discipline during the past decades. The days of autocratic, near tyrannical discipline are gone: "In general, law enforcement agencies are well-structured for formal disciplinary processes—they have direct lines of supervision, policy-driven operations and well-defined methods to assess performance and infractions" (J. Harris, 2007, p.3).

Imposing some form of discipline is invariably part of a law enforcement manager's responsibilities, one the manager must be prepared to exercise when necessary. Most people assume that when discipline is discussed, it refers to punishment, but discipline is far broader than punishment.

Collins and his research team (*Good to Great*) found that the great companies had one thing in common: a "culture of discipline" where all employees showed extreme diligence and intensity in their thoughts and actions and focused on implementing the company's mission (Wexler et al., 2007, pp.7–8). The opposite of a culture of discipline is a bureaucracy, which Collins says arises to compensate for incompetence and lack of discipline, the result of having the wrong people on the bus in the first place.

Most chiefs inherit their managers and officers, making it difficult to create the culture of discipline Collins talks about: "So the police department that wants to move in the direction of constant improvement must find a middle ground between having a culture of discipline and being willing to impose controls on employees who need it because they lack internal discipline and they cannot be forced off the bus" (Wexler et al., 2007, p.38). As more departments adopt community policing and problem solving, which require more creative, responsible officers, they have come to view honest mistakes resulting from well-intentioned acts as teaching moments, moving beyond simply telling officers what their job description dictates: "Discussion rather than description is used to help an officer who has made a mistake consider alternative behaviors or approaches." (Wexler et al., pp.38–39). Whereas a description is, more or less, a black-and-white account of essential qualities and characteristics of a specific entity, a discussion is an open dialogue for brainstorming and problem solving.

CHAPTER at a GLANCE

This chapter begins with a definition of discipline, followed by a description of positive, constructive self-discipline and a look at the importance of knowing the rules, regulations and expected behaviors of a law enforcement department. Then policies and procedures are briefly revisited, followed by a discussion of the tension often present between clarity of role and creativity. The challenge of managing problem employees is examined next, followed by an explanation of the need for negative discipline/ punishment when positive discipline proves ineffective. The chapter concludes with a discussion of comprehensive discipline and a brief description of a fair disciplinary system.

DISCIPLINE DEFINED

Discipline is training expected to produce a desired behavior—controlled behavior: "Discipline in an organization has two purposes. The disciplined leader not only focuses on what the organization needs to do but also uses discipline to focus on—and eliminate—those things the organization should not do" (Wexler et al., 2007, p.39). Discipline should never be an end in itself. It should be used to develop highly trained, efficient law enforcement officers. Those officers with the highest performance have a high level of determination, pride, confidence and self-discipline—a set of self-imposed rules governing a person's self-control. Leaders throughout the world set degrees of discipline, as do religions. Discipline can be a form of voluntary obedience to instructions, commands or expected demeanor.

Discipline is closely related to morale. As discussed in Chapter 9, morale is a state of mind, an employee's attitude. Discipline, in contrast, is a state of affairs, or how employees act.

> *Morale* is how a person feels; *discipline* is how a person acts.

Morale and discipline are closely related because the level of morale affects employees' conduct. The higher the morale, the fewer the discipline problems. Conversely, the lower the morale, the more likely discipline problems will erupt.

> The purpose of discipline is to promote desired behavior, which may be done by encouraging acceptable behavior or punishing unacceptable behavior.

The root of the word *discipline* is *disciple*: "A disciple is one who is cultivated and molded in the image of the teachers. A disciple is someone who can then take up the mission when that instructor passes on. Consequently, discipline is about education and mentorship" (Wyllie, 2009). All too often, however, discipline is punitive rather than constructive or instructive. An officer dismissed from work for five days without pay will learn little about how to correct the behavior that led to the disciplinary measure in the first place. The terms *corrective* and *disciplinary*, although often used interchangeably, are *not* synonymous, and understanding the differences can help clarify the distinction between negative and positive discipline:

> While I agree that there are certain offenses that absolutely require disciplinary action, there are far more instances where a more positive approach in the form of corrective action would bear more fruit. In order to be effective, both must be used appropriately, which involves both supervisory and line personnel understanding the difference. For example, if a form marked "corrective" action is filled out simply documenting an employee's tardiness and stating that he or she needs to come to work on time in the future, very little corrective action is taking place. In this and similar cases, the perception will be that "corrective" equals "disciplinary" because the employee sees that he or

discipline

training expected to produce a desired behavior—controlled behavior or administering punishment; also a state of affairs or how employees act, in contrast to morale, which is how employees feel.

she was reprimanded and that now there is a paper trail in the file. In contrast, if an employee is tardy and the supervisor talks with the employee, determines a root cause for the tardiness, assists in formulating a plan to overcome the issue, and then documents the conversation on a "corrective" action form, this record becomes a road map for the employee to successfully navigate the situation in the future. . . .

All too often, errors are concealed for fear of disciplinary measures. Errors can be a powerful learning tool, not just for the person who made the mistake but for the entire agency. Sharing an error or near error in a way that promotes learning and a collegial culture can do as much good as simply writing someone up can do harm. On the other hand, repeat offenders and others whose behavior does not improve through the use of nonpunitive measures must have additional or different, perhaps even punitive actions taken. . . .

Management under fear of discipline is negative reinforcement, while corrective action with a focus on solving the root cause of the incorrect behavior will have longer-lasting and more positive results. Employees should not be frustrated by the fear of consequences for incorrect behavior; they should be motivated by a desire to do the job correctly and be given the support needed to establish and maintain a positive approach. In short, negativity breeds resentment and more negativity, whereas positive reinforcement encourages positive results. (Brophy, 2007, pp.43–44)

Thus, the disciplinary system should not be feared but, rather, respected for its primary function or purpose, which is to create a high functioning, efficient and effective organization.

POSITIVE, CONSTRUCTIVE SELF-DISCIPLINE

Positive, constructive self-discipline, like self-motivation, is usually most effective. Positive discipline uses training to foster compliance with rules and regulations and performance at peak efficiency.

It is to law enforcement managers' advantage to maintain a high degree of self-discipline within themselves and within their subordinates. When employees willingly follow the department's rules and regulations and put forth full effort to accomplish their individual and departmental goals, positive discipline prevails. The Navy would call this a "taut ship." But officers need to know the rules and what is expected of them.

KNOWLEDGE OF RULES, REGULATIONS AND EXPECTED BEHAVIORS

Everybody should understand what he or she can and cannot do. The more employees know, the more able they are to conduct themselves as expected. To inform employees, managers might post rules on bulletin boards, distribute standard operating procedure (SOP) manuals and discuss the rules at meetings. Some departments find it beneficial to provide their SOP manuals on the agency intranet, which allows officers to reference this information easily from their squad car computers.

Officers should have input on rules. If they have a voice in establishing the rules, they are more likely to support them. Having a few rules that everyone supports is better than having many rules that are violated.

Typical Rules and Regulations for Law Enforcement Departments

Rules and regulations are often established by civil service boards and will vary with each department. Officers should be aware of all rules and regulations, and all members of the agency are subject to disciplinary action if they violate these.

General Conduct

Officers are expected to report for duty at the designated time and place. They must not engage in disorderly conduct or accept gifts from suspects, prisoners or defendants. Officers must refrain from using unnecessary force on any person. Officers must object to and refuse to obey an immoral or illegal order.

Performance of Duty

Officers must preserve the law; protect life and property; and enforce federal statutes, state laws and county and city ordinances. Officers are required to discharge their duties calmly and firmly, to act together and to assist and protect each other to maintain law and order. Any officer who fails to comply, by act or omission, with any order, procedure, rule or regulation of the department or who acts in the performance of official duties in a way that could discredit himself or herself, the department or any other member of the department may be considered in neglect of duty. Officers must be courteous and respectful in dealing with the public and respond promptly to all calls for assistance from citizens or other officers.

Restrictions on Behavior

Officers must not knowingly make a false report, either oral or written. For unionized law enforcement organizations, relevant provisions of the labor agreement must be considered. Some supervisors fear that with a union contract they cannot make discipline stick. This is *not* true. No union contract protects workers from discipline when a valid work rule is violated.

 Maintaining discipline is a fundamental management right.

Policy versus Discretion

Although clear policies and procedures are necessary, they can be overdone. Too often the policy and procedure manual collects dust on the shelf because it is just too big. Effective managers recognize when control is necessary and

FIGURE 10.1
The Continuum of Policy: Levels and Examples

Source: Geoffrey P. Alpert and William C. Smith. "Developing Police Policy: An Evaluation of the Control Principle." *American Journal of Police*, Vol. 13, No 2, 1994, p.9. Reprinted by permission.

Strict control	Structured guidelines	Summary guidance
← Use of force	Domestic violence	Telephone contacts →

when discretion should be allowed. Policies should be made to cover high-risk, low-frequency police functions, for example, use of deadly force and high-speed pursuits. Other police functions, such as most domestic dispute calls, require discretion within guidelines. Yet other functions, such as telephone contacts with citizens, may actually be hindered by controlling policies. Figure 10.1 shows a continuum on which control and discretion may be viewed.

POLICIES AND PROCEDURES REVISITED

 An agency's policy and procedure manual is the foundation on which most discipline must be based.

Policies and procedures were introduced in Chapter 3. At the heart of an effective discipline system and high morale are clear written policies and procedures that guide officers yet allow discretion in unique circumstances. Most SOP manuals are broken down into sections covering policies, general procedures and general orders, to be discussed shortly.

The writing style should be concise and understandable by all personnel. The tone of the language used can influence the organizational culture (Orrick, 2008, p.214). If the manual has a negative tone, for example, using *shall not* and *will not* or *forbidden*, the policy may be seen as unreasonably restrictive rather than empowering: "The text of the manual should avoid focusing on prohibited acts, but rather emphasize conduct the department expects and supports of officer"(Orrick, p.214). A properly developed and implemented SOP manual gives staff members the information they need to act decisively, consistently and legally, and it promotes confidence and professional conduct among employees (Orrick, p.209).

Finally, policies and procedures must reflect federal, state and local laws, and they must comply with the Americans with Disabilities Act (ADA). Further, policies and procedures should reflect applicable court decisions, the local government's charter and collective bargaining agreements.

Updating policies and procedures should be regularly scheduled, at least annually, rather than as a reaction to some crisis. In addition, managers must ensure that policies are being followed: "What gets inspected is what gets done" (Orrick, 2008, p.215). If the work is not being done according to the policy, the policy is meaningless and increases the department's exposure to liability.

General Orders

general orders
written directives related to policy, procedures, rules and regulations involving more than one organizational unit; typically have a broad statement of policy as well as the procedures for implementing the policy.

General orders are "written directives related to policy, procedures, rules and regulations involving more than one organizational unit. General orders typically have a broad statement of policy as well as the procedures for implementing the policy" (Orrick, p.209).

General orders formalize a department policy on a specific issue and are a central mechanism to law enforcement leadership confronting recurring and potentially problematic enforcement issues. Often, however, discrepancies exist between the formal policies and actual practices, referred to as **decoupling**: Decoupling occurs when an organization adopts a new policy but never really implements it to change how the work gets done. General orders should be based on accurate, simple descriptions of the situations to which they apply and be clear, inclusive, credible and durable.

decoupling
discrepancies between an agency's formal policies and informal practices; occurs when an organization adopts a new policy but then never really implements it to change how the work gets done.

CLARITY OF ROLE VERSUS CREATIVITY

Specific rules and regulations leave little doubt about what is expected of officers. This emphasis on formal rules is the result of three developments: the need for due process in discipline, protection against civil litigation and the accreditation movement. Despite this emphasis on rules and regulations, questions arise: Do such written directives help officers learn the correct way to do law enforcement work and motivate them to do so, or do they send a message to officers that they are not trusted? And what responsibility does an employee have to know and practice the agency's policies, versus the management's responsibility to ensure employees know and adhere to policies?

An excessive number of rules may discourage innovation, risk taking, imagination and commitment to the department's mission. The trend in business is just the opposite. Control is achieved not through formal, written rules and regulations but by developing team spirit and a commitment to shared values.

The administrator's challenge is to lead by instilling the desired values and culture within the organization. This might include gearing recruiting, selecting and socializing toward basic departmental values and basing assignments, promotions and other rewards on these basic values.

DEALING WITH PROBLEM EMPLOYEES

Administrators also sometimes deal with problem behaviors. "A growing number of researchers have indicated that approximately 10 percent of officers can cause, or have caused, 90 percent of the problems in law enforcement" (Hughes and Andre, 2007, p.164).

 The 10/80/10 principle divides the work force into three categories: 10 percent self-motivated high achievers, 80 percent average achievers and 10 percent unmotivated troublemakers who cause 90 percent of management's problems.

Employees have many reasons for exhibiting objectionable behavior. A formerly excellent employee may change behavior because of physical illness or emotional or mental breakdown. This may not be exhibited violently or suddenly but subtly and over a long period. A change in behavior may also occur in response to disruptive and objectionable changes in department rules or regulations.

A key question is, Are problem employees too costly to retain, or is it wiser to change their behavior? Research by C. Harris (2009, p.210), involving analysis of citizen complaints against more than a thousand officers, suggests the latter: "Problem behaviors peak quickly and early in officers' careers and begin a steady decline thereafter. It is likely this curve represents difficulties officers have in mastering the craft of policing early on." But officers grow in skill as they gain experience. Harris' study also found support for the 10/80/10 principle in that, although persistent problem behaviors are infrequent, a few officers receive the bulk of multiple complaints.

It is generally accepted that changing behavior is usually more cost effective than replacing employees, so managers must learn more about employee assistance programs (EAPs) and their underlying philosophy. Many law enforcement agencies operate their own EAPs. Others contract with outside agencies to provide services such as counseling and peer support, as discussed in Chapter 12.

 A problem employee exhibits abnormal behavior to the extent that the behavior is detrimental to organizational needs and goals as well as to the needs and goals of other law enforcement personnel.

Such behavior reduces the department's effectiveness and the desired professional level of law enforcement service to the community and results in numerous conflicts. When personal quirks irritate others or derail the success of those who display them, career consequences can be disastrous in a highly demanding profession such as policing (Miller, 2003, p.53).

marginal performer

employee who has demonstrated ability to perform but who does just enough to get by.

A **marginal performer** is an employee who has demonstrated the ability to perform but does just enough to get by. Sometimes a seasoned officer has difficulty adjusting to new technologies or is suffering burnout. Sometimes a newer officer is feeling disappointed by the reality of the job. Whatever the reason, a manager must deal with unproductive subordinates. Lack of productivity must be addressed and documented. Repeated warnings and direction without any consequences for failure to comply can create an entitlement attitude in an unproductive employee that can negatively affect the work unit, with the other members of the unit knowing who the "slug" is and expecting management to do something about it: "Your job as a supervisor is to deal directly and effectively with anyone in a position to destroy team cohesiveness" (Glennon, 2009).

Often employees themselves are responsible for their problems because of their mental attitude, physical condition and emotional well-being. The manifestations of such problems are laziness, moodiness, resistance to change, complacency, absence or tardiness and disorganization. These problems could probably be altered with changes in attitude, physical condition or emotional well-being.

Many factors affect employees and determine their behavior. New law enforcement employees enter the field with expectations of becoming professionals and often already have some college education or a college degree.

In addition, new officers expect law enforcement education courses that are more directly related to their career while on the job. Many of today's officers plan to attend college-level criminal justice courses after employment. With education come higher expectations of special tasks, promotions, specialized assignments and higher salaries.

Dealing with Difficult Personalities

Personality problems such as hostility, excessive sensitivity or bad attitudes can disrupt a law enforcement organization. In severe cases it may be necessary to refer an employee to outside counseling or assistance. With hostile employees it is best to listen and make arrangements to discuss the matter later when emotions have subsided. During later discussion managers should make it clear that the behavior is unacceptable because of its effect on other employees and operations.

Conflict often results from personality clashes. Personality types can be placed on a continuum ranging from those who are always in total agreement to those who are always in total disagreement. In the middle are those who are noncommittal, never taking one side or the other (see Figure 10.2).

Difficult people include yes people, passives, avoiders, pessimists, complainers, know-it-alls, exploders, bullies and snipers.

Yes people are vocally supportive in a manager's presence but rarely follow through. They smile, nod and do nothing. They have excuses when a deadline rolls around. Yes people have a high need for acceptance and usually avoid open conflict. They tell you what they think you want to hear. Tactfully confront the no-action behavior. When you make an initial request, give them time to say no. If they do not, have them put the commitment in writing or say exactly when they will complete the project. Do not allow them to make unrealistic promises. Build incremental steps, deadlines and checkpoints. Follow up and monitor the expected results. Show your approval when the promised action is taken.

Passives are silent, unresponsive people who seldom offer their own ideas or opinions, keeping their thoughts to themselves. Their responses are usually short and noncommittal. Some will put in writing what they will not say. Working with passives can be frustrating. The major coping strategy is to get

FIGURE 10.2
Personality Types

© Cengage Learning 2012

them to open up and talk to you. Comment on their quietness. Help reduce their tension. Ask open-ended questions and wait for them to answer, and then thank them for their ideas.

Avoiders put things off; they procrastinate or physically absent themselves to avoid getting involved. To deal with indecisive avoiders, find out why they are stalling. Probe. Question. Listen. Move away from vagueness toward specificity. Express the value of decisiveness. Explore alternatives. Help them make decisions, and then give support after they have made a decision.

Pessimists always say "no," are inflexible and resist change. Structure their work relationships so they have little contact with other workers. Closely related to pessimists are *complainers*—those who find fault with everything and everyone. These people continually gripe but take no personal responsibility for anything. Some people are basically negative about everything. Griping has become a habit—a chronically dismal way of looking at one's department, supervisor and fellow officers. Some people just are not happy unless they are complaining. Managers who have such subordinates should recognize the problem and make a concerted effort to at least not let the negative attitude affect others. Among the tactics managers might use are the following:

- Do not overreact to the negativism. When possible, ignore it.
- Relax tension. Negative people often make those around them feel stressed. Do not let that happen. Break the tension with a little humor.
- Promptly undo any damage. Negative workers often stir up their peers and disrupt the department or work group. If this happens, send the negative person out of the common work area and get everyone else back on track.
- Make your expectations clear. Have a heart-to-heart talk with the negative person. Try to find out why he or she is so negative. Let the person know you expect the negativism to be kept out of the department.
- Set an example. Be as optimistic and upbeat as possible. Encourage your subordinates to act positively, too.
- Confront them, interrupt the complaining and have them describe the problem. Acknowledge and understand the complaint, but do not agree with it, argue about it or accept blame for it.
- Discuss the realities of the situation and focus on solving it.

Know-it-alls are highly opinionated, egotistical, speak with great authority, are sure of themselves, have all the right answers (or think they do) and are impatient with others. Know-it-alls have a strong need for order and structure, to be right (or at least to never be wrong), to be seen as competent and to be admired and respected. Use the know-it-alls' expertise and at the same time be sure your ideas are fully considered and used. Acknowledge their expertise, but help them see their effect on others. Show them how their ideas are helpful and yet not necessarily the only way to view an issue. Avoid being a counter-expert and know your facts. Raise questions without confrontation. Let them save face.

Exploders yell and scream. They are overemotional and sometimes even hysterical. Because you cannot talk to people who are yelling and screaming, first disarm the anger. Stand up and face them squarely. Do not let them go on for more than 30 seconds, but do not tell them to calm down. Put your hand out to stop them. Call them by name and keep repeating the name until they stop yelling. Validate their feelings: "I understand you are angry. I want to work with you but not this way." Help them regain self-control. Let them cool off. Ask, "What do you need right now?" As a last resort, simply walk away from them.

Bullies attack verbally, a form of psychological abuse, using threats and demands to get their way. They are like steamrollers, using unrelenting, hammering arguments to push people to back down: "Bullying can cross all the lines of your organizational chart. Not only can a supervisor bully a subordinate, but we often see peers bully each other, and sometimes an 'untouchable' subordinate will bully and intimidate members of management" (Brantner-Smith, 2009, p.35). Bullies have a strong need to be correct, are impatient with others and usually have an excuse if their "bad behavior" is called out, such as claiming to be having a bad day or to be just kidding. A person who complains about being bullied may be seen as a weakling, a whiner or as not being a team player. Bullying can decrease morale and productivity and may also cost an agency thousands of dollars in litigation and lost work time (Brantner-Smith, 2009).

To deal with bullies, stand your ground without being aggressive, and avoid a head-on fight. Do not argue or worry about being polite. Use low-key persistence. Do not let them interrupt. Establish eye contact, call them by name and be clear about what you do and do not want.

Snipers are hostile, aggressive people who do not attack openly like exploders and bullies but rather engage in guerrilla warfare, using subtle digs, cheap shots and innuendos. Like exploders and bullies, snipers have a strong judgmental view of how others should think and act, but they choose to stay hidden and attack covertly. Neutralize sniping without escalation into open warfare. Meet in private and avoid countersniping. Bring them out into the open while avoiding a direct confrontation by saying things such as, "Are you trying to make a point?" and "What are you trying to say?"

To deal with problem people, get their attention, identify the problem behavior, point out the consequences, ask questions, listen and explain expectations. Avoid defensiveness.

Dealing with Problem Behaviors

In local law enforcement agencies, the most frequent charges are intoxication on the job, insubordination, frequent tardiness, negligence, prohibited moonlighting, incompetence or unsatisfactory performance, improper handling of evidence, violation of a municipal ordinance, conduct unbecoming an officer, use of abusive/racial/ethnic language, failure to report for duty or leaving duty without permission, abusive actions against prisoners or people under arrest and careless operation of a vehicle.

Among the most challenging problem behaviors are abuse of sick leave, substance abuse, corruption, insubordination, sexual harassment, use of excessive force and misconduct off duty.

Abuse of Sick Leave

Although the abuse of sick leave may seem relatively insignificant compared with such problem behaviors as corruption and use of excessive force, the abuse of sick leave can cost a department at least an additional 150 percent over the budgeted amount to cover the vacancies with overtime pay. In additional to the financial impact, abuse of sick leave has an organizational impact, reducing the effectiveness and efficiency of the department.

To effectively manage sick leave, managers need a good records system that tracks when employees take leave and the reasons for the absence.

Substance Abuse

Nationwide, employers lose thousands of work hours every year because of drug- and alcohol-related ailments. In addition to the health hazards, substance abuse on the job weakens morale, judgment and safety.

Preventing substance abuse in the workplace, including drugs and alcohol testing, can protect employees and the public and can lower an organization's operational costs. Federal or state law, collective bargaining agreements and contractual obligations may enter into the decision as to which drugs to test for. Federal regulations allow testing for alcohol and five controlled substances: marijuana, cocaine, amphetamines, opiates and phencyclidine (PCP), collectively referred to as the Department of Health and Human Services-5 (DHHS-5).

Telltale signs of substance abuse in the workplace include an increase in absenteeism, employee grievances, employee theft, accidental injuries and workers' compensation claims. Other signs include a decrease in job interest, productivity and quality of work.

Managers should recognize the symptoms of alcohol or drug abuse. If they suspect an employee is abusing alcohol or drugs, they should not accuse the employee of doing so, because this could open the manager and department to a slander or defamation of character lawsuit. Rather, focus on job deficiencies and corrective action. Show a genuine concern for the employee's problem and attempt to refer him or her to a qualified specialist. Give officers ample opportunity to seek assistance. Follow up if an employee enters a treatment program.

Corruption

The problem of corruption was discussed in detail in Chapter 8 and is only briefly reviewed here. Corruption is of concern because officers in the field are exposed to numerous opportunities to benefit personally from actions they take against criminals. Officers may be offered bribes or come across huge amounts of drugs or cash. They may feel overworked, underpaid and therefore entitled to take what they consider just compensation for the risks they face on the job. Yet, whenever one member of a police department is found to be corrupt, the hundreds of thousands of honest, hardworking officers suffer. The problem of police corruption affects agencies of all sizes, in all areas of the country.

Insubordination

Policing has traditionally followed a quasi-military structure, with higher-ranking officers authorized to give lawful orders to lower-ranking officers that must be obeyed, whether they personally agree with them or not. Failure to carry out such direct, lawful orders can expose an officer to discipline for **insubordination**.

Sexual Harassment

Sexual harassment has increased in visibility and has resulted in numerous lawsuits. Sexual harassment is a type of sex discrimination prohibited by Title VII of the Civil Rights Act of 1964, as well as by most state laws. The federal government defines **sexual harassment** as "unwelcome sexual advances, requests for sexual favors, and other verbal or physical conduct of a sexual nature" ("Preventing Sexual Harassment," no date, p.1).

The Equal Employment Opportunity Commission Web site states, "Unwelcome sexual advances, requests for sexual favors, and other verbal or physical conduct of a sexual nature constitutes sexual harassment when submission to or rejection of this conduct explicitly or implicitly affects an individual's employment, unreasonably interferes with an individual's work performance or creates an intimidating, hostile or offensive work environment" ("Sexual Harassment," 2009). The commission notes that sexual harassment can occur in a variety of circumstances, including but not limited to the following:

- The victim as well as the harasser may be a woman or a man. The victim does not have to be of the opposite sex.
- The harasser can be the victim's supervisor, an agent of the employer, a supervisor in another area, a coworker or a nonemployee.
- The victim does not have to be the person harassed but could be anyone affected by the offensive conduct.
- Unlawful sexual harassment may occur without economic injury to or discharge of the victim. The harasser's conduct must be unwelcome.

There are two legally recognized types of sexual harassment. One type, *quid pro quo harassment*, usually involves a supervisor's demand for sexual favors from an employee in return for a job benefit, such as passing probation, getting a promotion, getting a good performance evaluation, not being written up for doing something wrong and so on.

The second type, *hostile-environment harassment*, as the name implies, involves a hostile environment (whether created by co-employees or by supervisors). According to the National Center for Women and Policing

insubordination
failure to obey a lawful direct order from a supervisor.

sexual harassment
unwelcome sexual advances, requests for sexual favors, and other verbal or physical conduct of a sexual nature that explicitly or implicitly affect an individual's employment, unreasonably interferes with an individual's work performance or creates an intimidating, hostile or offensive work environment.

(www.womenandpolicing.org): "A hostile environment consists of unwelcome sexual behavior, such as jokes, cartoons, posters, banter, repeated requests for dates, requests for sexual favors, references to body parts, or physical touching that has the purpose or effect of unreasonably interfering with an individual's work performance or creating an intimidating, hostile, or offensive working environment. Isolated acts that are not severe will not rise to the level of a hostile environment." Two conditions determine liability for employers in cases of hostile environment sexual harassment: (1) The employer knew or should have known about the harassment, and (2) the employer failed to take appropriate corrective action.

Sexual harassment may occur as "indirect" or "third party" when one employee witnesses the repeated sexual harassment of another or when an employee is not directly harassed but the harassment of others adversely affects the workplace. Third-party sexual harassment may be either quid pro quo or hostile environment. Quid pro quo third-party sexual harassment occurs when employees who are not the target of harassment lose potential job benefits to other less qualified employees who submit to harassment. Hostile environment third-party sexual harassment occurs when employees who are not themselves harassed must work in an atmosphere where such harassment is pervasive. If employees who grant sexual favors are given preferential treatment, other employees' motivation and performance may suffer.

The police environment may be more conducive than others to sexual harassment because of the nature of the work, for example, investigating sex crimes and pornography rings. Some evidence also suggests that sexual harassment is significantly higher in male-dominated occupations. Keep in mind that, although sexual harassment occurs more commonly against women, men are not immune to such abuse. An officer who reports sexual harassment runs the risk of the situation getting worse or of other officers refusing to talk to him or her or to provide timely backup when called. Retaliation against an employee who opposed sexual harassment or made a charge or participated in an investigation is prohibited under Title VII. However, as the National Center for Women and Policing cautions, such retaliation does occur in such forms as the following:

- Shunning/ostracizing—no one will talk to the officers, or they are prevented from receiving information important to the performance of their job or important to their personal safety.

- Stalking/harassing incidents—obscene telephone calls, telephone calls where the caller says nothing, hang-up calls at all hours of the day and night, threatening or harassing letters or notes, damage to the officers' automobiles, articles left on the officers' desks or in their work area that are intended to intimidate or harass.

- Becoming the subject of rumors of sexual activity or other demeaning information.

- Being held to a higher standard of performance—the officers' evaluation reports become more critical, and they are held to a different standard than others.

- Harassing internal affairs complaints are filed against the officer by members of the organization or by citizens who have been enlisted to help the harasser.

- ◉ Denial of training opportunities.
- ◉ Denial of transfer to specialty jobs.
- ◉ Denial of promotion.
- ◉ Failure to provide backup in emergency situations. This is the ultimate form of retaliation. When it becomes apparent that the officer will not receive timely backup, the officer often leaves the organization out of fear for his or her life.

To prevent charges of sexual harassment, departments need a clear policy that identifies conduct that may constitute sexual harassment. The policy should also include a statement that such conduct will not be tolerated and that those found guilty of prohibited conduct will be subject to appropriate disciplinary action.

First-line supervisors are key in the battle against sexual harassment. How a manager investigates a sexual harassment complaint may determine the outcome of a harassment lawsuit. Managers should take every sexual harassment complaint seriously and collect all the facts from both sides, keeping the investigation confidential. As they investigate, they should document everything: memos, conversations, reports and the like. If the charge of harassment is substantiated, appropriate discipline should be undertaken, according to department policy.

Use of Excessive Force

Use of excessive force has always been a cause of problems, resulting in numerous lawsuits. Use of force is sometimes a necessary part of the job, but determining what is reasonable is highly subjective. Luna (2005, p.4) provides the following definitions:

- ◉ *Force.* Any nonnegotiable use of police authority to influence citizen behavior. Includes low-level force options (verbal commands, use of restraints) through high-level force options (deadly force). The mere presence of an officer, because of the implied authority of the uniform, is included.
- ◉ *Justifiable force.* Force used in accordance with law; force that was reasonable in light of the circumstances faced and known by the officer at the time it was used.
- ◉ *Excessive force.* The illegal or unreasonable use of force, with reasonableness determined by whether a reasonably prudent officer would have used the same amount of force in the same situation, in light of the information available to the officer at the time.
- ◉ *Deadly force.* Force likely to cause serious bodily injury or death.

Of the 43.5 million people who had contact with police in 2005, an estimated 1.6 percent had force used or threatened against them during their most recent contact, a rate relatively unchanged from 2002 (Durose et al., 2007, p.1). In 2002 and 2005 Blacks and Hispanics experienced police use of force at higher rates than did Whites. Of those who had force used against them in 2005, an estimated 83 percent felt the force was excessive.

The landmark case in use of force is *Graham v. Connor* (1989), in which the Court said the right to make an arrest or investigatory stop carries with it the right to use some degree of physical coercion or threat thereof to effect it. The Court also held, "The calculus of reasonableness must embody allowance for the fact that police officers are often forced to make split-second judgments— in circumstances that are tense, uncertain, and rapidly evolving—about the amount of force that is necessary in a particular situation." The standard established by this decision is the "reasonably objective officer." The more "heinous" a person's activities or threat level, the more force an officer may justifiably use. Sometimes shooting someone or striking them with a baton is absolutely necessary and reasonable and must be considered in any use-of-force policy.

Officers' decisions to use some type of force depend on the type of call, offense and level of perceived authority over the suspect. Reviews of the literature show that use of force is most likely to occur when the suspect shows signs of alcohol or drug intoxication or engages in hostile or disrespectful behavior.

The majority of excessive force claims are filed against police officers and agencies under Section 1983. Claims arise in three major areas: arrests and seizures of criminal suspects, post-arrest or pretrial detention and postconviction confinement.

Perhaps the best known use-of-force case to date is the 1991 beating of Rodney King by four Los Angeles police officers. Both the city and the officers involved were sued under Section 1983. In addition, other officers who stood by and did nothing to prevent the alleged wrongful acts were involved under the **nonactor liability** provisions. That is, officers who were present at a scene where use of force was in question or where force was obviously excessive yet did nothing to prevent it have also been held liable by the courts.

The key to avoiding a charge of excessive force is being able to justify the type and amount of force used. All use-of-force reports must be accurate and complete, for internal investigations as well as for criminal and civil liability suits and public relations.

nonactor liability

when an officer present at a scene where use of force is in question and is obviously excessive and the nonactor officer did nothing to prevent it, that officer is also held liable by the courts.

Recruits practice handcuffing techniques during training at the New York City Police Academy. Training must not end once the academy is complete. Regular, ongoing training of sworn officers by certified instructors is a critical element in developing an effective police force and in defending against claims of excessive force.

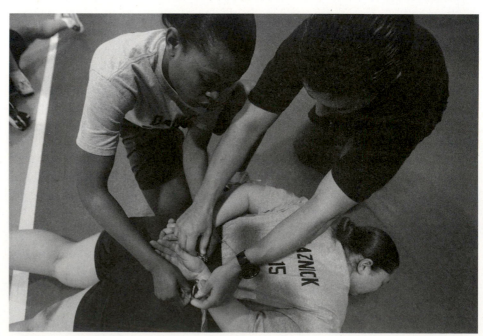

© Mario Tama/Getty Images

One way to reduce the force needed might be using K-9s. However, police canine tracking or searching for a wanted subject is a serious use of force and must be properly managed. Department policy should state when a canine can be used and against whom.

Use-of-Force Continuums

Use-of-force continuums have been evolving for more than three decades and are used to explain the complex, inflammatory realm in which police are faced with using force. Many departments use a linear, incremental force continuum, suggesting that officers work through a series of alternatives, ascending the continuum until they use the most appropriate response. Figure 10.3 shows a linear use-of-force continuum.

Critics of such linear use-of-force continuums contend that these tools imply that an officer must exhaust all efforts at one level on the continuum before proceeding to the next. Furthermore, they are complex and difficult to remember, potentially leading to dangerous delay by an officer during a critical incident.

To counter such complaints, some departments have instituted circular use-of-force models to replace the linear continuum. Figure 10.4 illustrates a circular use-of-force model. Many circular use-of-force models place the force options in random order to prevent any implication that officers escalate to greater force in a given sequence. Whether a department uses any type of force continuum, it should not replace a carefully crafted use-of-force policy.

Law enforcement managers need three essential elements in dealing with use of force in their agencies: (1) a sound policy, (2) effective mechanisms for enforcing the policy and producing accountability and (3) integrated training that teaches officers when and how to use force appropriately. The question of use of force often arises in situations involving demonstrations and sit-ins.

Passive Resistance

Passive resistance is a form of civil disobedience reflecting a philosophy of nonviolence. Protestors and demonstrators using passive resistance can pose a substantial challenge for police officers, who often face civil lawsuits alleging excessive force following such events. Young (2008, p.30) notes, "As every cop knows, the difference between a peaceful protest and a full-blown riot is razor thin. A peaceful crowd can become a mob."

Departments should establish clear policies on how passive resistance is to be approached. Because nonviolent protestors generally pose no immediate threat to the safety of officers or others, law enforcement officers must carefully select use-of-force tactics and control their application as specified in department policy. For example, the Metro Los Angeles Police Department (LAPD) uses 40mm foam baton rounds containing dye marker packets that help officers identify instigators (Schreiber, 2009). Metro LAPD has also altered its response protocol for protest events, replacing motorcycles with mounted units because the motorcycles were not nimble enough to turn around rapidly when officers needed to retreat quickly. Another modification was the

passive resistance

a form of civil disobedience reflecting a philosophy of nonviolence; often used by protestors and demonstrators.

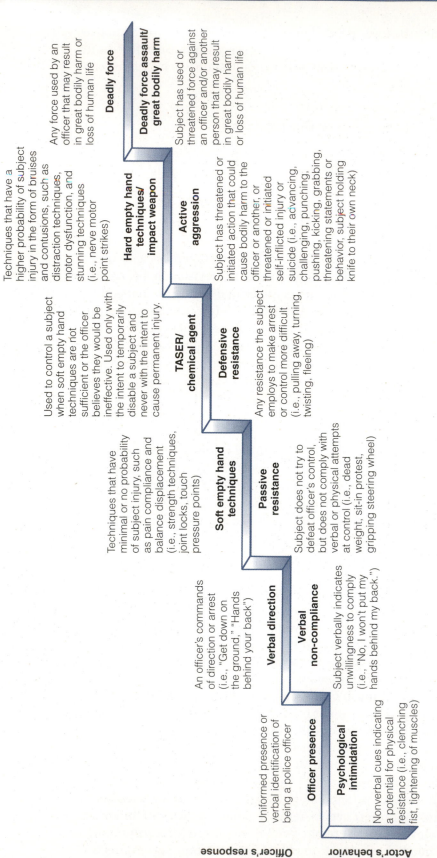

Officer's response

Actor's behavior

Officer presence

Uniformed presence or verbal identification of being a police officer

Psychological intimidation

Nonverbal cues indicating a potential for physical resistance (i.e., clenching fist, tightening of muscles)

Verbal direction

An officer's commands of direction or arrest (i.e., "Get down on the ground," "Hands behind your back")

Verbal non-compliance

Subject verbally indicates unwillingness to comply (i.e., "No, I won't put my hands behind my back.")

Soft empty hand techniques

Techniques that have minimal or no probability of subject injury, such as pain compliance and balance displacement (i.e., strength techniques, joint locks, touch pressure points)

Passive resistance

Subject does not try to defeat officer's control, but does not comply with verbal or physical attempts at control (i.e., dead weight, sit-in protest, gripping steering wheel)

TASER/ chemical agent

Used to control a subject when soft empty hand techniques are not sufficient or the officer believes they would be ineffective. Used only with the intent to temporarily disable a subject and never with the intent to cause permanent injury.

Defensive resistance

Any resistance the subject employs to make arrest or control more difficult (i.e., pulling away, turning, twisting, fleeing)

Hard empty hand techniques/ impact weapon

Techniques that have a higher probability of subject injury in the form of bruises and contusions, such as distraction techniques, motor dysfunction, and stunning techniques (i.e., nerve motor point strikes)

Active aggression

Subject has threatened or initiated action that could cause bodily harm to the officer or another, or threatened or initiated self-inflicted injury or suicide (i.e., advancing, challenging, punching, pushing, kicking, grabbing, threatening statements or behavior, subject holding knife to their own neck)

Deadly force

Any force used by an officer that may result in great bodily harm or loss of human life

Deadly force assault/ great bodily harm

Subject has used or threatened force against an officer and/or another person that may result in great bodily harm or loss of human life

NOTE: Subject may enter the continuum at any level. Officer may enter at any level that represents a reasonable response to the perceived threat posed by the subject.

FIGURE 10.3 A Linear Use-of-Force Continuum

Source: Owatonna (Minnesota) Police Department Use of Force Report.

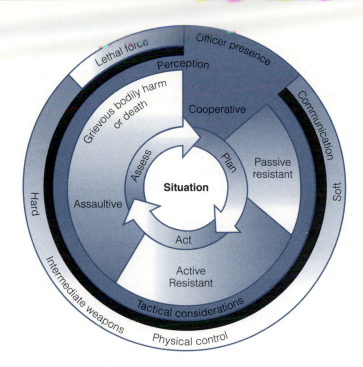

FIGURE 10.4
A Circular Use-of-Force Continuum

Source: Lorie A. Fridell. "Improving Use-of-Force Policy, Policy Enforcement and Training." In *Chief Concerns: Exploring the Challenges of Police Use of Force*, edited by Joshua A. Ederheimer and Lorie A. Fridell. Washington, DC: Police Executive Research Forum, April 2005, p.50.

discontinuance of using shields, as the department found such shields actually encouraged people to throw things at the officers, and holding the shields limited offices to having only one arm free for other functions.

Misconduct Off Duty

Although it may not seem fair, law enforcement personnel are held to a higher standard of conduct in their private lives than are ordinary citizens. More than 40 years ago, in *Gardner v. Broderick* (1968), the Supreme Court held that law enforcement agencies could legitimately have more stringent conduct rules, including rules regulating off-duty behavior because a police officer is "directly, immediately and entirely responsible to the city or state which is his employer. . . . He is a trustee of the public interest, bearing the burden of great and total responsibility to his public employer" (Kruger, 2008, p.12). This higher standard applies to an officer's off-duty sexual activity, a matter usually considered private.

Having looked at some of the most serious problem behaviors managers might confront, consider next what options managers have for dealing with the behaviors. Often some form of negative discipline or punishment is called for.

NEGATIVE DISCIPLINE/PUNISHMENT

Law enforcement managers at all levels will sometimes find it necessary to use negative discipline, including reprimands and punishments for wrong behavior, in an effort to compel expected behavior. In nonemergency situations, managers should make reasonable efforts to gain voluntary compliance. If that fails, managers must exercise the disciplinary responsibilities of their position.

The purpose of negative discipline is to help offenders correct their behavior and to send a message to others that such behavior is not acceptable. The ultimate decision to bring a disciplinary action may arise because an employee commits a number of minor violations or an obviously serious one. Those being disciplined must fully understand what they are being disciplined for and why. Managers must have the authority to exercise discipline and be willing to proceed through hearings and appeals if necessary. The discipline recommended should fit the offense and be neither excessively harsh nor overly lenient.

> **A primary rule of effective discipline is that it should be carried out as close to the time of the violation as possible.**

This proximity in time between the violation and the disciplinary measure is referred to as *celerity*. Delays cause further problems. Witnesses may have left employment, different versions may be manufactured or facts may have been forgotten.

Disciplinary actions should be carried out in private to avoid embarrassment and defensiveness. One exception to the privacy rule is if an employee openly confronts a manager in front of others. In such cases the manager must take immediate, decisive action to maintain respect and control.

Most cases of misconduct involve errors in judgment and do not rise to the level of ethical or criminal transgression requiring severe discipline. In such instances, most employees welcome the chance, at the earliest possible time, to come forward, admit their mistake, accept a reasonable sanction for the mistake and move forward in their careers. When discussing the corrective action to be taken, managers should address the problem behavior, not the officer's character, using open-ended questions to help individuals find within themselves the most appropriate answers and sanctions. Because managers have different experiences and personalities, they should not give advice, because what works for one person may not for another. Asking the right questions, at the right time, can lead people to find their own answers suited to their needs and circumstances.

Any initial disciplinary action should be *corrective*. Only when corrective discipline, training and counseling have little or no effect should disciplinary action be punitive. Punishment has the disadvantage of showing what should not be done, rather than reinforcing what should be done.

Supervisors first need to identify which officers, through their actions or lack thereof, deserve punishment or other disciplinary action. Supervisors must then determine which action is most appropriate and how to administer it.

Identifying the Problem Performer— Early Intervention Systems

Although most officers in a department readily cooperate with supervisors and their performance requests, some resist supervisory requests by repeatedly challenging and questioning orders, and still others outright fail to perform.

These problem performers need to be identified as soon as possible. Early intervention systems (EISs), commonly referred to in the past as early warning systems (EWSs), are data-driven management tools used to identify police officers with performance problems and intervene to correct those problems (Walker et al., 2005, p.5). EIS is a powerful, multifaceted tool that typically exists in the form of an electronic database (Walker et al., 2005, p.1). Among the common data elements recorded are officer's use of sick leave, the number and type of community complaints and the number and type of use-of-force incidents. Five guiding principles of EISs are (Walker et al., 2005, pp.5–6):

1. An EIS should be part of an agency's larger effort to support and improve officer performance.

2. First-line supervisors are the lynchpin of EISs.

3. For EISs to be effective, intervention options should vary to meet the wide range of officers' needs.

4. The chief executive ultimately is responsible for the success or failure of EISs.

5. EISs are a valuable administrative tool that can enhance accountability and integrity in a law enforcement agency.

The power of an EIS is its ability to identify patterns of officer performance, allowing supervisors to intervene early in an effort to prevent more serious problems from developing (Walker et al., 2005, p.14). However, the success and effectiveness of an EIS depends heavily on the level of supervisor buy-in and support (Walker et al., 2005, p.10).

Departments must carefully consider the criteria used to select EIS candidates. Research has found, for example, that the number of use-of-force complaints against an officer is *not* a good predictor, although departments frequently use this metric: "While the officers who did qualify for the early intervention program were frequent force users, their weighted force factor values were strongly positive, thus suggesting they tended to limit their use of force even when encountering relatively higher levels of resistance" (Bazley et al., 2009, p.122).

The availability of a range of interventions is also critical to an EIS. Counseling by an officer's immediate supervisor is the most common intervention. Other effective interventions include training, professional counseling, peer support groups, crisis intervention teams, reassignment and relief from duty (Walker et al., 2005, p.21). The many benefits of EISs include improved supervision, help to officers in overcoming personal or professional problems that affect job performance, earlier identification of potential problems with personnel, a strengthened culture of integrity and accountability within agencies, improved community relations, reduced litigation costs and adoption of proven best practices that help bring agencies to the forefront of the field (Walker et al., 2005, p.47).

The Community Oriented Policing Services (COPS) Office and the Police Executive Research Forum (PERF) have published *Strategies for Intervening with Officers through Early Intervention Systems: A Guide for Front-Line Supervisors* (Walker et al., 2006). This guide provides practical strategies for frontline supervisors to work with employees identified as needing assistance to correct deficiencies in behavior. If interventions are unsuccessful, penalties may be imposed.

Determining Penalties

Many variables enter into penalty determination; for example, is it a first offense or a repeated offense? Are there extenuating circumstances? Each case must be decided on its own facts, and penalties must be assessed in the same way. No single penalty will fit every set of circumstances. The penalty should have a legal and moral basis and should include an appeal process. Penalties should also be reasonable. If they are viewed as too lenient, they likely will not be enforced because it is not worth the effort. If they are too harsh, they may not be enforced because they are too severe.

 The offense and offender, how the offense was committed and the offender's attitude and past performance are important considerations in assessing penalties.

Most law enforcement departments have either departmental or civil service rules and regulations that define which behaviors are violations and the penalty for each. Punishments vary from warnings to termination of employment. Some departments use a table of offenses, penalties and application of appropriate disciplinary actions. Appendix A contains a sample of such a table. Such tables are not to be used automatically. Supervisors must consider the specific circumstances carefully when evaluating offenses and penalties, including the employee's work history, contribution to the agency and probability of rehabilitation. *Each case must be considered individually.*

In addition to policies and procedures, rules and regulations, most agencies now have a code of ethics to provide a broader conceptual statement of expected agency goals and officer conduct: "Running afoul of your department's ethical code can have as much potential impact upon an officer's career as a violation of a departmental regulation" (Dwyer, 2008).

The most common disciplinary actions in law enforcement departments are oral or written reprimands, efficiency rating demerits, summary punishment for minor offenses, withholding part or all of an officer's salary for a specified time, decrease of seniority rights, a fine, suspension, demotion in rank or dismissal.

Progressive Discipline

Many departments operate under the concept of progressive discipline. The primary objective of progressive discipline is to give employees a chance to voluntarily improve performance and to clearly inform employees that stronger disciplinary actions will be taken if they do not correct the behavior. Employees are usually given a light penalty for the first infraction of a rule, a more severe penalty for the next infraction and so on.

Progressive discipline uses disciplinary steps based on the severity of the offense. The steps usually are

- Oral reprimand.
- Written reprimand.
- Suspension/demotion.
- Discharge/termination.

progressive discipline

uses disciplinary steps based on the severity of the offense and how often it is repeated; steps usually are oral reprimand, written reprimand, suspension/ demotion, discharge/ termination.

reprimand

formal criticism of behavior; may be oral or written.

The most frequent type of penalty is an oral or a written *warning* or **reprimand**. An *oral reprimand* is a conversation between a supervisor and an employee about a specific aspect of the employee's performance. It informs employees that continued behavior or level of performance will result in more serious action. The supervisor must provide specifics. Employees should know what to correct and how, and they must have sufficient time to make the correction before other action is taken. Normally employees cooperate, and the problem behavior is eliminated.

If the warning is important, the supervisor should make a written record and place it in the personnel file. A *written reprimand* is a formal written notice to the employee regarding significant misconduct, specific inadequate performance or repeated offenses for which the employee has received an oral reprimand. The same conditions apply as for a warning. The violation should be stated in detail, along with what actions will correct the behavior, a time limit, whether there have been previous oral warnings for the same conduct and what will occur if the employee does not correct the violation. A written reprimand is usually recommended for a violation that must be corrected immediately. It should be given by at least a first-line supervisor and perhaps a middle-line manager, with the supervisor as a witness. The employee should receive a copy of the written reprimand.

A warning or a reprimand sends a signal to employees that management has disapproved. It is best to handle all employee penalty matters in person. The procedure may permit the employee to state his or her position before management takes final action.

A *suspension*, being barred from a position, is the next most serious punishment. Suspensions may be with or without pay. Normally, suspensions are given after consultation with the middle manager and the executive manager. Suspensions with pay normally are given to provide time for management to investigate a situation. It is not in any way a finding of wrongdoing. For example, an officer who shoots and kills a suspect may be suspended with pay while the matter is investigated. A coroner's jury will probably convene, and management will consider its findings in making a final decision. If the officer's action was justified, the officer is returned to duty as though no action had been taken. Suspensions may usually be appealed to the executive manager, city manager, civil service board or a special board. They may also be a matter for union support or denial.

The most serious forms of punishment are *demotion* and *dismissal* or *termination*. These actions are taken by the head of the law enforcement department or the government jurisdiction and are subject to appeal. These actions are end-of-the-road punishments, administered in very serious first offenses or in situations in which the employees have disregarded other warnings, reprimands and suspensions. A *demotion* places an employee in a position of lower rank and pay and can seriously impede the remainder of the employee's career. *Dismissal* or *termination* is the most serious penalty. It is used when management decides strong action must be taken in the best interests of the organization and its other employees. Termination is necessary when employees do not respond to attempts to correct behavior that violates written rules and regulations and of which the employee was provided proper notice. Incompetence and inability to get along with other employees are two major reasons for termination. Other major reasons are dishonesty or lying and insubordination.

Technically, dismissal and termination are slightly different. *Dismissal* is an action taken by a hiring and firing authority. It is not voluntary by the employee. It is, in effect, a discharge or firing. *Termination* is also an end to employment, but it may be voluntary or involuntary. Employees may terminate employment because of illness or accepting a different job. The differences are basically a matter of semantics.

Terminations are costly to the organization. Replacement selection costs are high, and training is a long-term commitment. Unfortunately, in some situations termination is the only recourse. Most managers will say that firing an officer is one of their most distasteful responsibilities.

Although firing someone is seldom easy, it is almost always easier than keeping that person. Normally termination occurs only after a serious offense; after repeated offenses by the same employee; or after a series of the same type of offense where warnings, oral and written reprimands, suspension or similar previous disciplinary actions went unheeded.

Wrongful termination lawsuits have been rising in the past decade. These actions arise from the due process clause of the Fourteenth Amendment, which prohibits persons acting as agents or employees of the state or its political subdivisions from depriving a person of property or liberty without due process. A person has the right not to be terminated from employment except for good or just cause. Title 42, U.S.C., Section 1983, provides a procedure by which a person employed by a state, county or municipal government can bring suit against a department or supervisor for violating the person's constitutional rights in the termination process. Due process requires a valid reason for termination, procedural action, notification of the person to be terminated and an opportunity for a hearing.

Difficult as termination is for police managers, it remains their responsibility. Failure to exercise it when justified results in the ultimate failure of manager effectiveness. Should a manager fail to terminate an officer when justified, and the officer does anything "wrong" in the public's eyes, the manager and the entire department could be sued for **negligent retention**.

Discharge should be presented so that employees can retain self-esteem, if possible. They should be told whether they can expect references for what they did well while on the job, when the termination takes effect, how the announcement will be made and whether they can resign voluntarily for the

negligent retention

failing to terminate an employee when justified.

record. Any actions taken should center on the behavior or offense rather than on the individual.

Summary Punishment/Discipline

Not all disciplinary actions fall within the realm of progressive discipline. Managers must have the authority to exercise *summary* discipline when certain infractions occur. **Summary discipline**, or **summary punishment**, is discretionary authority used when a supervisor thinks an officer is not fit for duty or when, for any reason, the supervisor thinks immediate action is needed.

Summary punishment may require officers to work a day or two without pay or may excuse them from duty for a day without pay. Officers who receive summary punishment have a right to a hearing.

summary discipline/ punishment

discretionary authority used when a supervisor feels an officer is not fit for duty or for any reason the supervisor feels a need for immediate action.

Education-Based Discipline

An innovative alternative to traditional punitive disciplinary measures, such as suspensions without pay, is education-based discipline (EBD), an approach developed by Los Angeles County Sheriff Lee Baca: "Fundamental fairness is a primary component of the Department's Core Values statement. Sheriff Baca believes that offering an educational alternative instead of the standard discipline of unpaid suspension days is beneficial to the employee and the Department" (Cobos, 2009, p.2). EBD is offered as an optional avenue for officers facing a 1- to 30-day suspension but is not available to those facing demotion, dismissal or termination.

Officers who agree to such behavior-focused education alternatives are then required to participate in any combination of the following: attending classes, attending training, conducting briefings, authoring a research paper or participating in an activity that addresses the behavior that led to the discipline (Cobos, 2009, p.2). EBD thus is viewed as a creative intervention option that strives to address underlying problem behaviors and attitudes in an effort to avoid future disciplinary measures. It is hoped that such interventions will reduce management-employee conflict and embitterment caused by withholding employee pay; will enhance organizational communication and employee character, competence and trust; and promote a more comprehensive and successful outcome (Parker, 2009, p.14).

Guidelines for Administering Negative Discipline

When you use negative discipline, what you do *not* do is often more important than what you do. Officers may become defensive and less concerned with listening than defending themselves. Communication tactics are essential in these situations, and the corrective conversation must focus on the goal of rebuilding a specific behavior positively, avoiding generalizations (Thompson and Walker, 2007, p.123). Supervisors should be especially cautious against using such words as *never* and *always*, because people rarely "never" or "always" do things, and using such words opens the way for defensiveness (Thompson and Walker, p.130). The following guidelines may also apply when using negative discipline:

- Get the facts first. Consider the circumstances. Was the misbehavior accidental? Did the person know the rules? Was this the first offense? Keep adequate records.
- Know your powers as outlined in your job description.
- Check on precedents for similar offenses.
- Criticize in private.*
- Be calm. Allow tempers to settle. Avoid sarcasm. Do not threaten, argue or show anger.
- Be sure the person is attentive and emotionally ready to listen.
- Focus on the behavior, not on the person. Be sure the behavior is something the person has control over or can change.
- Do not ascribe intent to the behavior or imply it was done on purpose. Focus only on the behavior.
- Be clear, specific and objective. Use actual examples of problem behavior.
- Check for understanding by asking questions. How is the person taking the criticism?
- Respect the employee's dignity.
- Suit the disciplinary action to the individual and the situation. Know each subordinate and his or her record. The severity of the discipline should match the seriousness of the offense.
- End with expectations for changed behavior.
- Set a time frame.
- Follow up.

Effective discipline is more easily maintained with a written set of guidelines such as the preceding. Managers should coordinate their disciplinary efforts. Every manager should enforce every rule, regulation and policy equally. Unenforced or unenforceable rules should be changed or cancelled. Further, managers should set the example, letting their subordinates know they mean what they say.

Using the three-letter word ACT, Furey (2009, p.38) describes the ACT of negative discipline by breaking it down into three critical parts. The first concern should be the **A**ccuracy of facts: "As a manager, make sure that everyone in your chain of command looks under each and every rock before making an official comment. And, make doubly sure that everyone under you carries out this level of observation before presenting the 'facts' to you."

---

*Sometimes it is necessary for a manager to stop inappropriate behavior immediately without preserving the offender's ego, for example, stopping use of excessive force at the end of a pursuit. Criticizing in public when a situation demands it can have a positive effect on the entire organization. However, "In the daily responsibility of improving performance or correcting minor deviations from professionalism, the principle of 'chew out in private' can be the best way to go" (Vernon, 2008, p.76).

The second concern is Consistency: "Given a similar set of situations, any employee who violates the same rule should receive equal punishment." A similar set of situations includes similar incidents, with similar outcomes as well as similar employees with similar tenure and disciplinary histories. The discipline imposed should stand up to the test of fairness and the results perceived by employee as equitable.

The third concern is Timeliness: "Taking corrective action as soon as possible after the infraction has a much greater impact than delaying the inevitable. Quick and positive ACTion sends a clear message to the offender—and to the entire staff—that a certain standard of behaviors is expected, and that violations will come with consequences."

Supervisors should avoid the **gunnysack approach** to discipline, accumulating negative behaviors of a subordinate and then dumping them all on the officer at the same time rather than correcting them as they occur. Accumulated, they may be serious enough to warrant dismissal. However, handled one at a time, the officer might have had a chance to change.

Steps in Administering Negative Discipline

To apply discipline, write down your main goal in taking disciplinary action—change the employee's behavior and reduce the chances of the behavior happening again. Write down the violation and what conduct was involved, much the same procedure used in making a charge against a citizen. State the reason for the action, specifically, what has been violated and how. Show how the behavior creates a problem. State how you feel about it.

Listen to the employee's explanation. Remember that to err is human. To blame somebody else is even more human. Anticipate this and help employees sort out their responsibilities. Also recognize that if an excuse is good enough, it becomes a reason. Managers and supervisors cannot know everything. They, too, can make mistakes. If this happens, managers must openly admit their mistake and offer a sincere apology for the *misunderstanding*.

Suggest corrective action and, if possible, involve the person in the suggestion. Be firm but fair. Fairness does not mean treating everyone equally. A rookie will make mistakes that might not be tolerated if made by a veteran officer. State exactly what action you are going to take and explain that further violations will bring more severe results. Offer assistance in resolving the present problem. Describe how you value the person as an individual and as an important part of the work group and the entire department. Secure a commitment to future positive behavior.

The final step is to tell the individual how to appeal the decision. The right to appeal should be inherent in any disciplinary action.

Appeal

An **appeal** is a request for a decision to be reviewed by someone higher in command. The most frequent appeals are to a review board or department disciplinary board. Appeals can also be made to a civil service board review,

gunnysack approach
occurs when managers or supervisors accumulate negative behaviors of a subordinate and then dump them all on the employee at the same time rather than correcting them as they occurred.

appeal
request for a decision to be reviewed by someone higher in the command structure.

a district or high court and, in some cases, a management–labor board. Many departments use an internal review procedure, including the following steps.

- ◉ **Step One.** The employee requests a face-to-face meeting with the immediate supervisor within a specified number of working days, for example, within five working days. The supervisor and employee meet, and the supervisor decides to withdraw or stand by the disciplinary action.

- ◉ **Step Two.** An employee who is not satisfied with the results of Step One presents the written reasons for dissatisfaction to the department head within another predetermined number of days. The department head sustains or rescinds the disciplinary action within a certain number of working days.

- ◉ **Step Three.** An employee who is not satisfied with the results of Step Two presents the written reasons for dissatisfaction with the department head's response to the top-level manager of the jurisdiction. Within a certain time frame, the manager or representative either sustains or rescinds the disciplinary action. This is the final step.

Departments may also have a process for employees to appeal disciplinary actions to a civil service commission. This process usually involves the employee appearing for a hearing before a board that rules in the matter. Such hearings may be closed to the public. The decision and findings of the commission are in writing and are considered final.

Legal Considerations

Disciplinary actions are subject to specific procedures as established by civil service or department rules and regulations. If an officer is charged with a criminal offense, the legal procedure is the same as for any citizen. In these cases, violation of civil service rules and regulations of the law enforcement department would, in all probability, await the outcome of the criminal action even though they are completely separate actions.

In general, violations of department rules and regulations are investigated using the same basic procedures as those accorded criminal violations. All facts must be carefully documented. Search warrants should be obtained when legally required to secure evidence. Gathering evidence, taking statements, seeking witnesses and adhering to legal procedures of handling evidence are all important.

Civil service hearings are similar to criminal hearings. Legal procedures vary, but the charges are read in an open hearing, witnesses are called and the employee is present. Employees may or may not testify because they are not required to give incriminating evidence against themselves.

Past personnel records may be introduced into evidence if relevant. Proper, detailed documentation of the facts supporting any violation of department rules and regulations is the key to justice. Most disciplinary action cases overturned by the courts have involved situations in which proper documentation was lacking, prejudice was involved, the violation was based on an action deemed a discretionary matter by the officer or violations of due process procedures were involved. Formal investigations of officer behavior and the legal issues involved are discussed in Chapter 11.

AWAY FROM THE DESK: The Role of Supervisors in Upholding Conduct and Related Discipline

There is probably no area in supervisor–subordinate relationships that creates more of a challenge than the administration of discipline. The ability to maintain a high level of employee discipline is, in the eyes of superiors, by far the most appreciated trait of a good leader. Discipline means strict and regular training for obedience and efficiency; a system of planning, orderly control, and appropriate conduct; and the use of rewards and progressively more severe punishments. Discipline must be insisted upon and sustained before there can be any continuous and cooperative effort to accomplish the organization's mission, goals, or objectives. On the other hand, the growing emphasis on employee rights and freedom in the workplace runs counter to the prerogatives of management in the area of behavior control.

The major responsibility for administrating both positive and negative discipline belongs to the sergeant rank or first-line supervisors. The first-line supervisor is the key in the disciplinary process, as this leader works day to day with those under his or her span of control and, as a result, is in the best position to witness subordinate behavior, both that which is favorable to the workplace culture and that which is in opposition to related standards.

For example, when a matter brought before the first-line supervisor is serious in nature, such as one involving excessive use of force, a violation of a citizen's constitutional rights, or unethical behavior, formal disciplinary action is a must. As a result of such actions, the procedural steps should be firmly structured within the agency and known to supervisors. However, minor infractions should allow for some discretion, with disciplinary measures determined individually based on facts of the situation. Personnel observation reports or performance matter reports should accompany all situations for purposes of consistency and fairness.

The best corrective actions are most often determined by the full breadth of facts surrounding the issue at hand, past employee performance, past disciplinary matters, attendance records for matters concerning misuse of sick time or sick call-ins, etc. These factors are often best known to the first-line supervisor and, thus, it is imperative that they fully understand the necessity of the disciplinary process as well as the need to address these matters, rather than ignoring infractions and allowing these issues to compound on the individual as well as the organization. The lack of prompt disciplinary action has permitted incompetents, malcontents, and criminals to remain on the public payroll in critically important positions.

Effective disciplinary action is always based on just cause, is appropriate in terms of the offense and the needs of the offender, and becomes progressively more severe if the subordinate fails to change his or her behavior.

(*continued*)

Personal and Vicarious Liability

We work in a highly complex, litigious society. Civil liability for failure to supervise is a serious issue in law enforcement, and exposure to such liability should be a significant concern for any first-line supervisor and agency manager. The risks of failing to properly supervise or to provide adequate training include injury or death to citizens and officers.

Federally, a police supervisor's authority to control the subordinate employee does not, by itself, make that supervisor liable for the acts of his or her subordinates; additional conditions must be proven to exist. In *Rizzo v. Goode* (1976), the court ruled that supervisors may be held personally liable for a violation of Section 1983 if the plaintiff proves that the supervisor: (1) received notice of a pattern of unconstitutional acts committed by subordinates; (2) demonstrated deliberate indifference to or tacit authorization of the offensive acts; (3) failed to make sufficient remedial action; and his/her failure to act proximately caused the claim for the injury.

Government officials performing discretionary functions generally are shielded from liability for civil damages insofar as their conduct does not violate clearly established statutory or constitutional rights of which a reasonable person should have known. Qualified immunity is an entitlement not to stand or face the other burdens of litigation. It is immunity from suit rather than mere defensive immunity. Qualified immunity gives room for ample mistakes in judgment but does not protect the plainly incompetent or those who knowingly violate the law.

In summary, failure to sustain a disciplinary action against an employee puts the supervisor at risk for a subsequent civil suit. Public employees have always been liable for their own negligent or wrongful acts. If the litigant can show by preponderance of the evidence that the police department failed to train, supervise, or discipline errant, disruptive, or deviant employees properly, the department may be held liable. The agency will pay for the misconduct of its personnel when that misconduct—violation of policies, procedures, rules, or regulations—causes injuries to others. Recent monetary judgments have been enormous. Some local governments have been forced into bankruptcy because of such lawsuits. It is in the police department's best interest, then, to promote only competent employees to the rank of sergeant and to strengthen the internal disciplinary system.

The challenge is clear: It is up to the first-line supervisor—the sergeant—to maintain control while encouraging self-discipline, and to take the appropriate disciplinary action in such a way as not to threaten but to enhance the employee's self esteem, sense of worth, and job-related productivity. The goal is total quality management.

—*Chief Shaun E. LaDue*

COMPREHENSIVE DISCIPLINE

Comprehensive discipline uses both positive and negative discipline to achieve individual and organizational goals. Several specific approaches to comprehensive discipline have been developed, including the balance of consequences analysis, the PRICE method, the one-minute management approach and the stroke approach.

> **comprehensive discipline**
>
> uses both positive and negative discipline to achieve individual and organizational goals.

The Balance of Consequences Analysis— Wilson Learning Corporation

Building on Skinner's reinforcement theory and Vroom's expectancy theory, Wilson Learning Corporation developed the balance of consequences analysis.

 The balance of consequences analysis considers behavior in terms of what positive and negative results the behavior produces and then focuses on those results.

For example, Officer Jones is a popular foot patrol officer. He spends lots of time chatting with citizens on his beat, having made friends with shopkeepers and owners of business establishments as well as area residents. The problem is that he is always late with his incident reports. Investigators complain that they do not have the reports when they need them. Further, Jones often has to put in unpaid overtime to get his paperwork done.

His sergeant does not want to lose him because he is a skilled officer, and his friendliness and popularity are assets to the department. But the lateness of his reports is causing problems. The sergeant analyzes the consequences operating in this situation.

First, what are the rewards Jones receives from socializing?

- Pleasant visits with citizens
- Satisfaction from knowing people like him
- Praise from peers and superiors for being people oriented

Against this list, the negative consequences of the behavior must be looked at. These include

- Complaints from the investigators
- Overtime (unpaid)
- Reduced chances for promotion

Next consider what positive results would occur if Jones stopped socializing and got his reports done on time:

- Investigators would stop complaining
- Unpaid overtime would stop
- Chances for promotion would increase

FIGURE 10.5
Officer Jones' Balance of
Consequences Analysis

Source: Steve Bucholz. *The
Positive Manager.* p.125.
Copyright ©1985 by John
Wiley & Sons, Inc., New York.
Reprinted by permission.

Behavior	
Undesired (current) • Late reports	**Desired** • Reports on time
Positive consequences • Pleasant visits • Satisfaction • Praise	**Positive consequences** • Less criticism • Less overtime • Promotion more likely
Negative consequences • Criticism • Overtime • Promotion less likely	**Negative consequences** • No pleasant visits • Less praise • More work

On the other hand, what negative consequences might result?

⦿ Miss the good times socializing

⦿ Miss the praise for being people oriented

⦿ More actual work to do

The balance of consequences grid would look like Figure 10.5.

A final piece of information is needed to complete the analysis—the strength of the consequences. Consequences fall into one of three either/or categories. Every consequence is either:

⦿ Personal or organizational (P or O)

⦿ Immediate or delayed (I or D)

⦿ Certain or uncertain (C or U)

 Personal, immediate and certain (PIC) consequences are stronger than organizational, delayed or uncertain (ODU) consequences.

Look at Jones' positive consequences for the undesirable behavior:

⦿ Pleasant visits with citizens—personal, immediate, certain (PIC)

⦿ Satisfaction from knowing people like him—personal, immediate, certain (PIC)

⦿ Praise from peers and superiors for being people oriented—personal, delayed, certain (PDC)

Compare this with the positive consequences if he should do less socializing and get his paperwork done on time:

⦿ Investigators would stop complaining—personal, delayed, certain (PDC).

⦿ Overtime (unpaid) would stop—personal, delayed, certain (PDC).

⦿ Chances for promotion would increase—personal, delayed, uncertain (PDU).

The positive consequences for the *undesirable behavior* are stronger than those for the desirable behavior. The same is true for the negative consequences. The negative consequences associated with the undesirable behavior are delayed and uncertain. The negative consequences for less socializing are immediate and certain. The message for management:

 Change the balance of consequences so that employees are rewarded for desired behavior and punished for undesired behavior—not vice versa.

Managers can change the balance of consequences by:
- Adding positive consequences for desired behaviors.
- Adding negative consequences for undesired behaviors.
- Removing negative consequences for desired behaviors.
- Removing positive consequences for undesired behaviors.
- Changing the strength of the consequences—that is, changing an organizational consequence to a personal one, a delayed consequence to an immediate one or an uncertain consequence to a certain one.

Consider the following situation: A law enforcement department is doing an analysis of its efficiency and has asked all officers to complete time sheets at the end of their shifts. One shift sergeant is having difficulty getting her officers to turn in their sheets. The officers see the sheets as busywork, interfering with efficiency rather than helping to improve it, so they often leave work without completing them. The sergeant then has to track them down the next day to get them to fill them in. As a solution to the problem, the sergeant gets on the P.A. system at the beginning of the shift, reads the names of those who did not complete their time study and asks them to report to the front desk to fill them in. Examine the following list of consequences of the described behavior.

- Filling out the sheets takes a few minutes past quitting time.
- This results in getting caught in a traffic jam.
- Officers may get chewed out by the sergeant if they do not fill in the sheets.
- Officers are given time at the beginning of their next shift to fill in the sheets.
- Officers get their names read over the P.A. system.
- Colleagues clap and cheer when the names are read.
- The efficiency study will not be reliable if all officers do not complete the time sheets.
- The sergeant has to spend time getting officers to comply with the request.

This problem can be looked at using the balance of consequences analysis. A key to using this tool is to look at the behavior through the eyes of the beholder—in this instance, the problem officers. The analysis will look like the chart in Figure 10.6. In this case it is obvious that reading the names over the P.A. system is positively reinforcing the undesired behavior, not punishing it. Peer pressure might be brought to bear on those who do not participate. Or those who turn their sheets in as desired could be rewarded in some way.

FIGURE 10.6
Balance of
Consequences
Analysis—Time Sheet
Problem

Behavior	
Undesired (current) • Not filling in time sheets	**Desired** • Filling in time sheets
Positive consequences • Get time next shift (PIC) • Get name announced (PIC) • Collegues cheer (PIC)	**Positive consequences** • NONE
Negative consequences • Make supervisor unhappy (ODC) • Unreliable survey results (ODU)	**Negative consequences** • Caught in traffic (PIC) • Name will not be read (PIC)

© Cengage Learning 2012

The PRICE Method

The PRICE method, developed by Blanchard (1989, p.18), is a five-step approach to employee performance problems such as attendance.

The PRICE method consists of five steps:
- **Pinpoint**
- **Record**
- **Involve**
- **Coach**
- **Evaluate**

The five steps are applicable to most problem behaviors. The first step is to *pinpoint* the problem behavior and make certain the employee knows about it. Say, for example, an officer frequently uses profanity in public. This unacceptable behavior needs to be changed. Exactly what constitutes profanity must be specified.

The second step is to *record* how often and when the problem behavior occurs. Under what circumstances does the officer use the profanity? Who else is usually present? What triggers it? How often does it happen? At any certain time of day? This record establishes the behavior as problematic and provides a baseline from which to work.

Third, *involve* the officer in setting a goal to eliminate the problem behavior and deciding on specific strategies to meet this goal. The strategies should include a specific timeline as well as incentives for specific accomplishments toward goal achievement.

Fourth, *coach* the officer regularly and consistently: "This is the most critical part of the plan. It is also the step where managers most frequently stumble" (Blanchard, 1989, p.18). Provide positive reinforcement whenever the officer substitutes an acceptable word for what would normally elicit a profanity. Enlist the aid of other officers to help provide positive reinforcement. Make certain others do not use profanity without being criticized. Double standards will undermine the PRICE method.

Finally, *evaluate* the performance according to a predetermined schedule to monitor progress.

One-Minute Managing

The *One Minute Manager*, for which Blanchard is perhaps best known, suggests that managers can use one-minute managing, including both praise and reprimands, to get their subordinates to perform at peak efficiency with high morale.

 Both praise and reprimands can be effectively accomplished in one minute.

Blanchard and Johnson (1981, p.44) suggest that *one-minute praising* works well when managers:

1. Tell people *up front* that you are going to let them know how they are doing.
2. Praise people immediately.
3. Tell people what they did right—be specific.
4. Tell people how good you feel about what they did right and how it helps the organization and the other people who work there.
5. Stop for a moment of silence to let them "feel" how good you feel.
6. Encourage them to do more of the same.
7. Shake hands or touch people in a way that makes it clear that you support their success in the organization. (Any such physical contact should be done in a way that could never be construed as sexual harassment.)

One-minute reprimands work well when managers:

1. Tell people *beforehand* that you are going to let them know how they are doing in specific terms.

The first half of the reprimand:

2. Reprimand people immediately.
3. Tell people what they did wrong—be specific.
4. Tell people how you feel about what they did wrong—in specific terms.
5. Stop for a few seconds of uncomfortable silence to let them *feel* how you feel.

The second half of the reprimand:

6. Shake hands or touch them in a way that lets them know you are honestly on their side. (Again, with any physical contact, avoid any appearance of sexual harassment.)
7. Remind them how much you value them.

8. Reaffirm that you think well of them but not of their performance in this situation.

9. Realize that when the reprimand is over, it's over. (Blanchard and Johnson, 1981, p.59)

Figure 10.7 illustrates how one-minute praisings and reprimands constitute a comprehensive disciplinary approach.

Simply knowing the secrets of one-minute praising and reprimanding is not enough: "To use these tools well, you must understand some specific management techniques. . . . Giving an equal amount of praise and criticism may not be enough to save you from being thought of as a bad boss. In most groups, there's a need for four times as many positive interactions—that is, praising—as negative interactions (Blanchard and Johnson, 1981).

A reprimand has such a powerful effect that it takes four positive words to balance one negative word.

FIGURE 10.7
The One-Minute
Manager's "Game Plan"

Source: Kenneth Blanchard and Spencer Johnson. *The One Minute Manager.* p.101. Copyright © 1981 by William Morrow and Co. Used by permission of William Morrow and Company, Inc., Publishers, New York.

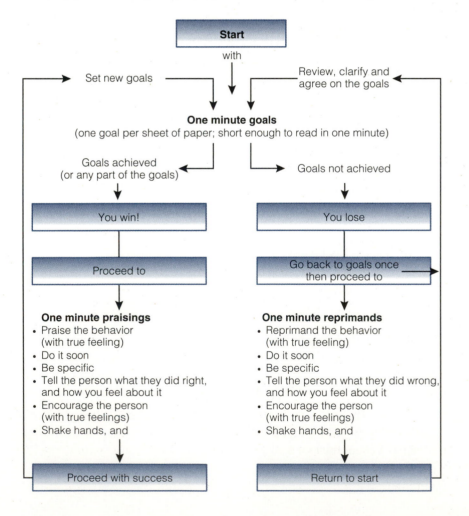

A very brief summary of
The One Minute Manager's Game Plan
How to give yourself and others the gift of getting greater results in less time.
Set goals, praise and reprimand behaviors, encourage people, speak the truth, laugh, work, enjoy and encourage the people you work with to do the same as you do!

An effective manager usually gives four times more praise than blame.

Blanchard describes a corporation he worked with where criticism and praise were approximately equal. The employees thought their relationship with their boss was "totally negative." Even when the ratio was changed to two praisings for every one reprimand, people still thought their boss was "all over them." Only when the ratio became four praisings to one criticism did the employees feel they had a "good relationship" with their boss. Managers need to "catch" their subordinates doing something well.

The Stroke Approach

The Better Than Money Corporation is founded on the principle that management has available to it several options that are "better than money" to motivate employees. This principle carries over into the corporation's main business, consulting on excellence in customer service. Its stroke approach includes five kinds of strokes:

- Positive—any sincere, positive comment or expression. Clearly a warm fuzzy.
- Negative—any negative action or word that is clearly a cold prickly.
- Absent—lack of any word or recognition.
- Crooked—a positive stroke followed by a negative one, for example, "That's a nice gun. What little old lady did you take that off of?"
- Plastic—a comment given as a ritual, for example, "How are things going?"

 Managers can give strokes that are positive, negative, absent, crooked or plastic. They should focus on positive strokes.

To use strokes effectively, managers should concentrate on the positive strokes as much as possible. Figure 10.8 shows how a manager might set "stroking objectives" each day.

A FAIR DISCIPLINARY SYSTEM

A fair, equitable disciplinary system has the following characteristics:

- Reasonable and necessary policies, procedures and rules to govern employees' conduct at work and promote both individual and organizational goals. Regular review of these standards.
- Effective communication of these policies, procedures and rules as well as the consequences for noncompliance.
- Immediate, impartial and consistent enforcement of the policies, procedures and rules.
- An appeals procedure.

FIGURE 10.8 Using Strokes to Discipline Positively

Source: Copyright © 1980 by John Tschohl, Better than Money Corporation. Courtesy of Service Quality Institute, Minneapolis, MN. Reprinted by permission.

Stroking objective for _____ Date: _____

1. Give out two positive strokes per day.
   • Genuine
   • Sincere
   • Specific
   • Timely

2. Identify one top performer in your work group.
   Name _____

   Give two positive strokes per week. (Do not combine with #1).

3. Identify one marginal performer in your work group.
   Name _____

   Give two positive strokes per week. (Do not combine with #1).

SUMMARY

Discipline and morale are closely related. Morale is how a person feels; discipline is how a person acts. The purpose of discipline is to promote desired behavior, which may be done by encouraging acceptable behavior or punishing unacceptable behavior. Maintaining discipline is a fundamental management right. An agency's policy and procedure manual is the foundation on which most discipline must be based.

The 10/80/10 principle divides the workforce into three categories: 10 percent self-motivated high achievers, 80 percent average achievers and 10 percent unmotivated troublemakers who cause 90 percent of management's problems. A problem employee exhibits abnormal behavior to the extent that the behavior is detrimental to organizational needs and goals as well as to the needs and goals of other law enforcement personnel. Difficult people include yes people, passives, avoiders, pessimists, complainers, know-it-alls, exploders, bullies and snipers. To deal with problem people, get their attention,

identify the problem behavior, point out the consequences, ask questions, listen and explain expectations. Avoid defensiveness. Among the most challenging problem behaviors are abuse of sick leave, substance abuse, corruption, insubordination, sexual harassment, use of excessive force and misconduct off duty.

A primary rule of effective discipline is that it should be carried out as close to the time of the violation as possible. The offense and offender, how the offense was committed and the offender's attitude and past performance are important considerations in assigning penalties. Progressive discipline uses disciplinary steps based on the severity of the offense. The steps usually are (1) oral reprimand, (2) written reprimand, (3) suspension/demotion and (4) discharge/termination.

The balance of consequences analysis considers behavior in terms of what positive and negative results the behavior produces and then focuses on those results. Personal, immediate and certain (PIC) consequences are stronger than organizational, delayed or uncertain (ODU) consequences. Change the balance of consequences so that employees are rewarded for desired behavior and punished for undesired behavior—not vice versa.

The PRICE Method consists of five steps: (1) pinpoint, (2) record, (3) involve, (4) coach and (5) evaluate. Both praise and reprimands can be effectively accomplished in one minute. An effective manager usually gives four times more praise than blame. Managers can also give strokes that are positive, negative, absent, crooked or plastic. They should focus on positive strokes.

CHALLENGE TEN

The new Greenfield police chief has asked Captain Blair to review and update the policy and procedure manual. The current manual is several inches thick, steeped in fine details and includes rules and procedures for nearly every circumstance. It was initially modeled after a manual written in the 1960s for a large police department in another part of the country.

Captain Blair knocks the dust off her copy of the manual and starts reading. She realizes that she hasn't read the entire manual since she was hired as an officer 20 years ago. Some language and policies in the manual are unrelated to the activities of the Greenfield Police Department. Captain Blair knows that most members of the department aren't familiar with all the policies and procedures in the manual and certainly aren't complying with them.

Captain Blair notes that the policy on breaks at restaurants requires officers to sit facing the entrance door for officer safety. The policy regarding traffic stops requires officers to approach vehicles with their hand on their gun as they listen for noise from the trunk and visually check back seats. An entire section of the manual is devoted to riot control, something the Greenfield Police Department has never experienced.

1. Do lengthy and detailed policy and procedure manuals enhance tight discipline?
2. Do lengthy and detailed policy and procedure manuals protect departments from litigation?
3. What basic changes should Captain Blair consider if she rewrites the manual?
4. How should she change the tone or philosophy of the manual?
5. What is a good strategy for gaining officers' acceptance of a new manual?
6. Should all policies and procedures be written with the same detail?

DISCUSSION QUESTIONS

1. Why is discipline a broader term than punishment?
2. What level of law enforcement manager should investigate the majority of discipline problems?
3. What is constructive discipline?
4. For what areas do you think written departmental rules and regulations are necessary?
5. What behaviors would be severe enough violations to warrant termination?

6. What would be a constructive law enforcement department philosophy for discipline?

7. Are there too many departmental rules and regulations? Not enough? What are the most important ones?

8. Why is discipline necessary for individual functioning? For organizational functioning?

9. Choose a problem behavior you would like to change and do a balance of consequences analysis. Are there changes you can make to reduce or eliminate the problem behavior?

10. As a manager, what types of positive and negative discipline would you be inclined to use?

 REFERENCES

Bazley, Thomas D.; Mieczkowski, Thomas; and Lersch, Kim Michelle. "Early Intervention Program Criteria: Evaluating Officer Use of Force." *Justice Quarterly*, March 2009, pp.107–124.

Blanchard, Kenneth. "A PRICE That Makes Sense." *Today's Office*, September 1989, p.18.

Blanchard, Kenneth, and Johnson, Spencer. *The One Minute Manager*. New York: William Morrow and Company, 1981.

Brantner-Smith, Betsy. "Bad Behavior in the Station: Dealing with Workplace Bullying." *Law Officer Magazine*, May 2009, pp.34–35.

Brophy, John R. "Corrective v. Disciplinary Action." *9-1-1 Magazine*, November/December 2007, pp.42–44.

Cobos, Al. "A New Era for the Discipline Process: Education-Based Discipline." Review of a presentation by Sheriff Leroy D. Baca at Harvard Law School, April 2009.

Collins, Jim. *Good to Great: Why Some Companies Make the Leap and Others Don't*. New York: Harper Collins Publishers, 2001.

Durose, Matthew R.; Smith, Erica L; and Langan, Patrick A. *Contacts between the Police and the Public, 2005*. Washington, DC: Bureau of Justice Statistics Special Report, April 2007. (NCJ 215243)

Dwyer, Terrence P. "Codes of Ethics and Officer Discipline." *PoliceOne.com News*, October 13, 2008.

Furey, Barry. "The ACT of Discipline." *9-1-1 Magazine*, June/July 2009, p.38.

Glennon, Jim. "Problem Children: Dealing with Whiney, Crybaby Malcontents in Your Ranks." *PoliceOne.com News*, June 29, 2009.

Harris, Christopher J. "Exploring the Relationship between Experience and Problem Behaviors: A Longitudinal Analysis of Officers from a Large Cohort." *Police Quarterly*, June 2009, pp.192–213.

Harris, Jack. "A 'Back to Basics' Approach to Employee Discipline." *Subject to Debate*, July 2007, pp.3,7.

Hughes, Frank, and Andre, Lisa B. "Problem Officer Variables and Early Warning Systems." *The Police Chief*, October 2007, pp.164–172.

Kruger, Karen J. "Investigating and Disciplining Off-Duty Sexual Conduct: Is There a Right to Privacy?" *The Police Chief*, September 2008, pp.12–13.

Luna, Andrea Morrozoff. "Introduction." In *Chief Concerns: Exploring the Challenges of Police Use of Force*, edited by Joshua A. Ederheimer and Lorie A. Fridell. Washington, DC: Police Executive Research Forum, April 2005, pp.1–20.

Miller, Laurence. "Police Personalities: Understanding and Managing the Problem Officer." *The Police Chief*, May 2003, pp.53-60.

Orrick, Dwayne. "A Best Practices Guide for Developing a Police Department Policy-Procedure Manual." In *Police Chiefs Desk Reference: A Guide for Newly Appointed Police Leaders*, 2nd ed., edited by International Association of Chiefs of Police and U.S. Bureau of Justice Assistance. Boston: McGraw-Hill Learning Solutions, pp.209–216.

Parker, Mike. "Education-Based Discipline: A New Approach." *Sheriff*, May/June 2009, p.14.

"Preventing Sexual Harassment." St. Paul, MN: Equal Opportunity Division, Department of Employee Relations, no date.

Schreiber, Sara. "Tools of the Riot Control Trade." *Law Enforcement Technology*, September 2009, pp.74–79.

"Sexual Harassment." Washington, DC: The U.S. Equal Employment Opportunity Commission, 2009. http://archive.eeoc.gov/types/sexual_harassment.html

Thompson, George J., and Walker, Gregory A. *The Verbal Judo Way of Leadership: Empowering the Thin Blue Line from the Inside Up*. Flushing, NY: Looseleaf Law Publications, Inc., 2007.

Vernon, Bob. "Chew Out in Private." *Law Officer Magazine*, October 2008, p.76.

Walker, Samuel; Milligan, Stacy Osnick; and Berke, Anna. *Supervision and Intervention within Early Intervention Systems: A Guide for Law Enforcement Chief Executives*. Washington, DC: Officer of Community Oriented Policing Services and the Police Executive Research Foundation, December 2005.

Walker, Samuel; Milligan, Stacy Osnick; and Berke, Anna. *Strategies for Intervening with Officers through Early Intervention Systems: A Guide for Front-Line Supervisors.* Washington, DC: Police Executive Research Forum, 2006.

Wexler, Chuck; Wycoff, Mary Ann; and Fischer, Craig. *"Good to Great" Policing: Application of Business Management Principles in the Public Sector.* Washington, DC: Community Oriented Policing Services and the Police Executive Research Forum, 2007.

Wyllie, Doug. "IACP Digest: The 'Traffic School' Approach to Officer Discipline." *PoliceOne.com News*, October 6, 2009.

Young, Dave. "Get Ready to Read the Riot Act." *Police*, May 2008, pp.30–34.

CITED CASES

Gardner v. Broderick, 392 U.S. 273 (1968)

Graham v. Connor, 490 U.S. 386 (1989)

Rizzo v. Goode, 423 U.S. 362 (1976).

CHAPTER ELEVEN

Complaints, Grievances and Conflict

> *A complaint is an opportunity to prove the kind of stuff you and your department are made of, a chance to cement a relationship so solidly it will last for years. That's much more important than who's right and who's wrong.*
>
> —Anonymous

DO YOU KNOW?

- Who may register a complaint?
- What categories of law enforcement misconduct are often included in external complaints?
- How complaints might be reduced?
- What the most common causes of internal complaints are?
- How job satisfaction, communication and performance are related?
- What the Pinch Model illustrates?
- When complaints do not need to be taken seriously?
- What two functions are served by a careful complaint investigation?
- How officers may protect themselves legally when under investigation?
- What the majority of grievances concern?
- What the outcome of a complaint or grievance might be?
- Whether conflict must be negative?
- What possible benefits conflict might generate?

- What major sources of conflict exist in the law enforcement organization?
- What management's responsibility in conflict situations is?
- How conflicts that arise during crises should be dealt with?
- What the confrontation technique is and what to expect from it?
- What the keys to maintaining healthy conflict are?
- What the intersubjectivity approach to resolving conflict involves?

 ## CAN YOU DEFINE?

arbitration
complainant
complaint
conflict
confrontation technique
crunch
exonerated
Garrity protection
grievance
grievant
intersubjectivity approach
mediation
pinch
Pinch Model
principled negotiation
reframing
sustained
unfounded

 ## INTRODUCTION

Chapter 10 discussed problem behaviors perceived by managers. This chapter reverses the perspective and looks at problems perceived by subordinates and by those outside the law enforcement organization. These perceived problems might result in complaints or grievances.

Most law enforcement supervisors must deal with complaints as part of their responsibilities. How supervisors react to complaints will directly affect the organization's ability to function effectively. If complaints are not dealt with promptly, thoroughly and fairly, the result will be serious negative consequences for the entire organization.

Managers must also deal with conflict, both internal and external. One reason is that our society has become increasingly complex. Choices used to be simpler. What kind of weapons? Squad cars? Investigative equipment? Another reason conflict is inevitable is that managers deal with people, and within the law enforcement agency people have strong egos and are used to speaking their minds and getting their way. But they are also people who depend on each other to get results—sometimes to stay alive. A third reason conflict is inevitable is that resources are limited, and the law enforcement organization is no exception. Choices must be made regarding allocation of human resources (who is assigned to what shift) and monetary resources (salaries, perks).

Indeed, all organizations, including law enforcement, will have conflict. Individual and organizational goals; differences in employee lifestyles and individual needs; varied interpretations of rules and regulations; physical, social and psychological differences; and variations in viewpoints all exist and contribute to disagreement and conflict.

 ## CHAPTER at a GLANCE

This chapter begins with definitions that differentiate between complaints and grievances. It then examines the difference between external and internal complaints, as well as complaint policies and how complaints are handled and investigated, including the role of internal affairs investigations, the legal rights and procedures for officers named in disciplinary actions, and the controversial use of civilian review boards. Next, grievances are discussed, including how they are resolved, followed by a look at the processes of mediation and arbitration and an examination of the disposition of complaints and grievances. The chapter then takes a closer look at the conflicts law enforcement managers must deal with, including some contrasting views of conflict, sources of conflict and the responsibility of managers to reduce negative conflict and make positive conflict work for the organization's benefit. Next is a discussion of recognizing and acknowledging conflict, managing crisis conflict, and handling personal attacks. Then the probability of role conflict and disagreements between coworkers is examined, followed by a look at external conflicts and internal and external politics. The chapter concludes with a discussion of maintaining healthy conflict and the importance of conflict resolution skills.

COMPLAINTS AND GRIEVANCES DEFINED

A **complaint** is a statement of a problem. A **grievance** is a formally registered complaint. By definition, a complaint and a grievance are basically synonymous. Either can be described as a criticism, charge, accusation or finding of fault. Complaints and grievances may also be described as circumstances or conditions thought to be unjust.

A complaint or grievance is an action taken by someone against a person or an organization for a perceived wrong. Whether real or imagined, the wrong is sufficient enough in the mind of the person complaining that the matter must be brought to the attention of the proper authority. The action taken may be an oral criticism, a written statement, a listing of wrongs, a civil service procedure, a meeting demand, a hearing demand or formal legal action.

> **complaint**
> a statement of a problem.

> **grievance**
> a formally registered complaint; a claim by an employee that a rule or policy has been misapplied or misinterpreted to the employee's detriment.

COMPLAINTS

Complaints are an unavoidable part of being a manager. Even the most effective managers get their share of complaints.

 A complaint may be made by the general public, by people arrested or by employees of the law enforcement department, including peers or managers. The person or group filing the complaint is called the complainant.

> **complainant**
> a person or group filing a complaint.

Complaints may be external or internal.

External Complaints

External complaints are those made by citizens against a law enforcement officer or officers, a supervisor, support staff or the entire department. The complaint may be made by an individual or a group. It may be as "trivial" as a citizen receiving what he or she perceives to be an unjustified parking ticket or as serious as a charge of brutality or racism.

Studies have found that complaints are not filed evenly by people across demographic parameters. A complainant profile generated by such studies shows that non-White, unmarried, low-income males under age 30 are most likely to complain about the police. Nearly 75 percent of all complaints against officers come from this group. Studies also revealed that the officers most likely to receive complaints against them were those under age 30 with fewer than 5 years of police experience, only a high school education and assigned to uniformed patrol duties. A study of use-of-force complaints, based on data from the Bureau of Justice Statistics, found (1) rates of force complaints were higher among agencies having greater spatial differentiation, internal affairs units and higher violence crime rates; (2) the percentage of complaints sustained was higher among agencies characterized by greater formalization and lower where collective bargaining was authorized for officers; and (3) minority representation was unrelated to complaint rates or to the percentage of complaints sustained (Hickman and Piquero, 2009, p.3).

People who call in complaints without leaving a name are generally not as credible as are those who identify themselves. This does not mean, however, that anonymous complaints should be ignored. With the drug problem as serious as it has become, and considering that those who provide information to the police are often threatened with intimidation, injuries and in some cases death, it is understandable that people may not want to give their names.

Law enforcement departments exist to serve their communities. With this basic premise, citizens can be thought of as consumers of law enforcement services, and, like any business, departments should "aim to please." Research suggests that customers who have bad experiences tell approximately 11 people about it; those with good experiences tell just 6. Managers should recognize that it is impossible to please everyone all the time. Some citizens, rightly or wrongly, will perceive a problem and register a complaint.

An employee who receives a complaint should obtain all possible information about the incident. Sometimes the complainant may be under the influence of alcohol or other drugs and, if interviewed later, may give a considerably different story. Many departments have dispatcher complaint forms. Others automatically record all calls into and out of the department.

The Police Executive Research Forum (PERF) has published a model policy statement for handling citizen complaints. The intent of the policy statement is to provide precise guidelines to ensure fairness to officers and civilians alike. It seeks to improve service quality in three ways: (1) by increasing citizen confidence in the integrity of law enforcement actions, (2) by permitting law enforcement officials to monitor officers' compliance with department procedures and (3) by clarifying rights and ensuring due process protection to both citizens and officers.

Causes of External Complaints

Specific categories of misconduct subject to disciplinary action need to be clearly defined.

Categories of officer misconduct often included in external complaints are crime, excessive force, false arrest, improper entry, unlawful search, harassment, offensive demeanor and rule infractions.

Reducing External Complaints

Preventing misconduct is a primary way to reduce complaints. Agencies should make every effort to eliminate organizational conditions that may foster, permit or encourage improper behavior by officers.

Complaints can be reduced through effective recruitment and selection, training, policy and procedures manuals, effective supervision, community outreach and data collection and analysis.

Data collection and analysis might reveal problem behavior before complaints are registered. If complaints do occur, mediation is often successful in resolving the problem.

Mediation

Mediation is a form of alternative dispute resolution (ADR): "Mediation is a process of dispute resolution in which one or more impartial third parties intervenes in a conflict or dispute with the consent of the participants and assists them in negotiating a consensual and informed agreement" ("What Is Community Mediation?" no date). Table 11.1 summarizes the potential benefits of mediation.

The National Association for Community Mediation (NAFCM) is a Washington, DC–based organization that promotes community mediation and maintains an extensive library of resources on conflict resolution and

> **mediation**
> a process of dispute resolution in which one or more impartial third parties intervenes in a conflict or dispute with the consent of the participants and assists them in negotiating a consensual and informed agreement.

TABLE 11.1 Potential Benefits of Mediation

Benefits for Police Officers
1. Better understanding of interactions with citizens.
2. Opportunity to explain actions to citizens.
3. Greater satisfaction with complaint process.
4. Empowerment.
5. Chance to learn from mistakes.
Benefits for Citizen Complaints
1. Greater opportunity to meet goals.
2. Greater satisfaction with complaint process.
3. Better understanding of policing.
4. Empowerment.
Benefits for Police Accountability
1. Greater responsibility for one's action.
2. Positive changes in police subculture.
Benefits for Community Policing
1. Goals consistent with those of community policing.
2. Problem-solving process.
3. An opportunity for dialogue.
Benefits for Complaint Process
1. More efficient complaint process.
2. Cost savings.
3. Higher success rate.
Benefits for Criminal Justice System
1. More trust in justice system.
2. Lower crime rate.

Source: Samuel Walker, et al., *Mediating Citizen Complaints against Police Officers: A Guide for Police and Community Leaders.* Washington, DC: Community Oriented Policing Services Office, 2002, p.5.

training. It reports great national growth in community mediation, with more than 550 mediation programs, 19,500 volunteer community mediators and 76,000 citizens trained by community mediation programs. More than 97,500 cases are referred annually.

The Denver Police Department (DPD) community–police mediation program is an example of how to improve police-community relations and establish the truth or falsity of misconduct allegations through a voluntary process allowing community members and officers to sit down face to face in a neutral, confidential setting to discuss their issues in a forum facilitated by a professional mediator (Clemons and Rosenthal, 2008, p.32). In 2005 the department administered a survey to all officers and community members who had filed a complaint within the previous three years. Almost three-quarters (74.5 percent) of community members reported dissatisfaction with the complaint process, and 63.5 percent of officers reported dissatisfaction. Following implementation of the mediation program, dissatisfaction figures have plummeted to 10.7 percent and 3.7 percent, respectively: "The benefits of a community-police mediation program so vastly outweigh the costs that every metropolitan police department should offer it as a service to its community and its own officers" (Clemons and Rosenthal, p.32).

Internal Complaints

Complaints by officers or employees, internal complaints, are generally brought to the attention of the next highest manager. If the complaint is against a manager, it is brought before the next highest manager. If the complaint is against the department head, it is brought before the city manager or other head of local government, following the chain of command.

When investigating internal complaints against specific employees, the primary purpose should be to correct the behavior and make the employee a contributing member of the department. Employees are a tremendous investment. Everything reasonable should be done to reach a conclusion satisfactory to management and the employee.

The following guidelines might assist in handling internal complaints: Always be available, listen carefully and gather all the facts. Address the problem, and if an apology is called for, do so immediately. Explain your decision and why it was made as well as how it can be appealed.

A manager's attitude toward complaints can mean the difference between a temporarily rocky road and a permanent dead end. Recall that many complaints may be symptomatic of low morale or of problems with employees' feelings of self-worth.

Causes of Internal Complaints

Law enforcement officers usually pride themselves on being tough, disciplined and able to take whatever they need to. They may, however, be harboring feelings of dissatisfaction that manifest themselves in observable behaviors. A number of conditions can cause officers to complain.

Most internal complaints are related to working conditions or management style.

Officers may be dissatisfied with safety conditions, condition of vehicles, lack of equipment needed to do the job or other work conditions. They may also think their managers are too strict or too lenient, have too high or too low standards, oversupervise or undersupervise, give too little credit and too much criticism, will not accept suggestions, show favoritism or make unfair job assignments. The discussions of motivation and morale in Chapter 9 include signs that officers are unmotivated or experiencing low morale—instances in which complaints and grievances are likely to appear.

One challenging area of internal complaint managers sometimes must deal with is a charge of disability discrimination under the Americans with Disabilities Act (ADA). Possible reasonable accommodations include such changes as job restructuring, modified work schedule and modification of equipment, policies or training. Employers should be flexible and reasonable, but they do not need to meet the accommodation request of a disabled employee if it would present an "undue hardship." The ADA is discussed further in Chapter 15.

Reducing Internal Complaints

When signs of employee dissatisfaction appear, preventive action is needed. When managers sense that "things are not going right," it may be time to set up a personal talk or a shift or department meeting. Determine the type of discontentment and the cause. Pay special attention to what employees are saying in small groups. Talk with individual officers. Make it known that you are available to discuss matters formally or informally.

For years researchers have looked for a correlation between satisfaction and performance (Buchholz and Roth, 1987, pp.70–71). Studies have examined satisfaction levels with self, job, peers, management and organizations and have found a person could be satisfied with all of these and still not perform well (hygiene factors). A breakthrough came when satisfaction was correlated to communication as follows:

Satisfaction	Communication	Performance
High	High	Highest
Low	High	High
High	Low	Low
Low	Low	Lowest

Satisfied employees who talked about it performed the best; dissatisfied employees who did not talk about it performed the worst—findings you might expect. Surprisingly, however, those who were satisfied but did not talk about it were ranked lower in overall performance than were those who were dissatisfied but talked about it. This means that even people who may not be fully satisfied but have an environment where they can *communicate* about their dissatisfaction perform better than those who may be satisfied but are in a climate that lacks open communication.

Pinch Model

illustrates the importance of communication in dealing with complaints and the consequences of not communicating effectively; a pinch, a minor problem, can turn into a crunch, a major problem.

pinch

a minor problem.

crunch

a major problem.

 Communication is directly related to job performance. Those who are dissatisfied on the job and communicate their discontent perform better than do those who are satisfied and do not communicate.

Open communication will help employees be more satisfied and help identify problems before they become major. This is illustrated in the **Pinch Model**, Figure 11.1, which illustrates the importance of open communication and the likely consequences of its absence.

A **pinch** is a small problem between individuals, a situation in which an individual or individuals feel something is wrong. It's not a full-blown problem—yet. Pinches result from such things as the supervisor changing the rules, changing the schedule, failing to provide expected support or feedback or failing to keep a promise. They can also result from misunderstandings and failure to clarify expectations on the job. If small problems are handled effectively, major problems can be avoided. If they are not dealt with, they may accumulate and disrupt performance and relationships, usually leading to a major confrontation, or **crunch**.

FIGURE 11.1
The Pinch Model

Source: Steve Buchholz and Thomas Roth. *Creating the High Performance Team*, p.73. Copyright 1987 by John Wiley and Sons, Inc. Reprinted by permission.

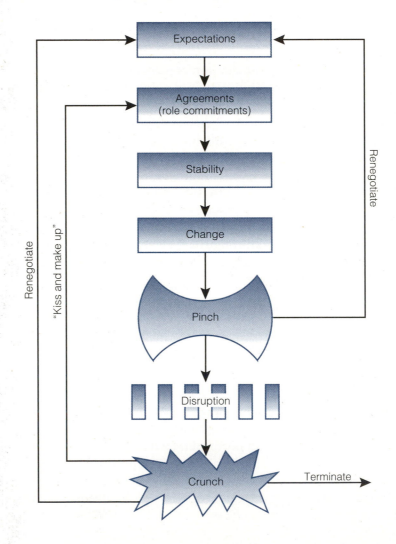

A crunch occurs when the problem becomes serious. It is marked by strong emotional reactions from both sides. This may be a heated argument or total avoidance. At this point two alternatives often exist. First, those involved in the crunch may "kiss and make up" but without dealing with the root problem. This results in a vicious cycle, with pinches leading to crunches and more confrontation. Or it may result in transfer or termination. The Pinch Model suggests that when pinches or crunches occur, managers and subordinates need to renegotiate, starting with an open discussion of expectations.

 The Pinch Model illustrates the importance of communication in dealing with complaints and the consequences of not communicating effectively.

The Pinch Model of communication can be seen as analogous to the broken-window theory discussed in Chapter 2, in that small issues, if ignored or discounted, can evolve into larger, more difficult challenges that require more effort and output of resources to correct.

In addition to keeping communication lines open and encouraging subordinates to express their concerns, managers can help reduce complaints in other ways. They can help employees improve their education and their work conditions; inspect and improve equipment and determine what additional equipment can be requested in the next budget; and give praise when it is deserved. When criticism is deserved, they can make it constructive criticism delivered in private.

Often people with complaints have tunnel vision and have not considered points on the other side. A complaint is usually nothing personal. Regard it as a chance for successful change. Be positive rather than negative. Surprisingly, most complaints can be worked out if they are not allowed to proceed too far. Complaints handled inappropriately often become grievances.

COMPLAINT POLICIES

Any manager who wants to operate efficiently and maintain high morale must take every complaint seriously. It is essential that citizens support and have confidence in the police department. No matter how trivial or unreasonable a complaint may seem to a manager, it does not appear that way to the person making it. Administrators should consider a no-nonsense, bright-line rule regarding complaints: "A simple declaration stating that ALL complaints against any member of the police department will be received and investigated leaves little room for dispute" (Orrick, 2008, p.185). Some departments require a sworn statement from complainants, but this practice can discourage honest people who may be skeptical or reticent.

 A basic rule: *Never* take a complaint lightly. All complaints must be investigated.

Every police department should have a written complaint review policy explaining procedures used to investigate complaints, the roles and responsibilities of the supervisors and the officer complained against, the function of internal affairs, possible dispositions and the appeal process. A complaint policy establishes a plan and states the department's philosophy regarding public complaints. Police administrators know that police–civilian encounters will inevitably cause problems. Police have unique authority in the community, as well as considerable discretionary power. The agency, community, employee and complainant all benefit from a fair, open investigation policy of complaints against the police.

HANDLING AND INVESTIGATING COMPLAINTS

Regardless of its origination, whether external or internal, the complaint must be investigated and resolved. Complaints can be received from any source, in person, by mail or by phone. Even complaints from juveniles, anonymous sources and arrestees should be accepted if the facts warrant.

Making a complaint should be easily accomplished. A clearly marked, easily accessible office should be open from early morning until evening. Often this is the internal affairs (IA) office. Phone complaints should be accepted any time. Whenever possible, complaints should be in writing. If this is not possible, the department should complete a complaint description form and send it to the complainant to be reviewed, signed and returned to the agency.

A complaint against an officer, support staff or the entire department must be investigated thoroughly, following the same principles as in a criminal investigation. This is true whether the complaint is from someone outside or within the department. The investigation and adjudication of complaints will depend on the specific charge and on the past record of the officer involved. The investigation process should have a definite time limit, such as 120 days, with a one-time, 30-day extension possible.

 A careful investigation of a complaint instills confidence in management's fairness and protects those accused of wrongdoing.

Complaints require action. In some cases the basis for the complaint is readily discernible and easily verified. In other cases, however, the facts are not clear or may be in dispute. These matters are considerably more difficult to resolve. In yet other situations the complaint is completely irrational, but it must be dealt with rationally. Figure 11.2 provides an overview of the complaint process: "It is incumbent on the police department to make its citizens aware that a complaint process exists, how to file a complaint, and how the agency processes and investigates complaints" (*Building Trust between the Police and the Citizens They Serve*, 2009, p.20).

Most complaints about minor infractions such as discourtesy or sarcasm can be investigated by the accused officer's first-line supervisor. In general, it is not recommended that senior officers investigate junior officers, as this can cause hard feelings among the ranks (Orrick, 2008, p.185). More serious allegations should be assigned to the department's internal affairs department, discussed shortly.

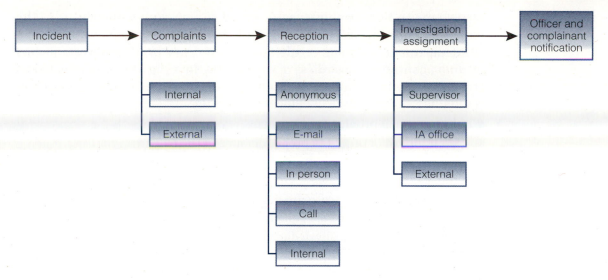

FIGURE 11.2 The Complaint Process

Source: *Building Trust between the Police and the Citizens They Serve: An Internal Affairs Promising Practices Guide for Local Law Enforcement.* Alexandria, VA: International Association of Chiefs of Police, November 10, 2009, p.20. IACP

In dealing with complaints, determine the exact nature of the complaint. What specifically occurred that caused the complainant to take action? An investigation must support the specifics and must involve the person complained against.

If a police officer is charged with a violation of rules and regulations and thinks the charge is unjust, the officer can request a hearing. If the charge is upheld at the hearing, the appeal procedure will vary from department to department. The hearing may be with the city manager, city council, police complaint board or civil service commission. If upheld by one of these hearing authorities, it may be possible to appeal to the district court. Officers' rights regarding complaints and grievances are discussed later in the chapter.

The person assigned to the investigation must be able to draw a conclusion from the specifics of the complaint. All complaints against law enforcement employees must be investigated within the constraints of the legal process. Inquiries must be objective. Conclusions and final decisions should be avoided until all facts are available.

Despite their seemingly minor nature, complaints may have a major impact on department morale if not investigated properly. It is necessary to investigate complaints to clear the person complained against as well as to serve the interests of justice. Considerations in the investigation include investigating immediately and collecting both positive and negative facts; interviewing those complained against as well as the complainant; and taking written statements, if necessary, checking personnel records of those accused as well as previous complaints of the person accusing and then conducting a fair hearing.

Good complaint investigations protect the reputation of the department and any accused employee and provide an opportunity for the complainant to be heard and the public to be notified of the results. Immediate disposition of such incidents builds public confidence, law enforcement morale and a general sense of justice.

Actions to be taken, offenses deemed to be wrongs, the status of the employee until the case is decided and other matters are often defined in the department rules and regulations or grievance procedures established by union contracts. Regardless of whether the investigation is conducted by supervisors, internal affairs or through mediation or arbitration, minimum standards for adjudication include the following:

- The burden of proof is on the agency.
- The standard of proof is a preponderance of the evidence.
- The standards of evidence are those of administrative law, not criminal law.
- No presumptions of truth are made regarding facts in disputes or witness credibility; all persons are equally creditable.
- Conclusions are logically deduced from the evidence (*Standards and Guidelines for Internal Affairs: Recommendations from a Community of Practice*, 2009, p.52).

These minimum standards, although developed for internal affairs, apply equally to other investigations as well.

INTERNAL AFFAIRS INVESTIGATIONS

The IIA department has the unenviable task of investigating itself and its own officers while not appearing biased to the public. Internal affairs investigators protect the public from abusive police, but they also tread the fine line of protecting individual officers from unfounded allegations. Internal affairs sections traditionally are reactive, responding to citizen complaints and reports of misconduct and policy violations from other department members. Figure 11.3 illustrates how an issue can flow through the system to become an IA investigation. As shown, issues come to the attention of the department at the *intake* stage from internal (other officers) and external (the public) sources. At intake, a first-line supervisor, usually a sergeant, determines if the issue is a concern or a complaint. Complaints are further sorted as minor, serious or criminal, with the cases involving serious administrative policy concerns being those processed into the IA division.

There are three major legal considerations in the complaint process: criminal, internal and civil. If there is even a hint of criminal behavior by the employee, the matter should be separated into both a criminal and an internal investigation. The criminal investigation should be conducted first, including the *Miranda* warning if applicable. This is followed by the administrative investigation, including a *Garrity* warning if applicable. A third consideration is a civil lawsuit brought by the complainant, where a third set of rules apply.

The first step is to review all evidence. Next, obtain copies of all associated elements of the case. These can include a copy of the crime or arrest report, a computer printout of the call-for-service, a copy of radio transmissions and any other retrievable items. A fundamental component of most investigations is interviewing all involved parties.

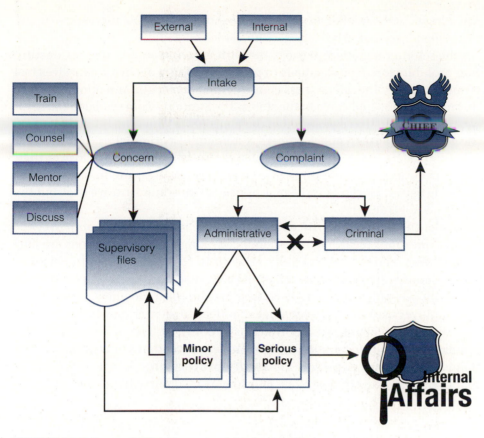

FIGURE 11.3 Internal Affairs Investigations Sorting Chart

Source: Deputy Chief Todd Sandell, Richfield (Minnesota) Police Department, 2009. Reprinted by permission. Use of this chart without expressed written consent of its originator is strictly prohibited.

OFFICERS' RIGHTS AND LEGAL PROCEDURES

The nature of police work makes officers vulnerable to a variety of legal actions. The National Association of Police Organizations (NAPO) provides legal resources to police defendants and their attorneys. Established in 1978 to protect officers' legal and constitutional rights, it attempts to put police officers on a level playing field with everybody else. NAPO represents more than 2,000 police unions and associations, 236,000 sworn law enforcement officers, 11,000 retired officers and more than 100,000 citizens ("Welcome to NAPO," 2009).

A variety of legislation has also protected due process rights of officers involved in disciplinary hearings and other court actions. In addition, several states have enacted Law Enforcement Officers' Bills of Rights (LEOBR). In other jurisdictions, contracts resulting from collective bargaining provisions may affect the investigative process when police officers are involved.

In general, a police officers' bill of rights gives law enforcement officers, sheriffs and correctional officers the right to be notified of any pending disciplinary action within a reasonable time before the action takes effect, to be treated with a specific minimum standard of fairness while under investigation, to request a hearing if an investigation results in a recommendation of disciplinary action and to advance review and comment on any adverse material being placed in the officer's personnel file.

The self-incrimination clause of the Fifth Amendment to the U.S. Constitution prohibits forcing individuals to provide evidence against themselves in a criminal matter. The due process clause of the Fourteenth Amendment makes this requirement applicable to the states. The Supreme Court ruled in *Garrity v. New Jersey* (1967) that a violation of the Fourteenth Amendment occurs when the government uses a police officer's statement in a criminal trial against that officer. Officers accused of misconduct can be threatened with loss of their jobs if they do not cooperate with an internal investigation. In other words, anything used in a criminal trial may be used in an administrative trial, but the reverse is not true.

Under the *Garrity* rule: "An employer has the right to require employees to answer questions regarding their conduct as long as those questions are narrowly drawn and directly related to the duties they were hired to perform. The employer may use these statements in disciplinary actions involving the employee which could result in termination of employment." However, if the employer uses *Garrity* to compel an officer to answer questions, they are prohibited from giving this information to police or having it used during a criminal trial. The officer must request *Garrity* protection. Officers can protect themselves by getting in writing a **Garrity protection**, a written notification that they are making their statement or report involuntarily:

> On (date) at (time) at (place), I was ordered to submit this report (give this statement) by (name and rank). Consequently, I submit this report (statement) involuntarily and only because of that order as a condition of continued employment.

> I believe the department requires this report (statement) exclusively for internal purposes and will not release it to any other agency or authority.

> I hereby specifically reserve my constitutional rights to remain silent under the Fifth and Fourteenth Amendments. Further, I rely specifically upon the protection afforded to me under the doctrines set forth in *Garrity vs. New Jersey* (1967).

This protects the officer should the matter become a criminal issue. The statement or report could not be used against the officer. It might also help break the code of silence.

Garrity protection
a written notification that an officer is making his or her statement or report in an internal affairs investigation involuntarily.

 While under investigation, officers may find legal protection from a Law Enforcement Officer Bill of Rights (LEOBR), if one has been enacted in that state, and under the *Garrity* protection.

CIVILIAN REVIEW BOARDS

In some communities, civilian review boards have been designated to investigate and dispose of complaints against law enforcement officers. Law enforcement agencies usually have opposed such civilian review boards on the grounds that they erode the authority of the responsible law enforcement manager. At the heart of the debate regarding the civilian review boards is the question of whether police possess the ability, the structure and the will to police themselves. Those in favor of review boards think they take pressure off the police to investigate their own and help reduce public belief that the police will whitewash wrongdoing within the agency. Further, because the review board is an external agency, it can be more independent in its investigation. In addition, review board membership can represent more elements of a diverse community.

Police, on the other hand, believe that the department can police its own, that it has its own complaint-handling procedures through existing department policies and that the police have governed themselves in the past and will continue to do so. Many police executives think that civilian review boards substantially reduce the effectiveness of the police agency administration. Accountability is the essence of the issue. Police believe they have accountability through the existing structure of first-line supervisor; middle manager; upper-level manager; and, finally, chief of police.

Despite the controversy, many larger cities have civilian review boards. According to one account, approximately 100 municipalities throughout the country use civilian panels to investigate complaints.

Civilian review boards typically have the power only to make recommendations to the police chief executive, not to impose discipline. Some, however, advocate modifying such boards, from a strictly reactive body to one more involved in preventing incidents leading to complaints.

It is conceivable that citizens might expect more sympathy from a panel of other civilians, yet such findings support the notion that civilian review boards are capable of making fair, objective, unbiased decisions regarding complaints, not automatically and disproportionately siding with the citizen complainant to the detriment of the officer or the department.

© AP Images/Mel Evans

U.S. Attorney General Alberto Gonzales, right, listens to New Orleans Police Chief Warren Riley, left, as St. Bernard Parish Sheriff Jack Stephens, center, looks on. They met in Chalmette, Louisiana, Thursday, Oct. 20, 2005, at the Disaster Recovery Center set up in the parking lot of a Walmart Store that was closed by flooding. Rapid, well-coordinated responses to emergencies and natural disasters, as well as listening to the concerns and immediate needs of residents in the wake of such crises, is critical to avoiding citizen complaints and keeping public support for the department high.

A study of the implementation of a new citizen oversight agency in a mid-sized Western city found that although the oversight agency improved citizen's satisfaction levels with certain aspects of the complaint process, such as the quality of communication and the thoroughness of the process, the implementation did not have a statistically significant direct effect on either citizens' level of satisfaction with the complaint process as a whole or their satisfaction with the complaint outcome (De Angelis, 2009, p.214).

GRIEVANCES

Grievances are as much a part of law enforcement managers' responsibilities as complaints are. Grievances can come only from law enforcement employees, not from the public. A grievance is a claim by an employee that a rule or policy has been misapplied or misinterpreted to the employee's detriment. The person filing the grievance is known as the **grievant**.

grievant

the person or group filing a grievance.

Grievances are a right of employees. Formal grievance procedures are not provided to cause problems but rather to promote a more harmonious, cooperative relationship between employees and management.

Managers' decisions are not always correct. Different interpretations can be made of rules, regulations, policies and procedures. The grievance procedure provides a means of arriving at decisions concerning these varied interpretations. In most instances the final decision may be more satisfactory to all parties involved because it involves input from a number of sources and is not just one person's opinion. Law enforcement managers should not treat employees who file grievances any differently from any other employee.

 Dissatisfaction with physical working conditions and equipment causes most grievances. Almost a third are caused by dissatisfaction with management's actions.

Vehicle condition, quality and timeliness of repair, equipment used in emergencies, lighting conditions, office space, excessive reports, type of acceptable firearm, protective equipment such as armored vests and tear gas and other physical items are the subject of much debate and dissatisfaction. Law enforcement supervisors need to discuss these matters at staff meetings because they are generally budget items that depend on decisions made by higher-level managers.

Roughly 30 percent of grievances result from some management behavior or action. This includes plural standards of conduct, failure to recognize good work, obstinate dealing with subordinates, failure to use procedures uniformly and fairly, use of obscene language, discrimination and other types of objectionable manager behavior.

Grievances concerning rules, regulations, policies and procedures center primarily on violations of civil rights. In the early years of policing, requirements were harsh concerning hairstyle, facial hair and off-duty employment. Employees realize some rules and regulations are necessary for the common good of management, employees and the community. They object, however, to what they consider overregulation. Many also object to off-duty conduct regulations. They believe that stricter regulations should not apply to officers simply because of their profession.

Civil and criminal actions against law enforcement officers have tended to force standardized procedures in these areas. In general, objections are low if the rules and regulations are communicated to the entire department and a two-way discussion is held concerning limitations and reasons.

The management's failure to do what employees expect also causes employee dissatisfaction. Employees, in general, want to do a good job and resent too many impediments. Among perceived impediments are

- Failure to communicate and to train employees to do the job effectively.
- Failure to explain procedures and then blaming employees for not doing it right.
- Failure to praise when it is deserved.
- Managers' failure to set a good example for subordinates.

Managers should not penalize employees for actions not directly related to performance of duty or to the best interest or safety of other department employees and not specifically in the rules, regulations, policies or procedures.

RESOLVING GRIEVANCES

Most noncontractual grievances are resolved at the first-line supervisor level. These are matters not associated with salaries, fringe benefits or conditions negotiated by the labor union or an employee group representative. The first-line manager talks to the grievant or the group filing the grievance. Through two-way communication, an objective approach by both sides, common sense, fair play and discussion of all issues and alternatives, the matter may be resolved at this level.

If the matter is not resolved at the first level, a formal grievance is filed and forwarded to the next level manager. If not resolved at this level, it proceeds to the head of the department. If it fails to be resolved at this level, the matter proceeds to voluntary arbitration, civil service board proceedings or other assigned hearing boards. Figure 11.4 illustrates the chain of command a grievance may go through.

Many law enforcement departments have ordinances, statutes or formal procedures for handling grievances. Following is an example of a grievance ordinance. Keep in mind that the "five working day" requirement stated in the procedure is only example. There is nothing universal or inherently superior about a five-day limit; it is simply the length of time used in this sample procedure:

> *Informal Grievance Procedure.* Any employee or group of employees having a grievance should first discuss the grievance with their immediate supervisor within five working days of the occurrence that caused the grievance. Within five working days, the supervisor should reply. If the supervisor's answer does not satisfactorily adjust the grievance, the employee should follow, within five working days, the formal grievance procedure outlined in the next section.

FIGURE 11.4
Grievance Chain of
Command

Source: "Conflict Management
and the Law Enforcement
Professional in the 1990s."
Law and Order, May 1994.
Reprinted by permission of the
publisher.

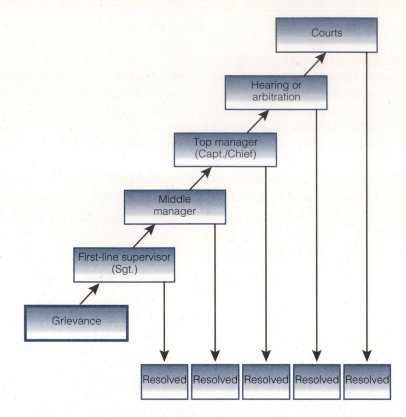

Formal Grievance Procedure. The following steps are used in the formal griev-ance procedure.

Step 1. The grievance is submitted in writing to the employee's immediate supervisor. The supervisor meets and discusses the grievance with the em-ployee and/or the employee's representative, if any, and replies in writing to the employee within five working days.

Step 2. If a settlement is not reached, the written grievance will be presented within five working days to the next level of supervision. The second level su-pervisor or his or her representative has five working days to investigate and render a written decision.

The procedure continues in this fashion, going up the hierarchy to the de-partment head, the city manager and finally the civil service commission.

The ordinance provides employees an opportunity and right to bring dis-satisfactions to management. It does not necessarily mean the grievance is justified, but it provides a procedure for having the matter heard and decided. It is an orderly procedure that applies to all employees equally and is free from interference, restraint, coercion or reprisal. The intent is to make grievances an aboveboard matter for discussion rather than a behind-the-back approach to problems.

The ordinance's wording makes it clear that employees have a chance to be heard. Grievance procedures are provided to avoid having problems fester, grow and become unmanageable. The results of such a procedure are most of-ten positive for employees, management and the organization.

MEDIATION AND ARBITRATION

Sometimes mediation or arbitration is used to settle grievances. Mediation, as previously discussed, brings in a neutral outside third party who tries to reconcile the two sides after hearing both and recommending a solution, which is not binding on either party.

Arbitration also brings in a neutral outside third party who, like the mediator, listens to both sides. The arbitration hearings may be informal or formal. After hearing both sides, the arbitrator recommends a solution. Unlike the mediator's recommendation, however, the recommendation of the arbitration is often binding, meaning it carries the weight and authority of a court ruling and must be adhered to.

arbitration
turning a decision over to an individual or panel to make the final recommendation.

DISPOSITION OF COMPLAINTS AND GRIEVANCES

 A complaint or grievance investigation usually results in one of four findings: sustained, not sustained, exonerated or unfounded.

A **sustained** complaint or grievance is one in which the investigative facts support the charge. If the investigative facts are insufficient, that is, the evidence does not support the accusations, the complaint or grievance is *not sustained*. An **exonerated** complaint or grievance is one in which the investigation determines that the matter did occur but was proper and legal. An **unfounded** complaint or grievance is one in which either the act did not occur or the complaint was false.

sustained
complaint or grievance in which the investigative facts support the charge.

exonerated
a complaint or grievance in which the investigation determines that the matter did occur, but was proper and legal.

Most cases are disposed of in a relatively short time, either as sustained or not sustained. A surprisingly small number have little basis for further action. If a complaint or grievance is sustained against an individual, progressive discipline such as that discussed in Chapter 10 is recommended. If corrective measures are necessary, they must be executed as soon as possible. At a set future time, the matter must be rechecked to determine whether further action is needed.

In addition to the challenges of complaints and grievances, managers often face less clearly defined problems in the form of conflict.

unfounded
complaint or grievance in which the act did not occur or the complaint/grievance was false.

CONFLICT

Conflict is normal in all organizations and becomes negative only when not effectively managed. **Conflict** is a struggle, a mental or physical fight, a controversy, a disagreement or a clash. Conflict can range from an internal struggle within a person over whether to smoke a cigarette or take a drink to armed combat between nations over boundaries or religious beliefs: "Conflict itself is not inherently bad and occurs anytime there is a difference of opinion" (Sharp and Yamashita, 2009, p.110). Controversy and conflict can be

conflict
a mental or physical fight.

fleeting or prolonged, conscious or subconscious, destructive or constructive. Conflict may be

* *Approach–approach conflict*—selecting one of two positive alternatives.
* *Approach–avoidance conflict*—selecting one positive alternative that will also produce a negative consequence.
* *Avoidance–avoidance conflict*—selecting one of two negatives, commonly referred to as "the lesser of two evils."

Because conflict is inevitable for managers and supervisors, they must have the skills to manage it effectively.

CONTRASTING VIEWS OF CONFLICT

Conflict has always existed between people and organizations. Most people believe conflict is always negative because they see the destructive results of conflict in wars, in marriages, in organizations and among individuals. Law enforcement departments also have traditionally regarded conflict as inherently bad. Administrators note its damaging effects. Morale decline, lower productivity, lack of creativity, poor performance and many other ills have been blamed on negative conflict. The prevailing attitudes are to avoid or eliminate conflict by adding more and more rules and regulations. Law enforcement agencies in which conflict reigns are regarded as poorly administered. In departments in which conflict is poorly handled, it is a destructive force. Excessive conflict without resolution *is* negative and can lead to disunity in individual and organizational purpose, decreased morale and lower productivity.

This need *not* be the case, however. Conflict does not have to be destructive. If it is recognized for what it is, conflict can be a positive influence because it can bring attention to problems that need to be resolved. Positive conflict can result in personal or organizational growth.

 How managers approach conflict determines whether it is a negative or a positive force within the organization.

Although organizations with badly managed conflict are hamstrung with dissension, those with *no* conflict are in an equally unproductive situation. Organizations with no conflict are dormant, static, unimaginative, unable to change and in danger of becoming obsolete.

 A healthy amount of conflict, properly handled, motivates individuals and organizations. It exposes problems, defines causes, obtains input from those involved toward constructive solutions and may develop new outlooks.

Conflict is constructive if it

* Encourages better decision making or change.
* Makes life more interesting.

- Reduces irritation.
- Enriches a relationship.
- Increases motivation to deal with problems.
- Is stimulating.

Conflict can be agitating and exciting, indicating organizational vigor. It can keep a groove from turning into a rut.

> **Conflict that opposes without antagonizing can be extremely beneficial to law enforcement organizations, keeping them innovative and responsive to change.**

It is usually not disagreement that creates anger and hostility; rather, it is the manner in which the disagreement is handled. As George Bernard Shaw noted, "The test of breeding is how people behave in a quarrel." The challenge to managers is not to suppress conflict but to minimize its destructiveness and to transform the anger often associated with it into positive, creative forces.

SOURCES OF CONFLICT

Conflict originates from several sources. In law enforcement organizations the most common forms of conflict are internal, between two or more individuals, between organization and officer, between groups within the organization (intra-organizational) or between officers and other agencies and the public (interorganizational).

> **Conflict may come from individual, interpersonal or job-related sources as well as from sources outside the organization. Change is a major source of conflict.**

Individual Sources

Individual, internal conflict exists because of uncertainty, lack of knowledge, criticism, pressures of superiors or the organization, differing opinions on organizational goals or the fear of doing something wrong. Personal problems at home can be brought to the workplace, for example, problems with children, financial matters, one's spouse and the like.

Interpersonal Sources

Interpersonal sources of conflict result because personnel come from differ-ent cultures, have different backgrounds and have different dominant needs. Many conflicts arise because of personality differences and may be the result of prejudices or biases or of different perceptions and values. Much conflict results from the various ways people view the world—ways that reflect the individual's upbringing, culture, race, socioeconomic class, experience and education. Such conflict is often expressed this way: "He has never done anything to me, but I just can't stand him."

As discussed in Chapter 7, several different generations of employees are found in law enforcement departments. The work ethic of each generation can lead to a number of conflicts. Refer to Table 7.1 for a review of intergenerational diversity among law enforcement officers. Police departments have a contingent of the "old guard" and a much larger contingent of the "new guard," which is predominately younger and better educated. The old guard may feel unappreciated, pushed aside and, consequently, threatened by the new guard. The two groups may mistrust and compete with each other, presenting a major challenge to management.

Sometimes a large group is dissatisfied, usually as a result of factors such as low pay, inadequate benefits, poor working conditions or exceptionally strict discipline. Frequently, whole group dissatisfaction arises during contract negotiations, and management must communicate openly during such times.

Job-Related Sources

Job-related conflicts usually involve organizational and administrative objectives, goals, rules and regulations; the hierarchy structure; differences on how to use resources; and conflicts between personnel and groups. Groups within the organization may be promoting self-interests ahead of organizational interests. Internally, departments such as administration, dispatch, juvenile, investigation and patrol compete for allocated budget funds, leading to intraorganizational conflict.

Competition also adds to conflict. Most officers seek recognition and promotion, which may result in extremely destructive interpersonal conflicts. Conflict may arise when an officer of less seniority is promoted over an officer of more seniority, when a patrol officer turns over a case to an investigator and never hears anything more about the case or when one officer does the work and the shift manager takes the credit. Conflict may also arise when a senior patrol officer gets a smaller salary than a starting detective does, when a senior officer is assigned to patrol in a new squad car or when officers are given preferential shift assignments.

Sources of Conflict External to the Law Enforcement Organization

Municipalities have limited resources to operate the total city government. The law enforcement organization is one agency competing for a share of these resources. If law enforcement personnel perceive they are not obtaining sufficient resources for reasonable operation, interorganizational conflict will arise. If, for example, the fire department receives more money than the law enforcement department or vice versa, heated disagreement is likely.

RESPONSIBILITY FOR CONFLICT MANAGEMENT

Law enforcement agencies have a number of levels at which conflict may be resolved. Supervisors are the front line to resolve conflict at its source and are directly responsible for most personnel. Personnel are the most frequent source of conflict, and personnel conflicts should be resolved at this level when possible. To this end, management should write sound policies on negotiating, educate and train officers on how to apply conflict management skills, and evaluate officers on their ability to use those skills. Without such an approach, sergeants are left in the untenable position of playing mediator for adults who cannot work out their own issues (Sharp and Yamashita, 2009). Furthermore, refereeing between officers diverts sergeants from their daily duties, delaying them from completing their own tasks.

Supervisors are also essential to conflict management because they are usually the first to know that conflict exists in the ranks. It is their responsibility to mediate these conflicts unless they believe the conflicts are deeper and more involved than the shift level of management can handle. Group conflicts may have to proceed to middle or upper management. Using higher-level authority sometimes resolves a situation temporarily but may not always identify the problem.

If there is conflict in the relationships of manager and subordinates, such as a past problem or personal prejudices, the matter should be sent to the next management level. If conflicts exist between supervisors, responsibility shifts to middle-management level. All conflicts could potentially shift to the executive manager, city manager, civil service proceedings or the courts. Resolution at the lowest level is preferable.

RECOGNIZING AND ACKNOWLEDGING CONFLICT

Regardless of the level of intervention, the best method to resolve conflict is usually to deal directly with those involved, determine the cause of the conflict and seek a solution. Delaying the inevitable only increases the probability of a worse problem.

 A manager's responsibility is to recognize conflict when it occurs, have a system for reporting conflict and take action as soon as possible.

Evading an issue does not resolve the conflict. Transferring or isolating individuals does not identify a conflict either and may interfere with the entire organization's operation. Some managers avoid conflict by seeking out employees who are not apt to "rock the boat"; using the authority of their position autocratically; increasing feelings of agreement but never actually agreeing; or stalling for time, hoping the problem will go away.

MANAGING CRISIS CONFLICT

Conflict is a constant concern of management. Usually it is best handled through discussion, exploration of causes and alternatives and participatory leadership. In crises, however, such conflict management is not possible.

 Conflicts that arise during crises must be managed by following established procedures and the chain of command.

Crisis management is usually reactive rather than proactive. Procedures must be established to minimize conflicts and to resolve those that occur during a crisis. The following guidelines might assist:

- Anticipate the kinds of conflict and who might be involved. Establish precedents.
- Make certain one person is clearly in charge.
- Make certain all officers know what they are responsible for doing.
- Let no one shirk assigned responsibilities.
- Keep lines of communication open. Keep everyone involved informed, including your superior, but also control the flow of information.
- Make decisions that allow the most options.
- If the crisis is prolonged, be sure personnel get rest and can attend to personal needs.
- If the crisis is prolonged, put someone in charge of routine duties that still must be performed while the crisis continues.
- As the crisis winds down, expect delayed stress reactions (depression, irritability, irrational outbursts). Hold debriefings.
- Return to normal operations as soon as possible.
- Evaluate performance and identify conflicts that should have been avoided or handled differently.

HANDLING PERSONAL ATTACKS

If you find that you are becoming angry, acknowledge it out loud: "This is starting to really irritate me." This gives the other person fair warning that you may blow up and is another way to buy time while you maintain control. *Respond* to the person rather than *react*. Listen to what the person is asserting. Could it be right? Ask clarifying questions. State your own position clearly.

Defuse the other person's anger. Get on the same level physically: sit if the person is sitting; stand if the person is standing. Be quiet and allow the person to vent. Empathize by saying something such as, "I can see how you might feel that way." But do not patronize.

Focus on the present and the future, on resolving the conflict rather than on placing blame. It takes two people to make a conflict. Open the lines of communication and keep them open, but do not exceed your level of authority. Make only promises that you can keep.

If the person continues to be angry and confrontational, ask, "What do you expect me to do?" or "What do you want?" Such statements may disarm a vindictive troublemaker. They may also help you discover a person's genuine concerns. If the person asks for something you cannot deliver, say so.

If all the preceding fail, accept that this person must want the conflict to continue for some reason. At this point seek intervention from a higher level of authority or suggest that the attacker get help from another source. Distance yourself from people who seem intent on making your job more difficult, and limit their access to you.

It is probably a truism that no one truly "wins" an argument. This is illustrated by the law enforcement lieutenant who was hardworking, conscientious and highly skilled but had not received a promotion in 10 years. Asked to explain his failure to advance, he replied, "Several years ago I had an argument with the chief. I won."

HANDLING DISAGREEMENTS BETWEEN OTHERS IN THE DEPARTMENT

The first step in handling disagreements between two subordinates is to decide whether intervention is wise. Some conflicts are truly personality clashes rather than problem centered. In such cases it is fruitless to intervene and will only weaken your leadership when conflicts involve true problems rather than simply personalities. Some managers rely on the confrontation technique to handle such disputes.

The confrontation technique, which insists that two disputing people or groups meet face-to-face to resolve their differences, may effectively resolve conflicts or it may make them worse.

confrontation technique
insisting that two disputing people or groups meet face-to-face to resolve their differences.

Sometimes those in conflict will resolve their differences themselves. Often, however, the differences intensify, positions harden, people become angry and defensive and logic gives way to personal attacks. Those in conflict refuse to back down on any points. The adversaries bluff, not wanting to show their true feelings.

Managers might intervene in conflicts if employees cannot reach a solution or the solution does not end the conflict. Managers should intervene if the conflict is disrupting the department. Once you decide it would be beneficial to intervene, meet with each person privately to discuss issues and to confirm the willingness of both parties to resolve the conflict. Then select a neutral meeting location.

If the conflict is truly disruptive, consider using the power of your position and issue an ultimatum to stop the bickering: "Come to an agreement by the end of the shift, or I'll come up with one for you that neither of you will probably like." At other times one subordinate may be clearly in the right on a given issue. In such instances an effective manager will serve as a mediator between the conflicting employees to resolve the conflict as rapidly as possible.

Most often, however, both subordinates are partially right and partially wrong. In such instances, the following guidelines may be helpful:

⊙ Listen to both sides to understand the issues.

⊙ Do not take sides.

⊙ Separate the issue from personalities.

⊙ Do not speak for one to the other.

⊙ Get the parties to talk with each other and to listen.

⊙ Point out areas of misunderstanding, but place no blame.

⊙ Get the parties to reverse roles to see the other's point of view.

⊙ Search for areas of agreement.

⊙ Allow both to save face in any solution reached.

⊙ Stress the importance of resolving the conflict.

⊙ Monitor any solution agreed upon.

⊙ If no solution can be reached, suggest a third-party mediator or negotiator.

Whether to use mediation to manage conflict often depends on the specific circumstances.

DEALING WITH EXTERNAL CONFLICTS

External conflicts can be with other agencies or with the public.

Conflicts with Other Agencies

External conflict may exist between law enforcement organizations at municipal, county, state and federal levels, as well as with private police and security agencies. Disagreements over jurisdictional authority, powers of arrest, who is in charge at the scene of an incident involving several jurisdictions, specialized and technological duties at the scene of a crime and many other issues cause conflict. Often it is the same basic conflict that exists internally within a law enforcement organization, that is, a lack of understanding and communication that deteriorates into a personality conflict. The goal of providing the best possible public service is lost.

Conflicts with the Public

Law enforcement personnel often come into conflict with angry citizens with complaints, people being arrested or given a citation or citizens angry about a general law enforcement situation they have heard about. The potential for conflict between officers and the public exists because officers' perception of their duties may differ from that of the public's. Officers on traffic patrol may enforce speeding laws. Offenders given citations may ask, "Why are you picking on me for going 5 miles over the speed limit on this open stretch of road? I'm not hurting anyone. Why aren't you over by the school where you could do some good?" Or "Why aren't you picking up criminals?" Officers rarely see vehicle crashes happen, but they are expected to determine who is in the wrong—a potential for conflict of opinion.

New York City police officers block a wall of angry antiwar protesters near the United Nations Headquarters on February 5, 2003. Law enforcement personnel often come into conflict with angry citizens and must try to diffuse the situation.

© AP Images/Diane Bondareff

Dispatchers or desk personnel are often on the receiving end of such complaints. How they handle them may be important to present and future public relations. Over the years a number of approaches for handling angry complainants have been developed.

People involved in these conflicts have learned that the first stages are important to defusing the situation. Except when the complainant is intoxicated or emotionally or mentally disturbed, the defusing phase takes from one to five minutes. Things have either calmed down by that time or the complainant is not going to be satisfied with anything you try to do.

DEALING WITH INTERNAL AND EXTERNAL POLITICS

Dealing with conflicts, internal or external, can be hazardous to managers, even if they are not directly involved. Intra-agency and interagency conflicts inevitably involve politics. People take sides; battle lines are drawn. Managers who attempt to stay out of conflict may be perceived as wishy-washy or fence sitters. In the midst of the conflict, managers have to keep their employees functioning efficiently.

To do so, managers should first separate their responsibility from the political games going on, focusing on the tasks to be accomplished. They should refrain from discussing any politically sensitive situation with subordinates. This is quite a different matter from keeping your people "in the know." Managers should also respect the chain of command even if they tend to side with the position taken by someone lower in the hierarchy. In addition, managers should say the same thing to everyone involved. They must remain honest and objective and not simply tell people what they want to hear. Finally, when the conflict ends, as it inevitably will, managers must help smooth the return to normalcy. When it's over, it's over.

Police chiefs should become politically active in supporting political issues affecting delivery of law enforcement services.

MAINTAINING HEALTHY CONFLICT

Law enforcement managers seek to control destructive conflict, but at the same time they should maintain healthy conflict to improve performance and productivity. Healthy conflict challenges the status quo and offers constructive alternatives. Healthy conflict breeds change and improvement. In fact, bringing conflict into the open is often one of the healthiest things you can do because it clarifies issues, reduces stress, clears the air, stimulates decision making and brings things to a forum where they can be dealt with, enabling relationships to continue to grow. Such opposition is a help. Kites rise against the wind, not with it.

 Keys to maintaining healthy conflict include open, two-way communication, receptivity to new ways of doing things and encouragement of risk taking.

Healthy conflict in law enforcement organizations may include

- Brainstorming sessions to develop new techniques for patrol and investigations.
- Contests for creative and innovative ideas on law enforcement projects and programs.
- Idea-developing sessions for improving task performance.

The secret in organizational conflict is establishing a balance between none and too much. Law enforcement departments with a balance of conflict are active, progressive organizations.

Avoiding the Suppression of Conflict

Some managers avoid conflict, preferring instead to always act as peacemakers. This is certainly appropriate in many instances, but sometimes it may result in delaying the resolution of arguments or finding the best solution to problems. Recall the discussions of the Abilene Paradox and groupthink in Chapter 5. Reasons that subordinates do not speak up include fear of making their superior mad, not wanting to appear as though they are trying to usurp their superior's authority, a lack of confidence in their own objections such that it keeps them from mentioning them or a simple lack of time to engage in a productive discussion (Smith, 2009). Such reasons should not be allowed to suppress disagreement.

Understanding

A key to positive conflict is to pursue agreement with understanding. Those involved should agree to agree or agree to disagree, but understanding is a must. The classic failure in interpersonal communications is the failure to recognize

the other person's right to believe in the good sense of his or her point of view.
A problem-solving approach to conflict would include the following:

- Understand each party's views.
- Identify underlying needs and concerns.
- Search for potential solutions.
- Enumerate probable consequences.
- Select manageable alternatives that satisfy all parties.
- Develop mechanisms to monitor and adjust.

Learning more about each other and about the task required of those involved in a conflict is helpful. Lack of understanding of each other's jobs increases conflict. Some departments rotate officers between shifts and patrol zones to provide a broader understanding of the total problems of the community. This also applies to divisions. For example, transferring some patrol personnel to investigations may help patrol understand problems of the investigating division.

Another solution is to have each person or group state what they would do if they were the other person or group in the conflict. In other words, force them to perceive the issue from the other side. It is much the same approach as having others state how they perceive you and comparing this with how you perceive yourself. Such an approach can be very revealing.

Another approach to solving group conflict is intersubjectivity. This refers to people mutually understanding and respecting each other's viewpoints, a kind of reciprocal empathy. In this approach, each person's most important ideas about the problem and its solution are recorded on separate 3-by-5-inch cards. From the total set of cards, about 40 are chosen to represent all contributions.

The group involved in the conflict meets, and each person is given a set of cards and asked to organize them in a meaningful way. Most people arrange their cards on the table in plain view, and discussion arises as to how each is sorting and arranging. The power of the exercise is not in what each person does with the cards but in the discussion it produces. This provides a basis for deepening mutual understanding and for the eventual merging of different perspectives.

 The **intersubjectivity approach** uses 3-by-5-inch cards as a means to get people in conflict to share their most important ideas about a problem and to come to a mutual understanding of and respect for each other's viewpoints.

> **intersubjectivity approach**
> uses 3-by-5-inch cards as a means to get people in conflict to share their most important ideas about a problem and to come to a mutual understanding of and respect for each other's viewpoints.

CONFLICT RESOLUTION SKILLS

Because conflict is inevitable, managers must learn to deal with it effectively and manage it positively. Conflict resolution skills should be part of every officer's training because they are invaluable on the streets as well as in interactions within the organization. Conflict management skills training should be part of annual in-service training, including problem solving, conflict de-escalation skills, mediation skills, negotiation skills and an emphasis on cultural awareness and ethical behavior throughout.

Conflict can result in one of three situations: win-lose, lose-lose and win-win. In *win-lose situations*, the supervisor uses command/control authority, giving orders and expecting them to be carried out. The subordinate must either obey or face disciplinary action. This is how conflicts have traditionally been managed within law enforcement organizations. Win-lose can produce frustration.

In *lose-lose situations*, a conflict is settled through an ineffective compromise, with neither side feeling they have accomplished their purpose. The underlying philosophy is that "something is better than nothing" and that direct confrontation should be avoided. Such short-term solutions may result in even greater conflict in the future.

In *win-win situations* the focus is on the basic merits of each side rather than on interpersonal haggling. Research from the Harvard Negotiating Project has resulted in a method known as **principled negotiation**, a higher-level approach to effective mediation that focuses on mutually satisfying options. One key is separating the people from the problem. The participants should see themselves as working together to solve a particular problem.

Principled negotiation proceeds in four basic steps, each involving both theory and practice, as Figure 11.5 illustrates. First, clearly identify the prob-

---

principled negotiation

pays attention to basic interests and mutually satisfying options; avoids positional bargaining that tends to produce rushed agreements that can lead to damaged relationships.

FIGURE 11.5
The Steps in Principled Negotiations

Source: Joseph Billy, Jr., and Ronald J. Stupak. "Conflict Management and the Law Enforcement Professional in the 1990s." *Law and Order*, May 1994, p.39. Reprinted by permission of *Law and Order*.

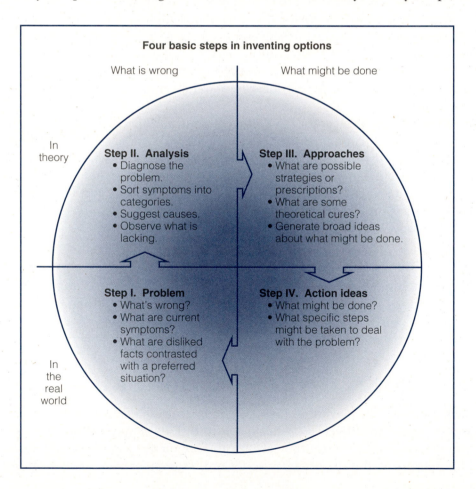

Four basic steps in inventing options

What is wrong — What might be done

In theory

Step II. Analysis
• Diagnose the problem.
• Sort symptoms into categories.
• Suggest causes.
• Observe what is lacking.

Step III. Approaches
• What are possible strategies or prescriptions?
• What are some theoretical cures?
• Generate broad ideas about what might be done.

Step I. Problem
• What's wrong?
• What are current symptoms?
• What are disliked facts contrasted with a preferred situation?

Step IV. Action ideas
• What might be done?
• What specific steps might be taken to deal with the problem?

In the real world

lem. Is the problem actually the heart of the conflict or merely a symptom of a deeper problem? Once you have identified the problem, analyze it to determine its underlying causes. The third step is to discuss alternative approaches to resolving the conflict. Fourth, reduce these alternative approaches to action ideas—steps that you can implement to resolve the conflict.

Another conflict resolution skill is **reframing**, a psycholinguistic technique that shifts a person's perspective. Many factors influence the direction of personal and organizational perspective, including an individual's unique life experiences and the workplace culture. Reframing relabels something, casting it in a different light and giving it new meaning. For example, rather than talking about *racial* profiling, relabel it as *racially biased* policing, or rather than talking about conflict *resolution*, call it conflict *management*.

> **reframing**
> a conflict resolution skill; a psycholinguistic technique that shifts a person's perspective to recast conflict as a positive, rather than a negative, force.

SUMMARY

A complaint may be made by the general public, by people arrested or by employees of the law enforcement department, including peers or managers. The person or group filing the complaint is called the *complainant*.

Categories of officer misconduct often included in external complaints are crime, excessive force, false arrest, improper entry, unlawful search, harassment, offensive demeanor and rule infractions. Complaints can be reduced through effective recruitment and selection, training, policy and procedures manuals, effective supervision, community outreach and data collection and analysis.

Most internal complaints are related to working conditions or management style. Communication is directly related to job performance. Those who are dissatisfied on the job and communicate their discontent perform better than do those who are satisfied and do not communicate. The Pinch Model illustrates the importance of communication in dealing with complaints and the consequences of not communicating effectively.

A basic rule: *Never* take a complaint lightly. All complaints must be investigated. A careful investigation of a complaint instills confidence in management's fairness and protects those accused of wrongdoing. While under investigation, officers may find legal protection from a Law Enforcement Officer Bill of Rights (LEOBR), if one has been enacted in that state, and under the *Garrity* protection.

Dissatisfaction with physical working conditions and equipment causes most grievances. Almost a third are caused by dissatisfaction with management's actions.

A complaint or grievance investigation usually results in one of four findings: sustained, not sustained, exonerated or unfounded.

How managers approach conflict determines whether it is a negative or a positive force within the organization. A healthy amount of conflict, properly handled, motivates individuals and organizations. It exposes problems, defines causes, obtains input from those involved toward constructive solutions and may develop new outlooks. Conflict that opposes without antagonizing can be extremely beneficial to law enforcement organizations, keeping them innovative and responsive to change.

Conflict may come from individual, interpersonal or job-related sources as well as from sources outside the organization. Change is a major source of conflict. A manager's responsibility is to recognize conflict when it occurs, have a system for reporting conflict and take action as soon as possible. Conflicts that arise during crises must be managed by following established procedures and the chain of command. The confrontation technique, which insists that two disputing people or groups meet face-to-face to resolve their differences, may effectively resolve conflicts or it may make them worse.

Keys to maintaining healthy conflict include open, two-way communication, receptivity to new ways of doing things and encouragement of risk taking. The intersubjectivity approach uses 3-by-5-inch cards as a means to get people in conflict to share their most important ideas about a problem and to come to a mutual understanding of and respect for each others' viewpoints.

CHALLENGE ELEVEN

Lieutenant Smith is in charge of the investigations unit of the Greenfield Police Department. He received a phone call from a citizen complaining about Detective Smug. The citizen did not want to give his name or file a formal complaint, but wanted to report that Detective Smug was rude and obstinate. The caller said he was the victim of a crime, and Detective Smug was assigned the case. The citizen hung up without giving further details.

Lieutenant Smith had fielded many complaint calls from angry citizens. He understood that detectives didn't always have the luxury of treating everyone courteously. He also felt that officers deserved the benefit of the doubt when complainants refused to identify themselves. Lieutenant Smith jotted a note to himself about the call and went on with his business.

Later that day, Lieutenant Smith had a meeting with Sergeant Davis. Sergeant Davis was recently promoted and is Detective Smug's direct supervisor. Lieutenant Smith mentioned the anonymous complaint in passing, and Sergeant Davis nodded. Lieutenant Smith detected concern in Sergeant Davis' response and asked if something was troubling her. Sergeant Davis said that during the previous month she had received several similar complaints from citizens about Detective Smug. She said he had also made rude comments to a couple of the other detectives. Sergeant Davis said she tried to talk to Detective Smug about his behavior, but he was dismissive and gave her the brush-off. Since no one had filed an actual complaint, she dropped the issue. She thinks Detective Smug's rude behavior may be the result of being passed over for the detective sergeant position even though he had more seniority and experience than Davis.

1. Was it appropriate for Lieutenant Smith to discuss an anonymous complaint regarding a minor infraction with Detective Smug's supervisor?

2. Why should the Greenfield Police Department be concerned about something as minor as a complaint of rude behavior?

3. Should Lieutenant Smith direct Sergeant Davis to personally address Detective Smug's behavior?

4. Is it a good idea to keep complaints and their resolutions a secret?

5. How should Lieutenant Smith deal with Detective Smug?

6. What should Lieutenant Smith do if he continues to receive complaints about Detective Smug's rude behavior?

DISCUSSION QUESTIONS

1. How are complaints and grievances similar? Different?

2. Why is it important to investigate complaints immediately?

3. Can you think of an example of some pinches in your work? Crunches?

4. What are some steps to reduce conflict?

5. What are examples of destructive conflict? Constructive conflict?

6. What are sources of conflict among law enforcement agencies at different levels of government?

7. What are possible sources of conflict between the police and the public?

8. What are some examples of reframing that you are aware of?

9. Do you know of instances in which conflict has produced positive results? Would these results have been accomplished without conflict?

10. How do the behaviors discussed in this chapter relate to those discussed in Chapter 10?

REFERENCES

Buchholz, Steve, and Roth, Thomas. *Creating the High-Performance Team.* New York: John Wiley and Sons, 1987.

Building Trust between the Police and the Citizens They Serve: An Internal Affairs Promising Practices Guide for Local Law Enforcement, Alexandria, VA: International Association of Chiefs of Police, November 10, 2009.

Clemmons, Ajenai, and Rosenthal, Richard. "Mediating Citizen Complaints." *The Police Chief,* August 2008, pp.32–36.

De Angelis, Joseph. "Assessing the Impact of Oversight and Procedural Justice on the Attitudes of Individuals Who File Police Complaints." *Police Quarterly,* June 2009, pp.214–236.

Hickman, Matthew J., and Piquero, Alex R. "Organizational, Administrative, and Environmental Correlates of Complaints about Police Use of Force: Does Minority Representation Matter?" *Crime & Delinquency,* January 2009, pp.3–32.

Orrick, Dwayne. "A Best Practices Guide for Recruitment, Retention and Turnover in Law Enforcement." In *Police Chiefs Desk Reference: A Guide for Newly Appointed Police Leaders,* 2nd ed., edited by International Association of Chiefs of Police and U.S. Bureau of Justice Assistance. Boston: McGraw-Hill Learning Solutions, 2008, pp.209–216.

Sharp, Kelly, and Yamashita, Kim. "Conflict Management in the Workplace." *Law and Order,* September 2009, pp.110–114.

Smith, Betsy Brantner. "Conflict Resolution, Being a Team Player, and Other Stupid Clichés." *PoliceOne.com News,* July 31, 2009.

Standards and Guidelines for Internal Affairs: Recommendations from a Community of Practice. Washington, DC: Office of Community Oriented Policing Services, August 21, 2009.

"Welcome to NAPO." National Organization of Police Organizations Web Site, 2009. http://napo.org/

"What Is Community Mediation?" National Association for Community Education Web Site. http://www.nafcm.org/

CITED CASE

Garrity v. New Jersey, 385 U.S. 493 (1967)

CHAPTER TWELVE

Stress and Related Hazards of the Job

Your day-by-day—sometimes minute-by-minute—contact with criminals, complainants and citizens alike who are crying, cursing, bleeding, puking, yelling, spitting . . . and just plain crazy subjects your system to repeated onslaughts of disturbance.

—Charles Remsberg
The Tactical Edge

DO YOU KNOW?

- Whether stress must always be negative?
- What common sources of stress are?
- What the four categories of stress are?
- What a major source of stress may be?
- Which law enforcement officers face stress from additional sources?
- What physical problems stress is related to?
- What posttraumatic stress disorder (PTSD) is? Who is most at risk for PTSD?
- What the symptoms of burnout are?
- How managers can help prevent burnout?
- What possible major negative effects of stress might be?
- How stress can be reduced?
- How alcohol, drugs and smoking relate to stress?
- What programs can reduce stress?
- What departments can provide to help officers?

CAN YOU DEFINE?

acute stress

afterburn

blue flame

burnout

burst stress

chronic stress

circadian system

critical incident

critical incident stress debriefing
  (CISD)

CSI effect

cumulative stress

distress

diurnal

employee assistance program (EAP)

eustress

homeostasis

posttraumatic stress disorder (PTSD)

resiliency

sleep inertia

split-second syndrome

stress

traumatic stress

type A personality

type B personality

INTRODUCTION

"The nature of law enforcement is such that officers often experience higher levels of stress for more prolonged periods of time than those in other professions, which can result in chronic stress. Due to this unique factor, officers should have available to them a variety of resources and training to help them recognize and cope with job demands. An unfortunate reality is that all too often officers do not have the resources they need to enhance their resiliency and work hardiness. To proactively address officer resilience and work hardiness, the agency should develop comprehensive and effective awareness, prevention intervention and response programs" (Orrick, 2008, p.191).

Police officer stress can manifest itself in many ways that can hurt officers, their loved ones, their department and the public: burnout, lower tolerance levels, poor judgment, substance abuse, health problems, deteriorating relationships with family and friends, low productivity, high turnover, use of excessive force, citizen complaints and increased rates of workers' compensation claims, to name just a few.

CHAPTER at a GLANCE

This chapter begins by defining stress and identifying some major sources of stress as well as sources of stress specific to the law enforcement profession. Next is a discussion of reactions to stress or the symptoms likely to be present, including physical, psychological, behavioral and on-the-job. The results of excessive levels of stress are then described, including divorce, alcohol problems, depression and suicide. Next, the chapter examines ways to cope with stress and how stress levels can be reduced. The chapter concludes with descriptions of how organizations can reduce stress, effective programs to manage stress and an examination of the manager's/supervisor's role in minimizing the negative effects of stress.

STRESS DEFINED

Stress means different things to different people. To a mechanical engineer, it means the point at which objects break or deteriorate from excessive pressures or physical tension. Stress is not that different in humans. A single high-stress incident or recurring minor stress can cause the mind or physical body to deteriorate or break down completely. **Stress** is generally thought of as tension, anxiety, strain or pressure. It is the body's internal response to a situation a person perceives as threatening.

Hans Selye, MD (1907–1982), the father of the stress field, originally defined *stress* as the body's nonspecific response to any demand placed on it. He later said stress was simply the wear and tear caused by living (Selye, 1956). Stress, like conflict, has both a positive and a negative aspect.

 Stress can be helpful (eustress) or harmful (distress), depending on its intensity and frequency, as well as how it is mediated.

Eustress is positive stress that enables people to function and accomplish goals. It allows law enforcement officers to react instantaneously in life-threatening situations, to feel the excitement, the energy and the heightening of the senses. **Distress**, in contrast, is negative stress that can lead to numerous diseases, including depression. Through training and practice, officers can identify and replace dysfunctional beliefs and stressors (distress) with appropriate aggression (eustress): "There's no physiological difference between getting mugged and winning the lottery. It ultimately comes down to your self-talk, belief or perception that serves as the proving grounds for developing a sense of control that can, with practice, bullet-proof the mind" (DeYoung, 2008, p.39). We all have a "golden mean of anxiety" in which our performance increases as anxiety increases, but if anxiety begins to exceed the optimal level, performance declines dramatically and cognitive distortions and errors are likely (DeYoung). Through training, officers can learn to identify their own levels of optimal stress and recognize when they are exceeding them.

Although stress can be positive, most people equate stress with distress. Most of this chapter uses the term in this sense because managers must try to manage the negative stress effectively. Lost hours, illness and reduced performance are costly to an organization. Law enforcement workers' compensation claims have increased substantially because of stress-related disorders. Too many high-stress incidents are occurring at home and at work with no chance to "come back to normal" between incidents. Stress can become overpowering.

The biological concept of homeostasis helps explain how stress occurs. **Homeostasis** is the process that keeps all bodily functions, such as breathing and blood circulation, in balance. To see homeostasis at work, run in place for a few minutes and then sit down. The running mildly stresses your body, temporarily putting it out of balance. After you rest, however, your body returns to normal. The same thing happens in acute stress.

Acute stress is severe, extremely intense distress that lasts a limited time, and then the person returns to normal. It is sometimes called **traumatic stress**. Acute stress is temporary and may result in peak performance.

stress

tension, anxiety or worry; can be positive, eustress, or negative, distress.

eustress

helpful stress, stress necessary to function and accomplish goals.

distress

negative stress.

homeostasis

the process that keeps all the bodily functions in physiological balance.

acute stress

severe, intense distress that lasts a limited time, and then the person returns to normal; sometimes called *traumatic stress*.

traumatic stress

severe, extremely intense distress that lasts a limited time, and then the person returns to normal.

Adrenaline rushes through the body; heart rate increases; blood pressure, brain activity, breathing rates and metabolic rates increase—preparing the body for fight or flight. Thousands of years before we became "civilized," our bodies were faced with the challenge of simple survival, for which either a "fight or flight" response was appropriate. Table 12.1 presents an explanation of the anatomy of stress: the physical and psychological changes that occur, how they were previously advantageous and how they now have become detrimental.

Cortisone, which is released into the body during times of stress, has the negative effects of breaking down muscle tissue and encouraging fat storage and weight gain, properties that were beneficial when survival under extreme conditions was at stake but that have become unnecessary in today's modern society.

In contrast to acute stress, **chronic stress** is less intense but continues and eventually becomes debilitating. It is sometimes called **cumulative stress**. Many of the sources of stress are continuous and may not even be noticed.

chronic stress

less severe than acute stress, but continuous; eventually becomes debilitating; sometimes called *cumulative stress*.

cumulative stress

less severe but continues and eventually becomes debilitating.

TABLE 12.1 The Anatomy of Stress

Natural Response	Original Benefit	Today's Drawback
Release of cortisone from adrenal glands.	Protection from an instant allergic reaction or from a dustup with an attacking foe.	If chronically elevated, cortisone destroys the body's resistance to the stresses of cancer, infection, surgery and illness. Bones are made more brittle by cortisone. Blood pressure can be elevated.
Increase of thyroid hormone in the bloodstream.	Speeds up the body's metabolism, thereby providing extra energy.	Intolerance to heat, shaking nerves to the point of jumpiness, insomnia, weight loss and ultimately exhaustion or burnout.
Release of endorphin from the hypothalamus.	Identical to morphine, a potent painkiller.	Chronic, relentless stresses can deplete levels of endorphin, aggravating migraines, backaches and the pain of arthritis.
Reduction in sex hormones—testosterone in the male and progesterone in the female.	Decreased fertility. In wartime, decreased libido made both partners' lives more bearable.	Obvious anxieties and failures when intercourse is attempted. Premature ejaculation in male, failure to reach orgasm in female.
Shutdown of the entire digestive tract. Mouth goes dry to avoid adding fluids to the stomach. Rectum and bladder tend to empty or jettison any excess load prior to battle.	Acts as a vital "self-transfusion," allowing person to perform superordinary feats of muscular power.	Dry mouth makes it difficult to speak with authority. The drawback of the "jettison response" is obvious.
Release of sugar into the blood, along with an increase in insulin levels to metabolize it.	Quick, short-distance energy supply.	Diabetes can be aggravated or even started.

Source: Adapted from Peter G. Hanson. *The Joy of Stress*, 1995, pp.19–27. Reprinted by permission of Peter G. Hanson.

SOURCES OF STRESS

Stress comes from several sources, many of which are work related.

 Stress commonly arises from change and uncertainty, lack of control and pressure.

Change and uncertainty are an unavoidable part of life and of law enforcement. Officers responding to a call often have no idea what awaits. They may be unsure of who they can trust or believe. *Lack of control* may be seen when law enforcement officers apprehend suspects they believe to be guilty and then see these suspects not prosecuted or found not guilty. Officers must work with assigned partners they did not select. They must be polite to surly citizens. *Pressure* is also abundant in law enforcement, with work overloads, paperwork, sometimes unrealistic expectations from the public and the responsibility to protect life and property and to preserve "the peace."

In addition to these general categories of stressors, sources of stress can also be found by looking at a person's lifestyle, personality and job. The rank order of 14 stressor variables is shown in Table 12.2.

Many lists of stressors have been generated, including stressors specific to the police profession. Most of the stressors fall into four main categories, although some overlap exists.

TABLE 12.2 Rank Order of 14 Stressor Variables (N = 415) (5 = highest; 1 = lowest)

Stressor	Mean
Child Beaten/Abused	4.39
Harming/Killing Innocent Person	3.93
Conflict with Regulations	3.90
Harming/Killing Another Police Officer	3.89
Domestic Violence Calls	3.89
Another Officer Killed	3.71
Hate Groups/Terrorists	3.67
Poor Supervisor Support	3.64
Riot Control	3.43
Public Disrespect	3.41
Barricaded Subjects	3.28
Shift Work	3.08
Another Officer Hurt	3.08
Hostage-Takers	2.96

Source: Dennis J. Stevens. "Police Officer Stress." *Law and Order*, Vol. 47, No. 9, September 1999, p.79. Reprinted by permission.

Sources of stress for police officers include
- Internal, individual stressors.
- Stressors inherent to the police job.
- Administrative and organizational stressors.
- External stressors from the criminal justice system, the citizens it serves, the media and the family.

Internal, Individual Stressors

Internal stressors vary greatly and can include officers' worries about their competency to handle assignments as well as feelings of helplessness and vulnerability. An especially pertinent source of stress today is that generated by an officer's racial or gender status among peers, discussed shortly. Some common stress producers of daily living are changing relationships, a lifestyle inconsistent with values (too committed), money problems (debt, poor investments), loss of self-esteem (accepting others' expectations) and fatigue or illness (poor diet, lack of sleep or exercise).

Personality may also affect stress levels. Psychologists often divide individuals into two types: **type A personality**, an aggressive, hyperactive "driver" who tends to be a workaholic; and **type B personality**, who has the opposite characteristics. The type A person is more likely to experience high stress levels.

type A personality

describes people who are aggressive, hyperactive "drivers" who tend to be workaholics.

type B personality

describes people who are more laid back, relaxed and passive.

Stress Related to Police Work

Stressors inherent in police work include constant threats to safety, entering dark buildings in which armed suspects are believed to be hiding, high-speed pursuits, continual exposure to victims in pain as well as unsavory criminals, the immense responsibilities of the job, the authorization to take a life, the ability to save a life and the need to remain detached yet be empathetic.

The police role itself is often vague and contradictory, with few, if any, accurate methods to assess performance. Many people become police officers to fight crime, not to do social work. They are surprised to see how much "service" is actually involved in police work. They are also surprised to learn that their efforts are often not appreciated and that their uniform is an object of scorn and derision. The police badge may weigh only a few ounces, but it carries a heavy weight to those who wear it.

Death Notifications

One of the "heaviest" tasks officers face is giving a death notification. About 45,000 people are killed in car crashes in the United States every year; another 32,000 commit suicide and an additional 17,000 more are murdered (Page, 2008, p.18). In most of these cases, law enforcement officers are responsible for notifying the next of kin: "Death notification is considered by police officers to be the least desirable job they have. It is also the one for which they are least trained" (Page, p.18). Delivering a death notification can be both physically and emotionally exhausting: "Officers are expected to express the right words, anticipate and understand family emotions and respond with empathy" (Page, p.18).

Law enforcement agencies should have a clearly defined policy for making such notifications. Death notification should be done in person (notification by phone is "callous and insensitive"), in pairs, in private, in plain language and in time—before it makes the news (Page, 2008, p.20). Do not be afraid to use the "D" words—*dead, died* or *death*. Avoid terms such as *expired, passed on* or *lost,* which are words of denial (Page).

Many agencies have police chaplains to help make death notifications. However, in some situations, such as a violent crime, police detectives commonly do not welcome the participation of a police chaplain (Page, 2008, p.24). Because many homicides involve spouses or family members, involving a third party who is not trained to be sensitive to how the family members react to the notification might affect the course of the investigation.

A death notification becomes even more difficult if it involves an officer killed in the line of duty. One of the greatest on-the-job stressors for police officers is being responsible for one another's life; a line-of-duty death has been ranked as the number one stressor in some police departments.

Line-of-Duty Deaths

More than 18,300 law enforcement officers have been killed since the first line-of-duty death was recorded in 1792 (Remsberg, 2008). In 2008, 41 officers were feloniously killed, a decrease from 2007 ("In the Line of Duty," 2009). In the first half of 2009, the 66 officer line-of-duty deaths were a 20 percent increase over the 2008 midyear figure of 55 ("Law Enforcement Officer Deaths," 2009). According to the National Law Enforcement Officers Memorial Fund, the average age of officers killed in the line of duty in 2009 was 39, and the average number of years of service of these fallen officers was 10.5 years (2009, p.3). Table 12.3 shows the number of law enforcement officers killed in the past 10 years. Figure 12.1 shows the causes of officer deaths in 2008.

Line-of-duty deaths place a tremendous strain on a department. Although any line-of-duty death will affect an agency, the death of a partner can be especially devastating. Every department should be properly prepared to handle such tragedies: "An established policy or general order will help ensure that the agency's response in the aftermath of the tragedy is professional, comprehensive and compassionate for all survivors" (Armitage, 2009, p.6).

Written policies should detail how to notify the family, assist with funeral arrangements, help the family complete paperwork required to receive benefits and provide continuing support to the survivors. Officers should understand the Public Safety Officers' Benefits (PSOB) program, which was designed to offer peace of mind to men and women seeking careers in public safety and to make a strong statement about the value American society places on the contributions of those who serve their communities in potentially dangerous circumstances. The program awards death, disability and education assistance benefits to the survivors of law enforcement officers killed or permanently and totally disabled in the line of duty.

TABLE 12.3 Law Enforcement Officer Line-of-Duty Deaths, 2000–2009

Year	Felonious Deaths	Accidental Deaths	Total Deaths
2000	51	84	135
2001	142	78	220
2002	56	77	133
2003	52	80	132
2004	57	82	139
2005	55	67	122
2006	48	66	114
2007	57	83	140
2008	41	68	109
2009*	49	76	125
Total	608	761	1369
Average	**(60.8 per year)**	**(76.1 per year)**	**(136.9 per year)**

*Based on preliminary information

Sources: Federal Bureau of Investigation, *Uniform Crime Reports: Law Enforcement Officers Killed and Assaulted* for 2000 through 2008 (www.fbi.gov/ucr/ucr.htm#lekao), and the National Law Enforcement Officers Memorial Fund, *Law Enforcement Officer Deaths: Preliminary 2009*, Research Bulletin, December 2009 (http://www.nleomf.org/assets/images/reports/law_enforcement_officer_fatalities_2009_end_year_report.pdf

FIGURE 12.1
Causes of Law Enforcement Officer Deaths, 2008
(*n* = 853)

Source: National Law Enforcement Officers Memorial Fund

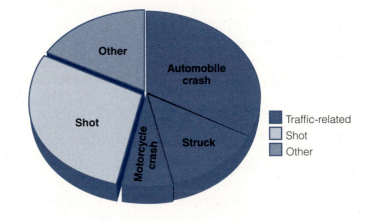

Critical Incidents

Frequently line-of-duty deaths are part of a critical incident, another source of extreme stress for many officers. A **critical incident** is any event that elicits an overwhelming emotional response from those witnessing it and whose emotional impact goes beyond the person's coping abilities. (One such impact known as posttraumatic stress disorder (PTSD) is discussed in greater detail later in the chapter.) Officers need to be in constant emotional control. They also experience what is referred to as **burst stress**, that is, having to go from relative calm to high intensity, sometimes life-threatening, activity in one "burst."

critical incident

any event, such as a mass disaster or a brutally murdered child, that elicits an overwhelming emotional response from those witnessing it and whose emotional impact goes beyond the person's coping abilities.

burst stress

to go from complete calm to high activity and pressure in one "burst."

This is closely related to what Fyfe (1986) refers to in his classic **split-second syndrome** that affects police decision making in crisis. The split-second syndrome asserts that if a person has intentionally or unintentionally provoked or threatened a police officer, at that instant the provoker rather than the police should be viewed as the cause of any resulting injuries or damages. In such situations, all that can reasonably be asked is that officers respond quickly and that a high percentage of inappropriate decisions should be expected and accepted.

A critical incident need not be a life-and-death situation, nor must it necessarily involve a *crisis*. A broader definition that seems to apply well to those in law enforcement is "any situation in which an individual believes that justice has not been served for that individual or another" (Conroy, 2009). This expanded definition of *critical incident* includes such things as a criminal going free on a technicality.

Officers routinely deal with incidents involving confrontation and violence, which create stress equal to or higher than that in most occupations. Many participants in these incidents have been involved in violence before the officers arrive, and often the violence continues after they arrive. Domestic disputes, disorderly conduct, rape and gang activities are examples of such confrontations.

During emergencies, officers receive orders and act on them, or they give orders, but they seldom have a chance to discuss events during the crisis. The quasi-military nature of law enforcement structure prevents them from questioning orders. Although officers have legal authority and responsibility to carry out their duties, they often have to repress how they feel when dealing

> **split-second syndrome**
>
> a condition that affects police decision making in crisis; asserts that if a person has intentionally or unintentionally provoked or threatened a police officer, at that instant the provoker rather than the police should be viewed as the cause of any resulting injuries or damages.

© AP Images/Danny Johnston

Police are under sudden and excessive stress, and frequently investigate incidents involving confrontation and violence. Little Rock, Arkansas, police officers comfort Tory Kennedy, 10, center, after he was held hostage in a Little Rock neighborhood in 2002. The child, one of four, escaped through a window before the other three were released by the man holding them.

with the public. For example, intoxicated persons often verbally abuse officers, and although the officers may make an arrest, they normally accept such verbal abuse as part of the job. Because most of these situational feelings can be discussed only with other officers, police officers tend to feel isolated from the rest of society, which can produce stress.

Officer-involved shootings have been identified in numerous studies as critical incidents that cause considerable stress in officers. Officers involved in shooting incidents may experience a wide range of reactions, including perceptual disturbances such as tunnel vision, sense of time slowing down or speeding up, sense of sounds diminishing or increasing in volume and memory loss. Muscular control may also be affected. Leg muscles can tremble or lock, hands can shake and muscles in the upper back and shoulders can go into spasm. Perhaps the most traumatic aspect of an officer-involved shooting involves the treatment of the officer after the incident because they often face uncertainty about criminal charges, job security and civil litigation (Conroy). Adding to the stress is that many departments lack a policy for how to treat officers following a shooting.

Especially traumatic for officers are confrontations with individuals who want to die. These extremely dangerous people generally fall into three classes: (1) terrorists on a suicide mission, (2) criminals who won't be taken alive and (3) emotionally disturbed people who want to take their own lives and choose a police officer to help them out, known as "suicide by cop" (SBC) incidents. A study by the Force Science Research Center based on some 700 shootings found that suicide by cop is "shockingly" on the rise ("New Study Yields Best Profile," 2009). The study "disabuses the widely held but false belief that suicidal subjects do not present a substantial risk of homicide. In fact, the opposite appears to be true: A suicidal individual poses a greater risk of homicide or at least violence toward others, than a nonsuicidal individual," because of the "high degree of desperation, hopelessness, impulsivity, self-destructiveness and acting out" of these subjects.

No matter how the death is classified, the officer who pulls the trigger is likely to experience tremendous stress, guilt and self-defeating second-guessing in the form of thoughts such as "I should have been able to see this coming and stop it" (Conroy, 2009). This self-doubt can haunt an officer for a long time.

No matter what size the department is, officers are always only one incident away from a deadly force situation, an event that could be the most traumatic experience the involved officers ever have (Mehlin, 2008, p.42). Noting how police departments go to great lengths to train and retrain their officers to protect themselves and the public, Chudwin (2008b, p.53) asks, "When [officers] act within the law at great need, why do some administrators suddenly consider them suspect? They did exactly as trained." He (2008a, p.58) stresses, "For those agencies mired in past ways of 'investigating' an officer-involved shooting (OIS), it's time to recognize that in almost every case your officer is *not* a criminal and must not be treated as one. They've acted in the very manner they've been trained to act when under threat of death or great bodily harm to themselves or others. Sadly, some agencies still have not planned or prepared to deal with such events, and the officers who place their lives on the line pay the price."

The worst response a manager can give to the media is to say a dismissively curt "The matter is under investigation, no further comments," or to say nothing at all: "Such a response is suspect on its face, and it gives no information or confidence to the public. And once the damage is done to public confidence and to the officer's reputation, it can't be undone" (Chudwin, 2008b, p.53). A better response would be to state that the matter is under investigation, all aspects of the incident are being examined, and that details will be released once they have been confirmed, as long as they do not compromise the open investigation.

Fear of a Lawsuit

Another source of stress for officers is fear of legal action against them and their agency. Every use of force or arrest is a possible basis for a lawsuit. Once publicized, a lawsuit suggests that the officer was wrong even though the suit may have no legal basis. Some officers choose to be less aggressive in confrontational situations, and others have been reluctant to use the necessary physical force to subdue violent criminals for fear of a lawsuit.

Fatigue and Shift Work

Yet another stressor, one that seldom makes headlines but has been clearly identified as harmful to officers, is fatigue. As a general rule, no single factor is solely responsible for police officer fatigue; it is typically the result of a combination of factors. "Commuting, family obligations, shift work, overtime and extra jobs are all significant contributors to police fatigue. Each one places an officer in grave danger while behind the wheel. An Alertness Solutions survey found that 85 percent of officers reported that they inadvertently fell asleep while on duty" (Yates, 2008). One study found that more than 90 percent of officers surveyed reported being routinely fatigued and 85 percent drove while "drowsy."

The dangers of driving while sleep deprived have been documented: "Researchers have shown that being awake for 19 hours produces impairments that are comparable to having a blood alcohol concentration (BAC) of .05 percent. Being awake for 24 hours is comparable to having a BAC of roughly .10 percent. This means that in just [five] hours—the difference between going without sleep for 19 hours versus 24 hours—the impact essentially doubles. (It should be noted that, in all 50 states and the District of Columbia, it is a crime to drive with a BAC of .08 percent or above.)" (Vila, 2009). The absolute minimum amount of sleep needed to live is 4 hours per 24-hour cycle, but that amount, night after night, is unhealthy and will not allow a human to thrive as it cannot support renewal, learning and memory functions (Slahor, 2008, p.61).

Humans are naturally day-oriented (**diurnal**) in their activity patterns. They are equipped with a complex biological timekeeping system (the **circadian system**), the major function of which is to prepare the body for restful sleep at night and active wakefulness during the day. The circadian system has a resetting mechanism that realigns it, but that mechanism is designed to cope with a "fine tuning" of *only* one hour or so per day. It is *not* designed to cope with the gross changes characteristic of moves to and from night work. The brain relies

diurnal
day-oriented; humans are by nature diurnal in their activities.

circadian system
the body's complex biological timekeeping system.

on outside influences, such as daylight, social contact, regular meal times and sleep, to keep its circadian rhythm functioning effectively. When these time-keeping clues are altered through shift work, the body's circadian rhythm is negatively affected and fatigue can result.

Fatigue may wear down the body's defenses, thus magnifying the effects of other stressful events. Fatigued officers use more sick leave, practice inappropriate uses of force more frequently, experience more accidental injuries, have more difficulty dealing with community members and other law enforcement agencies and have a higher likelihood of dying in the line of duty (*Officer Work Hours, Stress and Fatigue*, 2009). Overtime can also cause fatigue, and studies have indicated that officers who work overtime have a greater number of complaints filed against them.

A study of factors influencing fatigue in frontline officers found that most of the participants stated without hesitation that shift work was the primary reason for fatigue in their department (Senjo and Dhungana, 2009, p.129). The fatigue brought on by shift work, particularly rotating shifts, creates numerous other hazards and stressors: "Shift workers have weaker immune systems. They are more likely to have emotional problems and experience higher rates of divorce and social relationship difficulties. Shift workers make more mistakes than day workers, lack ability to focus and pay attention, and have a higher rate of traffic accidents—all potentially life-threatening factors for those in law enforcement" (Slahor, 2008, p.62). Monthly shift rotations necessitate not only physical adaptations such as getting used to sleeping different hours, but also adaptations in officers' social and personal lives. Thus, shift work may contribute to isolation from family and friends and to the "blue wall" and "code of silence" perceptions some have. This social isolation compounds the stress brought about by fatigue.

To address the problem of officer sleep deprivation, managers might do the following (Vila, 2009):

◉ Review policies that affect overtime, moonlighting and the number of consecutive hours a person can work. Make sure the policies keep shift rotation to a minimum and give officers adequate rest time.

◉ Give officers a voice in decisions related to their work hours and shift schedules. People's work hours affect every aspect of their lives. Increasing the amount of control and predictability in one's life improves a host of psychological and physical characteristics, including job satisfaction.

◉ Formally assess the level of fatigue officers experience, the quality of their sleep and how tired they are while on the job as well as training supervisors to be alert for signs that officers are overly tired and on how to deal with those who are too fatigued to work safely.

◉ Create a culture in which officers receive adequate information about the importance of good sleep habits, the hazards associated with fatigue and shift work and strategies for managing them.

An analysis of the relationship between department-level approaches to policy on secondary employment, overtime, court appearances and other job-related activities that affect the fatigue of line officers found the "reality of a tired work force but a low-level desire among agency chiefs to have fatigue reduction policy. Where such policy exists, a business-like managerialism dominated executive conceptualization rather than citizen safety or liability orientations. Informal controls, rather than formal rules, emerged as applicable tools used to address and reduce officer fatigue" (Senjo and Dhungana, 2009, p.123). Managers are reluctant to institute policies that might reduce fatigue because they need their officers to work more, not less. Furthermore, officers might reject such policies because they want the overtime or the extra shifts. Nonetheless, "Law enforcement agencies have fatigue-reduction opportunities—if they decide to take them. Proactive steps, of course, are highly preferable to accident-prompted or fatality-prompted changes" (Senjo and Dhungana, p.135).

Departments can use traditional methods, such as analyzing on-the-job accidents, coupled with newer technologies, such as actigraphy bracelets that produce valid, reliable data on fatigue levels, sleep duration and circadian rhythm patterns, to distinguish between well rested and fatigued officers.

Managers should also alert officers to the hazards of sleep inertia which, according to research conducted at the University of Colorado (UOC), can be even more impairing than sleep deprivation: "**Sleep inertia** is defined as the grogginess, the period of hypovigilance, impaired cognitive and behavioral performance that we experience upon wakening" (Sexton, 2008, p.56). An on-call officer jolted awake by a phone or pager may experience sleep inertia. According to the UOC, research shows that within the first three minutes of waking, decision-making performance can be as low as 51 percent of the person's best decision-making ability, the same as someone with a 0.10 BAC. Decision-making ability may still be 20 percent below optimum performance 30 minutes after waking: "Officers called from bed by dispatch should NOT try to remember incident details and should NOT make decisions on the phone" (Sexton, p.57). Officers should have pen, paper and a bright light ready for answering call-outs. They should take a few minutes to get dressed, gather their gear and then ask for details when in the car.

> **sleep inertia**
> the grogginess, the period of hypovigilance, impaired cognitive and behavioral performance that is experienced upon wakening.

Change

Yet another job-related source of stress is change. In law enforcement work, change is constant—a change of shift, assignment to a new manager, change of patrol partner, new computer software in the squad car, new training techniques and equipment, new laws to uphold—many types of changes affect officers. When change occurs in administration or operations, managers tend to be more involved with the organizational aspects of the change than with human reactions. The organization changes, but the organization is people. It is how people react to change that is important.

The first reaction to change is usually reluctance to accept it or fear it will not work. Management must explain changes and provide training so personnel can make a successful transition. Failure to explain change will bring resistance. Managers should explain that a change will be made and that input from employees is desired and that there will be follow-up and assessment.

Administrative and Organizational Stressors

Often the most significant stressor on law enforcement officers is administrative stress, for although line-of-duty deaths and other critical incidents do happen, they are relatively uncommon, whereas administrative and organizational forces are omnipresent and pervade every aspect of the job: "Although common sense may suggest that the primary source of police stress is the hazardous and at times horrific nature of law enforcement duty, researchers have reported otherwise: that the 'routine' administrative, bureaucratic and organizational aspects of police work are actually thought to be more stressful than critical incidents" (Best, 2009, p.9). In one recent survey, 534 officers responded to the question, "What is your biggest pet peeve about police work?" Fifty-one percent responded "the bureaucracy" ("*PoliceOne* Poll," 2009). This was followed by lack of funds (28 percent), bogus alarms (16 percent) and coworkers/personality tics (5 percent).

 A major source of employee stress may be upper-level management.

Many management practices and organizational factors can cause stress specific to law enforcement. Stress frequently arises from having to operate from a set of policies and procedures drawn up by individuals who do not have to carry them out. Seldom is the frontline officer's opinion on operational policies and procedures sought, even though the individual officer must carry out these policies and procedures. Research has found that a lack of control over work activities and how policing is accomplished stands out as an important predictor of stress: "Officers who felt stressed said they could not influence the way policing was done and could not influence department policies and procedures" (Morash et al., 2006, pp.35–36).

Other common criticisms of the work environment are internal politics, favoritism and interpersonal treatment. Internal surveys reveal that working in a paramilitary structure may depersonalize and marginalize people from top to bottom, treating them as numbers rather than as individuals. Lack of support from administration when a questionable action is taken, the unavailability of needed resources and the poor condition of equipment also cause stress for officers. Other stressors include excessive paperwork, adverse work schedules, unfair discipline and lack of promotional opportunities.

One study of law enforcement officers' stressors identified 12 major sources of administrative stress:

1. Feeling of inadequate support—hampered by the court system, public misunderstanding and lack of administrative support.

2. Unfair or unequal treatment—in shift assignments, time off, promotions.

3. Decisions overruled—higher authorities, especially sergeants, overrule a decision made by a patrol officer on the street, often in regard to an arrest.

4. Civil suits—often the policy is a "negotiated settlement," deciding it is more cost effective to settle, leaving the impression the officer was in the wrong.

5. Mixed messages—officers are expected to fight crime (be reactive) and at the same time engage in community policing efforts (be proactive).

6. Department policy versus discretion—a two-inch thick rule book lays out all the policies and procedures, but officers are expected to use discretion. A violation of any policy is grounds for disciplinary action. However, if following policy results in a negative circumstance that could or should have been avoided had the officer used discretion, the officer is again in trouble.

7. The administration as an adversary—this is worse than an administration being viewed as nonsupportive. Patrol officers are most often likely to feel this way, with middle management caught in the middle. It is also a common complaint of officers who represent the department for the union.

8. Hiring standards lowered—as the pool of candidates decreases, some departments have, indeed, lowered their standards. Affirmative action hiring also causes problems when less-qualified individuals are hired because they are members of a minority group.

9. Differing goals—officers may see themselves trying to alleviate victims' pain, but see administrators as trying to sway politicians. Officers see themselves as trying to save lives and administrators as trying to save dollars.

10. Miscommunication—administration may communicate one thing to officers and another thing to the public. The court notification process also causes friction, with officers being told to show up on a certain day, but not at a certain time, often during their time off.

11. Punitive transfers—often officers who are very satisfied in their present positions are transferred because of some minor infraction or because they do not get along with their supervisor.

12. Lack of input—the administration often makes decisions without consulting those who are expected to carry them out—in most instances the patrol officer (Conroy and Hess, 1992, pp.176–185).

Although the research was conducted over a decade ago, these administrative sources of stress still exist in many departments throughout the country (Conroy, 2009).

External Stressors

The criminal justice system and society at large also can induce stress in police officers. Officers are often faced with prosecutors who decide not to prosecute a case, exclude police officers during plea bargaining and fail to exhibit any appreciation for the role of law enforcement; a court that is perceived as too lenient and that schedules officers to appear to give testimony while off duty; defendants who "get off" because of a loophole in the law; the early release of offenders on bail or parole; and corrections' failures to rehabilitate criminals, resulting in "revolving door" justice. One police officer put it this way:

"I think the crowning blow was to see that it's almost futile to go out there and do anything about it. You keep putting 'em away, and they keep letting 'em out. And then new people come along, and it just doesn't stop, and it will never stop" (Conroy and Hess, 1992, p.29).

Not only do the failures of the criminal justice system cause stress for police, these failures are often perceived as partially the fault of law enforcement officers. In addition, law enforcement officers are seen as authority figures. People deal with them differently and treat them differently. Officers often are isolated. Wearing a badge, uniform and gun separates a law officer from society. An additional stressor is that many citizens have unrealistic expectations of what law enforcement officers can do, based on a distorted view of police work presented by the media and entertainment industry.

Approximately one third of regular television programming deals with some aspect of the criminal justice system. If a TV cop can solve three major crimes in an hour, why can't the local police at least keep prostitutes off the street or find the person who vandalized the school? This heightened expectation by the public of what police can do and the tools available to them is referred to as the **CSI effect**, a testament to the popular series and others like it that draw and, consequently influence, millions of American viewers each week.

A survey of juror expectations revealed that 46 percent expected to see some kind of scientific evidence in *every* criminal case, 22 percent expected to see DNA evidence in *every* criminal case, 36 percent expected to see fingerprint evidence in *every* criminal case and 32 percent expected to see ballistic or other firearms laboratory evidence in *every* criminal case (Shelton, 2008). Fortunately, these expectations have not been shown to translate into an actual prerequisite of jurors in finding defendants guilty (Shelton). Perhaps more problematic for law enforcement is that "The National Academy of Science (NAS) says studies show C*SI* viewers—and even judges and lawyers—are under the impression that the techniques they see on the show are science at work. They aren't" (Temple-Raston, 2009). The NAS has called for a "total overhaul" of the nation's crime labs.

As previously discussed, another potential source of stress is that duty-related tasks can carry over into family life and other personal pursuits. Officers miss family birthday parties as well as their children's school conferences, concerts, plays and sporting events. Even when officers' schedules allow them to attend important family events, they may not be able to transition as easily into "after-hours" activities as people who work in other professions. When they go off duty, they need to "come down" from having been hypervigilant during their shifts, but family life and the day-to-day activities require them to continue pushing.

In addition, the aftermath of a stressful incident can greatly affect an officer's family and leave damaging emotional scars, a phenomenon identified as **afterburn**. Risk factors that make a police family vulnerable to stress include limited knowledge of police work among family members, a conflict between job and family priorities and isolation felt by the officer and spouse. Protective factors that may help police families better handle the stress of police work include an awareness of job-related stress factors, a negotiated family structure with clear roles and responsibilities, conflict resolution skills and a social support system.

CSI effect
the heightened expectation by the public, often the result of watching popular television series such as *CSI*, of what police can do and the tools available to them in solving crimes.

afterburn
a stressful incident that greatly affects an officer's family and leaves damaging emotional scars.

The Interplay of Stressors

A survey of more than 1,000 police officers was conducted regarding the amount of stress caused by various organization, job-related and external sources, and the results were ranked on a scale of 1 (low level) to 100 (high level) (Garcia et al., 2004). Table 12.4 summarizes the mean (average) amount of stress from most to least. Interestingly, no organizational factors ranked

TABLE 12.4 Police Officer Stressors Ranked by Mean

	Organizational	Job-related	External	SD
Fellow officers being injured or killed		54.42		31.04
Public criticism of police			53.62	29.85
Family demands			51.36	31.09
Making important on-the-spot decisions		49.39		26.99
Fellow officers not doing their job		48.57		30.52
Responding to a felony in progress		43.33		29.30
Incompatible partner		41.13		35.10
Job conflict with rules (i.e., by the book vs. the situation		40.70		29.41
Exposure to death		37.88		27.29
Sustaining a serious physical injury on the job		37.73		29.55
Threat of lawsuit			37.00	34.42
Situations requiring use of force		36.53		30.69
Assignment of increased responsibility	35.98			26.91
Transfer to another assignment area	35.01			30.85
Department/unit recognition	33.62			26.87
Promotion competition	33.30			33.48
Racial conflicts			33.20	30.21
Subject of internal affairs investigation	28.79			33.54
Shift work		27.38		32.99
Undercover work		22.45		26.26
Personal thoughts of suicide*			9.56	21.35
Scales total/means			36.81	18.04
		37.93		18.25
	33.10			20.35
Total index 35.43				16.80

*Although not significant among the stressors, 20% of respondents (i.e., 210 officers) indicated having some thoughts of suicide during the previous 12 months, and 7% (i.e., 73 officers) specified that it had caused them moderate or high levels of stress.

Source: Luis Garcia, Dale K. Nesbary, and Joann Gu. "Perceptual Variations of Stressors among Police Officers during an Era of Decreasing Crime." *Journal of Contemporary Criminal Justice*, February 2004, Table 2, p.38. © 2004. Reprinted by permission of SAGE Publications.

among the top 10 stressors. It is also of interest that only three sources of stress had a mean of more than 50. The researchers conclude that their results indicate generally moderate levels of stress.

LAW ENFORCEMENT PERSONNEL WITH ADDITIONAL STRESSORS

Some officers are placed in high-stress assignments such as narcotics, undercover work and special weapons and tactics (SWAT) units. Stress levels vary tremendously depending on the assignment, the area and the shift.

 Additional stress is often experienced by women officers, minority officers, officers in small towns and rural areas, investigators and managers.

Women Officers

"Female police officers must walk a fine line between fitting in and making their own way in law enforcement" (Basich, 2008, p.44). In addition to the stress experienced because of the job they have selected, female officers have some stressors not faced by their male counterparts, for example, male chauvinism, lack of respect and support, higher rate of turnover, citizen negativism and sexual harassment. Additional stress for females is caused by lack of acceptance by predominantly White, male forces with subsequent denial of information, alliances and protection as well as a lack of role models and mentors.

Another stressor on female officers, seemingly more so than for males, includes personal issues related to home life and the issue of who is expected to care for family members. Further, "Convincing the public to look beyond gender and respect a woman's authority as a police officer is also an uphill battle. And it's not always clear how to win" (Basich, 2008, p. 44).

The good news, according to Basich, is that it is sometimes easier for women to deal with stress because they tend to express themselves, to not hold things in, especially with family members and close friends.

Minority Officers

Minority police officers may experience more stress than majority police officers because they are expected to be more tolerant of community problems within their minority population, yet are also expected to enforce the law impartially. They may also be expected to join a minority organization within the department, separating them from the majority of the force. And, like their female counterparts, minority officers face the additional stress of lack of acceptance by a predominately White force with subsequent denial of information, alliances and protection as well as a lack of role models and mentors.

Rural and Small-Town Officers

Stressors not commonly reported among larger departments but rating high in rural and small-town departments are lack of department resources; inadequate equipment and training; coming into conflict with a well-known community member; pulling over, arresting or citing a personal acquaintance (relatives and friends); being contacted by the public while off duty; and a longer time spent waiting for backup to arrive because of larger areas and distances patrolled. Another stress factor is long hours of inactivity, more so than in a larger department. Officers in small departments are essentially on-call 24/7. The stress that comes from never being able to get away from the job can be overwhelming (Conroy, 2009).

The geographical isolation of rural areas and limited number of officers on duty in smaller agencies means rural officers may face more stress related to their personal safety and security. Rural officers may struggle with patchy or intermittent radio and cell phone communications, making it difficult to call for assistance if they run into trouble. They may also frequently encounter hunters who, not surprisingly, have weapons (Novesky, 2009).

Investigators

Several stressors accompany the responsibilities of being a criminal investigator. They may have to investigate several cases at once, often within short time frames, because suspects can be incarcerated for only a short time without sufficient evidence. Many investigators work long hours, often on their own time, which can lead to fatigue and eventually burnout. They commonly take their cases home with them, which can cause severe tension in their family lives. Furthermore, for investigators working undercover, long hours away from family compound their stress and deep immersion into the criminal world can lead to intense internal conflict (Conroy, 2009).

Investigators may also become frustrated with the court system and the perception of a revolving door criminal justice system. In addition, they may be under constant scrutiny of citizens who expect cases to be solved rapidly. Investigators may not get needed backup or may have less sophisticated equipment than the criminals they are investigating. Finally, they may question society's values as they deal with horrible, inhumane crimes.

Managers/Supervisors

When officers are promoted, they assume the added stress of being managers. Promotion often involves managing officers who formerly were peers. Sometimes these relationships are difficult because of close, even social friendships, or prior antagonistic relationships. Most officers, however, understand what is required of the law enforcement manager position. They know that managers have to discipline and correct.

The amount of stress managers face varies with the position, level and assigned duties. First-line supervisors often work in the field with the officers they supervise, performing the same duties, especially in smaller departments. They need to learn to manage people rather than trying to handle situations. It is easiest to return to what is familiar and for the supervisor to handle situations, incidents and calls for service, but supervisors need to have faith in their officers and help them develop their skills.

Managers are responsible for themselves and for every officer they supervise or manage, which produces stress. The higher the level of law enforcement manager, the more stress there is in developing programs, preparing budgets, making speeches, settling personnel grievances and complaints, resolving citizen complaints and many other duties. Top managers have more control over their work and less stress from lack of control. Middle and first-line managers generally have more stress because of lack of control over their work.

EFFECTS OF STRESS—AN OVERVIEW

It is difficult to assess the total effect of going from boredom to high stress, dealing with conflict and confrontation, coping with the criminal element, facing the adversity of courtroom tactics, dealing with the spin-off effects on family members, writing tedious reports, handling criticism by managers and many other everyday pressures of the job. Stress demands a response, which may range from minimal to serious. Stress affects people in numerous ways: physical, emotional and psychological.

Physical

The average life expectancy in the United States is 77.8 years—75.6 years for men and 80.4 years for women (Arias, 2007, p.30). However, a 40-year study found that police officers with 10 to 19 years of service had an average age of death of 66 years. Officers with 30 years on the job increased their mortality rate more than three times (Violanti, 2002). This research found a "significantly increased risk of digestive and hematopoietic cancers among police officers who have 10 to 19 years" on the job, agreeing with other studies theorizing the link between cancer and stress (p.3). This same employment period linked stress with such maladaptive behaviors as alcohol and tobacco use and with significantly higher risk of death from esophageal cancer as well as significantly elevated risk of cirrhosis of the liver.

Law enforcement managers need to recognize signs of stress in their subordinates and in themselves. Symptoms of stress appear differently in different people.

 Stress is related to heart problems, hypertension, cancer, ulcers, diabetes, chronic headaches, anxiety-related disorders, asthma, excessive eating, decreased sex drive, fatigue, dizziness, muscle aches and tics and backaches.

Stress can cause these medical conditions, or the conditions can be prolonged, increased in severity or aggravated by stress. Living in our complex, fast-paced society results in many stress-related diseases. An estimated 85 percent of all illnesses are stress related.

Psychological

Every day those in law enforcement at all levels "do battle with the evils without, while often times not effectively defending against the evils within" (Murray, 2008, pp.65–66). Chief among the evils within is stress. Psychological symptoms of stress include boredom, defensiveness, delusions, depression, apathy, emotional illness, hostility, loneliness, nervousness, paranoia, sudden mood changes and tension. One of the most debilitating psychological effects is posttraumatic stress disorder.

Posttraumatic Stress Disorder (PTSD)

As they wage war on crime and violence, law enforcement personnel may have a problem similar to that experienced by military combat personnel. During World War I, soldiers were *shell-shocked*. In World War II, they suffered from *combat fatigue* and *battle stress*. More recently, those exhibiting similar symptoms after deploying to fight in Iraq, Afghanistan or other areas of armed conflict have been diagnosed with combat-operational stress disorder (COSD). Psychologists gradually came to realize that civilians involved in major catastrophes such as earthquakes, fires and rapes experienced similar stress disorders. Traumatic events such as these (1) are likely to be sudden and unexpected, (2) threaten officers' lives, (3) often include loss (partner, physical ability or position) and (4) may abruptly change officers' values and self-confidence.

 Law enforcement officers may experience posttraumatic stress disorder (PTSD), a clinical name associated with a debilitating condition suffered by war veterans.

posttraumatic stress disorder (PTSD)
a psychological ailment following a major catastrophe such as a shooting or dealing with victims of a natural disaster; symptoms include diminished responsiveness to the environment, disinterest, pessimism and sleep disturbances, including recurrent nightmares.

No amount of police machismo can deflect the cold, hard reality of PTSD. Like a relentlessly corrosive force if left unattended, PTSD can gnaw away at one's psychological bridges until they collapse.

The first phase after a traumatic incident, the initial impact phase, may last a few minutes or a few days. Attention is on the present, with the officer stunned or bewildered and having difficulty coping with normal situations. This phase may be followed by the recoil phase of wanting to retell the experience and attempt to overcome it through this retelling. The need is for support from fellow officers. Personal reactions may be withdrawal, apathy, disinterest, anxiety, hopelessness, pessimism, insomnia and nightmares. Other reported symptoms commonly experienced are flashbacks, depression, sexual dysfunction, obsessive behavior (particularly with alcohol and drugs) and fear.

Those who can be of greatest assistance are fellow officers; immediate supervisors; unit commanders; peer counselors; chaplains; mental health professionals; the officer's family; and, in some cases, the media and citizens. Those who assist should be good listeners, show empathy and concern, offer reassurances and support and provide group grief sharing.

Officers in larger law enforcement departments and those assigned to more difficult and violent tasks, such as murders, SWAT teams or narcotics teams, are the most likely candidates for PTSD.

In addition to the maladaptive response of substance abuse, some officers choose to forego what could be lifesaving, or at least career-saving, counseling because they fear being diagnosed with mental illness (PTSD) and the impact such a diagnosis would have on subsequent job assignments, promotional opportunities or civil litigation (Conroy, 2009).

Behavioral

Behavioral symptoms of stress include accident-proneness, anger, argumentativeness, blaming others, drug or alcohol abuse, excessive violence, irritability, inability to concentrate, lack of control, neurotic behavior, nail biting, obsession with work, rage, rapid behavior changes, uncontrollable urges to cry and withdrawal. Most people, after reading about the common symptoms of stress just discussed, would probably comment, "I've had all these symptoms." Only when the symptoms appear in excess or several appear simultaneously do problems arise.

On the Job

Stress reactions found among police officers include repression of emotion, displacement of anger, isolation and unspoken fears. In addition, police officers may behave inappropriately under stress, for example, becoming verbally or physically abusive, looking for any excuse to call in sick, arguing with other officers, placing themselves in danger or engaging in "choir practice" (heavy drinking with peers). They may argue with supervisors, criticize the actions of fellow officers and supervisors, lose interest in the job or sleep on duty. At its most extreme, stress may result in burnout.

Burnout

burnout

occurs when someone is exhausted or made listless through overwork; results from long-term, unmediated stress; symptoms include lack of enthusiasm and interest, a drop in job performance, temper flare-ups, and a loss of will, motivation or commitment.

When stress continues unremittingly for prolonged periods, it can result in the debilitating condition referred to as **burnout**, which occurs in a person who is used up or consumed by a job, made listless through overwork and stress. A once-motivated, committed employee experiences physical and emotional exhaustion on the job brought about by unrelieved demands. The person experiences a persistent lack of energy or interest in his or her work: "The road to burnout is a long and lonely stretch. It does not happen overnight. It is not a condition cased by one or two incidents, nor is it unique to certain personality types. It is a road traveled at one time or another by most law enforcement professionals, often midway through their career" (Carlton, 2009, p.64). Officers who are burned out are at extremely high risk of being injured or killed on duty because they are usually not safety conscious. They are also at risk for depression or suicide.

 Symptoms of burnout include lack of enthusiasm and interest; decreased job performance; temper flare-ups; and a loss of will, motivation or commitment.

Those most likely to experience burnout are those who are initially most committed. You cannot burn out if you have never been on fire. To those in police work, the **blue flame** is the symbol of a law enforcement officer who wants to make a difference in the world. The enthusiasm shown by rookie officers as they recover their first occupied stolen vehicle or make their first arrest is like a torch being lit. The key is knowing how to keep the flame burning throughout the many stresses of an entire law enforcement career.

Burned out employees can often be helped by a change—something to motivate them. Sometimes changes in the job itself help—adding new dimensions to old tasks. Expert assistance is usually needed at this level, and counseling may be necessary.

> **blue flame**
> the symbol of a law enforcement officer who wants to make a difference in the world.

 To avoid burnout, keep the work interesting, give recognition, provide R and R (rest and relaxation), avoid "other duties" and limit the assignment.

OTHER POSSIBLE MAJOR EFFECTS OF STRESS

 Police officers' stress may cause alcohol and substance abuse problems, higher rates of domestic abuse and divorce, depression and even suicide.

Alcoholism and Substance Abuse

According to the results of one study, for those officers who drank heavily, cirrhosis of the liver was elevated after only nine years on the job (Violanti, 2002). In addition, officers who use alcohol and other drugs to deal with stress often cannot perform their duties adequately. Substance use often results in progressive lateness and absenteeism.

Management must ensure that the department does not downplay, rationalize or deny the seriousness of drug abuse or its existence. Supervisors should be alert to signs of substance and alcohol abuse, including officers whose physical appearances deteriorate, who are frequently out sick or injured, who are shunned by their peers, who have more than their share of vehicle crashes or who receive frequent civilian complaints. Debt overload can also lead to alcohol abuse. Abuse of alcohol and other drugs can also play a role in domestic violence and divorce.

Divorce

Another common effect the high-stress lifestyle of policing has on officers is divorce. The national divorce rate is 50 percent, but research shows police officers suffer a substantially higher divorce rate, with estimates ranging between 60 and 75 percent. Some estimate that police officers divorce twice as often as the national average.

Depression

Depression is a serious, life-threatening medical illness that can affect anyone. Unfortunately our society places a stigma on having depression or seeking help for it. As with PTSD, a diagnosis of depression may affect an officer's future. And because many officers are skeptical about the confidentiality of medical records, they resist seeking professional help (Conroy, 2009). Because depression is a medical illness, an imbalance of chemicals in the brain, medication can often be prescribed to treat it. But often people do not recognize the symptoms.

Symptoms of depression include significant changes in appetite and sleep patterns; irritability, anger, worry, agitation and anxiety; loss of energy and persistent lethargy; unexplained aches and pains; feelings of guilt, worthlessness or hopelessness; inability to concentrate; indecisiveness; inability to take pleasure in former interests; social withdrawal; pessimism or indifference; prolonged sadness or unexplained crying spells; excessive consumption of alcohol or use of chemical substances; recurring thoughts of death; or suicide.

Depression must be treated because it is one of the leading causes of suicide. In at least 90 percent of all suicides, untreated depression is believed to be the major factor.

Suicide

Data from the National Police Suicide Association shows that the number of officers who take their own lives each year is two to three times higher than the number who are feloniously killed (Murray, 2008, p.65). Alcohol, family problems, the breakup of relationships and stress all contribute to the high rate of police suicide, about 30 percent higher than what is found in the general population. Some authorities feel that police suicides are underreported because fellow officers are usually the first on the scene and may cover up the suicide to save the family further pain or embarrassment or for insurance purposes.

The following factors contribute to officer suicide: alcohol abuse, posttraumatic stress disorder, failing relationships, suspension from the force, internal investigations into corruption or other malfeasance, career stagnation and clinical depression. Officer suicide may also be rooted in control issues: "Sometimes it is the only thing the officer has control over, and we know how important control is to cops" (Conroy, 2009). Retirement also appears to be a precipitant of suicide, as research shows retired law enforcement personnel were 10 times more likely to commit suicide than were age-matched peers (Honig and White, 2009). It is important for officers to have lives outside the department throughout their careers, and it becomes very important when officers retire (Perin, 2009, p.53). Retired officers need a plan for what they are going to do with the rest of their lives.

Among the warning signs of suicide, several of which are the same as symptoms of alcohol or substance abuse, are a high number of off-duty accidents, an increase in citizen complaints, a change in personality, the dispersing of gifts and writing a will. Miller (2007) adds to this list: verbal self threats, for example, "I'd be better off eating my gun"; threatening others; behaving insubordinately with no regard for the consequences, for example, "What's he gonna do, fire me?"; acting recklessly; or expressing feelings of being overwhelmed.

Managers should be tuned into such signs and proactively intervene should they appear in a fellow officer: "It's entirely possible that someone close to you might be one desperate decision away from self-termination" (Murray, 2008, p.64). Such intervention should include the fundamental principles of crisis intervention: identifying the problem with the officer, ensuring the officer's safety and providing support (Miller, 2007). As the saying goes, the best form of crisis intervention is crisis prevention. Miller suggests,

> First and foremost, the problem needs to come out in the open. Both command and line officers need to educate themselves as to the nature of police stress, syndromes of impairment, and good and bad ways of coping.
>
> Next, officers should receive training in crisis intervention skills that they can apply to fellow officers in a similar way as they do with distressed citizens on patrol. This is, in fact, the rationale behind the peer counseling programs that have been set up in many departments.
>
> Also supervisors must be alert to signs of depression and other problems that are affecting the officers under their command. Finally, there has to be a convenient and non-stigmatized system for referring distressed officers for psychological help, and this must be framed in health-maintenance context, not as a disciplinary procedure.

Having looked at the major sources of stress and possible reactions to it, consider what managers can do for themselves, their subordinates and department.

INDIVIDUALLY COPING WITH STRESS

No one escapes stress. How people *deal with* it determines whether they cope and develop or deteriorate. Much of the literature on stress management is about lowering the demands placed on the individual, an approach that does not work for police officers: "Stress cannot be eliminated in law enforcement. Officers need to be able to handle the high demands placed on them. From a management perspective, officers lacking in coping skills have a significant negative impact on their police agencies. The more resilient officers are, the more productive they will be" (Coulbeck, 2009, p.88). **Resiliency**, the ability to adapt to significant adversity or trauma, is the key to stress management. Research has identified seven ineffective habits—"enemies of sanity"— common in the policing culture that can harm officers' abilities to deal with

resiliency
the ability to adapt to significant adversity or trauma; is the key to stress management.

stress, each of which can be mitigated by a learned "resiliency factor" (Coulbeck, pp.89–96):

Enemy #1: Isolation. Resiliency factor: support systems.

Enemy #2: Negative worldview, cynicism. Resiliency factor: sense of optimism.

Enemy #3: Overuse of stimulants and depressants. Resiliency factor: Healthy diet.

Enemy #4: Giving up on exercise. Resiliency factor: Fitness.

Enemy #5: Tying self-worth to position or assignment. Resiliency factor: Finding meaning in life.

Enemy #6: Taking oneself too seriously. Resiliency factor: A sense of humor.

Enemy #7: Lack of sleep. Resiliency factor: Sleep and rest.

Coulbeck (2009, p.96) concludes, "In the stressful environment of law enforcement, it is up to the agency to promote and support training and programs that will increase officers' resiliency. By doing so, it will fulfill the duty of care that ethical organizations have toward employees and also create a more productive organization where officers are able to effectively handle the demands place on them, ultimately improving their quality of life."

Managers should take definite steps to reduce stress and encourage their subordinates to do the same. Most people need to work to earn a living but may need to change their attitudes about their work or about the people they work with. The symptoms of stress are often obvious, but its cause is more difficult to determine and even more difficult to change. Unfortunately, we tend to treat the symptoms rather than reduce the causes of stress.

> **Stress levels can be reduced through physical exercise, relaxation techniques, good nutrition, taking time for oneself, making friends, learning to say no, staying within the law, changing one's mental attitude, keeping things in perspective and seeking help when it is needed.**

Seek help if you need it. Law enforcement officers deal with life-threatening situations as part of their job. If you need help coping with the job's dangers, seek counseling. Talk about the problem with other officers and see how they deal with it. It is as real to them as to you. Mental stress is often more difficult to deal with than physical stress. Officers should be encouraged to seek confidential counseling even without a diagnosis of a mental illness (Conroy, 2009).

Other ways to reduce stress include getting plenty of sleep, setting personal goals, making a "to-do" list and taking things one at a time, smiling and laughing to lighten your day, saying positive things to yourself, taking time to recharge by taking mini time-outs, volunteering or helping others. A study by the Ontario Police College examined 218 experienced police officers and found that officers who reported the highest levels of job satisfaction "appear to handle the day-to-day cumulative stressors of police work by being involved with their families and their communities, pursuing self-development and following a healthy lifestyle" (Barath, 2009, p.119). Finally, *do NOT smoke*, and if you drink, *drink in moderation*. *AVOID drugs* to control stress unless recommended by a qualified physician.

 Alcohol, drugs and smoking increase stress over time and can seriously affect physical health.

HOW THE ORGANIZATION CAN REDUCE STRESS

The law enforcement administration can do much to reduce employee stress. Managers must pay attention to the victims of stress and to the conditions that created it. In law enforcement the source may be an incident, a citizen, a manager, a fellow officer or other sources. Having identified the source of the stress, study all methods of relieving stress and determine what might work best.

Implementing a stress management and prevention program may require increased use of personnel and resources, but such a program can lead to long-term cost savings, high productivity and morale and enhanced community–police relations. Therefore, concern for an officer's ability to manage stress should be a consideration in the selection process.

Testing and Selection

Administrators can continue the strong testing already in use to select candidates most likely to cope well with stress by being physically fit, mentally stable and emotionally well balanced. Law enforcement employees who start healthy have a good foundation for remaining healthy during their careers. Administrators need to demand tests designed specifically for the needs of law enforcement personnel selection.

Law enforcement budgets provide training, weapons and vehicles, and they should provide funds for keeping fit. As in the medical profession, those in law enforcement must sometimes cope with emergency situations that demand immediate yet highly analytical responses. In both professions life may depend on the actions taken. Psychological testing and interviews can help screen out mentally and emotionally weak or unstable applicants. Doing so is good for the department and is best for the candidates, even though they may not believe so at the time. The department benefits by less sick leave and absenteeism, greater productivity, better employee relationships, fewer resignations, fewer new hirings (with the associated costs) and more work hours available because of less new officer training time.

Managers can also learn to recognize the common physical, emotional and behavioral warning signs of individuals under stress both during the selection process and after employees are hired. Common physical symptoms include nausea, fatigue, dizziness, muscle tremors, chest pain, difficulty breathing, grinding of teeth, backaches, headaches and blackouts. Common emotional symptoms include anxiety, severe panic, depression, fear, irritability, guilt and anger. And common behavioral symptoms include withdrawal, pacing, para-noia, sleep disturbances, emotional outbursts and substance abuse (Conroy and Hess, 1992).

Training

Programs to train field training officers and supervisors in tactical decision making under stress can help eliminate many of the errors made in the field by teaching all personnel to control their judgment and decision making under crisis conditions. The agency's liability costs will also be substantially lowered when law enforcement personnel are experts in managing stress exposure, without any degradation in their performance or health.

Officers should be trained in countermanding the negative effects of stress, that is, how to control their reactions to stressful events in real time. Such training should build self-confidence as they see themselves control conditions in which they initially would probably be unprepared. Officers who are practiced and conditioned to peak performance in stress-exposure management under adverse conditions will respond properly to difficult or problematic conditions. Such training must be ongoing because, like physical fitness, stress-exposure management techniques are highly perishable skills.

Establishing and Supporting Fitness Standards

Oldham (2009, p.10) asks, "In what other endeavor do we even begin to think that a 50-year-old can, or even should, compete with a 21-year-old in any physical activity?" He also asks, "How is it that a 50-year-old can ever expect to survive in the physically demanding world in which all officers live?" Experience and cunning help, but "There must be a threshold limit as to exactly how out of shape an officer can become." Supervisors, especially line supervisors, probably will not be able to change agency policy, but they can have a significant effect by setting the tone for their officers, leading them by example: "The physical fitness level of a supervisor affects the level of confidence the officers have in the judgment and standards of that particular supervisory officer" (Oldham, p.10).

Ongoing Psychological Support

The field of police psychology has evolved significantly since psychology first partnered with the law enforcement community nearly 100 years ago (Corey and Honig, 2008, p.138). From initially being restricted to helping select qualified police offers, the discipline now involves nearly 60 services organized into four distinct core domains and competencies: assessment-related activities, intervention services, operational support and organizational/management consultation.

Periodic psychological fitness-for-duty evaluations are important. Psychological reviews should be available for employees who have developed mental or emotional problems after employment. They should also have psychological assistance available after a killing or other severely traumatic event while on duty.

Some agencies have full-time police psychologists. Others have regular access to confidential psychological services. Many agencies are now using self-help groups for police plagued with problems such as alcoholism and PTSD. In addition some areas have treatment centers for law enforcement personnel with job-related stress disorders and other types of psychological problems. Some agencies use a psychologist jointly with the county or state. Smaller departments may obtain the assistance of a retired psychologist in the community as a volunteer or on a small retainer.

Officers may resist psychiatric help because they view it as a sign of weakness. They may be reluctant to admit they have stress-related problems for fear of losing their coworkers' respect or lessening their chances for promotion. For these reasons, ensuring privileged communication is essential in working with officers after a trauma.

PROGRAMS TO PREVENT/ REDUCE STRESS

The business world has implemented stress-reduction programs such as athletic club memberships, physical activities, flex time, free time and company gripe sessions. Some of these programs might be options for law enforcement organizations. The Cleveland Police Department has developed a leadership training program for sergeants and lieutenants to learn how to minimize stress in their line officers: "Laminated pocket cards were provided which summarized warning signs of operations stress, self-care and partner-care actions and leadership strategies to treat early warning signs of operational stress. Based on focus groups with police supervisors, an incentive system was developed and implemented to reward officers seeking help or assisting other officers in managing operational stress, which could change the culture of keeping silent about problems and remove the stigma attached to help seeking" (Chapin et al., 2008, p.338).

Other programs include peer support groups, critical incident stress debriefing, organizational consultant programs and chaplain programs.

Peer Support Groups

Police departments of all sizes are implementing peer support programs to help officers deal with stress and emotional difficulties.

 Peer support groups are a particularly effective type of stress-reduction program.

Through such support groups, veteran members may advise new members on available financial benefits and can shepherd them through the complex paperwork and procedures. Veteran members can make referrals for local services for everything from a funeral home to a counselor. Support groups may hold regular meetings during which problems and issues can be discussed.

Dr. Richard Weinblatt, a former police chief known as "The Cop Doc," discusses a police shooting event and how such incidents contribute to police stress. Prompt and appropriate departmental response is crucial in helping officers successfully manage the range of physical and emotional stressors that follow such incidents.

Courtesy Richard Weinblatt

Critical Incident Stress Debriefing

critical incident stress debriefing (CISD)

officers who experience a critical incident such as a mass disaster or crash with multiple deaths are brought together as a group for a psychological debriefing soon after the event.

Critical incident stress debriefing (CISD) is another effective way to prevent or reduce stress by bringing together as a group those officers who experience a critical incident together, such as a mass disaster, a crash with multiple deaths or a particularly grizzly murder, and providing a psychological debriefing soon after the event. A trained mental health professional leads the group members as they discuss their emotions and reactions. This allows officers to vent and to realize they are not going crazy but are responding normally to a very abnormal situation.

A CISD should take place within 24 to 72 hours after a critical incident. Earlier is usually too soon for full emotional impact to have occurred. If only one officer is involved in the critical incident, he should be joined in the CISD by volunteers from the department who have experienced a similar incident or have been trained in PTSD.

To overcome officers' reluctance to participate in a mental health program, attendance at a CISD should be mandatory. A CISD should not become an operational critique. The groups should be small and everything said kept confidential.

employee assistance program (EAP)

may be internally staffed or use outside referrals to offer help with stress, marital or chemical-dependency problems.

 Law enforcement departments should include an **employee assistance program (EAP)** or provide referrals to outside agencies for psychological and counseling services and to assist officers with stress, marital or chemical dependency problems.

Topics and issues commonly addressed through EAPs include alcoholism and substance abuse; depression; anxiety; attention deficit disorder; fear of being fired, sued or charged criminally; social withdrawal; sleep apnea; fear; guilt; and a host of other personal and family problems. An ingredient missing from many EAPs is the orientation and preparation of family and friends for new officers' transition into the police culture. By providing such knowledge and insight, departments can help families and friends of new officers understand the potential pitfalls of policing, acquire insight into the potential attitudinal and behavioral changes in the new officer, be alert to personality and behavioral changes that may require action and be familiar with resources available for intervention if family relationships deteriorate.

The orientation might include the swearing-in ceremony and reception for new officers, a packet with material on stress and how it can be dealt with, a tour of the department and a ride-along. Such an orientation program can demonstrate that the department cares about the new police families while introducing them to police work and the possible pitfalls as well as the rewards of a law enforcement career.

Help for those at risk of suicide within the department includes counseling units, peer counseling groups and police chaplains. Outside the department help might be sought from physicians; priests, ministers, rabbis, etc.; attorneys; and family.

Chaplain Corps

When troubled or stressed, many people turn to their faiths for guidance and solace. Some departments make chaplains available to officers who need a place to turn in times of stress. However, these chaplains must be trained in police work and must know the difference between spiritual guidance and religion (Conroy, 2009).

When officers need someone to talk to, a chaplain provides that resource where officers can go be sure their confidentiality will be respected (Weiss and Davis, 2008). Chaplains can also accompany officers who are delivering a death notification to the next of kin; provide emotional support during hostage negotiations; serve ceremonial functions at memorial services, funerals and award ceremonies; make hospital visits; and consult on religious fraud issues.

Other Stress Management Programs

 Health programs and stress management seminars are another means to help law enforcement officers prevent destructive stress or at least reduce it.

Health programs include medical and psychological services and fitness programs. Law enforcement administration can also provide in-service health and fitness training and weight control classes.

Law enforcement management should provide an opportunity for employees to attend stress management seminars. All personnel, including dispatchers, should attend. A distinct benefit from attending such seminars is a better understanding of the nature of stress and ways to prevent, cope with or reduce its effects. The FBI has all new agents complete a Stress Management in Law Enforcement (SMILE) course to help them better understand the stress they may encounter on the job. Through such exposure they become more aware of the emotional and psychological dangers of the job, beyond the physical ones most expect to find in law enforcement.

THE CRITICAL ROLE OF THE MANAGER/SUPERVISOR

In addition to promoting the programs just described, law enforcement managers have a critical role in minimizing the effects of stress in themselves and their subordinates. Law enforcement managers should keep in close touch

AWAY FROM THE DESK: The Manager's Role in Surviving Critical Incidents

Fortunately, most officers and many departments do not have to experience the stress of an officer-involved shooting. However, other officers and departments have experienced these difficult situations on more than one occasion. Often in these types of situations, the police are second-guessed even though circumstances of this nature are life threatening and require split-second decision making. Most people's careers don't demand these types of abilities, and often people are given adequate time and supporting data to make informed decisions. For example, accountants have month-end, quarterly and annual reports to support corporate decisions. Those who report the weather are often inaccurate and still get paid even when they are wrong, yet they are rarely ridiculed or scorned by the public to the level of a police officer who is involved in a critical incident.

The stress and emotion surrounding officers and their department following a critical incident in general, and an officer-involved shooting in particular, often change the lives of those involved to the point where they are never the same. It is critical for all supervisors, both new and seasoned, to make every effort to, first, manage these types of incidents in the field and, second and equally important, understand the need to work with family members of the officer(s) involved, the community and the department for as long as necessary—several hours, days, months and even years—following an incident of critical magnitude. It is imperative that all law enforcement leaders, regardless of position held, fully understand what needs to take place and in what order to be effective in the eyes of the officers, their families and the community. Failing to do so can be devastating to everyone involved and can have long-lasting or permanent negative impacts on the organizational culture and its leadership if not handled properly.

—*Chief Shaun E. LaDue*

with their subordinates and recognize the symptoms of stress. If an officer shows such symptoms, the manager should be ready to assist and reduce to whatever level possible the degree of stress. Sometimes just having someone to talk to is the most helpful. If counseling or psychological assistance is needed, it should be provided or information furnished regarding local sources of assistance. Managers must also "walk the talk," keeping themselves physically and mentally fit as role models.

Evaluating subordinates' fitness for duty, which is defined as an employee's ability to safely or effectively perform his or her job duties, is an important role of supervisors and managers. Attending to fitness-for-duty (FFD) concerns ensures safe and efficient operations and helps departments and officers avoid liability. Such fitness encompasses both physical and mental aspects and includes employee performance, misconduct, general behavior and personal appearance.

 ## SUMMARY

Stress can be helpful (eustress) or harmful (distress), depending on its intensity and frequency, as well as how it is managed. Stress commonly arises from change and uncertainty, lack of control and pressure. Sources of stress for police officers include internal, individual stressors; stressors inherent to the police job; administrative and organizational stressors; and external stressors from the criminal justice system, the citizens it serves, the media and the family. A major source of employee stress may be upper-level management. Additional stress is also often experienced by women officers, minority officers, officers in small towns and rural areas, investigators and managers.

Stress affects people in numerous ways: mental, physical, emotional and psychological. Stress is related to heart problems, hypertension, cancer, ulcers, diabetes, chronic headaches, anxiety-related disorders, asthma, excessive eating, decreased sex drive, fatigue, dizziness, muscle aches and tics and backaches.

Law enforcement officers may also experience posttraumatic stress disorder (PTSD), a clinical name associated with a debilitating condition suffered by Vietnam War veterans. Officers in larger law enforcement departments and those assigned to more difficult and violent tasks, such as murders, SWAT teams or narcotics teams, are the most likely candidates for PTSD. Officers may also experience burnout. Symptoms of burnout include lack of enthusiasm and interest; decreased job performance; temper flare-ups; and a loss of will, motivation or commitment. To avoid burnout, keep the work interesting, give recognition, provide R and R (rest and relaxation), avoid "other duties" and limit the assignment.

Police officers' stress may cause alcohol and substance abuse problems, higher rates of domestic abuse and divorce, depression and even suicide. Stress levels can be reduced through physical exercise, relaxation techniques, good nutrition, taking time for oneself, making friends, learning to say no, staying within the law, changing one's mental attitude, keeping things in perspective and seeking help when it is needed. Alcohol, drugs and smoking increase stress over time and can seriously affect physical health.

Peer support groups are a particularly effective type of stress-reduction program. Law enforcement departments should include an employee assistance program (EAP) or provide referrals to outside agencies for psychological and counseling services and to assist officers with stress, marital or chemical dependency problems. Health programs and stress management seminars are other means to help law enforcement officers prevent destructive stress or at least reduce it.

CHALLENGE TWELVE

Lieutenant Smith is meeting with Detective Smug to discuss several complaints concerning Smug's rude behavior toward citizens and other detectives. Smug has been with the department for 15 years and a detective for 10 years. He has a good service record and is generally liked by his peers. He has no history of behavior problems. During the past several months, he has offended citizens with his obstinate attitude and curt remarks. A fellow detective has privately told Lieutenant Smith that Smug is quick to anger and often condescending. Smug's behavior seems out of character for him.

Before the meeting, Lieutenant Smith learned that Detective Smug's wife left him six months ago for an officer in a neighboring department. Smug has not shared this with other officers, but the rumors spread quickly. Smug was also recently passed over for detective sergeant. A younger female detective with less experience was promoted.

Lieutenant Smith begins the meeting by telling Detective Smug about the series of complaints. He asks Smug if he is aware of the behavior and what may be causing it.

Detective Smug is defensive and denies being rude to anyone. He says if there is a problem, it's the new chief and all the changes he's throwing at people. Smug says he's heard rumors that the detectives are going to rotate shifts every month.

Lieutenant Smith observes that Detective Smug seems withdrawn and tired. He's usually a snappy dresser, but now he's a bit disheveled. His attendance record shows an increased use of sick time.

1. As a skilled manager, Lieutenant Smith should be cognizant of potential signs of stress. What indicators are apparent in Detective Smug?

2. Identify three obvious sources of stress in Detective Smug's life.

3. If Lieutenant Smith suspects that stress is the root cause of Detective Smug's problem behavior, should he excuse it?

4. How can Lieutenant Smith and the department help Detective Smug deal with his stress?

5. Police officers face a variety of job-related stressors. Discuss one that is unique to Detective Smug's job.

DISCUSSION QUESTIONS

1. What do you consider the five most stressful aspects of work in law enforcement?

2. What are major stressors in your life right now?

3. How could you reduce your level of personal stress?

4. Has your level of stress changed with job changes? Age changes? Changes because of a singular incident? Changes caused by a series of similar incidents?

5. Have you taken any psychological tests? Which ones?

6. Are you a type A or a type B personality? What significance might that have to your career choice?

7. Have you ever participated in a support group? How effective was the experience?

8. Do you know anyone who has burned out? Can you explain why?

9. How does stress at the management level differ from that at the line level?

10. Does your local law enforcement agency have an EAP or other forms of employee support to reduce stress?

REFERENCES

Arias, Elizabeth. "United States Life Tables, 2004." *National Vital Statistics* Report. Atlanta, GA: Centers for Disease Control, December 28, 2007, p.30.

Armitage, Paul. "Preparing for the Unexpected: Line-of-Duty Deaths." *Big Ideas*, Spring 2009, p.6.

Barath, Irene. "Stress Management Research at the Ontario Police College." *The Police Chief*, August 2009, pp.112–121.

Basich, Melanie. "Women Warriors." *Police*, June 2008, pp.44–49.

Best, Suzanne. "Proactive Stress Management for Police Executive." *Big Ideas*, Spring 2009, pp.9–10.

Carlton, Jerry. "Preventing the Long and Lonely Ride to Officer Burnout." *Law Enforcement Technology*, March 2009, pp.64–70.

Chapin, Mark; Brannen, Stephen J.; Singer, Mark I.; and Walker, Michael. "Training Police Leadership to Recognize and Address Operational Stress." *Police Quarterly*, September 2008, pp.338–352.

Chudwin, Jeff. "Response to Officer-Involved Shootings: Part 1." *Law Officer Magazine*, June 2008a, pp.58–61.

Chudwin, Jeff. "Response to Officer-Involved Shootings: Part 2." *Law Officer Magazine*, July 2008b, pp.50–55.

Conroy, Dennis L. Personal correspondence with the author, review of the chapter, November 2009.

Conroy, Dennis L., and Hess, Kären M. *Officers at Risk: How to Identify and Cope with Stress*. Placerville, CA: Custom Publishing, 1992.

Corey, David M., and Honig, Audrey L. "Police Psychology in the 21st Century." *The Police Chief*, October 2008, p.138.

Coulbeck, Brad. "Seven Solutions for Stress." *Law and Order*, September 2009, pp.88–96.

DeYoung, Bob. "Bullet Proofing the Mind: Applying Stress Inoculation to Law Enforcement." *Law Officer Magazine*, March 2008, pp.38–40.

Fyfe, James J. "The Split-Second Syndrome and Other Determinants of Police Violence." In *Violent Transactions*, edited by Anne Campbell and John Gibbs. New York: Basic Blackwell, 1986.

Garcia, Luis; Nesbary, Dale K.; and Gu, Joann. "Perceptual Variations of Stressors among Police Officers during an Era of Decreasing Crime." *Journal of Contemporary Criminal Justice*, February 2004, pp.33–50.

Honig, Audrey L., and White, Elizabeth K. "By Their Own Hand: Suicide among Law Enforcement Personnel." *Community Policing Dispatch*, April 2009. http://www.cops.usdoj.gov/html/dispatch/April_2009/suicide.htm

"In the Line of Duty." Washington, DC: Federal Bureau of Investigation, Headline Archives, October 19, 2009.

"Law Enforcement Officer Deaths: Mid-Year 2009. After 48-Year Low, Officer Deaths Rise 20% in First Half of 2009." National Law Enforcement Officers Memorial Fund, Research Bulletin, July 2009. http://www.policeone.com/policeone/data/pdfs/2009MidYearReport.pdf

Mehlin, Keith. "Officer Involved Shootings." *Law and Order*, January 2008, pp.42–47.

Miller, Laurence. "Police Officer Suicide: Recognizing the Signs and Helping Our Colleagues in Distress." *PoliceOne.com News*, May 16, 2007.

Morash, Merry; Haarr, Robin; and Kwak, Dae-Hoon. "Multilevel Influences on Police Stress." *Journal of Contemporary Criminal Justice*, February 2006, pp.26–43.

Murray, Ken. "The Will to Live: Surviving the Emotional Pain behind the Badge." *Law Officer Magazine*, September 2008, pp.64–66.

National Law Enforcement Officers Memorial Fund. *Law Enforcement Officer Deaths: Preliminary 2009.* Research Bulletin. Washington, DC: National Law Enforcement Memorial Fund, December 2009. http://www.nleomf.org/assets/images/reports/law_enforcement_officer_fatalities_2009_end_year_report.pdf

"New Study Yields Best Profile Yet of Suicide-by-Cop Offenders and Their Threat." *Force Science News*, Transmission #126, July 3, 2009.

Novesky, Pat. "Policing Rural America: Lone Officer Vehicle Contacts." *PoliceOne.com News*, May 22, 2009.

Officer Work Hours, Stress and Fatigue. Washington, DC: National Institute of Justice, 2009. http://www.ojp.usdoj.gov/nij/topics/law-enforcement/stress-fatigue/welcome.htm

Oldham, Scott. "The Fat Farm." *Law and Order*, November 2009, pp.10–12.

Orrick, W. Dwayne. "Improving Officer Resiliency." In *Police Chiefs Desk Reference: A Guide for Newly Appointed Police Leaders*, 2nd ed., edited by International Association of Chiefs of Police and U.S. Bureau of Justice Assistance. Boston: McGraw-Hill Learning Solutions, 2008, p.191.

Page, Douglas. "Death Notification: Breaking the Bad News." *Law Enforcement Technology*, March 2008, pp.18–25.

Perin, Michelle. "The Health in Hobbies." *Law Enforcement Technology*, October 2009, pp.46–53.

"*PoliceOne* Poll: What Is Your Biggest Pet Peeve about Police Work?" *PoliceOne Member News*, March 16, 2009. http://www.policeone.com/polls/1354587-What-is-your-biggest-pet-peeve-about-police-work/

Remsberg, Charles. "10-8: Life on the Line." *PoliceOne.com News*, May 19, 2008.

Selye, Hans. *The Stress of Life.* New York: McGraw-Hill, 1956.

Senjo, Scott R., and Dhungana, Karla. "A Field Data Examination of Policy Constructs Related to Fatigue Conditions in Law Enforcement Personnel." *Police Quarterly*, June 2009, pp.123–136.

Sexton, David. "Sleep Inertia and Callouts." *Law and Order*, April 2008, pp.56–57.

Shelton, Donald E. "The CSI Effect: Does It Really Exist?" *NIJ Journal*, March 2008. (NCJ 221501)

Slahor, Stephenie. "Not Enough Sleep Is Dangerous." *Law and Order*, April 2008, pp.58–64.

Temple-Raston, Dina. "Call for Forensics Overhaul Linked to 'CSI' Effect." National Public Radio, February 19, 2009. http://www.npr.org/templates/story/story.php?storyId=100831831

Vila, Bryan. "Sleep Deprivations: What Does It Mean for Public Safety Officers?" National Institute of Justice, March 27, 2009.

Violanti, John M. "Study Concludes Police Work Is a Health Hazard." *American Police Beat*, November 2002.

Weiss, Jim, and Davis, Mickey. "Establishing a Chaplaincy Program." *Law and Order*, April 2008, pp.81–86.

Yates, Travis. "Police Driver Fatigue: 'Our Dirty Little Secret.'" *PoliceOne.com News*, March 28, 2008.

Deploying Law Enforcement Resources and Improving Productivity

The deployment of police strength both by time and area is essential.

—Basic Tenet of the Peelian Reform Act of 1829

DO YOU KNOW?

- How area assignments are determined?
- How patrol size is determined?
- Why rapid response may be important?
- What basic premise underlies random patrol?
- What the Kansas City study of preventive patrol found?
- What methods of patrol might be used?
- What the crime triangle is?
- How to most effectively channel resources to fight crime?
- What predisaster plans should include?
- What the strategic goals of the Department of Homeland Security include?
- What the first line of defense against terrorism is?
- How law enforcement productivity can be measured?
- How law enforcement productivity has traditionally been measured?
- How law enforcement productivity may be improved?
- What the single most important factor in high productivity and morale is?

CAN YOU DEFINE?

aggressive patrol
civilianization
cone of resolution
crime triangle
hot spots
lag time
management information system
    (MIS)
productivity
proportionate assignment
quota
random patrol
shift
triage
watch

INTRODUCTION

Law enforcement agencies exist for a purpose—to fulfill a specific mission. Management, in conjunction with line personnel, sets forth this mission and the requirements for accomplishing it. Missions mean little without action, and in most businesses, including law enforcement, that means schedules. The link between mission and schedules is illustrated in Figure 13.1.

The sergeants, lieutenants and captains convey the department's mission to those who will accomplish it. A key middle-management function is determining allocation of personnel. The characteristic that distinguishes law enforcement personnel allocation from most business and industrial situations is the manner in which tasks are generated. In most non–law enforcement situations, the tasks to be performed are known in advance, and the number of people required to complete them is easily determined. For example, if a shoe manufacturing plant needs to produce 10,000 pairs of shoes next week to meet orders, the number of people needed to produce them can be determined.

Some law enforcement tasks are also predictable. For example, escorting distinguished visitors or maintaining order along a parade route are services known ahead of time. Most law enforcement tasks, however, can be predicted only in terms of the likelihood of their occurring at a specific time and place. Such tasks make up the bulk of law enforcement work and are the basis of the personnel allocation problem.

CHAPTER at a GLANCE

This chapter begins by examining the key management function of deploying personnel, including how the response to calls for service is most effectively handled. Next is a look at the various kinds and methods of patrol currently in use. Then ways the law enforcement personnel pool might be expanded are discussed, including involving citizens. Next is a discussion of deploying resources to fight crime, for emergencies and to enhance homeland security. The discussion then turns to an examination of law enforcement productivity, and the chapter concludes with a return to previous discussions of leadership, discipline, motivation and morale as they relate to productivity.

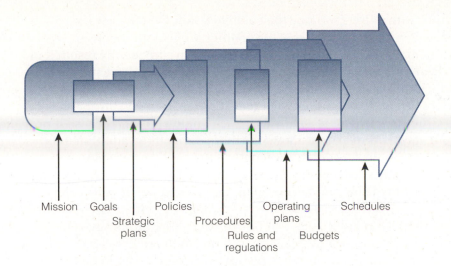

FIGURE 13.1

How Plans Interlock: From Missions to Schedules

Source: Lester R. Bittel. *The McGraw-Hill 36-Hour Management Course.* New York: McGraw-Hill Publishing Company, 1989, p.77. Reprinted by permission.

Mission   Goals   Policies   Operating plans   Schedules

Strategic plans   Procedures

Rules and regulations   Budgets

DEPLOYING PERSONNEL

The largest division in any law enforcement agency is the uniformed patrol unit, which provides services 24/7. Other specialized divisions, such as investigations, narcotics and juvenile, have fewer officers and often provide services for only portions of the day. Specialized personnel are assigned by demand based on frequency of incidents and cases requiring a specific service. Patrol is typically scheduled based on an analysis of service call data.

Police Logs

When managers analyze service call data, they can easily observe variations in how patrol officers are being deployed. Personnel assignment should match those variations as much as possible. Time logs provide information for studying the types of incidents that occur and how to assign personnel where they are needed most. The logs need not be complicated. They can simply list requests for services, time, nature of the request and time the incident was completed. However, it is becoming increasingly more common for departments to use computer software programs for such analysis.

The ideal work schedule does not exist. Among the variables affecting scheduling are staffing shortages caused by illness, injury, vacations, training and court time. Nonetheless, managers must schedule personnel to accomplish the department's mission. Again, software programs now make this once labor-intensive juggling act a thing of the past in most departments. Scheduling software streamlines the process of making shift assignments, and can manage related tasks such as tracking time off, sick time, vacation time and requests, assigning and managing overtime, tracking training hours, ensuring adequate coverage, and making special duty assignments (Mills-Senn, 2008, p.62).

Shifts

A **shift** is simply the time span to which personnel are assigned. Some departments call it a **watch**. Traditionally patrol was divided into three 8-hour

shift or watch

time span to which personnel are assigned.

shifts, with officers working their assigned shift five days a week, with two days off, much like the work schedule of other professions. In recent years 10- and 12-hour shifts have become common and have frequently resulted in higher officer satisfaction and easier scheduling. Ultimately, departments must select which shift plan makes the best use of available resources to meet the community's demands and the agency's goals.

The *10-hour shift* is an attractive scheduling option because it provides a four-day workweek and allows for more days off (52 additional days a year) than do 8-hour schedules. The length of the workdays are more tolerable than 12-hour shifts, and the staggered 10-hour shifts increase the number of officers on duty while the shifts overlap. These overlapping shifts can be matched to the periods of greatest activity on the streets, better matching coverage to workload. Ten-hour shifts can be effective in maintaining proper coverage around the clock while reducing overtime, eliminating overstaffing and ensuring acceptable service levels: "A tactical advantage to the 10-hour shift plan [is] that it provides regular shift overlapping that can be used for training, power shifts or scheduling flexibility to reduce overtime" (Solar, 2009a). However, from an efficiency standpoint, 10-hour shifts are the most costly to implement among the 8-, 10-, and 12-hour shift options (Solar, 2009a).

The *12-hour shift* is gaining popularity among officers and managers alike because it allows for nearly 80 more days off each year and has been shown to reduce overtime costs by nearly 25 percent (Solar, 2009a). Rank-and-file officers have been particularly receptive to 12-hour shift plans because such schedules often provide a more favorable work-life balance, which can lead to greater job satisfaction and higher departmental morale (Sundermeier, 2008). The primary concern with 12-hours shifts is officer fatigue, which can be damaging to officer safety and lead to a host of other problems, as discussed in Chapter 12. Although officer fatigue is not an inevitable consequence of 12-hour shifts because fatigue resistance and susceptibility varies by officer, managers who adopt extended shift plans must be vigilant to the possible effects of fatigue and adjust departmental policies and procedures accordingly.

Some police administrators are recognizing the benefits of allowing officers to take short naps during long shifts. This recharge period can help maintain officer alertness and effectiveness: "Officer fatigue should be a concern to all police managers—a risk-management issue as daunting as the use of force. Fatigue is not something inherent in the 12-hour shift plan. It will be present whenever officers endure surprise overtime assignments, rotate shifts frequently or when departments are chronically understaffed. Transition to an extended shift plan presents an opportunity for innovation to combat fatigue, including mandatory downtime (power naps), alternative shift assignments for those not well-suited to the long hours and flexible schedules" (Solar, 2009b).

Many departments rotate shifts and area assignments or both. The three general shift rotation options are nonrotating, forward (with the clock) and backward (against the clock). Not rotating remains a popular option because almost any change in daily sleep routines tends to increase fatigue. Backward shift rotation is the hardest to adapt to because the body's circadian rhythm is slightly predisposed to rotating forward. Frequent shift rotations (those occurring more often than every 12 weeks) and disruptions to shift schedules also cause adaptation problems and decrease officer effectiveness (Solar, 2009b).

Yet many police administrators consider shift rotation an important way to fight stagnation within the organization and to outfit officers with an understanding of how to function on various shifts because the shifts are all very different.

Some departments simply divide personnel into three equal shifts, but this is seldom effective. Rarely should personnel be equal on all shifts. Assignment of personnel by day of week and determining days off should be based on data. Assignments must maintain a balance between actual needs and the effects of some assignments on morale. Because computers allow rapid statistical data to be developed, personnel changes can be made at any time from one area to the other, resulting in proportionate assignment.

Proportionate Assignment

 Area assignments are determined by requests for services based on available data. This is called proportionate assignment. No area should be larger than the time it takes a car to respond to emergency calls in a reasonable time.

AWAY FROM THE DESK: Scheduling

As the police chief for a medium size (36 sworn personnel) department in the Midwest, I used our Scheduling Committee to develop a work schedule that would allow for 24/7 coverage, including overlapping shifts and establishing shift minimums for officer safety. The results of this effort led to 10-hour shifts, giving our officers 52 more days off per year than the traditional 8-hour shift and providing ample time off on the weekends, as well as setting a maximum of five continuous shifts before a minimum of 4 consecutive days off. Our officers get two full (4-day) weekends off per month.

The benefit to the city and community is that there are two days per rotation that are considered "All Work Days" or "Directed Work Days," which allows the department to train all of its officers consistently without paying overtime. It also allows our officers to work on community or neighborhood projects without the added responsibilities of taking calls. This work schedule allows for increased visibility in our neighborhoods as we have twice the resources available on certain days, and it keeps our officers interested by providing time and opportunity to address community problems outside the norm of traditional policing. The benefits to the taxpaying citizens are that our overtime is kept under control, we are able to train and proactively resolve issues in our community at a reasonable cost, and we are able to provide a timely response to citizens' concerns and requests for service. Further, our officers enjoy higher job satisfaction because we are not only respecting their need for time away from the job, we are providing an efficient method for service delivery in which they have a considerable amount of authority in implementing lasting solutions.

—*Chief Shaun E. LaDue*

Area boundaries should be primary arteries, if possible, to provide faster access. Patrol assignments generally follow the size of the areas to be patrolled and the frequency of requests for services in those areas.

A number of factors determine proportionate assignment. A first step is to list those items requiring time and to weigh the importance of each. For example, felonies are generally weighted heavier than misdemeanors. In recent years gang and drug offenses and related problems have required specialized personnel and increased training of regular officers. Even more recently homeland security efforts have become a priority.

 To determine patrol area size, consider square miles, street miles, amount of crime and disorder and response time.

THE RESPONSE

Two important factors managers consider when making decisions about appropriate responses to calls for service are how rapid the response should be and who should respond.

Response Time

Most statistical breakdowns provide information on patrol areas and response times. A federal study released in the 1960s stated that a response time of one minute or less was needed to increase arrests at crime scenes. Few law enforcement departments can guarantee a response time of less than three minutes on all calls for service. Reasons other than on-scene arrests, however, also require rapid response.

 A response as rapid yet as safe as possible builds public confidence in law enforcement capabilities and competence. It also places officers at the scene to protect evidence before people or the elements destroy it. Rapid response increases the chances of locating witnesses and making arrests. Further, it increases the chances of providing lifesaving emergency first aid to crime victims.

Other considerations in response time are barriers to patrol such as ditches, hills, water, number of officers available, total patrol area size, types of offenses, and types and quantity of service requests. Safety is of utmost importance. The response should not pose a more significant threat to society than does the incident to be investigated.

An even more important factor than police response time is the time between the occurrence of the incident and the report to the police, commonly referred to as **lag time**, over which police have no control. Another time factor important to total response is the time between when the dispatcher receives the call and dispatches it to a patrol car. Perhaps the most important factor, however, is citizen expectation.

lag time

time elapsed between the occurrence of an incident and it being reported to the police; often more important than response time.

The Kansas City Response Time Analysis study found that a large proportion of crimes were not discovered until some time after they occurred and were therefore unaffected by rapid police response. The Police Executive Research Forum (PERF) replicated the Kansas City study over three years and confirmed the findings. This information is the basis for many agencies using differentiated response.

Differentiated Response

It is only logical that the type of call influences the response. After a literature review and a survey of more than 200 police departments serving jurisdictions of more than 100,000, a group of police practitioners and researchers were charged with developing a model for police response to citizen calls for service. The result was the Differential Police Response Strategies model, which consists of three key components:

- A set of characteristics to define an incident type
- A time factor to identify the relationship between the time the incident occurred and the time the police received the call
- A full range of response strategies, going from an immediate response by a sworn officer to no response, with numerous alternatives in between.

KINDS OF PATROL

Patrol officers are often engaged in either random preventive patrol or directed aggressive patrol.

Random Preventive Patrol

During preventive patrol, officers frequently establish a pattern, which can become known to criminals and used to their advantage. To overcome this potential problem, many departments use **random patrol**, that is, computer-generated, unpredictable patrol routes. Criminals may think once an area has been patrolled, it will not be patrolled again, but this is not necessarily true.

> **random patrol**
>
> officers on patrol are unsystematically (randomly) assigned areas to cover.

 The basic premise of random patrol is to place officers closer to any potential incident or request for service before it happens, based on data provided by experience, but without any predictable pattern. Goals are to provide a police presence, observe suspicious activity and reduce response time.

Randomizing schedules is important to avoid the vulnerability that results from predictability (Page, 2009, p.76). A game theory–based randomizing scheme called Assistant for Randomized Monitoring Over Routes, or ARMOR, uses advanced mathematical algorithms to assist police in anticipating future criminal behavior based on the analysis of past behavior, while randomizing police behavior to lessen or eliminate predictability of deployments and operations (Page).

The Kansas City Preventive Patrol Experiment

Although the Kansas City Preventive Patrol Experiment was conducted more than 35 years ago (1972), it remains the most comprehensive study of preventive patrol. The experiment divided 15 beats in Kansas City into three groups, each having five beats:

Group 1—Reactive beats: no preventive patrol, responding only to calls for service

Group 2—Control beats: maintained their normal level of preventive patrol

Group 3—Proactive beats: doubled or tripled the level of preventive patrol

 The Kansas City Preventive Patrol Experiment found that increasing or decreasing routine preventive patrol had no effect on crime, citizen fear of crime, community attitudes toward the police on delivery of police services, police response time or traffic accidents (Klockars, 1983, p.160).

Klockars' (1983, p.130) conclusion: "It makes about as much sense to have police patrol routinely in cars to fight crime as it does to have firemen patrol routinely in fire trucks to fight fire."

Research has found that, on average, more than three quarters of a patrol officer's shift is unassigned (Famega et al., 2005). During this time most officers patrol routinely or back up other officers on calls to which they were not dispatched. Only 6 percent of unassigned time was directed by supervisors, dispatchers, other officers or citizens. When supervisors did provide directives, they were often vague and general, not proactive, problem oriented or community policing oriented. Two conclusions are drawn from these findings: (1) a significant proportion of patrol officer time is spent uncommitted and could be better used doing proactive, problem-oriented policing activities, and (2) supervisors need to provide much more detailed directives, based on sound crime analysis, to capitalize on the underutilization of patrol officer time (Famega et al., p.540). This implies that officers' activities should be more proactive, where police take the initiative to prevent problems, rather than being reactive and responding to calls only as they come in.

Although proactive activities are often associated with community policing and reactive activities with traditional or "professional" policing, this is a common misconception. In reality, both policing models engage in both kinds of activities. An analysis of the time allocated to proactive and reactive activities by traditional (post) and community police officers found that traditional officers had time to engage in proactive activities even though they are primarily for responding to calls for service; 50 percent of their time is spent on proactive activities, 29 percent engaged in administrative and personal activities, and 21 percent on reactive activities (Famega, 2009, pp.97–101). Traditional officers spend more time than community officers engaged in proactive patrol and backing up other officers. They spend less time than community officers engaged in proactive crime-related activities and order maintenance,

Many agencies are looking for ways to stretch limited resources, cut fuel costs and deploy more "eco-friendly" patrol methods. Here, officers of the South Pasadena (California) Police Department patrol on their electric-powered T3 personal transporters.

© Michael Newman/PhotoEdit

service and traffic activities. Traditional officers spend time on several order-maintenance activities that community officers do not: surveillance of people and juvenile disturbances (aggressive order-maintenance strategies), domestic arguments or family trouble, and casual conversations. Both traditional and community officers are likely to also use directed aggressive patrol.

Directed Aggressive Patrol

Rather than driving around randomly, officers might concentrate on locations where high numbers of crashes are occurring, areas of the beat with the highest incidences of crime or calls for service, and critical infrastructures that are potential targets for terrorists. **Aggressive patrol** focuses on preventing and detecting crime by focusing attention on problem areas and by investigating suspicious activity.

The premise behind aggressive patrol is that through purposeful contact with individuals, officers will build an intelligence base of information regarding who lives and works on their beat, where problems are occurring and possible reasons for the problems. An application of such patrol is aggressive traffic enforcement of suspicious vehicles (those driving at night without headlights, speeding or weaving through traffic), which often leads to arrests. Criminals use America's highways as escape routes, as a place to find victims, and as a way to traffic drugs, guns, stolen property and cash.

In addition to differing kinds of patrol that might be used, departments have a variety of methods of patrol from which to select.

aggressive patrol
focuses on preventing and detecting crime by investigating suspicious activity; also called *proactive patrol*.

METHODS OF PATROL

Given the wide range of circumstances encountered during patrol, a variety of patrol methods have been devised. The most common remains automobile patrol. Table 13.1 provides a summary of patrol methods.

TABLE 13.1 Summary of Patrol Methods

Method	Uses	Advantages	Disadvantages
Foot	Highly congested areas Burglary, robbery, theft, purse snatching, mugging	Close citizen contact High visibility Develop informants	Relatively expensive Limited mobility
Automobile	Respond to service calls Provide traffic control Transport individuals, documents and equipment	Most economical Greatest mobility and flexibility Offers means of communication Provides means of transporting people, documents and equipment	Limited access to certain areas Limited citizen contact
Motorcycle	Same as automobile, except that it can't be used for transporting individuals and has limited equipment	Maneuverability in congested areas and areas restricted to automobiles	Inability to transport much equipment Not used during bad weather Hazardous to operator
Bicycle	Stakeouts Parks and beaches Congested areas	Quiet and unobtrusive	Limited speed
Mounted	Parks and bridle paths Crowd control Traffic control	Size and maneuverability of horse	Expensive
Air	Surveillance Traffic control Searches and rescues	Covers large areas easily	Expensive
Water	Deter smuggling Water traffic control Rescues	Access to activities occurring on water	Expensive
Special-terrain	Patrol unique areas inaccessible to other forms Rescue operations	Access to normally inaccessible areas	Limited use in some areas
Segway scooter	Same as foot, but faster and less tiring	Close citizen contact, high visibility, quiet and maneuverable	Limited access to certain areas, not used during bad weather

Source: From HESS. *Introduction to Law Enforcement and Criminal Justice*, 9th edition. © 2009 Delmar Learning, a part of Cengage Learning, Inc. Reproduced by permission. www.cengage.com/permissions

Common methods of patrol include automobile, bicycle, motorcycle and foot patrol. Other methods include air, mounted, water, special-terrain and Segway patrol.

Managers may need to consider several issues involving automobile patrol, namely whether to use one-officer or two-officer patrol units and whether the department should implement a take-home policy for squad cars.

One-Officer versus Two-Officer Patrol Units

Officer safety is at the core of the argument favoring two-officer patrol units, which also make a shift less boring and provide a chance for officers to develop working relationships. However, officer productivity and operational efficiency are increased using one-officer patrol units. If two officers are needed, two squads can be sent on a call.

Using one-officer units with appropriate delay procedures for another car to arrive at a scene is an effective administrative and budgeting procedure. The use of electronic patrol vehicle locators can enhance officer safety in a one-officer unit. Such locators are also of great value in deploying patrol personnel.

The one-officer unit offers several advantages, including cost-effectiveness in that the same number of officers can patrol twice the area, with twice the mobility, and with twice the power of observation. In addition, officers working alone are generally more cautious in dangerous situations, recognizing that they have no backup. Officers working alone also are generally more attentive to patrol duties because they do not have a conversational partner. The expense of two cars compared with one, however, is a factor.

Experiments by the Police Foundation using both types of unit staffing in a large city police department revealed that officers in two-officer units were more likely to be assaulted by a citizen, be injured in the line of duty and have a suspect resist arrest. Studies that have looked at the frequency of assaults and injuries to patrol officers have upheld these findings that single-officer units tend to be safer.

Some districts may require two-officer units and, under specific instances and for short periods, more than two. Sometimes union contracts dictate that two-officer units be used, which can seriously hinder management as it plans for the most effective deployment of personnel.

Take-Home Patrol Cars

Another controversial area is whether officers should be allowed to take their patrol cars home. Allowing officers to take their patrol cars home through an assigned vehicle program (AVP) offers many advantages to officers and their agencies. These officers tend to take better care of their cars and be more responsible with them, resulting in lower maintenance and repair costs. Officers do not lose time at the beginning and ending of each shift for equipment change-out, vehicle inspections and equipment and equipment checks, which can add up to nearly 2 weeks of lost patrol time annually (Repecki, 2010). Take-home programs also increase the visibility of police officers in their neighborhoods. One of the biggest advantages is that officers with take-home cars are readily deployed to critical incidents while off duty.

Take-home car programs are not without disadvantages, however. While the officer is off duty, the car is not in service, necessitating a much larger vehicle fleet. Also of concern is the security of the car and its contents. Take-home vehicles can also draw unwanted attention to where officers live (Lauria, 2007, p.193).

INVOLVING CITIZENS WHILE EXPANDING THE LAW ENFORCEMENT PERSONNEL POOL

Some departments seek to improve productivity by involving citizens while expanding their personnel pool. The importance of involving citizens in making their neighborhoods safer has long been recognized: "Sustaining a crime reduction requires a critical mass of community involvement" (Kelling, 2008, p.5). An example is seen in the steepness and persistence of the decline of crime in New York City (NYC) as a result of the fervent pursuit of self-interest by a critical mass of public and private agencies operating out of a congruent understanding of the nature of the problems. When joined by the New York Police Department (NYPD) under the leadership of Commissioner William J. Bratton, this critical mass reached a tipping point. This critical mass is needed to reach a tipping point that can change a city's culture. In the case of NYC, the largest influence on the reduction in crime was arguably the implementation of CompStat policing (Kelling, p.6). In other jurisdictions, it may be the result of the implementation of community policing.

A study of the influence of community policing on citizens' crime reporting behavior found, "Although third-party police notification is more likely in cities with large numbers of full-time COP [community oriented policing] officers, victims residing in such cities are significantly less likely to report to the police than they are to report to nonpolice officials. However, in cities where the training of police officers in COP is relatively extensive, victims demonstrate a preference for police notification (relative to both non-police notification and non-reporting)" (Schnebly, 2008, p.223). Police involvement in COP was also found to have less influence on the reporting behaviors of residentially unstable victims who probably lack strong social ties to the communities in which they live, leading some researchers to conclude that COP may be most effective, perhaps *only* effective, in neighborhoods that need it least (Schnebly, p.247).

In addition to involving citizens in protecting their own neighborhoods, many agencies have used this citizen involvement to expand their personnel pool through the use of citizen police academies, citizen patrols, reserves and volunteers within the department—frequently retired individuals, including retired police officers. Another trend is the civilianization of certain law enforcement functions.

Citizen Police Academies

Several police departments seeking to implement community policing have started citizen police academies (CPAs). Since the organization of the first recorded U.S. CPA in Orlando, Florida, in 1985, many communities have developed their own academies, each with its own unique focus. Many academies also include ride-along programs for participants. The various goals of CPAs include educating citizens on the basics of the law enforcement profession, developing positive rapport between citizens and police, recruiting potential employees (both civilian and sworn), and recruiting a strong volunteer base that can stretch the resources of the police agency and increase overall productivity (Barlow et al., 2009).

A logical extension of the CPA is the Citizen Police Academy Alumni Association (CPAAA), an organization that can further deepen community relationships and leverage local volunteer resources. Often those who have participated in a CPA become active in citizen patrol.

Citizens on Patrol

In many jurisdictions community policing strategies include citizen patrols. A resource of departments interested in citizen patrols is the National Association Citizens on Patrol, founded in 1999. It now supports more than 5,000 citizen patrol volunteers in 80 cities ("National Association Citizens on Patrol," 2009).

An example of a successful endeavor is the citizen patrol operating in Fort Worth, Texas, which encourages community residents to patrol their own neighborhoods and be directly responsible for reducing crime. The program currently has more than 2,000 patrollers, representing more than 87 neighborhoods in the city.

In Delray Beach, Florida, a city with a population of 50,000, the police department's largest volunteer project is the Citizens Observer Patrol (COP), whose three primary goals are to

- Effectively reduce crime and disorder in selected communities.
- Establish a working relationship between the Delray Beach police and its citizenry.
- Empower people to take ownership of their communities to reduce crime.

The Delray Beach Citizens Observer Patrol has 850 members in 21 sectors. Crime has markedly diminished in every area.

The Guardian Angels, founded in 1979 in New York City by Curtis Sliwa, are probably the best known of the citizen patrols, having 135 chapters in 13 countries. They wear red shirts and caps and patrol the streets when asked to. They also provide educational school programs designed to prevent bullying and raise gang awareness ("Guardian Angels," 2009). The Guardian Angels have faced opposition from many police departments throughout the country, but as community policing is becoming more prevalent, they are becoming more accepted.

Reserves

Reserve officers, sometimes called part-timers, auxiliaries, specials or supernumeraries, are valuable assets to police departments in the effort to expand law enforcement resources. The number of reserve officers is increasing throughout the country as agencies use this cost-effective means to add personnel. In 2004 there were approximately 400,000 sworn law enforcement reserve officers (volunteer and paid) in the United States. Numerous benefits derive from a well-trained and equipped auxiliary force (Ferguson, 2008, p.87):

> They become additional uniformed personnel in times of need, i.e., riots, natural disasters, major exhibitions, fairs or festivals. They provide added uniformed police presence. Sometimes it is just nice for people to see marked police cars and uniformed officers any time they turn a corner. It is also nice when the bad guys see them, too.

> Auxiliary units convert a one-officer car into a two-officer unit, freeing other one-officer cars for additional calls for service in a timely manner. More

mundane tasks (prisoner transports, hospital guarding details, delivery of paperwork, etc.) can be performed by auxiliary officers, leaving a patrol unit available to continue to handle calls for service and maintaining shift strength.

Reserve officer programs vary considerably from department to department. In some jurisdictions reserve officers have powers of arrest and wear the same uniform as law enforcement officers except for the badge, which says "reserve." They may even purchase their own firearm and ballistics vest and drive their personally owned vehicles during operations. Some jurisdictions recruit reserves from those retiring from their full-time ranks. Many reserve units function in specialized roles, for example, search-and-rescue operations. Reserve officers are an effective force multiplier by performing such duties as crowd control, they free up sworn personnel for more pressing operations.

Although reserve officers are usually assigned to the patrol division, management should also consider using reserve detectives to perform such functions as assisting with property room management, evidence collection, case investigation, and researching; delivering and retrieving documents from other government agencies and from crime victims; interviewing victims; and taking notes and serving as a "gofer" at crime scenes (Webster, 2008).

Using reserves can improve productivity and help departments "do more with less," and the practice can save agencies money in most instances. For example: "In Macomb County [Michigan], Sheriff Mark Hackel said reserves put in 24,000 hours during the 2005–2006 fiscal year and said the hours worked were worth about $1.2 million to his office" (Donaldson, 2007).

Issues exist regarding the use of reserves, particularly in labor and liability concerns. To allay labor concerns, some departments have a contract with full-time officers stating that reserves are used only if a regular officer turns down the overtime or wants to take "comp" time off. To address liability issues, most agencies require reserves to complete rigorous training courses. Some, in fact, require reserves to go through the full basic academy, not accepting the reserve academy training as adequate: "Obviously, the best defense to some type of inappropriate action by a reserve officer is a proper hiring and screening program; thorough background check; psychological aptitude battery of exams, continuous, job-specific training; and continual monitoring by full-time officers with the teaching skills to train reserve officers in appropriate responses to situations" (Ferguson, 2008, p.90).

Volunteers

The three groups of law enforcement personnel just discussed—citizen police academy participants, citizen patrols and reservists—consist primarily, if not solely, of volunteers. And their numbers are increasing. Similar to reserves, volunteers supplement and enhance existing or envisioned functions, allowing law enforcement professionals to do their jobs more effectively. They can provide numerous benefits to a department, including maximizing existing resources, enhancing public safety and services, and improving community relations. Other services volunteers may provide include fingerprinting children, patrolling shopping centers, checking on homebound residents, and checking the security of vacationing residents' homes. Additional functions volunteers might perform include clerical and data support, special event planning, search and rescue assistance, grant writing, and transporting mail between substations.

Kanable (2009, p.40) describes how the Roselle (Illinois) Police Department is using volunteers to address the single greatest citizen complaint to police departments and city councils throughout the United States—speeding in residential neighborhoods. This department, like many others in the country, has enlisted the help of volunteers to run radar.

According to the Roselle chief of police, "A citizen radar program is an excellent community-oriented policing tool to establish collaboration between the police and the residents to solve a neighborhood quality-of-life problem." In the Citizen Assisted Radar Enforcement (CARE) Program, volunteers are issued a radar unit and taught to use it. They then monitor vehicles' speed and time on a log sheet. If they see a violation, they document the vehicle's description and license plate number. Usually letters are then mailed to the registered owners advising them of the observed violation. The volunteers don't issue tickets or appear in court, but the letters send a strong message to speeders, many of whom live in the neighborhood. In addition to local programs enlisting the aid of volunteers, national programs exist to help departments set up and maintain volunteer programs.

Founded in 2002 as a result of the September 11, 2001 (9/11), attacks, Citizen Corps entails several programs and partners to give citizens the chance to get involved in an initiative helping to make communities across America safer, stronger and better prepared for emergencies of all kinds. Coordinated nationally by the Department of Homeland Security's Federal Emergency Management Agency (FEMA), the mission of Citizen Corps is to harness the power of every individual through education and outreach, training and volunteer services ("Citizen Corp Programs and Partners," 2009).

Also in 2002, the Volunteers in Police Service (VIPS) initiative was created as a joint effort of the U.S. Department of Justice and the International Association of Chiefs of Police in partnership with Citizen Corps. The VIPS program works to enhance the capacity of state and local law enforcement to use volunteers and serves as a gateway to resources and information for and about law enforcement volunteer programs. To date, more than 1,980 law enforcement volunteer programs, representing more than 225,000 volunteers, have registered with the program ("VIPS Registered Program Analysis Results," 2009).

Another program of Citizen Corps is the Community Emergency Response Team (CERT) program, also managed by the Department of Homeland Security and created to provide opportunities for individuals to assist their communities in emergency preparation through volunteering. CERT educates citizens about disaster preparedness for hazards that may affect their area and trains them in basic disaster response skills, such as fire safety, light search and rescue, team organization, and disaster medical operations. Today there are more than 1,100 CERT teams across the country ("Community Emergency Response Teams [CERT]," 2009).

Establishing and maintaining a volunteer program is not cost free, but the return on the investment is substantial. Effective agency-provided volunteer training and periodic refresher sessions are important in decreasing costs and liabilities and increasing the effectiveness of volunteer resources. As with the concern over using reserves, some paid, full-time officers are hesitant to embrace volunteers. To overcome staff resistance to volunteer programs, managers should emphasize that volunteers are used to make officers' jobs easier, not to take work away from them. Keeping officers on the streets is what a volunteer program is about.

Explorers

Yet another way to expand and or support sworn officers' efforts is through an Explorer program. Law Enforcement Exploring is a worksite-based program for young men and women who have completed the eighth grade and are 14 years old, or who are 15 years old but have not yet reached their 21st birthday. Explorer posts help youths gain insight into a variety of programs that offer hands-on career activities. The objectives of the program are

- To provide a program of training that educates young adults on the purpose, mission and objectives of law enforcement agencies.
- To provide an opportunity for service, practical experience, competition and recreation.
- To help Explorers become better citizens and community members through character development, physical fitness, good citizenship and patriotism ("Law Enforcement Exploring," 2009).

Several approaches are used to achieve the objectives, including meetings and ride-alongs. Most departments provide extensive training in personal conduct, first aid, police procedures, weapons familiarization, crime scene investigation, traffic control, interpersonal communication, criminal law and specialized police duties.

Civilianization

civilianization

hiring citizens to perform certain tasks for law enforcement agencies.

Civilianization, which has been occurring during the past 40 years, is the hiring of nonsworn personnel to replace or augment the work of sworn police officers. Civilians have typically been employed in such functions as dispatch, forensic services, planning and research, budget and finance, information systems, legal counsel, jail/corrections, human resources and public information.

Civilianization is a cost-effective way to make use of the numerous and varied capabilities of citizens, while freeing up law enforcement personnel to concentrate their efforts on tasks they have been specifically trained for. Many routine functions performed by officers do not require their expertise or their special authority and arrest powers. Animal-control officers, dispatchers, jailers and others might be civilians, rather than sworn peace officers. One function glamorized by television programs is that of the crime scene investigator, who may or may not be a sworn law enforcement officer.

The economic crisis facing the entire country has resulted in police department budget cuts that tend to eliminate civilian jobs in policing, a "de-civilianization" of policing that some see as a big step backward (Wexler, 2009, p.2):

Today many departments use civilians to help drive some of their most significant initiatives in areas such as administration, research, technologies, human resources, finance, grant-writing and crime analysis. These civilians have earned the respect of other command staff and are an integral part of a chief's management team.

These civilians have tremendous depths of knowledge about the jobs that they do.

And what will happen when civilian positions are eliminated, as most chiefs will tell you, is that the work that was done by these civilians will not go undone. Chiefs will end up taking officers or command-level personnel off the street and putting them where civilians were. . . . This can be a false economy. It can be terribly inefficient and counterproductive to put police officers in areas that demand skills that are not related to the officers' core competencies.

In one case, a city let go a lower-level civilian clerk who kept crime statistics, and the city wound up being late in turning in its crime figures to the FBI, which cost the city millions of dollars in Byrne grant funding. . . .

To paraphrase Jim Collins' book *Good to Great*, we have come too far in "getting the right people in the right seats on the bus" to go back to a time when civilians weren't even allowed on the bus.

Having looked at various ways departments have involved citizens in an attempt to improve productivity and conserve resources, consider how specific reasons personnel might be deployed beyond general patrol.

DEPLOYING RESOURCES TO FIGHT CRIME

Many individuals in law enforcement and probably most of the citizens they serve consider crime fighting as a primary responsibility of their agency. Advances in technology have enhanced these efforts, especially advances in crime analysis, such as mapping crime.

Mapping Crime

Law enforcement's ability to understand the extent of crime and its patterns is continuously evolving, and with it has come an enhanced capacity for police to tailor their response to suit a community's specific crime problems. Crime tends to cluster, forming **hot spots** in certain geographic areas. Hot spots are found at the neighborhood level, which helps local law enforcement allocate patrols to areas most in need of a police presence. Individual commanders should be given expanded responsibility, authority and discretion to assign officers to hot spots where the most criminal activity is occurring (Grossi, 2008).

Networks and their associated databases have also allowed law enforcement to expand their use of geographic information systems (GIS) beyond crime mapping, enabling them to use generic Web browsers, or Intranets, to share information and resources more rapidly and cost-effectively. In addition,

hot spots
specific locations with high crime rates.

CompStat has been successfully implemented in several major metropolitan jurisdictions throughout the country, as discussed in Chapter 2.

The Crime Triangle

One tool to help law enforcement tackle crime through problem solving is the crime triangle, shown in Figure 13.2. The basis for the crime triangle is Cohen and Felson's Routine Activities Theory, which proposes that crime occurs at the intersection, in time and space, of motivated offenders and suitable victims (or targets), under circumstances of absent or inadequate guardianship. Crime is presumed amenable to suppression if any of the three legs of the triangle is removed or neutralized.

---

crime triangle

a model illustrating how all three elements—motivated offender, suitable victim and adequate location—are required for crime to occur.

 The **crime triangle** is a model that illustrates how all three elements—motivated offender, suitable victim and adequate location—are required for a crime to occur.

One side of the crime triangle, the offender, is most often the focus of crime-fighting efforts.

Focus on Criminals

Just as managers are beginning to tap into the resources of their community, they are also beginning to do more partnering with other agencies to apprehend criminals. A prime example of such a partnership is that between the Metro-Dade Police Department in Miami and the Bureau of Alcohol, Tobacco and Firearms (ATF), Miami District Office. The program is called Project Achilles because they target career criminals who are known to possess firearms. This possession of firearms makes them vulnerable, putting them within

FIGURE 13.2
The Crime Triangle

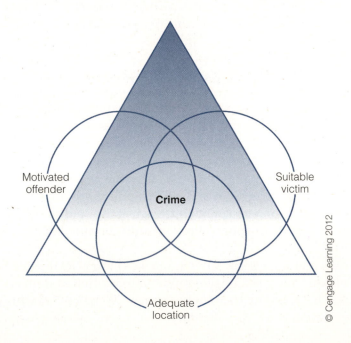

© Cengage Learning 2012

both the state and the federal criminal justice system. The program grew out of studies that indicate that 6 percent of the criminals arrested commit as much as 70 percent of all serious crime. Recidivists account for most crime in society. Intelligence-led and predictive policing extends the application of technology by using data to enter into the decision cycle of offenders, thus affording a degree of anticipation or prediction as to where crime might occur next (Beck and McCue, 2009).

Focusing on career criminals is a logical approach to fighting crime. Equally promising in crime-fighting efforts is a focus on high-crime locations.

Focus on Location

In the crime triangle, location is a critical element. Some criminal justice researchers and practitioners have begun to focus on *places* where offenses occur, identifying *hot spots*, a term borrowed from geology to designate a region of potentially volatile geologic, or volcanic, activity. A hot spot can be a single address, a cluster of addresses, part of a block, an entire block or two or an intersection. To organize data about crime over time at various levels of analysis, criminologists have applied the concept of the **cone of resolution** (Figure 13.3), this time borrowing from geography.

Another way of viewing location as an element of crime causation is to consider incivilities, or signs of disorder. Wilson and Kelling's classic brokenwindow" theory suggested that such incivilities lead to higher crime rates, victimization rates and residents' perception of the fear of crime. A focus on the third side of the crime triangle—the victims and reducing their suitability as targets—brings community policing into the scene.

cone of resolution

narrowing in on the geographic locations of crime.

DEPLOYING RESOURCES IN EMERGENCIES

During normal deployment, law enforcement managers have time to use statistics and studied judgment to determine allocation requirements, but during emergencies, present circumstances and experience largely dictate which

FIGURE 13.3
The Cone of Resolution

Source: Ralph B. Taylor. "Crime and Small-Scale Places: What We Know, What We Can Prevent, and What Else We Need to Know." In Taylor et al. *Crime and Place: Plenary Papers of the 1997 Conference on Criminal Justice Research and Evaluation*, July 1998, p.2.

Time

Regions

Communities

Hot Spots within Communities

personnel are deployed. Results depend on what managers in the field decide during those first minutes at the scene. Such actions should not be spontaneous but rather should be based on carefully formulated plans ahead of time: "As the saying goes, 'Failing to plan is planning to fail.' You must plan now to succeed later. Your department's disaster plans can help your community, businesses and institutions get up and running again and can aid those directly affected by the disaster. Good disaster planning also can save money because people are prepared to respond effectively" (Slahor, 2009, p.32).

Law enforcement managers must be trained in emergency procedures, including medical emergencies, earthquakes, tornados, hurricanes, flooding, radioactive waste accidents, hostage taking, bomb threats, terrorist attacks, aircraft crashes, large fires, gas leaks, riots or other large crowd disturbances and snipers. Managers must be familiar with civil emergency preparedness plans and the availability of assistance locally and from other agencies. Managers must be aware of the availability of emergency equipment and the location of area hospitals and rescue squads. This information should be condensed into written predisaster plans.

Predisaster Plans

Unfortunately, many managers place emergency planning as a low priority, thinking that such emergencies are unlikely to happen in their jurisdiction. But they could, and when they do, most citizens expect their law enforcement agencies to alert them, deal with it and keep them informed.

Predisaster plans should include the following:
- **Which emergencies to prepare for**
- **What must be done in advance (supplies on hand, agreements with other agencies, etc.)**
- **What specific functions must be performed during the emergency and who is responsible for performing them, including outside organizations and agencies that might help**
- **What steps need to be taken to restore order after an emergency has ended**
- **How to evaluate the response**

A comprehensive disaster plan should include lists, check-off/timetable guide, building plans/blueprints, maps, diagrams, shut-down procedures, and resource lists of help available in the community, who to contact to get that help, and other mutual aid and regional assistance (Slahor, 2009, p.33). Personnel should be designated by job position, not name, stating what each position entails. Alternates should be designated and volunteers and reserve officers should be included. An official spokesperson (and alternate) should be designated for media contact. The plan should be made by top management in conjunction with those who would be involved in implementing it, including government officials, fire department personnel, health care personnel and so on.

Many jurisdictions use a three-level approach, with *Level 1* for minor events that can usually be handled by on-duty personnel. *Level 2* is for moderate-to-severe situations requiring aid from other agencies and perhaps other jurisdictions. *Level 3* is for catastrophes in which a state of emergency is proclaimed, and county, state and perhaps federal assistance is requested. In such instances the National Guard may be called. The emergency plan should identify the levels of emergencies that might occur and the level of response required. Increasingly, law enforcement agencies across the country are devising and implementing Incident Command Systems (ICSs) to coordinate their emergency response.

Managers should have predisaster plans and *practice* them and should be familiar with establishing command posts, furnishing information to the press and obtaining intelligence information on which they can make decisions. Accurate information is needed to know whether to evacuate, provide extra security, treat injured people, prevent looting, put up barricades or redirect traffic. Most law enforcement departments have experienced managers who have been involved in similar incidents. No fixed rules will serve in every situation, but there are guidelines. A great deal of independent decision making occurs in these moments. Law enforcement decision makers must be prepared for short, intense incidents or long-term sieges involving many hours. A unified command structure should include all departments within the jurisdiction responsible for critical services, including law enforcement, fire, emergency medical services, power and gas, streets or highways departments, water services, sewer, the city manager and the media. Managers should also be familiar with federal assistance available for emergency planning and response.

Available Assistance

The National Incident Management System (NIMS), introduced in Chapter 3, can also be of assistance in planning for and responding to emergencies. Mutual aid agreements are a key component of the NIMS and must be updated regularly so that officers know exactly what they have the authority to do. Mutual aid agreements are comprehensive, formalized, far-reaching formal arrangements to sharing resources and services during periods of natural or manmade disasters. Such sharing during unusual circumstances is far more efficient and cost effective than having overlapping and duplicative services in each jurisdiction that may be infrequently or sparsely used.

Another source of assistance in emergencies is FEMA, whose mission is to reduce loss of life and property and protect our nation's critical infrastructure from all types of hazards through a comprehensive, risk-based, emergency management program of mitigation, preparedness, response and recovery. On March 1, 2003, FEMA became part of the Department of Homeland Security with three strategic goals:

1. Protect lives and preventing the loss of property from natural and technological hazards.

2. Reduce human suffering and enhance the recovery of communities after disaster strikes.

3. Ensure that the public is served in a timely and efficient manner ("About FEMA," 2009).

FEMA recommends communities address the following functions in disaster plans: (1) communication, (2) transportation, (3) public works, (4) firefighting, (5) intelligence efforts to assess damage, (6) mass care for those people displaced from their homes, (7) resource support (contracting for the labor needed to assist in a disaster), (8) health and medical, (9) search and rescue, (10) hazardous materials, (11) food or feeding and (12) energy. Communication should be the number one priority ("About FEMA," 2009).

Some emergencies can, and should, be anticipated, as was the case with Hurricane Katrina. In such instances the prep work may start slowly, with line officers making mental notes of the personnel gear they will need while middle management starts thinking about scenarios and contingencies, recognizing that the primary mission during the first 72 hours will be search and rescue but that officers will be expected to provide law enforcement and humanitarian services as needed. Furthermore, every level of the organization has a different function that depends on the levels above and below.

Responding to an Emergency

The first law enforcement manager at the scene must take control, regardless of rank. Stalling for a manager of higher rank to take over could be fatal to people who need evacuation or rescue or to people being threatened. Normally, time is on the side of law enforcement in criminal or hostage situations. Subterfuge to gain time is important. Direct confrontation should be avoided unless it is the last resort. Each incident of this type has individual elements to consider, and no matter how many incidents an officer has been called on to resolve, a surprise element usually requires a considered, different decision.

Triage

triage

rapidly, systematically and effectively sorting victims in a multiple casualty incident.

All first responders must be trained in **triage**, rapidly, systematically, and effectively sorting victims in a multiple casualty incident (MCI). A four-level sorting system, sometimes color-coded, that is commonly used is (Dickinson, 2009, p.54):

1. *Minor:* The "walking wounded," who may help treat and move more seriously injured victims.

2. *Delayed:* May have serious injuries and require aid, but are not at a high risk of death from those injuries.

3. *Immediate:* Require immediate medical assessment, intervention and transport for survival.

4. *Deceased:* Already dead or expected to die given the available resources.

Triaging can help calm and bring order to a chaotic situations. Knowing the triage system used by local emergency medical services (EMS) providers can make patient care more effective and efficient, prevent confusion in the transporting of victims, and help eliminate hostility between the police and EMS over who should be treated and transported first (Dickinson, 2009, p.55).

Technological Aids

A variety of technological devices are helping law enforcement better cope with resource deployment during and following emergencies. For example, in the hurricane-vulnerable region of the Florida Keys, rugged PC mobile laptop computers were used by sheriff's deputies during an evacuation to help with radio time, security-sensitive data and prioritizing who needed to be evacuated from the barrier island chain first. PDAs can put everything officers need in the palms of their hands, including computer-aided dispatch information, while away from their cruisers.

Another technological aid that helps law enforcement handle medical emergencies is the automated external defibrillator (AED). Because medical research has shown that as many as half of all sudden cardiac arrest (SCA) deaths could be prevented with early defibrillation, and officers commonly arrive on the scene of an SCA before paramedics or other personnel, many departments believe it makes sense to have AEDs and officers trained in their use. The American Heart Association (AHA) says that first responders must administer care to a person within eight minutes of a sudden cardiac arrest for the person to have more than a 4 percent chance of survival.

After the Emergency

After the emergency, the focus should be on returning to normalcy as soon as possible and on attending to the mental health needs of those who responded. Critical incident stress debriefings as discussed in Chapter 12 are essential.

Cross-Trained Responders and an All-Hazards Approach

Agencies might consider cross-training public safety employees to perform as police officers, firefighters and emergency medical first responders. Many

Technology has made the job of patrol officers more efficient and safe. Here, Los Angeles Police Department (LAPD) commanders keep an eye on a protest via electronics. A total of about 10,000 people, in three major marches, converged near downtown Los Angeles and marched up Broadway Avenue, carrying U.S., Mexican and Central American flags to show support for immigrant rights. The mostly peaceful march was in stark contrast to the previous year's police riot where several members of the news media were beaten, along with many parade marchers.

© Ted Soqui/Corbis

local governments look at cross-training personnel because of the financial benefits: "The general rule of thumb is that a group of cross-trained personnel can perform the same tasks that would require 60 percent to 80 percent more personnel to perform as single-discipline personnel" (Miller, 2009, p.59). Challenges to a cross-trained system center around three areas: maintaining multiple training regimens and required job proficiencies, maintaining sufficient personnel to safely and professionally respond to major incidents, and maintaining the safety of responders and those they serve despite the schedules most responders work under: "Adding the rigorous training schedule for the three disciplines into the mix, it is easy to see that while 'doing more with less' may save money, there is little potential for down time and a greater possibility of errors induced by lack of sleep under such an arrangement" (Miller, p.60).

Many of the management responsibilities related to deploying personnel in emergencies are similar to what would be needed during and after a terrorist attack. In addition, managers must be knowledgeable of their responsibilities in homeland security.

DEPLOYING RESOURCES FOR HOMELAND SECURITY

Time has passed since 9/11. Yet, as a starting point, it is important to understand the Department of Homeland Security (DHS) and how it affects law enforcement management.

Terrorist Attacks

The DHS (Figure 13.4) serves in a broad capacity, facilitating collaboration between local and federal law enforcement to develop a national strategy to detect, prepare for, prevent, protect against, respond to and recover from terrorist attacks within the United States.

 Among the strategic goals of the Department of Homeland Security are prevention of, protection from, response to and recovery from terrorist attacks.

Prevention of and Protection from Terrorist Attacks

On October 26, 2001, President Bush signed into law the Uniting and Strengthening America by Providing Appropriate Tools Required to Intercept and Obstruct Terrorism (USA PATRIOT) Act, giving police unprecedented ability to search, seize, detain or eavesdrop in their pursuit of possible terrorists. The law expands the FBI's wiretapping and electronic surveillance authority and allows nationwide jurisdiction for search warrants and electronic surveillance devices, including legal expansion of those devices to e-mail and the Internet.

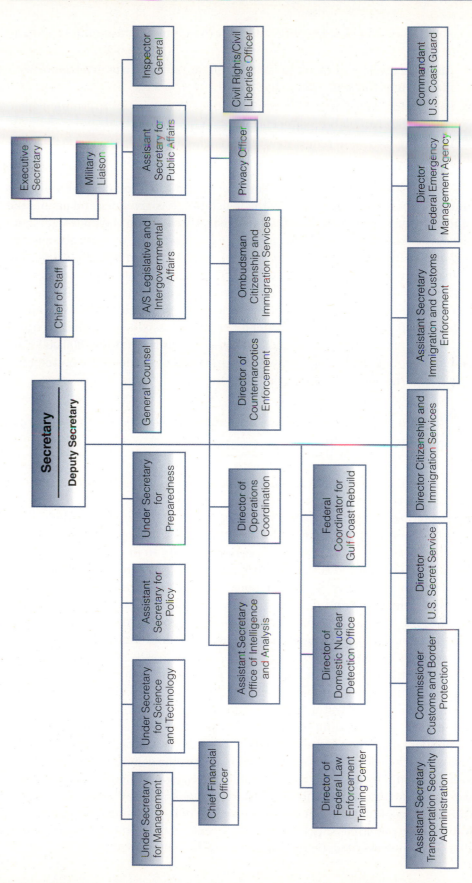

FIGURE 13.4 Organizational Chart for the Department of Homeland Security

Source: Department of Homeland Security, www.dhs.gov

The USA PATRIOT Act significantly improves the nation's counterterrorism efforts by:

◉ Allowing investigators to use the tools already available to investigate organized crime and drug trafficking.

◉ Facilitating information sharing and cooperation among government agencies so they can better "connect the dots."

◉ Updating the law to reflect new technologies and new threats.

◉ Increasing the penalties for those who commit or support terrorist crimes.

The PATRIOT Act has come under attack from some members of Congress and civil liberties groups who say the legislation has given federal agents too much power to pursue suspected terrorists, threatening the civil rights and privacy of Americans. However, after an extension from its expiration at the end of 2005, the Senate voted 29–10 to renew the act on March 2, 2006. The House followed suit on March 7, voting 280–13, days before the law was set to expire on March 10. On March 9, 2006, President Bush signed into law the USA PATRIOT Improvement and Reauthorization Act. Although this law was aimed at federal efforts, these efforts depend heavily on assistance from the cop on the beat in jurisdictions throughout the country, as the nation's 800,000 state and local police are the country's "first preventers"—who can stop terrorist acts before they occur (Kelling et al., 2007).

 The first line of defense against terrorism is the local patrol officer in the field.

Local police possess strengths that position them as valuable contributors to national counterterrorism efforts: "The strengths of U.S. local law enforcement agencies are drawn from the powers of search, seizure of evidence, and arrest; a community policing infrastructure; the growing ability to manage, share, and analyze information; the proven ability to identify and interpret suspect behaviors; and established relationships that can carry an investigation from inception to completion. Local police also add the critical elements of speed, resources and numbers to any situation. They are able to deploy rapidly and can quickly summon more forces if needed. Managers in the field are accustomed to making decisions in dynamic and high stakes incidents" (Downing, 2009, p.30).

In preparing for multipronged attack such as those that occurred in multiple locations across Mumbai, India, in November 2008, leaving 170 dead, law enforcement administrators must recognize that patrol officers will be "the tip of the spear," and first-line supervisors will have the greatest impact on the direction and ultimate outcome of any event of this magnitude (Reynolds, 2009, p.48). In such incidents, "patrol supervisors will be the generals of the street, and individual initiative will rule the moment. No centralized command structure can assimilate the issues and actions fast enough to give off-site commands to those first responders who have only second to make decisions. We must therefore prepare our street supervisors and officers to take initiative and recognize that their choices will determine the outcome" (Chudwin, 2009, p.51).

Since the 9/11 attacks, all agencies in the United States regardless of size or location have become responsible for homeland security and, as such, should have a counterterrorism mind-set as part of their mission and a focus on building and enhancing their counterterrorism capability. Rural emergency responders—law enforcement, fire, EMS and hazardous materials (hazmat)—are equally important in the preparation of dealing with homeland security incidents of terrorism: "Many times the rural responders are the first to arrive on the scene at an event or a disaster. In addition, rural responders represent a surge capacity to increase the capability of other jurisdictions during large-scale disasters" (Brosius, 2009, p.56). Unfortunately, recall from Chapter 2 that research has found that small agencies, most often rural, perceived their risk of a terrorist attack to be low; consequently, little seems to have changed since 9/11 in instituting homeland security measures in small departments (Schafer et al., 2009, p.283). This is especially worrisome if small police departments are responsible for the security of any critical infrastructures.

Our country's critical infrastructure—those deemed most vital to national public health and safety, governance, economic and national security, and retaining public confidence—now include agriculture, banking and finance, chemical and hazardous waste, defense industrial base, energy, emergency services, food, government, information and telecommunications, transportation, postal and shipping services, public health and water. Key assets now include national monuments and icons, nuclear power plants, dams, government facilities and commercial assets. Each locality should identify its own critical infrastructures and assets, assess their risk potential and keep a watchful eye on them through directed patrol.

In addition, because the private sector owns and protects 85 percent of the nation's infrastructure, law enforcement–private security partnerships can put vital information into the hands of those who need it.

Best Practices in Homeland Security: An Overview

In the years since 9/11, agencies throughout the country have focused efforts on homeland security, efforts that usually fall into one of four phases: mitigation (lessening the threat), preparedness, response and recovery. Table 13.2 summarizes approaches that have been identified as effective in each of the four areas.

Mutual Aid Agreements

Mutual aid agreements, commonly used to prepare for emergencies, can play a greater role in preventing and responding to the threat of terrorism. Such agreements were discussed earlier in the chapter.

Terrorism and Crime

Downing (2009. p.30) notes, "The crime-fighting model used to investigate organized crime, gangs and narcotics trafficking enterprises—their structures, the players and their strategies—is being applied regularly to the investigation

TABLE 13.2 Best Practices and Trends in Homeland Security by Phases of Emergency Management

Mitigation	Preparedness
Federal assistance programs	Assignment of emergency management responsibilities
U.S. Homeland Security Advisory System	Emergency plans and possible hazards
Threat assessment	Mutual aid agreements
Building design and physical structures	Simulated-disaster exercises
Municipal and county building codes	Training for local government employees
Nonstructural safety measures	Use of the Incident Command System
	Pedestrian and vehicular evacuation routes

Response	Recovery
Contributions and donations management	Crime scene security
Damage assessment practices	Crisis counseling
Early-warning notification systems	Disaster assistance to property owners and citizens
Emergency shelters and assistance	Management of fatalities
Evacuation practices	Rebuilding private structures and spaces
Geographic information systems	Restoration of public infrastructure and open spaces
Medical services and equipment	
On-site command and control	
Public information and the news media	

Source: Roger L. Kemp. "The Future of Homeland Security." In *Homeland Security: Best Practices for Local Government*, edited by Roger L. Kemp. Washington, DC: International City/County Management Association, 2003, p.136.

of terrorist networks." Crime fighting and counterterrorism efforts often go hand in hand. For example, several of the 9/11 hijackers had contact with law enforcement officers in various parts of the country before the attacks. Ziad Jarrah (Pennsylvania crash) was stopped by police in Maryland for speeding, issued a ticket and released two days before the attacks. Hani Hanjour (Pentagon crash) was stopped by police in Arlington, Virginia, issued a ticket for speeding and released. Mohammed Atta (north tower of the World Trade Center) was stopped in Tamarac, Florida, for driving without a valid license and issued a ticket. When he didn't pay the ticket, an arrest warrant was issued. A few weeks later he was stopped for speeding but let go because police did not know about the warrant.

On a more positive note, three officers—Diana Dean, Charlie Hanger and Jeff Postell—were doing the jobs of regular uniformed law officers when they captured three of the most dangerous terrorists our country has known: Dean was conducting a routine customs interview at a Northwest border station and prevented an airport bombing by Ahmen Ressam. Hanger was conducting a routine traffic stop and captured Timothy McVeigh, the Oklahoma City bomber.

Postell was conducting a routine security check behind a small North Carolina convenience store and captured Eric Rudolph, who had been on the FBI's Most Wanted List for domestic terrorism for more than five years (Stockton, 2008).

If local law enforcement hopes to be successful in meeting the challenges posed by terrorism, it must combine prevention efforts with prediction efforts through a "convergent strategy" that simultaneously fights crime and disorder while creating a hostile environment for terrorists: "The theme of convergence illustrates the coupling of local resources, namely police, with the ability to recognize ordinary crimes that terrorists have been known to commit in preparation for their operational attack: committing traffic violations, obtaining fake identification papers, smuggling, human trafficking, counterfeiting, committing piracy, drug trafficking, or participating in any other criminal enterprise that intersects with terrorists' needs. Local police serve as the eyes and ears of communities; as such, they are best positioned to observe behaviors that have a nexus to terrorism" (Downing, 2009, p.28).

Despite the ever-present threat of a terrorist attack, many of the nation's law enforcement agencies are not prepared. Although the events of 9/11 unquestionably expanded the scope of law enforcement's responsibility, it did not automatically include a corresponding increase in personnel or resources to fulfill the responsibility. Consequently, law enforcement productivity—already a considerable management concern—has endured new scrutiny and encountered unprecedented challenges.

LAW ENFORCEMENT PRODUCTIVITY

Productivity from the law enforcement department, one of the most costly municipal services, is expected. Managers' effectiveness is judged by the results they obtain using the available resources. **Productivity** is converting resources to achieve results efficiently and effectively. Productivity measures results gained from a specific amount of effort. An efficient use of resources alone may not be effective or meet a desired need. An effective use of resources may not be efficient or sufficient in overall impact. Productivity planning helps balance efficiency and effectiveness guided by an overall desire for value.

> **productivity**
> converting resources to achieve results in the most efficient and effective way possible.

Measuring Law Enforcement Productivity

Law enforcement services are not as measurable as production-line efforts. Production lines measure productivity in units manufactured; businesses measure it in profits.

 Law enforcement productivity is measured by the quality and quantity of services provided.

Increased productivity is a high priority. A balance between management and worker expectations has to be achieved without abandoning the concept that work must be productive. Reasonable standards must be determined. Desired management productivity and employee performance capability must be balanced. Once this balance is determined, employees have a standard against which management can measure them. If accurate records are kept, employees will know where they stand in relation to what is expected and to all other employees who perform the same functions.

 Law enforcement productivity has traditionally been measured by arrests, stops, traffic citations, the value of recovered property and reduction of crashes and crime.

The main concern with these productivity measurements is that law enforcement officers may not have much control over them. Reduction in crashes or crime may be short term, or there may be no reduction at all, but this does not necessarily mean that officers are not productive.

Quotas versus Performance Standards

quota
a specific number or proportional share that each officer is expected to contribute or receive.

Productivity normally involves setting minimum standards, which, in law enforcement, brings up the question of quotas. A **quota** is a specific number or proportional share that each is expected to contribute. It is difficult not to use arrests, tickets issued, number of service calls answered and number of reports and activities initiated by officers as a basis for productivity because these are what officers do. But also important are how these tasks are executed, the quality of reports and the public's perception of the officers.

Productivity Problems

Symptoms of productivity problems are similar to those of motivation/morale problems: high absenteeism and turnover, high levels of waste, high accident rates and unreasonable complaints and grievances. The Internet is often a time waster. Server logs record all Internet activity on a network, including who visited what Web site, how long they stayed, what they looked at, what they searched for and where they went next. Examining server logs can reveal whether employees are less productive because of time spent on nonwork-related Internet activities. Other problems that hinder productivity reside in employee attitudes, efforts, and unwillingness to self-initiate or to focus on the department's mission and vision, including the agency's strategies, goals and objectives.

Improving Productivity

Often the difference between promising ideas and productive results is a good manager. Productivity is directed from the top and accomplished at the bottom of the organizational hierarchy. Such productivity can be improved by

- Clearly explaining organizational goals.
- Permitting more decisions to be made at the "doing" level.
- Supporting creativity and innovation.
- Increasing individual control over the tasks for which officers are responsible.

Furthermore, managers and supervisors at all levels must set performance expectations and then insist that those they oversee meet these expectations. Each department level must hold the next level accountable.

Law enforcement productivity can be improved by
- **Training and experience.**
- **Rewards and incentives.**
- **Improved equipment.**
- **Technology.**

Training and experience can improve productivity by helping people do tasks more efficiently. Productivity can also be increased through a reward system. Deserved praise, commendations and personal recognition are rewards. Monetary rewards, although effective, may not be as effective as personal rewards that build self-esteem and self-worth. All the concepts in Chapter 9 related to motivating employees are relevant.

In addition, improved law enforcement productivity can be accomplished by introducing improved equipment. An up-to-date communications and computer center can assist officers; however, the equipment should be procured based on a realistic cost assessment in relation to expected benefit. Many smaller, less costly pieces of equipment can increase patrol productivity. For example, cell phones for each unit, radar installed in most beat cars and a car desk or lighted clipboard for report writing are small items that can increase productivity.

Implementing mobile computing systems has several benefits, including higher crime-solution rates, greatly reduced clerical costs and, most important, increased officer safety. Such systems are excellent examples of ways in which technology can increase productivity.

Technology

Productivity can be increased without adding employees by using technology presently or soon to become available. Taping reports to be recorded later by clerk typists, using computers, installing improved 911 and computer-assisted dispatch (CAD) systems, superhighway police information systems and a host of other future technologies will vastly enhance police productivity.

Computers can be used in a variety of ways to enhance productivity, for example, record keeping, data analysis, word processing, investigating, inventorying property rooms and maintaining stolen-property files. One way computers are improving departments' productivity is by facilitating the organization of data through a **management information system (MIS)**, which provides data for planning and decision making. MIS procedures include collecting, analyzing and reporting past, present and projected information from within and outside the organization. Figure 13.5 illustrates the components of a management information system.

management information systems (MIS)

software programs that organize data to assist in decision making.

FIGURE 13.5

Components of a Management Information System (MIS)

Source: Lester R. Bittel. *The McGraw-Hill 36-Hour Management Course.* New York: McGraw-Hill Publishing Company, 1989, p.234. Reprinted by permission.

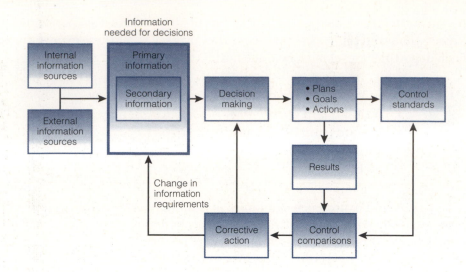

Integrated justice systems are improving the productivity of law enforcement and that of the entire criminal justice system. The goal is to have the original information, collected by the officer on the street, flow into every other application used by every other step in the justice system.

To keep up with technology, managers might use the National Aeronautics and Space Administration's (NASA) Technology Utilization Program, established in the early 1960s by congressional mandate to promote the transfer of aerospace technology to other areas. For example, a Pennsylvania police department called upon NASA's ability to enhance ATM films so the images were sufficiently sharpened to identify a car and driver, resulting in the arrest of a kidnapper/murder.

LEADERSHIP, DISCIPLINE, MOTIVATION AND MORALE REVISITED

An anonymous quote reads, "Interest and attention are just as important to people as grease and oil are to a machine. Without it they don't run smoothly, never reach top speed and break down more frequently." Developing a spirit to perform is one of management's jobs. Law enforcement managers use four motivating techniques: redesigning the law enforcement job; providing productive work and an opportunity for achievement and recognition; stating clear, concise and achievable goals; and providing some form of reward and enticement system for excellent performance. Intrinsic as well as extrinsic rewards can be used.

 The quality of management in the organization is the single most important factor for high productivity and morale. They are integrally related.

A management approach that creates high performance organizations through employee empowerment can greatly enhance an agency's productivity. The department's mission is accomplished through the line officers. It is up to management to provide this bridge between mission and accomplishments.

SUMMARY

A key management function is deploying personnel to patrol the jurisdiction. Area assignments are determined by requests for services based on available data. This is called proportionate assignment. No area should be larger than the time it takes a car to respond to emergency calls in a reasonable time. To determine patrol area size, consider square miles, street miles, amount of crime and disorder and response time. A response as rapid yet as safe as possible builds public confidence in law enforcement capabilities and competence. It also places officers at a scene to protect evidence before people or the elements destroy it. It increases the chances of locating witnesses and making arrests. Further, it increases the chances of providing lifesaving emergency first aid to victims of crimes.

Most law enforcement departments use some form of random patrol, the basic premise of which is to place officers closer to a potential incident or request for service before it happens, based on data from experience, but without any predictable pattern. Goals are to provide a police presence, observe suspicious activity and reduce response time. However, the Kansas City Preventive Patrol Experiment found that increasing or decreasing routine preventive patrol had no effect on crime, citizen fear of crime, community attitudes toward the police on delivery of police services, police response time or traffic accidents. Common methods of patrol include automobile, bicycle, motorcycle, and foot patrol. Other methods include air, mounted, water, special-terrain and Segway patrol.

Managers are expected to fulfill their responsibility to deploy resources to fight crime. The crime triangle is a model illustrating how all three elements—motivated offender, suitable victim and adequate location—are required for crime to occur. Focusing on career criminals is a logical approach to fighting crime. Equally promising in crime-fighting efforts is a focus on high-crime locations.

Managers also must be prepared to deploy resources during times of emergency and, therefore, should have carefully formulated predisaster plans. Predisaster plans should include, at minimum:

- Which emergencies to prepare for
- What must be done in advance (supplies on hand, agreements with other agencies, etc.)
- What specific functions must be performed during the emergency and who is responsible for performing them, including outside organizations and agencies that might help
- What steps need to be taken to restore order after the emergency has ended
- How to evaluate the response

A relatively new area of responsibility is participating in homeland security efforts. Among the strategic goals of the Department of Homeland Security are prevention of, protection from, response to and recovery from terrorist attacks. The first line of defense against terrorism is the local law enforcement officer on patrol.

Law enforcement productivity is measured by the quality and quantity of services provided. It has traditionally been measured by arrests, stops, traffic citations, the value of recovered property and reduction of crashes and crime. Law enforcement productivity can be improved by training and experience, rewards and incentives, improved equipment and technology.

The quality of management in the organization is the single most important factor for high productivity and morale. They are integrally related.

CHALLENGE THIRTEEN

The Greenfield Police Department has changed its mission statement to reflect the city's current service needs. The new mission emphasizes community-based, problem-solving policing. As the new police chief, you have reviewed the performance of the different units within the department. The detective unit is primarily reactionary and investigates crime reports taken by the patrol unit. Detectives also conduct frequent prostitution stings at a local hotel, for which they have received several commendations. Records for the previous five years indicate no citizen complaints regarding prostitution. The only reports of prostitution were generated during the sting operations. The arrested prostitutes all worked for outcall services in other cities and traveled more than 20 miles to reach the hotel where they were arrested.

The patrol division devotes most of its time to preventive patrolling. They have an excellent response time to emergency calls. Patrol officers have been evaluated by the number of arrests they make and the number of tags they issue. Officer Swanson, a patrol officer for 20 years, has never received a service award.

He has received several poor evaluations for spending too much time on calls and not writing enough tags. Officer Swanson knows everyone in town and often stops to chat at local businesses. He sometimes takes long coffee breaks at the senior citizens' home and has been seen dropping kids off at school. Citizens often specifically ask dispatch to send Officer Swanson to assist them. Although he receives consistently low evaluations from his supervisors, his file is packed with positive letters from citizens.

1. Is it possible for officers to do an excellent job at the tasks they are assigned and be unproductive?

2. Do you recognize a potential problem with the detectives' emphasis on prostitution stings?

3. Considering the Kansas City Preventive Patrol Experiment, why not reduce the strength of patrol shifts?

4. How can Greenfield's patrol strategy be changed to reduce preventive patrol and enhance community policing?

5. Is it possible that Officer Swanson may be more productive than his supervisors realize?

DISCUSSION QUESTIONS

1. What factors should be considered in determining personnel assignment to shifts?

2. What is your opinion of the random patrol method of deploying law enforcement personnel?

3. Do you favor one- or two-officer patrol units? Why?

4. Does your law enforcement agency use civilianization? If so, for what positions? Could this be expanded?

5. What emergencies should be planned for in your jurisdiction?

6. Have you ever been involved in a disaster or emergency that required law enforcement officers? If so, how effectively did they perform?

7. What proportion of resources do you feel should be allocated to "fighting crime"?

8. What innovative ideas can you think of to increase effectiveness and productivity?

9. How does your law enforcement agency use computers?

10. When are you highly productive? What factors are present during those times?

 # REFERENCES

"About FEMA." Accessed December 6, 2009. http://www.fema.gov/about/index.shtm

Barlow, Scott; Branch, Jim; and Close, Gary. "Citizen Police Academies: A Model for Smaller Agencies." *The Police Chief*, March 2009, pp.44–45.

Beck, Charlie, and McCue, Colleen. "Predictive Policing: What Can We Learn from Wal-Mart and Amazon about Fighting Crime in a Recession?" *The Police Chief*, November 2009, pp.18–24.

Brosius, Jo. "The Rural Domestic Preparedness Consortium." *The Police Chief*, November 2009, pp.56–63.

Chudwin, Jeff. "Terror, Again." *Law Officer Magazine*, January 2009, pp.50–55.

"Citizen Corps Programs and Partners." Accessed September 26, 2009. http://www.citizencorps.gov/

"Community Emergency Response Teams CERT." Accessed December 4, 2009. http://www.citizencorps.gov/cert/

Dickinson, Eric. "Sort Victims, Save Lives: What Every Cop Must Know about Triage." *Law Officer Magazine*, August 2009, pp.51–55.

Donaldson, Stan. "Police Reserves Multiply Forces." *Detroit Free Press*, January 4, 2007.

Downing, Michael P. "Policing Terrorism in the United States: The Los Angeles Police Department's Convergence Strategy." *The Police Chief*, February 2009, pp.28–43.

Famega, Christine N. "Proactive Policing by Post and Community Officers." *Crime & Delinquency*, January 2009, pp.78–104.

Famega, Christine N.; Frank, James; and Mazerolle, Lorraine. "Managing Police Patrol Time: The Role of Supervisor Directives." *Justice Quarterly*, December 2005, pp.540–559.

Ferguson, John. "Auxiliary Police Officers . . . Just Add Training." *Law and Order*, April 2008, pp.87–90.

Grossi, Dave. "Patrol Tactics: What Works Best?" *Law Officer Magazine*, September 2008, pp.26–29.

"Guardian Angels." Accessed November 30, 2009. http://www.guardianangels.org/about.php

Kanable, Rebecca. "Citizens on Radar Patrol." *Law Enforcement Technology*, January 2009, pp.40–50.

Kelling, George: "Sustaining a Crime Reduction Requires a Critical Mass of Community Involvement." *Subject to Debate*, September 2008, pp.5–6.

Kelling, George L.; Eddy, R. P.; Bratton, William J. "The Blue Front Line in the War on Terror." *City Journal*, September 20, 2007. Accessed September 21, 2007. http://www.city-journal.org/printable.php?id=2367

Klockars, Carl B. *Thinking about Police: Contemporary Readings*. New York: McGraw-Hill, 1983.

Lauria, Donald T. "Cost-Benefit Analysis of Tacoma's Assigned Vehicle Program." *Police Quarterly*, June 2007, pp.192–217.

"Law Enforcement Exploring." Accessed December 4, 2009. http://www.learningforlife.org/exploring/lawenforcement/main.html

Miller, Michael. "All-Hazard Approach and Cross-Trained Responders." *Law and Order*, October 2009, pp.58–61.

Mills-Senn, Pamela. "Right on Schedule." *Law Enforcement Technology*, March 2008, pp.62–70.

"National Association Citizens on Patrol." Accessed November 30, 2009. http://www.nacop.org/

Page, Douglas. "Police Behaving Predictably: The Other Enemy." *Law Enforcement Technology*, February 2009, pp.74–78.

Repecki, Tiffany. "Study: Police Vehicle Take-Home Policy Cheaper Than Car Pool." Cape-Coral-Daily-Breeze.com, September 18, 2010. http://www.cape-coral-daily-breeze.com/page/content.detail/id/519369.html Retrieved October 5, 2010.

Reynolds, Luther. "Preparing for a Mumbai-Style Attack." *The Police Chief*, November 2009, pp.46–54.

Schafer, Joseph A.; Burruss, George W., Jr.; and Giblin, Matthew J. "Measuring Homeland Security Innovation in Small Municipal Agencies: Policing in a Post–9/11 World." *Police Quarterly*, September 2009, pp.263–288.

Schnebly, Stephen M. "The Influence of Community-Oriented Policing on Crime-Reporting Behavior." *Justice Quarterly*, June 2008, pp.223–251.

Slahor, Stephenie. "Disaster Planning Means Plan to Succeed." *Law and Order*, October 2009, pp.32–34.

Solar, Patrick. "The Economics of Patrol Scheduling, Part 1." *Law and Order*, September 2009a.

Solar, Patrick. "The Economics of Patrol Scheduling, Part 2." *Law and Order*, October 2009b, pp.74–79.

Stockton, Dale. "Intervene and Prevent." *Law Officer Magazine*, February 2008, p.8.

Sundermeier, Jon. "A Look at the 12-Hour Shift: The Lincoln Police Department Study." *The Police Chief*, March 2008, pp.60–63.

"VIPS Registered Program Analysis Results." Accessed November 30, 2009. http://www.policevolunteers.org/

Webster, James. "The Benefits of Reserve Detectives." *Law and Order*, February 2008, pp.279–280.

Wexler, Chuck. "'De-Civilianization' of Policing: A Big Step Backwards." *Subject to Debate*, June 2009, p.2.

PURPOSES OF BUDGETS

Budgets control and guide how resources are used and make those in charge of them responsible for their wise use.

Budgets serve as a plan for and a means to control resources.

Budgets establish financial parameters for department needs. Most plans and projects of the department depend on finances. Budgets permit decision making at lower levels to work upward through the law enforcement hierarchy. First-line supervisors can present budget ideas that may ultimately be transformed into street operations. For example, the supervisor who develops an accident-prevention program and receives funding to put the program into action must be mindful of budget controls during the entire program.

Budgets also help reduce the tendency for divisions of a department to build their own little empires by establishing a maximum line item for each division. The detective division, the patrol division and the juvenile division may each have an allotted amount of funds. Any one division can spend only the funds approved for that division. Without budgeting, serious competition for total funds could be detrimental to the department's overall objectives.

Budgets provide an opportunity to compare expenditures with services provided. For example, the investigative division can compare personnel and other operational costs with the number of cases investigated, cases successfully closed, arrests made and property recovered.

Budgeting is a continuous process and a written commitment. Budgets are a law enforcement agency's work plan transformed into dollars, which translate into salaries, fringe benefits, equipment and special projects. Expenses are constantly balanced against the approved budget allocations. Budgets control available resources and assist in their efficient use. In essence, budgets are a monetary Bible whose First Commandment is "Thou shalt not spend more than is herein allocated."

Not less than monthly, executive managers receive itemized expenses and a statement of the balance remaining in each budget category. Some communities operate on a **bottom-line philosophy**, which permits departments to shift funds from one category to another as long as the total budget bottom line is not exceeded. Other communities consider each category as separate line items. Any shifting of funds from one category to another must be approved.

Budgets also reflect the political realities of law enforcement agencies and their jurisdictions. More effective managers are more likely to obtain approval for their programs and projects than are less effective managers or those with less political clout.

bottom-line philosophy

allows shifting funds from one expense category to another as long as expenses do not exceed the total amount budgeted.

RESPONSIBILITY FOR PREPARING THE BUDGET

Budget preparation may be the responsibility of the records department, a financial officer assigned to planning, or, in large departments, a separate division. In smaller law enforcement agencies, executive managers may prepare the budget. In larger departments, a person of next lower rank, a staff person or a special fiscal division is assigned to prepare the budget details and present it to the executive manager, who then holds staff meetings or budget workshops to complete the budget.

Executive law enforcement managers should encourage managers in all divisions and at all levels to monitor budget expenditures and justify expenses within their assigned responsibilities. Such a policy encourages budget preparation participation because managers can visualize the total process.

Executive managers or assigned staff need input from all employees. Requested budget information at various levels should be in a form and language understandable to people not directly connected to preparing the final budget. In a problem-oriented department, the budgeting process will be more participatory and bottom-up than it is in a traditional department.

The all-levels process of budgeting preparation is becoming common in many agencies. First-line supervisors know the needs of street-level law enforcement services and will include potentially overlooked items.

Managers at each level should be responsible for the budget they need, based on input from their subordinates. This results in all-levels budgeting.

all-levels budgeting
everyone affected by the budget helps prepare it.

If all levels of employees and managers have input into the budget, they will understand it and be more aware of revenue and expenditure balancing. They also become part of the process of budget preparation, the goal development on which the budget is based and the subsequent budget review and possible revisions.

What people help to create, they are likely to support. The budget is one area in which support is critical. Normally the employees' most active interests will be in the areas of salaries and fringe benefits. In reality, some other budget items more severely affect their day-to-day work activities. Effective managers demonstrate this to employees and ensure that subordinates do not focus solely on budget areas that directly affect them but rather on the whole picture.

Budgets will be more accurate and complete if they are prepared using a logical process beginning with the department's lowest levels and working upward. If the total budget exceeds the amount approved for the agency, the budget must be reviewed line item by line item, and items must be eliminated that will have the least effect on total services provided. Support of all involved is needed to make such cuts without negative effects.

Budget development usually starts at the level of area commands where budget requests originate. Such requests may be (1) funded within the department's base budget, (2) disapproved or (3) carried forward for management review. At the division level, managers review the area requests, make needed adjustments and submit a consolidated request to the budget section.

Within two to three months, the budget section identifies proposals for new funding that have department-wide impact and passes them on to the executive level. The commissioner and aides review the figures along with those from other city departments and agree on a budget to submit to the city manager.

THE BUDGETING PROCESS

Developing a budget is an art, not a science. Although budgeting is not a complicated process, it is a critical one for police organizations: "It is a learned skill that requires ingenuity, creativity, attention to detail and good communication skills" (Orrick, 2008, p.208). It also demands that police managers and administrators forge strong working relationships with policy makers because these are the people who determine core service priorities.

Each agency has developed guidelines, budget forms and formats. In addition, many computer software budgeting programs are in use by law enforcement agencies at all governmental levels. The year-round budgeting process begins with the department's mission, goals, objectives and work plans and the resources needed to carry them out.

Determining Personnel Costs

Personnel costs make up the largest item in an agency's budget, so determining staffing levels is a critical step. Once staffing levels are determined, the cost of personnel services can be calculated by obtaining information on base

Records help police officers identify areas where expenditures are needed. Using facts, officers can present their budget requests to their superiors. Input from all levels results in the best budget, and it helps make the budget acceptable to officers at all levels.

© Joel Gordon

salary, merit or longevity increases, cost of living increases, Federal Insurance Contributions Act (FICA—7.5 percent of salary withheld and matched by employer), worker's compensation, retirement, health/dental/life insurance, overtime and any other compensation-related benefits.

Review of Last Year's Budget

Budget preparation often includes a review of the previous year's budget. These expenditures were approved and likely apply to the new budget. Accurate figures of total costs related to successful accomplishment of past goals provide a foundation for future predictions. These figures are then adjusted to allow for increased costs caused by inflation and reduced costs resulting from wider use, greater availability of the product or competition. The figures should be placed on a computer spreadsheet so revisions can be easily made.

The next task is to compare cost increases, line item by line item, and adjust, eliminate or add items. These changes should be based on carefully thought-out assumptions. Each year new items and programs appear, and the total amount of available funds varies, but the main budget format remains.

 Most law enforcement budgets are developed by revising the previous year's budget based on logical assumptions.

Most budget items are short term, that is, applicable to current-year activities. Because estimated costs are more stable over short periods, short-term expenditures are easier to plan for than long-term expenses. Carryover, or continued items or programs from previous budgets, must include inflationary costs, including cost-of-living salary increases, additional fringe-benefit costs and spin-off costs from increased vacation or sick-leave programs.

Law enforcement budget preparation is a series of events involving hearings, city council workshops, input meetings, cost estimating and a host of other technical details. The process generally involves presentation by the finance department at a governmental entity department staff meeting or by written instructions sent to the department head. Sample forms for preparing budgets are included. Dates are set for various levels of preparation, discussions and workshops.

Law enforcement agencies repeat the process with their own personnel. Any changes in procedure from previous budgets are discussed. Dates and times for different levels of completion must be established, or procrastinators will submit at the last minute, resulting in lower-quality preparation and consideration. This may lead to omitting items important to continued effective operations.

Law enforcement agencies operate for extended periods with tasks and functions varying from day to day, month to month and year to year. It is difficult to foresee all situations that eventually must be converted into cost factors. For example, who can predict whether a squad car will be involved in a crash and "totaled"; or whether 20 inches of sleet and snow will fall, creating numerous crashes; or whether a natural disaster or a terrorist attack will

contingency funds

money allocated for unforeseen emergencies.

occur, requiring hundreds of hours of overtime? **Contingency funds** are set aside for such unforeseen emergencies, but the precise total of allowable expenditures is difficult to ascertain.

Priorities must be weighed. Rarely are revenues sufficient to support all requests, and rarely are all requests justifiable. Justification includes the reasons the item is needed and the effect it would have on the department's operations if eliminated. Items that can be accurately cost-determined should include the source of the cost estimate. The more specific the cost and justification, the less likely the expense is to be criticized.

Some items are mandated by state and federal regulations, collective bargaining agreements and the Fair Labor Standards Act. Some items are directly linked to safety issues, increasing chances a proposed expenditure will not be cut. Sometimes prices have risen, for example, fuel costs. Training is a common target for cuts because training is an abstract category that can't be seen or touched. A suggested rule of thumb to increase funding chances is that the department gets a return of 10 dollars for every dollar spent on training (Orrick, 2008, p.205).

Even if all requests are justifiable, final decisions must be based on available revenues. Tough decisions are often mandatory. Moreover, not all factors can be measured in dollars. Budgets involve intangibles, such as cost in morale and performance. In some budget preparations, the manager closest to the origin of the financial request is given the total list of requests, the estimated costs and the maximum funding available. Managers are asked to decide what to eliminate.

line-item budgeting

identifies specific categories (line items) and dollars allocated for each, and usually based on the preceding year's budget and anticipated changes in the upcoming year.

This prioritization often involves consulting with all employees for whom the manager is responsible. If priorities are set with employees' input, they are more acceptable. Further, employees understand the total budgeting process, which ultimately translates into their everyday operational capabilities for the budget year. Input may be given at one or several stages of the budget process.

Budget preparation should be an ongoing process of planning, setting goals and objectives, itemizing, obtaining input on needs and comparing the data with past budgets. Information to be used in developing the budget should be collected continuously.

line items

specific expense categories, for example, personnel, maintenance, training.

 All law enforcement employees should contribute ideas related to budget items as specific needs arise.

BUDGETING SYSTEMS

performance budgeting

allocates dollars based on productivity.

Law enforcement budgets may take several forms. One of the most common is **line-item budgeting**, initiated in the 1900s and still popular. In this system, specific categories (**line items**) of expenses are identified and dollars allocated for each. Line-item budgets are usually based on the preceding year's budget and a comparison between it and actual expenses.

program budgeting

identifies programs and allocates funds for each.

Performance budgeting allocates dollars based on productivity. Those divisions that perform most effectively are allotted a greater share of the budget. **Program budgeting** identifies the various programs an agency provides and allocates funds for each. A percentage of administrative costs, support costs and **overhead** (operating expenses exclusive of personnel) are assigned to each program. This budgeting approach requires much paperwork, and many managers feel it is unproductive. However, it can help preserve programs in the face of budget cut pressure. **Activity-based costing (ABC)** is a modern version of the program budgeting system, except that rather than breaking down costs by program, the approach breaks down costs by activity. Activity-based management (ABM) is a logical outgrowth of this approach to analyzing costs. ABC breaks up overhead into neat little cost drivers, the factors that determine the final cost of an operation.

Zero-based budgeting (ZBB) requires justifying all expenditures, not just those that exceed the prior year's allocations. All budget lines begin at zero and are funded according to merit rather than according to the level approved for the preceding year. Zero-based budgeting requires management to articulate objectives and then identify alternative methods of accomplishing those objectives, systematically analyzing the effects of various funding levels. Such an approach to budgeting makes comparison of competing programs easier.

BUDGET CATEGORIES

Regardless of the budgeting system, the budget is usually divided into two classes of expenses: **variable costs**, which will change depending on the level of service provided, and **fixed costs**, or overhead, which are relatively constant. Within these two categories, subcategories of expenses can be identified.

 Common budget categories include salaries and wages, services and supplies, training and travel, contractual services and other or miscellaneous.

The miscellaneous category should not be treated as a catchall but should be used for small items such as journal subscriptions or books. Budgets also often contain special one-time requests for capital equipment, such as new police vehicles or investigative equipment.

In most budgets, salaries and wages account for the largest expenditures, typically 80 to 85 percent. Of this amount, fringe benefits usually amount to 25 percent of the allocation.

 Personnel costs usually account for at least three fourths of the operating budget.

Salaries and wages predominate primarily because of the personnel needed to provide extended-time law enforcement services. Equipment is also used for the same extended time and consequently must be replaced more frequently. For example, a simple item such as a dispatcher's chair used 24/7 is going to need replacement much faster than one used during a 5-day, one-shift week. Figure 14.1 shows a typical public safety department's expenditures.

---

overhead

expenses that do not vary in total during a period even though the amount of service provided may be more or less than anticipated, for example, rent and insurance.

---

activity-based costing (ABC)

a modern version of the program budgeting system, except that rather than breaking costs down by program, the approach breaks down costs by activity.

---

zero-based budgeting (ZBB)

begins with a clean slate, justifying each expenditure anew and based on merit, rather than being based on the preceding year's funding level.

---

variable costs

costs that will change depending on the level of service provided, for example personnel.

---

fixed costs

costs that are relatively constant, for example, rent or insurance; also called *overhead*.

FIGURE 14.1
A Typical Public Safety Department's Allocation of Resources

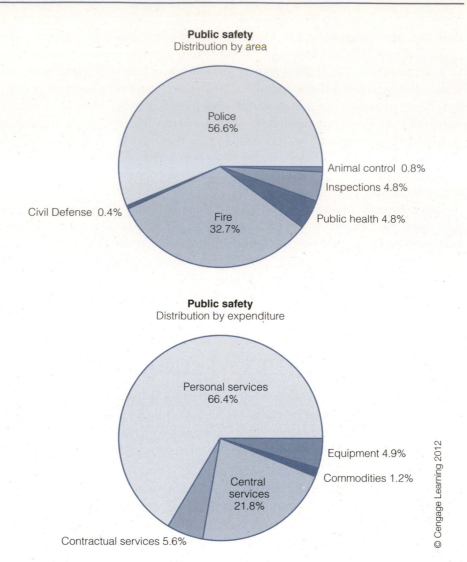

Public safety
Distribution by area

Police 56.6%

Animal control 0.8%

Inspections 4.8%

Civil Defense 0.4%

Fire 32.7%

Public health 4.8%

Public safety
Distribution by expenditure

Personal services 66.4%

Equipment 4.9%

Commodities 1.2%

Central services 21.8%

Contractual services 5.6%

COMMUNICATION AND BUDGET SUPPORT

Open, meaningful communication with neighborhood groups, citizens, elected officials, other departments and agencies and line officers is critical to securing an adequate budget. Of particular importance is effective communication with elected officials, the public and line staff when dealing with financial matters. Police administrators should encourage those elected officials with budgetary authority to ride with patrol officers to see firsthand what officers face and hear what citizens want.

To increase the likelihood of budget approval, those preparing the budget should consider forming an advisory committee representative of the community and the local governing body to ensure a diversity of viewpoints and information. They might also consider surveying the community to provide back-up and provide information to counter any claims by hostile officials.

PRESENTING THE BUDGET FOR APPROVAL

The law enforcement budget process generally culminates in presentation to the city council or city manager. Here it competes for revenues with all other departments. Many factors come into play at this point—some factual, some political.

Budget presentations should be made realistically and honestly because the law enforcement budget must be sold to a higher body for final approval. Political decision makers need accurate information. Padding the budget is often discussed, but city managers, city councils and finance departments are well aware of this tactic. Managers must request funds based on needs, provide a spirit of cooperation and candor and try to avoid serious conflicts. Without factual, accurate information, decisions will likely be made based on personal contacts, innuendo and community pressure. Finally, budget presentations should include both facts and emotions. The competencies needed in both areas are summarized in Table 14.1.

After the budget is approved, it must be implemented by converting dollars and cents into law enforcement services rendered. It is the manager's responsibility to make sure these dollars are used wisely as budgeted.

MONITORING

The budget is a *tool*, not a document to be approved and then filed. After the budget is passed, the most important task is to monitor spending. Budget execution can be compared with firing a weapon (Orrick, 2008, p.207). The sight alignment and trigger squeeze may be correct, but rounds may be grouped to one side at the 7-yard mark. If no corrective action is taken, the officer will miss the target from 15 or 25 yards. The same is true with a department's budget. If a line item is 2 percent over budget after the first month and no corrective

TABLE 14.1 Art of Winning Minds and Hearts: Leadership Competencies Needed

Art of Winning Minds	Art of Winning Hearts
Objective: Convincing people—make them understand the purpose	*Objective:* Moving people—increase their commitment/motivation
Medium: Information	Medium: Emotion
Relevance	Authenticity
Cogency	Empathy
Showmanship	Listening
Questioning	Rapport
Dialogue	Optimism
Promotion of discovery	Trust in intuition
Atmosphere of intellectual safety	Atmosphere of emotional safety

Source: From M. R. Haberfeld. *Police Leadership*, © 2006. Reproduced by permission of Pearson Education, Inc., Upper Saddle River, New Jersey.

action is taken, it may be 24 percent over at the end of the year. Expenditures must be monitored monthly. However, remember that budgeting is a guideline, not an infallible indicator of the future. No one can do better than an estimate, and variances *will* arise.

variance analysis

comparing actual costs against what was budgeted and examining the differences.

Variance analysis consists of comparing actual costs against what was budgeted and analyzing differences. Variances in the budget are caused by one or a combination of three things: (1) price change (either higher or lower), (2) volume (using more or less of a line item) or (3) efficiency of operation (equipment is operating more or less efficiently than anticipated) (Orrick, 2008, p.207). Differences should be contained in a variance report and made known to everyone who directly or indirectly influences the costs. A variance is not necessarily a sign the budget is wrong. Rather, it signals a need for control over income or expenses. Reporting budget variances is an opportunity to provide guidance to management. Variance reports should be made monthly. Problems or deviations should be identified and recommendations made for corrective action.

CUTBACK BUDGETING

The country is going through a financial crisis of monumental proportions, affecting the budgets of all localities, which, in turn, affects the budgets of law enforcement agencies. Most departments are being asked to provide more services with fewer funds. Whether called budget reduction, cutback budgeting or reduced expenditure spending, it means added frustration and anxiety for police managers.

cutback budgeting

providing the same or more services with less funding; also called *budget reduction* or *reduced expenditure spending.*

 Cutback budgeting means providing the same or more services with less funding.

"Doing more with less" is the mandate of the future for most law enforcement agencies. Even successful programs have been discontinued because of lack of funding. To a large extent, budgets control an organization's potential and capabilities.

Causes of Cutback Budgeting

Cutbacks are caused by several factors, the most familiar being that the problem is considered solved. A second cause is erosion of the economic base, seen especially in older U.S. cities and the Northeast, in the growth of dependent populations and shifts from the Frostbelt to the Sunbelt. Other causes include inflation, taxpayer revolts and actual limits to growth. Whatever the cause, cutback management poses special challenges.

Ways to Do More with Less

Approaches to handling budget cuts include (Orrick, 2008, p.204)

- Cut all requests for personnel increases.
- Cut equipment viewed as luxuries.

- Use precedent—cut items that have been cut before.
- Recommend repair and renovation, not replacement.
- Recommend a study to defer the costs.
- Cut all costs by a fixed amount (for example, 5 percent).
- Cut departments with a bad reputation.
- Don't cut when the safety of staff or the public is involved.

Common cost choices that management must make include whether to
- **Resist or smooth cuts.**
- **Make a deep gouge or small decrements.**
- **Share the pain or target the cuts.**
- **Budget for efficiency or equity.**

In each case, the best choice from a management viewpoint may not make sense politically or from a team-building viewpoint. Possible solutions include reassigning functions to other entities: "Some services can be 'privatized' by installing fees, user charges and contracting arrangements for special skills, and some services can be consolidated to achieve economies of scale. Services can be 'civilianized' through the use of volunteers and nonsworn personnel. Some services can be reduced or eliminated by careful monitoring of the differences between citizen 'needs' and citizen 'wants.' And expenses can be trimmed through overtime control, 'downtime management,' self-insurance and new pension arrangements" (Levine, no date, p.10).

Three steps that managers facing cutback budgeting might consider are (Levine, no date, pp.11–12)

1. Assume a positive attitude toward innovation; be willing to experiment.

2. Become convinced that fiscal stress can be managed; prioritize services and projects.

3. Develop a marketing strategy to convince taxpayers of the importance and quality of public services.

A PERF survey (*Violent Crime and the Economic Crisis*, 2009a, p.6) reports the following actions taken by police managers to lessen the impact of economic changes: eliminated/changed take-home car policy (27 percent); initiated/increased use of bicycles (23 percent), of hybrid vehicles (18 percent), of foot patrols (17 percent), of two-person cars (15 percent) and of Segways (13 percent); and adjusted work hours of staff (12 percent).

A follow-up PERF survey (*Violent Crime and the Economic Crisis*, 2009b) found even more drastic measures being taken. In response to how they were planning to apportion cuts in their upcoming budgets, managers indicated, on average, that 31 percent of the dollar cuts would come out of funding for sworn personnel; another 15 percent from funding for civilian personnel; and 12 percent out of overtime funding. Ironically, the respondents showed the strongest level of agreement with the statement: "Sworn officer positions should be the last thing cut in the budget." Yet these positions were most often at the top of the budget cut list: "Thus, it is apparent that even though most police chiefs believe that their last resort should be cutting sworn personnel, the economic crisis is so severe that many chiefs are finding it difficult or impossible to avoid cutting sworn officers" (*Violent Crime and the Economic Crisis*, 2009b, p.2). The report says the reason for this incongruity is that for most police departments, personnel typically account for at least 80 percent of total budget funding and may be as high as 95 percent or more in some departments.

Although police officials were planning budget cuts for the next fiscal year, many had already trimmed funding in the following areas (*Violent Crime and the Economic Crisis*, 2009b, pp.1–2): overtime (62 percent), hiring freezes (53 percent), increasing fees (52 percent), technology (49 percent), training (47 percent), take-home cars (29 percent), attrition (24 percent) and layoffs and furloughs (19 percent). Figure 14.2 shows how police departments are planning to cut their budgets for the upcoming fiscal year.

Each government agency has its sources of revenues and its requirements for services. When revenue sources do not meet the cost of requirements for services, a cutback budgeting situation develops. New revenues must be designated or services cut. Cost reductions might include cutting overtime, reducing capital outlay purchases, reducing travel, initiating hiring freezes, or, in extreme instances, laying off personnel or promoting early retirement.

Seeking new revenues is another solution. A combination of cutback budgeting procedures and new revenues may be necessary. Managers might look at how budgeting is done in the private sector, with requests for proposals and bidding an integral part of major purchases. Many businesses also use cooperative purchasing, joining together for better pricing. The same can be done in law enforcement. For example, several agencies could go together in purchasing police vehicles, thereby getting a better price.

FIGURE 14.2

Planned Budget Cuts for PERF Respondents

Source: *Violent Crime and the Economic Crisis: Police Chiefs Face a New Challenge, Part II.* Washington, DC: Police Executive Research Form, May 2009b, p.3.

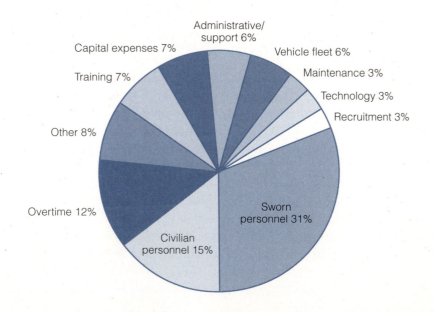

AWAY FROM THE DESK: The Importance of Budgeting within the Broader Police Function

The most important obligation of government is to provide for the safety of our residents. This is why a major portion of a police department's annual budget is dedicated to core services such as public safety and related programs. The satisfaction I have in budget oversight comes from having the opportunity to be part of a responsive, dynamic, organization within a vibrant and progressive community.

Budgeting within a police department should focus on existing services and all future programs and services. This focus should be based on the belief that continuous improvement as an agency, and, as individuals within an agency, are necessary to go from "Good to Great." This ongoing process includes setting "stretch goals" both organizationally and personally. The primary goal is very simply to be the very best at delivery of public safety services to our community, despite the social issues that, by default, have become the responsibility of the police.

Over the course of the past five years we have worked together to support the needs of public safety as a core service. As a public service agency, we are required to address the demands of our community by operating 24/7/365. Yet we must never compromise the safety of the officers by working short and further exposing the department and community to the liabilities that dictate and control our operations. We must continue to build on what has been started as a means of meeting the service capacity demands that are thrust upon us. In the past year we have witnessed the cost ineffectiveness of not filling vacant positions as well as the drain on everyone in the organization as we attempted to respond to budget and resource shortfalls throughout the city. In many circumstances, the services we provide cannot wait until the next day and often our emergency calls for service cannot and should not be handled by one officer.

Presently, we have been able to sustain our current level of services because we have prioritized shift minimums, thereby allowing us to be prepared to respond to whatever calls for service we may receive; however, this may not be the case in the near future. Therefore, we continue to utilize personnel who have uncommitted time to work with our community in solving neighborhood problems and further increasing our visibility so as to advertise to potential criminals that this is not an appealing community for crime. For example, our patrol response efforts have proven effective in saving the citizens approximately $30,000 annually from damages to our parks. Today, we spend less than $5,000.00 per year fixing and or repairing damaged property. I feel that this is attributed partly to a strong presence of our police force.

(continued)

> Despite significant progress in establishing adequate budgets, important challenges remain. Our challenges may be new, the solutions by which we answer them may be new, but those values upon which our success depends—Children and Youth, Diversity, Education, Excellence, Integrity, Justice, Partnerships, Quality of Life, Respect for Life, and Teamwork—are time honored.
>
> —*Chief Shaun E. LaDue*

MANAGING COSTS CREATIVELY

Perhaps without even realizing it, you have already learned about one of the most creative ways to manage costs—managing time. People and their time are a manager's greatest resource. The following discussion assumes that the manager is already paying careful attention to this aspect of budgeting.

Identifying Common Cost Problems

 The first step in solving cost problems is to identify waste areas.

Benjamin Franklin once stated, "Beware of little expenses; a small leak will sink a great ship." Absenteeism and turnover are major cost problems in most organizations. Managers concerned with controlling costs should have a very clear idea of just how much each subordinate is worth in dollars per day. This figure, coupled with absenteeism, is very important to managers as they look at their budgets.

Other costs managers should target are equipment maintenance and services such as mail, duplicating, computer use and telephones. Are employees using these facilities and services for personal business? If so, might it make sense to establish a mechanism so they could pay for the convenience? This works well in many organizations. Meetings are another area, already mentioned, where much waste occurs. Many resource management experts suggest that at least one fourth of all time (and dollars) spent on meetings is wasted. Paperwork is another obvious, yet frequently overlooked, area of waste.

 All employees are responsible for reducing costs.

Employees should understand where waste is occurring and how they might help reduce it. In addition to this reactive approach to cost containment, a more proactive approach might also be used.

Employee Cost Improvement
Suggestion Programs

The idea of a suggestion system is certainly not new; such systems have been successfully operating for decades in business and industry. A typical system includes guidelines for acceptable suggestions, a mechanism for making the suggestions and rewards for those suggestions selected as feasible.

 Employees can suggest ways to cut costs through an employee cost improvement suggestion program.

Successful employee suggestion programs share several common features, including clearly informing all employees of the program's details and procedures; providing fair, meaningful rewards; and continuously publicizing the program and its objectives. Such programs are in keeping with the team concept introduced in the first section of this text and emphasized throughout. Costs must be managed if law enforcement agencies are to provide the services citizens expect and require.

CREATIVE WAYS TO REDUCE COSTS

A financial crisis can also present opportunity as managers look for innovative ways to stretch existing budgets. Many law enforcement agencies are using the budget crunch as an impetus to conserve resources and develop new, efficient programs that may not ever have been developed.

 Reduce costs by sharing resources, using a regional approach or consolidating services, establishing community resource centers, contracting, using a Quartermaster system, using volunteers and privatizing.

Sharing Resources

One way agencies can share resources is to pass on or trade out extra equipment. For example, since 1995 the Defense Logistics Agency's Law Enforcement Support Office (LESO) has been responsible for transferring excess Department of Defense equipment suitable to counter-drug and counterterrorism activities to federal, state and local law enforcement. The LESO program has provided departments with such items as cars, surveillance equipment, uniforms and boots.

The Regional Approach
or Consolidating Services

Regional approaches to common problems allow multiple jurisdictions to pool their resources to form and share teams not needed full time, for example, SWAT, scuba, accident reconstruction and crime scene units. In addition, departments might make use of equipment from the Regional Intelligence Sharing System (RISS), a program funded by the Department of Justice that provides equipment and analytical support for law enforcement throughout the country. Many agencies are developing regional consortia: groups of departments with mutual interest in such things as funding a large-scale interoperability project.

Similar to the regional approach, consolidation allows jurisdictions to share staff and services. Cities and towns with small to medium police departments might consolidate emergency services. They might also share training rooms and actual training. Many communities have a single public safety complex where police, fire and emergency medical service (EMS) personnel are located. In other communities, firefighting and EMS functions are performed by one team.

Community Resource Centers

Another approach to reducing costs is to establish a community resource center, or more than one for large jurisdictions. Combining police services with social services can provide on-site counseling, educational tutoring, legal services, health care and after-school programs.

Contracting

Contracting, providing law enforcement services by one government entity to another, has come into its own. Departments should consider whether having one agency be responsible for all law enforcement activities is more efficient than having several separate special-purpose agencies. Organizational pride may play a role in this decision, as may community attitudes toward having an entity other than their local police provide law enforcement services.

The Quartermaster System

When examining the best way to equip a department and outfit their officers, many law enforcement administrators face a choice: provide officers with a uniform allotment or use the quartermaster system, where the agency keeps a storehouse of uniforms. Although stocking such inventory may have some drawbacks, such as limited flexibility for special needs, the quartermaster system has important advantages. Placement of a single large-quantity order provides a supply of identical stock from the same dye lot and usually affords higher level of quality for a lower price. Another consideration is that officers frequently are reluctant to spend their allotment on uniforms, spending it in other ways.

Research shows that 53.5 percent of police officers receive some kind of allotment to purchase essential gear, apparel or equipment. However, nearly 60 percent of officers from agencies with four or fewer officers do not receive allotments, perhaps because they tend to be union negotiated. Most agencies purchase ammunition and body armor, but most officers buy their own boots and footwear, either from their allotments or paying out of pocket.

Volunteers

Use of volunteers is increasing in law enforcement departments across the country, as discussed in Chapter 13. Using volunteers does more than just save money—it adds value to department services and enhances community policing efforts. However, there are initial budget implications to bringing volunteers into an agency, such as training and orientation, background checks and additional demands on current human resources to supervise these individuals. Data practices is another area of concern that managers must consider when using volunteers.

Privatization

An increasingly popular option among law enforcement agencies facing budget shortfalls and the need to cut expenses is to use private security personnel to replace service functions previously handled by sworn officers (Beck and McCue, 2009). This service alternative makes good sense since most of the critical U.S. infrastructure—nearly 85 percent, by some estimates—is already protected by private security companies: "The need for complex coordination, extra staffing and special resources after a terror attack, coupled with the significant demands of crime prevention and response, requires boosting the level of partnership between public policing and private security. The benefits are clear. Law enforcement agencies possess legal powers and training not normally available to the general public. Private industry, with approximately *triple* the personnel resources of the law enforcement community, is more advanced in the use of technology to prevent and detect crime and is uniquely able to address certain crimes, such as workplace violence or computer crimes" (Carter, 2007, p.6).

Areas where private security might help public police include investigating internal theft and economic crimes, responding to burglar alarms, examining evidence from law enforcement in private crime lags, conducting background checks, protecting VIPs and executives and controlling crowds and traffic at public events. Agencies might also consider using private security agencies to transport prisons and private correctional facilities to cut costs (Hess and Orthmann, 2009, p.75).

A prime example of effective use of private security is the response to burglar alarms, which in many communities has become the top call for police service: "In most communities a small percentage of citizens own alarms, which are subsidized by a large number of citizens [because] most alarm calls are false—typically 95 percent or higher" (Kanable, 2009, p.57). The cost of responding to false alarms is enormous and can have negative economic consequences for police agencies and the communities they serve (Petrocelli, 2008). It is estimated that each false alarm response consumes 20 minutes of police time, typically involving two officers, and costs the public millions of dollars (Sampson, 2007, p.7). To provide a specific example, the Orlando (Florida) Police Department reports that 99.9 percent of its burglar alarm calls are false, a total of 28,448 false alarms a year, costing the department 20,704 work hours of response time and a financial cost of $216,000 ("Orlando Police Department,"

2009). Additional concerns are that if most such calls are false, responding officers may endanger lives on the way to the call and may not be as alert as they should be in their response. Knowing that most alarm calls are false and unlikely to result in any enforcement action can lead to officer complacency, a serious threat to officer safety when a call turns out to involve an armed intruder.

INCREASING REVENUE

In addition to reducing costs, managers should look for ways to increase revenues. Managers should examine variations between in-house and outsourcing costs for every task their department does. Avenues to explore include free training opportunities, becoming a warranty repair center for the department's vehicles, contracting police services for other municipalities and holding prisoners for other agencies. Talk to other departments to find out why they have money.

 Departments might increase revenue by fundraising, donations, charging for some services, using asset forfeiture statutes to their advantage, going green and seeking grants.

Fundraising

The primary source of revenue for law enforcement agencies is provided by the jurisdiction served by the agency. Local police departments, for example, are supported primarily by local tax dollars. Many police departments find they are able to increase the dollars available to them by raising funds themselves. Among the methods agencies have used to raise funds are dues to a crime prevention organization and seeking support from civic groups for specific projects, such as K-9 units.

One example of a successful fundraiser is the Crown Point (Indiana) Police Department's Adopt-A-Car Program, started in 1995 when this small department needed to purchase 10 new cars but found itself $125,000 short. A lieutenant came up with the idea of asking local businesses to donate $1,500 each (tax deductible) to equip the vehicles. In return, the department painted "This vehicle equipped by (business name)" in 1 1/2-inch high letters on the back of the car. In less than two days, the department had enough sponsors to outfit its new cars and refurbish the old ones. Not everyone supports such programs, however. As one police chief said, "Some things are too important to be for sale. Police are one of them."

In one midwestern community, the Bloomington (Minnesota) Citizen Crime Prevention Association (BCPA) has an annual used book sale, appropriately named "Book 'Em." Collection boxes are placed in businesses, schools and churches throughout the community, and citizens donate their used books. Each spring, space is donated by a local business, and volunteers conduct a weeklong book sale. Their 17th-anniversary sale in 2009 earned more than $98,000. This allowed the BCPA to award $75,000 in grants in 2009.

Among community programs receiving grants were the police department's Explorer Post, National Night out, Kids Safari, Cornerstone (domestic abuse emergency shelter), Kennedy High School Afterschool Programs, Crime Stoppers, High School Activity Center, Neighborhood Watch and Normandale Community College Scholarships (*Bloomington Crime Bytes*, 2009). One purchase made with the funds from a previous year was a K-9 for the police department. The officers named the dog "Books."

Some police departments secure funds to purchase automated external defibrillators (AEDs) for their patrol cars from local chambers of commerce, insurance companies, civic organizations such as the Rotary Club and the Lions Club, banks and hospitals. The American Heart Association and the American Red Cross provided training on their use. Putting AEDs in patrol cars can save countless lives from sudden cardiac arrest.

Donations

Accepting money or donations from local businesses or community members might appear to be a simple, obvious solution to budget shortfalls. However, accepting monetary donations can be politically and ethically questionable. Nonetheless, many departments gladly accept donated bicycles, helmets, AEDs and the like.

An increasing number of departments are using nonprofit foundations to solicit funding for new initiatives. The first police foundation was introduced in New York city as a tax-exempt entity to help the New York Police Department (NYPD) close some of the gap between what the department had and what it needed to have to operate optimally and promote experimentation (Delaney and Carey, 2007, p.16). Currently the NYPD is using funds from such entities as Pfizer, Motorola and other donors to the New York City Police Foundation, a charity whose marriage of private philanthropy and public security is being replicated nationwide. Police and foundation officers acknowledge that the mix of private money and policing has inherent risks, particularly the possibility that wealthy donors can gain undue influence.

Charging for Services

Some agencies have begun charging for traditional services, such as driving under the influence (DUI) arrests, or for emergency responses that include fire services and rescue squads dispatched to accidents. Other departments are billing the hosts of loud parties if the police are called back to the party within 12 hours. In addition to raising revenues, some departments have noticed a 75 percent reduction in second calls about loud parties. Other departments are recouping their costs for extraordinary police services, that is, police services rendered during parades and athletic events or in natural disasters or criminally caused catastrophic events such as bombings or hostage incidents. Some departments are charging fees for extra after-hours security to local organizations and businesses. Other jurisdictions are charging sentenced prisoners an incarceration fee to help offset the costs of their confinement and supervision.

Other options for creative managers to increase revenues include selling department products or assets, for example, auctioning surplus equipment or unclaimed items from the property room. Departments might also charge fees for services such as reports, photographs, fingerprinting, license checks and responding to alarms, particularly false alarms. Besides collecting such fees, departments may also economize by taking advantage of the rapidly expanding electronic commerce technologies available over the Internet or via networked kiosks similar to ATMs. Such transactions might include ordering reports, issuing licenses and so on.

Some agencies have found that accepting credit cards rather than insisting on cash bail has increased revenues collected. Other departments have formed special police assessment districts.

Asset Forfeiture

One source of additional revenue is asset forfeiture. Asset forfeiture describes the confiscation of assets by the state, which are either the proceeds of a crime or the instrumentalities of a crime. The practice of attaching guilt to objects used in committing a crime may have originated with Greek and Roman law. If, for example, a sword was used to kill a man, it was believed to possess an evil quality independent of the killer. The sword would be confiscated and sold, with the proceeds used for good deeds.

Asset forfeiture as a way to combat crime gained momentum during the 1980s and 1990s and is now a commonly accepted practice among law enforcement agencies: "Although it is an enforcement tool, asset forfeiture can assist in the budgeting realm by helping to offset the costs associated with fighting crime. Doing what it takes to undermine the illicit drug trade is expensive and time consuming. Forfeiture can help agencies target these difficult problems, sometimes without the need to seek additional outside resources to offset their costs" (Worrall, 2009, p.2). Other areas for which forfeiture might provide a remedy are nuisance properties, street racing, drunk driving and drivers with revoked driver's licenses, all of whom might have their property or vehicles seized (Worrall).

Administered by the U.S. Marshals Service, the asset forfeiture program has three goals: enforcing the law while stripping criminals of their ill-gotten gains, improving law enforcement cooperation, and enhancing law enforcement through revenue through equitable revenue sharing ("Asset Forfeiture Program," 2009). Under the Equitable Sharing Program, the proceeds from sales are often shared with the state and local law enforcement agencies that participated in the investigations leading to the forfeiture of the assets.

The main factors in forfeiture decisions are the connection between the asset and the crime and the asset's value. Assets seized have included vehicles, boats, electronic equipment, furniture/household items, jewelry, precious items, drugs, cash, firearms, real property, businesses and financial instruments. In 2006 the value of seized assets totaled $6 billion (*Return to FY2006 Asset Forfeiture Funds Reports*, 2007). Currently the U.S. Marshals manage almost $1.7 billion worth of property ("Asset Forfeiture Program," 2009).

Forfeiture is not without its critics: "Critics point to the 'drug war's hidden economic agenda' and refer to the means by which forfeiture compromises due process protections and encourages law enforcement blunders. Critics further claim that forfeiture circumvents proper appropriations channels, threatens due process protections and guarantees a conflict of interest between effective crime control and creative financial management" (Worrall, 2009, p.15).

One defense of asset seizure is the Innocent Owner Defense—the assets of an owner who had no knowledge of the prohibited activity, either by act or omission, are not subject to forfeiture. This defense was created by the Civil Asset Forfeiture Reform Act of 2000, which also shifted the burden of proof from the property owner to the government, requiring the government to prove by a preponderance of the evidence that property is subject to forfeiture. The Supreme Court has ruled that asset forfeiture is governed by the Eighth Amendment and, as such, must not be so severe as to constitute cruel and unusual punishment.

> **The Supreme Court considers asset forfeiture to be governed by the Eighth Amendment, which forbids cruel and unusual punishment. It is up to the states to make this determination.**

Going Green

Another relatively new approach to saving costs that is being implemented by many agencies across the country is the effort to "go green." Law enforcement agencies nationwide are faced with budget cuts ranging from thousands to millions of dollars, often involving slashing personnel budgets: "With budget cuts of this magnitude in their sights, many police agencies are finding that changing their methods and procedures to make them more environmentally green can save another kind of green: dollars" (Garrett, 2009, p.44). Incongruously, it often takes spending money to save money:

> The bad news is that not every department has the means to build a green structure to save money, both now and in the future. The good news is there are many smaller environmental initiatives that can help any department save money now. Green IT purchases, hybrid vehicles, squad car propane conversions, and other green innovations are now being viewed as investments that pay for themselves quickly then add more cash to the bottom line.

> While the cash saved through these initiatives may land back in city coffers, the savings puts departments in a prime position to ask for more money and get it. They can certainly say, "We just saved you a half million dollars, can we at least hire three more officers?" (Garrett, 2009, p.44)

The Jackson County (Georgia) Sheriff's Department outfitted half its patrol fleet with propane conversion kits (using confiscated drug money), allowing the department to save almost $100,000 in fuel costs in a single year. In addition, propane provides the longest driving range of all clean burning fuel alternatives, resulting in two to three times longer service life (Garrett, 2009, pp.44–45).

The Concord (Massachusetts) Police Department added a hybrid Ford Escape to its fleet and saved $5,000 in a year in fuel costs compared with the Ford Explorer it replaced: "The potential for fuel savings has departments across the country shelling out the extra $3,000 to $5,000 for hybrids vs. traditional squads" (Garrett, 2009, p.45).

Other ways departments might save money by going green include going paperless, recycling battery radios and adding energy efficient computer systems. However, given that retrofitting or conversion of existing equipment, or purchasing of new "green" equipment, carries considerable upfront costs, many departments find it cost prohibitive, despite the anticipated long-range fiscal savings, to implement greener alternatives without receiving a grant or some type of seed money for such efforts.

Grants

Numerous grant opportunities exist for law enforcement agencies at both the federal and state levels. To improve the chances of receiving a grant, it is important to understand the types of grants available and which federal, state and local agencies fund such grants. There are two basic types of grants: a **formula** or **block grant**, which is awarded to states or localities based on population and crime rates, and a **discretionary grant**, which is awarded based on the judgment of the awarding agency.

Federal Grant Money

Formula and block grant programs are awarded to states or local government units according to an established formula based on population or crime statistics. The main clearinghouse for federal grants is a Web site called www.grants.gov, which makes available billions of dollars of grant money each year (Slahor, 2009).

 www.grants.gov is the logical starting point for grant research because, by law, it is to be the clearinghouse of all federal grant information.

Other helpful websites including the following (Slahor, 2009, pp.84–86):

- ◉ www.recovery.gov—lists information about money available under the American Recovery and Reinvestment Act of 2009 (ARRA), with about $14 billion
- ◉ www.dhs.gov/xgovt/grants—the Department of Homeland Security (DHS) has billions of dollars available for homeland security efforts
- ◉ www.fema.gov/government/grant/index—the Federal Emergency Management Agency (FEMA) has about $3 billion to offer for disaster-specific grants
- ◉ www.GrantWritingUSA.com—a leader in courses about grant writing and grant management

Grant writing is discussed shortly. A key to grant hunting is getting on government mailing lists for up-to-date information on federal grants. The federal

formula grant

awarded to states or localities based on population and crime rates; also called a *block grant*.

block grant

awarded to states or localities based on population and crime rate; also called a *formula grant*.

discretionary grant

awarded based on the judgment of the awarding state or federal agency.

government's fiscal year ends September 31, so October is a good time to start researching new grant opportunities.

 The Department of Justice's (DOJ) Office of Justice Programs (OJP) is the lead federal funding agency for law enforcement.

The most significant of the programs are the Edward Byrne Memorial State and Local Law Enforcement Assistance Formula Grant Program (Byrne Formula Grant Program) and the Local Law Enforcement Block Grants (LLEBG), both federal grant programs.

The Bureau of Justice Assistance (BJA) has three primary sources of funding. LLEBG, created by Congress in 1994, provides funds to local government units to support projects to reduce crime and improve public safety. Funds go directly to local jurisdictions, distributing approximately $500 million per year. It is a 10 percent matching program; that is, for every $9 the government provides, the recipient must match it with $1.

The Byrne Formula grants were first funded under the Omnibus Crime Control and Safe Streets Act of 1968. Grants are awarded in 28 purpose areas and support a comprehensive range of projects to improve the criminal justice system, with an emphasis on drug-related crime, violent crime and serious offenders. The Edward Byrne Formula Grant Program is based on a state's population. States receive .25 percent of approximately $500 million as a base proportion. After that, the grant size is based on population and crime rate. Byrne formula grants represent the single largest source of law enforcement–related funding Congress makes available to states. This is a 25 percent matching program.

The third program, the Edward Byrne Discretionary Grant Program, grants about $50 million to innovative programs that are within the government's high priority areas. The Byrne Discretionary Grants Program focuses on training and technical assistance for crime and violence prevention and control, with grants awarded to states, local government units, tribes and tribal organization, individuals, educational institutions and private nonprofit organizations. The BJA also has a Bulletproof Vest Partnership (BVP) grant that pays as much as 50 percent of the cost of National Institute of Justice (NIJ)–approved vests.

The BJA Web site (www.ojp.usdoj.gov/BJA/) offers information on everything from counterterrorism training to partnerships and programs to help departments with limited financial resources.

Another important source of funding is the Community Oriented Policing Services (COPS) office. The COPS program, established in 1994, has been controversial but has already distributed more than $8.8 billion dollars in grants to help fight crime in high-risk areas. COPS grants have consistently contributed between 10 and 13 percent to the yearly reductions in violent crime at the height of their funding (*Interim Report on the Effects of COPS Funds*, 2005, p.11). A broad, exhaustive survey of 13,133 local law enforcement agencies found "clear, significant statistical links between COPS grants increasing the number of sworn officers, preventing crimes by having more officers on the beat and encouraging the adoption of new police practices" (*Interim Report*, p.11). The survey also found that COPS grant funds were associated with significant increases in average reported levels of community policing–style practices, including problem-solving, place-oriented practices, crime analysis and community collaboration. The stimulus bill passed on February 17, 2009, included $1 billion in COPS funding for hiring or rehiring of local police officers. This should fund between 5,000 and 5,500 officers; however, the office received 7,263 applications, with 39,314 officers being requested and $8.3 billion in funding (Quinn, 2009, p.1).

Another federal funding source, the Weed and Seed program, provides small grants to community organizations to reduce crime, gang activity and drug abuse in more than 260 neighborhoods across the country. The grants help communities *weed* out crime from designated neighborhoods, moves in with a wide range of crime and drug prevention programs and then *seed* these neighborhoods with a comprehensive range of human service programs that stimulate revitalization ("Weed and Seed," 2009).

The availability of discretionary grants is advertised in the Federal Register, the official daily publication for rules, proposed rules and notices of federal agencies and organizations offering grants. This source, published Monday through Friday, also provides the application criteria and details about the grants. Most major libraries subscribe to this publication.

The National Criminal Justice Reference Service (NCJRS) is another valuable source of information for funding available at the federal level. An agency can request to be put on the NCJRS mailing list for proposal solicitations and other information, and the agency will then receive all solicitations disseminated by OJP and the COPS office.

As previously noted, the federal government's fiscal year runs from October 1 through September 30. The deadline for most federal grant applications is some time in April, half-way through its fiscal year, so preparations should be made early in each calendar year.

State Grant Money

Funding may also be sought at the state level. The governor's office generally houses contact points for law enforcement–related grants. Managers must be aware that the appropriate "administrative agency" for grants varies from state to state (Shane, 2003, p.19). In New Jersey, for example, it is the State Division of Criminal Justice; in California it is the Office of Criminal Justice Planning. The state's administrative agency is responsible to pass federal funds through to local jurisdictions (Shane). In addition, almost every state has a grant specialist in the attorney general's office or in the state emergency preparedness office. At a minimum, each state has a contact point for the BJA's Edward Byrne Formula Grants Program.

The 670-page No Child Left Behind (NCLB) Act has poured billions of new federal dollars into education and, in recognizing that youths commit most street crime and are victims of many of them, has made funds available to law enforcement, giving a proportional share to each state. The list of programs authorized in the education bill provides many opportunities and hundreds of millions of dollars to solve both problems.

The NCLB Act provides block grants in which each state gets a share. States, in turn, must give 95 percent of their share in grants to local communities for programs to provide homework help, counseling, recreation and mentoring. Police-sponsored Boys and Girls Clubs, Police Athletic Leagues, YMCA and other community organizations qualify for such funding. States can provide grants for three to five years, with a $50,000 minimum. This is another area law enforcement departments might want to explore at the state level, especially if they have police liaison officers in the schools.

To improve the chances of receiving any of the multitude of grants available, managers must acquire skills in writing grant proposals.

Writing a Grant Proposal

Donahue (2009, p.62) cautions, "Writing a grant application is tough, tedious and plain hard work. A successful application will be the result of multiple drafts and rewrites. There will be many people involved in its preparation. . . . A last minute all-nighter is probably a waste of time. Simply said, generalities don't cut it. Assertions must be supported with statistical facts as backup."

Many departments waver on pursuing grants because the process is labor intensive and requires significant human resources to manage every grant. Most departments do not have the extra personnel to do this. Furthermore, the new COPS grants are extremely labor intensive, which often translates into little or minimal success for small to medium departments in being awarded grant money.

Proposals should not be written in a vacuum but, rather, should be collaborative efforts, including people from different agencies. The more people and agencies that have input and stand to benefit, the greater the chances of receiving funding are. It does not hurt to have the endorsement of the mayor, the governor and maybe even a congressional representative. Becoming a pilot project to benefit many other agencies and stakeholders in the public and private sectors can also enhance funding success.

The first step in writing a grant proposal is to read the solicitation carefully and follow the instructions exactly. Where applicable, graphs and charts should be included to help communicate ideas and present data. Showing local support is also important. It is often advisable to partner with a local university. Professors skilled in grant writing can lend credibility to the project.

The six components of most proposals, unless otherwise specified, are (1) a statement of need, (2) how this need can be met—the objectives of the project, (3) who will accomplish the tasks, (4) what timeline will be followed, (5) what the cost will be and (6) how the results will be evaluated.

Do not be discouraged if your proposal is turned down. The key to successful grant writing is to learn from your mistakes. Hindsight can lead to insight and then to foresight. Many worthwhile and successful programs were rejected repeatedly before eventually being funded. Grant seeking takes knowledge, preparation, patience and endurance. It is challenging, and the competition is keen, but the effort can be rewarding. Specific information regarding writing grants is beyond the scope of this text and contingent on the type of grant being applied for. However, ample resources are available on the Internet.

Other Sources of Funding

Other sources of funding for law enforcement include direct corporate giving programs, usually foundations and community-service groups such as the Rotary, Kiwanis and Elks that focus on crime prevention programs, child abuse, drug abuse, senior citizen safety and the like.

Additional income may be obtained from company-sponsored foundations, private foundation funds, individual gifts of equipment or money and individual operating foundations. Thousands of private foundations fund hundreds of program areas each year. These can be found on the Internet or in the library, or through a research company such as Research Grant Guides. A quick, easy way to find grant information is via the Internet. Check any of the OJP offices by indicating the office at the end of their Web address. For example, the BJA would be found at www.ojp.usdoj.gov/BJA/. Information may also be obtained by calling the OJP Grants Management System hotline at 888-549-9901.

SUMMARY

Budgets serve as a plan for and a means to control resources. Managers at each level should be responsible for the budget they need, based on input from their subordinates. This results in all-levels budgeting. Most law enforcement budgets are developed by revising the previous year's budget based on logical assumptions. All law enforcement employees should contribute ideas related to budget items as specific needs arise.

Common budget categories include salaries and wages, services and supplies, training and travel, contractual services and other or miscellaneous. Personnel costs usually account for at least three fourths of the operating budget.

Cutback budgeting means providing the same or more services with less funding. Common cost choices that management must make include whether to resist or smooth cuts, to make a deep gouge or small decrements, to share the pain or target the cuts and to budget for efficiency or equity. The first step in solving cost problems is to identify waste areas.

All employees are responsible for reducing costs. Employees can suggest ways to cut costs through an employee cost improvement suggestion program. Reduce costs by sharing resources, using a regional approach or consolidating services, establishing community resource centers, contracting, using a Quartermaster system, using volunteers and privatizing.

Departments might increase revenue by fundraising, donations, charging for some services, using asset forfeiture statutes to their advantage, going green and seeking grants. The Supreme Court considers asset forfeiture to be governed by the Eighth Amendment, which forbids cruel and unusual punishment. It is up to the states to make this determination. www.grants.gov is the logical starting point for grant research because, by law, it is to be the clearing-house of all federal grant information. The Department of Justice's Office of Justice Programs (OJP) is the lead federal funding agency for law enforcement.

CHALLENGE FOURTEEN

Captain Jones is responsible for preparing the budget for the Greenfield Police Department. The new chief has asked her to review the entire budget and find long-term and short-term cost reductions. He wants to shift some resources to community policing projects and would like to create an undercover drug unit. He encourages her to be creative and bold because he does not anticipate any increases in the budget during the next few years.

The Greenfield Police Department is a medium-sized suburban department. Three neighboring cities have comparable departments performing similar functions. Each of the four departments has its own booking and short-term holding facility and its own dispatch center. The county sheriff's department operates a detention center for felons and long-term prisoners. Arresting officers transport their prisoners to the county facility and are often out of service for several hours during this process.

Each city has its own special weapons and tactics (SWAT) team. The teams' equipment was purchased through a federal grant, but the personnel costs are each department's responsibility. The teams train frequently, but the cities do not often have incidents that require a SWAT response. The county sheriff's department also has a SWAT team that responds when requested by local police departments. None of the departments has an undercover drug unit. They refer drug cases to state and federal agencies, but those agencies are often too busy for a timely response.

A review of the Greenfield Police Department activity logs reveals that officers spend considerable time standing by for vehicle tows, directing traffic at civic functions and delivering documents to city council members.

1. How should Captain Jones begin the process of preparing a new budget?
2. Assuming that the Greenfield officers are still relying on preventive patrol, how could a change in strategy benefit the budget?
3. Suggest some major long-term cost savings Captain Jones could consider regarding dispatch and booking services.
4. Is the continued support of a seldom-used SWAT team a good use of Greenfield Police Department resources?
5. What other sources of creative funding may be available to support a drug unit?
6. How could Captain Jones use volunteers and reserve officers to increase human resources?

DISCUSSION QUESTIONS

1. Do you have a personal budget? If so, what are your main categories?
2. Do you belong to any organizations that have a budget? If so, what are their main categories?
3. How do budgets restrict? Provide freedom?
4. What things in addition to money might a law enforcement agency budget (e.g., space)?
5. Is your law enforcement department functioning under cutback budgeting?
6. What percentage of a city's total budget goes to the law enforcement department?
7. Which department gets the largest share of the city's budget?
8. What methods might be used to raise funds for your local law enforcement agency?

9. What suggestions do you have for cutting the cost of providing law enforcement services?

10. Do you agree with allowing "advertising" on patrol vehicles as a way to raise funds?

REFERENCES

"Asset Forfeiture Program." Washington, DC: U.S. Marshals Service. Accessed December 9, 2009. http://www.justice.gov/marshals/assets/assets.html

Beck, Charlie, and McCue, Colleen. "Prediction Policing: What Can We Learn from Wal-Mart and Amazon about Fighting Crime in a Recession?" *The Police Chief*, November 2009, pp.18–24.

Bloomington Crime Bytes, Fall 2009. Accessed September 26, 2010. http://bcpamn.org/uploads/2009BCPAnewfall.pdf

Brock, Horace R.; Palmer, Charles E.; and Price, John Ellis. *Accounting Principles and Applications*, 6th ed. New York: Gregg Division, McGraw-Hill Publishing Company, 1990.

Carter, Joseph C. "Public-Private Partnerships: Vital Resources for Law Enforcement." *The Police Chief*, September 2007, p.6.

Delaney, Pamela, and Carey, Donald L. "Police Foundations: Partnerships for 21st-Century Policing." *The Police Chief*, August 2007, pp.16–20.

Donahue, Jim. "Going after a Piece of the Pie." *Law Enforcement Technology*, May 2009, pp.62–65.

Garrett, Ronnie. "Saving Green by Going Green." *Police*, October 2009, pp.44–48.

Hess, Kären Matison, and Orthmann, Christine Hess. *Introduction to Private Security*, 5th ed. Belmont CA: Wadsworth Publishing Company, 2009.

Interim Report on the Effects of COPS Funds on the Decline in Crime during the 1990s. Washington, DC: Office of Community Oriented Policing Services, 2005. Accessed December 24, 2005. http://www.gao.gov/new.items/d05699r.pdf

Kanable, Rebecca. "When Policing Doesn't Pay." *Law Enforcement Technology*, September 2009, pp.54–58.

Levine, Charles H. "Cutback Management in an Era of Scarcity: Hard Questions for Hard Times." *Executive Police Development*. Washington, DC: Department of Justice, National Institute of Justice and the FBI, no date.

"Orlando Police Department Burglar Alarm System Guide." December 10, 2009. Accessed December 10, 2009. http://www.cityoforlando.net/POLICE/administration/alarm_prevention.htm

Orrick, Dwayne. "A Best Practices Guide for Recruitment, Retention and Turnover in Law Enforcement." In *Police Chiefs Desk Reference: A Guide for Newly Appointed Police Leaders*, 2nd ed., edited by International Association of Chiefs of Police and U.S. Bureau of Justice Assistance. Boston: McGraw-Hill Learning Solutions, 2008, pp.209–216.

Petrocelli, Joseph. "Patrol Response to False Burglar Alarms." *Police*, June 2008, pp.20–21.

Quinn, Tim. "Tim Quinn of COPS Office Faces an Unusual Challenge: Stretching $1 Billion." (Interview) *Subject to Debate*, April 2009, pp.1,5.

Return to FY2006 Asset Forfeiture Funds Reports. Accessed September 26, 2010. http://www.usdoj.gov/jmd/afp/02fundreport/2006affr/report3.htm

Sampson, Rana. *False Burglar Alarms*, 2nd ed. Washington, DC: Community Oriented Policing Services, March 2007.

Shane, Jon M. "Writing a Winning Grant Proposal." *FBI Law Enforcement Bulletin*, May 2003, pp.12–21.

Slahor, Stephenie. "Grants Guide." *Law and Order*, September 2009, pp.68–86.

Violent Crime and the Economic Crisis: Police Chiefs Face a New Challenge, Part I, Washington, DC: Police Executive Research Forum, January 2009a.

Violent Crime and the Economic Crisis: Police Chiefs Face a New Challenge, Part II. Washington, DC: Police Executive Research Forum, May 2009b.

"Weed and Seed." Accessed December 8, 2009. http://www.whitehouse.gov/omb/expectmore/summary/10000176.2004.html

Worrall, John L. *Asset Forfeiture*. Washington, DC: Community Oriented Policing Services, March 6, 2009.

Recruitment efforts should not overlook a department's civilian employees as well as participants in its programs such as the reserves, Explorers or citizen police academies.

Branding and the Internet

branding

the process an organization uses to distinguish itself from other employers; a brand image immediately triggers a mental image of a product of service's quality.

Branding is the current leading strategy in private-sector-marketing: "Branding is the process an organization uses to distinguish itself from other employers. . . A brand image immediately triggers a mental image of a product of service's quality. For example, what images come to mind when one thinks of Mercedes versus Yugo, or Nordstrom versus Walmart?" (Orrick, 2008a, p.27).

The first step to developing an effective brand image is to identify the agency's current strengths and weaknesses and how incumbents, potential candidates and the public view the agency—the self-assessment discussed earlier (Orrick, 2008b, p.34). Agencies need to ask, "What makes our agency unique, special and better than any other employer? Why would someone want to work for our department?" (Orrick, 2008c, p.15). Brand consistency is composed of three elements: "First is the agency's identity, which is how the department wishes to be seen or the desired brand image. Second is officers' performance, which is how employees actually perform. Third is the public image, which is how the public perceives officers and the department's performance" (Orrick, 2008c, p.15).

The most effectual images have a tag line of six word or fewer, such as "Make a Difference, Join Us." The bottom line for tapping the power of branding is, "Departments must take responsibility for communicating the unique characteristics that make their agency an employer of choice. Prospective employees must view this branding campaign accurately, consistently and frequently" (Orrick, 2009a, p.23).

One of the best channels for getting this message across is the agency's Web site: "To effectively recruit through the department website, it must be accessible, functional, interesting and accurate. . . . It must capture the viewers' interest with the unique characteristics of the department and how employment at the agency will meet the individual's personal needs" (Orrick, 2009b, p.18). It should also include a direct phone number and e-mail address for candidates to talk to an actual person and be frequently updated. Agencies might also consider posting a link on social networks such as MySpace and Facebook to guide prospective applicants to their Web site (Orrick, 2009c, p.20).

Recruiting for Diversity

As departments recognize the value of diversity within their ranks, recruitment efforts often focus on attracting ethnic minorities and women.

Recruiting Racial/Ethnic Minorities

"According to conventional wisdom among police leaders, non-Whites are likelier than Whites are to associate police with the civil rights abuses of years gone by and with present-day bias and unequal treatment, including racial and ethnic profiling. Some non-Whites may view policing as a White-dominated and racist profession and may reject the idea of working for the police because they fear being perceived by their peers as selling out" (*Law Enforcement*

Recruitment Toolkit, 2009). Although many minorities view police as the "enemy" and would never consider joining their ranks, others view law enforcement as a way to a better life. An African American police lieutenant from Atlanta explains why he became a police officer: "You got out of my neighborhood without ending up dead or in prison by either becoming a minister or a cop. I always fell asleep in church so I decided to become a cop."

The Delaware State Police uses troopers from throughout the state in their recruiting efforts, sending officers into minority community centers and developing its own job fair. Other likely places to recruit are Latino festivals, urban leagues, National Association for the Advancement of Colored People (NAACP) meetings and minority churches. The Sacramento (California) Police Department taps and trains interested minority citizens to recruit potential officers in their neighborhoods. In addition to finding qualified candidates, the citizen recruiters sponsor their recruits if selected, meeting with them during the academy, meeting with their family to offer support and participating in the academy graduation ceremony.

Recruiting Immigrants

Police in many countries around the world are corrupt and commonly engage in brutality. Consequently, people who have recently immigrated to the United States from such places may naturally be suspicious and distrusting of American government in general, and law enforcement in particular (*Law Enforcement Recruitment Toolkit*, 2009). In addition, many immigrants have limited proficiency in written and spoken English. The same strategies used in recruiting minorities might be applicable with this group of potential applicants.

Recruiting Women

Recruiting, hiring and retaining female officers is vital to a balanced, effective department. However, tests of physical strength often wash out qualified candidates, especially women. In addition, "Law enforcement leaders . . . suspect that women generally see law enforcement as a male-dominated culture where women are not welcome and that women fear sexual harassment, fear being ostracized and stereotyped by colleagues and supervisors, believe that they'll be steered away from higher-prestige assignments (such as SWAT and detective services) and believe that a law enforcement career is incompatible with raising a family because of work scheduling and related issues" (*Law Enforcement Recruitment Toolkit*, 2009). Such concerns should be addressed in any recruiting efforts targeting women.

Strategies specific to recruiting women include revising recruiting brochures to include photos of female officers; organizing career fairs specifically for women; and displaying recruiting posters in gyms, grocery stores and other places women are likely to see them. Departments should reach out to physically active women by posting flyers in places such as gyms; locker rooms of women's sport teams; and facilities for rock climbing, karate and similar activities. Women might also be recruited at community colleges, especially those with criminal justice and social service degree programs.

Recruiting advertisements geared to the crime fighting, law-enforcing aspects of the profession and the warrior image may be ineffective. In contrast, an emphasis on the service aspects of the job might be very appealing. Departments must take care, however, not to turn off highly qualified male applicants.

If recruiting efforts are successful, the law enforcement agency will receive numerous applications from which to select those best suited for their particular agency.

THE SELECTION PROCESS

A person wanting to become a police officer must usually go through several steps in the selection process. Although procedures differ greatly from agency to agency, several elements are common to most selection processes.

 The selection process is based on carefully specified criteria and usually includes completing an application form, undergoing a series of tests and examinations, passing a background check and successfully completing an interview.

A typical sequence of events in the employment process is illustrated in Figure 15.2 Unfortunately, this process is sometimes lengthy, and the best-qualified candidates are not willing to wait months for a decision.

FIGURE 15.2
Typical Employment Process

Source: J. Scott Harr and Kären M. Hess. *Seeking Employment in Criminal Justice and Related Fields*, 6th ed. Belmont, CA: Wadsworth, a part of Cengage Learning, Inc. 2010, p.236. Reproduced by permission. www.cngage.com/permissions

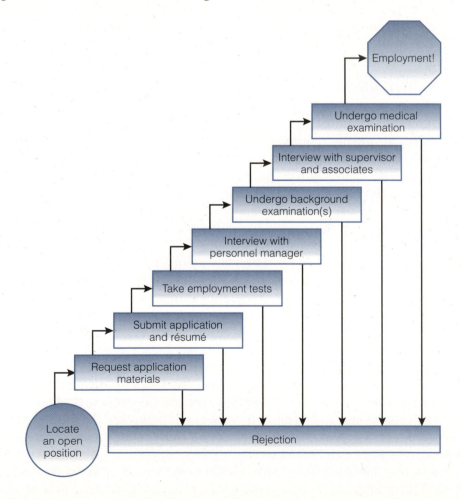

The Application

The initial application is an important document to determine a candidate's competence for the job. The consent statement provides the right to verify any information on the application. The application should also have an employment-at-will provision indicating that no contract guarantees permanent employment.

Many law enforcement departments use a civil service–type application and selection process. An increasing number of agencies now require all applications be done online. A sample application is contained in Appendix B.

Restricted Subjects

The following subjects are *not* allowed for either an application form or an employment interview: race, religion, national origin, gender, age (you may ask whether the applicant is between the ages of 18 and 70), marital status and physical capabilities. Administrators must be able to show that all questions are relevant to the position they are seeking applicants for.

Testing/Screening

Applicant testing usually progresses from the least expensive method, the written examination, to the most expensive, the background investigation, with the number of qualified recruits being narrowed at each step. Because several trips are needed to complete the process, the selection process is difficult for anyone living any distance from the hiring agency. Some agencies have revised their selection process so that it can be completed in one trip.

 The most common screening methods for selection are basic skills/written tests, medical examinations, background investigations, psychological examinations, physical fitness tests and oral interviews.

Other methods used with less frequency include polygraphs, assessment centers (discussed in Chapter 9), chief's or command interviews and writing tests.

Written Tests

Basic skills in math and reading can be assessed using standardized tests. Writing skills are also important to assess. Although report writing skills can be taught, they do take time to develop and master. A recruit who already possesses strong written communication skills can help a hiring manager decide between two or more otherwise equally qualified candidates. Writing skills can be tested by having candidates write an autobiography or an essay explaining why they want to become a law enforcement officer. Although many conventional written test formats are available, some departments are using innovative written exam alternatives to assess applicants' basic skills as well as their compatibility with the profession. In addition, more departments are now requiring officers to complete a report based on a scenario watched on a computer so that applicants' computer skills can also be assessed.

The Medical Examination

The medical examination assesses overall applicant health and includes more specific tests for vision, hearing and cardiovascular fitness. Departments do allow applicants to have corrected vision with glasses or contact lenses; however, an emerging issue that many agencies are wrestling with has been whether to permit vision correction by laser surgery. The debate centers on the as-yet-unknown long-term effects of laser correction surgery. Drug testing may be part of the medical examination.

Background Investigations

background check

investigating references listed on an application as well as credit, driving record, criminal conviction, academic background and any professional license required.

Candidates should undergo a thorough **background check**, usually conducted by a member of the agency. Background checks can prevent many potential problems and save the cost of training an unsuitable employee.

The background check includes past employers and references. The person who conducts the background check should contact every reference, employer and instructor. No final candidates should be selected until reference checks are made. Reference checks should be done from those who provided letters of recommendation and others as well. The same inquiries should be made for each candidate, and the questions must be job related.

The background check might also include queries regarding credit, driving record, criminal conviction, academic background and any professional license required. Most states have passed laws making it difficult, if not impossible, for ex-offenders to acquire employment as police officers. Candidates might be asked to sign a release and authorization statement such as that illustrated in Figure 15.3. A request should also be made for documents such as diplomas, birth certificates and driver's licenses. Applicants should be photographed and fingerprinted. Military duty should be confirmed, along with a copy of discharge papers.

FIGURE 15.3
Sample Release and Authorization Statement

Source: © 1991 American Society for Industrial Security, 1655 North Fort Myer Dr., Suite 1200, Arlington, VA 22209. Reprinted by permission from the April 1991 issue of *Security Management*.

Sample release and authorization statement

In connection with this request, I authorize all corporations, companies, former employers, credit agencies, educational institutions, law enforcement agencies, city, state, county and federal courts, military services, and persons to release information they may have about me to the person or company with which this form has been filed and release all parties involved from any liability and reponsibility for doing so.

I also authorize the procurement of an investigative consumer report and understand that it may contain information about my background, mode of living, character, and personal reputation. This authorization, in original or copy form, shall be valid for this and any future reports or updates that may be requested. Further information may be available on written request within a reasonable period of time.

_____   _____
Applicant's signature   Date

One controversial area explored during the background check is past experience with controlled substances. A related concern is whether applicants who smoke cigarettes should be disqualified. Some departments notify potential recruits of their tobacco-free policy. Other departments have no such policy, fearing it would greatly reduce the number of applicants.

Psychological Examinations

The IACP Psychological Service Section recommends that preemployment psychological assessments should be used as one component of the overall selection process. Nearly all departments recognize a need for psychological screening of final candidates for a police position, but because of cost or lack of suitable psychologists, it may not be done. Only the leading candidates are evaluated psychologically to keep costs down. The IACP guidelines state, "Except as allowed or permitted by law, only licensed or certified psychologists trained and experienced in psychological test interpretation and law enforcement psychological assessment techniques should conduct psychological screening for public safety agencies."

The psychological tests often include cognitive ability, quantitative and language reasoning, and the Minnesota Multiphasic Personality Inventory (MMPI), the most widely used psychological assessment test in the country. Most psychological tests measure social maturity and self-control, social tolerance, emotional stability/stress tolerance, confidence/assertiveness, personal insight, empathy, effectiveness in work relationships, conventionality and tendency to abide by rules, nondefensiveness, health and achievement/motivation.

Psychologists who work with police departments must be familiar with validity and reliability measures of tests and the legal requirements imposed by affirmative action and the ADA, as well as pertinent case law and guidelines. When a candidate's psychological tests indicate abnormalities, a department must consider these seriously before hiring. When testing indicates unsuitability or lack of stability, it is best not to hire.

Physical Fitness Tests

Frequent and critical physical tasks required of law enforcement officers include running long distances, up and down stairs and over uneven terrain; heavy lifting and carrying; dragging objects; extracting and dragging victims; pushing heavy objects such as cars; jumping or vaulting over obstacles; climbing fences; using hands and feet in self-defense; and short- and long-term use of force.

Fitness can become a legal issue too. The people and property the police are paid to protect depend on officers being able to do their job. If they cannot, they could be sued. In *Parker v. The District of Columbia* (1988), the jury awarded $425,046 to a man shot by a police officer who was arresting him. As part of its ruling, the court noted, "Officer Hayes simply was not in adequate physical shape. This condition posed a foreseeable risk of harm to others."

Research has found a striking lack of agreement regarding the physical capabilities that should be tested. Physical agility tests are most often of the

FIGURE 15.4
Physical-Agility Course

Source: Criminal Justice Institute, Broward Community College, Ft. Lauderdale, FL. July 1989. Reprinted by permission.

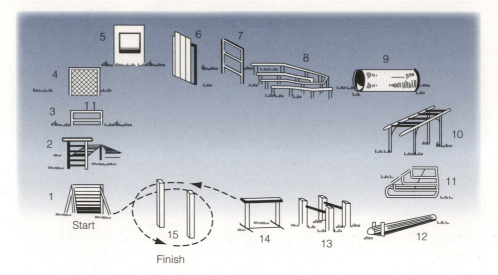

1) Start – 6' Wall
2) Ladder climb – Run across flat landing and down ramp
3) Hurdle – Use hands only!
4) Chain link fence climb – Reach, lift and climb over fence
5) Window climb through
6) Wooden gate – Open fence gate door, go through and close door
7) Hurdle – Climb over
8) Running maze – Enter at left. DO NOT touch siding!
9) Tunnel crawl – Crawl through. DO NOT dive!
10) Hand bar walk – Reach with hands, walk across
11) High stepper – Lift feet high
12) Log walk – Slanted, walk across
13) Horizontal hand walk – Use hands, push off ground and walk across bars
14) Short wall – Jump up and over
15) Pole run – Run to your right, go $1\frac{1}{2}$ times around. DO NOT touch poles!
    FINISH

military type and frequently include an obstacle course. The Broward Community College Criminal Justice Institute's testing center, for example, uses the physical-agility course shown in Figure 15.4.

In addition, Broward uses the following strength and endurance tests:

◉ Trigger pull—strong hand 18, weak hand 12

◉ Ten push-ups

◉ A standing jump based on the person's height

◉ Three pull-ups (from dead hang, palms facing away)

◉ Vehicle push—20 feet (push from rear of vehicle)

◉ Mile run (5 minutes maximum time)

Whether the criteria for passing should be the same for males and females is open to debate. If different standards are set, then the Civil Rights Act of 1991 might be used to claim disparate treatment. This act states, "It shall be an unlawful employment practice . . . in connection with the selection or referral of applicants or candidates for employment or promotion, to adjust the scores of, [or] use different cutoff scores . . . on the basis of race, color, religion, sex or national origin."

Other Issues

Other controversial areas that managers might need to consider when selecting new recruits concern the presence of tattoos and piercings. Given how prevalent this new form of art is among younger generations, departments are well advised to develop policies to address the handling of these issues, lest a discrimination suit arise from the non-hiring of someone with visible tattoos or piercings.

The Interview

In-person interviews may be held at different stages of the selection process, depending on agency protocol. Generally, a filtering process allows only a certain percentage of applicants to be interviewed at each of the various stages of the entire hiring process. For example, a finalist interview generally will consist of the top three remaining candidates, although preliminary interviews may occur before this final selection stage. During such interviews, the department can explain the nature and benefits of the position to be filled, and the applicant, in return, can explain his or her interest in law enforcement and, specifically, the hiring department. Managers should provide an opportunity for the applicant to ask questions because most have questions about salary, benefits, overtime, promotions, uniform allowances and the like.

Civil Service Commission representatives or other selection board personnel usually conduct the final interview. Whether an individual or a panel conducts the interview, those responsible should be familiar with what they can and cannot ask. The same questions prohibited on the application are also prohibited during the interview. Interviewers should also take certain steps before, during and after the interview to make it most effective.

Before the Interview

Interviewers should review the application forms, letters of recommendation, references, notes and all other application materials. They might be asked to do a preliminary ranking of specific factors. Such materials and information should not be discussed with others in the organization and should be kept secured.

Decide the questions to ask or general areas to cover as well as who will ask each question or cover each area. The questions should be designed to determine the "fit" between the candidate and the position. Consider asking the following questions:

- Why do you want to become a law enforcement officer?
- What do you think you will contribute to the department?
- What do you think are the most significant trends in law enforcement?
- How have your education and experiences prepared you for this position?
- What plans do you have for self-development in the next 12 months?
- Why did you select this department/agency?

In framing the questions, consider the following general guidelines:

- Avoid asking questions that call for yes or no answers (closed questions).
- Ask open-ended questions. Interviewers want to hear how candidates think and to see their ability to do so under stress.
- Avoid asking leading questions. Instead ask questions that use "why," "how," "what" and "describe" or "tell me about."
- Avoid asking about any of the prohibited information protected by the Equal Employment Opportunity Act (to be discussed shortly).
- Keep questions job related.

During the Interview

The first step is to establish rapport, a feeling of mutual understanding and trust. A warm greeting, friendly handshake, sincere smile and some small talk are appropriate to establish a relaxed atmosphere.

The next step is usually to explain how the interview will proceed or to set the agenda, including a general time frame. Next the job and the organization are described, followed by the asking of predetermined questions.

During the question/answer portion of the interview, an interviewer's listening skills are critical. Some suggest that interviewers should talk no more than 25 percent of the time. Candidates should do most of the talking. Silences should not be sources of anxiety because candidates often need time to formulate their responses. Wait patiently.

Consider tape recording the interview if several are to be conducted. This can help refresh your memory later. Candidates whose interviews you are recording should be notified of this before the interview begins. Recording all applicants and then listening to them in one sitting allows for better comparisons.

To ensure that interviews are nondiscriminatory:

- Ask the same general questions and require the same standards for all applicants.
- Treat all applicants fairly, equally and consistently.
- Be professional and consistent in addressing men and women. If using first names, do so for all candidates.
- Never indicate a particular interest in hiring a woman or minority person to improve the agency's Affirmative Action/Equal Employment Opportunity profile. It is unlawful and insulting to apply different standards based on a candidate's gender or minority status.

Maintaining eye contact, listening carefully and taking notes are ways to show candidates you are paying attention to their responses. It is often best to take notes on a clipboard held in your lap so candidates do not see what you are writing.

Do not form an opinion early in the interview. Stay neutral throughout. Avoid the **halo effect**—the tendency to assume that candidates who are strong (or weak) in one area will also be strong (or weak) in other areas. Allow time at

halo effect

the tendency to assume that candidates who are strong (or weak) in one area will also be strong (or weak) in other areas.

the end of the interview for candidates to ask questions. Conclude the interview with a thank you and an indication of when you might make a decision.

Some agencies use interview rating forms such as that in Appendix C.

After the Interview

After the successful candidates are selected, notified and have accepted the position, all other candidates should be notified of the decision. All selection process materials such as ratings, reference check notes and the actual application files should be returned immediately to the personnel office or other appropriate location. Successful candidates are usually required to pass a stringent medical examination before the job offer is final.

Selection is an expensive, time-consuming process for any agency. It is also a time-consuming and frustrating process for candidates. Often eligibility lists are obtained even though no actual position may be open. Elapsed time between taking an examination and obtaining a position may vary from weeks to years.

Some states have considered giving statewide examinations, permitting any participating law enforcement agency within the state to draw candidates from this list. This would eliminate much individual recruiting and selecting and reduce costs. However, a strong desire for local testing based on local needs remains. A future consideration could be metropolitan, regional or statewide examinations, with each community making its final selections from this list.

EDUCATIONAL REQUIREMENTS

One employment requirement that may pose difficulties is requiring a certain level of education. As far back as 1916 August Vollmer, father of modern policing, emphasized education for officers. In 1937 the Wickersham Commission and in 1967 the President's Commission on Law Enforcement and the Administration of Justice recommended education beyond high school. Yet most local police departments require only a high-school diploma or its equivalent. In some states, such as Minnesota, a two-year college degree is required, and a four-year degree is highly desired. A U.S. Department of Justice study reported that in 2000, approximately 37 percent of large police agencies required applicants to have some college when applying, compared with 19 percent requiring some collage just 10 years earlier.

The most common reason for not requiring higher education is the fear the requirement would be challenged in court or through labor arbitration. A landmark case was *Griggs v. Duke Power Company* (1971), in which Griggs, an African American employee, claimed that the requirement of having a high school diploma and passing two aptitude tests discriminated against him. The court ruled that any requirements or tests used in selecting or promoting must be job related.

A similar case occurred in *Davis v. City of Dallas* (1985). The Dallas Police Department at the time required applicants to have completed 45 semester hours of college credit with a "C" average. In this case the court ruled in favor of the police department, because the city introduced evidence supporting the educational requirement. Numerous nationwide studies have examined setting education requirements for police departments with favorable conclusions.

Not everyone agrees that college education enhances patrol officer performance. The biggest objections are that there are not enough promotions to satisfy a college-educated employee, the college-educated employee would be less likely to accept authority and that such a requirement would lower the pool of applicants for police positions and would be detrimental to potential minority applicants. Another objection is that life experience provides education in itself, and that much of what officers deal with must be learned on the streets, not in a classroom. Still, the advantages of advanced education appear to outweigh the disadvantages.

Various recruitment and scholarship programs have been developed throughout the country to attract and educate those who are interested in criminal justice professions. One national scholarship program, the Police Corps, recruits and trains college graduates to serve as community police officers.

One concern of those seeking higher education while employed as officers is how to pursue a course of study without taking time off from work. A solution is available through the Internet and distance learning, as discussed in Chapter 7. A question facing applicants and administrators alike is, if a degree is sought, what type of degree is most beneficial? Should it be a degree in liberal arts or in criminal justice? Opinions are mixed on this issue.

A bachelor of arts degree emphasizes problem solving, develops understanding of how perceptions influence behavior, increases a person's comfort with ambiguity and assumes the things going on the world are fluid and interrelated. A bachelor of science degree, in contrast, emphasizes collecting verifiable facts and drawing conclusions based on those facts. Perhaps the type of degree does not matter. The difference may be the type of person who chooses to pursue a bachelor of arts degree rather than a bachelor of science degree.

Another item of contention is how much advanced education is recommended for officers of varying ranks. Some experts think that experience in other law enforcement agencies should substitute for education. What this ratio of experience to education should be is not clear. An officer who has both education and experience is obviously the most desirable. And an officer who possesses a wealth of life experiences is in an even better position.

LAWS AFFECTING EMPLOYMENT

Civil Rights Act of 1964

prohibits discrimination based on race, color, religion, gender or national origin by private employers with 15 or more employees, governments, unions and employment agencies.

Because managers hire and promote, they must be thoroughly familiar with laws related to employment. Several laws affect employment, including the following:

- The *Equal Pay Act of 1963 (EPA)* prohibits discrimination in wages on the basis of gender for all employers.
- The **Civil Rights Acts of 1964** *and 1970* prohibit race discrimination in hiring, placement and continuation of employment for all private employers, unions and employment agencies.

Title VII of the Civil Rights Act of 1964, as amended by the Equal Employment Opportunity Act (EEOA) of 1972, prohibits discrimination based on race, color, religion, gender or national origin for private employers with 15 or more employees, governments, unions and employment agencies.

- The *Age Discrimination in Employment Act (ADEA) of 1967*, amended in 1978, prohibits discrimination based on age for people between the ages of 40 and 70.

- *Title IX of 1972 Education Amendments* prohibits discrimination in education benefits based on race, color, religion, gender and national origin.

- The *Rehabilitation Act of 1973*, amended in 1980, prohibits discrimination against handicapped individuals for federal contractors and the federal government.

- The *Pregnancy Discrimination Act of 1978*, an amendment to Title VII, prohibits discrimination in employment on the basis of pregnancy, childbirth and related conditions for all private employers with 15 or more employees, governments, unions and employment agencies.

- The *Civil Service Reform Act of 1978* requires a federal government "workforce reflective of the nation's diversity."

- The *Immigration Reform and Control Act of 1986* prohibits discrimination against qualified aliens or on the basis of national origin.

- The *Americans with Disabilities Act (ADA) of 1990* prohibits discrimination based on physical or intellectual handicap for employers with 15 or more employees.

The legislation guaranteeing rights for people with disabilities provides only for fair and equal treatment in the workplace based on ability. Private employers or government agencies are not required to hire candidates for employment who are not qualified to perform essential job functions. The ADA is discussed in detail following this overview.

> **Equal Employment Opportunity Commission (EEOC)**
>
> enforces laws prohibiting job discrimination based on race, color, religion, gender, national origin, handicapping condition or age between 40 and 70.

The Equal Employment Opportunity Commission (EEOC) enforces laws prohibiting job discrimination based on race, color, religion, gender, national origin, handicapping condition or age between 40 and 70.

> **adverse impact**
>
> when the *rate* of selection is different for special classes than for the most selected class of applicants; the rule of thumb is that an adverse impact occurs when the selection rate, or percentage passing, of any special class of persons is less than 80 percent of the selection rate of the top scoring group.

If a department has a selection standard or requirement that results in rejection of a greater percentage of a certain class of applicants such as minorities or women, an adverse impact has occurred. An **adverse impact** is when the *rate* of selection is different for special classes than for the most selected class of applicants. The rule of thumb is that an adverse impact occurs when the selection rate, or percentage passing, of any special class of persons is less than 80 percent of the selection rate of the top scoring group.

To comply with Equal Employment Opportunity requirements and avoid legal problems, law enforcement agencies must hire personnel to meet very specific standards directly related to the job. A **bona fide occupational qualification (BFOQ)** is one that is reasonably necessary to perform a job. An example of a bona fide occupational qualification in law enforcement might be that the applicant has normal or correctable-to-normal hearing and vision or that the person be able to drive a vehicle.

> **bona fide occupational qualification (BFOQ)**
>
> a requirement reasonably necessary to perform the job; it may on the surface appear to be discrimination.

The Family and Medical Leave Act of 1993

The Family and Medical Leave Act of 1993 requires companies of 50 or more employees to allow employees 12 weeks a year of unpaid leave of absence for parenting or medical reasons.

The Uniformed Services Employment and Reemployment Rights Act of 1994

The Uniformed Services Employment and Reemployment Rights Act (USERRA) of 1994 provides that returning service members are to be reemployed in the job they would have attained had they not been absent for military service, with the same seniority, status and pay as well as other rights and benefits. USERRA also requires that employers provide COBRA-like continuation of group health coverage for as long as 18 months for employees on military leave and their covered dependents who would otherwise lose their coverage.

The Americans with Disabilities Act of 1990

The Department of Justice (DOJ) estimates that about 20 percent of Americans have disabilities and that this figure will rise (Kanable, 2008, p.68). Among this population, it is likely that some will apply for positions within law enforcement agencies. The ADA of 1990, Title I, became effective in 1992. Title II, which involves discrimination in employment practices, went into effect in 1994 and applies to all agencies with 15 or more employees.

The ADA Amendment Act of 2008 (ADAAA), which went into effect on January 1, 2009, retained the basic three-part ADA definition but broadened the meaning of *disability* and other key terms. The purpose of the amendment is to reinstate a "broad scope of protection" by expanding the definition of the term *disability*, to include many types of impairments not previously covered, including epilepsy, diabetes, multiple sclerosis, intellectual disabilities, major depression and bipolar disorder. Although it may take several years to determine what effect the ADA amendment will have on police departments and municipalities, "Most experts agree that an increase in the number of ADA-related lawsuits is likely to result" (Collins, 2009a, p.12).

 Law enforcement is directly affected by the ADA's goal of guaranteeing individuals with disabilities access to employment and to governmental programs, services and activities.

TABLE 15.1 Terms Associated with the ADA

The ADA uses numerous terms to describe its requirements and the obligations of those covered by the law. Here is a brief index and short explanation of some of the key words and phrases commonly used in the ADA, updated by the ADAAA* ("Questions and Answers," 2009).	
Disability	(1) A mental or physical impairment that substantially limits a major life activity; (2) a record of having such an impairment; (3) being regarded as having such an impairment. (When an entity such as an employer takes an action prohibited by the ADA based on an actual or perceived impairment.*) The ADAAA states that the term *disability* shall be construed broadly.
Impairment	A physiological or mental disorder. The ADAAA states that impairments that are episodic or in remission are disabilities if they would be substantially limiting when active.*
Substantial limitation	When compared to the average person: (1) an inability to perform a major life activity; (2) a significant restriction on how or how long the activity can be performed; or (3) a significant restriction on the ability to perform a class or broad range of jobs. The ADAAA excludes the common cold, common influenza, sprained joints, broken bones, appendicitis and seasonal allergies.*
Major life activity	Basic functions that the average person in the general population can do with little or no difficulty such as walking, seeing, hearing, breathing, speaking, procreating, learning, sitting, standing, performing manual tasks, working or having intimate sexual relations. In addition to a nonexhaustive list of major life activities the ADAAA adds the operation of major bodily functions, including functions of the immune system, normal cell growth, digestive, bowel, bladder, neurological, brain, circulatory, respiratory, endocrine and reproductive.*
Otherwise qualified	A person with a disability who satisfies all of the requirements of the job such as education, experience or skill and who can perform the essential functions of the job with or without reasonable accommodation.
Essential functions	The fundamental, not marginal, duties of a job.
Reasonable accommodation	A change in the application process, work environment, or job descriptions involving marginal functions of the job, or the use of modified or auxiliary devices that enable a person with a disability to perform the essential functions of the job without causing an undue hardship or direct threat to the health and safety of herself or himself or of others.
Undue hardship	Significant difficulty or expense relative to the size and overall financial resources of the employer.
Direct threat	A significant risk of substantial harm based on valid, objective evidence and not mere speculation.

Source: Paula N. Rubin. *The Americans with Disabilities Act and Criminal Justice: An Overview.* Washington, DC: National Institute of Justice, Research in Action, September 1993, p.4. Updated 2009, "Questions and Answers on the Notice of Proposed Rulemaking for the ADA Amendments Act of 2008,*" Washington, DC: Equal Opportunities Employment Commission, September 23, 2009.

The ADA prohibits employers from discriminating against a *qualified individual with a disability (QID)* in all areas of employment, including hiring, training, promoting, terminating and compensating. It also prohibits discrimination in nonemployment areas and requires accessibility to all services and facilities of public entities. Table 15.1 contains a brief explanation of key terms commonly used in the ADA. Notice especially the definitions for *disability* and *otherwise qualified.*

The ADA also establishes the following excluded disorders that are not caused by a physical impairment and thus are not considered disabilities: bisexuality, compulsive gambling, exhibitionism, gender-identity disorders, homosexuality, kleptomania, pedophilia, pyromania, sexual behavior disorder, transsexualism, transvestism and voyeurism.

Employment Issues

This act has had a significant impact on the recruiting process. Most agencies have had to reorganize some of their recruiting procedures. To be in compliance, administrators should identify "essential functions" in job descriptions.

Based on these, they should next develop selection criteria—ways to measure an applicant's ability to perform each essential job function.

 The ADA prohibits medical inquiries or evaluations, including some psychiatric evaluations, until after a job offer has been made.

The medical examination remains an important part of the application process, however. Serious consequences could arise as a result of a police officer not having the ability to perform essential job functions. Thus, "After evaluating the applicant, and once the employer decides this is a desirable person to hire, a conditional offer of employment is made; the condition being that the applicant is physically and mentally capable of performing the essential job functions. Then, at that time, and only at that time, would the employer be permitted to make medically related inquires" (Mayer, 2009, p.14). If an applicant's disability would cause a direct threat to the applicant or public safety, the risk must be identified and documented by objective medical evidence as well.

Not all psychological examinations are disallowed under the ADA. Only those tests or scales specifically designed to disclose an impairment are disallowed. The ADA does not address polygraph tests and does not consider physical agility tests to be medical examinations; therefore, such tests are not governed by the ADA. Applicants may be subjected to drug testing. Further, employers may hold illegal drug users and alcoholics to the same performance standards as other employees.

Reasonable Accommodations

Employers must make "reasonable accommodations" for any physical or mental limitations of a QID unless the employer can show that such accommodation would create an undue hardship or could threaten the health and safety of the QID or other employees. Reasonable accommodations might include modifying existing facilities to make them accessible, job restructuring, part-time or modified work schedules or acquiring or modifying equipment. However, reasonable accommodations are not required when providing them causes an undue hardship for the agency.

It is unlikely that police agencies will be required to make substantial accommodations in the hiring process because the nature of police work requires some degree of fitness that can be substantiated through a job analysis. However, a reasonable accommodation goes beyond modifying job descriptions. It also means making buildings accessible to the physically disabled. Accessibility applies to employees and to non-employees as well and involves parking lots, the building itself, the front desk, the elevator and staff. Appendix D contains an accessibility checklist.

Nonemployment Issues

The ADA regulates all services and programs provided by public entities, which includes law enforcement agencies. Police agencies report that the greatest difficulties they face when responding to people with disabilities are citizens' misunderstanding of the police role in dealing with persons with disabilities; difficulty reaching help on weekends and evenings; and mistaking disabilities for antisocial behavior.

The ADA does not prohibit officers from enforcing the law, including use of force necessary to protect officer or public safety. However, the ADA does require officers who question suspects at the police station to provide communication and to delay questioning hearing-impaired suspects or witnesses until such assistance is available.

Enforcement of the ADA

The regulating agencies for the ADA are the Department of Justice (DOJ), the Architectural Transportation Compliance Board (ATCB), the Equal Employment Opportunity Commission (EEOC) and the Federal Communications Commission (FCC). Agencies out of compliance may face civil penalties as high as $50,000 for the first violation and $100,000 for subsequent violations, in addition to being ordered to modify their facilities to be in compliance.

AFFIRMATIVE ACTION

Employers must avoid discrimination in the hiring process, and in some instances they must actively seek out certain people and make certain they have equal opportunities to obtain jobs.

An **affirmative action program (AAP)** is a written plan to assist members of traditionally discriminated against minority groups in employment, government contracts and education.

affirmative action program (AAP)
a written plan to ensure fair recruitment, hiring and promotion practices.

The Supreme Court has held that mandatory quotas established to meet an affirmative action plan's racially motivated goals are unlawful and thereby unconstitutional under federal law. In *Griggs v. Duke Power Company* (1971) the Court ruled that racially based quotas violated federal law.

In 1978 the Supreme Court, in *Regents of University of California v. Bakke*, allowed use of race as a factor among many in admissions to achieve diversity. Alan Bakke, a 37-year-old White male engineer, was denied admission to the medical school at the University of California at Davis, although his Medical College Admission Test score and grade-point average were higher than those of several of the 16 minority students admitted under a set-aside. In a 5–4 decision, the Court voted to invalidate the UC Davis quota system and admit Bakke to medical school. However, it endorsed affirmation action in principle.

During the 2002–2003 term the Supreme Court handed down two landmark decisions regarding affirmative action. In *Grutter v. Bollinger* (2003) the Court upheld the University of Michigan's law school admissions' racially based affirmative action plan which permitted race to be one factor used in the admissions process. However, in *Gratz v. Bollinger* (2003) the Court declared unconstitutional the University of Michigan's undergraduate admissions program because it made race a "final and critically decisive factor" and used a point system in which the race of an undergraduate applicant was factored into the final score upon which final admission was predicated.

Affirmative action programs are mandated by several employment laws. Their intent is to undo the damage caused by past discrimination. The affirmative action policy of one agency states,

> The Anytown Police Department realizes that discrimination and the prejudice from which it results are deeply ingrained within our culture. Concentration on the mere prevention of discrimination can result in the implementation of practices that provide only superficial equality. Such practices, while possibly within the letter of the law, do not enact the full intent of the federal and state legislation, presidential and gubernatorial executive orders or the courts' interpretation of these mandates. It is, therefore, the intent of the Anytown Police Department to organize and implement policies, procedures, practices and programs that aid in overcoming the effects of past discrimination in regard to all of the protected groups.

special employment groups

groups included in affirmative action programs such as African Americans, Asians, the elderly, Eskimos, Hispanics, homosexuals, immigrants, individuals with acquired immune deficiency syndrome (AIDS), individuals with disabilities, Middle Easterners, Native Americans, religious group members, substance abusers, war veterans, women and youths.

reverse discrimination

giving preferential treatment in hiring and promoting to women and minorities, to the detriment of White males.

Among the **special employment groups** included in affirmative action programs are African Americans, Asians, the elderly, Eskimos, Hispanics, homosexuals, immigrants, individuals with acquired immune deficiency syndrome (AIDS), individuals with disabilities, Middle Easterners, Native Americans, religious group members, substance abusers, war veterans, women and youths.

From this listing, one conclusion is obvious: anyone can fit into a "special employment group." Those responsible for hiring must take precautions to be fair and unbiased. They should recognize existing biases and ensure that biases do not enter into the process—a difficult task. If, for example, an affirmative action plan requires that all members of certain groups, such as minority group members, be given a personal interview, this may cause members not within this group to claim reverse discrimination. **Reverse discrimination** refers to giving women and minorities preferential treatment in hiring and promoting to the detriment of White males.

Several court decisions have struck down affirmative action initiatives as discriminatory. In 1996 both Texas and California (Proposition 209) struck down race-based admissions policies in their universities. The Berger Court sought a middle ground regarding affirmative action, supporting the basic concept but rejecting rigid application. The Rehnquist Court took a more negative view of affirmative action but did not reject the concept totally.

Some departments use a form such as that contained in Appendix E to gather needed affirmative action data.

> **Equal employment opportunity and affirmative action policies begin with recruiting and selecting but are also important in assigning, training, promoting, disciplining and firing personnel.**

Title VII of the Civil Rights Act of 1964 prohibits two types of employment discrimination, whose prohibitions sometimes conflict with each other. The first type of prohibited discrimination is *disparate impact*, which refers to an employer's policy or practice that results in an *unintentional*, disproportionately negative effect on minorities. The second type is *disparate treatment*, which is intentional discrimination based on race, color, religion, sex or national origin. The second type is quite easy to recognize and avoid. Disparate impact is a different story because it is truly unintentional. A claim of disparate impact may be defended against by showing that the policy or practice is "job related for the position in question and consistent with business necessity": "Even if an employer's policy or practice has a disproportionate adverse impact on minorities, the policy or practice may nonetheless be lawful if the employer can establish its job-relatedness and business necessity" (Means and McDonald, 2009, p.21). The recent Supreme Court case of *Ricci v. DeStefano* (2009) dealt with a claim of reverse discrimination. Although the case involved firefighters, it applies equally to law enforcement:

> The city of New Haven, CT decided not to certify two promotional exams it had administered to its firefighters because the White and Hispanic candidates outperformed the Black candidates.

> The city's refusal to certify the test results denied the White and Hispanic firefighters who passed the exams the possibility of promotion. They filed this lawsuit alleging that the city's decision to discard the test results was based on the racial disparity of the test scores and was unlawful racial discrimination. The United States Supreme Court agreed with them, ruling that the city's refusal to certify the tests because of the racially divided scores was unjustified racial discrimination, violating Title VII of the Civil Rights Act of 1964. . . .

> The city of New Haven found itself in the precarious position of having to choose between certifying the exam results, permitting the disproportionate adverse effect on its Black candidates (disparate impact), and refusing to certify the exam results, an intentional race-based decision that would deny the White and Hispanic candidates promotions (disparate treatment). In its attempt to avoid liability for disparate impact discrimination, the city used race as the determining factor in its decision to throw out the test results, thereby committing disparate treatment discrimination. . . .

> The question for the Court then was whether it is permissible to commit one form of discrimination in an effort to avert potential liability for another form of discrimination. The Court's answer was a somewhat qualified "no." The Court explained that the mere fear of litigation is not sufficient to justify the race-based decision to reject the test results. (Means and McDonald, 2009, pp.18, 21–22)

Justice David Souter contended that the situation put New Haven in a "damned-if-you-do-damned-if-you-don't" predicament. Managers in law enforcement are all too familiar with such predications, but decisions must be made.

Because these EEO and AA policies are important in so many areas of management, it is critical that managers understand their own policies as well as the policies and ordinances or statutes of their municipality, state and the country. Such knowledge is critical during the selection process. Possible resources are the director of personnel, the city attorney, law enforcement advisory boards, other law enforcement agencies and the International Association of Chiefs of Police.

In addition to laws related to hiring, many managers also must take into consideration restrictions imposed by unions.

LABOR LAWS AND UNIONS

A **union**, in the broadest context, is any group authorized to represent the members of the law enforcement agency in negotiating matters such as wages, fringe benefits and other conditions of employment. Most states require by statute that certain conditions be met to be recognized as a union or bargaining unit. A **union shop** refers to a situation in which people must belong to or join the union to be hired.

Several laws ensure fair compensation standards as well as employees' rights to bargain collectively with management. Unions have existed in the United States for more than 200 years, beginning in 1792 when shoemakers formed a local union in Philadelphia. In 1932, the **Norris–LaGuardia Act** was passed to regulate employers' use of court injunctions against unions in preventing work stoppages. The act also made yellow-dog contracts illegal. A **yellow-dog contract** forbids new employees to join a union. To do so would be grounds for discharge.

Another major law, sometimes called the "Magna Carta of organized labor," was enacted in 1935.

 The **National Labor Relations Act of 1935 (Wagner Act)** legalized collective bargaining and required employers to bargain with the elected representatives of their employees.

This act sets forth rules and procedures for both employers and employees. Its intent was to define and protect the rights of employees and employers and to encourage collective bargaining.

The **Fair Labor Standards Act (FLSA) of 1938** established the 40-hour week as the basis of compensation and set a minimum wage. Police officers generally are covered by the FLSA. The FLSA requires covered employees to be compensated for overtime at the rate of one and one-half times their regular hourly wage. Time spent engaged in training, which primarily benefits the employer or is done at the employer's direction, is compensable. Employees may be given one and one-half hour compensatory time off for every hour of overtime worked, but public safety employees may be allowed to accumulate only 480 hours of compensatory time. In *Christensen v. Harris County* (2000) the Supreme Court ruled that the FLSA allows a public employer to order an employee to take compensatory time off whenever the employer chooses to do so. The FLSA does not require a public employer to allow its employees the use of comp time on days specifically requested by the employee. It requires

Sidebar glossary

union

any group authorized to represent the members of an agency in negotiating such matters as wages, fringe benefits and other conditions of employment.

union shop

must belong to or join the union to be hired.

Norris–LaGuardia Act

regulated court injunctions against unions and made yellow-dog contracts illegal.

yellow-dog contract

makes union membership illegal under the penalty of discharge.

National Labor Relations Act of 1935 (Wagner Act)

legalized collective bargaining and required employers to bargain with the elected representatives of their employees.

Fair Labor Standards Act (FLSA) of 1938

established the 40-hour week as the basis of compensation and set a minimum wage.

only that comp time be permitted within a reasonable time after the employee requests its use.

Generally, time spent on-call is not compensable under the FLSA unless the employees are required to remain at the employer's premises or are so restricted they cannot engage in personal activities. Time spent commuting from home to work is not compensable, nor is time spent caring for equipment. In addition, volunteers are not covered by the FLSA.

Police managers should review all positions to ascertain which are exempt from the FLSA's overtime pay requirements because "street cops" designated as "first responders" and detectives are *not* exempt and must be paid overtime if they work beyond their FLSA threshold (Collins, 2008). Specialists and others with supervisory ranks *may* be exempt if their salary is at least $455 a week and their primary duties meet the applicable exemption requirements of "exercise of discretion" and "independent judgment."

The **Taft–Hartley Act of 1947** was passed to balance the power of unions and management by banning several unfair labor practices, including closed shops. A **closed shop** prohibits management from hiring nonunion workers. In effect, this act allowed states to pass their own **right-to-work laws**, making it illegal to require employees to join a union. In addition, the **Landrum–Griffin Act of 1959** required regularly scheduled elections of union officers by secret ballot and regulated the handling of union funds.

 The **National Labor Relations Board (NLRB) is the principal enforcement agency for laws regulating relations between management and unions.**

When relationships between management and labor unions are successful, it is the result of hard work by two committed, value-based leaders: the police chief and the union president. A respectful relationship, despite differences that will inevitably arise, is in the best interest of the department and the union.

Strong feelings for and against unions are common in the general public and among those in law enforcement. For many law enforcement agencies, unions are a positive force; for others, they create problems and dissension; and in yet others, they are nonexistent. Even in agencies without unions, however, the possibility of employees becoming unionized is always there. Managers need to understand the current nature of unions and how they can benefit from the mission of a law enforcement agency.

Unions are often the result of poor management because management practices may antagonize employees and cause them to seek more control over the workplace through collective bargaining.

Collective Bargaining

 The primary purpose of unions is to improve employment conditions through collective bargaining.

Taft–Hartley Act of 1947

balanced the power of unions and management by prohibiting several unfair labor practices, including closed shops, which prohibited management from hiring nonunion workers.

closed shop

prohibits management from hiring nonunion workers.

right-to-work laws

make it illegal to require employees to join a union; established by the Taft-Hartley Act of 1938.

Landrum–Griffin Act of 1959

required regularly scheduled elections of union officers by secret ballot and regulated the handling of union funds.

National Labor Relations Board (NLRB)

the principal enforcement agency for laws regulating relations between management and unions.

Police officers stand in support of their union representative during a city council meeting, at which council members were proposing a 6.5 percent pay cut for police officers as a way to help the city resolve its financial crisis.

© AP Images/Denis Poroy

collective bargaining

the process whereby representatives of employees meet with representatives of management to establish a written contract setting forth working conditions for a specific time, usually one to three years.

Collective bargaining is the process whereby representatives of employees meet with representatives of management to establish a written contract that sets forth working conditions for a specific time, usually one to three years. The contract deals with wages and benefits and with hours of work and overtime, grievance procedures, disciplinary procedures, health and safety, employees' rights, seniority and contract duration. Most states have laws restricting officers from going on strike.

Law enforcement managers must recognize that officers have a right to join a union and to negotiate with management. Unions have caused administrators to reexamine their roles in negotiations, roles that have varied from remoteness to direct involvement at the bargaining table. In more recent years both sides have engaged outside experts to represent their positions in negotiations, both at the bargaining table and during arbitration proceedings.

Collective bargaining legislation has been proposed in the past, with the International Association of Chiefs of Police (IACP) opposing such legislation. The IACP sent an alert to its members stating, "Safe streets and safe neighborhoods require well-trained and well-managed police departments that are responsive and accountable to the communities they serve. The IACP believes that the provisions of H.R. 980 would effectively federalize state and local governmental labor-management relations and as a result, make these goals harder to achieve" (Mays, 2007, p.8). However, the bill is strongly supported by groups representing rank-and-file officers (Greene, 2008, p.4). About 20 states do not fully protect public safety employees' collective bargaining rights, and Virginia and North Carolina prohibit public safety employees from collectively bargaining.

The House of Representatives passed the Public Safety Employer-Employee Cooperation Act of 2007 (HR 980), but it was defeated in the Senate. Similar legislation, the Public Safety Employer–Employee Cooperation Act (H.R. 413), has been introduced in the 2009 congressional session, with the IACP continuing to strongly oppose it:

> Briefly, H.R. 413 would effectively federalize state and local government labor-management relations and deprive state and local governments of the necessary flexibility to manage their public safety operations in a manner that they choose. By mandating a "one-size-fits-all" approach to labor-management relations, H.R. 413 ignores the fact that every jurisdiction has unique needs and therefore requires the freedom to manage its public safety workforce in the manner that is determined to be the most effective.
>
> The bill has previously passed the House of Representatives by overwhelming majorities. In the Senate, several attempts have been made to pass the bill, but to date, all have been unsuccessful. (Mays, 2009, p.12)

This bill was referred to the House Committee on Education and Labor on January 9, 2009 ("H.R. 413, The Public Safety Employer–Employee Cooperation Act of 2009"). On March 10, 2010, the bill underwent hearings held by the Subcommittee on Health, Employment, Labor, and Pensions, after which it was again referred to committee, where it presently exists.

Most state collective bargaining statutes divide the scope of bargaining into three categories: (1) voluntary subjects that may be negotiated if both parties agree, (2) mandatory subjects that must be negotiated and (3) forbidden subjects that cannot be negotiated. *Voluntary topics* include issues such as safety, union security and productivity. *Mandatory subjects* usually include all matters directly affecting wages, hours and terms and conditions of employment. *Excluded subjects* generally include the mission and functions of the agency, how the work is to be done and the equipment that will be used.

The union is obligated to protect the union employees' interests. Management is obligated to manage and control the agency. The ultimate goal of both should be excellent law enforcement services. At times the relationship develops into a struggle for power, with each assuming an adversarial position. By working together, management and unions can achieve the agency's mission to provide effective service to the community.

Key Contract Clauses

Although all clauses of the contract are important, five clauses deserve special attention: (1) a management rights clause, (2) the definition of a grievance and the procedure for filing one and a procedure for handling disciplinary matters, (3) a no-strike provision, (4) a "zipper clause" and (5) a maintenance-of-benefits clause.

Managements' rights clauses usually include the right to plan, direct and control all police operations and set department policy, goals and objectives. This includes the right to hire, discipline, promote, train, fire, determine standards of conduct and the like.

just cause

principle stating that
a disciplinary case
must be presented
in two distinct parts:
(1) management must
first prove that the act
in question was actually
committed in violation
of an agency policy
and (2) management
must show that the
discipline imposed was
not arbitrary, capricious,
unreasonable or
discriminatory.

zipper clause

clearly states that the
contract is a complete,
full agreement between
the two parties and
neither party is obligated
to negotiate on other
items during the term of
the contract.

Grievance clauses generally define what constitutes a grievance, the steps in the process and time limits. In collective bargaining, part of the disciplinary process is the basic principle of **just cause**. Under the just cause principle, a disciplinary case must be presented in two distinct parts. First, management must prove that the act in question was actually committed and that it violated some rule or policy. Second, management must show that the discipline imposed was not arbitrary, capricious, unreasonable or discriminatory.

No-strike clauses put the union on record as being against strikes and, properly written, could allow the department to seek monetary damages from the union in case of a strike. A **zipper clause** clearly states that the contract is a complete, full agreement between the two parties and neither party is obligated to negotiate on other items during the term of the contract. A *maintenance-of-benefits clause* identifies and describes in detail the specific benefits that will be maintained under the new contract.

Midterm Bargaining

In states with collective bargaining, if management wants to make material changes to existing rules or implement new rules, it should involve the union bargaining unit before the effective date of the new rules or regulations.

Types of Law Enforcement Unions

Many law enforcement labor organizations simply evolved. A social group would be formed to discuss the interrelationships of a department and plan social events for the year, often including family members. Over the years these groups started discussions concerning perceived department problems and eventually grew into benevolent associations. Today, law enforcement labor representation groups include local department benevolent associations that act on behalf of personnel, independent unions with a regional or state affiliation and nationally supported and organized labor unions such as the American Federation of Labor–Congress of Industrial Organizations (AFL-CIO).

One highly debated issue concerning union membership has been who should belong. What ranks should be included? Should managers and supervisors belong to the same union as line officers because their interests in wages and benefits are largely the same? Is there a conflict of interest?

Some studies indicate that 85 percent of law enforcement unions include both patrol officers and sergeant levels or above, which means that only 15 percent consist solely of patrol-level officers. As long as issues are mainly concerned with wages and benefits, this is not a problem. But when issues involve taking more control of what management considers its rights, such as one-officer versus two-officer patrol cars, transfers and promotions, working-hour assignments and the like, conflict can occur. Some agencies have formed separate management-level units within the same umbrella as the rank-and-file union to overcome the objections to a single unit.

Some managers would rather not have unions. If unions are to exist, most managers would rather they be local and independent. Local union membership provides opportunity for personal, face-to-face discussions about local department problems; lower dues; more control over who is to represent the department; and control over all expenditures.

On the other hand, national union representation allows national research on wages, benefits and other issues; outside representation at discussions; and greater political influence. Legal assistance is often available. Outside representation prevents union conflict issues spilling over into everyday performance and personal relationships. The main national union groups are

- *International Union of Police Associations*—affiliated with the AFL-CIO.
- *Fraternal Order of Police*—the oldest police organization in the United States; emphasizes collective bargaining in some areas and socializing in other areas.
- *National Association of Police Officers*—consists of police unions opposed to affiliation with the AFL-CIO.
- *International Brotherhood of Police Officers*—founded in Rhode Island in 1969; emphasizes collective bargaining.
- *International Brotherhood of Teamsters*—a private union.
- *American Federation of State, County and Municipal Employees*—a union for public employees founded in 1936, affiliated with the American Federation of Labor.

The National Association of Police Organizations (NAPO) is a coalition of U.S. police unions and associations serving the interest of law enforcement officers through legislative and legal advocacy, political action and education: "Founded in 1978, NAPO is now the strongest unified voice supporting law enforcement officers in the United States. NAPO represents more than 2,000 police unions and associations, 241,000 sworn law enforcement officers, 11,000 retired officers and more than 100,000 citizens who share a common dedication to fair and effective crime control and law enforcement" ("Welcome to NAPO," 2009).

Each organization decides what kind of union to have and often bases its selection on past local management–rank-and-file relationships. Attitudes toward management have often been as much a reason for union membership as other conditions of employment.

Reasons for Joining Law Enforcement Unions

A common reason for joining a union is a perceived lack of communication, inaction or deliberate disregard for the feelings and reasonable desires of the majority of employees. Other frequently mentioned reasons are lack of concern for the employees' general needs, lower wages and fewer benefits than comparable departments, peer pressure, general frustration, conditions of equipment or employment, imagined wrongs, lack of concern for legitimate grievances, badly handled personnel problems, inadequate communications, favoritism, lack of formal grievance procedures, distrust between management and the rank and file, disregard of job stress factors, past bad-faith bargaining and negotiating, lack of recognition for a job well done and a lack of leadership by management.

People join unions to ensure fair treatment, to improve their economic situation and to satisfy social needs.

Management versus Employee Rights

Controversy between management and unions revolves largely around what is perceived as reasonable management and employee rights or demands. Managers must have specific functions reserved. On the other hand, management depends on employees to do the job. The better law enforcement tasks are performed, the better the managers and employees are perceived by the community they both serve. The better the community perception and rating of the agency, the greater the acceptance of law enforcement needs in terms of wages, benefits and general support.

The most frequently reserved management rights are determining staffing and staffing levels; determining work schedules, patrol areas and work assignments; controlling police operations; establishing standards of conduct on and off duty; establishing hiring, promoting, transferring, firing and disciplinary procedures; setting work-performance standards; establishing department goals, objectives, policies and procedures; and establishing training programs and who should attend. Management should not have these rights unreasonably infringed upon at the bargaining table. Contracts are long-term instruments that affect future managers as well as the present regime. Management must possess sufficient rights to fulfill the agency's mission to the community.

The most desirable way to avoid management–employee conflict is to resolve issues at the lowest level possible. Primarily, this means between first-line supervisors and patrol officers (or equal rank). Most issues should be resolved at this level, and the first-line supervisor must have the responsibility and authority to do so.

Others perceive a more basic conflict—a distinct difference between the professional law enforcement stance and that advocated by unions. The professional model: We look to lateral entry and professional skills rather than time on the job in our selections. We want to expand the entire profession. The union model: We protect our people no matter what happens. If we have to pick between the young, educated professional and the old, established worker, we go with the old one every time.

Management, Unions and Politics

Management would like to believe that it can administer a law enforcement agency without being involved in politics. Many administrators say, "I try to stay out of politics." If "politics" is perceived as actively supporting candidates during political campaigns, it is possible. But to remove oneself from all politics is virtually impossible. Locally elected government officials approve law enforcement budgets. Passage of desirable ordinances and statutes depends on elected officials. Gaining the respect and support of these officials after they are elected is a necessity to law enforcement administration. In some cities, unions are also very active in elections and in supporting specific candidates.

Law enforcement management involvement in politics is less likely in communities with a council/manager form of government because the chief executive officer reports directly to the city manager. The city manager is a buffer between law enforcement managers and the city's elected officials.

City management has many departments and varied personnel concerns. Even though city government may sympathize with law enforcement demands, it must balance the demands of all departments. City administration may resist binding arbitration for this reason. Final decisions are made by people not associated with the local government and who have no personal stake in how the decision may be implemented financially or managerially.

Levels of Bargaining

Bargaining may take place at various levels ranging from discussion to court settlements. At the most cooperative level, *open discussion* resolves issues and results in a win-win situation, with a contract that both sides consider fair. If discussion does not resolve all the issues, the next level may be *mediation*, bringing in a neutral third party to assist in the discussion. A mediator helps the two sides reach an agreement.

If the negotiation process stalls, the matter may be referred to *arbitration*, with the consent of all parties. Usually three arbitrators are appointed, and a majority makes the decision. Either a statute or agreement of all parties determines the method of selection. Arbitration should be a last resort. Beyond arbitration, the matter can sometimes be appealed to the courts.

 Negotiations usually proceed through discussion, mediation, arbitration and the courts.

Management and Unions Working Together

Carpenter and Fulton (2010, p.115) note, "Too many supervisors at all levels of police management don't fully understand their relationship with the unions, nor their obligations under the union/management contracts." Managers, regardless of rank, must work within the confines of the contract, and remaining ignorant to the contract's terms or ignoring them is to invite problems into their command and bring possibly seriously harm to their careers. Consequently, the following guidelines are recommended for all managers (Carpenter and Fulton, pp.115–117):

- Know the contracts.
- Comply with the contracts.
- Treat employees fairly.
- Know the steward.
- Follow the grievance procedure.

Law enforcement management/union decision making may involve mayors, councils, city managers and often outside negotiators, arbitrators, grievance committees and even the courts. Although law enforcement officers usually do not have the right to strike, they may accomplish similar results through actions such as "blue flu" or slowdowns. Bargaining units of some type are a fact of administrators' lives. It is better to form good relationships that lead to positive results for both sides than to begin with adversarial attitudes. Working within the confines of the written contract is important at all levels of supervision and management, from sergeant to chief.

Open communication, reasonable expectations, honest cooperation, upfront presentations, a sincere desire to negotiate and common objectives are all evidence of good-faith bargaining. Both sides should avoid delaying tactics such as failing to disclose important demands until the end; deliberately withholding information; deliberately providing misinformation, untruths or distortions; providing only information that weakens the others' position; or deliberately exhibiting unwillingness to resolve the issues so as to throw the process into binding arbitration.

Successful management/union negotiations begin with a positive atmosphere within the agency during everyday activities and normal routine, for it is here that the tone for mutual respect is established. Everyday problems have a way of developing into grievances, which may then become issues in management/union negotiations. When first-line supervisors have open dialogue and communication about problems and this continues up the hierarchy, an avenue is established for later openness in labor relations as well.

Negotiations should be entered into far ahead of budget deadlines. Timing should also avoid city and union elections. Both sides should agree on rules for negotiation procedures; maintain open channels of communication; present logical, reasonable justification for their positions; and prepare areas of agreement as well as disagreement. Areas of agreement should be disposed of as soon as possible to focus energies on differences. Both sides should recognize the emotions involved and resist overreactions. Officials on both sides should be aware that off-the-cuff, unsupportable statements can stop negotiations. Items for negotiation should not be discussed outside negotiation proceedings. No individual department head should have the authority or responsibility for final settlement. Lay the past contract and the proposed contract side by side and compare wording, additions and deletions, word for word, page by page.

The most equitable negotiations take place in an atmosphere of openness, cooperation, faith and trust. Seek fairness and focus on the main goals of both sides.

Collective Bargaining, Arbitration and the CEO

Chief executive officers (CEOs)—such as chiefs of police, sheriffs, superintendents, directors of public safety or any other title denoting head of an agency—might take several positions in collective bargaining negotiations. At the very least, CEOs should be available to describe how a prior contract has affected the agency or how changes in the community or the agency require changes in

AWAY FROM THE DESK: The Effects of the Economy on Unions and Union Contracts

I have been the chief of police in a medium-size midwestern community for six years. During this time I have yet to operate under a union contract for either officers or supervisors, which has given me an opportunity to address operational issues. In fact, the lack of opportunity to review contract issues has been a large struggle in this organization, as only wages and insurance have been arbitrated in the last six years. I inherited a department that was in need of change, and the labor contracts play a large part in whether or not one can be successful, particularly when one is hired from the outside to help make change. The recent troubles with our economy have led to a lack of funding to support union requests, thus preventing opportunities for government policy makers to work closely with their labor groups. As a result, it has become very difficult as a leader to implement change or address inefficiencies or ineffectiveness because often the attitude, effort and morale are significantly impacted, and it takes a great deal of relationship building and luck to make progress in today's environment. One cannot underestimate the necessity of strong management and labor relationships. As a change agent, I have found that it is essential.

—*Chief Shaun E. LaDue*

the new contract. During negotiation stages, the CEO or the management representatives should be informed about how matters under discussion might affect their operations.

In some instances CEOs may be facilitators or advisors. In this role they can tell negotiators how specific actions would affect management's ability to administer the agency. In other instances CEOs may actively participate in the pre-negotiation stages but become interested bystanders during actual negotiations, or they may actively participate in the negotiations.

In all discussions, mediations and arbitrations, retain careful records. What occurs at one level of negotiations is likely to be reviewed at the next level. In addition, what is stated at any time in the process is usually subject to appeal. After the negotiation process is complete, a contract is written containing the specific terms of the agreement. Everyone affected by the contract should receive a copy and understand its terms. In this way, agencies can head off conflict and potential lawsuits.

Avoiding Conflict and Potential Lawsuits

Collins (2009b, p.12) cautions, "There are few changes involving or affecting working conditions that a public employer can make without giving notice to, and if requested, discussing the matter first with the employees' elected representative." The following suggestions are offered as a way to avoid conflict and promote good management-labor relations (Collins, pp.12–13):

- Dealing directly with employees on matters that are properly the subject of negotiations.
- Hiring and creating a new position are not subject to a bargaining obligation. Requiring a certain level of education or a drug or alcohol test of applicants is outside the scope of bargaining.
- New rules and practices require giving the union notice and the opportunity to bargain. Examples of mandatory bargaining include changing hours an employee is required to work, job descriptions, promotion criteria, performance evaluation systems and dress and grooming regulations.
- Changing schedules to avoid overtime requires employers to provide advance notice to the union and, if requested, bargain in good faith.
- Contracting out unit work to save money or improve efficiency depends on whether the agency is expressly barred from doing so in the collective-bargaining agreement.

Wexler (2008, p.2) notes, "Like everything else, labor relations in policing are a function of the quality of leadership on both sides. There will always be inherent differences between a police chief and a police union leader in the nature of their responsibilities, their priorities and their constituencies." The more effective the leadership on both sides, the better the labor relations will be.

SUMMARY

Selection of law enforcement personnel is a critical management function. The selection process is based on carefully specified criteria and usually includes completing an application form, undergoing a series of tests and examinations, passing a background check and successfully completing an interview. The most common screening methods for selection are basic skills/written tests, medical examinations, background investigations, psychological examinations, physical fitness tests and oral interviews.

Selection is often affected by laws related to equal employment, affirmative action and labor (unions). Title VII of the Civil Rights Act of 1964, as amended by the Equal Employment Opportunity Act (EEOA) of 1972, prohibits discrimination based on race, color, religion, gender or national origin for private employers with 15 or more employees, governments, unions and employment agencies. The Equal Employment Opportunity Commission enforces laws prohibiting job discrimination based on race, color, religion, gender, national origin, handicapping condition or age between 40 and 70. Law enforcement is directly affected by the ADA's goal of guaranteeing individuals with disabilities access to employment and to government programs, services and activities. The ADA prohibits medical inquiries or evaluations, including some psychiatric evaluations, until after a job offer has been made.

An affirmative action program (AAP) is a written plan to assist members of traditionally discriminated against minority groups in employment, government contracts and higher education. Equal employment opportunity and affirmative action policies begin with recruiting and selecting but are also important in assigning, training, promoting, disciplining and firing personnel.

The National Labor Relations Act of 1935 (Wagner Act) legalized collective bargaining and required employers to bargain with the elected representatives of their employees. The National Labor Relations Board (NLRB) is the principal enforcement agency for laws regulating relations between management and unions.

The primary purpose of unions is to improve employment conditions through collective bargaining. People join unions to ensure fair treatment, to improve their economic situations and to satisfy social needs. Negotiations usually proceed through discussion, mediation, arbitration and the courts.

CHALLENGE FIFTEEN

The Greenfield Police Department's hiring process has not changed in many years. Officer applicants, without exception, must have a two-year law enforcement degree to be eligible to apply. Applicants are initially screened with a standardized written exam testing general knowledge. The test uses language not specific to the Greenfield Police Department and appears to be a test developed decades ago by another department. The test includes outdated references to technology and police procedures. The test emphasizes officer qualities suited for a traditional "crime fighting" strategy.

The interview portion of the hiring process consists of a panel of police managers reading general questions to the applicants. Each applicant is given a certain amount of time to respond. Follow-up questions are discouraged, and the managers are provided with the preferred answers to use in assessing the applicant.

Successful applicants are required to pass a rigorous physical fitness test. The applicants are tested for strength, endurance and agility. It is common knowledge within the department that many of the current officers could no longer pass the test.

You have recently been promoted to captain. The new chief has asked you to study the hiring procedure and to offer suggestions for updating it. The chief wants a process that reflects the department's emphasis on community and intelligence-led policing.

1. The Greenfield Police Department has a requirement that applicants must have a two-year degree in law enforcement. Can you think of any potential negative consequences resulting from this requirement?

2. What changes should you suggest for the written exam?

3. What are the benefits of adding an essay to the written test?

4. How could you improve the interview portion of the hiring process?

5. Do you see any pitfalls with the physical fitness test?

DISCUSSION QUESTIONS

1. During which stages of the selection process is discrimination most likely to occur?

2. Compare and contrast the Equal Employment Opportunity Act and an affirmative action plan.

3. Have there been any civil suits related to law enforcement employment in your area in the past few years? In your state?

4. What is the most difficult part of the selection process?

5. What questions would you ask during an employment interview?

6. How much education should an entry-level position in law enforcement require? A management position?

7. What are other bona fide occupational requirements for an entry-level position in law enforcement? For a management position?

8. Have you ever belonged to a union? If so, what were your reactions to it?

9. Do you favor unions for law enforcement employees? What are the advantages and disadvantages for management?

10. Do you feel H.R. 431 should be passed? Why or why not.

REFERENCES

Carpenter, Michael, and Fulton, Roger. *Law Enforcement Management: What Works and What Doesn't.* Flushing, NY: Looseleaf Law Publications, Inc., 2010.

Collins, John M. (Jack). "Salary Exempt Employees under the FLSA." *The Police Chief*, January 2008, pp.10–11.

Collins, John M. (Jack). "Americans with Disabilities Amendments Act: What It Means for Law Enforcement Agencies." *The Police Chief*, January 2009a, pp.12–13.

Collins, John M. (Jack). "Thirteen Ways to Lose a Labor Case." *The Police Chief*, November 2009b, pp.12–13.

Greene, Kevin E. "2007 Legislative Year in Review." *Subject to Debate*, January 2008, p.4.

Griffith, David. "The Thinning Blue Line." *Police*, January 2008, pp.45–51.

Haberfeld, M. R. *Police Leadership.* Upper Saddle River, NJ: Pearson, Prentice Hall, 2006.

"H.R.413, the Public Safety Employer–Employee Cooperation Act of 2009," WashingtonWatch.com. 2009. Accessed December 17, 2009. http://www.washingtonwatch.com/bills/show/111_HR_413.html

Kanable, Rebecca. "ADA Compliance." *Law Enforcement Technology*, January 2008, pp.68–75.

Kohlhepp, Kim, and Phillips, Tracy. "A Nationwide Online Recruiting Resource for the Law Enforcement Profession." *The Police Chief*, January 2009, pp.46–47.

Law Enforcement Recruitment Toolkit: COPS/IACP Leadership Project. Washington, DC: Community Oriented Policing Services, June 2009.

Mayer, Martin J. "ADA and the Hiring Process," *The Police Chief*, September 2009, pp.14–15.

Mays, Meredith. "House Approves Collective-Bargaining Legislation." *The Police Chief*, September 2007, p.8.

Mays, Meredith. "Collective Bargaining Legislation Still Looming." *The Police Chief*, October 2009, p.12.

Means, Randy, and McDonald, Pam. "Firefighters Case . . . 'Reverse' Discrimination: The Final Answer." *Law and Order*, September 2009, pp.18–22.

Orrick, Dwayne. "Developing Brand Recognition, Part 1." *Law and Order*, September 2008a, p.27.

Orrick, Dwayne. "Developing an Employee Brand, Part 2." *Law and Order*, September 2008b, pp.34–35.

Orrick, Dwayne. "Creating the Desired Brand Image, Part 3." *Law and Order*, December 2008c, p.15.

Orrick, Dwayne. "Marketing the Employer Branding, Part 4." *Law and Order*, June 2009a, p.23.

Orrick, Dwayne. "Improving the Department's Website." *Law and Order*, June 2009b, pp.18–19.

Orrick, Dwayne. "Developing a Strong Web Presence, Part 2." *Law and* Order, April 2009c. pp. 20–22.

Vest, Gary. "Closing the Recruitment Gap: A Symposium's Findings." *FBI Law Enforcement Bulletin*, November 2003, pp.13–17.

"Welcome to NAPO." The National Association of Police Organizations. Accessed December 17, 2009. http://www.napo.org/

Wexler, Chuck. "Labor Relations Will Be a Critical Issue as Chiefs Work through the Economic Crisis." *Subject to Debate*, December 2008, p.2.

Williams, Brandt. "Mpls. Police Chief Blames Economy for Recruit Layoffs." Minnesota Public Radio News, December 18, 2009. Accessed December 18, 2009. http:/Minnesota.publicradio.org/display/web/2009/12/17/Minneapolis-officer-graduation/

Wilson, Jeremy M., and Grammich, Clifford A. *Police Recruitment and Retention in the Contemporary Urban Environment: A National Discussion of Personnel Experiences and Promising Practices from the Front Lines.* Santa Monica, CA: RAND Corporation, 2009.

CITED CASES

Christensen v. Harris County, 529 U.S. 576 (2000)

Davis v. City of Dallas, 777 F.2d 205 (5th Cir. 1985), cert. denied

Gratz v. Bollinger, 539 U.S. 244 (2003)

Griggs v. Duke Power Company, 401 U.S. 424 (1971)

Grutter v. Bollinger, 539 U.S. 306 (2003)

Monell v. New York City Department of Social Services, 436 U.S. 658 (1978)

Parker v. The District of Columbia, 850 F.2d 708 (D.C. Cir. 1988)

Regents of University of California v. Bakke, 438 U.S. 265 (1978)

Ricci v. DeStefano, 557 U.S. _____ (2009)

of their subordinates and to reward those who are performing well and counsel, reassign or terminate those who are not. "Until police agencies invest the effort to produce valid and reliable instruments for measuring the real work of policing, it will remain very difficult to move nonperformers or poor performers out of the organization based on regular evaluations" (C. Wexler et al., 2007, p.24).

 CHAPTER at a GLANCE

This chapter begins with an overview of evaluation and a look at the specific purposes of evaluation. This is followed by a discussion of inspections and performance appraisals. The chapter then examines evaluating the teams within a department as well as evaluating the entire department. Next is a discussion of recognizing value in policing, measuring citizen satisfaction with police services and a look at evaluation and research. The chapter concludes with a short example of how challenging the status quo can benefit productivity.

EVALUATION: AN OVERVIEW

Evaluation and *appraisal* are synonyms. Both refer to measuring performance or outcomes. To **evaluate** means to determine the worth of something, be it an individual's performance, a training program or an agency.

> The basic purpose of evaluation is to determine how well individuals within an agency and the agency itself are accomplishing its mission and how to make improvements.

The importance of having a stated mission has been stressed throughout this text. Evaluation assesses how well individuals, teams, units and the entire department are contributing to this mission. Integral to this assessment are the training efforts and the innovations a department undertakes as well as perceptions of the citizens an agency seeks to serve and protect.

Evaluation can be as informal as a manager pointing out to a subordinate a job well done or as formal as an annual performance review. Evaluation can be as simple as an inspection of the patrol officers at roll call before they hit the streets or as complex as the process involved in seeking accreditation.

Evaluations must be objective, seeking to identify strengths and weaknesses. Only through such objectivity can improvements be made. As improvements are made, their effectiveness should also be assessed, resulting in a cycle of evaluation.

For evaluation to be effective, the results must be used. Evaluation must be perceived as a means to determine strengths and weaknesses of individuals as well as programs within an agency and how well each is contributing to total agency efforts. The evaluation cycle is diagrammed in Figure 16.1.

PURPOSES OF EVALUATION

Evaluation provides an objective assessment of how individual officers and managers are performing. It can provide an objective assessment of teams or units within the department as well as innovations and training efforts being

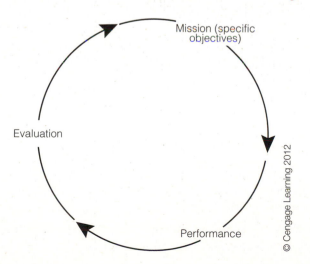

FIGURE 16.1
Evaluation Cycle

implemented. Evaluation can provide an assessment of the entire agency to determine whether it is accomplishing its stated mission. It can also provide an assessment of citizen satisfaction. Further, evaluation can provide information related to the budget, help defend against lawsuits, assess citizen satisfaction with the service provided and enhance recruiting and branding efforts. One of the most common types of evaluation used in law enforcement agencies is the inspection.

INSPECTIONS

All officers, from those on the front line to those behind desks, should take responsibility to inspect their own appearance and whatever equipment they are responsible for. Barring unusual circumstances, they should be able to pass inspections wherever and whenever they occur.

 The three typical forms of inspections are line inspections, spot inspections and staff inspections.

Line Inspections

A line inspection is the day-to-day review of a subordinate's appearance. Such an inspection serves two purposes: (1) it lets the supervisor know that the subordinate's uniform and equipment or business attire meet established standards, and (2) it provides supervisors a chance to demonstrate to subordinates that they are interested in how subordinates look and that the supervisors are going to adhere to established standards.

A type of line inspection often missed by supervisors is direct observation of officers performing day-to-day tasks by riding along with an officer from time to time.

Spot Inspections

Spot inspections are like line inspections but are done by someone other than the inspected person's chain of command. They are unannounced and give the inspectors a true picture of how things are actually being done. They also assess if a supervisor is handling reports and other paperwork properly. Spot inspections may lead to discipline, but they usually document an officer's or supervisor's good work.

Staff Inspections

Staff inspections are more formal than line or spot inspections. Staff inspections are proactive and complement and augment the line inspection. Most staff inspections have six objectives:

1. To determine whether the department's procedures and policies are being properly implemented

2. To determine whether the department's procedures and policies are adequate to attain the department's goals

3. To determine whether the department's resources (such as personnel) are being used fully and sensibly

4. To determine whether the department's resources are adequate to attain the department's goals

5. To discover any deficiencies in integrity, training, morale or supervision

6. To help operating line units plan their line inspections

A correctly conducted staff inspection can uncover potential problems before they reach proportions that negatively affect the department. The focus should be on how things are being done, not necessarily on the people who are doing them. Such a distinction can negate the common perception that staff inspections are spy operations intended to detect personnel shortcomings.

Every unit and activity should be inspected, but certain areas need regularly scheduled attention: human resources; crime reporting and statistics; evidence handling and storage; firearms, drugs, money and other valuables; agency vehicles, interior and exterior; emergency equipment in patrol vehicles; personal defense and restraint systems; unit work stations; case presentation and officers' testimony; overtime payments; and accuracy of roll-book entries.

PERFORMANCE APPRAISALS

In addition to inspections, one of the most important types of evaluation is the performance appraisal. A field training officer provides continuous informal evaluation while helping rookies learn to perform tasks efficiently. The time comes, however, when the rookies will have to pass a test—a formal evaluation of their skills. Both types of evaluation are necessary.

Informal evaluation is thought by some experts to be better than formal evaluation, arguing that evaluating on a precise date, for example, every March 1, or every 6 months, is arbitrary and less effective and that it is better to make judgments whenever necessary. Thus, evaluation should be continuous. Careful, specific documentation of employee behavior at the present can avoid or help defend against lawsuits in the future. In addition, evaluating at the time behavior occurs is more apt to consider the behavior rather than the personality. Informal evaluations, such as a sergeant praising a patrol officer, can be motivating, as discussed in Chapter 9. Informal evaluations can also help identify behaviors that might become serious problems if not dealt with early, as discussed in Chapter 10.

Formal evaluations may be in the form of checklists and rating forms. A performance appraisal is intended to represent an accurate, objective accountant of an employee's performance during a stated period. There are various ways of measuring performance: quality of task performance, productivity measurements, attendance records or individual testing. Basically, managers need to know what subordinates are doing, how well they are doing it and how strong performance can be continued and weak areas improved.

Regardless of the rating form selected, managers must observe subordinates performing their assigned tasks and conduct a **performance appraisal**. Managers must find some form of comparison and measurement and assess

performance appraisal

formal evaluation of on-the-job functioning; usually conducted once or twice a year.

employees' development. Law enforcement managers' attitudes toward performance appraisals and their ability to assess are critical factors for a successful evaluation system. Will employees be rated as individuals, in comparison with other employees doing similar tasks or by state or national standards?

Managers who provide the most immediate direction of subordinates should do the evaluation.

Immediate supervisors can most directly observe employee behavior at the level at which most required tasks are performed. In most cases, the police sergeant evaluates patrol officers. The administrative sergeant or lieutenant evaluates dispatch personnel. The investigative sergeant or lieutenant evaluates investigative personnel.

If employees are transferred during a rating period, each responsible manager should put in writing the evaluation for the period of responsibility. A system to establish periods for evaluation and reminders should be devised, often based on the hiring anniversary date. Some type of immediate follow-up and feedback should be provided between formal ratings as needed. Law enforcement managers are motivators, and motivation is one reason for evaluation.

Purposes of performance appraisals include promoting common understanding of individual performance levels, needs, work objectives and standards; providing feedback and suggesting specific courses of action to improve, including training; setting objectives for future performance; and helping in making decisions about promotions, reassignments, disciplinary actions and terminations.

Performance appraisals are not intended to cause undue burdens to managers but rather to provide consistent criteria for improving employee performance. When employees understand how they are doing, know that what they are doing contributes to the organization and know what they are doing correctly, performance levels will justify the evaluation effort.

Most managers who do performance evaluations do not know how to do them correctly because they were never taught adequately. A trained evaluator has the skill and ability to successfully observe, accurately record and objectively articulate observed behaviors.

Some managers claim that evaluations take too much time, that employees resent it or that to do an evaluation is a "pain." The truth is, managers must evaluate employees—either by means of formal rating systems or informally. If managers correct employees on the job, they are evaluating task performance. If they fail to correct a situation that needs correcting, they are not accepting responsibility.

The main purpose of performance evaluation is to improve employee performance.

AWAY FROM THE DESK: The Sergeant's Role is the Key to Police Personnel Development

Performance appraisals serve a number of administrative purposes: they are used in employee development, promotion, assignment, and transfer decisions; merit pay programs; training needs identification; coaching and counseling; demotions and dismissals. They also assist employees in understanding their own strengths and weaknesses, serving as a foundation for improving their performance and the overall success of the police organization.

Evaluating employees is one of the most important tasks a sergeant has. Although each employee is informally evaluated daily, a systematic approach is needed on a planned and specific timeline in an effort to provide the department and employee with a written document of each individual employee's performance.

Performance evaluation or appraisal systems make for a harmonious and efficient workplace where attitudes of commitment, trust and teamwork predominate. As a result, employees develop a strong feeling that the organization has a philosophy and methodology of fairly and consistently evaluating the results of each individual employee. This creates a more committed employee to organizational goals. In turn, productive employees who fully understand the workplace expectations contribute to the creation of a trusted and reputable department that effectively represents the citizens employees have sworn to protect.

Finally, effectiveness of the performance evaluation process is often determined by the degree of talent, training, and people skills of those who hold the rank of sergeant in a police organization. These individuals set the tone for and protect the integrity of the evaluation process. Essentially, first-line supervisors maintain the quality of public service and safety and, frankly, are the determinants of an organization's success or failure.

—*Chief Shaun E. LaDue*

Performance Criteria/Standards

Performance appraisals must be based on clearly stated job descriptions and clearly stated performance standards. If job descriptions change, evaluations must reflect these changes. Evaluation forms and standards *must* fit the job. What tasks are rated? What level of performance is required? As many criteria as possible should be written. Separate criteria should be noted for patrol officers, detectives, supervisors and secretaries (Kurz and Kelly, 2007).

One important responsibility of a supervisor or commander is to maintain the standards that are set for the subordinates and department: "In some departments, the standards are set high originally, but then those high standards erode over time, due to tolerance or lack of due vigilance by command personnel. Sometimes these lowered standards can explode in short order, such as in a front-page case of police brutality. Other times, a slow erosion of professional standards eventually ends up in unprofessional conduct and public distain for the department and its members. And, the leadership of the department, at all levels, is to blame for such a failure" (Carpenter and Fulton, 2010, p.24).

The manager's job is to help everyone achieve his or her level of competence. Although some evaluation systems rank order employees, usually they should not be rated on a curve but individually. It is possible to have all excellent employees (or the reverse). Employees who meet established standards at the required level should be provided an acceptable rating regardless of how other employees perform.

standards

targets to be met, including level of performance.

Standards may involve quality of performance, quantity and meeting established goals. In law enforcement work, quality rather than quantity is usually most important. Competence and courtesy in handling requests for service are important factors. Without performance standards supervisors may be inconsistent and unfair in promotions, awards and discipline. Performance standards allow supervisors to be consistent and fair.

Performance standards should be mission related, measurable, attainable and practical to monitor. Such standards let officers know what to expect, remove personality from ratings and provide a basis for objective appraisal with minimal inconsistency.

 Job standards make it easier for employees to meet requirements and for managers to determine whether they have been met.

Numerical or quantity standards are easier to meet and evaluate, but many law enforcement tasks do not lend themselves to quantitative standards. Traditional measurements such as crime rates, clearance rates, tickets issued and the like measure only events, not whether the activities were completed efficiently and effectively. When standards are established, they must be communicated to employees so that they know what is expected. As noted, managers must accompany subordinates in the field periodically to know what they are doing and how well. They cannot do this from behind a desk.

Reports can also be used to measure performance. Activity reports indicate types and numbers of tasks performed. The number of citizen complaints or commendations also indicate performance quality.

A relatively new way to evaluate performance uses the audit capabilities of an in-car video camera system, which are now common in police cruisers. By providing enormous amounts of information on how stops and citizens contacts are conducted, this technology offers a benefit beyond its original intention of enhancing officer safety. For example, the audit detail can confirm or validate a citizen complaint and, in many cases, the camera has worked in favor of the officer.

Standards may include areas such as physical fitness to perform and emotional stability while performing law enforcement tasks; individual judgment; reliability; loyalty and ability to get along with the public, fellow employees and managers; creativity and innovation; attitude; knowledge of tasks; competence; and amount of management required.

Standards vary considerably among federal, state, county and municipal organizations.

Quotas

One controversial area related to performance standards is whether an agency uses a quota system to evaluate an officer's performance. A survey of 30 law enforcement agencies found that none had a quota system, nor had they ever had such a system for arrests and traffic stops. Nonetheless, programs such as "Click It or Ticket" (a program promoting use of seatbelts) lead to a persistent belief among citizens that law enforcement agencies *do* use quota systems. In the Click It or Ticket program, officers have to make contact with at least three violators per hour to receive federal funds. The manager of the Washington State program says it is not a quota but is rather a performance standard: "Officers must make three contacts an hour, but that doesn't mean writing three tickets."

The consensus of the survey respondents was that quotas in any form (e.g., points) should not be used as a motivational tool or to judge an officer's performance. As one respondent observed, the use of quotas elicits an atmosphere of quantity rather than quality.

Fitness-for-Duty Evaluations

Fitness-for-duty evaluations (FFDE) usually include physical and psychological fitness. This evaluation process is very detailed and complicated and requires significant experience. As such, this is an area of evaluation often left to human resource departments, which have greater specialization in this area of employment law. "In recent years, there has been a reduction in the health and fitness of law enforcement officers across the United States. This lack of fitness makes officers prone to on-duty injuries and illnesses, increases their exposure to liability and engenders a loss of respect from the community based on their appearance" (Quigley, 2008, p.62). Many agencies rely on in-house or contracted attorneys to help manage the risk liabilities associated with these types of cases.

Whether a law enforcement agency should have mandatory physical fitness standards (MPFS) is controversial. A poll of 32 agencies of various sizes revealed that MPFS are a concern but they are not a high priority. Even though 93 percent of the respondents said there should be mandatory standards for at least some department members, only 37 percent had in-service standards in place and, of those standards, only 30 percent were mandatory. The principal reason given for the lack of standards was insufficient funding.

In most law enforcement agencies, if an officer is not part of a specialty unit such as special weapons and tactics (SWAT), the agency does not require a set level of physical fitness for veteran officers (Oldham, 2009, p.10). And even in agencies that have such standards, the requirements to meet them are seldom as demanding as they should be, considering the numerous physical challenges officers may face on the street. Oldham (p.12) asserts, "There must be a threshold limit as to exactly how out of shape an officer can become."

Consider the following definition of "fit for duty": "If an officer can safely perform his or her duties in an effective manner without jeopardizing his or her life or the lives of others, including other officers, bystanders, even subjects and suspects, the officer is fit for duty" (Young, 2008, p.48). Being fit for duty goes beyond officer safety concerns: "It is the mark of a professional who is ready to fight to protect him- or herself, fellow officers and the public" (Young, 2008, p.49). Sanow (2008, p.95) takes it one step further, contending that police officers have an ethical obligation to each other to be physically fit and that failing to do so violates the police code of ethics: "The uniformed officer simply must be fit enough to offer backup assistance to a fellow officer. . . . If not, it is like showing up at a gunfight without a gun. Worse yet, not showing up at all because you can't help at all. . . . Ever hear of a lifeguard who couldn't swim? Then why is it that we must entice officers with compensation or comp days to become fit enough to pass voluntary fitness standards? Why is it that we end up in civil court defending task-based, job-relevant, mission-specific fitness standards?"

Numerous fitness standards are available, many of which have passed court challenges (Sanow, 2008). Some standards are prorated for age and gender and are complicated to administer, time-consuming to conduct and expensive to evaluate. All of the sophisticated, cross-validated physical fitness tests can be boiled down to a single paragraph (Sanow, 2008, p.95):

> Do 30 pushups, no time limit, and do 30 sit-ups in 60 seconds. That is the test for *upper body strength*. Run 1½ mile in 16 minutes, an *aerobic test*. This, in turn, predicts how well you can survive just 2 minutes of higher levels of exertion. Run 300 meters in 70 seconds, an *anaerobic* test, i.e., burst of strength. Finally, do a standing jump 15 inches higher than the standing reach, a *test of explosive leg strength*.

Physical fitness is important, not only for officer safety, but also to ensure that officers can perform their jobs effectively. The Cooper Institute for Aerobics Research (CIAR) has worked with law enforcement fitness programs since 1976 and suggests that agencies be concerned with fitness because it relates to

- The ability of officers to perform essential functions of the job.
- Minimizing the risk of excessive force situations.
- Minimizing the known health risks associated with the public safety job.
- Meeting many legal requirements to avoid litigation and have a defensible position if challenged in court. (*Physical Fitness Assessments*, 2009)

Current legislation requires that fitness standards and programs be job related and scientifically valid (*Physical Fitness Assessments*, 2009).

To demonstrate job relatedness, a fitness standard must be an underlying factor for performing essential or critical physical functions of the job and it must *predict* who can and cannot perform these functions.

As has been discussed, tests, standards and programs cannot discriminate against protected classes as established by the Civil Rights Acts of 1964 and 1991, the Americans with Disabilities Act (ADA) or the Age Discrimination in Employment Act (ADEA). However, the Cooper Institute stresses, "If job relatedness is established and documented, then the fitness tests, standards and programs *can* discriminate against anybody. It is important to implement tests/standards/programs that do discriminate between those *who can and cannot do the job* regardless of age, gender, race, or handicap condition" (*Physical Fitness Assessments*, 2009, p.11).

The Institute also suggests two levels of legal concern. The first concern involves *safety*. An agency must document that their policies and procedures meet the "standard of ordinary care" by following American College of Sports Medicine (ACSM) guidelines. The second area involves liability for an agency that does not have fitness tests, standards and programs. Agencies who do not address fitness requirements and needs of officers are susceptible to litigation for the following:

- Negligent hiring—failure to hire applicants who are fit to do the job
- Negligent training—failure to train recruits and incumbents so they are physically capable of doing the job
- Negligent supervision—failure to supervise incumbents to ensure they can meet the physical demands of the job
- Negligent retention—failure to reassign officers who cannot meet the physical demands of the job

 Law enforcement agencies that do not have fitness tests, standards or programs may face charges of negligence in hiring, training, supervision or retention.

In addition to physical fitness standards, most states have statutes that define *psychological fitness* for peace officers. The issue of mental stability comes under the purview of the ADA, whose primary benchmark is whether an individual's condition prevents him or her from performing "essential job functions." The pre-employment psychological assessment was discussed in Chapter 15. A psychological FFDE is a formal, specialized examination of an employee that results from (1) objective evidence that an employee may be unable to safely or effectively perform a defined job and (2) a reasonable basis for believing that the cause may be psychological. A psychological FFDE requires the informed consent of the person to be examined. Circumstances that may trigger a psychological FFDE include officer-involved shootings and any other critical incidents that might have profound psychological impacts.

In addition to assessing whether individuals are "fit for duty," performance assessments must measure how individuals actually have performed and are performing using various instruments.

Instruments for Performance Appraisals

Whether a department creates its own assessment instrument or adopts one from another department, the instrument should be objective, comprehensive, reliable and current. (See Appendix F for sample evaluation forms.) An objective evaluation form, for example, might rate an officer's proficiency on a numerical scale of 1 to 7, with 1 indicating least proficient and 7 most proficient. The values of 1, 4 and 7 are designated as "anchors," with 1 representing *unacceptable*, 4 *acceptable* and 7 *outstanding*. Raters need not comment on any factor unless it is rated 7 or less than 3.

by-the-numbers evaluation

makes evaluations more objective by using a numerical scale for each characteristic or dimension rated.

 By-the-numbers evaluation makes evaluation more objective by using a numerical scale for each dimension.

Promotability/assignment factors attempt to make the evaluation "count for something."

promotability/ assignment factors

an attempt to make evaluation "count for something."

 Evaluations should have consequences. Those who rate highly might be considered for promotions, special assignments or pay raises. Those who rate below the acceptable range might be given counseling, training, a demotion, salary reduction, probation or, in extreme cases, termination.

For instance, in the Redondo Beach (California) Police Department, a simple mathematical formula is used based on the individual ratings assigned to each factor. The rating counts toward 25 percent of the promotional process and 50 percent of the selection process for special assignments. In addition, the evaluation has other consequences, with those having acceptable or higher overall ratings being considered for special training.

pre-evaluation

a procedure to allow those being evaluated to have input by completing a form outlining their accomplishments.

Some departments opt to give employees a pre-evaluation form several weeks before their formal evaluation (Appendix G). **Pre-evaluation** is a procedure that allows those being evaluated to have input by completing a form outlining their accomplishments. The Redondo Beach Evaluation Manual (p.17) notes, "The prime factor in obtaining the best results of the performance evaluation is the supervisor's fair, impartial and sincere desire to help the employee grow and advance. *The performance evaluation process can either be the key link in the supervisor-employee relationship or a periodic source of irritation, depending on the way it is used.* Periodic performance evaluation and counseling is the very best method available in improving relationships with employees and helping them to fulfill their needs for satisfactory recognition and growth."

Information for Performance Appraisals

Law enforcement managers responsible for evaluation must record all information as soon as possible after an incident is observed. A form for each officer the manager rates should be maintained. It is impossible to remember such information over long periods. A simple form and notation are all that is required.

When it is time to complete the formal evaluation form, all the information will be available. This lessens the tendency for information gathered closer to the time of the formal evaluation to overshadow information gathered months before. The information may be about specific incidents such as a high-speed chase, a shooting by an officer or a public-relations-type incident. Enter such information immediately after the occurrence while facts are remembered.

Some departments have implemented quarterly or trimester reports, to be completed every three or four months, respectively, to adequately provide each employee with an assessment of their performance and how it compares or relates to others in their work group. Such reports can be effective in forcing supervisors to record more frequently the progress and problems of those under their span of control, making the annual performance evaluation more complete and easier to perform because there are three or four documents from the previous year's activities to reference. The result is that there are no evaluation surprises for the employee, and officers are given adequate notice before formal evaluation of any areas that need improvement.

Common Types of Performance Evaluations

Numerous types of performance evaluations are available to managers.

Among the types of performance evaluations are the following:
- **Ratings by individual traits or behaviorally anchored rating scales (BARS)**
- **Group or composite ratings**
- **Critical incident ratings**
- **Narrative, essay or description**
- **Overall comparison ratings**
- **Self-evaluation**

Opinions vary on the value of each type of evaluation. Any of the preceding common types of performance evaluations can be used to evaluate subordinates.

Ratings by Individual Traits

Behaviorally anchored rating scales (BARS) are individual trait ratings usually done by the manager immediately above the employee in rank. Various factors concerning individual employees and the job are rated on a scale of 1 to 5 or 1 to 10. For example, a factor such as dependability would be rated from 1 to 10, with 1 being poorest and 10 being outstanding or excellent. It is fairly easy to perform this type of rating. The Redondo Beach Evaluation Form in Appendix F is an example of this type of evaluation.

Differences arise over how to do individual trait rating. Some think managers should rate the first item for all employees before proceeding to the second item. Others think all factors for one employee should be rated at once before going to the next employee rating.

> **behaviorally anchored rating scales (BARS)**
>
> specific characteristics for a position are determined; employees are then rated against these characteristics by on-the-job behaviors in each area.

Unless department policy dictates otherwise, raters should try both ways to decide which works better. The total score is the composite rating. Some think that poor and excellent ratings should be justified by performance evidence. Trait categories fall into those related to *performance* measured by quantity and quality, accuracy, efficiency and amount of supervision required; *personal qualities*, such as personality, attitude, character, loyalty and creativeness; and *ability*, which involves knowledge of job, mental and emotional stability, initiative and judgment. The traits must be job related.

Group or Composite Ratings

Many departments are changing from individual to group ratings, in which traits are rated by a group instead of one manager. For example, rather than having a sergeant rate the patrol officers, a group of three or four people of different ranks in the department, including an officer from the same level as the person being rated, might evaluate the patrol officers. Varied percentage weights may be applied to different raters according to rank. Or employees could be rated by all members in the organization of the same rank or a selection of first-line supervisor, a higher manager, their peers or other group members. Some departments use a member of the personnel department to interview those associated with the employee, and this interviewer makes the rating for the personnel file. This method involves more time.

Critical Incident Ratings

Most managers keep *critical incident logs* that record all good and bad performances of employees. Although keeping such logs is time consuming, the information is of great value when it is time for the formal performance appraisal. If an officer did an excellent investigation or made an excellent arrest, this would be recorded. If the officer made a bad arrest or conducted a poor investigation, this would also be recorded. All incidents would be discussed with the employee.

Keeping track of how officers handle incidents can help a department reduce its risk of civil liability, identify situations where more officer training is warranted and keep track of outstanding officer performance so commendations can be awarded. Officers, and in some instances their direct supervisors, should update records whenever they are involved in incidents involving use of force, officer-involved shootings, vehicle pursuit, K-9 deployment, missed or tardy court appearances and civil or criminal actions.

Narrative, Essay or Description

In this method, raters use a written description of what they observed rather than a rating scale. It is also possible to combine numerical and narrative in the same form.

Overall Comparison Ratings

Managers review all their subordinates and then rate which one is top and which bottom. Managers then arrange the other subordinates on a comparative scale.

Self-Evaluation

Self-evaluation is becoming more popular. Self-evaluation forms allow subordinates to rate themselves. There is value in people comparing how they perceive themselves with how others perceive them. Self-evaluation assists in getting employees to accept other types of evaluations. In some instances, individuals are more self-critical than external raters, simply because they know things about themselves others do not. These ratings have substantial value and are increasingly used in conjunction with other rating types.

Evaluation of Managers and Supervisors by Subordinates

One form of performance evaluation allows subordinates to evaluate their supervisory and administrative personnel. This gives command personnel a new source of information and a reasonably accurate assessment of subordinates' perceptions.

Higher level managers and the chief or sheriff might also be evaluated by their subordinates using an instrument that includes management and leadership skills. Although subordinates evaluating managers is not common, it has value. Rating managers could help both managers and the organization, and the same rating method would be used for managers and subordinates. Subordinates should have as much right to rate their managers as managers have to rate their subordinates.

Performance Interviews

Performance interviews are private, one-on-one discussions of the performance appraisal by manager and subordinate. The performance interview should be based on comprehensive, accurate records and should focus on employee performance and growth. The appraisal form is the basis for the performance interview. Although rating forms and managers vary, it usually takes two to three hours of preparation time for each person rated. Many managers mark the evaluation forms lightly in pencil in case the interview brings facts to light that change the rating.

Managers should allow 45 minutes to an hour for each performance interview. They should prepare in advance so they do not omit important items. Planning includes the time and place, preventing interruptions and topics to be discussed. A starting point is to review the evaluation form.

Performance interviews open with a statement of purpose and should seek to make the employee feel at ease. Personalize the interview so it does not appear "canned." After rapport has been established, the employee's accomplishments are usually discussed. The appraisal form can serve as the foundation for the discussion. Compare it with the last appraisal. The tone throughout the interview should be positive. Ask employees to indicate what they see as their strengths and weaknesses. Ask what you, as manager, can do to help improve the weaknesses. Encourage participation. Interviews of this type may identify conditions; distractions; lack of resources, training or equipment to do

> **performance interviews**
> private, one-on-one discussions of the performance appraisal by manager and subordinate.

the tasks required; or other obstacles, none of which may have been known to the manager before the interview.

> **The performance appraisal interview should help employees do their jobs better and therefore improve individual performance and productivity.**

All employee performance interviews should be private. Employees are normally apprehensive about evaluation. They are concerned about the manager's perceptions and how these compare with their own. An interview is a chance for managers and employees to establish rapport. If the interview is conducted properly—inviting input from employees—it will decrease controversy. Emphasize strengths rather than weaknesses.

A positive approach is likely to produce positive responses. A negative approach normally generates defensiveness and lack of cooperation. This does not mean everything needs to be "hearts and roses." Criticism is necessary for development, but it should be constructive.

Law enforcement managers are employee problem solvers. During performance appraisal interviews, employees will be concerned about any low ratings and individual problems. They should be encouraged to mention perceived problems. Explain precisely what makes performance unsatisfactory, and do not apologize for discussing the matter. As a supervisor or manager, correcting your subordinates is your responsibility. Ask whether the employee understands the problem and has any ideas about how to approach it. Offer help in resolving the problem. If the problem is resolved at the first meeting, follow up by further monitoring. Congratulate the employee if the problem is corrected. Some departments use a Performance Improvement Plan to help redirect those employees who are not meeting department expectations. To see an example of a Performance Improvement Plan, visit www.cengagebrain.com and log into the CourseMate website that accompanies this text.

If the employee's position is one you cannot immediately discuss further or resolve, tell the employee of your next step. Set a time and place to continue the discussion. Explain that in light of what you have been told, you will investigate further and will reach a decision as soon as possible. Follow through within a day or two.

In some extreme cases of intentional misbehavior, for instance, an officer who abuses alcohol or drugs, it may be necessary to suggest termination if immediate remedies are not available.

Agree on important issues discussed, set future expectations, discuss training opportunities available for personal improvement and summarize the entire meeting with a positive ending. If you agree to do certain things, follow through.

The Redondo Beach Evaluation Manual (pp.14–15) contains the following suggestions, based on experience and research:

- Plan the appraisal interview in advance. Define your objectives and outline the key points you want to cover.

- Plan and schedule the interview for a time and place that will give you and the employee privacy and allow your undivided attention to be devoted to the subject.

- Get right into the appraisal at the outset, but encourage the employee to address any portion of the appraisal the employee thinks is incorrect or unfair.
- Listen to the employee during the interview—especially immediately after negative feedback has been given.

Your attitude and interest regarding the employee are more important than any counseling technique you might use. If employees see that your prime objective is to help them do a better job, the appraisal is on its way to a successful result. If you put yourself in the role of a judge and the employee is the defendant, the appraisal will in all likelihood be a waste of time.

The appraisal interview should not be the only time you talk with employees about performance. Appraisal, to be effective, must be continuous.

 The most common recommendation for frequency of performance appraisals is twice a year and more frequently for employees performing below expectations.

When the interview is completed, managers should make appropriate meeting notes immediately. These should be part of the permanent personnel file. Another file should contain any agreements reached that must be performed before the next appraisal, along with the date of the next appraisal.

Generally, appeals regarding ratings can be made to the next higher manager and on up to the department head. There may even be provision for an appeals board. The decision of the appeals board is usually final. Appeals should be required within a specified time and hearings held as quickly as possible.

Guidelines for Conducting Performance Appraisals

The following guidelines are summarized from the Redondo Beach Police Department Evaluation Manual:

- Communicate your expectations in advance.
- Appraise performance for the entire period. Critical incident reports can highlight performance over the entire rating period.
- Keep the appraisal job related. Don't let your attitude toward individuals or their personal attitudes bias your evaluations.
- Employees should participate. During the appraisal interview, the supervisor may choose to alter his or her appraisal after the subordinate provides additional information and insights regarding performance.
- Avoid the halo effect.
- Use descriptive statements to support your evaluations. Describe the performance on which you base your evaluations. Any rating of "not satisfactory" or "exceeds standards" should have very specific explanatory comments and examples.

Problems of Performance Appraisals

Every employee evaluation system has shortcomings. Some problems of performance appraisals are the following:

- Lack of faith in any appraisal system
- "Late-inning" results count most
- The halo or horn effect
- Inaccurate numerical or forced-choice methods
- Unfair percentage ratings
- Rating personality rather than performance
- Rater bias
- Rating at the extremes

Lack of Faith in Appraisal Systems

Some managers have a defeatist attitude about performance rating: "It won't work." "Employees should not be compared with one another." "It all depends on the rater." "Managers are not trained to be evaluators." "Employees don't like it." "The seniority system is good enough for me."

A defeatist attitude can arise from excessively high expectations about performance evaluations. Perfection is not the goal; growth and development are. Sometimes choosing the best method is a problem. Any formal performance appraisal is better than no appraisal if it is **valid**, meaning it is well grounded, sound, the factors rated are job related and the raters are trained.

valid

appraisals that are well grounded and sound in which the factors rated are job related and the raters are trained.

Late-Inning Results Count Most

When ratings are performed annually, the actions and performance in the final months of the rating period are often better remembered and given more weight. This works both ways. Employees may have a good first nine months and a bad last three months or vice versa.

The Halo and Horn Effects

The **halo effect** is the tendency to allow an employee's performance in one area to unduly influence the ratings in other areas. Some evaluation experts use a narrower meaning of the halo effect, reserving that term for allowing highly positive attributes in one area to carry over into rating all characteristics positively. When the opposite happens and a highly negative attribute causes other attributes to be rated low, this is called the **horn effect**.

halo effect

tendency to rate one who performs above average in one area above average in all areas or vice versa.

horn effect

allowing one negative trait to influence the rater negatively on other traits as well.

Inaccurate Numerical or Forced-Choice Methods

Numerical ratings do not provide the information needed for improving employee performance because they do not indicate specifics about individuals. Managers who do the ratings are not put to the test of really knowing their employees.

Unfair Percentage Ratings

When raters must place a percentage of employees in the upper, middle and lower third of ratings scales, they tend to be unfair. The same unfairness exists when raters place all employees at or near the average or middle of the scale. Employees should be rated on their actual performance, regardless of how many are upper, middle or lower. Some managers do not have the courage or training to do such ratings. In other instances, managers have a problem of being either high, low or middle raters.

Rating Personality Rather Than Performance

Some raters tend to use their personal prejudices to rate employees. Instead of looking at each task or criterion and considering it individually, raters use a personal opinion of the individual based on a single experience. They may also rate on prejudice based on education, race or other factors.

Rater Bias

Closely related to rating personality is allowing one's personal biases to interfere with the evaluation, for example, preferring men over women or nonminorities over minorities.

Rating at the Extremes

Some evaluators rate in extremes of too lenient or too strict. This is especially true with marginal employees. Rather than terminate an employee who is liked, managers give a higher rating than the employee deserves. The opposite is true if the rating supports termination because the employee is not a "yes" person but performs other tasks well.

Other rating problems arise when managers rate employees in higher-level positions higher than those in lower-level positions, especially when raters have no training in rating or when raters do not care about the process. Other problems arise when the instructions are unclear or the terms and standards are not clearly defined.

Benefits of Performance Evaluation

Kurz and Kelly (2007, p.2) cite numerous benefits of performance evaluation: "Performance evaluations have many positive outcomes including employees understanding their jobs, ensuring that they have the necessary training, and the reinforcement of satisfactory performance and correction of substandard performance. They allow critical feedback for both supervisors and subordinates; provide tools to evaluate performance on a formal, periodic basis; and create a mutual understanding of individual needs, work objectives and acceptable performance standards."

Performance evaluations benefit all levels of a police department. First, they benefit the *organization as a whole* by accurately assessing its human resources so informed decisions can be made about assignments. Evaluations provide a permanent written record of the strengths and weaknesses of the department, which can help determine salary changes, promotions, demotions, transfers, court evidence and so on.

Second, performance evaluations benefit the departments' *supervisors and managers* by giving them a clear picture of their subordinates' abilities and allowing supervisors input into officer development. Areas in which training is needed become more obvious.

Third, evaluations benefit the department's *officers* by letting each know exactly what is expected and identifying areas needing improvement. Once employees come to recognize personal weaknesses, they should be stimulated to set goals for self-improvement. Perhaps most important is that managers document officers' good work.

Using Performance Assessment Results to Recognize Excellence

Means (2008, pp.17–20) describes a "Ten Star" evaluation/recognition system in which "stars" are awarded in 10 rating categories. A gold star represents an "excellent" rating; a silver star represents a "good" rating. An officer who is rated good or excellent in all 10 ratings is recognized as a "Ten Star Officer," good or excellent ratings in nine categories would be awarded nine stars and on down. The "stars" are worn on service ribbons on the uniform as visible symbols of excellence.

Of the 10 categories, 4 are awarded for preparedness and include knowledge, human relations skills, level of physical fitness and tactical proficiencies; four are awarded for performance and include reliability, attitude, productivity and quality of work performed. Of the remaining two stars, one recognizes academic achievement (perhaps gold for a master's degree and silver for a bachelor's degree), the other recognizes community involvement outside on-the-job requirements. Means (2008, p.20) notes that only two of the 10 categories rely on partially subjective supervisory ratings, with 8 of the 10 categories being entirely in the control of the person being rated.

Another area that is frequently assessed is individual teams or units within an agency.

EVALUATING THE TEAM

Although it might be tempting to think that adding up all the individual performance ratings would be sufficient to evaluate the team as a whole, this is not the case. Periodically, managers and supervisors should formally assess the effectiveness of their teams. A form such as that in Figure 16.2 might be used.

Abilities to evaluate include how the group works together; effective use of individual skills; competence in addressing community issues; ability to engage the citizenry, other city departments and community groups in addressing local problems; adaptability to change; ability to function as part of the organization; ability to problem solve and reach a consensus on methods to define solutions; and the quality of solutions produced.

FIGURE 16.2
Team Evaluation

Teamwork Assessment

Listed below are characteristics of effective, productive work teams. This assessment seeks feedback about (1) how important you feel each characteristic is and (2) how well you feel your team exhibits the characteristic. Please use a rating scale of 1 to 10, with 1 indicating lowest rating and 10 highest rating.

Characteristic	Importance	Performance Rating
Officers work toward common goals, known and understood, that serve both individual officers and the agency.	_____	_____
Officers know their individual responsibilities as well as those of their team.	_____	_____
Officers have the skills and knowledge to accomplish the job.	_____	_____
Team morale is high. Officers are enthusiastic and upbeat.	_____	_____
Productivity is high. Officers work hard and perform to the best of their ability.	_____	_____
Officers have confidence and trust in their team members.	_____	_____
Officers cooperate rather than compete with one another.	_____	_____
Officers can disagree without being disagreeable.	_____	_____
Communication lines are open. Officers can openly discuss their ideas and feelings, and they also listen to their team members.	_____	_____
Officers are not threatened by change. They are eager to try new approaches to routine tasks.	_____	_____
Officers take pride in their team and its accomplishments.	_____	_____
The team frequently evaluates how well it is dong.	_____	_____

© Cengage Learning 2012

EVALUATING THE ENTIRE DEPARTMENT

Evaluation must also consider the entire agency and how well it is accomplishing its mission. Again, this cannot be done simply by looking at the performance of individual officers or even of the teams making up the organization.

Law enforcement agencies generally measure their results in terms of crime statistics and response times and, from a managerial perspective, such outcome measures have important disadvantages. Even if proper outcome measures are chosen, there is an enormous problem in measuring the police contribution to the results. First, outcome measures do not directly measure the value of the police. Second, clearance rates are notoriously unreliable and arrest data are suspect.

As managers evaluate the department as a whole, they should remember that people tend to use crime rates, number of arrests and case clearance rates to measure how the police are doing. Such measures have several problems:

◉ Low crime rates do not necessarily mean a police agency is efficient and effective.

◉ A high arrest rate does not necessarily show that the police are doing a good job.

Although responding to crime is an important function of police, the reality is that noncrime calls for service consume most of a patrol officer's time. Here an officer helps citizens in need. These positive officer-citizen interactions are extremely important because when an officer interacts with citizens, both may be informally evaluating each other.

© Joel Gordon

- A high ratio of police officers to citizens does not necessarily mean high-quality police services.
- Responding quickly to calls for services does not necessarily indicate that a police agency is efficient.

Rather than looking at crime rates, number of arrests and response time, evaluation should assess whether the agency is effective in fulfilling its responsibilities to the community and the value it provides to the community.

Evaluating Specific Departmental Efforts

The importance of evaluating training programs being implemented in an agency was discussed in Chapter 7. Projects undertaken within an agency should also be assessed as to their effectiveness. Roberts' (2007) *Law Enforcement Tech Guide for Creating Performance Measures That Work* is one resource for executives and managers.

In addition, Poulin (2009, pp.1,5) provides an overview of the performance measurement approaches of the U.S. Government Accountability Office (GAO), the Pew Center on the States and the Justice Research and Statistics Association (JRSA) and identifies elements "perceived to be important" for a strong performance measurement system, as shown in Table 16.1. According to this document, two types of measures should be collected for every program/project: process measures (how the program was implemented) and outcome measures (whether it accomplished its objectives) (Poulin, p.5).

Efforts to measure the performance of programs are consistent with the trend toward evidence-based policing (EBP), discussed in Chapter 2. Practicality is a vital element in assessing the effectiveness of innovative programs: "The bottom line is that EBP has to work in the real world. Sometimes this

TABLE 16.1 Key Components of a Strong Performance Measurement System by Organization

	GAO	Pew	JRSA
Preparation/Organization			
Infrastructure and capacity for performance measurement	✓	✓	✓
Checks on data and reporting accuracy	✓		✓
Willingness to share information		✓	✓
Process, outcome measures	✓	✓	✓
Data collection permits aggregation and breaking out			✓
System in place at program start			✓
Transparent	✓	✓	✓
Strategic planning and management	✓	✓	✓
Analysis			
Meets targets	✓	✓	✓
Time-series analysis	✓	✓	✓
Review of external factors impacting objectives	✓		✓
Cost savings	✓	✓	✓
Cross-program comparisons			✓
Performance budgeting		✓	
Results			
Useful information for stakeholders	✓	✓	✓
Timely/efficient reports	✓	✓	✓
Broad sharing of results	✓	✓	✓
Report usage	✓	✓	✓
Public access to information electronically	✓	✓	✓
Make recommendations for improvement	✓		✓
Checks to see if recommendations were implemented	✓		✓
Independent review	✓	✓	✓

Source: Mary Poulin. "Moving toward the Development of a Strong Performance Measurement System." *JRSA Forum*, March 2009, p.5.

may mean combining various pieces of evidence-based practice" (Rodriguez, 2008, p.1). An EBP approach must reconcile what research has proven in a controlled setting with what works in the real world (H. Wexler, 2008, p.2). To this end, the Bureau of Justice Assistance (BJA) has awarded almost $4 million to 10 agencies through the Smart Policing Initiative (SPI) to encourage the use of evidence-based practices to address contemporary public safety problems. This initiative seeks either to build on the concepts of offender-based and place-based policing by replicating evidence-based practices or to encourage

TABLE 16.2 Smart Policing Initiative Grantees

Smart Policing Initiative Grantees	
Agency (Research Partner)	**Crime Problem and Police Response**
Police Department, Boston, MA (Harvard University)	Robbery, burglary: Place- and offender-based policing
Police Department, Glendale, AZ (Arizona State University)	Crime-prone neighborhoods: Problem-oriented policing
Police Department, Lansing, MI (Michigan State University)	Neighborhood drug markets: Pulling Levers strategy
Police Department, Los Angeles, CA (Justice and Security Strategies)	Gun violence: Place- and offender-based policing
Police Department, Memphis, TN (University of Memphis)	Robbery, burglary: Place- and offender-based policing
Sheriff's Office, Palm Beach, FL (Florida State University)	Robbery: Victim-based (Hispanic) policing
Police Department, Philadelphia, PA (Temple University)	Violent crime: Place-, offender-, and holistic-based policing
Police Department, Reno, NV (University of Nevada)	Juvenile prescription drug abuse: Victim- and offender-based policing
Police Department, Savannah, GA (Savannah State University)	Violent, repeat offenders: Offender-based policing
Police Department, Winston-Salem, NC (Winston-Salem University)	Violence, drug markets: Intelligence-led policing

Source: Michael Medaris and Alissa Huntoon. "Smart Policing Initiative." *BJS Fact Sheet*, September 2009, p.2.

exploration of new solutions to public safety problems (Medaris and Huntoon, 2009, p.1). Recipients of these grants will enlist a research partner to assess the effectiveness of their efforts. Table 16.2 lists the 10 grantees and the crime problem and response they are researching.

Measuring a Department's Level of Community Policing

The Justice Department has developed a Community Policing Self-Assessment Tool (CP-SAT) that agencies can use to create a baseline measurement of their current state of community policing, track their progress over time in implementing community policing and educate residents and others about effective community policing (Taylor et al., 2009, p.6). Chapter 2 discussed the difference between transactional change, which affected strategies being implemented, and transformational change, which affected core values and mission statements. Many departments reporting that they are implementing community policing are still in the transactional period. The CP-SAT can help managers assess their current status based on a set of commonly accepted elements of community policing falling into three categories: community engagement and partnerships, problem-solving, and organizational transformation. CP-SAT includes surveys tailored for six types of agency stakeholders: officers, supervisors, command staff, civilian personnel, community partners and a cross-agency group comprising sworn and civilian police staff members at various levels and members of the community. These surveys are organized into an automated summary report. To many within the department and external to it, community policing efforts are of great value and should be recognized.

RECOGNIZING VALUE IN POLICING

Before looking at ways to measure the performance of the entire department, consider what valuable goals of policing are and measures associated with them:

- Reduce criminal victimization—reported crime rates; victimization rates.
- Call offenders to account—clearance rates; conviction rates.
- Reduce fear and enhance personal security—reported change in levels of fear; reported changes in self-defense measures.
- Guarantee safety in public spaces—traffic fatalities, injuries and damage; increased use of parks and other public spaces; increased property values.
- Use financial resources fairly, efficiently and effectively—cost per citizen, deployment efficiency/fairness, scheduling efficiency, budget compliance, overtime expenditures, civilianization.
- Use force and authority fairly, efficiently and effectively—citizen complaints, settlements in liability suits, police shootings.
- Satisfy customer demands/achieve legitimacy with those policed—satisfaction with police services, response times, citizen perceptions of fairness. (Moore et al., 2002, p.132)

An oft-stated truism of management is What gets measured is what gets done. If important values are not measured, the police will pay less attention to them than is desirable (Moore et al., p.71):

> Citizens need high-quality measures of police performance to determine whether their police department is performing well. As "owners" of the police, they need to see the extent to which the police department is producing results that matter to them, and whether the organization is positioning itself for even better performance in the future.
>
> At the moment police departments are being driven by performance measures that capture only a portion of the value they can contribute to their local communities. The systems can describe levels of reported crime, and efforts the police have made to respond to crimes with both arrests, and threats of arrest. They can describe the extent to which the police have been successful in calling offenders to account for their crimes.
>
> Missing from these measures is the contribution the police make to many other important purposes. These include preventing crime through means other than arrest, reducing fear, enhancing safety and security in public spaces, and providing responsive, high-quality services to citizens. . . .
>
> To improve the system [of assessing police performance], three conceptual steps must be taken.
>
> First, we must recognize the wide variety of valuable contributions that police departments make to their communities, and treat all these valuable effects as important, interlocking components of the police mission.
>
> Second, we must recognize that we are interested in economizing on the use of force and authority, as well as money, and that the police must be evaluated

in terms of the quality of justice they produce as well as the amount of safety and security. . . .

Third, we must recognize our interest in helping police departments strengthen their capabilities for the future, as well as perform well in the present.

Using Internal Surveys to Evaluate an Agency

An internal survey can be used as a catalyst for improvement ("Internal and Community Surveys," 2008, p.117). An internal survey might ask the following questions of all employees for specific areas within the agency, including prosecution; salary, benefits and human resources support; patrol operations; communications; parking enforcement; bike patrol; animal control; investigations; clerical staff, computerization and other technology; and special programs:

- How effective are we?
- What, if anything, should we change?
- What challenges do we face *now*?
- What challenges will we face in the *future?*

Surveys might be used to determine how effective a department is in doing the following (on a scale of 1 to 5, with 1 being ineffective and 5 being very effective): responding to employee ideas and suggestions, communicating important information through appropriate channels, treating employees fairly and consistently, praising employees for work well done, providing constructive criticism for work not so well done, providing appropriate training, providing informative and helpful work evaluations, and involving employees in decisions that affect them and involving employees in research and planning.

An internal survey might solicit employees' opinions on the importance of various department goals such as the following: technology improvements, increase support staff, increase number of sworn officers, increase racial/ethnic/gender diversity, increase community partnerships, broaden and enhance current training offerings, improve the field training officer (FTO) program, solicit community input on police operations, improve personnel evaluations procedures, increase pay/benefits, work towards accreditation, provide crime prevention services, provide family services, provide youth services. Surveys might also assess how employees perceive specific programs and innovations.

Evaluating an Agency's Integrity

Klockars et al. (2005) summarize research findings on police integrity and describe an assessment instrument that can measure integrity within an agency and pinpoint problems involving misconduct. The research is based on responses of 3,235 officers from 30 agencies across the country to questions about hypothetical scenarios related to misconduct.

Survey results suggested that, more than any other factor, officers refrained from reporting the misconduct of other officers out of concern for the welfare of their peers.

The researchers (Klockars et al., 2005, p.6) identified two practices to enhance integrity. First, consistently address relatively minor offenses with the appropriate discipline. Second, disclose the disciplinary process and resulting discipline to public scrutiny.

In addition to internal surveys, the department should also conduct a self-assessment, perhaps through a committee established for this purpose.

As with individual performance evaluations, the department evaluation should be a continuous cycle of evaluating performance, identifying areas to improve, making adjustments and evaluating the results.

In addition to the preceding ways to evaluate a department or agency, the decision might be made to seek an external evaluation of the department through the accreditation process.

Accreditation

Accreditation is a process by which an institution or agency demonstrates that it meets set standards. Schools, colleges and hospitals frequently seek accreditation as recognition of their high quality. Institutions that lack accreditation are often considered inferior.

accreditation
the process by which an institution or agency proves that it meets certain standards.

Accreditation consists of meeting a set of standards established by professionals in the field authorized to do so. Currently, accreditation may be granted by the Commission on the Accreditation of Law Enforcement Agencies (CALEA) or by some state agencies.

Accreditation provides a number of tangible benefits, including controlled liability insurance costs, fewer lawsuits and citizen complaints, stricter accountability within the agency and recognition of a department's ability to meet established standards. Intangible benefits include pride, recognition of excellence and peer approval. Everyone involved in the process gains a broader perspective of the agency, which ultimately leads to improved management. Accreditation was briefly introduced in Chapter 7.

Accreditation is not without its critics, however. In addition to the expense, some think that local and regional differences in agencies make a national set of standards unrealistic. Many agencies think the number of standards is simply overwhelming. Smaller agencies must usually meet 500 to 700 standards; larger agencies must usually meet more than 700 standards. Other critics contend that accreditation is like having a "big brother" overseeing their activities. Further, most of the standards deal with departmental administration rather than with its mission.

Accreditation and Certification of Forensic Personnel

In 2009, a report by the National Academy of Sciences (NAS) called for requiring mandatory accreditation of all forensic science provider operations and certification of the practitioners who work there, noting that most jurisdictions do not require accreditation of crime laboratories (*Strengthening Forensic Science in the United States*, 2009). The International Association of Chiefs of Police (IACP), however, was three years ahead of the NAS in calling for forensic science accreditation and certification (Fitzpatrick and Martin, 2009, p.26). The NAS and the forensic science community specifically recognize an international standard—ISO 17025—as the "gold standard" in forensic service provider accreditation. Fitzpatrick and Martin (p.27) assert, "No matter the cost of accreditation, it is always less than litigation. Eliminating shoddy work that exposes an agency to potential litigation is insurance." They also highly recommend that in addition to accreditation of the units within the agency or external to it, those within the agency who perform specialized forensic functions should be certified as experts.

Evaluation of the entire department should also be conducted by obtaining the views of those the department serves, the individual citizens and the various stakeholders in their jurisdiction.

EVALUATING CITIZEN SATISFACTION WITH SERVICES

Most citizens want to live in safe, orderly neighborhoods. Recall from the discussion of productivity in Chapter 13 that police are considered effective when they produce the perception that crime is under control. Reduction of fear is a very important measure. In fact, several important research studies have found that citizen fear of crime is a more important quality of life indicator than are actual crime levels. A fear and disorder index allows police to measure citizens' concerns and sends a message to citizens that the department is addressing their fear of crime and neighborhood disorder.

Citizen approval or disapproval is generally reflected in letters of criticism or commendation, support for proposed police programs, cooperation with incidents being investigated, letters to the editor, public reaction to a single police–citizen incident or responses to police-initiated surveys.

Citizen Surveys

One way to assess citizen approval or disapproval is through citizen surveys, which can measure trends and provide positive and negative feedback on the public's impression of law enforcement.

Community surveys are often a win-win situation—citizens are better served and officers receive positive feedback. Community surveys can also be key in establishing communication. One citizen survey developed by the Plainsboro Township (New Jersey) Police Department uses a closed-end form (answer yes or no), asking very specific questions to assess the performance of individual officers (see Figure 16.3).

Surveys can be conducted by mail or by phone. Mailed surveys are less expensive and reduce the biasing errors in phoned surveys caused by how the person doing the phoning comes across to the respondent. However, they

Call-for-service contact

We have started a Citizen Response Survey as part of our continuing effort to provide professional and efficient police service to the residents of Plainsboro Township and other individuals with whom our police officers come in contact. Your name has been selected at random from among those who have had recent contact with one of our officers.

Your response will be used internally to help us recognize potential deficiencies, acknowledge officers who continually perform in the manner expected and evaluate our procedures and methods. The feedback you provide will facilitate the improvement of future relations between the police and the public, aid in the evaluation of individual officers and provide an important means of acquiring additional citizen input into how we serve the community.

Please return the questionnaire in the enclosed envelope. It is the policy of this department to follow up unfavorable comments. However, if you do not wish to be contacted, please indicate in the space provided. Thank you.

Sincerely,

Clifford J. Mauler
Chief of Police

Citizen response questionnaire

1. Did the officer repond quickly to your call for service?   Y ____   N ____
   Appoximately how long did it take for the officer to respond
   after being called?_____
2. Was the officer courteous?   Y ____   N ____
3. Was the officer neatly attired?   Y ____   N ____
4. Did the officer identify himself by name?   Y ____   N ____
   If not, do you think he should have?   Y ____   N ____
5. Did the officer speak clearly? Were you able to understand him?   Y ____   N ____
6. Were you satisfied with the service provided by the officer?   Y ____   N ____
7. Did the officer appear knowledgeable?   Y ____   N ____
8. Did he obtain all information that would seem pertinent under the Y ____   N ____
   circumstances of this contact?
9. If applicable, did you feel satisfied with the supplemental investigation   Y ____   N ____
   conducted by the officer?
10. Upon completion of this police contact, did you feel satisfied with the   Y ____   N ____
    general quality of the service rendered?
11. Additional comments:
    _____
    _____
    _____

Signature _____   Date _____

FIGURE 16.3 Cover Letter and Citizen Response Questionnaire

Source: Elizabeth Bondurant. "Citizen Response Questionnaire: A Valuable Evaluation Tool." *The Police Chief*, November 1991, p.75. Reprinted from *The Police Chief*, Vol. LVIII, No. 11, November 1991, p.75. Copyright held by the International Association of Chiefs of Police, Inc., 515 N. Washington St., Alexandria, VA 22314, USA. Further reproduction without express written permission from IACP is strictly prohibited.

require that the person receiving the survey be able to read, which might not be the case. The major problem with mailed surveys is their low response rate. Phone surveys have a much higher response rate but are also much more expensive unless volunteers can be enlisted to make the calls. In addition, individuals who do not have a phone cannot be included.

No matter which form of survey is used, the expense is small relative to continued positive police–community relations. Citizen surveys might also help set organizational goals and priorities, identify department strengths and weaknesses, identify areas in need of improvement and training and motivate employees.

A study of patrol officers' attitudes toward a survey on citizens' satisfaction with their department's services found that 66 percent of the officers felt the survey was personally useful, more than 75 percent felt it was useful for the organization and 82 percent believed the survey was good for the citizens (Wells et al., 2005, p.171). However, the study also found that citizen feedback did *not* alter officers' performance, attitudes toward the communities they served or activities that put them in close contact with these communities. The researchers (pp.197–198) suggest that theories of information processing in organizations, such as **cybernetics**, help interpret these findings. The core principles of cybernetics suggest that organizations regulate themselves by gathering and reacting to information about their performance. The cybernetic perspective holds that perception, decision making and action are conceptually and functionally discrete. This decision-making perspective views systems, including organizations, as similar to organic brains, continually detecting, processing and reacting to information (Wells et al.).

In this context, citizen surveys are the preceptor element, providing information about how the organization is performing. The officers interpret the feedback and decide on the appropriate action. In this research, the response is no response. Wells et al. suggest that the response might be different if the information was routed through managers who decide on appropriate remedies and assign supervisors the job of ensuring that those remedies are carried out. Thus methods for processing citizen feedback and using it to implement meaningful change need to be developed and tested (Wells et al., 2005, p.201).

> **cybernetics**
>
> suggest that organizations regulate themselves by gathering and reacting to information about their performance.

Other Ways to Assess Community Perceptions

Another way to obtain community input is through focus groups, forums or roundtable discussions, which usually take about three hours and have three phases. First, citizens talk and management listens. Second, together they brainstorm ways to work together, using a 10/10 target (coming up with 10 creative ideas in 10 minutes). They then evaluate the ideas and select those with merit. Third, they focus on implementation, setting up teams or task forces to implement and track the ideas. Groups should be kept small—eight to twelve participants—and should exclude competitors and have a trained facilitator.

EVALUATION AND RESEARCH

This chapter has focused on evaluating individuals, teams and entire departments; training; and integrity and citizen satisfaction. Sometimes, however, administration wants to evaluate specific problems. In such cases, research is needed. One approach is using the SARA problem-solving approach introduced in Chapter 5, identifying problems, analyzing current responses and available resources, exploring alternatives and assessing the results of implementing alternatives.

Two kinds of statistics are generally helpful in such research: descriptive statistics and inferential statistics. **Descriptive statistics** focus on simplifying, appraising and summarizing data. **Inferential statistics** focus on making statistically educated guesses from a sample of data.

At other times administration wants to determine how well a specific program is working. In such instances administrators might want to familiarize themselves with the National Institute of Justice's (NIJ) "Research Partnerships in Policing." The NIJ partnership program in policing complements the basic premise of community policing: Working as partners achieves more than working alone. Such research partnerships typically consist of a local police department or other law enforcement agency and a local university and make extensive and effective use of graduate students. A valuable resource for departments wanting to undertake research is the Justice Research and Statistics Association (JRSA), whose Web site is www.jrsa.org.

Another resource is the Police Executive Research Forum (PERF) Center for Survey Research (LECSR). The center can assist departments in conducting neighborhood/community surveys, officer surveys, homeland security assessments and organizational climate surveys.

Much of the results from research fail to help managers improve the performance of their subordinates. For example, research on characteristics of high-performing patrol officers may be useful in the selection process, but managers need to deal with incumbent officers. Managers would welcome research on how to develop these characteristics. Partnerships between police leaders and academic researchers are critical to discovering and implementing best policing practices.

As has been stated, evaluation results must be analyzed and acted upon to be useful. Surveys, evaluations and research results often question the ways things have traditionally been done. Law enforcement managers and leaders must be willing to challenge the status quo when this occurs.

CHALLENGING THE STATUS QUO

Sometimes traditional practices are no longer productive. Consider the story of the four monkeys and the cold shower:

> In a conditioning experiment, four monkeys were placed in a room. A tall pole stood in the center of the room, and a bunch of bananas hung suspended at the top of the pole. Upon noticing the fruit, one monkey quickly climbed up the pole and reached to grab the meal, at which time he was hit with a torrent of cold water from an overhead shower. The monkey quickly abandoned his quest and hurried down the pole. After the first monkey's failed attempt, the other three monkeys each climbed the pole in an effort to retrieve the bananas, and each received a cold shower before completing the mission. After repeated drenchings, the four monkeys gave up on the bananas.
>
> Next, one of the four original monkeys was replaced with a new monkey. When the new arrival discovered the bananas suspended overhead and tried to climb the pole, the three other monkeys quickly reached up and pulled the

descriptive statistics

focus on simplifying, appraising and summarizing data.

inferential statistics

focus on making statistically educated guesses from a sample of data.

surprised monkey back down. After being prevented from climbing the pole several times but without ever having received the cold shower, the new monkey gave up trying to reach the bananas. One by one, each of the original monkeys was replaced, and each new monkey was taught the same lesson—don't climb the pole.

None of the new monkeys ever made it to the top of the pole; none even got close enough to receive the cold shower awaiting them at the top. Not one monkey understood why pole climbing was prohibited, but they all respected the well-established precedent. Even when the shower was removed, no monkey tried to climb the pole. No one challenged the status quo.

What implications do this story and its lesson hold for managers? The realization that precedents, enacted into policy manuals and training programs can far outlive the situational context that created them. Simply telling officers, "That's the way it's always been done" can do a great disservice to the organization as a whole. When officers don't know *what* they don't know and, worse yet, aren't even aware *that* they don't know, they are kept from empowerment, and problem-solving efforts are seriously compromised.

Encouraging officers to think creatively, tackle public safety issues through innovative problem solving and question the status quo if necessary are basic challenges facing law enforcement managers and certainly affect the future success of their agencies. This is the focus of the next chapter.

SUMMARY

The basic purpose of evaluation is to determine how well individuals within an agency and the agency itself are accomplishing its mission and how to make improvements. The three typical forms of inspections are line inspections, spot inspections and staff inspections.

Managers who provide the most immediate direction of subordinates should do the evaluation. Purposes of evaluation appraisals include promoting common understanding of individual performance levels, needs, work objectives and standards; providing feedback and suggesting specific courses of action to take to improve, including training; setting objectives for future performance; and helping in making decisions about promotions, reassignments, disciplinary actions and terminations. The main purpose of performance evaluation is to improve employee performance.

Job standards make it easier for employees to meet requirements and for managers to determine whether they have been met. Standards may include areas such as physical fitness to perform and emotional stability while performing law enforcement tasks; individual judgment; reliability; loyalty and ability to get along with the public, fellow employees and managers; creativity and innovation; attitude; knowledge of tasks; competence; and amount of management required. Law enforcement agencies that do not have fitness tests, standards or programs may face charges of negligence in hiring, training, supervision or retention. By-the-numbers evaluation makes evaluation more objective by using a numerical scale for each dimension.

Evaluation should have consequences. Those who rate highly might be considered for promotions, special assignments or pay raises. Those who rate below the acceptable range might be given counseling, training, a demotion, salary reduction, probation or, in extreme cases, termination.

Among the types of performance evaluations available to managers are ratings by individual traits or behaviorally anchored rating scales (BARS); group or composite ratings; critical incident ratings; narrative, essay or description; overall comparison ratings; and self-evaluation.

The performance appraisal interview should help employees do their jobs better and therefore improve individual performance and productivity. The most common recommendation for frequency of performance appraisals is twice a year and more frequently for employees performing below expectations.

In addition to internal surveys, the department should conduct a self-assessment, perhaps through a committee established for this purpose. Accreditation consists of meeting a set of standards established by professionals in the field authorized to do so. Currently, accreditation may be granted by the Commission on Accreditation of Law Enforcement Agencies (CALEA) or by some state agencies.

CHALLENGE SIXTEEN

The Greenfield Police Department requires performance appraisals at the end of each year. The appraisals use a numerical scale to evaluate several broad areas of performance. Categories include knowledge of policies, dependability and productivity. The appraisal forms provide room for optional narratives to explain numeric scores. Supervisors conduct appraisal interviews with their officers before forwarding the appraisals to the appropriate manager.

Detective Sergeant Bilko supervises 10 detectives. His detectives consider him a nice guy and a hard worker who often assists them with their cases. Sergeant Bilko is a fishing buddy of several of his detectives.

Detective Quick is one of the most talented detectives in the entire county. He takes on the most difficult and complex cases with a remarkable success rate. He is well liked in the community and by fellow officers. He is a credit to the department. Detective Delay does not make nearly the contribution that Detective Quick makes. He spends a good deal of time in several local coffee shops, and his fellow officers often say he missed his calling as a talk show host. Detective Delay is popular and entertaining, but not a great detective. He is usually assigned simple cases and often needs prodding to turn his cases in on time.

Sergeant Bilko asks his detectives to complete their own performance appraisal forms before their appraisal interview. He reviews the forms with them during the interviews and seldom questions the ratings. Every year his detectives all receive nearly identical above-average scores. Detective Quick's performance appraisal score is indistinguishable from Detective Delay's.

1. Sergeant Bilko is obviously doing an in-effective job of evaluating his detectives' performance. Is this a disservice to his detectives?

2. Are performance appraisals inherently more difficult for line supervisors such as Sergeant Bilko?

3. If Sergeant Bilko's evaluations of his de-tectives have all been nearly the same for several years, is someone else failing to do his or her job?

4. Does Detective Delay have a defense against any action the department may take against him for performance deficiencies?

5. Suggest some changes to improve the Greenfield Police Department's perfor-mance appraisal system.

DISCUSSION QUESTIONS

1. What are the advantages and disadvan-tages of informal evaluation? Formal evaluation?

2. What can law enforcement managers do to prepare for employee evaluation interviews?

3. What main change would you recommend for future performance evaluations?

4. Should performance evaluations be used for promotions? Transfers? New assign-ments? Pay increases?

5. Who should rate subordinates? One per-son or several?

6. What type rating do you like best?

7. What are some uses of performance evaluation?

8. Have you been formally evaluated? What was your opinion of the evaluation? Should such appraisals be retained?

9. What are the advantages and disadvan-tages of having subordinates evaluate their managers?

10. Do you favor or oppose national accredi-tation? State accreditation? Why?

REFERENCES

Carpenter, Michael, and Fulton, Roger. *Law Enforcement Management: What Works and What Doesn't.* Flushing, NY: Looseleaf Law Publications, Inc., 2010.

Fitzpatrick, Frank, and Martin, Kenneth. "The Need for Man-datory Accreditation and Certification." *The Police Chief,* September 2009, pp.26–27.

"Internal and Community Surveys." In *Police Chiefs Desk Ref-erence: A Guide for Newly Appointed Police Leaders,* 2nd ed., edited by International Association of Chiefs of Police and U.S. Bureau of Justice Assistance. Boston: McGraw-Hill Learning Solutions, 2008, pp.117–148.

Klockars, Carl B.; Ivkovich, Sanja Kutnjak; and Haberfeld, Maria R. *Enhancing Police Integrity.* Washington, DC: NIJ Research for Practice, December 2005. (NCJ 209269)

Kurz, David L., and Kelly, Sean. "Performance Evaluations and the Smaller Police Agency." *Big Ideas for Smaller Police Departments,* Fall 2007, pp.1–4.

Means, Randy. "Evaluation and Recognition Systems." *Law and Order,* July 2008, pp.17–20.

Medaris, Michael, and Huntoon, Alissa. "Smart Policing Initiative." *BJA Fact Sheet,* September 2009. (FS 000315)

Moore, Mark; Thacher, David; Dodge, Andrea; and Moore, Tobias. *Recognizing Value in Policing: The Challenge of Measuring Police Performance.* Washington, DC: Police Executive Research Forum, 2002.

Oldham, Scott. "The Fat Farm." *Law and Order,* November 2009, pp.10–12.

Physical Fitness Assessments and Norms for Adults and Law Enforcement. Dallas, TX: The Cooper Institute, 2009. Ac-cessed October 3, 2010. http://www.cooperinstitute.org/personal-training-education/law-fire-military-training/documents/Commonly%20Asked%20Questions%202010.pdf

Poulin, Mary. "Moving toward the Development of a Strong Performance Measurement System." *JRSA Forum*, March 2009, pp.1, 5–6.

Quigley, Adrienne. "Fit for Duty: The Need for Physical Fitness Programs for Law Enforcement Officers." *The Police Chief*, June 2008, pp.62–64.

Roberts, David J. *Law Enforcement Tech Guide for Creating Performance Measures That Work: A Guide for Executives and Managers.* Washington, DC: Community Oriented Policing Services Office, February 2007.

Rodriguez, Pamela F. "Understanding Evidence-Based Practice." *TASC New and Views*, Winter 2008, p.1.

Sanow, Ed. "Fitness Is an Ethical Obligation." *Tactical Response*, January/February 2008, pp.95–96.

Strengthening Forensic Science in the United States: A Path Forward. Washington, DC: National Academies Press, 2009.

Taylor, Bruce; Chapman, Rob; and Mulvaney, Rebecca. "Justice Department Develops Way to Measure a Department's Level of Community Policing." *Subject to Debate*, June 2009, p.6.

Wells, William; Horney, Julie; and Maguire, Edward R. "Patrol Officer Responses to Citizen Feedback: An Experimental Analysis." *Police Quarterly*, June 2005, pp.171–205.

Wexler, Chuck; Wycoff, Mary Ann; and Fischer, Craig. *"Good to Great" Policing: Application of Business Management Principles in the Public Sector.* Washington, DC: Community Oriented Policing Services Office and the Police Executive Research Forum, 2007.

Wexler, Harry K. "EBP: A Researcher's Perspective." *TASC (Treatment Alternative for Safe Communities) News and Views*, Winter 2008, pp.2–3.

Young, Dave. "Redefining Fit for Duty." *Police*, August 2008, pp.42–49.

Technical competence used to be most important. Now and in the years ahead, "people skills" are most important.

Woodward and Buchholz (1987, pp.13–14) explain it this way:

One way to visualize this tactical, people-oriented approach is with a bicycle. The two wheels of a bicycle have different purposes. The back wheel powers the bike; the front wheel steers it. Extending this analogy to an organization, "back-wheel" skills are the technical and organizational skills needed for the organization to function. "Front-wheel" skills are the interpersonal "people management" skills. Corporations tend to rely on their back-wheel, that is, their technical skills.

Typically, however, when change comes, the response of organizations is primarily back-wheel response—do what we know best. But the real need is for front-wheel skills, that is, helping people understand and adapt to the changing environment.

Winning coaches know that games are not won or lost in the fourth quarter or the ninth inning. The outcome of any game is determined by the amount of preparation. Law enforcement managers must possess a combination of technical skills and people skills to successfully guide their departments through the new millennium.

A Changing Law Enforcement Officer and Public to Be Served

Numerous social changes have affected law enforcement and will continue to affect it in the future. For example, when compared with police departments several decades ago, 21st century departments typically have more minority and women officers, better educated officers and officers from two or three different generations. Police departments have become more diverse, and the public they serve has grown increasingly diverse.

The public to be served will include more two-income families, more single-parent families, more senior citizens and more minorities. The educational and economic gap will increase, with those at the bottom becoming more disadvantaged and dissatisfied.

The high rate of divorce has changed family relationships. R. Morton Darrow, speaking at the National Press Club, stated, "With growing divorce and remarriage, the United States is moving from a nation in which parents had many children to one where children have many parents. This results in different needs and pressures in the family."

In addition, our population is aging. The baby boomers have turned 50, and in 2010 one-fourth of all Americans were at least 55 years old. More efforts will need to be spent on crime prevention and on support programs for older adults.

Another change is that the educational gap is increasing, with those at the bottom becoming even more disadvantaged. As the gap widens, economic opportunities dwindle and frustrations increase. The gap between the haves and the have-nots is widening significantly, with the likely result being social unrest.

The smokestack America of the early 1900s has been battered by the most accelerated technological revolution in history. Computers, satellites, space travel, fiber optics, robots, biometrics, electronic data interchange and expert systems are only the most obvious manifestations. All of this has been combined with globalization of the economy, rising competition and many social and cultural changes as well.

Although the American public has grown increasingly diverse, the public has also become vitally important as a partner to law enforcement in the effort to attain peaceful and prosperous communities. Indeed, community policing and its emphasis on problem solving have taken hold in agencies across the country.

TRENDS SHAPING THE FUTURE OF POLICING

Cetron and Davies (2008), along with their associates at Forecasting International, describe 55 trends they have identified that help define the future environment to systematically identify discrete threats and capitalize on hidden opportunities. The goal stated in the "Preface" to their report (pp.ix–x) is "to analyze the trends that will affect policing in the United States and project their impact over the medium-term future. In this way it should be possible to anticipate changing demands for police service, future staffing and budgetary requirements, technological innovations on both sides of the law, and many other factors that police agencies large and small will have to cope with between now and, say, 2025." They (p.x) predict unprecedented challenges for police in the United States, as well as across most of the developed world, during the next two decades and suggest that police managers need not face the coming challenges unprepared; well-informed foresight can make a big difference in how successfully police departments meet the demands of the future.

Forecasting International (FI) has been studying trends in our changing world for more than four decades and has developed a track record for being able to assess whether sudden shifts indicate seismic transitions or mere fads. The FI trend report covers eight areas: economics and society; values, concerns and lifestyles; energy; the environment; technology; the labor force and work; management; and institutions. As noted, the forecasts cover to 2025 but do not speculate about long-range futures that are of little practical use. In the past, their forecasts have been more than 95 percent accurate.

Forecasting International rates technology as the most powerful of the many forces now changing law enforcement.

Cetron and Davies identified 55 trends shaping policing and then selected the top 10 most important trends for policing, described in approximate descending order. The following information regarding these top trends is adapted from the Forecasting International report.

Increasing Reliance on Technology

#1 Technology increasingly dominates both the economy and society (Trend 28, pp.9–11):

◉ New technologies are surpassing the previous state of the art in all fields, including policing, and technological obsolescence is accelerating.

◉ For most users, computers have become part of the environment rather than just tools used for specific tasks.

◉ Robots are taking over more and more jobs that are routine, remote or risky, such as repairing undersea cables and nuclear power stations and responding to and disarming bombs.

◉ By 2015, artificial intelligence (AI), data-mining and virtual reality will help most companies and government agencies to assimilate data and solve problems beyond the range of today's computers. AI applications include robotics, machine vision, voice recognition, speech synthesis, electronic data processing, health and human services administration and airline pilot assistance.

Assessment

Technologically related changes in society and business seen during the last 20 years are just the beginning of a trend that will accelerate at least through this century.

Implications for Policing

Networks of video cameras are just the first of many high-tech tools that will affect police operations in the years ahead.

Nanotech sensors capable of detecting explosives and chemical and biological weapons will be scattered around prime terrorist targets, such as major public gatherings, relaying the location of any possible threat to the local command center.

Intelligence analysts, already overwhelmed by the amount of data collected each day, will face a growing torrent of data in the years ahead. Until automated systems become available to help monitor incoming data, much of the information will be used more to provide evidence for prosecutions than to prevent or interrupt crimes.

The Supreme Court decision to block data mining by the Department of Homeland Security (DHS) is a major loss to U.S. security efforts.

Surveillance technology will have dramatic impacts, particularly in traffic enforcement. Traffic officers increasingly will become technicians and warrant servers as traffic enforcement, particularly regarding speeding and red light running, becomes fully automated.

Advances in forensics will dramatically transform the investigative function, requiring far more technicians and far better educations. Smart car technology will alter the traffic control function. Drug and bomb dogs will be replaced by electronic sniffers.

New technologies will contribute to improved officer safety. Beneficial technologies include less-lethal weaponry, protective tools, the use of video cameras to document on-the-job performance, unmanned aerial vehicles (UAVs) for surveillance, digital assistants and online data systems that help police to prepare for operations and anticipate problems.

Although technologic changes create tremendous tools for the profession, they also open new avenues for crime, including identity theft, white-collar crimes, scams and other forms of cybercrime. Technology offers extremely lucrative and easy means of criminal activity, forcing us to re-think how we will investigate crime and criminals and how laws must be changed or updated.

Technology has begun affecting the processing of cases, and the absence of technological tools can actually impede the successful prosecution of cases. For example, a driving while intoxicated (DWI) arrest made without the benefit of a video recording of this arrest may very well fail to hold up in court. The "*CSI* effect" discussed in earlier chapters is similar, in that juries expect to see results from high-tech forensic tests to help guide them in determining guilt and innocence. What this reliance on technology has done, in many cases, is to create an expectation of its availability and use and to undermine the credibility of law enforcement in its absence.

Changing Societal Values

#2 Societal values are changing rapidly (Trend 10, pp.12–13):

- Developed societies increasingly take their cue from Generation X and the Millennial generation (aka Generation Y or Generation Dot-com), rather than the Baby Boomers who dominated the industrialized world's thinking for most of four decades.
- Millennials value, and display, both self-reliance and cooperation.
- Post–September 11 fear of terrorist attacks has led Americans to accept, almost without comment, security measures that their traditional love of privacy once would have made intolerable.

Assessment

This trend will continue for at least the next two decades in the industrialized lands and two generations in the developing world.

Implications for Policing

Reaction against changing values is a prime motive for cultural extremism, in the Muslim world and parts of India, as well as in the United States and Europe, where it appears in the form of hate crimes against immigrants.

The spread of westernized Generation X and Dot-com values will provoke an even greater reaction from fundamentalists, likely making the anti-Western movement among Muslims even more violent and widespread.

The large generation gap is creating significant dissonance and affecting succession schemes in various organizations. Boomers have a strong sense of moral superiority; they look upon the youth with great consternation because they do not share the Boomers' values. In the coming decade, a leadership vacuum is likely to emerge because Boomers have failed to groom their successors.

Changing attitudes to authority and the lack of traditional authority figures and role models for many of the younger generation affect attitudes toward police officers. Police forces around the world have spent the last 20 years trying to move away from traditional "authority policing" to being the "friend of the citizen." With the changing perceptions and values in the light of increased terrorist threats, citizens may ultimately be happy with a return to traditional "authority policing."

Values change faster than the law can, and sometimes change for a time in ways the law must not follow. This could lead to the spread of activities that are criminal under the law, even though they may be accepted by a substantial portion of society.

An Integrated Global Economy

#3 The global economy is growing more integrated (Trend 8, p.14):

- Companies are increasingly farming out high-cost, low-payoff secondary functions to suppliers, service firms and consultants, many located in other countries, for example, parts for the new Boeing 787 "Dreamliner" are being constructed in at least eight countries around the world for assembly in the United States.
- The Internet continues to bring manufacturers effectively closer to remote suppliers and customers.

Assessment

This trend will continue for at least the next two decades.

Implications for Policing

International fraud, money laundering and other economic crimes (particularly carried out via the Internet) are a growing problem and one that can be expected to spread.

Entrepreneurial success in global markets could widen the gap between the rich and poor, worsening social strains in countries already vulnerable to separatist and extremist movements. This could strengthen criminal gangs that are likely to spread to the United States. It is also likely to worsen the problem of international terrorism.

We will be experiencing increasing levels of cross-national crimes, making investigations far more complex, expensive and legally challenging. As more products and services used in law enforcement originate overseas, security concerns rise.

Growth of Militant Islam

#4 Militant Islam continues to spread and gain power (Trend 9, pp.15–16):

- Muslim lands face severe problems with religious extremists dedicated to advancing their political, social and doctrinal views by any means necessary.
- According to the American intelligence community, al Qaeda was more powerful in 2007 than it had been before the so-called "war on terror" began—more dangerous even than it had been when it planned the attacks of September 11, 2001.
- American support for Israel has also made the United States a target for Muslim hatred.

Assessment

This trend may wax and wane, but it seems unlikely to disappear this side of a Muslim reformation comparable to those that transformed Christianity and Judaism.

Implications for Policing

The West, and particularly the United States, must expect more and more violent acts of terrorism for at least the next 20 years. Europe faces a significant homegrown Muslim extremist movement, and the United States may do so in the near future, largely because of waves of immigration since the 1980s that have made Islam the fastest-growing religion in both regions. This must be taken seriously because, for the first time, a Muslim country, Pakistan, has nuclear weapons.

Homeland security issues will have the single greatest impact on the law enforcement community for the next 20 years. Law enforcement will be expected to divide its current efforts focused on the traditional core mission of policing because it has augmented the existing job with the added expectation by the populace to develop prevention measures for domestic/homeland security.

Redistribution of the World's Population

#5 Mass migration is redistributing the world's population (Trend 6, pp.17–18):

- Immigration is quickly changing the ethnic composition of the U.S. population. In 2000, Latinos made up 12.6 percent of the U.S. population; by 2050, they will make up 24.5 percent.
- Higher fertility rates among the immigrant Latino population will accelerate this trend.

Assessment

As native workforces shrink in most industrialized lands, economic opportunities will draw people from the developing world to the developed world in growing numbers. Thus, this trend will continue for at least the next generation.

Implications for Policing

Even where terrorism is not a problem, the new wave of immigrants will require law enforcement agencies to cope with such challenges as diversity recruitment, the need to speak and understand many foreign languages and the possibility of colonization by foreign gangs and organized crime.

With increasing international movements of people, law enforcement will encounter difficulties in identifying and tracking perpetrators. This will require a closer working relationship between the police agencies of different nations.

Illegal immigrants will continue to enter the United States from the southern hemisphere. Local law enforcement may often be at odds with federal concerns of homeland security versus the local mission of serving and protecting communities. Local policing often focuses on gaining the trust and confidence of these groups to provide services to them, while the federal focus will be on enforcing immigration laws and closing the national borders. If these immigrant groups do not trust and have confidence in the police they will become fertile ground for the criminal class, and they will not provide any possible intelligence relating to criminal or terrorist activity.

Decline of Privacy

#6 Privacy, once a defining right for Americans, is dying quickly (Trend 17, pp.19–20):

* Internet communications, a basic part of life for many people, are nearly impossible to protect against interception, and governments around the world are working to ensure their unfettered access to them. Postings to blogs and Web forums are nearly immortal.

* Widespread surveillance of private individuals is technically feasible and economically viable. Increased surveillance has become socially acceptable in an age when many people fear terrorism and crime.

* The USA PATRIOT Act of 2001 sets aside the constitutional requirement of a search warrant for government officials who wish to search someone's home to thwart possible terrorism.

Assessment

Pessimists could say that privacy already is a thing of the past; society is merely coming to recognize its loss. We believe that enough effective privacy survives outside the most authoritarian countries to justify noting its continued erosion. However, this trend could easily reach its logical conclusion within 10 years.

Implications for Policing

It will be nearly impossible for criminals to operate without being observed, but as noted, until artificial intelligence systems "learn" to recognize suspicious activities, most data will be used in forensic reconstruction rather than in active crime prevention efforts.

The rules of evidence will change, and investigations will be able to rely on information seized in ways formerly illegal and considered unconstitutional. Any future terrorist strikes inside the United States will dramatically accelerate the willingness of people to surrender liberty, privacy and freedom in exchange for the perception of security.

We are becoming a fully recorded society through passive surveillance cameras, in-car video systems, citizens recording encounters with police and the like. Police activities will be traced via global positioning systems (GPS) on vehicles and perhaps on officers. Videos of officers' interactions will be used for accountability and lawsuit protection.

Longer Life Expectancies

#7 The population of the developed world is living longer (Trend 3, pp.20–21):

◉ Each generation lives longer and remains healthier.

◉ Medical advances that slow the aging process now seem within reach.

◉ Younger generations in the developed world are likely to routinely live beyond 100 years.

Assessment

Demographic trends such as this are among the most easily recognized and difficult to derail. Barring a global plague or nuclear war—wildcard possibilities that cannot be predicted with any validity—there is little chance that the population forecast for 2050 will err on the high side.

Implications for Policing

Longer life expectancies mean extended careers and longer retirements, raising pension costs for police departments. It may also encourage officers to remain on the job longer, making promotions difficult for younger officers. Retired officers may be brought back to work to carry out support, administrative and technical jobs. It may be necessary to have police work longer than the traditional 20 to 25 years.

This trend raises the potential for increased victimization as the elderly are the most vulnerable segment of society,

Continuing Urbanization

#8 Continuing urbanization will aggravate most environmental and social problems (Trend 27, pp.22–23):

◉ More than three fourths of the population in developed countries live in cities. The United States is an exception to the global urbanization trend where more Americans live in the suburbs than in the cities because of the nation's highway system and relatively little mass transit.

◉ As many as 1 billion city dwellers lack adequate shelter, clean water, toilets or electricity.

Assessment

Perhaps the world's oldest trend, after surviving for some 3,500 years, this trend is unlikely to disappear in the next 50.

Implications for Policing

Concentrating the poor and powerless in cities produces conditions ideal for the spread of petty crime, violence and the kind of religious extremism that lends itself to terror-prone political ideologies. As Americans become increasingly concentrated in urban centers, police will be called on to referee more disputes between haves and have-nots. Dispossessed, violent predators will grow in viciousness and number as they see themselves as having nothing to lose. An urban underclass will be subject to radicalism as mercurial gang leaders effectively organize and lead groups in more disciplined violent strikes. There will be more pitched firefights between police and highly organized and disciplined gangs.

Concentration of populations will exacerbate environmental problems, with urban police departments being asked to take on a greater role in enforcement of environmental regulations.

The Spread of Specialization

#9 Specialization continues to spread throughout industry and the professions (Trend 36, pp.23–24):

◉ For doctors, lawyers, engineers and other professionals, the size of the body of knowledge required to excel in any one area precludes excellence across all areas.

◉ Modern information-based organizations depend on teams of task-focused specialists.

Assessment

This process will continue for at least another 20 years.

Implications for Policing

Like the rest of society, policing is trending toward greater specialization. Many of the most highly specialized functions may be shared between agencies or outsourced to consultants. There will still be a need for senior managers to have an understanding of a spectrum of activities.

Increasingly, officers must receive special training and be accredited to undertake certain law enforcement tasks. More support positions not requiring sworn, armed law enforcement personnel are being civilianized. Included are crime scene investigation, crime analysis and dispatch. Police agencies may need to put special effort into developing a cadre of generalists with the broad skills to become managers and leaders.

A Vanishing Work Ethic

#10 The work ethic is vanishing (Trend 43, p.25):

- More than one third of U.S. workers reported calling in sick when they were not ill at least once in the past 12 months.
- Enron, WorldCom, Tyco International, Adelphia Cable and ImClone just begin the list of companies implicated in deceptive accounting practices, looting of corporate assets and other misdeeds. And the number of American political leaders either under investigation for corruption or convicted of it grows almost daily.

Assessment

There is little prospect that this will change until the children of today's young adults grow up to rebel against their parents' values.

Implications for Policing

A decline in the work ethic is already prevalent. Younger officers do not have the same loyalty, dedication and commitment as previous generations had. Senior law enforcement managers are already finding it harder to motivate younger employees.

New generations are taking over, and they are bringing with them new values that may fit poorly with standards long established in police agencies. These are Generation X, now in their late 30s and 40s and rising into senior positions in law enforcement; Generation Y or Dot-com, in their 20s and early 30s; and the Millennials, now just entering the work force. Throughout the world, members of these generations resemble each other far more than they resemble their parents. The single most obvious characteristic of these generations, reinforced with each successive age cohort, is a single-minded devotion to the bottom line—their own.

 The top 10 trends identified by Forecasting International as shaping the future of policing in descending order are (1) technology increasingly dominates both the economy and society, (2) societal values are changing rapidly, (3) the global economy is growing more integrated, (4) militant Islam continues to spread and gain power, (5) mass migration is redistributing the world's population, (6) privacy, once a defining right for Americans, is dying quickly, (7) the population of the developed world is living longer, (8) continuing urbanization will aggravate most environmental and social problems, (9) specialization continues to spread throughout industry and the professions and (10) the work ethic is vanishing.

Of all the changes affecting law enforcement now and in the future, many experts, including those contributing to the preceding report, point to the impact of technology.

THE IMPACT OF TECHNOLOGY, NOW AND IN THE FUTURE

The success of policing increasingly hinges on the ability of agencies to adapt to change, often rapidly, including the capacity to embrace technology and use it to analyze emerging trends in local communities (Wallentine, 2009). The most significant trend in law enforcement continues to be the application of technology to law enforcement, seen in every facet of policing: "Technology will help solve crimes, prevent crimes, and facilitate crimes that haven't yet been conceived" (Wallentine). "Technology is changing the way police departments operate, how grant requests are formatted, and what is requested in the local operating budget. Technologies funded today were not even common knowledge just a few years ago. . . . These technologies function as force multipliers that improve efficiency, effectiveness, and officer safety in a variety of ways. An additional benefit is that department personnel enjoy working with state-of-the-art equipment, which can boost morale" (Schultz, 2008, p.20).

Most individuals in law enforcement are capitalizing on the accelerated advances of technology, using daily such devices as cell phones, BlackBerry, PDAs, mobile data terminals (MDTs), video stream and countless other communication tools: "Couple that with the volume of new products, advances, and applications and you have the equivalent of a technology tsunami. It's difficult for even the most 'geeked' agency to keep up with" (Marshall, 2008). Keeping up is both a budgetary and a training challenge, and failing to keep pace can place the agency and community at a dangerous disadvantage: "There's danger to not technologically advancing in law enforcement. . . The cop on the street not having fingertip access to all the data-mining capacity is detrimental to law enforcement and the public at large" (Wethal, 2008, p.57).

Numerous "practical technologies" that even small agencies can use include crime lights (portable crime scene examination lights with preset wavelengths designed to detect body fluids, fibers, hair, etc.), in-car camera systems, photo enforcement systems (red light violations or speeding summons), graffiti cameras (some of which warn intruders they are breaking the law), thermal imaging, criminal investigations records systems, electronic white boards, laser spectroscopy (to determine the chemical composition of a substance within seconds), language translators, less-lethal technology, crime scene diagramming systems, crime mapping, automatic license plate recognition (ALPR) systems, GPS technology, and the list will expand (Schultz, 2008, pp.20–25). Managers must stay current in emerging technology, because "These technologies are not for the next generation—they are for this one" (Schultz, p.25).

The Advanced Surveillance and Protection (ASAP) program features a combination of technologies integrated into a station command center that may revolutionize law enforcement practices:

Imagine that a shooting has just occurred wherein the victim is injured or killed. Sensors immediately detect the gunshot and automatically pinpoint high-powered, night vision-capable cameras on the crime scene and send a live image of the fleeing suspect vehicle to the Los Angeles County Sheriff's Department (LASD) station command center. The license plate is recorded by the camera and then entered into a database. The suspect vehicle drives through an intersection equipped with surveillance cameras that automatically detect the suspect vehicle and alert the command center and nearby LASD cars. Live images of the fleeing vehicle are transmitted to the LASD cars, which then go into pursuit. During the pursuit, the command center takes control of the local traffic signals, turning them red in order to reduce the potential for collisions involving innocent drives. This is ASAP at work. (Edson, 2008, p.12)

Having looked at the "big picture" and the worldwide trends that are shaping policing, consider next some specific issues identified by police leaders and the Police Executive Research Forum as being "chief concerns, literally and figuratively," in the past decade.

CRITICAL ISSUES IN POLICING

A "close friendship" has developed between the Police Executive Research Forum (PERF) and Motorola during the past 20 years, beginning when Motorola wanted to contribute to communities' economic vitality by helping reduce crime using analytical tools pioneered at Motorola (Wexler, 2009, p.i). In the first Motorola/PERF collaboration, *Challenge to Change* (1998), the collaboration helped eight police agencies test whether process mapping could improve police departments' core operations, such as responding to calls, conducting investigations and solving crimes. This project's success led to further joint efforts by PERF and Motorola, in what became known as the "Critical Issues in Policing" series, the basic concept of which involves Motorola and PERF co-conducting research and bringing together police leaders to discuss the most difficult and important issues facing departments. To this end, PERF and Motorola conduct surveys to identify issues, hold summits to discuss the key issue identified and publish reports summarizing their findings. Following are brief summaries of the issues included in the series through 2009.

 Critical issues included in the Motorola/PERF Critical Issues Series are police use of force, strategies for resolving conflict and minimizing use of force, police management of mass demonstrations, violent crime in America, hot spots enforcement, patrol-level response to a suicide bomb threat, police planning for an influenza pandemic, local immigration enforcement, and violent crime and the economic crisis.

The following brief descriptions are from *Critical Issues in Policing: An Anthology* (2009).

Use of Force

Exploring the Challenges of Police Use of Force (Ederheimer and Fridell, 2005) reports, "Today, virtually all police agencies have policies on deadly force and less-lethal force, which are based largely on landmark Supreme Court opinions from the 1980s." Analysis of officer-involved shooting cases shows that a "critical period of 15 minutes" occurs between when a call comes into a department and when shots are fired: "If a supervisor arrives at the scene during the critical 15 minutes, the chances of an officer-involved shooting occurring decline dramatically" (p.10).

This critical issues report discusses use of force and the department's culture, improving use-of-force policies and training and the influence of U.S. Justice Department consent decrees, reducing use of force through hiring decisions, re-engineering use-of-force systems in a department, whether less-lethal weapons prevent lethal consequences, use of force investigations, handling the aftermath of a use-of-force incident in the community and officer aftercare programs (Ederheimer and Fridell, 2005, pp.3–4).

A MANAGER'S PERSPECTIVE:
Understanding the Language of Policy

A concern that police administrators should have is how many of their officers are trained beyond the basic language of the policy. For example, many use-of-force policies talk about the "amount of force necessary." The key word here is *necessary*; yet often officers do not fully understand, nor are they trained to understand, the meaning of the word as it applies to the policy. More emphasis must be placed on learning the meaning of each of those words used in departmental policies so that officers can adequately respond and further articulate their actions, which are increasingly being questioned by today's society.

A thought-provoking article by Jennifer Hunt (1985) explores how police officers come to hold different definitions for legal force, excessive force and normal force. What is particularly insightful about her research is that officers' standards for "normal" force vary, often significantly, from those held by the public. Through the socialization process, officers come to normalize the use of force in ways that people who do not do the police job may not understand or hold as legitimate. She (p.321) notes, "For a street cop, it is often a graver error to use too little force and develop a 'shaky' reputation than it is to use too much force and be told to calm down." Such variations in expected use of force can leave officers in discretionary limbo, despite policies that claim to address when officers are justified in using force. Hunt (p.338) concludes, "The organization of police work reflects a poignant moral dilemma: for a variety of reasons, society mandates to the police the right to use force but provides little direction as to its proper use in specific, 'real life' situations. Thus, the police, as officers of the law, must be prepared to use force under circumstances in which its rationale is often morally, legally, and practically ambiguous. This fact explains some otherwise puzzling aspects of police training and socialization."

The bottom line for police managers is that the socialization process may trump the message or intent of an ambiguous formal policy, particularly when training fails to help officers "fill in the blanks," so to speak, by providing an interpretation and understanding of the language of such policies.

Resolving Conflict and Minimizing Use of Force

Strategies for Resolving Conflict and Minimizing Use of Force (Ederheimer, 2007) provides multiple perspectives on the broad topic of how departments can most effectively make arrests, subdue resisting suspects and otherwise handle situations in which they may be required to use some type of force. The goal of using as little force as is necessary can be difficult to achieve in the world of day-to-day policing. The report has four sections: (1) building community trust around issues of force, (2) police use of force and people with mental illness, (3) less-lethal weaponry and less-lethal force decision making and (4) national studies regarding and guidelines for using conducted energy devices (Ederheimer, pp.11–12).

Management of Mass Demonstrations

Police Management of Mass Demonstrations: Identifying Issues and Successful Approaches notes the competing goals police face of maintaining order and protecting the freedoms of speech and assembly (Narr et al., 2006). This report details the tough lessons learned by police during the 1960s as well as in the aftermath of the World Trade Organization protests, stressing, "Learn from this experience or risk repeating it."

The key issues discussed include how to manage police resources to deal with very large numbers of people who are protesting (or people who may simply be gathering following an incident such as a major sports victory), how to work with business and community members who are not involved in the demonstration or celebration but who expect police to protect their property, how to gather information in anticipation of a demonstration and during the event and how to determine what levels of force should be used if demonstrators become violent (Narr et al., 2006, pp.5–6).

Violent Crime

A Gathering Storm: Violent Crime in America (2006) and *Violent Crime in America: 24 Months of Alarming Trends* (2006) reported Federal Bureau of Investigation (FBI) figures showing that violent crime was, indeed, increasing in the United States, a development PERF viewed with alarm. Sensing a need to move quickly, PERF began to sound the alarm with the news media and elsewhere about the "gathering storm" of violence, hoping to help local agencies understand what was happening and develop countermeasures. This idea of moving quickly to fight a crime trend was somewhat new in policing.

Noting how the country was facing a tipping point in violent crime, PERF strongly advocated a rapid intervention that "could prevent a return to the horrendous crime rates of the past and could save thousands of lives." PERF conducted its own surveys on violent crime because the FBI's massive Uniform Crime Reports required time to produce findings, time which PERF saw as critical. The results of PERF's surveys proved to be "remarkably" accurate, with FBI figures released months later confirming PERF's conclusions. PERF's members were not interested in waiting years for "rock solid" statistical trends before taking action (*Critical Issues in Policing*, 2009, pp.7–8).

Violent Crime in America: "A Tale of Two Cities" (2008) is a follow-up of the two reports on the increase in violent crime and how law enforcement rose to the challenge of facing a two-year nationwide spike in violent crime, explaining how police departments reversed the rising crime rate and brought it back to an overall downward trend. A PERF survey in 2007 revealed that gangs were considered the Number 1 factor contributing to violent crime, with 77 percent of responding agencies citing gangs as a factor. Other factors cited by more than half of the agencies included juvenile crime, impulsive violence and "disrespect" issues, the constant release of thousands of offenders from prison back into the community every month and an increased availability of guns.

The survey also showed that "hot spots" enforcement was the Number 1 strategy police agencies were using to address the increases in violent crime. Many agencies using such strategies reported seeing a decrease in violent crime, results borne out nationally by later data (*Violent Crime in America*, 2008, pp.15–16).

Hot Spots Enforcement

Violent Crime in America: What We Know about Hot Spots Enforcement (2008) was the fourth in a series on violent crime trends. Based on PERF survey results it became apparent that police departments across the country were having some success in driving violent crime rates back down, with substantial decreases between 4 and 8 percent in homicide, robbery, aggravated assault and aggravated assault with a firearm. The five most commonly used strategies to deal with homicide/shooting hot spots were problem analysis and problem solving (77 percent), community policing/partnerships (73 percent), enhanced traffic stops and field interviews (69 percent), targeting known offenders (69 percent) and directed patrol (65 percent). Targeting known offenders was most often identified as the most effective strategy (pp.19–20).

The Chicago Police Department's Targeted Response Unit (TRU) is a squad of 240 of the agency's youngest and most aggressive officers sent into the most troubled and crime-ridden neighborhoods of Chicago. The TRU has employed a new high-tech security system to help lower crime rates that uses citywide cameras and a computerized central database for patrol officers to view leads, mug shots and rap sheets.

© Ed Kashi/Corbis

Patrol Response to a Suicide Bomb Threat

Patrol-Level Response to a Suicide Bomb Threat: Guidelines for Consideration (Spahr et al., 2007) was based on nearly a year of research and two conferences, one at which participants drafted a proposed set of guidelines and a second at which they vetted these guidelines. In addition to the 68 guidelines presented, this report includes three essays offering suicide bomb threat perspectives—one each from London Metropolitan Police Commissioner Ian Blair; Michael Heidingsfield, head of the U.S. State Department Police Advisory Mission in Iraq from 2004 to 2006 and who was the target of four suicide bombing attempts; and Los Angeles Police Chief William Bratton—a glossary of terms and a chart providing the U.S. Army's estimates of dangers posed by 15 types of suicide bomb threats, ranging from small pipe bombs, suicide vests and briefcase bombs to large truck bombs, with suggested evacuation distances for each type (Spahr et al., pp.9–10).

Police Planning for an Influenza Pandemic

Police Planning for an Influenza Pandemic: Case Studies and Recommendations from the Field (2007) reports that police departments must prepare for a pandemic threat because a major outbreak of flu could bring new demands on departments such as enforcing quarantines at public places and maintaining security at hospitals as limited supplies of vaccine become available. At the same time, departments may be short staffed as police employees become infected and are required to stay home from work. The report notes, "When bad things happen, people call the police to answer their questions and solve their problems." This report outlines the elements to be included in pandemic flu plans and provides a set of recommendations as well as a list of resources for pandemic flu planning (pp.13–14).

Local Immigration Enforcement

Police Chiefs and Sheriffs Speak Out on Local Immigration Enforcement (2008) reports that the immigration issue is extremely complicated legally, politically and in terms of finding practical policies that "work." The goal of the report was to explore these issues and to work out some points of consensus on which the participating agencies could agree. The survey found that police executives' top concern about taking on responsibilities for helping to enforce federal immigration laws is that they do not have the manpower to do it. Nearly two-thirds of respondents expressed this concern, followed closely by a concern that immigration enforcement undermines the trust between immigrants and the police. The most common existing practice among local law enforcement agencies is that immigration status checks are conducted when police make an arrest. Sixty-five percent of participating departments did not have a written policy related to checking immigration status.

The summit on this topic produced three major points of consensus:

1. It is appropriate to check immigration status at the time of arrest and booking for serious offenses. (But there was no consensus about checking the status of misdemeanants.)

2. A national identification card based on biometric technology would be helpful, as the existing driver's license identification systems are considerably vulnerable to fraud.

3. The U.S. Congress needs to set policy for the nation. Many participants decried the lack of federal leadership on this issue and expressed resentment that local police are being forced to take the lead on what is a federal issue (*Police Chiefs and Sheriffs Speak Out*, 2008, pp.17–18).

Violent Crime and the Economic Crisis

Violent Crime and the Economic Crisis: Police Chiefs Face a New Challenge, Part I and Part II (2009) reflects PERF's commitment to respond to emerging issues and respond immediately to changing events in the work. In one survey, PERF shifted its focus from violent crime to the economic downturn and its impact on police operations, with "startling" results. These findings were discussed in Chapter 14 as they relate to staffing and budget cuts. The survey also revealed that 44 percent of agencies were experiencing increased crime levels that they believed resulted from changes in the economy, in particular burglaries from vacant homes and "opportunistic" property crimes such as thefts of GPS devices from cars (*Violent Crime and the Economic Crisis: Police Chiefs Face a New Challenge, Part II*, pp.21–24).

Up Next: Gangs and Guns

In May 2009 PERF held a summit on policing gangs and surveyed police agencies regarding gang issues and trends. The next Critical Issues report will focus on this topic. PERF is also planning a summit on guns and crime and is surveying local police agencies as well as field offices of the federal Bureau of Alcohol, Tobacco, Firearms and Explosives regarding local initiative to reduce gun crimes and illegal gun sales. A future Critical Issues in Policing will report the results of these surveys and the Summit on Guns and Crime.

OTHER MAJOR CHALLENGES FACING 21ST-CENTURY LAW ENFORCEMENT

Most of the significant trends and issues within law enforcement have been alluded to throughout this text. Some of the issues are relatively new. Others have been present for decades.

 Three challenges law enforcement managers faced before the 21st century continue as major challenges in the 21st century: drugs, gangs and terrorism.

The Drug Problem

The national and international drug problem has placed law enforcement officers on the front line, in enforcing drug laws and in establishing drug undercover operations and participative community programs. The drug

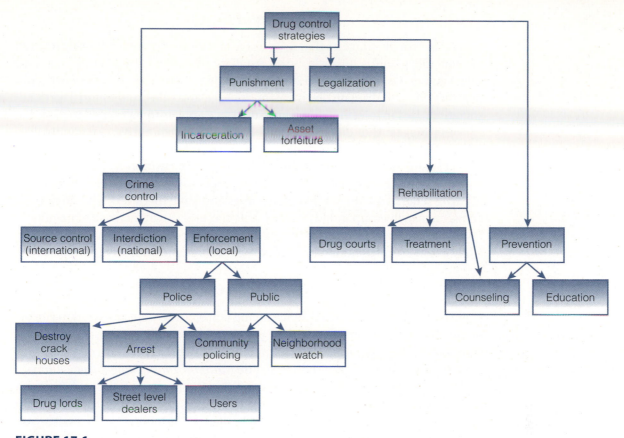

FIGURE 17.1
Overview of Drug-Control Strategies

Source: From HESS. *Introduction to Law Enforcement and Criminal Justice*, 9th ed. © 2009 Delmar Learning, a part of Cengage Learning, Inc. Reproduced by permission. www.cengage.com/permissions

problem is of such magnitude that no single individual, segment of society or government can resolve the problem, which means that no segment can move ahead alone. An attack on one segment of society must be accepted as an attack on all.

In 1989 the drug problem was the largest single issue and concern in the nation. The public still expects law enforcement organizations to deal with this problem. Many federal resources will have to be devoted to it, and law enforcement entities must develop new approaches to meet the local challenge. Resolving the problem may involve reducing individual civil liberties in the interest of overall social well-being.

Suggested approaches to address the drug problem include crime control, punishment, rehabilitation, prevention and legalization, as summarized in Figure 17.1. These approaches support the goals of the *National Drug Control Strategy* (2009): (1) stopping use before it starts: education and community action; (2) healing America's drug users: getting treatment resources where they are needed; and (3) disrupting the market: attacking the economic basis of the drug trade.

This is a war in which all willing and unwilling participants have been losers, either financially or in human distress and suffering. Drastic measures will be necessary to bring about a resolution.

Drugs and Gangs

Research strongly suggests that drug usage and violent crime are closely related. What is still in doubt, however, is the association between drugs (both usage and sales) and gangs. Bjerregaard (2010, p.3) studied the relationship between gang membership and drug involvement, both usage and sales, and found a weak association. This involvement, however, does not appear to be related to assaults: "Results suggest that gang membership is not determinative of drug involvement among a national random sample of youths." Other research has found that (1) gang members who sell drugs are significantly more violent than gang members that do not sell drugs and drug sellers that do not belong to gangs; (2) drug sellers who do not belong to gangs and gang members who do not sell drugs engage in comparable levels of violence; and (3) an increase in neighborhood disadvantage intensifies the effect of gang membership on violence, especially among gang members that sell drugs (Bellair and McNulty, 2009, p.644).

Gang Violence

Gang violence is another challenge facing law enforcement now and in the future. Despite the differences in data presented by various sources as to the estimated number of gangs and gang members, the threat posed to communities by gang violence is of great concern. The *National Youth Gang Survey Analysis* (2009), conducted by the National Youth Gang Center (NYGC), reports that the most recent estimate of 27,000 gangs is the highest since 1998. Their estimate of 788,000 gang members is a statistically significant increase over the 12-year low in 2001. An update of the National Youth Gang Survey reports that overall, the number of gangs in the study population increased 25 percent between 2002 and 2007 (Chambers, 2009).

The *National Gang Threat Assessment 2009* reports approximately 1 million gang members belonging to more than 20,000 gangs were criminally active within all 50 states and the District of Columbia: "Local street gangs, or neighborhood-based street gangs, remain a significant threat because they continue to account for the largest number of gangs nationwide. . . . Criminal gangs commit as much as 80 percent of the crime in many communities." Typical gang-related crime include alien smuggling, armed robbery, assault, auto theft, drug trafficking, weapons trafficking, extortion, fraud, home invasions, identity theft and murder. The *Assessment* also reports that few gangs have been found to be associated with terrorist organizations. Gang affiliation or not, terrorism is also a challenge facing law enforcement.

Terrorism

Until the attacks on American soil on September 11, 2001, terrorism was viewed as a federal challenge. On June 7, 1999, Osama bin Laden was placed on the FBI's 10 Most Wanted fugitives list for the murder of U.S. nationals outside the United States, conspiracy to murder U.S. nationals outside the United States and attack on a federal facility resulting in death. Bin Laden was wanted in connection with the 1998 bombings of two U.S. embassies that killed 224 and injured more than 5,000 people. A reward of as much as $25 million was

© Reuters/CORBIS

The need for homeland security was brought to the forefront by the events of September 11, 2001. A rescue helicopter surveys damages to the Pentagon Building as firefighters battle flames after terrorists crashed an airliner into the U.S. Military Headquarters outside Washington, DC.

offered for information leading directly to the apprehension or conviction of bin Laden. He remains on the FBI's 10 Most Wanted List, as does the reward offer ("Usama Bin Laden, FBI Ten Most Wanted Fugitive," 2009).

In July 2002, the first *National Strategy for Homeland Security* was released, providing direction for steps that can be taken by local and state law enforcement agencies, private companies and organizations and individual Americans. However, the problem of sharing information continues:

> Tremendous demands are being placed on local police agencies to feed information to agencies needing to develop intelligence on terrorism risks around the nation. . . . Local chiefs want access to timely and useful information about the risks of terror in their communities, and most bridle at the security restrictions placed upon them by federal agencies. And they sometimes are uncomfortable with the role federal agencies want them to play in seizing, interrogating, and otherwise controlling suspects and persons of interest—especially in areas where there are large numbers of persons who are thought to be in a "prime" suspect pool (e.g. immigrants and persons from parts of the world believed to produce and shelter active terrorist groups). (Mastrofski, 2007, pp.21–22)

The problem boils down to how *terrorism* is classified (Burton, 2009). Currently terrorism is considered a matter of national security, and details surrounding terrorism cases are classified, meaning the information is restricted from flowing across agencies. Further, state and local police typically do not have sufficient clearance for details involving investigations by FBI-led joint terrorism task forces (JTTFs). Because of this, state and local law enforcement officers are unaware of terrorism cases taking place in their own jurisdiction:

> As a result, law enforcement officers cannot share information they might have on a certain suspect, and they might not be aware of the threat an individual

poses when they confront that individual for unrelated reasons. The case of the Fort Hood shooter, U.S. Army Maj. Nidal Malik Hasan, is an example of this: An FBI JTTF team had investigated Hasan based on comments he had made but concluded that he did not pose any kind of threat, so details of the investigation were not disseminated. It is not clear that dissemination of those details would have prevented the attack, but combined with the knowledge of local base or military police, it could have lead to a more complete profile of Hasan. (Burton, 2009)

Another important aspect of terrorism and the war on it is the reentry of military personnel into American communities and how society responds to them and the issues they are dealing with. Equally important, as many soldiers are also police officers, is the reentry of these personnel into the ranks of law enforcement and the department's responsibilities for such officers after they return from war. This situation can present a considerable challenge for law enforcement supervisors who may be unprepared for the psychological aftermath these officers suffer following their wartime experiences.

How law enforcement will meet the special challenges ahead of it are addressed by futuristics.

FUTURISTICS

As a profession, law enforcement has relied too heavily on experience and not enough on innovation. This has begun to change, with the development of predictive analysis and other future-focused methodologies, but for the most part, policing remains heavily reliant on status quo techniques. Such a narrow and overly restrictive perspective can be broadened through the use of **futuristics**, a new tool for managers and leaders that involves the science of using data from the past to forecast alternatives for the future and to then select the most desirable alternatives.

futuristics

the science of using data from the past to forecast alternatives for the future and to then select those most desirable.

People who study the future use environmental scanning; that is, they identify factors likely to "drive" the environment. **Environmental scanning** has been defined as "a process for systematically examining and evaluating various trends that may have future significance for an organization" (Cowper and Jensen, 2003, p.127). Three categories of change are likely to affect the future criminal justice system:

environmental scanning

identifying the factors that are likely to "drive" the environment, influencing the future; includes social and economic conditions.

1. Social and economic conditions (size and age of the population, immigration patterns and nature of employment and lifestyle characteristics)

2. Shifts in the number and types of crimes and disorder challenges

3. Developments in the criminal justice system itself, including community involvement in all aspects of the system

Forecasting, a form of futuristics, is similar to the headlights on a car being driven in a snowstorm. The lights provide enough illumination to continue but not enough so the driver can proceed without caution. What lies ahead is still unknown. Futuristics is not something mystical or prophetic. It combines historical facts, scientific principles and departmental values with vision to imagine what could happen in the future. The Society of Police Futurists International (PFI) was founded in 1991 by Dr. William Tafoya. PFI is dedicated to futures research in policing and to stimulating new ideas on a variety of policing theories and practices.

Basic Principles of Futuristics

Futuristics rests on three basic principles or assumptions about the nature of the universe and our role in it (Tafoya, 1983, p.13).

The three basic principles of futuristics are
1. **The unity or interconnectedness of reality.**
2. **The significance of ideas.**
3. **The crucial importance of time.**

The *unity* or *interconnectedness of reality* suggests that we operate in a "holistic universe, a huge mega-system, the activities of whose systems, subsystems and components interface and interact in synergistic fashion" (Tafoya, 1983, p.13).

The *significance of ideas*, the second basic principle of futuristics, emphasizes the quest for new and better ways of doing things—exploring divergent new ways to deal with old problems and imagining new ways to anticipate potential problems.

The third basic principle, the *importance of time*, suggests a future focus. Rather than being absorbed with today's problems and holding on to traditions, futurists think five years ahead and beyond. Futuristics often uses the following time frames (Tafoya, 1983, p.15):

Immediate future	Present to 2 years
Short-range future	2 to 5 years
Mid-range future	5 to 10 years
Long-range future	10 to 20 years
Extended-range future	20 to 50 years
Distant future	50 years and beyond

Law enforcement managers tend to focus on the immediate future, dealing with problems that need resolution, trying to stay "on top of things" and "putting out fires." No wonder they do not notice a mere 2- to 4-percent annual increase in the crime rate. The crisis faced today is probably a minor one that was ignored yesterday. Time is significant. Do not let it be said of the future that it is "that time when you'll wish you'd done what you aren't doing now."

Fundamental Premises and Goals

Futurists also operate under three fundamental premises (Tafoya, 1983, p.15):

Fundamental premises of futurists are the following:
- **The future is not predictable.**
- **The future is not predetermined.**
- **Future outcomes can be influenced by individual choice.**

The third premise is critical to managers because the choices made today will affect law enforcement in the future. As has been said, "The future is coming. Only you can decide where it's going." How can futuristics be used in law enforcement management? Tafoya suggests three primary priorities or goals that deal with the possible, the probable and the preferable (1983, p.17):

> If people are to influence future outcomes, perceptions of the future must be formed. . . . Be alert to risks as well as opportunities. What is possible is what "could be"; this key role is characterized as *image-driven*. . . . What is required is breaking the fetters of one's imagination. It is the vital, creative goal of futuristics.
>
> Once new images have been generated, likely alternatives must be studied. The probable path to the future must be analyzed; quantitatively as well as qualitatively. . . . What is probable is what "may be"; this aim is characterized as *analytically driven*. It is the detached, systematic and *scientific* goal of futuristics.
>
> Having imagined the possible and analyzed the probable, it is necessary to make choices among alternatives. . . . What is preferred is what "should be"; this intent is characterized as *value-driven*. It is the *managerial, decision-making goal* of futuristics.

 Goals of futuristics:
  - **Form perceptions of the future (the possible).**
  - **Study likely alternatives (the probable).**
  - **Make choices to bring about particular events (the preferable).**

The Futures Working Group

The Futures Working Group (FWG), consisting of PFI and FBI members, stresses that the post–September 11 era of policing has made the role of the first responder to disasters and crises a high priority of police departments and that the homeland security function may have even more profound effects on policing.

The group also identified several possible futures for community policing. Community policing may evolve into community-oriented government. It is also possible that public–private partnerships may evolve to the point where policing in wealthy neighborhoods will be provided by private police forces. Another possibility is that a department may have a *proactive*, or quality-of-life, division and a *reactive*, or crisis, division coexisting. It may be that in the future police responses to disturbances and violence are largely responded to by robotic devices because nearly all public places will be under video surveillance monitored by computers.

Other Futures Envisioned

Wallentine (2009) sees several changes in policing in the coming decade:

- Expanded employment opportunities for and further professional development of police intelligence analysis, including new degree tracks in intelligence analysis.
- More use of public surveillance cameras and use of facial recognition software.
- Advances and simplification of DNA collection and more rapid testing methods.
- Court decisions that further guide eyewitness identification methods and changes to evidentiary rules that create an incentive to record interrogations.
- Improved technology in wearable cameras and significantly greater use of wearable cameras.
- Fewer younger violent criminals, but more white-collar criminals with rises in identity theft and financial crimes and new methods of fraud.
- Home-grown jihadists will increase. The massacre at Fort Hood may be just the beginning of terrorist attacks by jihadists trained in American mosques.

Jetmore (2009) envisions the following in the coming decade:

1. The polygraph will morph into a true lie detector with the same accuracy as fingerprints and DNA. The courts will rule that because it would instantly set an innocent person free it is an exception to the Fourth Amendment. Cops will carry lie detector units the size of cell phones and use them the same way we use "Stop and Frisk."

2. Computerized Droids will process all of our crime scenes and be able to instantly analyze DNA and ballistics. Robots will also be used for forced, high risk, entry.

3. We will use military type drones for surveillance and all activity in public will be videotaped.

4. All handguns will be illegal except for the military and the police. People will be allowed to keep their shotguns and rifles. No private ownership of automatic weapons will be allowed.

5. Babies born after 2020 will have a computer chip embedded under their skin. All medical and criminal records will be on the chip. The government will be able to scan the imbedded chips and add information, such as the fact the person is wanted for a crime. A black market will develop to mask scanner readings.

6. Local police departments will slowly be merged into larger and larger organizations until there is a national police department.

7. The death penalty will be abolished in favor of a mind-sweeping technique that eradicates criminal behavior. Eventually it will be used on all violent felons.

8. All drugs will be decriminalized. The addicted will be reprogrammed.

9. The police will drive hover vehicles having the same capability as helicopters, but closer to the ground. Surveillance devices will penetrate walls.

10. U.S. military forces will have law enforcement powers in our major cities and it may become difficult to distinguish between police officers and soldiers.

Jetmore acknowledges that some of what he foresees may sound like science fiction, but when looking to the future, one need only consider the mind-boggling changes that have occurred in policing since the beginning of this century to realize that what was once considered impossible has now become possible.

CHANGE REVISITED

Change occurs in several major areas directly affecting law enforcement. These include changes in the society itself, in technology, in the economy and in the environment, as well as political changes. Often, if things are going well for a department, it sees no reason to make a change. Recall the story of the monkeys, the banana and the cold shower told in the last chapter. Many managers believe, "If it ain't broke, don't fix it." However, managers who do not pay attention to the changes occurring around them do so at their own peril. Consider the boiled frog phenomenon.

The Boiled Frog Phenomenon

The boiled frog phenomenon rests on a classic experiment. A frog is dropped into a pan of boiling water and immediately jumps out, saving its life. Next, a frog is placed into a pan of room-temperature water that is gradually heated to the boiling point. Because the temperature rise is so gradual, the frog does not notice it and sits contentedly in the bottom of the pan. The gradually rising temperature initially makes the frog comfortable but eventually saps its energy.

As the water becomes too hot, the frog has no strength to jump out. It boils to death.

boiled frog phenomenon

based on a classic experiment, suggests that managers must pay attention to change in their environment and adapt—or perish.

 The **boiled frog phenomenon** suggests that managers must pay attention to change in their environment and adapt—or perish.

Resistance to Change

As discussed previously, resistance to change is natural. Consider the following statements:

"The horse is here to stay, but the automobile is only a novelty—a fad." Marshall Ferdinand Foch, 1911, a French military strategist.

"There is no reason for any individual to have a computer in his home." Ken Olsen, 1977, president of Digital Equipment.

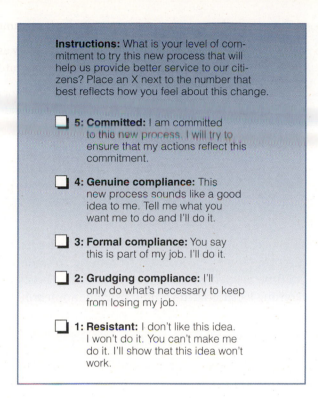

Instructions: What is your level of commitment to try this new process that will help us provide better service to our citizens? Place an X next to the number that best reflects how you feel about this change.

☐ **5: Committed:** I am committed to this new process. I will try to ensure that my actions reflect this commitment.

☐ **4: Genuine compliance:** This new process sounds like a good idea to me. Tell me what you want me to do and I'll do it.

☐ **3: Formal compliance:** You say this is part of my job. I'll do it.

☐ **2: Grudging compliance:** I'll only do what's necessary to keep from losing my job.

☐ **1: Resistant:** I don't like this idea. I won't do it. You can't make me do it. I'll show that this idea won't work.

FIGURE 17.2
A Sample Commitment Ladder

Source: Reprinted from *The Police Chief*, Vol. LXX, No. 10, p.57, ©2003. Copyright held by the International Association of Chiefs of Police, 515 North Washington Street, Alexandria, VA 22314 USA. Further reproduction without express written permission from IACP is strictly prohibited.

To overcome resistance and obtain commitment to change, consider who among those who would be affected by the change could help or derail the plan. Figure 17.2 shows a commitment ladder that could be used to begin the change process. Middle managers are important players in making changes, for if they are not properly prepared, they will not provide supervisors with the rationale for organizational change. The middle manager must excite change in supervisors, who in turn can excite the first-line officers who are responsible for implementation.

Next, consider where those affected by the change currently are. People usually fall into one of four categories: those who *resist* the change, those who *let it* happen, those who *help* it happen and those who *make* it happen. Then determine where they need to be to make the change happen. Figure 17.3 illustrates a commitment planning chart that can be used in this second step, with Xs indicating current level of commitment and Os indicating the level of commitment needed from each person.

It often takes a catastrophe such as the attacks on America on September 11, 2001, to bring about change. Without such an impetus, initiating change may be difficult.

Police organizations have considerable momentum. Having a strong personal commitment to the values with which they have "grown up," police officers may find hints of proposed change in the police culture extremely threatening. Often what is needed is change in the very culture of an agency. If the reality of an organization does not match its stated mission and goals, it is management's responsibility to change the organizational culture to meet the

FIGURE 17.3
Commitment Planning Chart

Key employee	Resist change	Let change happen	Help change happen	Make change happen
1.	X		O	
2.		X		O
3.		X	O	
4.				XO
5.			X	O
6.		XO		
7.	X	O		

desired goals and expectations. Change takes time, and it's what is done day by day that matters most.

The amount of time needed will vary from agency to agency, but managers should avoid becoming victims of the boiled frog phenomenon.

Acceptance of Change

Change is inevitable. No person or organization can stop it. Managers must accept that the only constant is change. Whether change is positive or negative is characterized by Enright (1984) this way:

> A branch floats peacefully down a river whose waters are high with the spring runoff. Although the branch is floating rapidly and occasionally bumps gently into a rock, it is almost effortlessly motionless in relation to the water it floats in.

> A similar branch has become wedged between some rocks and is thus resisting the swift flow of water around it. This branch is buffeted, whipped and battered by the water and debris floating past it, and will soon be broken by the pressures against it (unless it dislodges and "goes with the flow"). If branches could experience, the one wedged into the rocks would be experiencing change with intense pain and distress; the floating one would experience ease and, paradoxically, comfortable stability even in the midst of rapid motion.

 Change is inevitable. View it as opportunity.

> The future is not some place we are going to, but one we are creating. The paths are not to be found, but made, and the activity of making them changes both the maker and the destination.—John Schaar

The future never comes. It is like tomorrow. We can only function in today—but what we do today will influence all the todays to come. Managers and leaders must be forward looking, adapting as necessary to accomplish their mission.

AWAY FROM THE DESK: Pride to Carry into the Future

An organization with a culture of achievement is one where professional excellence is expected and where there is commitment to performance and accountability. It is our people who drive this culture by being professional, motivated and flexible in their approach.

These are key characteristics consistent with the intention of our future and strategies to take us into the future. These characteristics apply to individuals and the organization.

Police leaders are results-oriented, innovative, fair, passionate about policing and responsive to change. These qualities promote excellence and all of us are capable of displaying them in everything that we do.

An individual's qualities do not create a culture—the organization must also foster a climate where superior public service is standard practice, partnerships and collaboration are expected, supported respect is freely given and accountability is expected and accepted.

This organizational climate becomes effective when all individuals commit to these requirements. While many people commit daily, we all need to adopt this approach of maintaining pride in our personal achievement and in being part of the Owatonna Police Department on an ongoing basis.

In meeting the expectations of an achievement culture we will continue to grow and our collective pride in being part of the Owatonna Police Department will become our greatest strength!

—Chief Shaun E. LaDue

SUMMARY

Technical competence used to be most important. Now and in the years ahead, people skills are most important. The public to be served will include more two-income families, more single-parent families, more senior citizens and more minorities. The educational and economic gap will increase, with those at the bottom becoming more disadvantaged and dissatisfied.

Forecasting International rates technology as the most powerful of the many forces now changing law enforcement. The top 10 trends identified by Forecasting International as shaping the future of policing in descending order are (1) technology increasingly dominates both the economy and society, (2) societal values are changing rapidly, (3) the global economy is growing more integrated, (4) militant Islam continues to spread and gain power, (5) mass migration is redistributing the world's population, (6) privacy, once a defining right for Americans, is dying quickly, (7) the population of the developed world is living longer, (8) continuing urbanization will aggravate most environmental and social problems, (9) specialization continues to spread throughout industry and the professions and (10) the work ethic is vanishing.

Critical issues included in the Motorola/PERF Critical Issues Series are police use of force, strategies for resolving conflict and minimizing use of force, police management of mass demonstrations, violent crime in America, hot spots enforcement, patrol-level response to a suicide bomb threat, police planning for an influenza pandemic, local immigration enforcement, and violent crime and the economic crisis.

Three challenges law enforcement managers faced before the 21st century continue as major challenges in the 21st century: drugs, gangs and terrorism. In planning to meet the challenges facing law enforcement, managers can benefit from futuristics. Futuristics is the science of using data from the past to forecast alternatives for the future and to then select the most desirable. The three basic principles of futuristics are (1) the unity or interconnectedness of reality, (2) the significance of ideas and (3) the crucial importance of time. Fundamental premises of futurists are that the future is not predictable, the future is not predetermined and future outcomes can be influenced by individual choice. Goals of futuristics include

- Form perceptions of the future (the possible).
- Study likely alternatives (the probable).
- Make choices to bring about particular events (the preferable).

The boiled frog phenomenon suggests that managers must pay attention to change in their environment and adapt—or perish. Change is inevitable. View it as opportunity.

CHALLENGE SEVENTEEN

Your first year as the police chief of the Greenfield Police Department has been a resounding success. When you arrived the department was a traditional crime-fighting organization with a military command structure. Now the department is well on its way to implementing a community policing strategy and a participative management structure. You are confident the department's mission is in line with the current needs of the Greenfield community.

You cross your feet on your desk, clasp your hands behind your head, and take a deep, relaxing breath. You are proud of your leadership and the department's accomplishments. But then, a troubling thought creeps into your head.

What if community policing and participative management are outdated in 10 years? Will the next chief look back at you and wonder why you were entrenched in an antiquated paradigm of policing? Will you be the next generation's Chief Slaughter?

You want to be remembered as an innovator on the cutting edge of modern policing. You sit up in your chair and pull out a note pad. You write across the top, "My 10 Year Plan."

1. Should police leaders plan to make major changes in policing strategies every 10 years?

2. Anticipate some major changes in the population that will affect American policing in the near future.

3. Will the Internet affect local law enforcement?

4. How will the trend toward private security affect policing?

5. The rapid pace of technology will continue to change the way we police. Can you recognize ways technology is currently changing American policing?

6. What traits come to mind when you envision a police leader of the future?

DISCUSSION QUESTIONS

1. What should be law enforcement's role in the drug problem? In the gang problem? The challenge of homeland security?

2. Which of the top ten trends identified by Forecasting International do you think should be rated as Number One?

3. Which of the issues discussed in the Motorola/PERF Critical Issues Series is most important? Least important?

4. What trends do you foresee in the future of policing?

5. How far into the future should predictions be made?

6. Why is studying the past important in preparing for the future?

7. How would you meet the decline of law enforcement resources?

8. What changes do you think are needed in the selection of future officers?

9. What major changes have you experienced in the past year? The past five years? How well did you handle them?

10. How can you best prepare for the inevitability of change in your life and your career?

REFERENCES

Bellair, Paul E., and McNulty, Thomas L. "Gang Membership, Drug Selling and Violence in Neighborhood Context." *Justice Quarterly*, December 2009, pp.644–669.

Bjerregaard, Beth. "Gang Membership and Drug Involvement: Untangling the Complex Relationship." *Crime & Delinquency*, January 2010, pp.3–34.

Burton, Fred. "A Decade of Evolution in Police Counterterrorism Operations." *PoliceOne.com News*, December 21, 2009. Accessed December 24, 2009. http://www.policeone.com/pc_print.asp?vid=1981177

Cetron, Marvia J., and Davies, Owen. *55 Trends Now Shaping the Future of Policing*. The Proteus Trends Series. Forecasting International, Inc. February 2008. Accessed December 18, 2009. http://www.carlisle.army.mil/proteus

Challenge to Change: The 21st Century Policing Project. Washington, DC: Police Executive Research Forum, 1998.

Chambers, Benjamin. *Reclaiming Futures Every Day: Juvenile Justice: Updated National Youth Gang Survey*. National Youth Gang Center, September 29, 2009. Accessed January 6, 2010. http://blog.reclaimingfutures.org/?q=juvenile-justice-youth-gang-data-2009

Cowper, Thomas, and Jensen, Carl. "Emerging Technology." *Law and Order*, June 2003, pp.124–127.

Cowper, T.; Jensen, C; and Levine, B. "Let's Get with the Digital Age." *Law Enforcement Technology*, July 2003, pp.8–10.

Critical Issues in Policing: An Anthology. Washington, DC: Police Executive Research Forum, 2009.

Ederheimer, Joshua A., editor. *Strategies for Resolving Conflict and Minimizing Use of Force*. Washington, DC: Police Executive Research Forum, April 2007.

Ederheimer, Joshua A., and Fridell, Lorie A., editors. *Exploring the Challenges of Police Use of Force*. Washington, DC: Police Executive Research Forum, April 2005.

Edson, Scott. "Los Angeles County Sheriff's Department ASAP Program. *The Police Chief*, March 2008, pp.12–13.

Enright, John. "Change and Resilience." *The Leader Manager*. Eden Prairie, MN: Wilson Learning Corporation, 1984, pp. 59–73.

A Gathering Storm: Violent Crime in America. Washington, DC: Police Executive Research Forum, October 2006.

Hunt, Jennifer. "Police Accounts of Normal Force." *Urban Life*, January 1985, pp.315–341.

Jetmore, Larry F. "Yesterday, Today, Tomorrow: Changes in Police Careers over the Years." *PoliceOne.com News*, December 17, 2009. Accessed December 24, 2009. http://www.policeone.com/pc_print.asp?vid=1979409

Marshall, Mark A. "The Cutting Edge of Law Enforcement Technology." *PoliceOne.com News*, January 2, 2008. Accessed January 3, 2008. http://www.policeone.com/pc_print.asp?vid=1645861

Mastrofski, Stephen D. *Police Organization and Management Issues for the Next Decade.* Paper presented at the National Institute of Justice (NIJ) Policing Research Workshop: Planning for the Future. Washington, DC, November 28–29, 2006. Published May 2007.

Naisbitt, John, and Aburdene, Patricia. *Megatrends 2000: Ten New Directions for the 1990s.* New York: William Morrow & Co., 1990.

Narr, Tony; Toliver, Jessica; Murphy, Jerry; McFarland, Malcomb; and Ederheimer, Joshua. *Police Management of Mass Demonstrations: Identifying Issues and Successful Approaches.* Washington, DC: Police Executive Research Forum, 2006.

National Drug Control Strategy. Washington, DC: Office of National Drug Control Policy, January 2009. Accessed December 28, 2009. http://www.whitehousedrugpolicy.gov/publications/policy/ndcs09/index.html

National Gang Threat Assessment, 2009. Washington, DC: National Gang Intelligence Center, January 2009. Accessed July 3, 2009. http://www.usdoj.gov/ndic/pubs32/32146/index.htm

National Youth Gang Survey Analysis. Washington, DC: National Youth Gang Center, 2009. Accessed January 6, 2010. http:www.nationalgangcenter.gov/Survey-Analysis

Police Chiefs and Sheriffs Speak Out on Local Immigration Enforcement. Washington, DC: Police Executive Research Forum, April 2008.

Police Planning for an Influenza Pandemic: Case Studies and Recommendations from the Field. Washington, DC: Police Executive Research Forum, October 2007.

Schultz, Paul D. "The Future Is Here: Technology in Police Departments." *The Police Chief*, June 2008, pp.20–25.

Spahr, Lisa L.; Ederheimer; Joshua; and Bilson, David. *Patrol-Level Response to a Suicide Bomb Threat: Guidelines for Consideration.* Washington, DC: Police Executive Research Forum, April 2007.

Tafoya, William L. "Futuristics: New Tools for Criminal Justice Executives: Part I." Presentation at the 1983 annual meeting of the Academy of Criminal Justice Sciences, March 22–26, 1983, San Antonio, Texas.

"Usama Bin Laden: FBI Ten Most Wanted Fugitives." Washington, DC: Federal Bureau of Investigation, 2009. Accessed January 5, 2010. http://www.fbi.gov/wanted/topten/fugitives/laden.htm

Violent Crime and the Economic Crisis: Police Chiefs Face a New Challenge, Part I. Washington, DC: Police Executive Research Forum, January 2009.

Violent Crime and the Economic Crisis: Police Chiefs Face a New Challenge, Part II. Washington, DC: Police Executive Research Forum, May 2009.

Violent Crime in America: "A Tale of Two Cities." Washington, DC: Police Executive Research Forum, 2008.

Violent Crime in America: 24 Months of Alarming Trends. Washington, DC: Police Executive Research Forum, 2006.

Violent Crime in America: What We Know about Hot Spots Enforcement. Washington, DC: Police Executive Research Forum, May 2008.

Wallentine, Ken. "Law Enforcement Trends to Watch in 2010 and Beyond." *PoliceOne.com News*, December 7, 2009. Accessed December 24, 2009. http://www.policeone.com/pc_print.asp?vid=1974235

Wethal, Tabatha. "The Jurassic Park Effect." *Law Enforcement Technology*, February 2008, pp.52–57.

Wexler, Chuck. "Foreword." *Critical Issues in Policing: An Anthology.* Washington, DC: Police Executive Research Forum, 2009, p.i.

Woodward, Harry, and Buchholz, Steve. *Aftershock: Helping People through Corporate Change.* New York: John Wiley and Sons, 1987.

Offenses and Their Penalties— Progressive Discipline

Offense	Explanation	Penalties*		
		1st Offense	2nd Offense	3rd Offense
1. Failure to carry out assignment/insubordination				
a. Minor	Deliberate delay or failure to carry out assigned work or instructions in a reasonable period of time.	R	R to 5 days S	R to D
b. Major	Refusal to obey legitimate orders, disrespect, insolence and like behavior.	R to D	R to D	D
2. Absence without leave				
a. Minor	Unauthorized absence of 10 hours or less, repeated tardiness, leaving the job without permission.	R	R to 5 days S	R to D
b. Major	Unauthorized absence of more than 10 hours. (If misrepresentation is involved, see #8).	R to D	R to D	D
3. Neglect of duty				
a. Minor	Unauthorized participation in activities during duty hours that are outside of regularly assigned duties. The offense is usually considered minor when danger to safety of persons or property is not acute or injury or loss is not involved.	R	R to 5 days S	R to D
b. Major	The offense is usually considered major when danger to safety of persons or property is acute or injury or loss is involved.	R to D	D	
4. Careless workmanship or negligence				
a. Minor	When spoilage or waste of materials or delay in production is not of significant value.	R	R to 5 days S	R to D
b. Major	When spoilage or waste of materials or delay in production is extensive and costly; covering up or attempting to conceal defective work.	R to D	D	
5. Violation of safety practices and regulations				
a. Minor	Failure to observe safety practices and regulations and danger to safety of persons or property is not acute.	R	R to 5 days S	R to D
b. Major	Failure to observe safety practices and regulations and danger to safety of persons or property is acute.	R to D	D	
6. Loss of, damage to, unauthorized use or willful destruction of city property, records or information				
a. Minor	When loss or damage is of small value and such loss or damage is not knowingly perpetrated.	R	R to 5 days S	R to D
b. Major	When loss or damage is knowingly perpetrated.	R to D	D	

*Note: R means reprimand, S means suspension and D means dismissal.

[Continued]

[continued]

Offense	Explanation	Penalties*		
		1st Offense	**2nd Offense**	**3rd Offense**
7. Theft, actual or attempted, in taking and carrying away city property or property of others	Penalty will be determined in part by value of property.	R to D	D	
8. False statements or misrepresentation				
a. Minor	When falsification, concealment or misrepresentation has occurred, but has not necessarily been done deliberately.	R to 10 days S	D	
b. Major	Deliberate misrepresentation, falsification, exaggeration or concealment of a material fact, especially in connection with matters under official investigation.	R to D	D	
9. Disorderly conduct				
a. Minor	Rude, boisterous play that adversely affects production, discipline or morale; use of disrespectful, abusive or offensive language; quarreling or inciting to quarrel.	R to 5 days S	R to D	D
b. Major	Fighting, threatening or inflicting bodily harm to another; physical resistance to competent authority; any violent act or language which adversely affects morale, production or maintenance of discipline; indecent or immoral conduct.	R to D	D	
10. Gambling				
a. Minor	Participation in gambling during working hours.	R	R to 5 days S	D
b. Major	Promotion of, or assisting in, operation of organized gambling.	R to D	R to D	D
11. Use of intoxicants				
a. Minor	Drinking or selling intoxicants or controlled substances on duty or on city premises.	R to D	D	
b. Major	Reporting for duty drunk, under the influence of controlled substances or intoxicated and unable to properly perform assigned duties or posing a hazard to self or others.	5 days S to D	D	
12. Misconduct off duty	Misconduct which adversely affects the reputation of the employee or reflects unfavorably on the city.	R to D	R to D	D
13. Failure to honor valid debts	Garnishment of an employee's wages by an appropriate court order.	R[†]	R	R to D
14. Discrimination				
a. Minor	Any action or failure to take action based on age, sex, race, color, religion or national origin of an employee, former employee or applicant which affects their rights, privileges, benefits, dignity and equality of economic opportunity.	R	R to 5 days S	R to D
b. Major	If the discriminatory practice was deliberate.	R to 20 days S	20 days S to D	S
15. Fiscal irregularity	Misappropriation of city funds which came into the employee's possession by reason of their official position; falsification of payroll records for personal gain.	D		
16. Political activity	Engaging in types of political activity prohibited by these personnel policies.	R to D	R to D	R to D
17. Violation of code of ethics	Acceptance of gifts or favors influencing discharge of duties; use of position to secure special privileges or exemptions; disclosure of information adversely affecting the affairs of the city; transaction of city business where personal financial interest is involved; deliberately thwarting execution of a city ordinance, rule or official program.	R to D	D	

[†]The first offense requires more than one garnishment before applicable.

Offense	Explanation	Penalties*		
		1st Offense	2nd Offense	3rd Offense
18. Violation of the city charter or personnel or departmental personnel policies not already covered above				
a. Minor	Violation of a policy which has little adverse affect on production, employee morale, maintenance of discipline and/or the reputation of the city.	R	R to 20 days S	R to D
b. Major	Violation of a policy which adversely affects production, employee morale, maintenance of discipline and/or the reputation of the city in a direct way.	R to D	D	

Source: City of Boulder City, Nevada, Police Department. Reprinted with permission.

APPENDIX B

Sample Application Form

DEPARTMENT OF ADMINISTRATION
4801 West 50th Street • Edina, Minnesota 55424-1394
(612) 555-8861   TDD(612) 555-5461

DATE RECEIVED

OFFICE USE ONLY

Employment Application

THE CITY OF EDINA WELCOMES YOU as an applicant for employment. Your application will be considered with others in competition for the position in which you are interested. It is our policy to provide equal employment opportunities to all. Individuals are evaluated and selected solely on the basis of their qualifications.

Please furnish complete and accurate information so that the City of Edina can properly evaluate your application.

Be warned that the use of false or misleading information or the omission of important facts may be grounds for immediate dismissal. Also note that information you provide herein may be subject to later verification and/or testing.

You may attach to this application any additional information that helps explain your qualifications.

Please print clearly or type.

Personal Information

Name	Last	First	Middle	Previous
Present Address	Street	City	State	Zip Code
Permanent Address	Street	City	State	Zip Code
Telephone	Residence	Business	May we call you at work? ☐ Yes	☐ No
Are you between the ages of 16 and 70?		☐ Yes	☐ No	If "No", state date of birth:
Do you have a Social Security Number?		☐ Yes	☐ No	

Work Preferences

Position for which you are applying (or type of work in which you are interested):

Are you interested in . . .
☐ Full-Time
☐ Part-Time
☐ Seasonal
☐ Paid on call
☐ Volunteer
☐ Date available for work:
_____

616

General Information

Have you previously been employed by the City of Edina?   If "Yes," Dates   Position
  ☐ Yes   ☐ No

Do you have relatives or in-laws working for the City of Edina?   If "Yes," who:
  ☐ Yes   ☐ No

How did you hear about a job at the City of Edina?

  ☐ Came in on my own _____   ☐ Other (Specify) _____
  ☐ City employee _____   ☐ Newspaper (Specify) _____
  ☐ School (Specify) _____   ☐ Employment Agency _____
  (Counselor) _____   (Specify) _____

Have you ever been convicted of a crime for which a jail sentence   Have you ever been convicted of a felony?
of more than 90 days could have been imposed?

  ☐ Yes   ☐ No   ☐ Yes   ☐ No

You may answer "No" to these questions if the conviction or criminal records thereof have been annulled, expunged, sealed, set aside or purged, or if you have been pardoned pursuant to law. Before any applicant is rejected on the basis of a criminal conviction, he or she will be notified in writing and will be given any rights to processing of complaints or grievances afforded by Minnesota Statute Chapter 364. If the answer to this question is "Yes," please attach a separate sheet of paper giving full particulars.

If you are not a citizen of the United States, do you have a valid work permit?   Do you have a valid Drivers License?
  ☐ Yes   ☐ No   Number _____   ☐ Yes   ☐ No
                                        State: _____   Class: _____

Are you subject to a child support or spousal maintenance order?   If "Yes," are you subject to withholding for child
  ☐ Yes   ☐ No   support or spousal maintenance?
                                        ☐ Yes   ☐ No

Education

School Name and Location	Attendance Dates From (mo/yr) To (mo/yr)	Graduate	Type	Degree, Diploma or Certificate and Major/Minor	Academic Standing Grade Average, eg, (3.2/4.0)
High School last attended		☐ Yes ☐ No			
Vocational, technical school		☐ Yes ☐ No			
College or university		☐ Yes ☐ No			
College or university		☐ Yes ☐ No			
Other (skilled trade training, etc.)		☐ Yes ☐ No			

Please list academic honors, scholarships, fellowships, memberships in professional and honorary societies, and any other extracurricular activities:

Clerical Skills	What is your present speed per minute?	Typewriter	Shorthand	Speedwriting	Can you operate	Dictating equipment ☐ Yes ☐ No	Computer/terminal ☐ Yes ☐ No
	Other office equipment you can operate (including word processing, database management, spreadsheet and other software):						
	Do you have experience in a skilled trade? If so, please describe the extent/nature of experience.						

Skilled Trade Skills, Licenses, Certifications	Have you completed an apprenticeship in a skilled craft? ☐ Yes ☐ No	If yes,	What craft?	Where did you complete it?
	List all machines and equipment you have operated:			
	List all current licenses and/or certifications together with an identification of the granting authority:			
	Do you have Advanced First Aid, EMS First Responder, Crash Injury Management (CIM) or EMT certification? ☐ Yes ☐ No			

Employment History

Please give accurate, complete and part-time employment record. *Start with present or most recent employer.*

Company Name	Telephone ( )
Address	Employed (State month and year) From To
Name of Supervisor	Salary ☐ Hourly ☐ Monthly ☐ Yearly $
State job title and list your duties/responsibilities beginning with the duty that consumed the greatest proportion of your time:	Reason for leaving

Company Name	Telephone ( )
Address	Employed (State month and year) From To
Name of Supervisor	Salary ☐ Hourly ☐ Monthly ☐ Yearly $
State job title and list your duties/responsibilities beginning with the duty that consumed the greatest proportion of your time:	Reason for leaving

Company Name	Telephone ( )
Address	Employed (State month and year) From To
Name of Supervisor	Salary ☐ Hourly ☐ Monthly ☐ Yearly $
State job title and list your duties/responsibilities beginning with the duty that consumed the greatest proportion of your time:	Reason for leaving

Company Name	Telephone ( )
Address	Employed (State month and year) From To
Name of Supervisor	Salary ☐ Hourly ☐ Monthly ☐ Yearly $
State job title and list your duties/responsibilities beginning with the duty that consumed the greatest proportion of your time:	Reason for leaving

If you need additional space, please continue on a separate sheet of paper. Be certain to complete both sides of this application.

Public Safety Applicants (Please Respond)

Date and location of POST licensing exam   Date:

Skills course attended

Date of graduation from skills course

Are you currently licensed? ☐ Yes   ☐ No   If so, License Number

If you are currently licensed, status of license?   ☐ Active   ☐ Inactive   ☐ Part-time   ☐ Other _____

Additional Experience and/or Training

Describe any additional experience or training that qualifies you for this job.

Important facts concerning information on your application

MINNESOTA LAW AFFECTS YOU AS AN APPLICANT with the City of Edina. The following data is public information and is accessible to anyone: veteran's status, relevant test scores, rank on eligibility list, job history, education and training, and work availability. All other personally identifiable information is considered private, including, but not limited to, your name, home address and phone number.

If you are selected as a finalist for a position, your name will become public information. You become a finalist if you are selected to be interviewed by the City of Edina.

The information requested on the application is necessary, either to identify you or to assist in determining your suitability for the position for which you are applying. You may legally refuse, but refusal to supply the requested information will mean that your application for employment may not be considered.

If you are selected for employment with the City of Edina, the following additional information about you will be public: your name; actual gross salary and salary range; actual gross pension; the value and nature of your fringe benefits; the basis for and the amount of any added remuneration, such as expenses or mileage reimbursement, in addition to your salary; your job title; job description; training background; previous work experience; the dates of your first and last employment with the City of Edina; the status of any complaints or charges against you while at work; the final outcome of any disciplinary action taken against you, and all supporting documentation about your case; your badge number, if any; your city and county of residence; your work location and work telephone number; honors and awards; payroll timesheets and comparable data.

Anything not listed above which is placed in your application folder or your personnel file (such as medical information, letters of recommendation, resumes, etc.) is made private information by law. For further information, refer to Minnesota Statute, Chapter 13.

I understand that any false information on or omission of information from this application (including additional information required for Public Safety Applicants, if applicable), or failure to present the required proof, will be cause for rejection or dismissal if employed.

Public Safety Applicants Only: In consideration of being permitted to apply for the position herein, I voluntarily assume all risks in connection with my participating in any tests the City of Edina deems necessary to determine my fitness and eligibility, and I release and forever discharge the City of Edina, its officers and employees from any and all claims for any damage or injury that I might sustain.

Tennessen Warning. The purpose and intended use of the information requested on the application is to assist in determining your eligibility and suitability for the position for which you are applying. You may legally refuse to give the information. If you give the information, that information, or further investigation based on it, could cause your application to be denied. If you refuse to give the information, your application for employment may not be considered. Other persons or entities authorized to receive the information you supply are: Staff of Edina Police Department, Bureau of Criminal Apprehension, Hennepin County Warrant Office, Ramsey County Warrant Office, State of Minnesota, Driver's License Section, Hennepin County Auditor, and other governmental agencies necessary to process your application.

Applicant's Signature

Date

The City of Edina's policy and intent is to provide equality of opportunity in employment to all persons. This policy prohibits discrimination because of race, color, religion, national origin, political affiliation, disability, marital status, sex or age (except when sex or age is a bona fide occupational qualification).

The City of Edina is an equal opportunity/affirmative employer.

Sample Interview Rating Sheet

CITY OF ANYWHERE, U.S.A.
Oral Interview Board
Police Officer

Candidate's Name: _____

Total Score: _____

A. Interview Questions

Instructions: Do not permit candidates to give a "yes" or "no" answer to the following questions. Ask for justification or explanation of candidates' positions.

1. You and your partner have just stopped a driver for speeding. You observe the driver hand your partner some money and drive off. When your partner returns to your police vehicle, he offers you part of the money. What action would you take?

    1   2   3   4   5   _____

2. Give three good reasons why you have become a candidate for the position of police officer.

    1   2   3   4   5   _____

3. Do you think you could use deadly force, if necessary, to make an arrest? Justify your position.

    1   2   3   4   5   _____

4. What changes do you foresee having to make in your lifestyle to become a police officer?

    1   2   3   4   5   _____

5. What is the role of the police in crime prevention?

    1   2   3   4   5   _____

6. When did you decide to become a police officer? What preparations have you made toward that goal?

    1   2   3   4   5   _____

7. Is there anything else you would like to say about yourself with regard to this position?

NOTATIONS (FOR QUESTION 7 ONLY): _____

_____

_____

TOTAL SECTION "A": _____

B. Personal Characteristics

1. Appearance: Consider the candidate's personal appearance, bearing in mind the requirements of the position. Does the candidate give a satisfactory appearance as a representative of the local government?
   (Observe: dress, neatness, posture, sitting position, facial expressions, mannerisms)

       1   2   3   4   5   _____

2. Voice and ability to use the English language: Consider the quality of the candidate's voice in relation to the subject position. Does the candidate speak clearly and distinctly? Is his/her voice pleasant or harsh? Consider the candidate's choice of words, sentences, phrases, use of slang or needless technical jargon.
   (Observe: use of simple and correct English, logical presentation, coherence of thought)

       1   2   3   4   5   _____

3. Self-Confidence: Consider self-control. Is the candidate nervous or ill at ease? Is he/she poised and relaxed? Does he/she appear to be uncertain or hesitant about his/her ideas?
   (Observe: embarrassment, stammering, tension, poise, hesitation, confidence, timidness, over confidence)

       1   2   3   4   5   _____

4. Ability to get along with people: Consider the candidate's attitude toward the examiners. Does he/she seem over-sensitive? Is there antagonism, indifference, a cooperative attitude?

       1   2   3   4   5   _____

5. Suitability for this position: Consider whether the candidate will work out on the job. Does he/she reply readily to questions asked? Are his/her ideas original? Are statements convincing and appropriate? Is there evidence of leadership? Does he/she speak out voluntarily at proper times? Does he/she have a definite interest in this work?
   (Observe: alertness, responsiveness, tact, cooperation, enthusiasm)

       1   2   3   4   5   _____

TOTAL SECTION "B": _____

GRAND TOTAL: _____

REMARKS: _____

_____

_____

_____

_____

_____

SIGNATURE OF RATER _____

APPENDIX D

Accessibility Checklist for Complying with the ADA Regulations

Parking Lots

☐ Designated parking spaces should be located near the building, and they should not be occupied by maintenance trucks, employee cars or the cars of able-bodied guests.

☐ If parking spaces are not close to the building, valet service should be available at curbside.

☐ Verify that access from the parking lot to the building is free and clear. (No gravel or loose impediments.)

☐ The approach should be flat and smooth.

☐ If the weather is bad, is access to the building covered?

☐ Are curbs adjacent to designated parking spaces?

☐ Are the angles on the curbs sharp?

☐ Watch out for open stairs. Are handrails present?

The Building

☐ The approach to the entrance should be a hard surface at least five feet wide.

☐ There should be space for a wheelchair lift to be lowered flat to the ground (not on curb).

☐ Is the doorsill raised?

☐ How heavy is the door?

☐ If there are revolving doors, are the side doors unlocked and easy to open?

☐ A single-door entrance to the building must be at least 32 inches wide (a standard wheelchair is exactly 32 inches wide). The ideal width for a single-door entrance is 36 inches.

☐ A double-door entrance must be at least 48 inches wide.

☐ Once inside, is there signage? What is the height? Is it easily visible from a wheelchair?

The Front Desk

☐ Most front desks are uncomfortably high. If inaccessible for wheelchair users, can registration be moved to the concierge table, or to another table to the side of the front desk, or can the guest use a clipboard to complete registration forms?

The Elevator

☐ Are the control panels low enough to be accessible by wheelchair users?

☐ Are the floor numbers in Braille for the sight-impaired?

☐ Elevators must be a minimum of 48 inches deep and 22 feet square to permit the wheelchair user to turn around and face the door.

☐ The door must be at least 32 inches wide.

The Guest Room

☐ Door handles on the outside door and all inside doors should be levers.

☐ Once inside the room, all doors and hallways must be a minimum of 32 inches wide.

---

*By January 1993, any major construction required for public accommodations must comply with ADA standards. Both tenants and owners of facilities are responsible for insuring that areas of public accommodation and where public services are offered are accessible. This is a comprehensive checklist for use in site inspections to make sure your site meets ADA standards.

*Note: Although developed for meeting sites, this checklist can be used for any public facility, including police departments.

Source: Cindy Alwood. "Checklist: Does Your Meeting Site Obey the ADA?" *Successful Meetings,* December 1992, pp. 131–132.

Reprinted with permission from the MPI Education Research Foundation Research Center's "Americans with Disabilities Act & Meeting Planning" research subject package.

☐ Mirrors in a guest room should not be higher than 40 inches from the floor.

☐ In rooms with two beds, there should be a space between the beds or along the outside.

☐ Phones, remote controls and light switches should be located next to the accessible side of the bed.

☐ Maneuverability is important in a guest room, so check for poorly placed furniture.

☐ If the room has a thermostat, it should be no more than 40 inches from the floor.

☐ If the temperature controls are on the heating/cooling unit itself, make sure furniture does not block the unit.

☐ The closet bar should be 40 inches from the floor.

☐ The peephole in the outside door and all locks should be low enough for a person in a wheelchair.

The Bathroom

☐ There should be a cutaway under the sink to allow wheelchair users to roll up to the sink.

☐ There should be space to maneuver along the bathtub.

☐ The bathtub should be equipped with grip bars, ideally with both vertical and horizontal bars low to the tub.

☐ Check for stability of grip bars. Poorly mounted grip bars might not withstand a strong pull.

☐ Towels should be within reach of someone in a seated position.

☐ Toilets should not be higher than 29 inches off the floor, urinals should not be higher than 17 inches.

Lounge

☐ Is access to the restaurant/lounge a flat surface?

☐ Are there stairs or a ramp?

☐ Is there adequate space between tables for a wheelchair?

☐ Check out table heights.

☐ Is there access to the dance floor?

☐ Are the restrooms accessible by wheelchair?

☐ The upper edge of the drinking fountain should be no higher than 36 inches from the floor.

☐ Phones should feature coin slots that are no more than 54 inches off the ground.

☐ At least one phone should have hearing amplification in the handset.

☐ A phone equipped with TDD (telecommunications device for the deaf) should be available.

Meeting Rooms

☐ Aisles should be a minimum of 32 inches wide.

☐ If you are using a riser, consider its accessibility: Risers require ramps with a slope of no more than 1 inch vertical to every 12 inches horizontal.

☐ Noisy heating/cooling systems in older facilities can make hearing difficult.

☐ Chandelier and fluorescent lighting are hard on the eyes.

☐ If your meeting has recreation time built into it, recreation facilities—the pool, locker rooms, sundeck—should be accessible.

Staff

☐ Staff should be sensitive to greeting and working with persons with disabilities.

In the event of emergencies:

☐ Is there a sprinkler system?

☐ Are fire alarms 40 inches from the floor?

☐ Are there flashing lights to alert deaf or hearing-impaired guests?

☐ Is there a voice alarm for guests who are blind or sight-impaired?

☐ The door to the bathroom should open out. If the door does open out, make sure it does not block access to the outside door.

APPENDIX E

Sample Affirmative Action
Questionnaire

The following information is necessary for the city of Anywhere to evaluate its recruiting and hiring practices and to prepare reports required by law for the state and federal governments. We ask your help in filling in the blanks that apply to you. The Civil Rights Act, Title VII, makes it unlawful to discriminate in employment on the basis of race, color, religion, gender or national origin. Federal and state laws prohibit discrimination in employment on the basis of disability or age. This form will be detached from your application and the information will not be used to make any employment decisions that affect you.

_____ American Indian or Alaskan Native (All persons having origins in any of the original peoples of North America.)

_____ Black (Not of Hispanic origin): All persons having origins in any of the Black racial groups.

_____ Asian/Pacific Islander (All persons having origins in any of the original peoples of the Far East, Southeast Asia, or the Pacific Islands. This area includes, for example, China, Japan, Korea, the Philippines and Hawaiian Islands and Samoa.)

_____ Hispanic (All persons of Mexican, Puerto Rican, Cuban, Central or South American, or other Spanish culture or origin, regardless of race.)

_____ White (Not of Hispanic origin): All persons having origins in any of the original peoples of Europe, North Africa, the Middle East, or the Indian Subcontinent.

Birthdate: _____ Age _____ yrs. Sex: Male _____ Female _____

Do you have a physical, mental or addictive handicapping condition that substantially limits a major life activity?

Yes _____ No _____ If yes, explain: _____

Exact title of position for which you are applying: _____

DATE: _____ NAME: _____

Redondo Beach Sworn
Personnel Evaluation Form

Redondo Beach Police Department
Peace Officer Performance Evaluation

_____ _____ _____
Name (Last, First, Initial)   Job Classification   Serial Number
Assignment/division
Evaluation Type
( ) Probation   ( ) Semi-annual   ( ) Other (Specify)
_____
Evaluation Period: From: _____ To: _____
Rating Instructions: Rate observed behavior with reference to the scale below by
using the numeric value definitions contained in the evaluation program guidelines. Specific
comments are required for all ratings of 3 or less or 7.

Dimensions Rated	General Performance Factor	Levels Of Proficiency

Job Skills

1. Knowledge of legal codes and procedures 1 2 3 4 5 6 7
2. Neatness of work product, spelling, grammar 1 2 3 4 5 6 7
3. Oral expression 1 2 3 4 5 6 7
4. Planning and organizing work 1 2 3 4 5 6 7
5. Problem solving/decision making 1 2 3 4 5 6 7
6. Thoroughness and accuracy 1 2 3 4 5 6 7
7. Written expression 1 2 3 4 5 6 7

Productivity

8. Acceptance of responsibility 1 2 3 4 5 6 7
9. Initiative, resourcefulness, and observation skills 1 2 3 4 5 6 7
10. Quantity of work 1 2 3 4 5 6 7
11. Seeks training to enhance abilities 1 2 3 4 5 6 7

Work Conduct

12. Ability to follow instructions 1 2 3 4 5 6 7
13. Attendance 1 2 3 4 5 6 7
14. Care of equipment 1 2 3 4 5 6 7
15. Dealing with co-workers 1 2 3 4 5 6 7
16. Dealing with the public 1 2 3 4 5 6 7
17. Observance of rules, regulations, and procedures 1 2 3 4 5 6 7
18. Officer safety 1 2 3 4 5 6 7

Adaptability

19. Performance in new situations/acceptance to change 1 2 3 4 5 6 7
20. Performance under pressure 1 2 3 4 5 6 7
21. Performance with minimum instruction 1 2 3 4 5 6 7

Personal Traits

22. Appearance 1 2 3 4 5 6 7
23. Attitude toward police work 1 2 3 4 5 6 7

[Continued]

[continued]

Specific Job Classification Factors

Police Officer/Agent

24. Driving skill 1 2 3 4 5 6 7
25. Firearms 1 2 3 4 5 6 7
26. Interview techniques 1 2 3 4 5 6 7
27. Investigative skill 1 2 3 4 5 6 7
28. Radio procedures 1 2 3 4 5 6 7

Supervision/Management (Supervisory and Management Personnel Only)

29. Approachability 1 2 3 4 5 6 7
30. Budgetary management 1 2 3 4 5 6 7
31. Delegation 1 2 3 4 5 6 7
32. Disciplinary control 1 2 3 4 5 6 7
33. Evaluating employees' performance 1 2 3 4 5 6 7
34. Fairness and impartiality 1 2 3 4 5 6 7
35. Training and instruction 1 2 3 4 5 6 7
36. Supportive of policy and procedure 1 2 3 4 5 6 7

Total numeric rating: _____

Numeric average: _____*Promotability/assignment factor
(To second decimal place)   (numeric average × 3.58)

*Promotability factor to be applied as 25% of final selection process core for promotion and 50% of the overall score for assignment election.

RBPD Form 345 11/87

Redondo Beach Pre-Evaluation Form

Redondo Beach Police Department
Performance Pre-evaluation Form

Name ————————————————
Date ————————————————

You are encouraged to complete this form to provide a more meaningful exchange of information during the performance evaluation.

If you wish, you may provide a completed copy to your supervisor prior to being evaluated on your performance.

1. Describe individual accomplishments, noteworthy achievements and/or projects that you feel should be considered. Also, discuss those situations you feel required special consideration or which involved extenuating circumstances.

2. What personal/professional growth has there been during this time period?
   (a) For yourself?

   (b) For your staff? (Supervisors/Managers ONLY)

3. What additional experiences or training would you like to obtain to enhance your professional development and job proficiency?

4. Do you have any ideas or suggestions that would enable you to function more efficiently/effectively?

RBPD Form 344 5/86

GLOSSARY

Number in parentheses is the chapter(s) in which the term is discussed.

A

Abilene Paradox—begins innocently, with everyone in a group agreeing that a particular problem exists; later, when it comes time to discuss solutions, no one expresses a viewpoint that differs from what appears to be the group's consensus, even though many secretly disagree with it; finally, after the solution has been implemented, group members complain privately about the plan and look for someone to blame for its development. (5)

abstract words—theoretical, not concrete, for example, *tall* rather than *6'10"*. (4)

accreditation—the process by which an institution or agency proves that it meets certain standards. (16)

active listening—includes concentration, full attention and thought. (4)

activity-based costing (ABC)—a modern version of the program budgeting system, except that rather than breaking costs down by program, the approach breaks down costs by activity. (14)

acute stress—severe, intense distress that lasts a limited time, and then the person returns to normal; sometimes called *traumatic stress*. (12)

administrative services—supports those performing field services; includes recruitment and training, records and communication, planning and research and technical services. (2)

adverse impact—when the *rate* of selection is different for special classes than for the most selected class of applicants; the rule of thumb is that an adverse impact occurs when the selection rate, or percentage passing, of any special class of persons is less than 80 percent of the selection rate of the top scoring group. (15)

affirmative action program (AAP)—a written plan to ensure fair recruitment, hiring and promotion practices. (15)

afterburn—a stressful incident that greatly affects an officer's family and leaves damaging emotional scars. (12)

agenda—a plan, usually referring to a meeting outline or program; a list of things to be accomplished. (4)

aggressive patrol—proactive patrol, focuses on preventing and detecting crime by investigating suspicious activity; also called *proactive patrol*. (13)

all-levels budgeting—everyone affected by the budget helps prepare it. (14)

andragogy—principles of adults learning. (7)

anticipatory benefit—criminals may be deterred even before the efforts are implemented. (4)

appeal—request for a decision to be reviewed by someone higher in the command structure. (10)

arbitration—turning a decision over to an individual or panel to make the final recommendation. (11)

autocratic leadership—managers make decisions without participant input; completely authoritative, showing little or no concern for subordinates. (1)

B

background check—investigating references listed on an application as well as credit, driving record, criminal conviction, academic background and any professional license required. (15)

balanced performer managers—develop subordinates' and an organization's capabilities, empower others. (8)

balancing—unfairly stopping unoffending motorists to protect officers from the "statistical microscope" individually or collectively. (8)

behaviorally anchored rating scales (BARS)—specific characteristics for a position are determined; employees are then rated against these characteristics by on-the-job behaviors in each area. (16)

bifurcated society—a society in which the gap between the "haves" and the "have nots" is wide—that is, there are many poor people, many wealthy people and a shrinking middle class. (2)

block grant—awarded to states or localities based on population and crime rate; also called a *formula grant.* (14)

blue flame—the symbol of a law enforcement officer who wants to make a difference in the world. (12)

body language—messages conveyed by gestures, facial expressions, stance and physical appearance. (4)

boiled frog phenomenon—based on a classic experiment, suggests that managers must pay attention to change in their environment and adapt—or perish. (17)

bona fide occupational qualification (BFOQ)—a requirement reasonably necessary to perform the job; it may on the surface appear to be discrimination. (15)

bottom-line philosophy—allows shifting funds from one expense category to another as long as expenses do not exceed the total amount budgeted. (14)

branding—the process an organization uses to distinguish itself from other employers; a brand image immediately triggers a mental image of a product of service's quality. (15)

broken-window theory—suggests that if it appears "no one cares," disorder and crime will thrive. (2)

budget—a list of probable expenses and income during a given period, most often one year. (14)

burnout—occurs when someone is exhausted or made listless through overwork; results from long-term, unmediated stress; symptoms include lack of enthusiasm and interest, a drop in job performance, temper flare-ups, and a loss of will, motivation or commitment. (12)

burst stress—to go from complete calm to high activity and pressure in one "burst." (12)

by-the-numbers evaluation—makes evaluations more objective by using a numerical scale for each characteristic or dimension rated. (16)

C

capital budget—deals with "big ticket" items such as major equipment purchases and vehicles. (14)

chain of command—the order of authority; begins at the top of the pyramid and flows down to the base. (2)

channels of communication—the official paths through which orders flow from management to personnel who carry out the orders; usually follow the chain of command. (2)

chronic stress—less severe than acute stress, but continuous; eventually becomes debilitating; sometimes called *cumulative stress.* (12)

circadian system—the body's complex biological timekeeping system. (12)

civilianization—hiring citizens to perform certain tasks for law enforcement agencies. (13)

Civil Rights Act of 1964—prohibits discrimination based on race, color, religion, gender or national origin by private employers with 15 or more employees, governments, unions and employment agencies. (15)

closed shop—prohibits management from hiring nonunion workers. (15)

code of silence—encourages officers not to speak up when they see another officer doing something wrong. (8)

collective bargaining—the process whereby representatives of employees meet with representatives of management to establish a written contract setting forth working conditions for a specific time, usually one to three years. (15)

community policing—decentralized model of policing in which individual officers exercise their own initiatives and citizens become actively involved in making their neighborhoods safer; this proactive approach usually includes increased emphasis on foot patrol. (2)

complainant—a person or group filing a complaint. (11)

complaint—a statement of a problem. (11)

comprehensive discipline—uses both positive and negative discipline to achieve individual and organizational goals. (10)

CompStat policing—a method of management accountability and a philosophy of crime control. (2)

cone of resolution—narrowing in on the geographic locations of crime. (13)

conflict—a mental or physical fight. (11)

confrontation technique—insisting that two disputing people or groups meet face-to-face to resolve their differences. (11)

consideration structure—looks at establishing the relationship between the group and the leader. (1)

content validity—the direct relationship between tasks performed on the job, the curriculum or training and the test. (7)

contingency funds—money allocated for unforeseen emergencies. (14)

contingency theory—Morse and Lorsch's motivational theory that suggests fitting tasks, officers and agency goals so that officers can feel competent. (9)

convergent thinking—focused, evaluative thinking. Includes decision making, choosing, testing, judging and rating; opposite of *divergent thinking*. (5)

creative procrastination—delaying decisions, allowing time for minor difficulties to work themselves out. (5)

crime triangle—a model illustrating how all three elements—motivated suspect, suitable victim and adequate location—are required for crime to occur. (13)

critical incident—any event, such as a mass disaster or a brutally murdered child, that elicits an overwhelming emotional response from those witnessing it and whose emotional impact goes beyond the person's coping abilities. (12)

critical incident stress debriefing (CISD)—officers who experience a critical incident such as a mass disaster or crash with multiple deaths are brought together as a group for a psychological debriefing soon after the event. (12)

cross flow—message stating a problem and asking other units if they have encountered the same thing and, if so, what they did about it. (5)

cross tell—one department alerts other departments about a mistake revealed during inspection. (5)

crunch—a major problem. (11)

CSI **effect**—the heightened expectation by the public, often the result of watching popular television series such as *CSI*, of what police can do and the tools available to them in solving crimes. (12)

cultural awareness—understanding the diversity of the United States, the dynamics of minority–majority relationships, the dynamics of sexism and racism and the issues of nationalism and separatism. (8)

cumulative stress—less severe than acute stress but continues and eventually becomes debilitating. (12)

cutback budgeting—providing the same or more services with less funding; also called *budget reduction* or *reduced expenditure spending*. (14)

cybernetics—suggest that organizations regulate themselves by gathering and reacting to information about their performance. (16)

D

daily values—how people actually spend their time and energy. (8)

data mining—an automated tool that uses advanced computational techniques to explore and characterize large data sets. (5)

decentralization—encourages flattening of the organization and places decision-making authority and autonomy at the level where information is plentiful; in police organizations, this is usually at the level of the patrol officer. (2)

deconfliction—avoiding conflict when working with other agencies during an investigation; deployed with declassified and confidential investigations. (4)

decoupling—discrepancies between an agency's formal policies and informal practices; occurs when an organization adopts a new policy but then never really implements it to change how the work gets done. (10)

Delphi technique—a way to have individual input; uses open-ended questionnaires completed by individuals; answers are shared, and the questionnaires are again completed until consensus is achieved. (5)

descriptive statistics—focus on simplifying, appraising and summarizing data. (16)

discipline—training expected to produce a desired behavior—controlled behavior or administering punishment; also a state of affairs or how employees act, in contrast to morale, which is how employees feel. (10)

discretionary budget—funds available to be used as the need arises. (14)

discretionary grant—awarded based on the judgment of the awarding state or federal agency. (14)

dispersed leadership—the 21st century trend to not tie leadership to rank, but rather to instill leadership qualities through the department. (1)

distress—negative stress. (12)

diurnal—day-oriented; humans are by nature diurnal in their activities. (12)

divergent thinking—free, uninhibited thinking; includes imagining, fantasizing, free associating and combining and juxtaposing dissimilar elements; opposite of *convergent thinking*. (5)

doom loop—characterized by incessant restructuring, following fads, management by cheerleading without careful thought, and especially inconsistency, constantly running after new ideas. (3)

E

eclectic—blending the best teaching approaches to meet students' needs. (7)

employee assistance program (EAP)—may be internally staffed or use outside referrals to offer help with stress, marital or chemical-dependency problems. (12)

environmental scanning—identifying the factors that are likely to "drive" the environment, influencing the future; includes social and economic conditions. (17)

Equal Employment Opportunity Commission (EEOC)—enforces laws prohibiting job discrimination based on race, color, religion, gender, national origin, handicapping condition or age between 40 and 70. (15)

ethics—standards of fair and honest conduct. (8)

eustress—helpful stress, stress necessary to function and accomplish goals. (12)

evaluate—to determine the worth of, to find the amount or value of or to appraise. (16)

evidence-based policing—a methodological approach that uses empirically derived evidence—what has been shown, through scientific research, to be effective—and applies it to real-world policing. (2)

exonerated—a complaint or grievance in which the investigation determines that the matter did occur, but was proper and legal. (11)

expectancy theory—Vroom's motivational theory that employees will choose the level of effort that matches the performance opportunity for reward. (9)

F

face time—time spent in the agency or department long after a shift ends and on weekends when not on duty to make sure you are seen putting in extra time by those with the power to promote you. (6)

facilitators—assist others in performing their duties to meet mutual goals and objectives. (3)

Fair Labor Standards Act (FLSA) of 1938—established the 40-hour week as the basis of compensation and set a minimum wage. (15)

field services—directly help accomplish the department's goals using line personnel; main division is uniformed patrol; also includes investigations, narcotics, vice, juvenile and the like. (2)

field training officer (FTO)—an experienced officer who serves as a mentor for a rookie, providing on-the-job training. (7)

financial budget—a plan or schedule adjusting expenses during a certain period to the estimated income for that period. (14)

Firefighter's Rule—states that a person who negligently starts a fire is not liable to a firefighter injured while responding to the fire. (7)

fiscal year—the 12-month accounting period used by an agency. (14)

5P principle—proper planning prevents poor performance. (6)

fixed costs—costs that are relatively constant, for example, rent and insurance; also called *overhead*. (14)

flat organization—one with fewer lieutenants and captains, fewer staff departments, fewer staff assistants, more sergeants and more patrol officers. (2)

flywheel challenge—asks managers to imagine a huge, heavy flywheel about 30 feet in diameter, weighing about 5,000 pounds mounted horizontally on an axle; then to further imagine that management's task is to get the flywheel rotating on the axle as fast and long as possible, requiring time and the combined efforts of many people making many decisions and doing many things to get it going. (3)

force-field analysis—identifies forces that impede and enhance goal attainment; a problem exists when the equilibrium is such that more forces are impeding goal attainment than enhancing it. (5)

formative assessment—uses informative gathered during instruction to adjust and improve program content and training. (7)

formula grant—awarded to states or localities based on population and crime rates; also called a *block grant*. (14)

fusion center— an entity that pools the resources and personnel of multiple agencies into one central location to facilitate information sharing and intelligence development regarding criminal activities. (2)

futuristics—the science of using data from the past to forecast alternatives for the future and to then select those most desirable. (17)

G

***Garrity* protection**—a written notification that an officer is making his or her statement or report in an internal affairs investigation involuntarily. (11)

general orders— written directives related to policy, procedures, rules and regulations involving more than one organizational unit; typically have a broad statement of policy as well as the procedures for implementing the policy. (10)

geographical diffusion of benefit—properties immediately adjacent to the intervention implemented also experienced a reduction in burglary. (4)

ghosting—falsifying patrol logs to make the numbers come out right to avoid charges of racial profiling. (8)

GIGO—computer acronym for "garbage in, garbage out." (5)

goals—broad, general, desired outcomes; visionary, projected achievements; what business calls *key result areas*. (3)

grapevine—informal channel of communication within the agency or department. Also called the *rumor mill*. (4)

grievance—a formally registered complaint; a claim by an employee that a rule or policy has been misapplied or misinterpreted to the employee's detriment. (11)

grievant—the person or group filing a grievance. (11)

groupthink—the negative tendency for members of a group to submit to peer pressure and endorse the majority opinion even if it individually is unacceptable. (5)

guiding philosophy—the organization's mission statement and the basic values to be honored by the organization. (3)

gunnysack approach—occurs when managers or supervisors accumulate negative behaviors of a subordinate and then dump them all on the employee at the same time rather than correcting them as they occurred. (10)

H

halo effect—tendency to rate one who performs above average in one area above average in all areas or vice versa. (15, 16)

Hawthorne effect—workers are positively affected by receiving attention, which affects research efforts. (9)

hierarchy—a group of people organized or classified by rank and authority. In law enforcement, typically pyramid shaped with a single "authority" at the top expanding down and out through the ranks to the broad base of "workers." (2)

hierarchy of needs—Maslow's motivational theory that people have certain needs that must be met in a specific order going from basic physiological needs to safety and security, social, esteem and self-actualization needs. (9)

highlighting—using a special pen to graphically mark important written information; should be done after the initial reading of the information. (6)

holistic management/leadership— recognizes that both management and leadership skills are required for an agency to accomplish its mission and that all those within the organization are complete individuals who have answered a special calling and are part of the team. (3)

holistic personal goals—includes all aspects of a person's life: career/job, financial, personal, family/relationships and spiritual/service. (8)

homeostasis— the process that keeps all the bodily functions in physiological balance. (12)

horn effect—allowing one negative trait to influence the rater negatively on other traits as well. (16)

hot spots—specific locations with high crime rates. (13)

hygiene factors—tangible rewards that can cause dissatisfaction if lacking. (9)

I

impact evaluation—an assessment to determine whether a problem declined. (5)

incident—an isolated event that requires a police response. (2)

incident command—an organizational structure designed to aid in managing resources during incidents. (3)

incivilities—signs of disorder. (2)

inferential statistics—focus on making statistically educated guesses from a sample of data. (16)

initiating structure—looks at how leaders assign tasks. (1)

insubordination—failure to obey a lawful and direct order from a supervisor. (10)

integrated patrol—the end goal resulting from the combination of the two elements of community policing and aggressive enforcement. (2)

integrity—steadfast adherence to an ethical code. (8)

intelligence-led policing—a methodical approach to prevent, detect and disrupt crime, including terrorist activities; uses early detection of crime trends to allows police to be proactive in preventing continued crime. (2)

interactors—communicate with other groups and agencies: the press, other local government departments, the business community, schools and numerous community committees and organizations. (3)

interfacers—coordinate law enforcement agency's goals with those of other agencies within the jurisdiction. (3)

interoperability—the ability of public safety emergency responders to work seamlessly with other systems or products without special efforts. (4)

intersubjectivity approach—uses 3-by-5-inch cards as a means to get people in conflict to share their most important ideas about a problem and to come to a mutual understanding of and respect for each other's viewpoints. (11)

interval reinforcement—presenting information several times, with breaks between the repetition. (7)

J

jargon—nonsense or meaningless language, often called legalese, for example, "party of the first part, hereafter referred to as . . ."; also, specialized language of a field, for example, perpetrator. (4)

Johari window—a model to illustrate how people can learn more about others and themselves. (8)

just cause—principle stating that a disciplinary case must be presented in two distinct parts: (1) management must first prove that the act in question was actually committed in violation of an agency policy and (2) management must show that the discipline imposed was not arbitrary, capricious, unreasonable or discriminatory. (15)

L

lag time—time elapsed between the occurrence of an incident and it being reported to the police; often more important than response time. (13)

Landrum–Griffin Act of 1959—required regularly scheduled elections of union officers by secret ballot and regulated the handling of union funds. (15)

leadership—influencing, working with and through individuals and groups to accomplish a common goal. (1)

learning curve principle—states that grouping similar tasks together can reduce the amount of time each takes, sometimes by as much as 80 percent. (6)

left-brain thinking—primarily using language and logic. (5)

line-item budgeting—identifies specific categories (line items) and dollars allocated for each, and usually based on the preceding year's budget and anticipated changes in the upcoming year. (14)

line items—specific expense categories, for example, personnel, maintenance, training. (14)

line personnel—those who actually perform most of the tasks outlined in the work plan. (2)

lines of communication—similar to channels of communication; may be downward, upward (vertical) or lateral (horizontal) and internal or external. (4)

M

magnet phenomenon—occurs when a phone number or address is associated with a crime simply because it was a convenient number or address to use. (5)

management—the process of combining resources to accomplish organizational goals. (1)

management by objectives (MBO)—involves managers and subordinates setting goals and objectives together and then tracking performance to ensure that the objectives are met. (1)

management information systems (MIS)—software programs that organize data to assist in decision making. (13)

marginal performer—employee who has demonstrated ability to perform but who does just enough to get by. (10)

mechanistic model—divides tasks into highly specialized jobs where job holders become experts in their fields, demonstrating the "one best way" to perform their cog in the wheel (Taylorism); the opposite of the *organic model*. (1)

mediation—a process of dispute resolution in which one or more impartial third parties intervenes in a conflict or dispute with the consent of the participants and assists them in negotiating a consensual and informed agreement. (11)

micromanagement—oversupervising, providing oversight with excessive control and attention to details better left to the operational personnel. (1)

mission—the reason an organization exists. (3)

mission statement—a written explanation of why an organization exists and is the driving force for that organization, providing a focus for its energy and resources. (3)

modified Delphi technique—uses objective rather than open-ended questions. (5)

morale—a person or group's state of mind, level of enthusiasm and involvement with work and with life; how employees feel, in contrast to discipline, which is how employees act. (9)

motivation—an inner or outer drive or impetus to do something or to act in a specified manner; an inner or outer drive to meet a need or goal. (9)

motivator factors—intangible rewards that can cause satisfaction. (9)

N

narrow eye span—occurs when a reader focuses on one word at a time rather than taking in groups of words or phrases in one look. (6)

National Labor Relations Act of 1935 (Wagner Act)—legalized collective bargaining and required employers to bargain with the elected representatives of their employees. (15)

National Labor Relations Board (NLRB)—the principal enforcement agency for laws regulating relations between management and unions. (15)

negative reinforcement—increases a given behavior by removing an unwanted stimulus as a consequence of that behavior. (9)

negligent hiring—failure to use an adequate selection process resulting in hiring personnel unqualified or unsuited for law enforcement work. Often includes failure to check for prior offenses of misconduct. (15)

negligent retention—failing to terminate an employee when justified. (10)

nominal group technique—an objective way to achieve consensus on the most effective alternatives by using an objective ranking of alternatives. (5)

nonactor liability—when an officer is present at a scene where use of force is in question and is obviously excessive and the nonactor officer did nothing to prevent it, that officer is also held liable by the courts. (10)

nonverbal communication—messages conveyed by body language as well as tone of voice. (4)

norms—attitudes and beliefs held by a group of individuals. (8)

Norris–LaGuardia Act—regulated court injunctions against unions and made yellow-dog contracts illegal. (15)

O

objectives—specific, measurable ways to accomplish goals; more specific than goals and usually have a timeline. (3)

operating budget—contains projections for income statement items as well as expenses, including all expenses needed to run the department: salaries, insurance, electricity and the like. (14)

organic model—a flexible, participatory, science-based structure that will accommodate change; designed for effectiveness in serving the needs of citizens rather than the autocratic rationality of operation; the opposite of the *mechanistic model*. (1)

overhead—expenses that do not vary in total during a period even though the amount of service provided may be more or less than anticipated, for example, rent and insurance. (14)

P

paradigm—a model, theory or frame of reference. (2)

paradigm shift—a dramatic change in how some basic structure is viewed. (2)

Pareto principle—20 percent of what a person does accounts for 80 percent of the results. (6)

Parkinson's Law—the principle that work expands to fill the time available for its completion. (6)

passive resistance—a form of civil disobedience reflecting a philosophy of nonviolence; often used by protestors and demonstrators. (10)

performance appraisal—formal evaluation of on-the-job functioning; usually conducted annually. (16)

performance budgeting—allocates dollars based on productivity. (14)

performance interviews—private, one-on-one discussions of the performance appraisal by manager and subordinate. (16)

pinch—a minor problem. (11)

Pinch Model—illustrates the importance of communication in dealing with complaints and the consequences of not communicating effectively; a pinch, a minor problem, can turn into a crunch, a major problem. (11)

positive reinforcement—increases the likelihood that a behavior will occur in the future by introducing an appealing or pleasurable stimuli as a consequence of that behavior. (9)

posteriorities—tasks that do not have to be done, have a minimal payoff and have very limited negative consequences. (6)

posttraumatic stress disorder (PTSD)—a psychological ailment following a major catastrophe such as a shooting or dealing with victims of a natural disaster; symptoms include diminished responsiveness to the environment, disinterest, pessimism and sleep disturbances, including recurrent nightmares. (12)

pre-evaluation—a procedure to allow those being evaluated to have input by completing a form outlining their accomplishments. (16)

prerequisites—necessary background needed to master a given skill. (7)

principled negotiation—pays attention to basic interests and mutually satisfying options; avoids positional bargaining that tends to produce rushed agreements that can lead to damaged relationships. (11)

priorities—tasks that must be done, have a big payoff and prevent negative consequences. (6)

proactive—recognizing problems and seeking the underlying cause(s) of the problems. (2)

problem-solving policing—management ascertains what problems exist and tries to solve them, redefining the role of law enforcement from incident driven and reactive to problem oriented and proactive. (2)

process evaluation—an assessment to determine whether the response was implemented as planned. (5)

procrastination—putting things off. (6)

productivity—converting resources to achieve results in the most efficient and effective way possible. (13)

program budgeting—identifies programs and allocates funds for each. (14)

progressive discipline—uses disciplinary steps based on the severity of the offense and how often it is repeated; steps usually are oral reprimand, written reprimand, suspension/demotion, discharge/termination. (10)

promotability/assignment factors—an attempt to make evaluation "count for something." (16)

proportionate assignment—area assignments are determined by requests for services, based on available data. (13)

Pygmalion effect—what managers and supervisors expect of their officers and how managers treat officers largely determine officers' performance and career progress. (9)

pyramid of authority—the shape of the typical law enforcement hierarchy, with the chief at the peak and having full authority, down through managers (captains and lieutenants) and supervisors (sergeants), to those who accomplish most of the tasks (officers). (2)

Q

qualitative data—examines the excellence (quality) of the response—that is, how satisfied were the officers and the citizens; most frequently determined by surveys, focus groups or tracking of complaints and compliments. (5)

quantitative data—examines the amount of change (quantity) as a result of the response. This is most frequently measured by pre/post data. (5)

quota—a specific number or proportional share that each officer is expected to contribute or receive. (13)

R

racial profiling—any police-initiated action that relies on the race, ethnicity or national origin rather than the behavior of an individual or information that leads the police to a particular individual who has been identified as being or having been engaged in criminal activity. (8)

random patrol—officers on patrol are unsystematically (randomly) assigned areas to cover. (13)

reactive—simply responding to calls for service. (2)

reframing—a conflict resolution skill; a psycholinguistic technique that shifts a person's perspective to recast conflict as a positive, rather than a negative, force. (11)

regression—looking back over previously read material. (6)

reinforcement theory—Skinner's motivational theory that behavior can be modified by using positive and negative reinforcement. (9)

reprimand—formal criticism of behavior; may be oral or written. (10)

resiliency— the ability to adapt to significant adversity or trauma; is the key to stress management. (12)

reverse discrimination—giving preferential treatment in hiring and promoting to women and minorities, to the detriment of White males. (15)

right-brain thinking—primarily using images and emotions. (5)

right-to-work laws—make it illegal to require employees to join a union; established by the Taft-Hartley Act of 1938. (15)

rote learning—memorization, not necessarily with understanding. (7)

S

scanning—reading material rapidly for specific information. (6)

seagull management—manager hears something's wrong, flies in, makes a lot of noise, craps on everybody and flies away. (1)

self-actualization—refers to meeting individual goals and fulfilling one's potential, including expressing creative talents. (9)

self-fulfilling prophecy—the theory that people live up to expectations—if people believe they can do a job, they usually can, but if people believe they cannot do a job, they usually cannot. (9)

sexual harassment—unwelcome sexual advances, requests for sexual favors, and other verbal or physical conduct of a sexual nature that explicitly or implicitly affect an individual's employment, unreasonably interferes with an individual's work performance or creates an intimidating, hostile or offensive work environment. (10)

shift—time span to which personnel are assigned; sometimes called a *watch*. (13)

single handling—not picking up a piece of paper until you are ready to do something with it; applies particularly to the daily stack of mail. (6)

skimming—reading information rapidly for the main ideas, usually the first and last paragraph, the first sentence of all other paragraphs and the captions of any charts or figures. (6)

sleep inertia—the grogginess, the period of hypovigilance, impaired cognitive and behavioral performance experienced upon wakening. (12)

SMART goals and objectives—objectives that are specific, measurable, attainable, relevant and trackable. (3)

social capital—a concept to describe the level or degree of social structure within a community and the extent to which individuals within the community feel bonded to each other. Exists at two levels (local and public) and can be measured by *trustworthiness*, or citizens' trust of each other and their public institutions, and by *obligations*, or the expectation that service to each other will be reciprocated. (2)

sound bite—good information stated briefly; two essential elements are (1) that it contain good, solid nuggets of information, not speculation or opinion, and (2) that it is short. (4)

span of control—how many people one individual manages or supervises. (2)

special employment groups—groups included in affirmative action programs such as African Americans, Asians, the elderly, Eskimos, Hispanics, homosexuals, immigrants, individuals with acquired immune deficiency syndrome (AIDS), individuals with disabilities, Middle Easterners, Native Americans, religious group members, substance abusers, war veterans, women and youths. (15)

split-second syndrome—a condition that affects police decision making in crisis; asserts that if a person has intentionally or unintentionally provoked or threatened a police officer, at that instant the provoker rather than the police should be viewed as the cause of any resulting injuries or damages. (12)

staff personnel—those who support line personnel. (2)

stakeholders—those affected by an organization and those in a position to affect it. (3)

standards—targets to be met, including level of performance. (16)

strategic planning—long-term planning. (3)

stress—tension, anxiety or worry; can be positive, eustress, or negative, distress. (12)

subvocalization—the contraction of the tongue and other speech-related organs made during learning to pronounce each letter of the alphabet; becomes ingrained and can slow down adult readers. (6)

summary discipline—discretionary authority used when a supervisor feels an officer is not fit for duty or for any reason the supervisor feels a need for immediate action. Also called *summary punishment*. (10)

summary punishment—*see* **summary discipline.** (10)

summative assessment—involves tests given at the end of a predetermined period that assess proficiency: written exams, end-of-week quizzes, end-of-training exams. (7)

supervision—overseeing the actual work being done. (1)

sustained—complaint or grievance in which the investigative facts support the charge. (11)

synergy—occurs when the whole is greater than the sum of its parts; the team achieves more than each could accomplish as individuals. (3)

T

tactical planning—short-term planning. (3)

Taft–Hartley Act of 1947—balanced the power of unions and management by prohibiting several unfair labor practices, including closed shops, which prohibited management from hiring non-union workers. (15)

tickler file system—a set of file folders, organized by year, month and day, into which lists of tasks to be accomplished are placed. (6)

total quality management (TQM)—Deming's theory that managers should create constancy of purpose for improvement of product and service, adopt the new philosophy, improve constantly, institute modern methods of training on the job, institute modern methods of supervision, drive fear from the workplace, break down barriers between staff areas, eliminate numerical goals for the work force, remove barriers that rob people of pride of workmanship and institute a vigorous program of education and training. (1)

touchstone values—what people say is important to them. (8)

transactional change— various features of an organization may be altered, but the core framework is untouched; this evolutionary change intervenes in structure, management practices, and motivations. (2)

transformational change—intervenes in an organization's mission, culture and leadership style. (2)

traumatic stress—severe, extremely intense distress that lasts a limited time, and then the person returns to normal. (12)

triage—rapidly, systematically and effectively sorting victims in a multiple casualty incident. (13)

two-factor theory—Herzberg's motivational theory that employees' needs can be classified as hygiene factors (tangible rewards that can cause dissatisfaction if lacking) and motivator factors (intangible rewards that can create satisfaction). (9)

type A personality—describes people who are aggressive, hyperactive "drivers" who tend to be workaholics. (12)

type B personality—describes people who are more laid back, relaxed and passive. (12)

U

unconditional backup—dictates that other officers must take action, get involved and back each other up physically, psychologically, emotionally and ethically. (8)

unfounded—complaint or grievance in which the act did not occur or the complaint/grievance was false. (11)

unified command—allows agencies with different legal, geographic and functional authorities and responsibilities to work together effectively without affecting individual agency authority, responsibility or accountability. (3)

union—any group authorized to represent the members of an agency in negotiating such matters as wages, fringe benefits and other conditions of employment. (15)

union shop—must belong to or join the union to be hired. (15)

unity of command—means that every individual in the organization has only one immediate superior or supervisor. (2)

V

valid—appraisals that are well grounded and sound in which the factors rated are job related and the raters are trained. (16)

variable costs—expenses that will change depending on the level of service provided; for example, personnel costs. (14)

variance analysis—comparing actual costs against what was budgeted and examining the differences. (14)

vetting—a process in which policies are evaluated, examined and investigated thoroughly and expertly by sergeants, department attorneys and other stakeholders. (3)

vicarious liability—makes others specifically associated with a person also responsible for that person's actions. (5, 15)

vocoder—a device that is part of every digital radio that changes voices from analog to digital to be transmitted. (4).

W

Wallenda Effect—the negative consequences of fear of failure. (1)

watch—*see* **shift.** (13)

whole-brain thinking—using both the logical left side and the emotional right side of the brain together for best results. (5)

working in "silos"—when local government agencies and departments work quite independently of each other. This lack of partnering with other city and county agencies hinders problem-solving success. (2)

work plans—the precise activities that contribute to accomplishing objectives; detailed steps or tasks to be accomplished. (3)

Y

yellow-dog contract—makes union membership illegal under the penalty of discharge. (15)

Z

zero-based budgeting (ZBB)—begins with a clean slate, justifying each expenditure anew and based on merit, rather than being based on the preceding year's funding level. (14)

zipper clause—clearly states that the contract is a complete, full agreement between the two parties and neither party is obligated to negotiate on other items during the term of the contract. (15)

AUTHOR INDEX

SUBJECT INDEX